THE
ISO 14000
HANDBOOK

edited by

Joseph Cascio

Chairman, U.S. Technical Advisory Group to ISO/TC 207

ASQ Quality Press
Milwaukee, Wisconsin

The ISO 14000 Handbook

Edited by: Joseph Cascio
Chairman, U.S. Technical Advisory Group to ISO TC 207;
Vice President, Environmental Management Systems,
Global Environment and Technology Foundation

Published by: ASQ Quality Press
611 East Wisconsin Avenue, PO Box 3005
Milwaukee, Wisconsin 53201-3005
Tel: 800-248-1946, 414-272-8575; Fax: 414-272-1734

ISBN 0-87389-440-5

The authors have made every effort to verify the accuracy and completeness of the information contained in this report and do not accept responsibility for errors or omissions. This publication is designed to provide accurate and authoritative information regarding the subject matter covered. It is not intended to render legal, accounting, or any other professional services. If legal advice or other expert assistance is required, the services of a competent professional should be sought.

For permission to photocopy pages or sections from The ISO 14000 Handbook, contact the Copyright Clearance Center at
508-750-8400; Fax: 508-750-4470.

American Society for Quality

ASQ

Quality Press
611 East Wisconsin Avenue
Milwaukee, Wisconsin 53202
Call toll free 800-248-1946
http://www.asq.org
http://standardsgroup.asq.org

Content Summary

Table of Contents

CHAPTER 3

Tips on Interpretation and Implementation 156

by Cynthia Neve, The Victoria Group;
Michelle Blazek, AT&T Environmental Health and Safety Process;
Leilia McAdams, AT&T (currently with Lucent Technologies);
Marilyn R. Block, MRB Associates;
Phil Marcus, ICF Kaiser Inc.;
Marie Godfrey, Franklin Quest Consulting Group;
Edwin Pinero, EnSafe Inc.; and
Samantha Munn, Inchcape Testing Service/Intertek Services

CHAPTER 3

ISO 14040 Life-Cycle Assessment Standards 275

by Dr. Stanley P. Rhodes, Scientific Certification Systems, Inc., and
Linda G. Brown, Scientific Certification Systems

PART 6

Environmental Auditing 293

CHAPTER 1

The Evolution of Environmental Auditing 293

by Jean H. McCreary, Esq., Nixon, Hargrave, Devans & Doyle LLP,
Leader ST2 TG1 on General Principles of Environmental Auditing
Cornelius C. Smith, Jr., ML Strategies Inc.; Chairman, ST2 on Environmental Auditing;
Elizabeth A. Potts, ABS Quality Evaluations; and
Raymond W. Kane, Environmental Management Consulting

PART 7
Conformity Assessment 345

Preface

Welcome to the Challenge!

As the 21st century draws near, the consequences of how organizations provide activities, products, and services to the world's burgeoning population are critical. Few if any legacies worth passing on to future generations are more valuable than a healthful, sustained environment. Each of us in our own way — individuals, small enterprises, and corporations alike — is called to become a faithful steward of the world we live in. It is therefore incumbent upon us to be more proactive in our efforts.

Arguments against planning for sustainable development to improve both the environment and the bottom line are rare, if not extinct. For many organizations, the thorny question is: "How do we act on our responsibility to improve environmental performance and still remain competitive players in stressful economic times?"

The time to act is *now*, and the ISO 14000 series of international environmental management system (EMS) standards may well be a solution to enhanced internal management system efficiency, reduced waste, pollution prevention, improved environmental performance, and anticipating regulation with proactive environmental policy.

As the ISO 14000 series of standards becomes a reality, companies worldwide are moving rapidly to implement ISO 14001. Philips Components Lebring of Austria became the first organization certified to the committee draft (CD) of ISO 14001 in early 1995. In January 1996, SGS Thomson became the first United States site to certify to Draft International Standard (DIS) ISO 14001.

By early 1996, more than 200 companies were implementing ISO 14001 as a first step. Once implementation is complete, these companies plan to reassess their environmental and business goals. Among the companies adopting this strategy are Kodak, IBM, DuPont, Texas Instruments, Lucent Technologies, Polaroid, Motorola, and Alcoa.

More than 150 are already certified to the European Union's Eco-Management and Audit Scheme (EMAS), BS 7750, or a draft version of ISO 14001. And still others are committed to certifying their sites *worldwide*, including: Akzo Nobel, ARCO, Bahia Sul, Lucent Technologies, Philips Components, Radian Corp, SGS-Thomson, and Toyota.

These and numerous other companies, large and small, in developed and developing nations, have decided to accept the challenges posed by an as-yet-unproved international EMS standard. They will be among the first to discover the obstacles and advantages of undertaking what many are calling a "paradigm shift" in business management.

View From the Top

At a conference in San Jose, California, Peter Wilson, expert to the European Union in the European Commission Directorate General XI-Environment Nuclear Safety and Civil Protection was emphatic about the potential advantages of environmental management systems. The European Commission drafts proposals and directives that often become E.U. environmental policy.

Wilson stated, "The need to employ new and innovative approaches in pursuit of sustainable development is clearly identified in the environmental action program of the European Commission. Over recent years, the potential for voluntary regulation to play a role within the regulatory framework has become more widely accepted in Europe.

"The European Commission's Eco-Management and Audit Scheme is a good example of the application of this philosophy, and organizations registered in the scheme are looking forward to significant changes in their relationships with local regulators. Within EMAS a structured approach to environmental management through the application of an environmental management system plays a fundamental role as the means by which improvements in environmental performance are delivered.

"The potential for such standards as the ISO 14000 series of standards, suitably implemented and appropriately certified, to act as a vehicle by which genuine improvements in the environmental performance of organizations can be delivered is clear. Organizations of all sizes, wherever they are situated, should be encouraged to use environmental management system standards in this way as one step on the road to a sustainable future."

How to Use This Handbook

From the beginning, we committed ourselves to publishing a high quality handbook in the purest sense of the word: a useful tool you won't want to leave on the shelf. International standards issues can be complex. We have tried to simplify them for you in every way.

The book is divided into 10 topical parts and several reference appendixes, the most important of which is Appendix A. This contains the adopted version of ISO 14001, its annex, and ISO 14004. We recommend that you read this through at some point in your journey, and refer to it frequently as your roadmap to successful implementation.

Each part begins with an overview to set the stage and is written so it can be read independently from others. Throughout each part, chapter, and section we have numbered headings and listed references to other pertinent sections of the book. References are denoted by the symbol 📖.

In the margins, you will find annotations that draw your attention to key concepts and tips to guide you through the text.

Also, we added sidebars, tip boxes, and graphics to provide you with anecdotal examples and experiences of others; these are aimed at showing rather than telling you how to meet the challenges of ISO 14001 implementation.

Part 3 on planning and implementing ISO 14001 is the heart of the book. It offers hands-on, common-sense advice in logical implementation sequence. It tackles two of the thorniest problems — documentation and environmental aspects identification — head on., and provides a set of implementation tips from varying perspectives, denoted by icons for easy reference. And because implementation is as varied as companies themselves, in Part 4, the companion to Part 3, several authors and case studies show you how others have approached this new venture.

Finally, the appendices are filled with valuable resources. We know the frustration of having to interrupt work to dig up resources for making an informed decision, so we have provided you with the necessary information at your fingertips.

About the Editor and Key Authors

The ISO 14000 Handbook is your passage onto the spiral staircase leading toward environmental excellence. CEEM Information Services has collected a premier group of top-level industry managers and consultants from all over the world, many of whom were leaders of working groups and sub-working groups to the United States Technical Advisory Group (TAG) to ISO Technical Committee 207 on EMSs and to TC 207 subcommittees. These were the framers of the ISO 14000 series of standards. In fact, many of our contributors have lived, breathed, and toiled over the ISO 14000 series from its genesis.

Joseph Cascio

In particular, CEEM is privileged to share with our readers the extensive expertise of Joseph Cascio, chairman of the U.S. TAG to ISO TC 207 and lead negotiator for ISO 14000 on behalf of the American National Standards Institute. His passion for and constructive analyses of ISO 14001's mission comes from knowledge and experience gained over 26 years with IBM Corporation. At IBM, he held positions in engineering, marketing, and litigation prior to his becoming program director of environmental, health and safety standardization.

In the latter position, some of his many successful endeavors included:

- negotiating public policy issues relative to the environment;

- creating and developing management programs leading to the end of CFCs used in manufacturing;

- initiating solid waste reduction programs;

- managing IBM's involvement in the Superfund program; and

- leading efforts in chemical management and design for environmentally conscientious products.

In May 1996, Joe left IBM to become vice president of environmental management systems for the Global Environmental Technology Foundation, where he is managing director of the ISO 14000 Integrated Solutions Unit (ISS).

The ISS mission is to accelerate dissemination of the ISO 14000 message to the largest number of potential beneficiaries.

Joe is a true believer in the ISO 14000 series of standards. In his words, "ISO 14000 is the right approach at the right time. The world is ready for these standards, and the time is right to move beyond command-and-control. If we are to keep the ball rolling, ISO 14000 is the new force to keep momentum going to improve environmental protection." His introduction to this book and his other contributions are a lucid portrait of ISO 14000 and the world they will affect.

C. Foster Knight and Robert Ferrone

We are also pleased to share with you the knowledge and vision of C. Foster Knight and Robert Ferrone. Foster is managing director of Knight & Associates, a consulting group specializing in environmental management, law, and technology. Knight & Associates is helping Mexican companies in the United States and Mexico develop corporate environmental strategies and management systems. Foster also develops and instructs ISO 14000 courses for CEEM Inc.

Foster is an environmental attorney with more than 20 years' experience and has served as deputy general counsel of the President's Council on Environmental Quality and as deputy attorney general in the California Attorney General's unit. Before forming Knight & Associates, Foster was responsible for worldwide environmental compliance management systems as environmental counsel to Digital Equipment Corporation.

Robert Ferrone is president of the Ferrone Group, which specializes in integrating industrial design engineering, quality, manufacturing, and environmental management systems toward improved environmental and quality performance. The Ferrone Group provides training and technical support to companies preparing for ISO 14001, including integration of ISO 9000 quality and environmental management systems.

Robert Ferrone also is a lead course developer and instructor for CEEM Inc. His experiences include developing innovations in quality management systems for Fortune 500 companies and leading ISO 9000 certification efforts and a variety of technical initiatives for Digital Equipment Corporation. Bob regularly contributes to quality and environmental publications.

Betweem them, Bob and Foster have years of hands-on experience managing environmental systems at companies like yours. Their outstanding contribution on preparing, planning, and implementing ISO 14001 in Part 3 attests to the empathy they have for those faced with day-to-day EMS activities. You will find yourself nodding your head in agreement at the common-sense advice they offer.

There were more than three dozen eminent contributors to this handbook who deserve high praise and appreciation for the hours and expertise they provided. Absent room to acknowledge them all, please turn to Appendix K for their biographies.

ISO 14000 Series Overview

CHAPTER 1
Introduction

by Joseph Cascio,
Chairman, U.S. Technical Advisory Group to ISO/TC 207

Following on the heels of the ISO 9000 standards for quality management, the ISO 14000 standards hold out the promise to revolutionize environmental protection as we have known it in the past quarter century.

These standards embody a novel approach that relies on changes in organizational commitments, focus, and behavior rather than on coercion from governmental authorities. They are expected to provide the basis and the key to actualize strategic environmental management in organizations and redirect regulatory evolution to what is variously referred to as the "new paradigm," the "dual track," or the "cooperative model."

If we look back, for comparison, at the existing "command-and-control" regime, we see that it was not a failure in fostering organizational actions that led to improvement of the environment. In fact, the environment has improved rather noticeably since 1970 — the year our modern environmental movement began. Rivers no longer burn and air is much cleaner. Many toxins such as PCBs, phosphates, and lead have for the most part been removed as environmental factors.

Whether any other approach could have worked in 1970 or for much of the two decades that followed is a subject much debated. Some argue, persuasively I believe, that a voluntary, cooperative approach would not have worked in a world that by today's standards was lax in its environmental attitudes and convinced of its belief that environmental protection and economic development are antithetical. It was necessary, they would claim, to have imposed extremely detailed rules and technological prescriptions with sanctions and threats of punishment to discipline all but the most brazen and imprudent among us.

No one questions the value of our environmental gains since 1970. Rather, what is questioned is whether we went too far with the prescriptions, the threats, the costs, and the resulting climate of distrust, litigation, and ideological skirmishes. In my view, the more relevant questions today are whether we can build on what we have achieved to promote further progress in environmental protection, and what is the best model to follow under prevailing conditions?

prevailing
conditions

We should first ask, "What are today's prevailing conditions?" We can certainly start with the general and very popular desire to reduce government and bureaucracy. Some of this is already happening, and any reading of the tea leaves points to diminished resources and capability in coming years for all regulatory agencies.

For example, the U.S. Environmental Protection Agency's (EPA) ability to send out legions of inspectors and auditors to operating facilities continues to erode as funds are slashed. Furthermore, the job of the remaining inspectors has become ever more difficult and not just because of reduced funding. As the obvious sources of pollution were addressed by organizations, the ability of government inspectors to ascertain the more subtle threats to the environment became less certain. Much of the potential environmental improvement that can still be tapped is tied to improvements in the industrial processes themselves and not to the control of wastes after they have left those processes.

Government agencies worldwide — including the U.S. EPA — have acknowledged this reality by their growing focus on pollution prevention rather than pollution control. But success in this area is dependent on voluntary initiative by organizations. The U.S. EPA, for example, has neither the resources nor the competence to dictate to industry how industrial processes should be designed. Unless we employ an approach that stimulates voluntary action, we are not likely to see significant improvement in these processes.

Another factor adding to the momentum for change is the unacceptably low returns of the current approach. For example, the yearly tab for environmental protection in the United States is somewhere between $120 and $140 billion. While these expenditures have led to improvements, there is wide recognition that much of this sum is squandered on litigation, bureaucracies, paperwork, inspections, and unnecessary procedures.

Most of these expenditures mushroomed from the very approach that relied on detailed technical commands from government agencies, followed by close supervision, enforcement, and punishment of all infractions both substantive and administrative. Not surprisingly, command-and-control spawned a huge body of legal experts as organizations sought protection from what was often perceived as overzealous idealism, or worse, ideologues. It can be argued that this was the only approach feasible during the 1970s and 1980s. There is now, however, a great desire to cut waste so that we can reap greater returns from investments.

Fortunately, major advances in the acceptance of an environmental ethic within industry have made pursuit of cutting waste realistic and achievable. The compatibility of environmental protection and economic development is no longer seriously questioned. What is even more heartening is the growing realization that technological development that cuts down on pollution often results in greater profitability and competitiveness.

The recent popularity of voluntary environmental programs with both industry and government attests to the force behind these drivers for change. Examples of early versions of such programs include the Coalition for Environmentally Responsible Economies (CERES) principles and the International Chamber of Commerce *Business Charter for Sustainable Development — Principles of Environmental Management*. The U.S. EPA later came out with Green Lights, Energy Star, and many others. The Chemical Manufacturers Association adopted the Responsible Care® program, and other industry groups followed with their own versions of that approach. More recently, the U.S. EPA has proposed other pilot programs that seek higher environmental performance for various regulatory advantages such as the Environmental Leadership Program, the Common Sense Initiative, and Project XL.

ISO 14001 is structure

The ISO 14000 series of standards builds on these programs in a number of significant ways.

First, it provides the framework — through a series of specified elements — that takes the guesswork out of integrating strategic environmental management into company operations.

Second, it is universally expected that implementation will be verified through third-party audits to guarantee the actuality of good-faith endeavors.

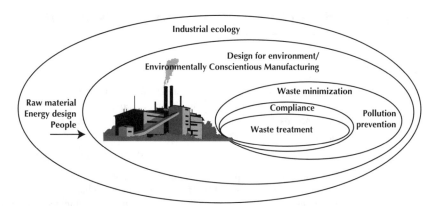

Figure 1.1 Moving beyond compliance.

Finally, the universality of ISO 14000 — created by consensus of delegates from nearly 50 countries over a five-year period — sets the ISO 14000 standards very far apart and above any of the existing programs.

That universality augurs well for the acceptance of ISO 14000 internationally, and all indications today are that the standards are being accepted very quickly on a broad front.

The great expectation is that ISO 14000 will become the engine for fostering the environmental ethic within organizations.

ramifications
The ramifications of such change are potentially vast as individuals begin to export their environmental sensitivity from their workplace to their homes and families. ISO 14000 has the promise to drive societies to realize the much desired but elusive goal of sustainable development. It will foster the development of clean technologies, greater environmental protection, and, for those with a bottom-line orientation, greater competitiveness.

The contributions in this volume aim to make understanding and implementation of an environmental management system easier. The authors have all been closely involved in the creation of the ISO 14000 standards or of associated programs that support implementation of management systems. Their views and suggestions should be of real value to those wishing greater understanding or who are planning to develop EMS systems in their organizations.

A minor word of caution — the views are those of the authors and are not official or unofficial interpretations of the standards. There was some effort on my part to ensure a degree of consistency and integrity in the text. The authors were not, however, given a specific line of thought to follow, so the views may not be totally compatible.

My thanks to all contributors for their excellent work and for their patience with my comments and suggestions.

To the readers, best wishes on your ISO 14001 efforts. You have embarked on a journey well worth taking!

CHAPTER 2
Background and Development of ISO 14000 Series

1.2.1 What Is ISO?

The International Organization for Standardization (ISO) is a worldwide federation founded in 1947 to promote the development of international manufacturing, trade, and communication standards. ISO is composed of national standards bodies from 118 countries. 📖 (See Appendix B for a list of ISO and other standards bodies.)

The American National Standards Institute (ANSI) is the United States representative to ISO.

fosters trade
ISO's stated goal is "to promote the development of standardization and related activities in the world with a view to facilitating the international exchange of goods and services and to developing cooperation in the sphere of intellectual, scientific, technological, and economic activity."

Until late 1970, ISO's work was largely technical in nature. It focused almost exclusively on product specifications and guidances geared toward performance attributes. But with the advent of ISO Technical Committee 176 on quality management and quality assurance in 1979, it began focusing attention on holistic business management systems that take into account horizontal functions and decision making.

shift to process orientation

In adding horizontal and process-oriented standards to its mix of vertical and product-oriented standards, ISO is reflecting a shift in thinking by business leaders. Today, these leaders are integrating and coordinating their operations to face stiff and sometimes unpredictable global competition. And many governments are seeking to boost national interests by fostering incentives for this kind of thinking. Given ISO's makeup, this new kind of standards development should be no surprise.

Before developing a standard, ISO receives input from government, industry, and other interested parties. More than 70 percent of ISO member bodies are governmental or quasi-governmental. Many offer input through a consensus process that seeks to include a broad array of interested parties, including manufacturing, consumer, laboratory testing, engineering, academic, and environmental organizations. Others are more closed in their deliberations.

voluntary standards

All standards developed by ISO are voluntary; no legal requirements compel countries to adopt them. However, countries and industries often adopt ISO standards as requirements for doing business, thereby making them virtually mandatory in these cases.

ISO develops standards in all industries except those related to electrical and electronic engineering. Standards in these areas are developed by the Geneva-based International Electrotechnical Commission (IEC), which has more than 52 member countries, including the United States. 📖 (See Appendix B for the list of countries.)

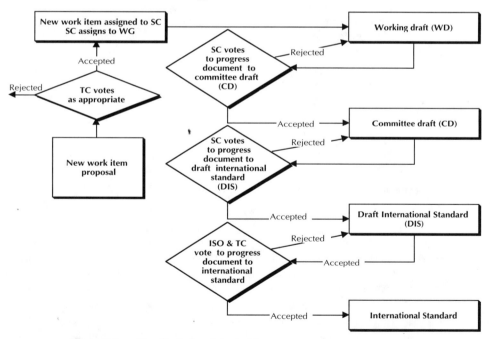

Figure 1.2 — Standards development process.

The ISO Process

A policy-level management board called the Technical Management Board (TMB) administers the technical work of ISO. The TMB, made up of 12 national body members is responsible for the organization, coordination, strategic planning and programming of ISO's technical work. The TMB examines all proposals for new fields of ISO technical activity and decides on the most appropriate path forward.

For example, the TMB decides whether to establish a technical committee (TC) and if so, what the TC's scope will be. Within this scope the committee determines its own program of work.

The actual technical work is carried out through TCs. TC members may participate at the following levels:

- national member bodies who are active participants in the work of a given technical committee and vote, or "P" members;

- member bodies who observe TC activities but do not vote, or "O" members; and

- member bodies who can represent either external organizations that meet the necessary criteria, or other IEC/ISO committees, or "L" members.

A proposal to begin work in a new field of technical activity such as OHSMS normally comes from within ISO itself, (e.g., national member or existing technical committee) but it may also originate from some other international organization. All new proposals are ultimately submitted for consideration to the ISO member bodies. If accepted, the appropriate existing technical committee or a new technical committee will be established to receive the new "work."

In the case of a straightforward proposal(s) (e.g., one that impacts only one sector of interests), a review is conducted to determine whether or not there is any existing standardization activity in place and, if not, the proposal is submitted to the national bodies to determine:

- national body support for the proposal (two-thirds of those voting are in favor of the proposal);

- interest in participating (at least five national bodies must agree to participate for a proposal to be accepted); and

- interest in assuming the Secretariat of the technical committee.

The results of this review are referred back to the TMB for a final decision.

In the case of a more complex proposal(s) (e.g., one that has broad impact on a number of sectors, such as OHSMS), the TMB examines the proposal and determines an appropriate course of action. Numerous options are available to the TMB and, depending on the situation, one will be chosen. For example, the proposal may have a direct impact on the work of one or more existing technical committees, and the TMB may decide to convene a meeting of the leadership of the affected TCs.

Once the TMB decides to establish a new technical committee with a given scope and to assign the Secretariat to a national body, the membership of the committee is determined and a first meeting is planned. At this meeting, the TC reviews its scope and decides on an initial structure and program of work. The TC may establish subcommittees (SCs) and working groups (WGs) to cover different aspects of its work. Each subcommittee formed is assigned a scope that must be within the scope of the TC, and a national body is assigned the Secretariat. In the case of working groups, a convener is appointed for each.

Development of an International Standard

An international standard is the result of an agreement among the member bodies of ISO. Normally, the development of an international standard is a multi-stage process.

A new work item proposal, accompanied optionally by an initial draft for consideration, is submitted for a three-month letter ballot of the committee members.

If approved (five member bodies must agree to participate actively), the item is assigned to the appropriate group for development and a project leader is appointed.

The initial draft will then progress to:

- a final working draft;
- a committee draft (CD — subjected to a three-month letter ballot review);
- a draft international standard (DIS — five-month letter ballot review); and
- a final draft international standard (FDIS — two-month yes/no vote, no comments permitted).

The entire process, from the formation of a TC to the publication of the final text of the international standard, can take anywhere from three to eight years. Most standards require periodic revision, and ISO has established the general rule that all ISO standards should be reviewed at intervals of not more than five years.

Exceptionally, and with the permission of the TMB, an existing standard may be submitted by a member body for fast-track processing. In this instance, the document starts at the DIS stage and can become an approved international standard in less than 12 months. Candidate fast-track standards are normally standards that have already achieved wide acceptance internationally.

U.S. Representation in ISO

The American National Standards Institute (ANSI) is the U.S. member of ISO and a permanent member of the TMB. Whenever ANSI participates on an ISO technical committee, it does so based on the recommendation of the affected U.S. interests. To support this participation, ANSI accredits a technical advisory group (TAG) and appoints a TAG Administrator. The TAG is responsible for developing U.S. positions for the technical committee and for selecting U.S. delegates to the TC meetings. The TAG administrator is responsible for the overall administration of the TAG and for ensuring adherence to the procedures governing its operation. The TAG is an open body made up of interested, materially affected parties from the United States.

Source: American National Standards Institute

The standards development process generally follows the following five-step process:

1) proposal stage;

2) preparatory stage;

3) committee stage;

4) approval stage; and

5) publication stage.

There are three levels of ISO membership:

full ISO
memeber

1) A full member of ISO is the national body "most representative of standardization in its country." Full members sit on the ISO General Assembly and are candidates for ISO Council membership. The Council governs ISO operations and consists of the principal officers and 18 elected member bodies. The Council also appoints the Treasurer, the 12 members of the Technical Management Board, and the Chairmen of the policy development committees. It also decides on the annual budget of the Central Secretariat. Full members can participate and vote in any ISO technical committee.

correspondent
ISO member

2) A correspondent member is usually an organization in a developing country that does not yet have its own national standards body. Correspondent members do not take active part in standards development, but are kept up-to-date about work of interest to them.

subscriber ISO
member

3) A subscriber member is a country with a very small economy that pays reduced membership dues, allowing it to maintain contact with international standardization activities.

(See Appendix B for a list of ISO members.)

As of early 1996, ISO had assigned standards and other document development to 213 technical committees (TCs). Generally, related documents are assigned to one technical committee. The ISO 14000 series of environmental management system standards has been assigned to TC 207.

1.2.2 What Is an EMS?

An environmental management system (EMS) is that facet of your organization's overall management structure that addresses the immediate and long-term impact of your company's products, services, and processes on the environment. An EMS provides order and consistency in organizational methodologies by allocating resources, assigning responsibilities, and continually evaluating your practices, procedures, and processes.

An EMS is essential to your organization's ability to anticipate and meet growing environmental performance expectations and to ensure ongoing compliance with national and international requirements. EMSs succeed best when corporations make environmental management among their highest priorities.

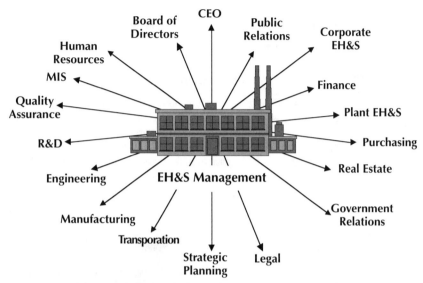

Figure 1.3 — The EHS challenge: holistically managing an array of elements.

Generally, environmental management systems should provide organizations with the
framework framework to do the following:

NEED TO WRITE

- establish an appropriate environmental policy, including a commitment to prevention of pollution;

- determine the legislative requirements and environmental aspects associated with the organization's activities, products, and services;

CHECK IN SPCC
WMP.

- develop management and employee commitment to the protection of the environment, with clear assignment of accountability and responsibility;

NEED TO DO
- encourage environmental planning throughout the full range of the organization's activities, from raw material acquisition through product distribution;

- establish a disciplined management process for achieving targeted performance levels;

- provide appropriate and sufficient resources, including training, to achieve targeted performance levels on an ongoing basis;

EDUCATION ⟶ establish and maintain an emergency preparedness and response program;

- establish a system of operational control and maintenance of the program to ensure continuing high levels of system performance;

Do NOT DO
- evaluate environmental performance against the policy, objectives, and targets, and seek improvement where appropriate;

- establish a management process to review and audit the EMS and to identify opportunities for improvement of the system and resulting environmental performance;

- establish and maintain appropriate communications with internal and external interested parties; and

- encourage contractors and suppliers to establish an EMS.

ISO 14001 can provide this framework.

1.2.3 What Is Driving the EMS Movement?

Public concern over the impact of industrial products and processes on the world's environment is increasing. Politically oriented bodies such as environmental advocacy organizations, watchdog groups, and the "green" parties that have established footholds in most European parliaments are urging businesses to take responsibility for their environmental effects. This pressure from the public sector has led to a rash of proposed and enacted environmental legislation worldwide.

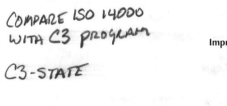

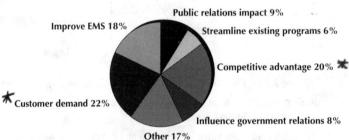

Figure 1.4 — Recent survey of 99 companies illustrates drivers of potential ISO 14001 certification.

However, recent reports are showing that companies choose to implement an EMS more for internal management system efficiencies, waste reduction, and proactive regulatory compliance than for any other purpose.

The list of reasons many companies are now adopting an environmental management system includes the following:

multitude of benefits

- Ease of trade — International standards obviate the need for and proliferation of national and regional standards that are more likely to hinder trade by erecting barriers and bureaucratic complexity and redundancies.

- Improved compliance with legislative and regulatory requirements — This includes requirements that certain information relating to environmental performance be made public.

- Credibility — Third-party certification ensures the credibility and substance of a commitment to regulatory compliance and continuous, institutional focus on environmental protection.

- Reduction in liability/risk.

- Regulatory incentives — Organizations can take advantage of incentives that reward companies showing environmental leadership through certified compliance with an EMS.

- Sentencing mitigation — It is likely that sentencing guidelines will accept corporate EMSs as mitigating factors in levying both individual and corporate fines.
- Pollution prevention and waste reduction — and attendant savings and expense reduction.
- Profit — Customers from consumers to governments are increasingly preferring to purchase "green" products.
- Improved internal management methods — and the efficiencies and savings that result.
- Pressure from shareholder groups — who are more likely than ever to look for environmental responsibility in investments and financial reports.
- Pressure from environmentalists — who bring a raft of legal precedents to bear on companies they consider poor environmental players, to stockholders.
- Community goodwill.
- A high-quality workforce — which is seeking empowerment and involvement along with healthy and safe working conditions.
- Insurance — Insurance companies are less willing to issue coverage for pollution incidents unless the firm requesting coverage has a proven environmental management system in place.
- Sustainable development — Management standards will become a stepping-stone for less developed countries (LDCs) to begin their progress toward an equivalent level of environmental protection found in their more developed neighbors. Since management standards require considerably fewer resources to implement, LDCs can reap the benefits of more focused and organized environmental protection activities now. Over time, as their economies grow in concert with environmental protections, they can acquire appropriate technologies to maximize environmental protection.
- Preference in bank loans — Some institutions, such as the World Bank, may view ISO 14000 as a test of a country's sincerity in its promotion of environmental protection and sustainable development.

1.2.4 How Did the ISO 14000 Series Evolve?

John Wolfe, former Secretary to ISO/TC 207, contributed to this section

Some observers trace the genesis of the ISO 14000 series to the United Nations Conference on Human Environment in Stockholm in 1972. More than 113 countries were represented by more than 1,000 delegates from some 350 non-governmental organizations. The United Nations Environment Program (UNEP) is a direct result of this conference, along with the World Commission on Environment and Development, headed by Gro Harlem Brundtland, who became prime minister of Norway in October 1981.

The 1972 conference resulted in a global action plan for the environment in which UNEP was charged with fostering worldwide environmental responsibility and awareness.

In 1987, the Brundtland commission published a report titled *Our Common Future*, which contained the first use of the term "sustainable development," calling for industry to develop effective environmental management systems.

By the end of 1988, more than 50 world leaders had publicly supported the report and were calling for a major international event to discuss and act upon it. In 1989, the UN decided to convene the United Nations Conference on Environment and Development (UNCED), also known as the Earth Summit. This conference was held in Rio de Janeiro in June 1992.

50 world leaders support global health

This period marked the beginning of ISO and IEC's involvement. In preparation for the summit, a Swiss industrialist, Stephan Schmidheiny, had been asked to provide business advice for the summit. He established the Business Council for Sustainable Development for this purpose. The council approached ISO and IEC because of their well-known consensus process in developing standards and other documents, asking to see what they were doing in the area of environmental management. As it happened, the ISO/IEC president's advisory board on technical trends was looking into this very issue.

strategic advisory group

In August 1991, ISO and IEC formally established the Strategic Advisory Group on the Environment (SAGE) to make recommendations regarding international standards for the environment.

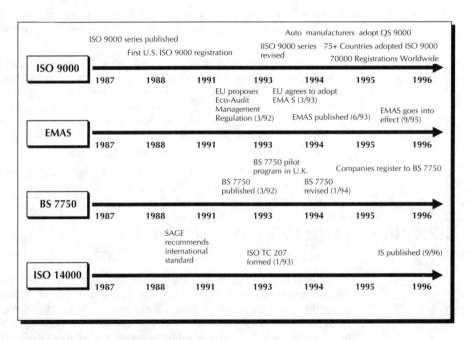

Figure 1.5 — Evolution of ISO 14001 (relative to ISO 9000).

SAGE was charged with considering the following:

- a common approach to environmental management similar to "quality" management (i.e., ISO 9000);

- enhancing the ability to attain and measure improvements in environmental performance; and

- using international standards to facilitate trade and remove trade barriers.

It was instructed not to consider environmental criteria such as levels of pollutants, health assessments/risks, technology specifications, or product/process criteria.

During its deliberations, SAGE spent more than a year studying the British Standards Institution (BSI) standard, BS 7750, *Environmental Management Systems*, and other national EMS standards as possible starting points for an ISO version. BS 7750 had been developed as a companion to the BS 5750 standard on quality management systems.

SAGE had also heard the call among ISO and IEC members for fewer duplicative — and sometimes competitive — corporate and governmental programs, and a call for a way to garner objective validation of industry commitment to effective environmental management.

SAGE's work produced a series of recommendations on environmental management submitted for consideration during preparations for the Earth Summit, and a recommendation that ISO/IEC create a new technical committee to develop standards in environmental management.

As a result, SAGE's call for better environmental management became a key element of two major documents that came out of the Rio summit: *Agenda 21*, the comprehensive policy guidance document, and the *Rio Declaration*, a set of 27 principles for achieving sustainable development.

And, in January 1993, ISO created Technical Committee 207, charged with developing a uniform international EMS standard and other documents for use as environmental management tools. Canada was awarded the secretariat.

TC 207's stated mission is "standardization in the field of environmental management tools and systems."

Excluded from its scope are:

- test methods for pollutants, which are the responsibility of ISO TC 146 on air quality, TC 147 on water quality, TC 190 on soil quality, and TC 43 on acoustics;

- setting limit values regarding pollutants or effluents;

- setting environmental performance levels; and

- standardization of products.

The committee met for the first time in Toronto in June 1993, at which point SAGE was disbanded. At TC 207's first meeting, some 200 delegates representing about 30 countries expressed a desire to move as rapidly as possible to complete a first draft of the EMS and auditing international standards. 📖 (See Part 1, Chapter 2, Section 8 for information on the structure of TC 207.)

The following years saw tremendous, and often contentious, work among dozens of industry experts to create standards that would be universally credible, usable, and effective. The next meeting was held April 17-20, 1994, in Surfer's Paradise, Australia.

At its June 24-July 1, 1995, meeting in Oslo, Norway, a record 500 delegates from 47 countries agreed to elevate the EMS standards and auditing standards to draft international standards with scheduled publication by the end of 1996. The environmental aspects in product standards guidance, the terms and definitions standard, one of the labeling standards, and the life-cycle assessment principles standard were moved substantially further along in the development process and were expected to become final by late 1996, but the others lagged behind.

BS 7750

Although much of BS 7750 was used as a starting point in the search for an international EMS standard, the draft ISO 14001 standard that emerged includes language from several other national standards in development, and input from each TC 207 member.

EMAS

Complicating development of these standards, in December 1990, the European Union's (E.U.) European Commission adopted the Eco-Management and Audit Regulation, which includes the Eco-Management and Audit Scheme (EMAS). EMAS establishes specifications for environmental management systems of companies doing business in the E.U.

In late January 1996, 15 of the 17 members of the European Accreditation of Certification (EAC) — a group of European accreditation bodies — signed a memorandum of understanding offering ISO 14001 accreditation services in most of the European Union. Most of these accreditation bodies were focusing on developing criteria for EMAS accreditation first. Since EMAS has requirements not included in ISO 14001, there has been speculation that a document covering remaining gaps would be written so ISO 14001 certification could be seen as equivalent to EMAS registration. (See Part 7, Chapter 3, Section 2 for more information on the bridge document for EMAS.)

U.S. standard

There were national EMS standard efforts underway in several other countries as well, including in the United States. In January 1996, the US Technical Advisory Group (TAG) to TC 207 approved adopting ISO 14001 verbatim as the U.S. national standard with NSF International, the American Society for Quality Control (ASQC), and the American Society for Testing and Materials (ASTM) as cosponsors. (See Part 8, Chapter 3 and Part 10, Chapters 2 and 5 for more information on U.S. pilot projects.)

When the international standard becomes final, the U.S. and the other national standards will as well. By becoming certified to the verbatim national standards, companies will be certified to ISO 14001.

To take advantage of experience gained with development of quality management systems, and to respond to the desire among companies for integrating systems wherever possible, TC 207 was directed in its scope "to have close cooperation with ISO TC 176 in the field of environmental systems and audits."

TC 176 liaison

ISO established a TC 176/207 liaison group to harmonize relevant standards in the ISO 9000 quality management systems series of standards and the ISO 14000 series of standards. According to a report the liaison group presented to both TCs, a high level of alignment between the two standards can be expected within "a reasonable time frame" (i.e., by 2000).

1.2.5 What Is the ISO 14000 Series of Standards?

ISO 14000 is an evolving series of generic standards being developed by ISO to provide organizations with the structure for managing environmental impacts. The TC 207 standards include a broad range of environmental disciplines:

✓• the basic environmental management system;

✓• environmental auditing criteria for use by both internal and third-party auditors;

• criteria for doing an environmental performance evaluation;

✓• environmental labeling criteria; and

⊙ life-cycle assessment methodologies.

Technical Committee 207 is made up of subcommittees (SCs) and their working groups (WGs), each assigned a set of related standards[1]. 📖 (See Part 1, Chapter 2, Section 8 for an organizational flowchart.)

Types of Documents

Two basic types — specification standards and guidance standards — form the ISO 14000 series.

specification, guidance

According to ISO TC 207, a <u>specification</u> standard "contains only those requirements that may be objectively audited for certification/registration purposes and/or self declaration purposes." A <u>guidance</u> is an international standard that "provides guidance on the development and implementation of environmental management systems and principles, and their coordination with other management systems." Both types are referred to as "standards."

guides, technical reports

ISO also develops "guides," not to be confused with "guidances." There is one guide in the ISO 14000 series: *ISO Guide 64 — Guide for the Inclusion of Environmental Aspects in Product Standards*. Several technical reports may be considered.

According to ISO, "<u>Guides</u> are intended for use as a voluntary, internal management tool and are not intended for use by EMS certification/registration as a specification standard. They are applicable to any organization, regardless of size, type, or level of maturity, that is interested in developing, implementing, and/or improving an environmental management system."

ISO also develops <u>technical reports</u> that are written under three different circumstances.

The first is in cases of doubt concerning consensus on an issue being taken up by a technical committee. In the foreword of the technical report, the technical committee would publish "the reasons why the required support could not be obtained."

The second is "when the subject is still under technical development or where for any other reason there is future but not immediate possibility of an agreement on an international standard."

The third is "when a technical committee or subcommittee has collected data of a different kind from that which is normally published as an international standard. . . . The technical committee or subcommittee may decide, by a simple majority vote . . . to publish such data in the form of a technical report. The document shall be entirely informative in nature and shall not contain matter implying that it is normative."

Generally, ISO assigns development of documents to a technical committee. Guides and technical reports are assigned to working groups that answer directly to the full technical committee. Standards or sets of standards are assigned to subcommittees for development, and subcommittees in turn may create working groups.

all but ISO 14001 are guidance documents

With the exception of ISO 14001, the specification standard that is a model for an EMS, all the ISO 14000 series of standards are guidance documents. This means that these documents contain descriptive guidelines, not prescriptive requirements. Your company will not become certified to ISO 14000 as a series; it will become certified to ISO 14001.

ISO 14000 Standard Categories

The standards can be classified according to their focus. They are divided into two categories: organization- or process-oriented standards, and product-oriented standards. See the chart below for the TC 207 groupings.

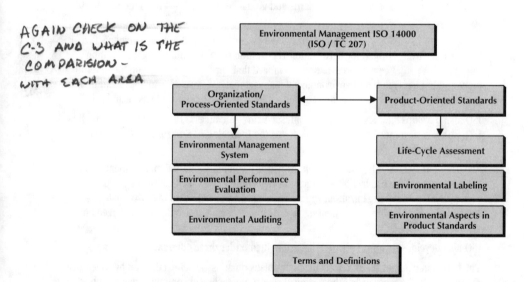

Figure 1.6 — ISO 14000 document categories.

The EMS and auditing standards were elevated to Draft International Standard (DIS) status in June 1995 and were published as final International Standards (ISs) in September 1996. ANSI was expecting to publish American national standards identical to the ISO standards in the same time frame. In spring 1996, the other standards were in various earlier stages of development.

In addition to the TC 207 EMS standards, other technical committees have developed standards that incorporate elements of an EMS, including:

1.2.6 What Standards Compose the Series?

The ISO 14000 series comprises a number of unique standards. Together, these documents provide the necessary guidance for implementing an effective environmental management system.

product-
oriented
standards

The product-oriented standards include environmental labeling, life-cycle assessment, and environmental aspects in product standards; the organization and process standards include environmental management systems, environmental auditing, and environmental performance evaluation.   📖 (See Part 1, Chapter 2, Section 7 for more information the ISO 14000 series of standards.)

Standards in development or under consideration by ISO TC 207 as of spring 1995 were:

This list of ISO 14000 standards may expand as new documents are developed and adopted when the need arises.

This document will list all definitions in ISO 14000 EMS and auditing standards and in other available ISO 14000 standards, with cross-references. Subcommittee 6's role at the TC 207 level is to help resolve differences in terminology as they arise among standards writing subcommittees. A draft international standard was planned by the end of 1996, but several critics were arguing that this standard's promulgation should await completion of several other standards or risk defining terms that will have changed between draft and final iterations.

1.2.7 How Do the Standards Interrelate?

ISO 14000 is the generic title to a series of environmental management standards that address six distinct but related subjects. These include:

- environmental management system (EMS)

- environmental auditing (EA)

- environmental performance evaluation (EPE)

- environmental labeling (EL)

- life-cycle assessment (LCA)

- environmental aspects in product standards (EAPS)

20 documents

In all, some 20 separate documents were being drafted under these six headings, and the obvious question is whether your organization must conform to all 20 to become certified to ISO 14000.

ISO 14001 is a
specification

The answer, quite simply, is "No." Only ISO 14001, the environmental management system specification, is a standard that you can be audited against — and it is voluntary. The other 16 documents are being offered to provide guidelines that support either the implementation of a management system or the analysis of product characteristics. Though useful, none of these others needs to be implemented or otherwise used by your organization for certification purposes.

Document	Responsible Group Schedule as of March 1996	Document	Responsible Group Schedule as of March 1996
ISO 14001 Environmental Management Systems - Specification with Guidance for Use	SC1 WG1 Tentative Schedule: Final IS: June 1996	ISO 14022 Environmental Labels and Declarations - Symbols	SC3 WG2 Tentative Schedule: Further work scheduled in 1996. DIS or IS date not set
ISO 14004 Environmental Management Systems - General Guidelines on Principles, Systems, and Supporting Techniques	SC1 WG2 Tentative Schedule: Final IS: August 1996	ISO 14023 Environmental Labels and Declarations -Testing and Verification	SC3 WG2 Tentative Schedule: Further work scheduled for 1996. DIS or IS date not set
ISO 14010 Guidelines for Environmental Auditing - General Principles on Environmental Auditing	SC2 WG1 Tentative Schedule: Final IS: August 1996	ISO 14024 Environmental Labels and Declarations - Environmental Labeling Type I - Guiding Principles and Procedures	SC3 WG1 Tentative Schedule: DIS expected late 1996. Final IS expected 1997.
ISO 14011/1 Guidelines for Environmental Auditing - Audit Procedures - Auditing of Environmental Management Systems	SC2 WG2 Tentative Schedule: Final IS: August 1996	ISO 1402X Type III Labeling	SC3 WG1 Tentative Schedule: NWIP proposed in Spring 1996. Work schedule developed after proposal is issued.
ISO 14012 Guidelines for Environmental Auditing - Qualification Criteria for Environmental Auditors.	SC2 WG3 Tentative Schedule: Final IS: August 1996	ISO 14040 Life Cycle Assessment - Principles and Framework	SC5 WG1 Tentative Schedule: Final IS: Summer 1997
ISO 14014 Initial Reviews	SC2 WG4 NWI proposal submitted in March 1996. Tentative schedule not established in March 1996	ISO 14041 Life Cycle Assessment - Life Cycle Inventory Analysis	SC5 WGs2-3 Tentative Schedule: DIS expected Summer 1997 Final IS expected 1998
ISO 14015 Environmental Site Assessments	SC2 WG4 Tentative Schedule: First WG draft: Winter 1997 CD for comment: Winter 1998 CD for ballot: Winter 1999 DIS for Ballot: June 2000 Final IS: June 2001	ISO 14042 Life Cycle Assessment - Impact Assessment	SC5 WG4 Tentative Schedule: DIS date not set Final IS date not set
ISO 14031 Evaluation of Environmental Performance	SC4 WGs1-2 Tentative Schedule Review of 4th WD: June 1996 CD for comment: November 1996 Pilot project using CD: November 1996 to June 1998	ISO 14043 Life Cycle Assessment - Interpretation	SC5 WG5 Tentative Schedule: Document in development in April 1996. Final IS date not set.
ISO 14020 Goals and Principles of All Environmental Labeling	SC3 WG3 Tentative Schedule: Further work scheduled for 1996	ISO 14050 Terms and Definitions - Guide on the Principles for ISO/TC 207/SC6 Terminology Work	SC6 WG1 Tentative Schedule: CD for ballot: Spring 1996 DIS: Fall 1996 IS: Fall 1997
ISO 14021 Environmental Labels and Declarations - Self Declaration Environmental Claims -Terms and Definitions	SC3 WG2 Tentative Schedule: CD for ballot/comment issued in fall 1995. Further work postponed until progress is made on symbols (14022) and testing and verification methodologies (14023).	ISO Guide 64 Guide for the Inclusion of Environmental Aspects in Product Standards	WG1, likely to disband Tentative Schedule Final ISO Guide: December 1996

Figure 1.7 — ISO 14000 documents and status.

Why, then, are they being drafted? What are their roles and how do they relate, if at all, to one another?

The ISO 14000 Family

The six subjects covered by ISO 14000 can be grouped into two categories, as shown in Section 1.2.5.

The standards in the first grouping — which include EMS, EA, and EPE — are used to implement your organization's environmental management system. As intended in ISO 14001, the term "organization" includes any body where there is organized human activity such as companies, agencies, factories, refineries, branch offices, libraries, etc.

The other grouping — which includes the EL, LCA, and EAPS standards — is useful for analyzing and characterizing the environmental attributes of products.

While the elements of ISO 14001 are key components of the specification, your EMS would not be complete without a process for ensuring it is conforming to the requirements you establish for it, be they in ISO 14001 or in your corporate program. You must have an audit or review to ensure the EMS is implemented and maintained, to assess whether management is reviewing the EMS properly, and to assess whether you are continuously improving the system.

No EMS can be audited if it doesn't contain measurable requirements. In addition, most companies wish to improve environmental performance as an EMS goal. For this reason, you are likely to need some sort of environmental performance evaluation process. The EPE measures performance improvements, provides a basis for reporting improvements and nonconformances, and offers a way of assessing qualitative and quantitative environmental indicators and techniques.

The audit and EPE standards — guidances, really — developed by ISO are aimed at helping you fulfill the requirements of an EMS, be it ISO 14001 or any other.

✳ ISO 14001 — EMS

Very much like ISO 9001, ISO 14001 specifies the framework for the management system that allows your organization to meet its environmental obligations reliably and consistently. Subcommittee 1 of ISO TC 207 developed this standard.

✳ take inventory

The approach used is straightforward and pragmatic. Your organization is required first to take an inventory of all the environmental "aspects" associated with its activities, products, and services. It determines which are significant and then proceeds to define and implement a management system that includes a policy, objectives and targets, resources, responsibilities, controls, maintenance, corrective action, education and training, management reviews, and audits.

integrate
responsibility

The most significant and difficult of these is the requirement to integrate environmental protection into all the activities of the enterprise. Unlike the practice of environmental protection under the command-and-control regime, this responsibility can no longer be relegated to the environmental engineering staff. The central thesis of ISO 14001 is that environmental protection is a collective responsibility that can be accomplished best through the awareness, commitment, and actions of the individual employer. Instilling an environmental ethic in the workforce is, therefore, the paramount challenge of ISO 14001. Is this not what the goal of environmental laws and regulations should have been from the very beginning?

ISO 14010, ISO 14011, ISO 14012 — EMS Auditing

Another element of ISO 14001 specifies the need to conduct periodic environmental management system audits. Subcommittee 2 of ISO TC 207 has prepared three guideline documents that can help your organization conduct audits to satisfy the ISO 14001 requirements. The use of these guidelines is not mandatory, however, so you may elect to use equivalents.

EMS quality control

By following the EMS audit guideline (ISO 14011) your organization can evaluate whether its system is complete and working, whether all required processes, including those for compliance, are being properly exercised, and whether the management reviews are capable of ascertaining the continuing adequacy, suitability, and effectiveness of your organization's EMS.

It is important to note here that the EMS auditor evaluates processes, not results, though he or she may sample results to ascertain that the processes are working. He or she may, for example, query the auditee on its record in maintaining compliance. If that record indicates that compliance is a problem or is getting worse, the auditor can come to a preliminary conclusion that the compliance process is not working.

In his or her audit of management reviews, the auditor evaluates the process and asks to see evidence that management has actually made a determination on the EMS. Again, ISO 14011 does not call for the EMS auditor to make that determination. As specified in ISO 14001, it is your organization's management that is charged with that duty.

ISO 14031 — Environmental Performance Evaluation

performance indicators

ISO 14001 expects your organization to do monitoring and measurement as part of its EMS. There is recognition that your organization should know where it stands relative to key performance markers and whether it is making progress in achieving its policy goals as well as its objectives and targets.

Subcommittee 4 of TC 207 is developing a guideline (ISO 14031) that will help your organization fashion a subsystem for the purpose of doing environmental performance evaluation. You will find following the guideline to create such subsystems useful in satisfying the ISO 14001 requirement.

As with the ISO 14011 audit guideline, the ISO 14031 performance evaluation guideline is not mandatory. Alternatively, your organization can simply follow some predetermined process for establishing its own unique and relevant subsystem for performance evaluation.

ISO 14031 will contain sample indicators of performance. Some of these are intended to measure elements of the management system while others will be applied to the performance of processes and operations. Still others are designed to measure the status of the environment itself, though the impracticality of doing this may obviate this portion of the guideline. Significantly, there are no mandatory indicators that your organization must use.

Which indicators are used will be dictated by your environmental aspects, as well as by your organization's set policy, goals, objectives, and targets.

Environmental Labeling and Life-cycle Assessment

symbols and terms

The remaining guidelines in the ISO 14000 family relate to the analysis of product characteristics — specifically to those that have some consequence on the environment.

assessing consequences

The environmental labeling guidelines address the symbols and terms used to communicate those environmental characteristics, as well as the procedures used to determine which set of attributes will produce superior environmental performance in a product. The life-cycle assessment guidelines provide principles and approaches for the assessment of the environmental consequences of a product throughout its life cycle.

no official EMS relationship

Clearly, life-cycle assessments should be a key factor in creating environmental labels. The question here, though, is what relationship does environmental labeling and life-cycle assessment have to an environmental management system? The short answer is "None." There is no requirement in ISO 14001 for either environmental labeling or life-cycle assessment. They are offered as optional tools for those organizations that wish to use them for their own purposes.

The largest classes of users of both tools are expected to be professional analysts and third-party labeling programs. Life-cycle assessment also may be used for environmental performance evaluation under appropriate circumstances. This use is limited, however, due to the current inability to conduct impact assessments that have scientific credibility

Environmental Aspects in Product Standards Guide

warnings and encouragement

This last member of the ISO 14000 family is an ISO guide intended to be used by product standards writers. The EAPS guide gives warnings and suggestions that help standards writers avoid specifications in standards that would be environmentally detrimental and to help them incorporate those that will be beneficial. This guide, too, takes a pragmatic approach and avoids listing environmentally questionable materials or elaborating on design-for-environment techniques.

Standards writers quickly realized that a practical guide for standards writers could not do justice to those approaches and techniques. Instead, the guide simply warns and encourages them to seek technical assistance from design-for-environment engineers and life-cycle analysts.

As with the environmental labeling and life-cycle assessment guidelines, there is no relationship between this guide and an EMS. More than that, there is no way for it to be used within the EMS.

1.2.8 What Is the U.S. TAG and What Is Its Role?

When the new work item on environmental management systems was proposed, ANSI, the U.S. representative to TC 207, formed a parallel structure to TC 207 called the U.S. TAG to TC 207.

ANSI also has appointed three groups to administer the U.S. TAG work: the American Society

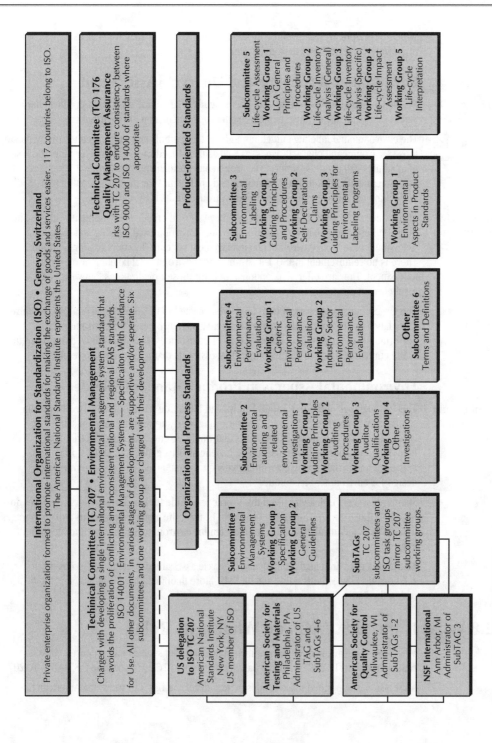

International Organization for Standardization (ISO) • Geneva, Switzerland
Private enterprise organization formed to promote international standards for making the exchange of goods and services easier. 117 countries belong to ISO. The American National Standards Institute represents the United States.

Technical Committee (TC) 176
Quality Management Assurance
rks with TC 207 to endure consistency between ISO 9000 and ISO 14000 of standards where appropriate.

Technical Committee (TC) 207 • Environmental Management
Charged with developing a single international environmental management system standard that avoids the proliferation of conflicting and inconsistent national and regional EMS standards. ISO 14001: Environmental Management Systems — Specificaiton With Guidance for Use. All other documents, in various stages of development, are supportive and/or seperate. Six subcommittees and one working group are charged with their development.

Product-oriented Standards

Subcommittee 5
Life-cycle Assessment
Working Group 1
LCA General Principles and Procedures
Working Group 2
Life-cycle Inventory Analysis (General)
Working Group 3
Life-cycle Inventory Analysis (Specific)
Working Group 4
Life-cycle Impact Assessment
Working Group 5
Life-cycle Interpretation

Subcommittee 3
Environmental Labeling
Working Group 1
Guiding Principles and Procedures
Working Group 2
Self-Declaration Claims
Working Group 3
Guiding Principles for Environmental Labeling Programs

Working Group 1
Environmental Aspects in Product Standards

Organization and Process Standards

Subcommittee 4
Environmental Performance Evaluation
Working Group 1
Generic Environmental Evaluation
Working Group 2
Industry Sector Environmental Performance Evaluation

Other
Subcommittee 6
Terms and Definitions

Subcommittee 2
Environmental auditing and related environmental investigations
Working Group 1
Auditing Principles
Working Group 2
Auditing Procedures
Working Group 3
Auditor Qualifications
Working Group 4
Other Investigations

Subcommittee 1
Environmental Management Systems
Working Group 1
Specification
Working Group 2
General Guidelines

SubTAGs
TC 207 subcommittees and ISO task groups mirror TC 207 subcommittee working groups.

US delegation to ISO TC 207
American National Standards Institute New York, NY
US member of ISO

American Society for Testing and Materials
Philadelphia, PA
Administrator of US TAG and SubTAGs 4–6

American Society for Quality Control
Milwaukee, WI
Administrator of SubTAGs 1–2

NSF International
Ann Arbor, MI
Administrator of SubTAG 3

Figure 1.8 — U.S. TAG/TC 207 structure.

for Quality Control for SubTAGs 1 and 2; NSF International for SubTAG 3; and the American Society for Testing and Materials for the other SubTAGs.

U.S. TAG structure

The U.S. TAG is broken down into Sub-Technical Advisory Groups (SubTAGs or STs), the sub-working group (SWG), and task groups (TGs) within the SubTAGs. Each of these groups has interest areas corresponding to TC 207 subcommittees and their working groups. They help form a national consensus for content and application of the environmental standards for advocacy at the international level. No U.S. position is advocated unless a consensus has been developed in support of it.

📖 (See Appendix I for more information on US Tag Administrators.)

U.S. TAG membership

As of April 1996, there were more than 600 members in the U.S. TAG, and this number was growing. Membership consists of representatives from:

- government organizations, including the Department of Defense, Department of Energy, Department of Commerce, and U.S. Environmental Protection Agency;

- industry, mainly Fortune 500 companies in the petroleum, electronics, communication, and chemical industries;

- consultants, including environmental services, CPA firms, management groups, and individuals;

- certifiers/auditors/standards bodies, including the Institute of Internal Auditors, Institute for Environmental Auditing, Environmental Auditing Roundtable, American Society for Testing and Materials, American Society for Quality Control, NSF International; and others;

- public interest groups, including the National Wildlife Federation, Environmental Defense Fund, Green Seal, and Clean Sites Inc.

Most of the members come from the ranks of large industry groups and environmental consultants. Public interest groups and the academic community are marginally represented. Some environmental public interest groups initially avoided participation because they said that, if they were out-voted on certain issues, their names would still appear on the roster and could imply endorsement. But interest among these groups was growing.

The election of an EPA official to the vice-chair position in September 1995 indicates strong EPA and TAG interest in forging links between government and industry in the ISO 14000 area.

U.S. TAG participation

Participating U.S. TAG members have the opportunity to review, comment, and recommend how the U.S. will vote on all new work item proposals and individual standards drafts. Each SubTAG is responsible for selecting a SubTAG chairperson, and once ballots have been distributed to all TAG members and are returned to the TAG administrator, the SubTAG chair assumes a number of responsibilities. The chair prepares:

- a summary of the vote;

- a brief summary of the issues, including objections and any actions taken to resolve the objections; and

- a recommended U.S. position based on the summary of the votes.

According to TAG procedures, the full TAG voting membership decides on and approves U.S. experts for membership in the international working groups directly under ISO TC 207.

CHAPTER 3
The ISO 14001 Standard

1.3.1 Overview

by Joseph Cascio,
Chairman, U.S. Technical Advisory Group to ISO/TC 207

As ISO 14001 becomes the prevailing model for environmental management systems, there is a danger that your organization's stakeholders will view it as just another level of environmental compliance. However, if they adopt this position, they will be missing the entire point of ISO 14001.

Everyone involved needs to take a step back from the standards development process and see ISO 14001 for what it really is: an initiative that will take your organization beyond compliance in the long run, but initially may cause you to fall out of compliance.

ISO 14001 establishes a new approach for protecting the environment, in contrast with the prevailing command and control model. It challenges your organization to explore and understand its environmental aspects and to take stock in them. Under ISO 14001, your organization will establish objectives and targets and commit to effective and reliable processes, including continual improvement of your EMS. The ISO 14000 standards also gather all your employees and managers into a system of shared and enlightened awareness and personal responsibility for your organization's environmental performance.

motivational,
not punishing

This new model relies on positive motivation rather than punishment of errors. It expects an understanding of consequences and a desire to "do the right thing" rather than blind obedience to regulation or corporate directives.

Over the long term, ISO 14001 conformance promises to establish a solid base for reliable, consistent management of environmental obligations. ISO 14001 is the foundation of the entire ISO 14000 series and includes, among other commitments, an obligation to comply with applicable laws and regulations. However, if you fall into the trap of over-emphasizing this legal compliance commitment, you will depreciate the value of ISO 14001, and, worse, you and your stakeholders will miss the real point and advantage of this standard.

ISO 14001 is more and bigger than mere compliance with the law. Not that compliance is unimportant; clearly it is. We have seen how companies that have been in consistent compliance with the law can still have catastrophic accidents such as oil spills and chemical disasters. But ISO 14001 is a whole that is more than the sum of its parts.

Preventive Health

Without a base of educated and committed employees, it only takes one major disaster to negate years of compliance to regulation.

Your organization need only consider the major environmental catastrophes of the last 10 years to exemplify this possibility. In each instance, the organization largely had been in compliance with regulations when its luck ran out. While an EMS may not have prevented these accidents, the standard does specify that your company have an emergency preparedness plan in place. This plan is designed to give you an opportunity to foresee and prevent an accident.

system transparency

The systemic failures that led to each catastrophe had less to do with regulatory transgressions than with process failures. In fact, it is true that, while your organization may have difficulty maintaining compliance to the minutia of the law, it still can have a thoroughly solid operational system to prevent tragedies or, perhaps less dramatically, to prevent routine environmental harm.

If compliance issues become overemphasized, the unfortunate results could be authorities rewarding your company for its regulatory record rather than for substantive achievement toward real protection. It is imperative, therefore, that authorities view ISO 14001 in the proper light and avoid trivializing it by setting its value only with reference to its impact on compliance. ISO 14001 is valuable for its own sake, independent of its ramifications for compliance, and must be valued separately by both users and regulatory authorities.

Easier Said Than Done

Even organizations with sophisticated programs should not be under the illusion that ISO 14001 will be easy to implement.

First, its reach goes much further than regulatory requirements. Your organization must inventory and then assess all environmental aspects of its operations, products, and services. While regulations may apply to many of these aspects, they are not likely to apply to them all.

The standard calls for a system that produces reliable and effective management. Regulations call for compliance but do not typically include requirements for management systems. ISO 14001 expects all your employees to be trained and competent on handling the environmental consequences of their work. This requires the infusion of environmental awareness and attitudes in all workers.

shift in culture

Broadly, what this produces over time is a shift in culture to one that is as sensitive to the environment as to production schedules and product design. Few regulations require such far-reaching changes in the mental attitudes of all employees.

It is also true, however, that the diffusion of environmental responsibility from the environmental engineering function to all your employees in the enterprise will be the biggest challenge and one that, in the short term, may carry the largest risk. In fact, one immediate impact of this shift may be an increase in administrative noncompliance with regulations.

However, if the goal is to broaden your organization's base of responsibility, you must be willing to accept the possibility of these types of errors during the early phases of implementation. Thus, you need to understand that conformance to ISO 14001 is not likely to result in an immediate change in your organization's compliance posture. But look for it in the long run.

1.3.2 Key Definitions

The following is a list of words most frequently associated with the ISO 14001 standard. These definitions are the foundation for the material throughout the rest of this book. Keep in mind that this list is not exhaustive. A complete list of terms is found in ISO 14001 Appendix A.

environmental management system
Environmental Management System (EMS) — "Organizational structure, responsibility, practices, procedures, processes, and resources for developing, implementing, achieving, reviewing, and maintaining the environmental policy."

EMS audit
EMS audit — "A systematic and documented verification process to objectively obtain and evaluate evidence to determine whether an organization's environmental management system conforms to the EMS audit criteria set by the organization, and to communicate the results of this process to management."

environmental aspect
Environmental aspect — "Element of an organization's activities, products, and services that can interact with the environment."

continual improvement
Continual improvement — "Process of enhancing the environmental management system to achieve improvements in overall environmental performance, in line with the organization's environmental policy. Note: The process need not take place in all areas of activity simultaneously."

1.3.3 The Plan-Do-Check-Act Cycle

The ISO 14001 environmental management system specification follows what is known as the "Plan-Do-Check-Act" cycle. It is designed for continual improvement of the EMS to foster improved environmental performance. Imagine ascending a spiral staircase. As you complete each upward spiral, you find yourself one level closer to your destination. Similarly, the Plan-Do-Check-Act cycle forms the structure for each ISO 14001 requirement to continually improve upon itself. No organization will ever reach environmental perfection; however, by applying this cycle, you will achieve continual improvement.

Commitment and Policy

First, your organization must commit to its environmental policy, the stated intentions and principles relative to your overall environmental performance. Committing to the environmental policy will help you set environmental objectives and targets. As you continue acting on your environmental policy's objectives and targets, your organization can and will experience continual improvement in the EMS and its objectives.

Plan

Planning is critical. As the axiom suggests: If you fail to plan, you plan to fail. The planning phase of the continual improvement cycle requires that you formulate plans to fulfill your environmental policy's objects and targets. According to ISO 14004 Sections 4.2. and 4.3, your environmental planning should take into account the following:

- identification of environmental aspects and evaluation of associated impacts;
- legal requirements;

- environmental policy;
- internal performance criteria;
- environmental objectives and targets; and
- environmental plans and management program.

Do

If you expect your organization's EMS to succeed, you must develop the capabilities to support it. The information in the Part 3 in this handbook on planning and implementing ISO 14001 goes into detail on this issue. In general, however, your organization must be responsive to the changing requirements of a broad array stakeholders, internal and external circumstances, and continual improvements. *ISO 14004 — Environmental Management Systems — General Guidelines on Principles, Systems and Supporting Techniques* advises your organization to consider:

- Resources — Human, Physical, and Financial (ISO 14004 Section 4.3.2.1);
- EMS Alignment and Integration (ISO 14004 Section 4.3.2.2);
- Accountability and Responsibility (ISO 14004 Section 4.3.2.3);
- Environmental Awareness and Motivation (ISO Section Clause 4.3.2.4);
- Knowledge, Skills, and Training (ISO 14004 Section 4.3.2.5);
- Communication and Reporting (ISO 14004 Section 4.3.3.1);
- EMS Documentation (ISO 14004 Section 4.3.3.2);
- Operational Control (ISO 14004 Section 4.3.3.3); and
- Emergency Preparedness and Response (ISO 14004 Section 4.3.3.4).

Check

Monitoring and measuring is one way to gauge the success of your organization's environmental performance and to make certain your EMS is meeting stated objectives and targets. Remember: what gets monitored gets measured and what gets measured gets managed. According to ISO 14004, your organization should evaluate:

- Measuring and Monitoring (Ongoing Performance) (ISO 14004 Section 4.2.2);
- Corrective and Preventive Action (ISO 14004 Section 4.2.3);
- EMS Records and Information Management (ISO 14004 Section 4.2.4); and
- Audits of the Environmental Management System (ISO 14004 Section 4.2.5).

Act

Finally, your organization's EMS is a framework that should be continually monitored. Additionally, you should subject it to periodic reviews. (See Part 6, Chapter 4 for more information on management review.)

Your organization must keep abreast with the dynamic internal and external factors that affect both environmental policy and environmental activities and improve your environmental performance. If you treat the management review as the final step in the EMS process, you are liable to suffer. Consider management review the beginning and end of the overall EMS process. Management review is essential because it reflects management's commitment to the EMS. The output of this review has to be top quality action if you expect your employees to buy in to the system.

1.3.4 Key Requirements

As noted in *Figure 1.10*, ISO 14001 has several key components. First, the entire system flows directly from the policy — which references goals and objectives — that your company develops and that top management embraces. Corporate management must commit to this policy; many companies require a signed policy statement to demonstrate this commitment.

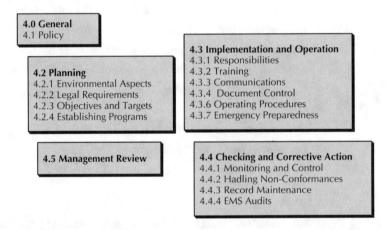

Figure 1.9 — ISO 14001 contents.

The requirements of ISO 14001 are the heart of this handbook. They are referenced throughout. 📖 (See Part 3, Chapter 2 on implementation for a practical guide on fulfilling these requirements.)

What ISO 14001 Is Not

ISO 14001:

- is not a product standard;
- is not a performance standard;
- does not establish values for pollutants or performance levels;
- does not establish test methods;
- does not require initial performance testing;
- does not require or establish a final performance goal;

- does not require you to reach zero emissions or surpass regulatory compliance limits;
- does not mandate best achievable technologies;
- does not require you to disclose performance levels;
- does not require you to disclose audit results; and
- is not required, period.

What ISO 14001 Is

NEED THIS FOR REPORT COMPARISION WITH C-3

ISO 14001:

- is a framework for managing significant environmental aspects you can control and over which you can be expected to have an influence;
- is for use by any company, any size, anywhere in the world;
- is a voluntary consensus, private-sector standard;
- is systems-based, placing reliance on the system, not on individual specialists;
- represents a "paradigm" shift toward holistic management and total employee involvement;
- represents a shift to proactive thinking and acting;
- urges employees to define their roles from the bottom up and requires top management backing, resources, and visibility to support them.

1.3.5 What Are Concerns Relating to ISO 14001?

ISO 14000 is attracting a lot of attention from all stakeholder groups. For the most part, all groups see the many potential advantages and benefits in an international standard for environmental management. Yet each group also harbors concerns over possible costs and impacts.

 costs

Some in industry are concerned that implementation of ISO 14001 will increase costs and administrative red tape without commensurate improvement in environmental protection or offsetting commercial regulatory advantages. This fear reflects a failure to understand that the major goal of ISO 14001 is to foster an environmental ethic in the workforce that justifies the efforts and brings long-term benefits to the organization. While the current practice of relegating environmental compliance to a specialized staff may achieve the short-term legal requirements, it is not the solution or the approach that leads to changed attitudes and behavior to safeguard the environment into the future. The concern expressed is valid if ISO 14001 is seen only in the narrow context of regulatory compliance. It is, of course, true that ISO 14001 is not needed to simply achieve compliance. Its real value, rather, is in its potential to change the organizational culture and the behavior of individuals. Those are the changes and benefits that make implementation worthwhile and ultimately justified.

need for compliance

Some regulators are concerned that emphasis on the management approach to environmental protection will de-emphasize command and control regulation. They believe that environmental performance can only be achieved through coercive measures and detailed legal requirements. Such attitudes betray a lack of understanding that environmental protection can only be guaranteed over the long term by behavioral change and institutional acceptance and integration. While holding a gun to someone's head will make that person behave as you want, you have not necessarily changed his views or attitude. This is the untenable situation we have today with environmental compliance, and it is regrettable that some regulators want to see this mode perpetuated. It seems reasonable that as these regulators begin to understand the significance of the ISO 14001 approach, they will embrace its use in alternative compliance schemes to create win-win situations for all parties.

false claims

Like regulators, environmentalists also worry that ISO 14001 may lead to relaxation of the command-and-control approach. They also worry that ISO 14001 registration will be used to denote environmental excellence of the organization or environmental superiority of the organization's products. Conformance to ISO 14001 does not necessarily equate to environmental excellence. It only reflects that the organization has a management system that satisfies the elements of ISO 14001. It would be a misuse as well to imply that the organization's products are environmentally preferable. This would confuse ISO 14001 registration with environmental labeling of products. These are valid concerns that are now being addressed by the leadership of Technical Committee 207.

All stakeholders are concerned about the credibility and integrity of conformity assessment. Conformity assessment that lacks integrity is useless as it can nullify any credit the organization expects to receive from customers, regulators, and environmental groups. A conformity assessment process that cannot assure that the organization is in conformance with the elements of ISO 14001 lacks integrity. Regulators are particularly concerned over this issue as they are under public scrutiny to treat all enterprises equally and not to give advantages to undeserving parties. The conformity assessment officials in many countries are taking great pains to ensure the integrity of their conformity assessment systems as stakes are quite high.

In general, some concerns are being addressed at various levels of TC 207 or as part of the conformity assessment process. Others, that stem from a failure to appreciate the potential of ISO 14001 to establish a new approach to environmental protection, are addressed by contributors in this handbook.

Conformity Assessment

The U.S. needs to establish a process for certification body (registrar) accreditation and for conformity assessment in accordance with ISO 8404. This 1994 standard on quality management and quality assurance defines conformity assessment as follows:

> "Conformity assessment includes all activities that are intended to assure the conformity of products to a set of standards. This can include testing, inspection, certification, quality system assessment, and other activities."

market access processes

In general, conformity assessment includes all market access processes for a product or service that must be followed to bring that product or service to a market. Governments and private organizations (e.g., ANSI, Register Accreditation Board (RAB), Underwriters Laboratories, and the National Institute for Standards and Technology use conformity assessment procedures to ensure that products sold in their countries meet their laws and regulations and to protect their citizens, public systems, and the environment from harm caused by products that enter their country. Some see it as vital that ISO 14000 standards be considered with this effort. (See Part 7, Chapter 1 for more information on this topic.)

U.S. Integration with National Regulatory Scheme

regulatory mitigation

U.S. companies are concerned that federal and state regulators remain active participants in discussing EMS policies and protocols so they end up buying into the standards themselves. If regulatory bodies such as the U.S. Environmental Protection Agency and the Department of Justice accept the validity and mission of an auditable ISO 14001 EMS, they are more likely to offer regulatory enforcement relief to certified companies, according to U.S. TAG members. The EPA has issued an auditing policy that offers reduced penalties for self-identified, reported, and corrected problems. Many see an ISO 14001-type EMS as a way to take advantage of this benefit. 📖 (See Part 8, Chapter 2 and Appendix D for more information.)

Use by Governments and NGOs To Require Performance Improvement

credibility

While companies are looking for government to give them credit for having a verified EMS in place, they also fear that government and pressure groups could insist on requiring proof of improved, if not perfect, environmental performance as a prerequisite to their accepting ISO 14001 as credible. This double-edged sword has resulted in some desire by industry that government and others step back from involvement until companies have a chance to implement the EMS and weigh the costs and benefits, and until the standards have a chance to make their mark on the marketplace.

Competitive Advantage

customers

Most companies involved with ISO 14001 development say that a compelling reason for implementing the standard is customer endorsement — and that might include government bodies in the U.S. and elsewhere. If these and other customers reduce the frequency of compliance audits or consider ISO 14001 companies as preferred suppliers, certification will be tempting. This is already happening in the United Kingdom, The Netherlands, and elsewhere.

Validation of ISO 14001 for EMAS

The main difference between the European Union's Eco-Management and Audit Scheme (EMAS) and the draft ISO 14001 standard is that EMAS is focused on corporate environmental *performance* in the absence of strong European regulations that might otherwise force acceptable performance levels. ISO 14001 is focused on ensuring that company systems and actions are in *conformance* with established company environmental management policies and objectives.

pressure for acceptance

Although EMAS doesn't really need a standard such as ISO 14001 to work because its authors designed it to stand alone, there is international pressure for the E.U. to accept the ISO 14001 standard, with the possible addition of a bridge document containing further requirements for companies with E.U. sites to follow. Nobody wants a proliferation of differing standards, and companies in the E.U. have said they would opt for an internationally accepted ISO 14001 as a recognized standard under EMAS. All indications were that the

E.U. would accept ISO 14001 with a "bridge." 📖 (See Part 7, Chapter 3 for more information on the "bridge" document.)

ISO 14001/ISO 9000 Harmonization

harmonization

Although the ISO 14000 documents are being developed with cooperation between TC 207 and TC 176 to identify areas of common interest, there will need to be a proactive effort to harmonize the two series of standards. According to ANSI, the short-term goal for the two committees is to explore the general structures of the specification standards and how they would relate to each other; the medium-term goal is to bring future editions of the standards closer together; and the long-term goal is for there to be no incompatibilities and, as much as possible, no differences in structure or specific clause wordings. This effort is being taken up among U.S. TAG members.

📖 (See Part 1, Chapter 3, Section 4 for more information on harmonization.)

Conversion to National Standards

parallels ISO 14001

As the ISO 14001 standard and the EMS auditing standards near adoption as international standards, the international and national standard synchronization process must be followed. Each member country of ISO must have an accredited standards body in place to adopt international standards as national standards.

In the U.S., ANSI formed a "Z1" subcommittee to work on such a process. The objective is to have an American national standard that parallels the ISO 14001 standard. On January 18, 1996, the U.S. TAG to TC 207 approved adoption of ISO/DIS as the U.S. national EMS standard. The standard then had to go through an ANSI approval process. A U.S. standard was published at the same time the international standard was published in September, 1996.

Scope of TC 207 — Expansion to OHS

integration

As a frequent joint function in many businesses, health, safety, and environmental matters could be integrated in an international standard. The ISO Technical Management Board is exploring the possibility of developing an occupational health and safety management standard. If the need for such a standard is established, ISO will have to decide whether TC 207 or some other committee develops it. 📖 (See Part 10, Chapter 6, Section 1 for more information on development of an OHS management system standard.)

1.3.5 What Gets Certified?

by Joseph Cascio,
Chairman, U.S. Technical Advisory Group to ISO/TC 207

Managers considering the advantages of certifying to ISO 14001 will ask themselves whether to seek a single certification for their entire enterprise, or to subdivide the enterprise into logical or physical units and seek multiple certifications.

For those managing smaller entities housed in one location, the answer is relatively obvious, and they likely will pursue one certification. Since there may be ramifications for both the costs and the realized value of certifications, managers of larger, multi-site entities will want to consider carefully how they proceed in this matter.

Experience with ISO 14001 reflects a management tendency to define "organization" more broadly than was done with ISO 9001 — the quality management standard. We may see enterprises that have 100 or more ISO 9001 certificates with fewer than ten ISO 14001 applications. There are reasons for this contrast that stem from the differences between quality and environmental management as well as from the acquired knowledge and experience gained by those who went through the ISO 9001 certification process.

Many organizations that implemented ISO 9001 did so at the departmental and sometimes at the individual process levels. One can, therefore, find ten or more certified sub-units at a single manufacturing plant. Adding to the complexity, these certifications were sometimes awarded by multiple certification bodies.

certification at
highest
sub-level

Individuals have attacked the standards themselves for allowing the proliferation of certifications in this fashion because it has proven to be expensive and disruptive. These disruptions have taken away time that could have been spent on improving the system and maximizing the advantages of process management. Needless to say, these organizations have learned from their past mistakes and have no intentions of repeating them. They are now planning certification at the highest sub-unit level that fits the logical or physical realities of their firms.

Fortunately, ISO 14001 allows total freedom in defining the "organization" unit seeking certification. As specified in ISO 14001, virtually any organized business activity such as companies, departments, plants, divisions, construction sites, refineries, mines, branch offices, administration centers, schools, banks, restaurants, fire houses, mills, etc., can be considered "organizations" capable of implementing an environmental management system.

Some large multi-site enterprises may choose to obtain a single certification even though it poses unique challenges for both the enterprise and the certification body.

Historically, large enterprises have concentrated their environmental focus on environmentally sensitive operations that are under regulatory scrutiny. Certification of the entire enterprise to ISO 14001 would also bring in administrative and sales offices that for the most part have escaped that scrutiny. Establishing an environmental ethic in such places would be much more challenging than in those areas where environmental issues have been prominent for years. This is particularly true where such offices are physically separate and remote from manufacturing activities. There also are logistical and resource challenges for the organization in this approach.

Prior to undertaking such an assessment, several key questions would require answers:

☑ Should one or more teams make the assessment?

• What is the optimum time to conduct the assessment?

• How can the assessment team guarantee consistency in its approach?

• What team expertise is necessary to cover a greater variety of situations, including the role and leadership from corporate headquarters?

• Would one certification for the entire enterprise require management reviews led by the CEO?

built-in
flexiblity

The drafters of ISO 14001 allowed for enterprise certification even though their expectation was that it would be predominantly applied to each location separately.

In certifying some of your locations as independent entities, there are a few critical issues to take into consideration. For example, a company's division may have many locations where the same product is manufactured or where different parts of a product are made and subsequently assembled elsewhere. Unless all locations of such a division are certified, it will be virtually impossible for your company to claim that any of the unit's products are manufactured in certified locations. Outsourcing poses additional problems for locations as they acquire product components from other manufacturers.

suppliers

Because your company is ISO 14001 certified does not mean the other manufacturers (suppliers) also must be ISO 14001 certified. It does mean, however, that your organization must take advantage of opportunities where it has influence to minimize the environmental consequences of its dealings with the supplier(s).

The advantage of a location focus is that site management usually has the requisite authority to promote a site-wide management system. The location focus is also appropriate since environmental protection cannot be segmented to lesser units. In keeping with the spirit of ISO 14001, it would not be appropriate to segregate an environmentally offensive operation within a location and claim that it is not a part of the organization for purposes of ISO 14001 conformances.

weigh options

When choosing how to certify your enterprise properly, carefully weigh the available options. For nearly all businesses, the most logical consideration will be location. For some, this may need to be rolled into a divisional aggregate to make product representations to customers easier. For small, single-location companies the proper unit will be the entire enterprise. Large, multi-location companies may choose a single company certification, but only if they commit to bringing all operations into line with the environmental ethic and to involving the corporate office in management reviews.

Because regulatory authorities must ensure environmental protection on a location basis, individual processes and operations within a location seldom will qualify as organizational entities. Whichever option you select, your managers should weigh a variety of factors to minimize cost and maximize the value of certification to your company.

2

Preparing for ISO 14001

CHAPTER 1
Making the Decision

by Dawne Schomer, Corporate EHS Audit and Systems Program Manager,
Texas Instruments Inc.; Leader ST2 TG3 on Auditor Qualifications and
Robert Kloepfer, Vice President, EHS Management Consulting Group, Haley & Aldrich Inc.

2.1.1 Overview

Quite simply, the first question a company, task force, or decisionmaker considering either implementing or pursuing certification to ISO 14001 must ask is, "Why do it?"

why do it? The pros and cons, pitfalls, resource implications, and potential cultural mismatches of ISO 14001 are many. The decision even to spend the time required to assess each of these should be predicated on the presence of a compelling "driver" or reason for your organization to take the first step.

"driver" needed The most talked about drivers for moving ahead with ISO 14001 have centered on international standardization, international trade, and the benefits of one worldwide standard. As more companies take up the idea of ISO 14001 EMS specification, however, more international and domestic reasons to pursue implementation have arisen. Let's look at some of the factors to weigh as you consider your decision on ISO 14001 from a variety of different perspectives.

2.1.2 You're a Large Company

Let's say you are a Fortune 500 company. You have 120,000 employees worldwide. You have facilities on five continents. You need to comply with environmental directives, policies, and regulations from 15 nations, including countries with strong enforcement mechanisms and countries where environmental regulation is almost unheard of. Many of your foreign competitors have far fewer environmental requirements placed on them, and you feel this gives them a big competitive advantage. Relatively recent environmental management standards in Europe have given you another layer of responsibilities, and other countries and nations are considering enacting their own, slightly different standards. Many of your divisions are ISO 9000 certified.

An organization such as yours may be supportive of ISO 14001 and consider implementation or certification for several reasons.

single standard
First, international acceptance of ISO 14001 may remove some of the redundancy of multiple international, national, and regional environmental standards, making it easier for you to meet one widely embraced standard.

level field
Second, to some degree it may level the playing field between you and some of your less regulated international competitors, setting at least a minimum procedural standard for managing environmental responsibilities.

small adjustment
Third, because your company already has many of the necessary environmental programs and procedures in place, you really only need to adjust your existing environmental management plan to look the way ISO 14001 wants it to look. It is likely that your company already has experience implementing ISO 9000, so you can probably do it even more efficiently this time.

market requirement
Finally, whether you like it or not, international acceptance of the new ISO standard may become a market requirement for doing business with certain pro-ISO 14001 companies — and governments — around the world, and perhaps in certain geo-economic regions.

Identify Overlaps

overlaps exist
For most large multinational firms/organizations, making the decision to meet ISO 14001 requirements is not an issue of great debate. If you are familiar with their common use, applying management systems techniques to your environmental endeavors makes good business sense. You likely are already performing many of your environmental efforts using these techniques.

Several practices typically in place at many companies of this size and visibility include:

- environmental compliance assessment and reporting;

- a mature ESH (environmental, safety, and health) compliance audit program;

- established interactions with regulators and community, an existing process of strategic planning, including setting and monitoring measurable goals and objectives; and

- existing participation in cooperative efforts, such as:
  - technology transfer;
  - pollution prevention; and
  - waste minimization.

The existence of these management system elements already may have provided some baseline for environmental excellence. Examples include:

- an organizational culture that supports good corporate citizenship;
- established ESH resources;
- some degree of integration of ESH into business units — or at least familiarity with ESH by them;
- a general foundation supporting further maturation and management system program development; and
- an awareness of the current level of environmental program maturity.

gap analysis   If your organization is in this position, ISO 14001 may be compared easily with existing management system elements and you can identify gaps. A gap analysis will help you include the missing elements of ISO 14001 into your organizational plans. 📖 (See Part 2, Chapters 2 and 3 for more information on gap analysis.)

2.1.3 You're a Smaller Company

Perhaps you are not quite that big. Maybe you have one or two plants in the U.S. employing about 5000 people. You don't do business overseas. The current regulatory requirements of U.S. Environmental Protection Agency and your state and local governments are more than enough of a burden on your time and overhead costs. ISO 9000 was very difficult and costly for you to implement, and you're not looking forward to going through that again. You have a good environmental program, an internal compliance audit run by your employees, and your record with the agencies has been exceptional. Your operating units were given enhanced control of their functions a few years ago, resulting in a marked increase in efficiency, and you do not want to impose many procedural requirements on them. That being the case, your biggest customer intends to be one of the first multinational U.S. companies to become ISO 14001 certified and has indicated that supplier certification will be a consideration in the award of work.

"trickle-down"   To the degree that large corporations around the world require conformance to ISO 14001
requirement   from their suppliers, there very likely will be a market driven "trickle down" of conformance by smaller companies over time. Firms such as yours may need to consider ways to meet the requirements of ISO 14001 in a cost-effective manner, addressing the marketplace requirements for conforming, if not certified, corporations.

why wait?   What if your organization is not currently blessed with the advantages of an existing formal EMS? Does this indicate you should wait until some future point to consider ISO 14001? On the contrary, it is a strong indicator that ISO 14001 should be incorporated into your company plan as a mechanism to drive change in your organization's perception of environmental issues.

initial review   If you fall in this category, some up-front evaluation and assessment beyond the gap/overlap analysis described above may be in order. This is where the European Union's Eco-Management and Audit Scheme (EMAS) concept of an "initial assessment" may be helpful. 📖 (See Part 9, Chapter 5 and Part 9, Chapter 6 for more information on EMAS, and 📖 Part 2, Chapter 2, Section 2 for more information on conducting an initial review.)

You Have Only One Facility

You have one U.S. facility employing 200 people. You don't do business with any big multinationals, and the chance that the marketplace will require you to embrace ISO 14001 is remote. Over the past few years, the agencies have been hammering you over a number of relatively minor regulatory violations, and just keeping up with that paperwork has been costly. Because of all the agency attention, some of your facility's neighbors have begun to get a little nervous about your operation and have been asking some questions about the risks posed by your plant. You have a good program, and you feel confident that your environmental exposures are being adequately controlled, but you do wonder why the same kinds of violations keep popping up year after year.

good
management
tool

Firms such as yours may want to consider implementing or conforming to the ISO 14001 standard without certifying to it, because it is a good environmental management tool. A structured program with clear responsibilities, procedures, and management systems may go a long way toward solving some of those nagging compliance problems.

stakeholder
assurance

Without the need for actual third-party certification, you may even find that the costs of developing such a program are not that high. The ability to "self-declare" conformance to the standard may serve as a big "green stamp" that your neighbors will like. 📖 (See Part 2, Chapter 3 for more information on stakeholders.)

government
incentives

Finally, a number of U.S. state and federal regulatory agencies are introducing initiatives to allow companies a greater degree of latitude in self-inspection, reporting, and correction if they develop formal environmental management programs along the lines of ISO 14001.

2.1.4 Basic Questions

For any organization considering "What to do about ISO 14001," a good starting point after the gap/overlap analysis may be to ask some basic questions, such as:

☑ What is the intended outcome of implementing each of these ISO 14001 elements? (What impacts, what changes, do you seek in incorporating an ISO 14001 element into your business culture?)

☑ How do each of the ISO 14001 elements fit in with my current "toolbox" (a.k.a. environmental management system elements)?

Your ISO 14001 Toolbox

If you have an idea of what tools you already use, it may help you to compare them with those found in ISO 14001. To help in this comparison, you may want to categorize each of the elements of ISO 14001 in this or a similar fashion.

Handwritten margin notes:
NEED TO HAVE AN ENVIRONMENTAL POLICY — WRITTEN ✓

BREAK OUT REPORT ON FRAMEWORK
2 INFORMATIONAL
3 PROGRESSIONAL
4) QUALITY

"Framework" Tools

Framework elements provide parameters and information on company culture, goals, and objectives. They also help define your organization's needs and requirements. They may include:

- a policy — providing the framework of expectation for environmental responsibility, created internally;

- legal, other requirements — providing a framework of expectation for environmental responsibility, created externally; and

- emergency planning, preparedness, and response capabilities — providing the framework of expectation for environmental activity related to emergencies, created internally, and may include requirements based on external regulations.

"Informational" Tools

Information elements provide specific guidance on issues related to environmental stewardship. The guidance may be internal, external, or a combination of both. The elements may include:

- environmental aspects and impacts — providing parameters and information that indicate where your organization is now regarding environmental stewardship;

- management program — providing specifics on activities, etc., needed to support the policy and requirements;

- operational controls — providing specifics on activities, etc., needed to support the policy and requirements;

- documentation/records — providing guidance to those following the internal and external requirements; and

- monitoring/measurement — providing "real-time" indicators of performance status, and potentially providing information that drives environmental goals and objectives.

"Progressional" Tools

Tools that help drive progress include:

- structure and responsibility — identifying job functions and accountability for the many environmental activities, which helps drive good performance;

- training, awareness, and competence — knowing what "skill set" is needed for the individual with environmental responsibility; identifying and fulfilling training needs to meet those skill set requirements; and providing general awareness training; and

- communication — providing a key activity for success through organized communication programs; driving involvement and awareness of environmental issues; and creating ownership of environmental stewardship.

"Quality" Tools

Quality assurance is an important part of the "Plan-Do-Check-Act" process. Some of the ISO 14001 elements that provide a method for review include:

- document control — ensuring that environment-related documentation is current, accessible, etc.;

- nonconformance and corrective and preventative action — closing the loop when issues are identified, and making sure the issues are permanently fixed;

- management systems audits — conducting periodic audits of the management system, providing information on areas where corrective/preventative actions are needed and where improvement opportunities exist; and

- management reviews — identifying areas where the organizational culture and the business needs meet — and where they don't — through a review by management of the whole environmental management system and how it functions relative to other business processes.

By looking at each element as a function that helps your organization meet requirements and goals, you may identify what you do to provide a framework to the business of environmental management, to supply feedback on the current status of environmental activities, to drive progress, and to check for system quality. The ISO 14001 elements that do not show up on your list of currently used methods may be those you want to focus on. This will give you an opportunity for improvement in your environmental management system.

Your ISO 14001 Expectations

expected
outcome

In exploring what you expect the outcome of implementing the above elements of ISO 14001 to be, you might ask the following questions:

Why have an environmental policy? A list of reasons may include things like:

- to increase visibility of your organization's position regarding environmental issues (is this internal visibility, external visibility, or both?);

- to emphasize an existing commitment to the environment (or to establish one);

- to provide a framework for behavioral expectations within your company.

Why identify environmental aspects? Ideas may include:

- to provide a baseline of information on where your organization is now in relation to potential improvement;

- to help prioritize plans for potential improvement; and

- to help meet regulatory requirements (are these existing requirements or future ones?).

Going through such an exercise with each element may help you define *why* your organization should consider implementing ISO 14001. More important, it may influence *how* your organization looks at such an endeavor.

Many of the ISO 14001 elements can be considered in more than one of these categories. The exercise above is designed to encourage further thinking about why each of the ISO 14001 elements is a value-added tool to your environmental management toolbox.

Collectively these exercises can help identify *what* and *why* your organization should consider ISO 14001. Viewed as a set of tools you can add to your toolbox, each ISO 14001 element can be considered for the results it will have on existing systems, and that's where the "rubber hits the road!"

2.1.5 Before You Commit

commitment

Assuming there are adequate reasons for your firm to investigate implementation of or certification to the ISO 14001 standard, your decision to actually take the plunge still needs careful consideration. You should recognize that today's environmental management issues potentially affect every aspect of a company's operations and can have significant direct and indirect impacts on your bottom line.

You should also note that ISO 14001 is a procedural standard. It is a process, not a product standard; thus, it may not replace your existing environmental program now in place. For many companies, especially those with advanced environmental management programs, an ISO 14001 certifiable program may need to exist in tandem with existing compliance and management vehicles.

standardization vs. decentraliztion

Corporate culture and approaches to environmental management also are key consider- ations. A certain degree of program centralization and a large degree of implicit financial resource commitment will be required to implement ISO 14001.

Constructing and maintaining basic guidelines or procedures addressing environmental management activities may result in a more standardized approach than many organizations have advocated in recent years. Though you could argue that management practices for environmental functions carry such high liabilities and are so dynamic that standardization and a degree of centralization are necessary, this approach may run counter to the increas- ingly decentralized approach of other operational areas that many companies now adhere to. Organizations where corporate or division personnel are reluctant to provide direction to first-line operating entities as guidelines will want to consider this aspect of ISO 14001 implementation.

You must also recognize that, beyond the more obvious costs of implementation as outlined by ISO 14001, maintaining an effective environmental management system will carry with it the implicit resource requirements of follow-up and corrective action.

"Don't look if you are not prepared to deal with what you find," has long been a basic tenet of good environmental audit programs. Although establishing procedures to ensure compliance and perform environmental management systems audits are only part of the 14001 specification, they are an important part, and one that is likely to drive both continual improvement and resource allocation needs.

dynamic process

In implementing or certifying to ISO 14001, you must realize that certification will be a dynamic process, and programs designed to support continual improvement likely will require dedicated continual resources to meet continually identified needs.

top commitment

Because of its likely wide-ranging impacts within your corporation, implementing ISO 14001 requires clear buy-in and support from the top, perhaps more so than any other environ- mental program.

modified
attitudes

Some consultants working with clients who are evaluating their approach to 14001 will not meet with any corporate unit — be it a facility, division, or the corporation itself — if the top person is not in the room. This requirement underscores the fact that ISO 14001, for any organization, will probably require modified approaches and attitudes toward traditional environmental management functions — and allocated resources to make them happen. In most organizations, such changes proceed slowly even with the commitment of top management and may be almost impossible without it.

current system
advantages

Certifying to the procedural ISO 14001 standard will not in itself guarantee environmental excellence. Some proactive companies may find that their existing internal environmental management programs and procedures are more effective than ISO 14001 for managing their environmental responsibilities. Such companies may find it necessary or advisable to consider whether they will need to create a "shadow-program" to their existing environmental management system that will serve to certify the company to the ISO standard but not represent the entirety of the company's system where current elements are more far-reaching.

ISO-izing your
program

Some larger companies with extensive international environmental management programs in place feel that there is a certain wisdom in constituting your auditable ISO program such that it will meet and be certifiable to the standard, yet not contain more information than is necessary. The costs of "ISO-izing" existing programs and procedures in cases such as these therefore may still be significant.

2.1.6 Implementation vs. Certification

A critical distinction can be made between implementation of and certification to the ISO 14001 specification. Implementation would require your organization to conform with the concepts of ISO 14001, though not necessarily to complete the third-party audit that may be necessary to achieve internationally accepted certification.

Implementation not only would be valuable in demonstrating your organization's commitment to proactive environmental management to various stakeholders including employees, regulators, stockholders, and the community — but likely would provide benefits in terms of program effectiveness as well.

implementation
is cheaper,
flexible;
certification is
credible

Implementation without certification would be less costly, and to the greatest degree possible would allow for flexibility in the way your organization accomplishes the goals of ISO 14001. However, this may not satisfy the international marketplace. If your organization has identified international trade requirements or requirements from customers who have trade-related motivations, you may find third-party certification necessary. In fact, on the international scene, it remains to be seen if the marketplace will accept self-declaration of conformance to the standard.

decision is
economic

Ultimately, gaining acceptance of the ISO 14001 specification from management hinges on the drivers behind your corporation's interests, the cultural fit of the standard within your organization, and the relative strength of the pros and cons of committing to implementation, including explicit and implicit costs and benefits. In the end, however, the decision to embrace ISO 14001 is an economic one, not a technical one. Organizations like yours are beginning to realize that some of the greatest bottom-line enhancements in their operations can come from improvements in the way they address environmental management.

The key challenge will be for organizations to create programs that meet the requirements of ISO 14001 yet are still not so cumbersome that they are useless in guiding effective results on the plant floor.

A reminder: ISO 14001 Section 4.3.2 requires that you identify training needs, among other things. This initial training excersise is a good place to start.

2.1.7 When to Seek Training

Whether your organization has just been introduced to the concepts of the ISO 14000 series of standards or you are on the verge of becoming the first company in your industry to implement ISO 14001, you must consider some critical training issues. "Training" can, and usually does, have more than one meaning and implication. And as with most issues that affect your bottom line, the axiom, "If you fail to plan, you plan to fail," holds true.

First, never let the obvious escape you. Consider using the resources you have available to the best of your ability. You may already have someone on staff who can offer a general understanding of the subject. Perhaps you subscribe to a variety of professional publications, or you monitor the latest news pertinent to your organization on the Internet. Your organization may be supported by a professional association. Do you have a consulting firm on retainer? Can your company's ISO 9000 registrar answer any of your ISO 14000 questions? Given the resources you have on hand, your first target should be to raise your awareness in the subject area. Get yourself educated.

Remember, the type and amount of training your company and implementation team receives will play a direct role in the implementation of your environmental management system and its success.

Awareness Training

If your organization has had no previous experience with ISO 14000, consider raising your level of awareness. Moving forward with ISO 14001 implementation may necessitate a complete shift in your existing constructs, moving from compliance to conformance, for example. Therefore, consider overview training for your decisionmakers prior to your decision to implement ISO 14001, well before you select an implementation team.

If you have only a few employees who need training or your employees are located at different sites, consider a management overview course. You will have to weigh the cost/benefit ratio to discern whether bringing a trainer into your facility or sending your employees to a public course is more prudent. The information goal of this initial training should be:

- to learn more about the subject in general;
- to consider major implications;
- to bring ideas for discussion back to management; and
- to bring ideas to the planning table.

If you want to extend your knowledge further, consider purchasing a management level instructional video training package to help you open communication lines for discussion with others.

Moving Forward

Once a "champion" (individual or group) has emerged, your organization must assess its total training needs. You may want to develop a training matrix like the example in Figure 2.1.

Ultimately, the more complex your company is, the more detailed your training matrix will be. The information gathered in this matrix will be helpful regardless of whether an outside consultant helps you determine your training needs or you determine them on your own.

Develop a Training "Wish List"

Create a training "wish list." Brainstorm every conceivable training need to fulfill your implementation plan. Don't forget to include training that benchmarks your company against others within your industry sector.

Realize your limitations. When your existing internal resources no longer can add value to your project or cannot meet extensive training requirements, look outside for help. Think with an eye and an ear focused on the future. You may have budgetary restrictions. Training cost is always a factor. But be aware of the damage that can be done by not using trainers who are well-versed in the topic area.

Skills needed	Number of employees who need training
Awareness	200
Developing an EMS	15
Implementing and EMS	15
Documenting an EMS	5
Internal Auditing	20
Additional Special Skills	etc.

Figure 2.1 — Training decision tool.

Assess the cost differential between the on-site or public training you need to complete your implementation needs. Comparison shop. This information should be readily available from a host of course providers. 📖 (See Part 2, Chapter 4 for more information on training.)

You may find benefits in hiring an outside consultant. 📖 (See Part 2, Chapter 5 for more information on hiring a consultant.) On the other hand, you may already have enough information to proceed on your own.

Training Your Team

If possible, train your cross-functional team together at one location. Obviously logistics and cost will factor into this decision as well, but having your entire team together may buy the philosophical continuity you will need to implement an EMS that demands top management commitment and total employee buy-in.

Training Others

Now that you have a cross-functional team in place, the time has come to execute your total training program. Whether you choose to use third-party trainers or in-house resources, a well-planned training program will save you time and money. It will also help ensure that your ISO 14001 environmental management system is more than a paper exercise.

CHAPTER 2

Gap Analysis Case Study — Caterpillar, Inc.

January 1996

Caterpillar, Inc. has 23 facilities worldwide that are registered to ISO 9001 or 9002, of which Mossville Engine Center (MEC) is one. The MEC site in Peoria, Illinois, has 4,300 employees and was registered in December 1992. Jim Winn, ISO 9001 management representative for MEC, has been with Caterpillar for 28 years. He offers the following advice based on his experience with ISO 9001.

Integrate the EMS with existing requirements. He explains that company procedures have always been benchmarked to stiff regulatory requirements. For this reason, the company did not start its ISO 9000 program from ground zero. "We had been audited by several international marine societies for years and they had pretty much pushed us to do all the right things that were in the ISO streams. We had very few areas that fell between the cracks."

Conduct internal audits early. Winn further recommends auditing early while there is time to correct potential gaps in the program. "The best training tool in your plant is an internal auditor standing face-to-face asking you questions. No amount of lectures, videos, and slides in the classroom means much until you're standing in the manager's office asking for evidence. The best internal training tool is internal auditing." As the first traditional Caterpillar site and the first major diesel engine manufacturer to become registered to ISO 9001 in the U.S., Caterpillar has always used internal auditing to conduct gap analysis surveys. "You have to do internal auditing. You have to write a quality system manual and you have to audit to assure that you're complying to the quality system," Winn says.

Audit to procedures regularly. Caterpillar's MEC has two internal auditors that do this kind of work on a regular basis. They use the quality system manual that is designed by the plant administration to follow a large number of procedures that are defined within the plant. They audit to the quality manual to assure that necessary procedures are defined, then use the procedures to audit to determine whether the company is doing what it says it is doing. Every functional area of the plant is audited once per year, depending on the complexity of the area and its involvement with the quality system. Areas where problems have occurred may be audited more frequently.

Build on current system. MEC is considering certifying to ISO 14000 as well, knowing it has an advantage with the ISO 9001 procedures in place. Many of these procedures have some of the same requirements, such as management review and document control. Winn further explains, "ISO 9000 is a way to manage business relative to quality. If you are adhering to the ISO 9000 scheme, this drives you to organize your business to adhere to any other requirements that you have, especially those that are customer- or regulatory-driven."

Walk the talk. "The whole ISO thing is about 1) say what you do and do what you're saying, and 2) know your customer requirements and have systems in place so that you can adhere to those. The whole structure is how to manage your business so you can make those things happen," Winn points out.

Define your status — Use ISO 14001, ISO 14004 guidance

To conduct a gap analysis, an organization must use some means to define the framework, criteria, and requirements of its current EMS — if one exists. ISO 14001 is silent as to an appropriate methodology for performing this task, as well as for conducting an overall gap analysis. However, some ISO 14001 related documents do provide some useful guidance — for companies with and without an EMS.

ISO 14001 Section A.4.2.1 of Annex A suggests that an organization without an existing EMS should undertake a "review" covering the following four areas:

1) legislative and regulation requirements;

2) an identification of significant environmental aspects;

3) an examination of all existing environmental management practices and procedures; and

4) an evaluation of feedback from the investigation of previous incidents.

Annex A recommends that the review address abnormal as well as normal operations, including potential emergencies. It also identifies "checklists, interviews, direct inspection and measurement, results of previous audits and other reviews . . ." as useful tools for conducting such a review.

ISO 14004 Section 4.1.3 on initial environmental review refers to such an examination as an "environmental review" and enlarges upon its potential scope to include nine possible areas of inquiry. These areas are:

1) identification of legislative and regulatory requirements;

2) identification of environmental aspects of its activities, products, or services to determine those that have or can have significant environmental impacts and liabilities;

3) evaluation of performance compared with relevant internal criteria, external standards, regulation, codes of practice, and sets of principles and guidelines;

4) existing environmental management practices and procedures;

5) identification of the existing policies and procedures dealing with procurement and contracting activities;

6) feedback from the investigation of previous incidents of noncompliance;

7) opportunities for competitive advantage;

8) the views of interested parties; and,

9) functions or activities of other organizational systems that can enable or impede environmental performance.

It also states that its "process and results . . . should be documented and opportunities for EMS development should be identified."

Use initial reviews as tools — Remember, they're not required

The **EMAS-environmental review** (EMAS) defines an "environmental review" as "an initial comprehensive analysis of the environmental issues, impact, and performance related to activities at a site." In Article 3(b), EMAS requires participants to conduct such an initial review, which must include an examination of the 12 environmental issues contained in its Annex I, Part C. **EMAS-Article 3(b); EMAS-Annex I, Part C; EMAS-Item 1, Article 5** 📖 (See Part 9, Chapter 5 for more information on EMAS.)

In Item 1 of Article 5, EMAS also states that registrants must base their first required public environmental statement on the results of the required initial review, and thereafter on required environmental audits.

While these initial review-related provisions of Annex A of ISO 14001, ISO 14004, and EMAS are excellent references for organizations wishing to define their current EMS, they are in no way binding on an organization seeking to demonstrate conformity with ISO 14001.

Initial reviews are required neither expressly nor by implication by the ISO 14001 specification. However, if your organization is seeking to implement ISO 14001 and does not have a formal EMS or has a very immature EMS, you might choose to use some form of an initial review as part of the gap analysis to help you define your EMS inputs and your current EMS.

Tread with caution — Legal marshes may lie ahead

Should your organization choose to conduct an initial review, a word of caution is necessary. After a look at the previously cited initial review references, it is reasonably clear that you should include an examination of your organization's compliance with applicable environmental laws and regulations within the scope of a gap analysis or initial review.

If your company does not do any periodic environmental compliance or systems auditing, a good possibility exists that an initial review including such an audit might uncover previously unknown noncompliance situations. Accordingly, you would be well-advised to consult with your attorneys about the feasibility of conducting the legal compliance segment of your initial reviews under an attorney/client privilege. 📖 (See Part 8, Chapter 1, page xx for more information about legal issues.)

Planning Your Implementation

by Connie Glover Ritzert, Environmental Issues Manager, Alcoa

Note: Before you begin, be sure you have read the ISO 14001 standard line by line.

Once the decision has been made to develop and implement an EMS based on ISO 14001, there are ten steps that any organization will need to take before implementation can begin, regardless of its size or whether an EMS is already in place. Some of these items have been addressed in detail elsewhere in Part 2. You will need to:

1) define the scope of the EMS you want to develop — the boundaries on the organization for which you will implement 14001;

2) review what you already have in place — what management system components and what environmental management processes and programs;

3) set some preliminary criteria for where you want to be — roughly, what will your system look like once it is designed to meet ISO 14001 requirements?

4) do a "gap analysis" — compare where you are with where you want to be;

5) prepare a preliminary plan for developing and implementing your EMS — estimate the actions, time, and resources needed to fill the gaps;

6) do a reality check — review your preliminary plan in light of your goals, gaps, and resources and confirm or adjust the plan;

7) choose a leader or leaders (and a team, if your organization is large enough) for the effort and assign responsibility and authority;

8) allocate sufficient resources to match your plan — financial and human resources;

9) communicate your plan to all affected parties — show your commitment and encourage the involvement and support you will need to be successful;

10) get started — put your plan into action.

To help illustrate gap analyses elements, the editors have included case studies throughout this chapter showing how companies have conducted gap analyses.

2.2.1 Scope

ISO 14001 provides a flexible blueprint that can be applied to whatever segment of your organization you choose, but this means you must make some decisions about the scope of your EMS before you begin the process.

define scope clearly

For large and complex organizations, this will be especially important, since the EMS can be designed for a single unit or an entire multi-unit corporation. Even for small organizations, however, clearly defining scope is important. A small business might consist of three units, two of which are similar and the third different in function — for example, two gas stations and a home heating oil delivery service. Such a business might choose to design an EMS for the two similar units separately from the third unit or it might combine the three, depending upon which approach suited the management style and situation better. Either approach is workable, but the scope should be clearly defined at the outset. 📖 (See Part 1, Chapter 3, Section 5 for more information on certification.)

scoping factors to consider

The scope of your EMS should not be chosen arbitrarily or without consideration of the implications. For many organizations, it will appear obvious that the scope of the EMS should cover the whole enterprise, but that decision should be made consciously. When choosing a scope, consider factors such as:

☑ Is your organization divided into units for any other management purpose?

☑ Is there an existing management system that covers all or portions of your organization?

☑ If there are multiple units, are their functions/products/ services alike or different?

☑ Does your organization have multiple locations?

☑ Is there a reason to implement ISO 14001 in phases across different units of your organization, e.g., do some units have a greater need in the near term?

☑ Is your organization multinational? Would it be more efficient to apply an EMS separately to units located in different countries? (This may or may not be the case.)

☑ Are some units of your organization clearly influenced by stakeholder considerations that are different than those that affect the rest of your organization, e.g., is there a particular unit whose customers have identified an EMS as a point of concern or a condition of doing business?

☑ Is there a unit (or units) that has an existing EMS that already approximates ISO 14001 and for which it would be relatively easy to implement the remaining pieces, adjusting the scope later to incorporate other units?

☑ Would the process of designing and implementing the EMS be more efficient for your organization — considering the existing structure and operating approach — if it were accomplished unit by unit, or more broadly, encompassing the entire organization? (e.g., is your organizational structure centralized? decentralized? networked? line-managed? team-structured? etc.)

☑ Since implementing an EMS will require some resources, is your organization prepared to fund development of the EMS for all units simultaneously or on a phased basis? Which approach will be most cost-effective?

☑ Are there any regulatory considerations for any of your units that would influence the scoping decision, either permanently or in terms of timing?

Your initial decision on scope doesn't have to be final; you will always have the option to revise it, and a phased approach may be appropriate. In most cases, it will be more efficient if you begin with a plan than reflects the right scope for your organization.

2.2.2 Initial Review

Most organizations pursuing an ISO 14001 EMS will not be starting from scratch. Almost all will have some management system(s) in place (e.g., to manage operations, finances, personnel, etc.) and most will have some type of environmental management program. The latter may or may not be a management system, and it may or may not be integrated with other aspects of management.

conduct initial review

In any case, the next step after defining the intended scope of your EMS is to review what systems and programs you do have in place. This is sometimes referred to as an "initial review." (The only circumstance in which an initial review would not be needed would be for new ventures — designing an EMS for a brand-new organization.)

Although the terms "initial review" and "gap analysis" are often applied as synonyms, there is a clear difference between the two. For the purposes of this discussion, an "initial review" is the examination of your existing processes, procedures, and practices in light of ISO 14001 requirements. A "gap analysis" builds on your initial review. It addresses all specific requirements in ISO 14001 and provides detailed point-by-point evaluation that leads to a clear action plan, that should include allocation of human and financial resources in a timetable for implementation.

Note: At this point, you will need to consider when to do your environmental aspects evaluation. In the initial review described here, you are only reviewing your system elements — identifying what you have — not doing an environmental aspects review. For some organizations, it may be efficient to do both at the same time, but it is important not to confuse the two.

A review of your management systems and what functions your organization is currently performing to accomplish environmental management is very different from identifying the aspects of your activities and products that interface with the environment. The latter is a much broader evaluation that produces much different information. Both are important to designing your EMS. This section focuses on the mechanics of preparing for implementation. Identifying environmental aspects is discussed elsewhere. ⬚ (See Part 3, Chapter 1, Section 4 for more information on aspects identification.)

evaluate environmental aspects

If you are designing an EMS for a new organization or one that has no EMS, you will want to begin with an environmental aspects evaluation, but consider some of the following sections on preliminary plans, leadership, and resources before you undertake that evaluation. If you elect to put off an environmental aspects evaluation until you are ready for implementation, make sure it is an early step in that process or tackle it in stages to ensure that input from environmental aspects is included in your EMS design. Much of the benefit of an ISO 14001 EMS comes from the value that an environmental aspects determination can provide.

Preliminary Checklist

initial review checklist

Before beginning your initial review, it may be helpful to set up a preliminary checklist covering the basic elements of the 14001 EMS specification. This will help ensure that you have a clear understanding of what the standard requires and what flexibility exists where decisions will have to be made. It can also help you organize your review into segments, and if your organization is large enough, help you in delegating review segments to appropriate individuals.

Systems Issues and Environmental Issues

It may be helpful to begin your review along two paths: existing management systems and existing environmental management programs. Look at your existing management systems — such as quality systems, financial management systems, and OHS systems — as models of management approaches and examine your approach to environmental issues and responsibilities separately.

No matter how small your organization, it has some system of management. Remember: A system is merely an organized way of doing something that links the pieces (or processes) together.

think "system"   If your organization has a fairly sophisticated system, the environmental issues will already be part of your management systems. If you are just beginning in environmental management, it is likely that environmental programs are less documented and less integrated into a systems approach. The process of developing an EMS will help you bring these issues into your management systems.

Existing Management Systems

One advantage to examining your existing management systems first: It should help you avoid "reinventing the wheel" — developing new environmental management system components or processes when similar processes already exist within your management system for other areas that could be adapted or expanded (for example, a financial planning process, a training records system, or a production objective setting process).

You will want to review your organization's overall management style and structure and consider how these factors will affect decisions on EMS design.

consider management style   A highly centralized organization will need a different approach to implementing an EMS than an organization with multiple units operating with considerable independence. Although these factors were considered in defining the scope of your EMS, they need to be examined in greater detail at this point to define "what you have in place."

record what's in place   Using a preliminary checklist or some other tool, you will want to identify what elements, processes, etc., you have in place in existing management systems that may be applicable (or relevant to) your EMS design. Most organizations will find it useful to capture a brief description of these systems elements at this time rather than just a "check-off." In whatever format is convenient for you, you will want to record what management system components are in place.

build on ISO 9000   For an organization with a formal quality management system in place, such as an ISO 9000 system, this aspect of the initial review is particularly important. There are many compatible and comparable elements of an ISO 9000 and ISO 14001 system. 📖 (See Appendix H for a comparison chart and Part 1, Chapter 3, Section 4 for more information on ISO 9000.)

The 14001 standard encourages integration with 9000 systems. Even if your organization has only begun to implement an ISO 9000 system, starting your review with those activities and maintaining close connections can pay off in efficiency of operation of both quality and environmental management. A table comparing ISO 9001 and ISO 14001 components appears directly in the ISO 14001 document as Annex C. You may want to expand on this table to specifically compare your ISO 900X system to ISO 14001.

If you do not have an ISO 9000 system in place, you still may want to develop a table comparing your management system components (e.g., production, finance, etc.) to ISO 14001 elements as a quick reference aid in further planning efforts. Try a couple of items to see if it makes sense. If it appears to be helpful, do it. If not, don't create data with no purpose. Capture what you need to know about your management systems in some other way.

Existing Environmental Programs

For best results — that is, to get the most useful information out of your initial review — take a critical look at the system or parts of a system you have in place. If you merely use some previously prepared summary of environmental programs for this purpose, you will be missing an opportunity to learn some things that could save you time later in the process.

"say what you do"

Your environmental programs may not have been designed as a system originally. For many companies, environmental management has grown over time as new regulations developed with new compliance requirements. In some cases, these functions have been molded into systems, but in many cases, activities are best described as a series of programs, usually by medium (e.g., water, air, waste), and some supporting functions such as training, communications, etc. Your task at this stage is to examine what is actually in place (actually implemented and working) and consider how each piece fits into an EMS.

Use your ISO 14001 checklist to evaluate methodically what you have in place. The level of detail in your checklist is up to you. At this stage, you may find that you need only work with broad categories. For instance, your organization may be very simple or you may have very few pieces of an EMS in place. For others, with a complex organization and many functions to evaluate, it may be better to work with a detailed checklist to avoid overlooking elements that need attention.

In some cases, a simple "yes, we do have that element in place," or "no, we don't have that element in place," will suffice. In many cases, however, you will find shades of gray. What you have:

- may be only partially developed;
- may or may not meet ISO 14001 requirements; or
- may not be fully implemented.

You may find it useful to use a preliminary grading system. This should be only a rough cut, such as a 1-2-3 scale, since you will be doing an actual gap analysis later, but it might help to get a preliminary picture of where you are. Rely on your own experience and judgment rather than hard data. Avoid getting bogged down in searching for details at this stage.

As with other management systems, you will probably not only want to check off items, or give them a simple "grade," but briefly describe how functions are performed and how they link to one another. The idea is to capture this kind of summary information while you are reviewing it and document it with your checklist. (Get used to documenting!)

Where to Look for Information

key personnel
top sources

For information on what you have in place, consider sources such as:

- quality system documentation;
- policy and procedures manuals;
- standard operating procedures (SOPs);
- work instructions;
- previous reports to management;
- environmental audit reports;
- employee orientation materials; and
- interviews with key personnel.

This last item on the list should not be overlooked as a source of useful information.

undocumented
processes exist

In many organizations, particularly smaller ones, some management processes are in place but have not been documented. The individuals who carry out various functions are the only reliable source of information on what actually is done. Don't assume that just because there is no formal documentation that there is no process or system. If management processes are in place and understood by those who need to know them, the effort to complete your ISO 14001 EMS will be much less than if you have to start from scratch. The challenge is to identify those processes so they can be evaluated and incorporated into the EMS.

Consolidating your Initial Review

Once you have gathered the information on what you have in place and done some preliminary evaluation, you will probably want to package what you know at this point. Try bringing together your checklists for general management systems and environmental programs, looking for overlaps, commonalities, disconnects, and opportunities:

- opportunities to build on good system elements from some other function;
- opportunities to learn from the experiences of those in other functions in your organization;
- opportunities for integration at some point in the future.

Consolidating your information at this point also will aid in the steps to follow, which require that you involve others in the development effort. Communication immediately becomes important.

2.2.3 Preliminary Design

At this point, you are not ready to design your EMS, but you should be ready to set some criteria for that design. Although the 14001 document specifies EMS requirements and a

Gap Analysis Case Study: Monsanto Chemical Company

December, 1995

Monsanto Chemical has 30,000 employees worldwide, with about 700 at the W.G. Krummrich Plant in Sauget, Illinois, where Tom Kreinbrook is quality manager. Monsanto's output covers a broad range of mostly intermediary products; that is, chemicals that go into the production of another product. Some of its well-known items include NutraSweet, Roundup Herbicide, Searle Pharmaceuticals, products for the automotive industry, plastics, Wear-Dated Carpet, and fibers for clothing. Kreinbrook offers the following advice to companies beginning the ISO 14001 implementation process.

ISO 14001 is inevitable. The W.G. Krummrich plant was one of the first sites in the United States to become ISO 9001 certified, so it is experienced in the realm of management systems. In June 1995 it was implementing ISO 14001. "Organizations that do not have ISO 9000 instituted will find it much more difficult to implement ISO 14000," Tom Kreinbrook suggests. He points out that although many people did not take ISO 9000 seriously when it became well-known in the U.S. in 1991, the standard has grown in popularity by leaps and bounds. "Companies using ISO 9000 feel the benefits have far exceeded both their own expectations and the effectiveness of other quality systems." He says that ISO 14001 will go through a similar, positive evolution with U.S. companies as it gains wider acceptance.

Benchmark audits against two systems. Kreinbrook explains that the company double-checks its systems by auditing two ways. (Its version of an audit may be another company's version of an initial review or gap analysis.) First, it audits its environmental management system against the requirements of ISO 14001. In addition, it audits its environmental management system against its corporate requirements. "Our corporate management system may exceed the requirements of ISO 14001," Kreinbrook says. "For a large chemical company like Monsanto, ISO 14001 gives us very few new requirements that we haven't already imposed on ourselves. For this reason, embracing ISO 14001 makes a great deal of sense to us."

Keep the environmental impact analysis broad. When auditing to ISO 14001, it is necessary to define the environmental impacts that products may pose. Keep this analysis broad by focusing on the impact on the community where the manufacturing takes place, the impact on other communities as the products are being transported, the impact the products could have in customers' hands, as well as the impact the products have in a final user's hands.

"If we are manufacturing chemicals to go into a product a consumer buys at the grocery store, we have to look at impacts throughout the whole life-cycle of that product and evaluate all of these," Kreinbrook explains. "I don't think we have been doing studies that are that broad." The life-cycle concept ties together aspects of the community, environmental issues, and business practices. "If we have any gaps in the ISO 14001 standard, this is one area where we do," Kreinbrook adds.

Make self-audits more stringent. "Another gap that we are now addressing is in the area of environmental auditing or self-auditing. According to the standard, EMS self-audits need to be much more stringent and more heavily documented than in the past. In fact, we are conducting our EMS audit as we do our quality system audit. In this area, our past experience with ISO 9000 has really paid off." The document control, auditing, management review, and corrective action systems that are requirements for ISO 14001 are already in place through ISO 9000. Monsanto will be able to expand its ISO 9000 systems to include ISO 14001 requirements, rather than developing another stand-alone system.

Kreinbrook indicates that past environmental audits included recommendations for improvements, but that there was no system in place to make sure that the improvements took place. "Now when we do audits, we don't necessarily make recommendations. We actually cite nonconformances within our own system and issue corrective action requests as we do for quality audits. In issuing corrective action requests, the people they have been issued to must, in fact, identify what the corrective actions will be.

"Once those corrective actions are identified as part of the system, it is a requirement that follow-up audits be done to ensure that identified nonconformances and corrective actions have been put in place and are really effective in solving the problem." This is much more efficient in practice than the old system because the company now knows whether specific, necessary changes have been made.

Give documentation a new image. "In the past," Kreinbrook points out, "people were very reluctant to do a lot of documentation around environmental audits." This is because companies could be cited for an omission, even if it had been corrected. "Now, that whole arena is changing. People are becoming much more comfortable in documenting nonconformances within their environmental system. Once a person becomes more comfortable with documentation, it is also possible to become more effective at implementing solutions and following through with them."

framework, it does not provide a fully designed EMS. That is left to each organization. Before you do a detailed design, it will be helpful at least to create a picture of what your system will look like — create the broad outline of what "should be."

Identifying Decision Points

To begin, use the information you have developed on existing systems (and environmental aspects, if you have begun that process) and the ISO 14001 requirements to identify the decision points in EMS design for your organization. Keep in mind that the EMS should be designed to carry out your organization's environmental policy, and therefore you should use that policy as your guide.

Note: If your organization does not have an environmental policy, work should begin on developing one now. 📖 (See Part 3, Chapter 1, Section 9 for more information on environmental policies.)

define decision points

Decision points are those points in the EMS framework where your organization must choose the approach it wishes to take — as opposed to those points that are prescribed by ISO 14001. For example:

- Setting objectives — A process for setting objectives is required, and some of the considerations in that process are prescribed, but your organization must decide what functions and levels within your organization will participate in the objectives process. (a decision point — what functions and levels of the organization should be involved in setting environmental objectives?)

- Organizational structure and responsibilities — Your organization must define roles, responsibilities, and authorities, but the way in which they are defined and the structure within which they operate must be decided by the organization. (a decision point — what type of structure and responsibility network will be best?)

The usefulness in identifying decision points at this stage is to understand where decisions must be made in the design of your system and where you must only interpret specific requirements in ISO 14001. This is not the appropriate time to start a detailed evaluation. Spend enough time to find the major decision points. You may want to highlight any of these that will require top management involvement.

Based on your organization's policies and circumstances, set at least some tentative guidelines for those decision points that could have a significant effect on your EMS development process. For example:

- EMS documentation — decision point: paper or electronic format — guideline for EMS development: goal is maximum use of electronic format;

- EMS audits — decision point: responsibilities for conducting audits — guideline for EMS development: build audit program around internal audit capabilities.

This exercise should not be extensive or time-consuming, but some consideration of management's intent in system design at this stage may avoid problems later.

Building on Existing Systems

As discussed elsewhere in Part 2, identify those opportunities to build on existing systems that you will use in your first-cut design, using information from the initial review. Consider the decision points above and the decision guidelines you selected. Those existing systems that appear to fill an ISO 14001 requirement, or could do so with modification and are consistent with the guidelines you selected, should be the starting point for your first cut.

The First Cut at "What Should Be"

Using the ISO 14001 checklist (or whatever form you find most convenient for a reference to requirements), your guidelines for decision points, and your starting set of existing system elements, construct a rough outline — or a diagram — of your EMS as you want it to be. This exercise should give you a more useful description of "what should be" for your gap analysis than just the ISO 14001 requirements list alone. The format is up to you. Choose a form that will allow you to depict the key elements and sufficient detail to capture all the requirements, but keep it simple. This should be a working document — not a report.

2.2.4 Gap Analysis

What is a Gap Analysis?

make
comparisons

In simple terms, a gap analysis is a process of determining the difference between what is and what should be. Its purpose is to identify where the gaps are and approximate the size of the gap — i.e., how much of a difference is there between what is and what should be? This information is then used to develop a plan to fill the gaps — to answer the question: What do we need to do to modify "what is" to meet the criteria established for "what should be"?

In this case, you will want to compare the environmental management system elements, processes, etc., you have in place with the first-cut EMS you have prepared from ISO 14001 requirements and the criteria specific to your organization. This will determine the gaps that need to be filled to create an EMS that meets your needs.

Identifying Gaps

In most cases, you will find it useful to perform this exercise on a spreadsheet of some sort. Any format is fine as long as it suits your needs for level of detail and flexibility. For each of the specific requirements of ISO 14001, you will want to ensure that you clearly identify any gaps. If you have questions about interpretation of the ISO 14001 requirement, you may want to seek outside help. Any such questions should be captured for later modification, if necessary. In addition, you will want to identify those gaps that relate to choices you have tentatively made based upon the organization's policies or preferences. For these items, you have another variable — the opportunity to modify your criteria. & See Part 4, Chapter 6, for a sample gap analysis chart.)

Information developed in your initial review should be directly usable in this gap analysis. Those data have been used in developing your "what is," but take another look at that consolidated review information for help in understanding the gaps.

You may find that you have some gaps in all elements of the EMS or that some elements are essentially complete, and your gaps are isolated in a few elements. These factors will influence your development and implementation plans, timing, resources, etc., so capturing this type of information now will be helpful.

Steps Toward Quantifying Gaps

estimate action
plan

Once you have identified where your gaps are, you will want to estimate the size of the gap, asking "What will it take to fill the gap?" It may be helpful to use a rating or grading system to either categorize or assign some relative values to the effort required to fill the gaps. You may have a head start on this approach if you used a rough grading scale in the preliminary review. Don't expect to be able to quantify the gaps fully at this point. Usually you will need more data than you have. The purpose is to estimate sufficiently the activities and the extent of effort required to put a plan of action together. It is not expected that you will be able to predict accurately the final outcome at this point. Once again, you will have to use your judgment.

At the end of this exercise, you should have the information you need to develop a plan of

Gap Analysis Case Study: Anheuser-Busch Inc.

January 1996

Anheuser-Busch Companies employs 42,600 people and encompasses 160 facilities worldwide that include breweries, SeaWorld parks, canning businesses, a railroad and railroad car manufacturing business, printing services, agricultural and food businesses, breweries in London and China, and joint venture breweries in Japan and Mexico. Of these sites, 78 have environmental management systems in place. Bill Sugar, director of environmental affairs for Anheuser-Busch Inc., offers the following advice based on his experience beginning the ISO 14001 process.

Research other systems. Sugar has researched environmental systems for several years. He worked on the Business Charter for Sustainable Development developed by the International Chamber of Commerce (ICC) that came together in Rotterdam, the Netherlands, one year before the Earth Summit in Rio de Janeiro in June 1992. This program operates under the auspices of the Global Environmental Management Initiative (GEMI). The charter's 16 principles have been endorsed by 1,200 companies worldwide. These principles deal directly with the environment but include health and safety issues as well. AB benchmarked to the 16 principles, deciding where it wanted to be in a few years and developing strategies to achieve its goals.

Build in corporate requirements. Anheuser-Busch created 23 corporate requirements, some of which focus on what senior management wants to do to protect the environment. In this way, AB was able to build its environmental management system into the corporate mission statement and policy, calling the EMS program "Commitment to Environmental Excellence." Sugar points out the logical link between its quality management system-integration quality and environmental programs: "AB has always had an interest in quality — not ISO 9000 — and calls our quality program "Commitment to Excellence." For this reason, he says, linking quality to environmental issues is a logical next step. "If you're doing the right thing for the environment, you're very likely doing the right thing for total quality. With total quality, you want to achieve integration." He feels that if each person does a share of the 23 corporate requirements, everyone is involved in the environmental issues as well.

Develop a delivery system that suits your needs. With AB's many diverse sites, dealing with a single EMS becomes a very complex issue. "We needed to have a delivery system and wrestled with that," Sugar explains. "Now we have an electronic quality manual that is built on a Lotus Notes platform. Each manual is developed as each audit is completed and incorporates federal, state, and local laws, regulations, and applicable parts of the corporate policy, all as they apply to the particular operation. One of the components of the computer program is a calendar linked with a compilation of responsibilities to be accomplished that week. The layers of the system allow integration of corporate functions and interactions with other groups."

Build support tools into the delivery system. Customized support tools need to be built into the EMS delivery system. Sugar explains some examples of this: "We have a model spill prevention plan that can be used to build a new spill prevention plan. In addition, we have a model permit form and model databases, all of which are an outgrowth of the 16 principles and gap analysis. TQM pulls it all together. If the lettering on a particular program screen is a certain color, the user can click on it and up pops a support tool to help do the job. This empowers the employee to get the job done."

action for developing and implementing an EMS that conforms to ISO 14001 and meets your organization's needs. Document what you have done and make sure that you will be able to communicate process and results to management and others working on the project.

2.2.5 Plan

Converting Your Gap Analysis Into Action Items

The gap analysis should tell you what needs to be done. Now you must determine how it can be done. This plan will be unique to your organization. It is not an ISO 14001 requirement and there are no "rules" other than the processes your organization employs for planning. You will want to identify:

- the steps that need to be taken, in the appropriate order;
- the decisions that will need to be made;
- the tools, input, etc., that will be needed; and
- feasible approaches to accomplishing the tasks.

There are many tools to assist in planning that can be found in general management texts. A good plan at this point will help you gain management support for the effort and improve chances of producing a workable system.

A common tendency is to jump directly into doing, rather than planning — that is, to begin developing and implementing portions of the EMS without going through the remaining preparation steps. That approach may work well for some, if the gaps are small, resources are not critical, and there already is good buy-in at various levels of the organization.

plan first-act later

However, in most cases, time spent on planning at this point will be worthwhile and will help you produce a more effective EMS more efficiently.

Even for small organizations, this step is useful and should not be overlooked. Your planning step does not have to be long or complicated. Like many components of the EMS itself, the scale of your effort should be consistent with the size and complexity of your organization. Your planning effort may be accomplished in less than an hour.

To construct a plan of action to go from your gap analysis to an actual EMS that can be both described and implemented, think through the questions that need to be answered. These might include:

☑ number of gaps to fill — Is this a major effort or a small project?

☑ size of gaps — Making many small program adjustments is very different from developing a few major components from scratch.

☑ how to fill the gaps — Do you already know what you want to implement or do you have a lot of development to do?

☑ unanswered questions; additional information needed — Does your plan need to include more investigation of the "what is"?

☑ how to get the necessary information — What sources? What is critical and what can be added later?

☑ management decisions required — Can you proceed with action steps or do you need additional approvals? Are there choices that management needs to make? Has management been made aware of its options?

☑ priorities — Are there some gaps that are critical and need to be filled first? Should you work on the EMS in stages? Should you tackle the easy parts first and schedule the more difficult or complex parts over time?

☑ deadline — Is there a goal for completion?

☑ timing — How much time do you estimate it will take to complete design? To implement?

☑ who should be involved — Do you know what resources you need to complete the EMS design? Do you know what resources are available?

☑ budget — Can you estimate costs? Has a budget been set?

The most important thing about your plan is that it be useful in accomplishing your objective — to develop and implement an ISO 14001 EMS. You must judge how much planning is enough.

Estimating Resources and Schedules

This is usually the most difficult part of the planning process. If you have never developed an ISO 14001 EMS before, estimating resources and timing can be very difficult. There is no magic formula. Even in the smallest organization, some estimate of people resources and other costs, together with a schedule with milestones and decision points, will be needed.

Suggestions:

- Use ISO 9000 experience — If your organization has implemented an ISO 9000 quality management system, you should have some good information on development costs. Although building an ISO 14001 EMS will not be identical, there should be both many similarities and many ways in which costs can be reduced by building on your ISO 9000 experience. 📖 (See Part 3, Chapter 3 for more information on building on ISO 9000 experience.)

- Try a "pilot" — Identify one segment of your operation or one portion of your EMS that could be approached as a trial, or pilot. By carefully tracking costs, resources, and timing associated with a small effort, you can get the data you need to better estimate the overall effort. 📖 (See Part 8, Chapter 2, and Part 10, Chapters 2 and 5 for more information on existing pilot programs.)

- Collaborate with others — If your organization belongs to a trade association or other group, it could be beneficial to share information on such things as resources — or to share resources, if that seems appropriate. The experience of others may not be directly applicable to your situation, but it could be useful as a starting point.

- Focus on the action plan to develop the EMS — Remember that the resources and schedule you are defining now are for the development stage first. Once your system is defined, you will need to address the broader issue of resources to carry out the functions of the EMS as part of the implementation process and of ongoing improvement of the system.

2.2.6 Reality Check

Revisit the purpose of your plan: a road map for developing and implementing an ISO 14001 EMS that meets the particular needs of your organization.

✦ do a quick check

Does the plan:

✓• address the scope you selected?

✓• consider the systems you already have in place?

✓• reflect your best estimate of the type of EMS you want to achieve?

✓• look realistic in terms of timing and resources?

✓ tell you what actions need to be taken, in what order, by whom, with what resources to develop and implement an ISO 14001 EMS that meets the needs of your organization?

The level of detail you want will vary with your organization. Some plans for this purpose can exist on one page and still be effective.

2.2.7 Leadership

Building an EMS and putting it into place is a project that will require a leader, or champion. This must be someone with the responsibility and authority to take the actions necessary and with the commitment to meet the organization's goals for an EMS. This could be one individual or more than one individual working as a team, depending upon the size and nature of your organization.

The leadership for the project should be identified as soon as possible to get the best results from the planning process. Keep in mind that the leader(s) of the effort to develop an EMS need not be the same as the individual(s) assigned responsibility for the operation of the EMS (although the operating staff should be included in the process).

For example, your organization might choose to assign a leader for the EMS development project from:

• the quality function, based on experience with ISO 9000;

• the environmental compliance function, based on experience with the current EMS and requirements;

• operations management, based on knowledge of the organization;

• an engineering function, based on experience with systems approaches and standardization; and/or

• the environmental, health, and safety staff, based on experience in integrating technical, regulatory, and policy considerations.

In many cases, a team approach will be most effective, particularly in organizations where the activities will require cooperation across functional lines. Since the EMS will operate throughout the organization, not just within an environmental department, it is important to bring the ideas, concerns, and information from multiple functions into the development process as early as possible, within resource limitations.

Whether leadership is provided by an individual or a team, it is important to be clear about responsibilities and authority — who will take responsibility for what part of the development effort and who has authority to make what types of decisions.

2.2.8 Resource Allocation

Your planning process has identified the resources needed, at least enough to get started. To ensure that the process of developing an EMS is carried out successfully, your organization's management must commit those resources to the project. This is a simple step, but one that needs to be clearly understood by all participating in the effort. If individuals in various functions will be called upon to provide information or assistance, they must understand how that time will be allocated. If external resources are to be used, such as outside consultants, provisions need to be made for contracting for those services.

Your organization may wish to capture costs for the project for future benefit/cost evaluation, for use in planning other similar projects, as preliminary information for capturing ongoing costs associated with environmental management, or for other accounting purposes.

In allocating resources, be sure to include the concept that specific skills or knowledge may be needed — not just the concept of cost. If there are key individuals in the organization whose input is essential to designing the EMS, you may want to get a commitment for their participation.

2.2.9 Communication

The key to success in most endeavors is good communication, at the right time, to the right people. Developing an EMS is no exception. If you consider communication an integral part of the project, rather than something tacked on at the end, your ability to successfully implement the EMS will be greatly improved.

Following the simple rules of effective communication, you will want to:

begin early
- Begin early in the process — Let people who may be affected by your process of investigating an EMS know what you are doing. Don't wait until the decision to move forward has been made. In most cases, you will need the cooperation of several people to gather information and develop an EMS that will work. Especially in small organizations, it would be difficult to build an EMS without involving people. When there are only a few people in an organization, it is more likely that things are accomplished through a common understanding of what needs to be done and how things should be done. In large organizations as well, early communication will pay off in better acceptance of the resulting system.

set objectives
- Set your communication objectives — Decide what you want to achieve in your communication. This will help you get the right message across without overwhelming people with too much communication, spending too much time, or missing the mark.

For example, at the beginning of the effort, what you really want to achieve may be to get management's approval for preliminary planning and cooperation from various departments in acquiring information. You can set such limited objectives at the outset, or, if you are confident that the project will move forward, you may want to set broader objectives that carry through the entire planning process.

target
- Target your communication — Based on your objectives, you will want to identify what to communicate and to whom. In many cases these two aspects are nearly inseparable — the what and the who. Consider which individuals or functions in the organization will need detailed information and which need only general concept information. For example, prospective members of the development team will need considerably more input than, for instance, the sales department, which may only be peripherally involved.

  Things you may want to communicate include:

  – what an EMS is;

  – the organization's interest in an ISO 14001 EMS;

  – who is working on the project;

  – your schedule;

  – information you will need;

  – the benefits you see from the EMS in the future; and

  – a variety of more specific things for those actually involved.

- Communicate regularly — To build support for the EMS that will be implemented, try to provide some communication on a regular basis. Some form of update mechanism works best for general interest, while those individuals who are participating directly will have differing needs for input.

Once you have initiated communication on the subject, don't let it drop without closing the issue, even if the project is discontinued. Some simple means of regular communication can usually be accomplished without strain on resources — for example, a bulletin board posting, E-mail messages, or articles in the organization newsletter. Don't forget to consider direct word-of-mouth communication, particularly in smaller organizations. Talking directly with key individuals at intervals may be the best mechanism for ensuring good communication.

You will want to use the type and frequency of communication that makes sense for your organization, keeping in mind that it is a tool to help you succeed in developing and implementing your EMS, not an end to itself.

2.2.10 Getting Started

Each organization will have a different approval cycle for taking action — a different set of hoops, so to speak. At this point in your preparation, you should be ready to proceed — to implement your action plan and develop your EMS — but this may be a crucial point in your organization's decisionmaking process. This may be the point at which a decision to go forward is needed. If so, you should be well prepared, having done your homework in the previous steps.

The Difference Between an Initial Review and Gap Analysis

—from International Environmental Systems Update, December 1995

"Too many U.S. companies are confused over the difference between the terms 'initial review' and 'gap analysis,'" according to Cornelius "Bud" Smith. Smith is director of Environmental Management Services for ML Strategies Inc., a management consulting firm in Danbury, Conn., and chairman of the U.S. TAG SubTAG 2 on environmental auditing,

While some experts may use the terms interchangeably, Smith explains why it is vital that companies understand the differences and the implications associated with each. According to Smith, this understanding could be the difference between going to prison or not.

Smith says every company or organization seeking to implement ISO 14001 will have to conduct some variation of a gap analysis that compares its current EMS with the criteria of ISO 14001. This procedure will help it identify the system improvements necessary to achieve conformity with the standard.

Every EMS, he notes, is a web of interrelated components, including such basic elements as a policy, planning and goal-setting, programs (e.g., training), measurement, auditing, reporting and communications, documentation and recordkeeping, and management review.

These components will vary from organization to organization depending on their relevant EMS inputs. In addition to ISO 14001, those EMS inputs may include requirements from environmental laws and regulations, industry commitments (e.g., the chemical industry's Responsible Care® initiative), and other applicable criteria such as organization internal requirements. Below he offers insights regarding the differences between an initial review and gap analysis, and points out relevant sections in ISO standards for guidance.

Define your inputs

The first steps in conducting an ISO 14001 EMS gap analysis are to define your organization's EMS inputs and to break each of them down into a comprehensive set of meaningful subcategories.

For example, you might subdivide reporting into internal and external communications, and then again into different audiences such as management, employees, shareholders, local communities, governmental agencies, etc. For each subcategory, you should develop a list of all applicable requirements of each identified EMS input.

Since the ultimate objective is the definition of "the organization's EMS" rather than a series of individual systems related to each EMS input, you should combine the systems elements into a single set of desired organization EMS requirements for each subcategory.

When the organization compares its desired EMS requirements with its current EMS requirements, the differences identified for each subcategory will be the "gaps," or the product of the gap analysis, which will have to be addressed by the organization in order to conform to ISO 14001. The amount of effort and the degree of difficulty of conducting a gap analysis will vary depending on the complexity of the organization and the quality of its current EMS.

Once you get the go-ahead, be sure to use what you have developed in this preliminary planning process. In some cases, a disconnect will develop between the original plan and the actions being taken. If a course correction is needed, make the change to your plan, not just to the actions you are taking. Refer to the gap analysis and supporting information as needed to help keep you on course.

It may be helpful to build in some early feedback to management and to other interested parties — indications that you are making progress, any unexpected developments, small successes, etc. As you move forward, you will want to begin the process of identifying opportunities for improvement as the first steps in your continual improvement process.

2.2.11 How Much Time Will All This Take?

If you have read through this section on preparing for implementation, you are probably wondering how much time all this preparation and planning will take. It doesn't have to take a lot of time. For a small organization, you might be able to go through all of the suggested steps in a day or two. For a large, complex organization, this pre-planning stage will be important and could have several decision loops in it. In that case, it could take a few weeks and cover an elapsed time of several weeks.

Just as ISO 14001 only identifies the components of an EMS but doesn't develop your system, this outline only suggests preparation steps that may be useful; it doesn't prescribe your preparation. The amount of time it takes to make adequate preparation will depend on your judgment and your choices.

CHAPTER 3
Gaining Stakeholder Acceptance

by Nancy Evans Stuckwisch, Consultant,
TECHNE Environmental Consulting

Under the terms of ISO 14001, developing and implementing a comprehensive program for involving stakeholders in your organization's EMS is a decision left virtually up to management discretion.

In **ISO 14001 Section 4.3.3** on communications it states, "The organization shall establish and maintain procedures for . . . receiving, documenting and responding to relevant communication from external interested parties regarding its environmental aspects and environmental management system. The organization shall consider processes for external communication on its significant environmental aspects and record its decision." 📖 (See Part 3, Chapter 2, Section 4 and Part 3, Chapter 3, Clause 4.3.3 for more information on this section.)

go beyond
requirements

If your organization were to include this element in its EMS program, you would satisfy the ISO guidelines. However, you would have lost a tremendous opportunity to add credibility, transparency, and value to your EMS by not going beyond the ISO recommended minimum and voluntarily implementing a comprehensive stakeholder program.

Gap Analysis Case Study — BF Goodrich

January 1996

Once known as a tire manufacturer, BF Goodrich has about 13,000 employees worldwide at 71 sites in ten countries and is now manufactures specialty chemicals and aerospace systems and components. The company also provides maintenance and overhaul services for large commercial aircraft. BF Goodrich designs instruments for aerospace, such as speed, air,and pressure sensors, landing gear, safety systems, brakes, and wheels. Its specialty chemical business manufactures a broad array of polymers, additives, and coatings with intermediate and final applications.

Ron Black, corporate director of health, safety, and environmental management systems for BFG, explains that throughout 1995, his company measured its existing HS&E site systems against company systems guidelines. At the same time we took a look at how our system stacked up against ISO 14001 specifications. Not only does our corporate systems guidelines parallel 14001, in some areas we excel.

The company wants to be positioned to make the shift to certifying to the standard if market factors favor registration. It has many facilities that are ISO 9000 certified. Black says, "one viable option is to integrate ISO 14000 and 9000 systems." However, most companies are viewing ISO 14001 basically as we are, that is, looking internally to see how they match up with 14001 and taking a 'wait and see' attitude in terms of registering to ISO 14001."

Combine ISO 14000 concepts with regulatory compliance issues. Black points out that while it was initially assumed that customers would drive 14000, his sense is that "the engine with a little more thrust is the regulatory engine." Some states, such as Pennsylvania, are looking for substitutes for compliance enforcement programs. Jim Seif, Department of Environmental Protection of Pennsylvania in testimony before the state Senate Environmental Resource and Energy Committee said, We see ISO 14000 and our new tools as a way to improve the competitiveness of our businesses in the global market place and to lower environmental compliance cost." States are considering programs that recognize ISO 14000 registrants as environmentally responsible companies. This would allow states to focus their limited resources on those companies needing assistance. "Some people in the EPA have said this was a possibility. If you look at all the potential stakeholders, such as governments, customers, enforcement agencies, and communities, it appears that the regulatory stakeholders have stepped up front." He adds that while customers and suppliers could become drivers of ISO 14000, that does not appear to be the case in the U.S. at this time.

Develop structures to deal with gaps strategically. Black explains that he sees gap analysis on two levels: 1) measurement or assessment of performance within the company's organization's sites, segments, or divisions as it relates to the company's environmental management systems

guidelines, and 2) identifying any differences between the company's EMS and ISO 14001 requirements. BF Goodrich has developed and implemented HS&E guidelines in the following key areas:

1) leadership and accountability;

2) stakeholder outreach and involvement;

3) strategic planning;

4) performance measurement;

5) procedures and controls;

6) audit and assurance;

7) reporting;

8) product stewardship; and

9) training.

"When we take these strategies and match them up against ISO 14001, we find significant alignment," Black notes.

Incorporate other programs into your EMS. ISO 14001 also requires that organizations fully
implement the requirements of programs to which they subscribe, such as the International
Chamber of Commerce Sustainable Development Charter or Responsible Care®. BF Goodrich has
added two specific areas: the Responsible Care Code and the Department of Justice Guidelines, both
of which are built into its systems' elements. "These systems will also be evaluated under ISO
14001," Black says. 📖 (See Part 8, Chapter 1, Section 3 for more information on DOJ Guidelines.)

The Responsible Care Code is part of the membership requirement for the Chemical Manufacturers
Association in the United States. It is made up of six codes: 1) distribution, 2) process safety, 3)
product stewardship, 4) pollution prevention, 5) Community Awareness and Emergency Response
(CAER), and 6) employee health and safety. The Responsible Care Code, which includes 26
principles listed under these six codes, is now implemented in the United States and 22 countries.

The Chemical Manufacturers Association not only collects data on Responsible Care, but also sends
out audit teams to verify systems implementation. In addition to this being a third-party audit, CMA
requires that a person from the community be on the audit team. "This has been extremely
successful," Black comments. "The people who have participated as representatives of the
community have written some really nice letters about how well they thought that program was
working."

National Wildlife Federation Perspective

by Nancy Evans Stuckwisch,
TECHNE Environmental Consulting and Barbara Haas, Director,
Corporate Conservation Council, National Wildlife Federation

The National Wildlife Federation (NWF) was the first environmental organization in the United States to become involved in the ISO 14000 negotiations. While NWF involvement does not automatically equate with endorsement of the final product, NWF has actively worked to bring more stakeholders to the ISO table in the United States. Publication of ISO 14001 marks an obvious and important turning point in the process from negotiation to implementation.

However, NWF believes that, for ISO 14001 to be as effective and credible as possible, the trend of stakeholder involvement begun in the negotiations must continue and intensify as individual organizations implement the standard. Collaborative efforts are necessary to address the environmental problems we all face. The National Wildlife Federation has been a long-standing advocate of this philosophy. In 1982, NWF established the Corporate Conservation Council, a cooperative joint venture between NWF and business leaders demonstrating that environmental protection and economic development need not be mutually exclusive. This same principle now needs to be applied by organizations using ISO 14001.

An environmental management system will be able to address the environmental aspects of an organization's operations and activities only if the organization has a clear conception of those issues. To get the entire picture, the input of all parties affected by or interested in those environmental aspects needs to be heard and considered. Application of this input from diverse stakeholders will strengthen the organization's environmental management system in the long run. If you apply this input from diverse stakeholders, you will only strengthen your environmental management system in the long run.

ISO 14001 was developed and is being implemented because organizations need to demonstrate to a wide variety of groups, not just environmental advocates, that they conduct themselves in an environmentally responsible fashion. Omitting the environmental concerns of a stakeholder group may lead other stakeholders to doubt the ability of an organization to manage its environmental issues. Conversely, the inclusion of stakeholders in the environmental management system process can add a breadth and depth of understanding to the environmental management system and will put the company in a much better position to effectively manage its environmental issues.

Below are some important issues you should consider regarding stakeholder relations. This chapter will address some reasons to involve stakeholders. It will examine three key aspects you will need to understand about stakeholders in order to build an effective relationship with them:

1) stakeholder identification;

2) understanding stakeholder interests and perceptions of ISO 14001; and

3) strategic suggestions for gaining stakeholder acceptance.

The term "stakeholder" referred to in the ISO 14000 series as "interested party" is defined as "an individual or group concerned with or affected by the performance of an organization."

When faced with such a broad definition, knowing where to begin gaining stakeholder acceptance may present a challenge. You should ask these two critical questions:

☑ Do you know your stakeholders?

☑ Which of your organization's activities and operating issues are the most critical in their minds?

Why Involve Stakeholders?

To begin with, should you attempt to gain stakeholder acceptance?

Under the terms of ISO 14001, the decision to communicate with stakeholders/interested parties is entirely one of internal management. In recent years, businesses have dramatically altered their perceptions of external group interest. Previously, stakeholder concern focused almost exclusively on an organization's financial performance. The emergence and growth of environmentalism have added a new dimension to that traditional focus. Environmental performance is increasingly an area of interested party pressure.

This demand for improved environmental performance has taken different forms.

pressure — One form of this pressure has been driven by environmental advocates who have pushed organizations to improve their environmental performance. Although there have been exceptions, these relationships have typically been adversarial. The tactics of environmental advocates have included drawing attention to a particular aspect of an organization's activities and using the resulting attention as leverage to force a change in behavior.

Another type of pressure has come from consumer demand. Many consumers have become more environmentally aware and have demanded that firms alter their operations that result in negative environmental consequences. The market potential of the "green consumer" is something that firms are not taking lightly.

Regardless of the source, environmental pressure on organizations has been growing for some time. Environmental issues are now a factor that no company can afford to disregard. The proliferation of EMS approaches and now the international harmonization of EMS guidelines under ISO 14001 offer evidence of the importance of managing environmental concerns in the business world.

Just as stakeholders played a vital role in creating the atmosphere leading to ISO 14001 role in success   development, they will also have a similar part in determining its success or failure. Including environmental stakeholders in the EMS process will allow individual organizations and interested parties to develop cooperative relations, with each party working to understand and address the concerns of the other.

ISO 14001 is intended to provide your organization with a means of effectively managing the environmental aspects of your operations and activities. Environmental advocates have been successful in raising the sensitivity of other interested parties to environmental issues. If external groups are excluded from the EMS implementation process and if they question the value of ISO 14001, they could damage its credibility before it is even given an opportunity to perform.

2.3.1 Identifying and Understanding Stakeholders

For your organization to gain stakeholder acceptance, you will need to pay careful attention to using the most complete and accurate information possible about your stakeholders. Almost every organization will have a wide array of external groups interested in it. These groups will not be homogenous. Each will have its priorities and perspectives.

Potential sources of stakeholder activity include:

- environmental advocacy groups;
- local community organizations;
- trading partners;
- customers;
- investors and insurers;
- the media; and
- employees.

bringing them in from the cold   Of all these groups, gaining acceptance from environmental advocates and local organizations likely will be the most challenging. These parties have traditionally worked from the "outside" and do not share the same interest in your organization as other stakeholders do. Therefore, the following information will focus on these two types of organizations. Stakeholder development programs aren't going to be "one-size-fits-all." Each organization will be faced with unique circumstances that will determine the specifics of its approach.

The first group is from the environmental advocacy community. These are likely to be regional, national, or international parties with an interest in one or more of the specific environmental impacts of your organization's activities and operations. Within this category of stakeholder there will be a great deal of diversity. Some groups will be confrontational and others more cooperative. However, the primary purpose of all of them is to advance environmental concerns and exert pressure for environmentally beneficial change.

U.S. TAG seeks stakeholder input   In an attempt to increase stakeholder representation on the U.S. Technical Advisory Group to TC 207, the National Wildlife Federation and the U.S. TAG have made a concerted effort to educate and involve more environmental groups in the ISO process. Interest was limited at first, but is growing slowly. Therefore, since 1994 a few of the advocacy groups have had some knowledge of ISO 14001; however, they were also likely to be skeptical of it. Some groups will continue to question the efficacy of a voluntary, management approach to environmental performance. That the ISO 14000 series is only a guideline that sets no performance standards is another source of concern for these groups. They will want to see conclusive results that lead to improved environmental performance.

The surrounding community almost certainly will be another source of stakeholders for your organization. These groups will represent the concerns of the population living in the immediate vicinity of your organization. This geographic area may contain more than one active group. Their catalyst for action is likely to be concern over the state of the local environment, rather than "environmentalism" per se.

Along with more general environmental concerns, a priority for community groups probably also will be specific risks and hazards the surrounding area and population may be exposed to as a result of business operations. Many other issues, such as environmental justice, may be brought into the mix. The range and nature of the issues community organizations want to address may be broader and less strictly "environmental" than those of advocacy groups. The community groups are concerned with the overall welfare of the people and places they represent, and their agendas will reflect their specific priorities.

Community-Right-to-Know regulations have significantly increased the amount of information available to local communities, and these groups are becoming increasingly active as they obtain information and demand action about the issues that affect them. Community groups probably will not have any direct experience with ISO 14001 since none of them were involved in its formulation in the U.S.

Once your organization has made an initial assessment of the type of interested parties it is likely to encounter, it should move on to the design of a program to bring stakeholders into its ISO implementation process.

- what frequency of delivery will be;
- what media will be used; and
- whose responsibility is it to see that the message will be delivered.

For example, your organization should have a clear strategy laid out to answer these questions when considering the spread of the message from top management, to mid-management, to staff. It is most likely that as the message is diffused throughout your organization the subject and frequency of the message will change, responsibility for its delivery will alter, and different media will be appropriate to use at different times.

Tailor the message

be sensitive

A second issue elaborates further on "from" and "to" of the last section. As the message is spread throughout your organization it should be divided into two parts. The first is done from the "top-down." This involves key managers (the CEO, etc.) repeatedly delivering and reinforcing the message about what your organization is trying to do. This will demonstrate that there is strong commitment to the project or program at the very highest levels of management.

An essential follow-up to that message of commitment should then be spread by representatives from functional areas. These individuals should spend more time delivering a tailored message as it applies to specific business areas. They should also be answering questions, concerns, and issues that staff members may have about how this program will affect them.

Repeat the message

The third component concerns the frequency of the message's delivery. When implementing a stakeholder program, or any other major change, the message must be delivered more than once and particularly at key times during the project's life.

For example, your organization may choose to address this issue in the following way. A first message may be sent prior to the initiation of the project to act as a "heads-up" to your organization. A second, reinforcing message could be sent at initiation to inform your organization of the formal structure, goals, and objectives of the program. Third, during the program, members of your organization need to receive the information on "what this means to me."

Deliver context

The fourth component provides some further context for the subject matter that is being delivered, the "what" of the road map. In addition to the traditional message of "project management" your organization should also be disseminating information that concerns this program in the context of "change management." Traditional project management messages concern issues like timetables and resources; while this message is necessary, it is not sufficient by itself. Members of your organization need to understand the greater context in which the project is occurring. Therefore, the "change management" aspect of your organization's communication needs to underpin and reinforce company strategies and change plans.

2) Establish a dialogue.

The next stage of the process is to establish dialogue with the stakeholders. You should view this as an opportunity to further refine your understanding of the various interests of the groups. Your organization should also make sure it does not unintentionally neglect to establish contact with a group.

Some sources to consider when making a good-faith effort to locate suitable stakeholders include:

- contacting local officials for suggestions;
- contacting a local planning agency for suggestions;
- asking your organization's own employees, including plant/site managers and public relations personnel;
- contacting local schools, community colleges, or universities; and
- contacting a national advocacy group to see if they can make any suggestions as to local or national groups who may be interested/suitable.

While your organization is communicating internally about its stakeholders, you must also inform the stakeholders about your organization. Depending upon your stakeholder groups'

talk about
company

prior knowledge of your organization, it may be necessary to further inform them about your activities. Your organization will certainly want to disseminate and discuss its environmental policy (as formulated under the EMS specification document) and make known its commitment to stakeholder relations. More specifically, you should also present the stakeholders information about ISO 14001 itself and the EMS program you are implementing.

As stated earlier, the amount of direct experience with ISO 14001 among the stakeholder communities may be limited. There is great potential for misperception about what EMS is and what its limitations are. If interested parties do not understand the ISO 14001 EMS, they may have unrealistic expectations of it. Not to educate the stakeholders and correct those misperceptions will only undermine credibility at some point and jeopardize attempts to bring external groups into the ISO implementation process.

Disseminate information

There are many methods of outreach to consider when attempting to inform stakeholders about your organization and its activities. These may include one or more of the following media for disseminating information:

- producing a fact sheet about your organization's activities, the EMS program, why and how your organization would like to include stakeholders;

- holding public meetings;

- establishing a phone line to answer questions, record concerns, etc.;

- scheduling tours of your organization; and

- going to local schools, community colleges, universities, or other local groups that may provide a focal point of interest about your organization.

two-way
process

Furthermore, you should also ensure that this dialogue is a two-way participatory process. The stakeholders will want to know that their comments and concerns are being listened to and taken into account. They will not accept ISO 14001 unless they think that your organization is genuinely and actively including them.

3) Evaluate Results.

The final step in this process is to assess and evaluate the results of the first two stages. All the parties will have an interest in seeing what the results of the dialogue and the EMS are.

☑ Were the goals set in a consensus-based manner that reflect the issues and priorities of all the parties?

☑ Were those goals met?

☑ If not, why not?

☑ How can what has been learned be applied in the future?

Just as the ISO 14001 process uses a feedback loop to strengthen your organization's EMS, the stakeholder involvement process should do likewise. Feedback to and from all parties is vital because a successful stakeholder program will have to be an ongoing effort. It will not be sufficient to go through one cycle and stop there. All the stakeholders will have evolving agendas and the dialogue must stay open in order to act on that information to everyone's benefit.

2.3.2 Stakeholder Program Checklist

The following checklist will provide some suggestions you should consider when setting up a stakeholder program. While this list is not exhaustive, it offers some important steps in understanding and matching the needs of stakeholder concerns:

☑ Develop a strategy for your stakeholder program.

- Why do you want to develop this strategy?

- What do you want to accomplish with a stakeholder or interested party program?

- What steps will your organization need to take to accomplish this stakeholder program?

☑ Identify potential stakeholders.

- Begin with initial information gathering — look for possible interests/priorities of potential stakeholders. You are not trying to create stakeholders; rather, you are trying to deal with those appropriately interested in your goods, products, or services. You should match up your environmental issues with the stakeholder concerns germane to those particular environmental issues.

☑ Contact stakeholders.

- Make a good-faith effort to contact/invite all appropriate groups to participate in your stakeholder program.

☑ Begin communicating.

- Find out their interests/priorities/concerns/advice.

- Educate them on your EMS and ISO 14001 program.

- Set up a mechanism for two-way participatory dialogue.

☑ Assess and evaluate.

- How successful was this program in reaching appropriate stakeholders, incorporating their concerns into the EMS, educating them about the potential of the EMS reaching objectives and targets?

- How can all the lessons of the last cycle be applied to the next?

2.3.3 Conclusion

prove yourself   Establishing a stakeholder program is neither going to be a simple task nor will it be a guaranteed success. However, it is worth trying. Stakeholders will be an important factor in determining the overall credibility of ISO 14001 and will also have a lot of insight and information to offer individual organizations that can benefit their own EMS programs. ISO 14001 is a major break from the traditional command-and-control approach to environmental protection.

Non-regulatory EMSs offer tremendous opportunities for innovative advances in environmental performance. For those advances to reach maturity, stakeholders must become a part of the process. Many stakeholders will be wary of this voluntary, market-based system, concerned that it will lead to a worsening of environmental performance. The best way for

Gap Analysis Case Study: Millar Western Pulp Ltd.

January 1996

Millar Western Pulp Ltd. in Whitecourt, Alberta, has been in business for seven years. It is a privately owned company that produces and supplies the world market with chlorine-free bleached chemithermal mechanical pulp for use in fine writing and tissue paper. Millar Western Pulp has 140 permanent employees.

In March 1995, Millar Western Pulp became the first North American company to become certified to BS 7750. Wendy Lyka, environmental coordinator, offers the following advice based on experience with this certification.

Consider indirect effects. "When we started developing this system, it was fairly straightforward and was strictly for our site," Lyka explains. "Then the whole indirect effects issue caught us by surprise. Our two different product types are hardwood and softwood. We get our softwood chips from the sawmill next door, which is run by Millar Western Industries, and our hardwood is chipped on-site.

"Because Millar Western Pulp and Millar Western Industries are two separate companies, wood harvesting became an issue. Indirect effects, such as wood harvesting and raw chemicals, have to be included in our EMS. We had defined indirect effects as those that are not controlled by site management, which was okay, but then we had to show the interface. We also had to show that we were aware of what their practices are. We felt we had run into a brick wall. We had it all there — the information — we just hadn't known we had to include it."

Develop procedures for environmental concerns. The implementation team also found Millar had gaps in responding to environmental concerns. "We didn't have anything in place," Lyka explains. "We just assumed that our receptionist, the guardhouse, and the initial responders to concerns knew where to direct the calls. We did some tests, and discovered they did not know this. We had to develop procedures to meet these needs."

The company now trains all its employees to know that a call may come in and the caller may not necessarily say, "I've got an environmental concern." The employee has to understand what the concern is — that is, whether it is a safety issue, a health and safety issue, or an environmental concern. The company's procedures now require that employees know who to give the call to and require that the caller not be put on hold or transferred until the right person to take the call is found.

Get help with standard interpretation. Millar Western Pulp began with two auditors who had initially been quality system auditors; one was the chief steam engineer and one was an operator. They were chosen as EMS auditors because they were both auditors and were independent from the environmental systems. However, when they began going through the standard, they had a difficult time interpreting it. "We tried to help as much as we could without biasing them," Lyka explains. "We brought an instructor on-site to conduct environmetntal auditor training. Understanding and being able to audit against the standard was a big pitfall for us. We had some difficulties with that."

Communicate, communicate. "When we initially went out to talk to employees in the mill and tried to sell this whole EMS, they wanted to know what was involved for them, — what did they have to do that was extra. We had a really hard time with that," Lyka explains. "Currently, we are struggling with the whole communication realm. We are still trying to sell our environmental management program to our own employees and to the community around us." She explains that the employees know there is policy somewhere in a book, but trying to get them to live and breathe and understand the concept is another issue.

"When it's not part of their job, we're not sure how to make it a part of their job and to get them interested in environmental issues. We are starting one-on-ones, where we go out and talk individually to each employee very informally. We ask how they feel about environmental issues, how they think we are doing, and what they think of the whole system. We began doing this in December 1995 and hope this activity will give us some really good feedback. This is very time-consuming, but will be very worthwhile in the end."

your organization to overcome stakeholder reservations about ISO 14001 is to demonstrate to them that it can accommodate stakeholder needs. For this to occur, you will have to establish credible programs that effectively build a participatory dialogue and produce results that stakeholders want to see.

CHAPTER 4
Training

2.4.1 Tip from Industry

A survey of companies of varied sizes, locations, and kinds of industry quickly reveals that there are almost as many approaches to training employees about ISO 14001 and training internal and external auditors as there are companies. These training approaches range from all in-house training to all outside training and every imaginable combination of the two. Because the training concepts outlined here are innovative, these anecdotal explanations may be of use to companies currently involved in or just embarking on ISO 14001 implementation. (see Part 2, Chapter 1, Section 2.1.8 for more on training.)

Expand upon existing systems.

"I don't like to go out and reinvent the wheel," comments Debra Reese, R/QA engineer and

ISO 9000 director of Matsushita Semiconductor Corporation of America in Puyallup, Washington. "Since employees are already familiar with quality policy and systems, we can expand that to include environmental management systems." She adds that employees are more receptive to and comfortable with expansion of existing systems than they are of applying new concepts.

Exchange education and training with vendors.

Matsushita doesn't bring in outside trainers, preferring to train with contractors who come to the site to work on projects that Matsushita designed. If contractors are installing equipment that Matsushita employees are not familiar with, the employees learn from the contractors and obtain their manuals. In some cases, engineers or technicians go to a contractor's facility for additional training on the equipment. Often, Matsushita assembles the training material as its own equipment is developed and designed, depending heavily on electronic media. This concept can be applied to ISO 14000 standards if contractors are used to help implement them.

Audit across functions for efficiency and effectiveness.

Matsushita certifies its own auditors for ISO 9002 and has one dedicated auditor in its facility. Systems audits that are required by ISO 9002 are conducted by Reese. If a system in her department requires an audit, another manager from another department who is certified to perform audits, audits Reese's group as an independent auditor. In turn, Reese grades the auditor's performance and uses the audit as an on-the-job recertification training tool.

The other manager can also evaluate Reese's performance as an auditor and can audit Reese's internal auditor. In addition, there is a trained backup for Reese, who can step in to be audited in her place and run her systems. She explains, "Being able to critique the systems from an audit perspective helps locate discrepancies. Then we can effectively judge the corrective action and determine its effectiveness."

Cultivate environmental awareness.

"Our number one focus of training is environmental awareness," says Richard Masterton, corporate manager of waste management and environmental training for CN North America Railroad in Montreal, Quebec. "We want to enlighten employees and management within the railway about the environment and why this is a concern for everybody. All employees go through a two-hour session and managers have a four-hour session."

Combine the skills of consultants and internal auditors.

Masterton explains that environmental compliance audits are all performed by consultants from Arthur D. Little in Boston. The same firm has trained 18 to 20 CN staff members to perform compliance audits. In this way, audits can be done on site using two Arthur D. Little consultants and two people from the company's CN training base. The same concept can apply to systems audits. "One of our stipulations is that the person from the site cannot be an auditor on his own site," Masterton explains. "This gives our auditing staff members an opportunity to see other sites across the country and see how they operate."

Get help from reputable training organizations.

Jim Winn, ISO 9001 management representative for Caterpillar's Mossville Engine Center (MEC) in Peoria, Illinois, explains that his site of 4,300 employees is certified to ISO 9001 and is considering certification to ISO 14001. Asked what he does when faced with training issues for employees, he says he contacts reputable organizations that conduct auditor training in the U.S.

"We sent three people from the company to receive internal auditor and lead auditor training," Winn explains, "and then those people came back to the facility and provided any training that was necessary. We did no formal ISO training classes in the facility." His criteria for future trainer selection include:

- Look for someone recognized in the certification field who has done real-world work with ISO standards.

- Listen to your customers in selecting an auditor for certification, and select one who is respected and has a historical presence in your industry.

Develop a staff of dedicated training personnel.

Tom Kreinbrook, quality manager of Monsanto Chemical Company at the W.G. Krummrich Plant in Sauget, Illinois, explains that its corporate environmental group provides training to individual plants and businesses in Monsanto. "We have a staff that researches and interprets new regulations and passes those interpretations along to the businesses that are affected by them. In every plant, there is a plant environmental group that includes environmental safety and health. At our plant, this group includes about 15 people who are responsible for taking information provided by the corporation to the next step. This includes interpretation and training. In addition to this group, there are nine people working full-time who do nothing but training for this plant in environmental, quality, safety, and operating procedures for hazardous materials."

Make sure employees go through effective training programs.

Environmental audits are done by employees at that particular plant who have gone through a five-day training session on quality audits presented by an outside consultant. A few people, such as Kreinbrook, have been through ISO 14001 training classes given by outside consultants. "Both ISO 9000 and ISO 14001 require that internal audits be conducted. The people doing those clearly need training in auditing techniques. One of the ways to do that is by using outside organizations to provide the training," Kreinbrook says.

"Within Monsanto as a company, we have put about 500 people through the lead auditor course for ISO 9000 through outside training organizations. We do not allow anyone to do any auditing for our EMS or quality system unless they have been through some auditor training course. Since March of 1993 we have done over 200 internal quality audits. We began doing our own internal environmental audits starting in June of 1995 and have done about 44 at this in early in the first quarter of 1996. Rather than do the once-a-year check recommended by ISO 14001, Monsanto conducts frequent internal audits."

When Monsanto first became involved with ISO 9000, it brought instructors from the U.K. to train its 500 internal auditors. However, with so many employees trained, this is no longer cost-effective, so the company now uses U.S.-based trainers for ISO 14001 auditor training and for training senior managers as lead auditors.

Combine a variety of approaches to training.

Ron Black, corporate director of health, safety, and environmental management systems at BF Goodrich in Akron, Ohio, explains, "If I had an internal staff that was trained to do compliance audits, I would send them out to get management systems audit training. In fact, they could take the ISO 9000 QMS training. That's a good combination. Alternatively, internal auditors trained to ISO 9000 could get some environmental training. Teams of internal auditors could also be formed with both EMS and QMS trained people on the team."

He adds that he has been involved in EMS audits in the U.S. and Europe since 1990 and has noted that pure compliance auditors without any supporting training who are performing EMS audits can easily fall back into a compliance mode. Conversely, when pure systems auditors conduct audits, they can find it difficult to locate the environmental aspects of the programs. Black says he feels that the answer is to find a person with both kinds of experience or to send out people that have the combined experience as a team. If a single auditor with a single background is to perform an audit, that person should have some cross-functional training.

Develop training videos involving executives and employees.

Bill Sugar, director of environmental affairs for Anheuser-Busch Inc., in St. Louis, Missouri, comments, "It's easier now to set up training programs and environmental training. We have Busch Media Group that produces many of the commercials on TV — not just beer commercials — so we have excellent video graphics people with great capabilities. Our CEO and CFO volunteered to be part of an environmental awareness video they prepared on environmental excellence. Then six different businesses within Anheuser-Busch were filmed with employees talking about the work they do." These videos were then sent out to all the facilities with a front-end piece that suggests ways the supervisor can present the video to employees.

Set high standards for environmental training.

In dealing with training issues, Sugar comments, "In most companies, training is one of the weakest links in the system. Anheuser-Busch has done the regulatory training as required by law for environmental professional people or for people who are closely attached to the issues so we can be in compliance. However, I don't think that's where I'm trying to drive this program." In addition to seeking a competitive advantage, Sugar wants AB's management system to be effective in terms of environmental and quality issues while fundamentally reducing cost structures.

Base training issues on corporate policy requirements.

"To do that," he points out, "there has to be a lot of awareness training." He says that sending documented environmental policies out to the sites does not mean that employees understand the concepts. He also says that his company needs a training program geared for all strata of the organization: business types in the corporation (the middle management layer), the plant managers and their direct staff, supervisors, and employees. Using their 23 corporate requirements that were developed as corporate policy, the company looks at the issues involved in each of these, and uses the components to develop training programs in-house.

Know how to respond to environmental concerns.

Wendy Lyka, environmental coordinator for Millar Western Pulp in Whitecourt, Alberta, explains that her company found it had gaps in responding to environmental concerns. "We didn't have anything in place," Lyka explains. "We just assumed that our receptionist, guardhouse, and the initial responders to concerns knew where to direct the calls. We did some tests, and discovered they did not know this. We had to develop some procedures for that. That was really, really interesting."

The company trains all its employees to know that a call may come in and the caller may not necessarily say, "I've got an environmental concern." The employee has to determine the nature of the specific concern, perhaps without much help from the caller. Possibilities range from a safety issue to a health and safety issue, to an environmental concern. The company developed procedures so employees know where to direct the call and how to keep the caller on the line until they have found the right person to take the call.

2.4.2 What the Trainers Say

Trainers who were asked what companies should look for in evaluating their training needs and selecting a trainer were able to shed light on training concepts that companies might not have considered. These insights may be a useful tool in establishing a corporate training program for ISO 14001 auditors or the audit team. 📖 (See Appendix J for more information on the trainers interviewed below.)

Gap Analysis Case Study: Westcoast Energy Inc.

January 1996

Westcoast Energy Inc. gathers, processes, and transmits natural gas and is involved in the co-generation business, in addition to having subsidiaries in other gas-related areas. It has 6,000 employees. The Pipeline Division operates five gas processing plants, three sulfur recovery plants, 33 compressor stations, and approximately 4,500 kilometers of gas pipeline. The corporate headquarters is in Vancouver, British Columbia.

Deborah Bisson, senior advisor on environmental legislation and risk assessment for Westcoast Energy, explains that the company has been working with the Canadian Standards Association (CSA) on an EMS pilot project for over a year. The pilot project is based on CSA's estimate of the final ISO 14001 document. In earning an MBA, Bisson, an attorney, developed a thesis on her company's environmental management system and its relationship to ISO 14001 specifications. Because Westcoast Energy has a strong commitment to environmental issues and is heavily regulated as a utility, many of the processes emerging in ISO 14001 have already been instituted. Following is advice on implementation based on experience with its current EMS.

Combine regulatory requirements and Total Quality Management (TQM). Bisson points out that there are two models for EMS programs. The first, which is based on regulations and due diligence/liability issues, encompasses many programs and can be extended far beyond compliance issues. The second model is based on the integration of TQM and environmental management. This model may have begun with the efforts of the Global Environmental Management Initiative (GEMI), which coined the term Total Quality Environmental Management (TQEM), an environmental management system built on the quality model. This model, much of which focuses on setting objectives and subsequent measurements to determine whether these objectives are being met, is based on continuous quality improvement.

Recognize that gaps must be closed over time. When Westcoast Energy had its first environmental management systems audit conducted by external management consultants a few years ago, it was audited against a due diligence model used by the consulting group. Upon receiving a description of gaps existing in its program, it immediately set to work to close these gaps. While many gaps were quickly closed, it soon discovered that others take more time. It was not possible to change the entire EMS right away.

Some aspects, such as developing training programs to meet its specific training needs effectively take a significant amount of time. Likewise, implementing a more sophisticated information management system is time-consuming because it requires developing a complete environmental management information system (EMIS). Development of an environmental policies and procedures manual is another project that took considerable time.

Crystallize corporate vision in EMS policy. One of the ways that Westcoast Energy crystallized its vision of where it wanted to go was to revamp its environmental policy statement (EPS), making it less compliance-oriented and more proactive, focusing on pollution prevention, waste minimization, resource conservation, and sustainable development. It had senior management support but wanted to cultivate environmental awareness at the field level. Just after the new EPS was drafted, Westcoast's president and senior vice president went into the field to talk with employees about the new environmental policy statement to increase awareness of environmental issues.

Change organizational structures and reporting. To stay on top of the environmental issues, organizational structures and reporting were changed so there were environmental coordinators/ technicians at all the major sites. Because of burgeoning environmental demands, the company also began developing a computerized EMIS to track permits, waste management, and other environmental information.

Strengthen policies and procedures. Bisson explains that Westcoast found it was weak in this area in 1992, and has been working hard to develop stronger policies and procedures. In 1995 it had completed an environmental policies and procedures manual that is used as an auditing tool. Keeping this manual up-to-date is a continuous process.

Track emergent regulatory requirements. Bisson tracks developing government legislation, regulations, guidelines, and policy. Environmental laws change frequently in Canada and are less prescriptive than in the U.S. She coordinates input from members of the environmental issues committee. These include technical experts from the company and from the field who can provide feedback on regulatory, environmental issues that Bisson then takes to the government body coordinating the consultation. It is now standard practice in Canada to cultivate input from the public and from private industry for new regulatory initiatives at the federal and provincial level.

Seek training that meets the specific needs of your organization.

Stanley Marash, chief technological officer of Stat-A-Matrix in Edison, New Jersey, suggests that you look at a broad range of training, not just lead auditor training, to meet the specific needs of your organization. He recommends evaluating training for concepts and philosophies, documentation development, and interpretation of the standards, in addition to technological and skill-set requirements.

 ## Create a qualification process for trainers.

People brought in to do testing or staff trained to do the work must also have to pass some sort of diagnostic qualification process that defines the skill levels that are necessary and methods for doing a diagnostic to be sure the skill levels have been attained. "This could be a written test, an oral test, or a demonstration. Somehow," Marash explains, "you have to get proof that the trainer has internalized the necessary information and knows how to do the job."

Get outside help when you need a customized program.

A properly designed training program will go through an alpha test and a beta test. In training just a few people, they will all be trained at once, but if there are 300 people needing training, it is possible to try the program out on a few first. In this way, the program can function as a pilot, get adjusted as needed, and then be rolled out to everyone else. Unfortunately, it is not always practical or possible to do this. "This is where it becomes really useful for companies to buy that skill outside," Marash suggests. "If you have a small number of people to train and this is something that can be standardized, you can buy it outside."

Develop training in sync with policies and procedures.

"We have clients all around the world who ask us to design their training programs for them. As they develop their procedures and instructions, we help them develop their training modules and their examination modules. In this way, as they are developing their management system, the training and testing methodologies are also developed," according to Marash.

Determine the characteristics wanted in an auditor.

The person doing the job needs to be able to listen and to ask questions and may need to have technological knowledge to do the job. Because many people who have dealt with quality issues may be expanding the scope of their work to environmental issues, they may not have environmental credentials. "Some people feel that an auditor can audit anything, and that is not valid," Marash points out. He refers to the nuclear energy industry, where teams with a variety of skills were used for audits as a reasonable solution, but the best possible auditors are those who have both industrial process and system management knowledge.

Ask for references from the trainer.

Find out who has taken the course, how long that company has been doing training, and what the individual skills of the trainers are, such as advanced degrees and teaching skills. Learn the pass/fail rate of people taking the course, as participants are graded both on exams and degree of participation in the class. Make sure the trainers have both environmental technology and management systems skills, Marash says.

Look for programs you can grow with.

Mary Crisler, EMS program manager for CEEM Training Services, a division of CEEM Inc., explains that if you were satisfied with courses you have taken before with a particular trainer, chances are you'll be satisfied with others. Therefore, she recommends, you should look for a company that offers a variety of course levels to suit the particular needs of your company — and that will allow you to return to get a higher level of training. These levels might include:

- courses in understanding the ISO 14000 series of standards;
- a class on developing and implementing an ISO 14001 conformance program;
- an internal auditor program for ISO 14001;
- in-house training that can be tailored to any organization;
- environmental management consulting for issues such as gap analysis, cost reduction, and ISO 14001 program implementation.

Gap Analysis Case Study:
Matsushita Semiconductor Corporation of America

January 1996

Established in February 1991 and located in Puyallup, Washington, Matsushita Semiconductor Corporation of America employs 350 people. The site area covers 92 acres and the facilities are 393,000 sq. ft. Matsushita's global semiconductor operations have diversified applications including the manufacturing of PCs, audio and video products, personal communications, multimedia products, and office equipment (fax/copier). Matsushita began its ISO 14001 gap analysis in July 1995, and is expected to conclude the analysis in March 1997. The company hopes to beat that target date however. Debra Reese, R/QA engineer and ISO 9000 director for Matsushita, offers the following advice.

Review the standard as a team. To avoid gaps in meeting ISO 14001 requirements, Reese recommends that you "sit down as a team and review the standard clause-by-clause. Cross-reference your existing EMS requirements with documents in your organization to be sure you have appropriate documentation. Then go over the elements of your existing EMS and compare it to the requirements of ISO 14001."

Her group felt its team approach was more effective and accurate than a single interpretation. Because representatives from all the management groups were involved, they could approach issues from several perspectives. Their cross- functional team was made up of upper management and direct staff, and representatives from finance, fabrication engineering, product engineering, facilities, equipment maintenance, quality assurance, manufacturing, and sales.

Interpret the standard clause-by-clause. "We took a clause a week so we didn't burn anyone out," Reese explains. "I typed it up and gave everybody handouts. We were familiar with the systems, such as document control, because we had already instituted ISO 9002." They interpreted the standard and determined whether it met with their existing system in their clause-by-clause management review. In this way, Reese says, they were able to avoid a potential later mindset of, "You came up with this and it doesn't work."

Keep the scope broad. "When we look for improvement in the systems, which we continuously do," Reese explains, "I ask how we can make it bigger — not more verbose or with more documents — but how we can have a broader scope. If the focus becomes narrow, something can be missed." She says it is important to expand horizons in the facility and in their industry. Because Matsushita's customers may have a completely different scope, they also want to evaluate customers' needs as a natural next step in expanding the scope of its management system.

Understand the functions of each system. "Everybody who works in this facility is using a system at some point for issues, such as documentation procedures, which is document control, or in dealing with equipment, which is preventive maintenance and calibration. Training, for instance, is involved in all of the systems." The team checks to see that each system meets the company's business goals. If any of the systems break down, the others are affected.

Make sure all the systems mesh. All systems must interrelate effectively. "If a facility looks at systems as independent, the systems don't mesh, and gaps occur," Reese explains. As an example, she points out that document revision affects document control. If employees on the plant floor are not aware of the change and have not been trained to the change, the revision is not effective and has no positive impact on the organization. None of the systems is isolated from the others. Everything has to work together.

Understand the intent of the systems. The audit team needs to understand the intent of the system, not just the requirements. If employees understand the purpose and goal of document control, when it is audited to determine whether or not it is being used, it easier to judge whether or not it is effective. "Many people miss that; they just note that a system is not being used. Maybe it isn't being used because it isn't good," Reese warns.

Audit and educate outside vendors. If vendors say they will meet the basic minimum, breakdowns in the systems can occur. Vendors who treat an EMS as a compliance document don't understand the concept. The value of an EMS is determined not only by compliance issues, but by whether or not it is appropriate and effective for that organization. Discrepancies in the management system need to be reported for the EMS to be effective. If there is an excursion on an environmental parameter, it needs to be reported and the staff involved need to understand how and why it occurred. It is also necessary to develop positive, corrective action to prevent reoccurrence. Understanding the original intent of that element of the EMS reaches beyond the basic criteria for certification.

Seek joint ISO 9000/14001 third-party audits for certification. "If we pursue registration for ISO 14001, I do not wish to have another set of auditors appear at this facility every six months, in addition to ISO 9002 auditors," Reese explains. Because the two ISO standards use similar systems and because ISO 14001 is a natural extension of ISO 9000, she says, the audits should be performed by the same auditors at the same time. As of January 1994, Matsushita used Underwriters Lab for certification audits.

Look for added value.

Look for courses that appeal to your organization's culture, Crisler says. For example, CEEM offers in-house courses in Spanish that can be taught by bilingual instructors, although the teaching materials are all in English. "This works well in Puerto Rico or Mexico where many of the personnel read and speak English but find it easier to communicate problems in their own language," Crisler explains.

Crisler explains that EMSs often are not implemented in a vacuum. You should look for training that offers implementation as an integrated business approach, for example. You might also seek a company that does ISO 9000 training to ensure that experience with that standard gets incorporated into the training program.

In addition, some companies offer video training to augment lessons learned in the classroom.

Sue Jackson, business development manager of environmental management systems at Excel Partnership Inc., in Sandy Hook, Connecticut, notes that if you have locations worldwide, finding a trainer with similar locations could save you money and time. So ask if the trainer offers courses in areas where you plan future ISO 14001 implementation. Excel, for example, offers training in Brazil, Hong Kong, Mexico, the U.K. and the U.S.

Look for regulatory knowledge and an EMS background.

Jackson recommends looking for EMS experience in a training organization. This may show up through a combination of environment and management systems. She also points out that the instructors also need to understand the environmental regulatory framework in the United States, which is unique in that the U.S. is the most heavily regulated country in the world. The desired level of environmental technology need not include advanced degrees, as she feels that heavy involvement in one aspect of environmental issues can ultimately result in a narrow evaluation of the issues.

Look for a strong business focus.

Jackson explains that a trainer should have a strong business focus related to the organization's specific business, not as a generic application. She adds that the trainer should ask the company if it has implemented ISO 9000 and should find ways to build the EMS on top of existing quality management systems.

Look for a trainer who keeps up with emergent issues.

Because ISO 14000 issues are changing so fast, Jackson says it is important to have a trainer who has ties to TC 207, the U.S. EPA, and the emergent certification system.

Jackson comments that course providers should continuously improve their training courses to remain current with developing international standards and market trends. Major recent changes at Excel, for example, involve an expanded use of an interactive adult learning approach with a focus on application to the client's own business.

CEEM's Crisler says you should look at the instructor backgrounds specifically to get a good mix for your needs. She explains that CEEM instructors have extensive EMS experience in industry, environmental engineering, and environmental law. "Because of their involvement in the U.S. TAG and TC 207, they are aware of all the changes taking place in the ISO 14000 arena and adjust course materials easily to meet these needs."

Determine which kinds of training to seek.

Samantha Munn, manager of environmental systems business development at Inchcape Testing Services — Intertek Services, points out that a company may need just basic awareness training, not in-depth auditor training, and that it's good to make this kind of determination up front. The awareness training could be a basic two-day course, while auditing may be a five-day in-depth lead auditor training. The first is for someone who just wants to get the general idea, while the latter is for people who plan to be involved in auditing.

Have trainers supply a detailed outline of the courses.

Munn suggests contacting trainers and asking for a detailed outline of the courses offered to determine whether the courses satisfy your company requirements. She explains that the Environmental Auditors Registration Association (EARA) of the U.K. has developed criteria for companies that are offering ISO 14001 and EMS training in the U.S. Auditors in the U.S. are now able to obtain points toward auditor certification under this program. In early 1996, several U.S.-based organizations also were developing course certification criteria. (See below for more on this topic.)

Ask what types of materials come with the courses.

"Some trainers offer a copy of the standard and a full course manual," Munn explains. She suggests asking for the qualifications of the trainers at the same time.

Make sure the trainer understands ISO 14000 and its history.

Ted Miller, partner, Miller-Rettew Associates in Lancaster, Pennsylvania, says it is important to understand how ISO 14000 came into being and why market forces make this a major issue. He says the trainer should be able to translate these issues to prospective students, explaining why they need ISO 14000 training, why the company needs the standard, and what it means.

Get a trainer who knows the implementation issues.

Miller explains, "When you look at the standard, you find basic good business practices, whether you are a one-person company or 100,000, and these should be included. Where interpretation of the standard really varies is with implementation. The responsibilities still need to be carried out and executed. The execution is considerably different in small and large companies."

Make sure the trainer can help participants learn to docu-

ment an EMS.

The participants need to be able to understand all the elements of ISO 14001 and how all the other sections of the standard relate to the auditing document. Miller also adds that the trainer should be able to let participants know the real significance of documentation.

Find out how the courses are designed.

Rita Grenville, competitive specialist at DuPont Safety and Environmental, which does a great deal of training but stopped offering ISO 9000 courses in early 1996, points out the importance of the trainer's style and approach. "The agenda of materials won't vary, but the philosophy of training will. How the course is designed can be very important," she says.

Get a trainer who can help you find out what you don't know.

"Most clients don't know what it is they don't know," Grenville explains. "The trainer needs to be able to explain the course materials they have in place and the significance of each of these components."

Make sure training is presented in logical phases.

Gregory P. Johnson, director of quality systems development, an associate at L. Marvin Johnson and Associates Inc. (QSD/LMJ), recommends that training be broken down into phases and that they make sense to you. For example, his company's development process is presented in eight phases:

1) commitment;
2) organization;
3) communication;
4) establishing objectives;
5) documentation for 14001;
6) implementation;
7) verification; and
8) certification/registration.

"When the training is over, ask what to do now to keep up-to-date," Johnson suggests. The trainer should have this information in the training material for participants.

Consider whether the course should be officially accredited.

As of March 1996, only one organization offered accreditation to training providers: the Environmental Auditors Registration Association of the U.K. However, several U.S.-based course accreditation bodies were developing criteria for U.S.-based syllabi that were due out in mid-1996.

EARA accredits both U.S.- and U.K.-oriented EMS courses. Because the course criteria for the U.S. courses had only just been released in March 1996, very few providers had had a

Gap Analysis Case Study: WMX Technologies Inc.

December 1995

WMX Technologies Inc., with headquarters in Oakbrook, Illinois, is a holding company that wholly owns or is majority owner of four major waste management and engineering services. These businesses encompass 136 solid waste landfills, hazardous waste landfills, hazardous waste incinerators, hauling companies, medical waste incinerators, waste-to-energy incinerators, and fuel-blending/solvent recovery facilities. These functions take place at more than 800 sites throughout the world.

WMX owns Waste Management Inc., Wheelabrator Technologies Inc., Rust Engineering, and Waste Management International, which provides a wide range of services in Europe, Asia, and Australia. Emerging markets include Indonesia, India, and Australia. The company also built a large hazardous waste plant and a landfill in Hong Kong.

Originally a garbage business 24 years ago, WMX has expanded to hazardous waste and environmental services, such as wastewater, sludge recovery, and regeneration. "There were no kind of equivalent waste management services when our company was incorporated," explains Bob Newport of the WMX corporate environmental audit department. "It proved to be a very timely business because there was a growing demand for waste services. We provide an integrated waste management business that allows for one-stop shopping for management and disposal of wastes and engineering services."

He offers ISO 14001 implementation advice below, based on his experience rolling out other environmental programs. Applying "phase approach" helps fine-tune the process and helps avoid a crisis during implementation.

Apply ISO 14000 to appropriate businesses. "We have a lot of different kinds of businesses," Newport points out. "To do a phased approach of ISO 14001, it is necessary to reflect the kind of business, the environmental systems used, the consistency of the systems used, and the anticipated customer demands." One of WMX's companies, Rust Federal Services, bids on projects for the Department of Energy (DOE) and similar other large-scale jobs. This company has already received one request for proposal (RFP) that stipulates it must have an ISO 14001 equivalent EMS as a requirement for bidding on the contract. This company will have to look at ISO 14001 right away.

"Other companies within our group are not as environmentally significant, such as our companies that just go around and pick up garbage as a trucking operation," he says. "Those would not be expected to have the same kinds of environmental impacts or customer demands, so they would be on a different track for implementation of ISO 14001."

During 1996, WMX will evaluate all its different businesses, working with a few that are top priority as pilot projects. Ultimately, a handful of different types of businesses will be registered to ISO 14001 so it can see if its systems improved and got stronger as it compared them to ISO 14001 and met the specifications. It will determine the benefits gained and the cost of documentation for certification.

Participate in innovative EMS enhancement projects. WMX Technologies Inc. is part of the EPA's Environmental Leadership Program (ELP) pilot that demonstrates a state-of-the-art environmental management system. WMX, which is demonstrating an environmental compliance management system, among other programs, has all necessary regulations on a computer software program that gives out related reference information and calendars with tasks for specific dates. Its self-audit program is a model for other companies. In addition, an outside consultant comes in every year and does an evaluation of the company. 📖 (See Part 8, Chapter 2, Section 3 for more information on the ELP program.)

Have EMS directly link company policy to compliance issues. Newport explains that company policy has 14 environmental principles that address issues such as protection of biodiversity, wise use of energy, and sustainable use of natural resources. The planning process each year sets goals related to the policy. The business groups prepare environmental plans, and a tracking system is used to make sure that they are achieving goals. Parallel to the policy is the environmental compliance program to make sure that applicable requirements are systematically met as well.

Combine management system evaluation and compliance verification. WMX uses a two-part audit system, the first part composed of a management system evaluation that includes analysis of self-audit, processes, and procedures. When WMX looks at facilities management systems, it delves into the environmental aspects of the business, management team activities, training, and ways that business ensures compliance to a wide range of requirements. An example might be asking the personnel at that site how they determine if incoming waste is hazardous and what they do with hazardous waste once they receive it.

The second phase of the audit, the compliance verification, involves examination of specific records, such as manifests and tank inspection forms, to see if the documentation is there to support effective functioning of the system.

Develop incremental steps for thorough assessment. The full range of assessments done by WMX includes four phases:

1) self-inspections and routine walk-arounds;

2) self-audits to checklists on all environmental requirements applicable to that business;

3) a corporate audit program, which includes management system evaluation and compliance verification; and

4) third party evaluation by an outside consultant.

In this way, it has relatively seamless checking on all environmental aspects of its businesses.

Have a third party auditor evaluate your system. The final phase of the WMX four-part assessment was to have consultants from Arthur D. Little in Cambridge, Massachusetts, come in to evaluate systems and verify that they were being implemented. Newport says of ADL's evaluation, "They confirm that we have compliance systems working across the company and evaluate the strengths and weaknesses of our compliance programs. We have a public environmental report that we issue every year, and Arthur D. Little writes an opinion statement that goes into the report about our environmental management systems. That is our confirmation that everything is happening the way it is supposed to be happening."

Gap Analysis Case Study — CN North America

December 1995

CN North America is a Canadian railroad with 13,000 employees that owns more than 6,000 pieces of property, including track laid from coast to coast in Canada. It also owns and operates the Grand Trunk Railroad, Canadian National's United States division, a line that extends into Chicago. Its corporate headquarters is in Montreal, Quebec. Richard Masterton, corporate manager for waste management and environmental training at CN North America, offers the following ISO 14001 implementation advice.

Set up a scoring system for identifying environmental aspects. Masterton explains that his company has developed a scoring system for its sites. This scoring, used in conjunction with risk analysis, creates a prioritization for remediation of its sites. "We are instituting a detailed measurement system that will measure EMS activities on site, such as wastewater systems, waste management, and storage tanks. This system is about 85 percent completed.

"This system will be put on a mainframe computer and will have all factors of the site taken into account, such as the size of the property and the risk associated, to provide a scoring system. This scoring system measures all aspects of environmental performance. The software program automatically tallies the results to give the site a score, which is then combined with other area site scores to give a provincial score. Then all provincial scores are combined for a national score." CN anticipated having all sites scored by mid-1996. It also planned to be in full compliance with ISO 14001 by 1999 and to have all 6,000 sites remediated by 2001.

The scoring system has negative ratings for environmental hazards or risks onsite, such as number of locomotives painted, number of locomotives fueled, volume of hazardous waste generated, or proximity to a river. These factors are balanced out against the controls. If the number of locomotives painted is a -100 score but all the controls are in place, the score would be a positive 100. The positive scores are based on controls, such as equipment, preventive maintenance program, or monitoring and sampling.

Eliminate unnecessarily hazardous materials. Following a systemwide survey of products used, CN has eliminated 86 of 95 products that contain chlorinated substances and replaced them with other, more environmentally safe products. Because of the complexities of decentralization, it has a low-key pollution prevention program, but is getting rid of all PCBs by mid-1996 and is researching the possible disposal of used railroad ties through co-generation at a utility power plant.

Develop an EMS that can survive changes in corporate culture. CN North America has been in the process of privatizing, decentralizing, and downsizing, and has lost some employees who were knowledgeable about environmental issues. In addition, procedures for handling wastes on each site had not been documented. "We wound up with weaknesses in the reporting relationships on, say, how to report waste management costs or how to deal with hazardous waste manifesting problems," Masterton explains. "We are struggling right now to institute a management system for handling waste management across the railway. We are about 60 percent there. The remaining 40 percent is all management structured and will be more difficult to accomplish."

Get more diverse groups of employees involved. Because CN's decentralization cost it some of the environmentally knowledgeable employees, it began offering detailed training to field-oriented personnel, such as those who repair locomotives and freight cars or who work with equipment shops or track gangs, on issues such as handling a barrel of oil and how it is manifested. This training extends to a wide range of topics and is being offered at all its sites across the country, Masterton says.

Gather employee comments and implement good ideas. When CN offered environmental awareness training to its 13,000 employees, including management, it gave out comment sheets at the end of the presentations, asking for employee ideas. "About 25 percent to 30 percent were pretty good ideas," Masterton notes, "which we grouped into functions, such as running the train or repairing the locomotive. Then we prioritized the comments. We evaluated the ideas for cost and environmental benefit, and reported back to the head of that CN department, pointing out the top 10 to 15 concepts that we felt should be considered. In this way, the department heads know what their employees are thinking and the employees buy into the environmental initiatives. It worked well. In December 1995 the top 15 ideas of each group were in the process of being implemented."

Employee ideas that emerge on the job also are heard. "We've tried to refocus waste as everyone's problem," Masterton points out. CN North America has some very aware employees who have expressed concerns about the environmental future of Canada and the world. "We're listening more to the grassroots people and using some of their ideas." For instance, an employee may have recommendations about recycling and take her ideas to her manager, who then suggests that the employee go ahead and make phone calls and inquiries on behalf of the railway.

chance to review the criteria and begin tailoring their courses accordingly, several course providers note.

There has been some debate over whether it would be better for U.S. course providers to await accreditation by a U.S.-based course accreditation body or use EARA's criteria. Several experts were saying there would be very little difference between any U.S. accreditor's criteria and EARA's, while others were saying the U.S. criteria would be geared more toward a U.S. interpretation of ISO 14001.

Whether to go for training by an accredited course provider at all is an issue that many experts say will be entirely up to the organization to decide. Some will want the "stamp of approval" offered by an accredited course and the points that lead to auditor certification. Others are more interested in excellent training, regardless of accreditation.

These experts note that ISO 14001 training is in its early stages, and organization certification itself is likely to be a long time in coming, so certified training at this stage may not be as important as it will be later, especially for internal auditors. At this stage, they say, most companies are more interested in training the implementation team. Those who seek to become third-party auditors will have to take accredited training courses at some point, these experts note.

CHAPTER 5
Hiring a Consultant

by Marilyn R. Block, President, MRB Associates

Once your organization has decided to implement ISO 14001, one of the first questions that you must answer is whether to interpret the standard using in-house staff or to bring in an outside consulting firm. Those who opt for in-house interpretation should review ISO 14004, a guidelines document created to provide assistance to organizations implementing or improving an EMS. It is organized around five principles:

1) Commitment and Policy — Your organization should define its environmental policy and ensure commitment to its EMS;

2) Planning — Your organization should formulate a plan to fulfill its policy;

3) Implementation — Your organization should develop the capabilities and support mechanisms necessary to achieve its environmental policy, objectives, and targets;

4) Measurement and Evaluation —Your organization should measure, monitor, and evaluate its environmental performance;

5) Review and Improvement —Your organization should review and continually improve its environmental management system, with the objective of improving its overall environmental performance.

Each of these five areas discusses specific elements from ISO 14001 in terms of key issues that you should consider and concrete actions that could help your organization fulfill the requirement of that element.

If your company is implementing an environmental management system for the first time, you should find ISO 14004 helpful. The sections on "issues to be considered" pose questions that encourage critical thinking about the intended purpose of EMS elements. Companies looking to improve existing EMSs, however, are likely to find ISO 14004 too elementary to be useful.

2.5.1 Advantages of Outside Help

If your organization elects to use in-house employees to implement ISO 14001, you certainly should not be discouraged from doing so. However, external expertise may provide a number of distinct advantages.

Specialized Knowledge

Although there are exceptions, consultants generally work within a specialized area (such as environmental management systems) and are able to bring a depth of understanding that may be lacking within an organization. Your company's environmental, health, and safety (EHS) staff is responsible for the multitude of environmental issues that affect your organization and are likely to have a more superficial understanding of voluntary initiatives such as ISO 14001.

Exposure to Diverse Applications

An experienced EMS consultant is likely to have provided assistance to organizations in a diverse array of industries. Such experience presents you with approaches that have been successful in other settings with which you may be unfamiliar.

Objectivity

Unlike your own employees, outside consultants are not hampered by personal knowledge about or relationships with others in your organization. The lack of "institutional memory" allows objective evaluation of whatever information is available for comparison to ISO 14001 requirements.

Credibility

Because outside consultants do not have a vested interest in the results of the work that they perform, a consultant who determines whether your company's activities adequately fulfill the requirements of a particular ISO 14001 element is far more likely to be believed than those with direct responsibility for such activities.

2.5.2 Attributes to Consider

Determining whether your company would benefit by hiring an outside consultant may be a relatively easy decision. A more difficult decision, however, is figuring out which consultant to hire. Generally, determining which consultant is right for your company or organization requires consideration of two sets of attributes: credentials and personal chemistry.

Credentials

Your company, the client, should obtain a clear understanding of the consultant's qualifications and ability to perform the work. You should ask the following questions.

*   *Who are the consultant's previous clients?*

Not every consultant has been hired by a Fortune-50 corporation, nor is this essential. You should evaluate your consultant's previous projects based on their similarity to your current situation. Mid-sized companies might find that experience with a number of similarly sized companies in different industries is preferable to experience with one large multinational corporation in the same industry. Alternatively, you should view experience with proactive companies, regardless of size, as highly desirable.

*   *What are the consultant's capabilities regarding ISO 14001?*

This is particularly important because the ISO 14001 standard is new. A number of consultants from two related areas — ISO 9000 quality management and environmental compliance — have begun to offer ISO 14001 services. You would be well advised to determine whether your prospective consultants have conducted projects pertaining specifically to environmental management.

A related issue concerns participation on the United States Technical Advisory Group (U.S. TAG) to TC 207. Critical to interpreting the standard in a manner that ensures effective implementation is a thorough understanding of the meaning of the language contained in each clause of ISO 14001, its annex, and the ISO 14004 EMS guideline. Consultants who served as United States technical experts to TC 207 and those who participated at the U.S. TAG level are likely to have an edge in this regard.

Personal chemistry

Professional qualifications should not be the sole criterion for hiring a consultant. Excellent capabilities are likely to be found within a number of consulting firms. They should provide the basis for consideration.

Equally important is the chemistry that exists between you and your consultant. Faced with an EMS assessment that requires significant interaction between your consultant and various employees, you must determine whether he or she will be able to work comfortably with your employees or vice versa in a potentially disruptive situation.

Personal chemistry is a legitimate criterion for selecting among similarly qualified consultants. Most of us have had the experience of working with an individual who was pompous, arrogant, self-centered, or otherwise unpleasant despite excellent professional qualifications.

Ultimately, hiring a consultant constitutes an act of faith. Even the most intensive due diligence effort is fraught with uncertainty. To help select the right consultant, look for:

☑ initiative

During your first meeting, does the consultant exhibit an understanding of your industry and organization? Or does he or she ask for basic information that could have been obtained in advance?

☑ ability to listen

Does the consultant ask questions about your specific situation and the problems that you are trying to solve? Or does he or she focus on his or her ability to solve your problems without knowing what they are?

☑ expertise

Does the consultant demonstrate a knowledge of ISO 14001 by discussing appropriate issues and asking relevant questions? Or does he or she tell you about his or her experience?

☑ conversational manner

Does the consultant elicit and share information in a manner that treats you as a contributing member of the project or group? Or does he or she employ a style that limits your participation?

☑ understanding of client pressures

Does the consultant exhibit an understanding of how and by whom your program is evaluated and your budget limitations? Or does he or she pursue wholesale change regardless of cost?

☑ flexibility

Does the consultant provide alternative methods of proceeding? Or does he or she employ a "one size fits all" approach?

☑ critical thinking

Does the consultant demonstrate a thorough knowledge of the contents and meaning of ISO 14001? Or has he or she obtained a superficial knowledge by reading articles and overviews?

A good consultant can provide an excellent return on your investment by focusing you and directing your orientation on significant environmental issues in a concentrated period of time. Unlike corporate EHS staff, who may be inundated with minutiae that preclude examination of the big picture, external consultants are able to see both the forest and the trees.

3

Planning and Implementing ISO 14001

CHAPTER 1
Preparations and Planning

by C. Foster Knight, Managing Director, Knight and Associates and
Robert Ferrone, President, The Ferrone Group

3.1.1 Overview

This section covers practical, cost-effective planning and implementation practices for enterprises that have made the decision to implement ISO 14001. ISO 14001 provides companies with considerable leeway in how they implement the standard. At the outset, we would like to advise our readers that this chapter contains planning and implementing approaches that may go beyond the minimum requirements of ISO 14001. Unless we specifically say so, we are not interpreting ISO 14001 requirements.

economic
performance

Our intent is to provide you with practical and effective directions that will yield substantial environmental as well as economic performance improvements from your EMS. We are convinced from years of experience in environmental management implementation that a

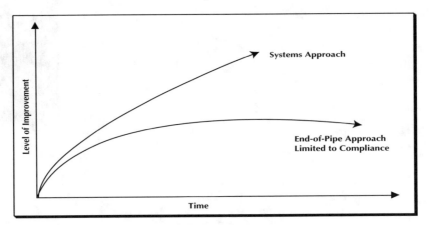

Figure 3.1 — Path toward excellence is a systems approach.

company or facility should not undertake a halfhearted or "minimalist" approach to ISO 14001. Either do it well, or don't waste your money and time.

While ISO 14001 is intended as an environmental management system specification for any kind of organization, we are focusing on industrial and commercial enterprises, with appropriate examples for small and medium firms.

The principal corresponding elements of the **ISO 14001** specification covered in this chapter are **Section 4.2** Planning, and **Section 4.3** Implementation and Operation. Planning and implementation necessarily also involve environmental policy, auditing, and measurement issues and overall management review, so this chapter also covers relevant features in **Section 4.1** Policy, **Section 4.4** Checking and Corrective Action, and **Section 4.5** Management Review.

most
implementation
is site-based

The "setting" for this discussion is an industrial facility or site. ISO 14001 envisions the possibility of a multi-site, enterprise-wide ISO 14001 certification process. But, as a practical matter, most industrial and commercial enterprises contemplating ISO 14001 will need to undertake the effort at the facility or site level, so that is how we are approaching ISO 14001 planning and implementation.

To avoid duplication where more than a reference to brief text of the standards (ISO 14001 and ISO 14004) or another element of ISO 14001 implementation is required, we may refer you to actual text of the standards as it appears in 📖 Appendix A.

3.1.2 Integrating Your EMS with Other Systems

integration is
practical

Many companies have found from experience the value of integrating environmental, health, and safety (EHS) management. Environmental aspects of a company's operations often are intertwined with occupational health and safety elements. Reducing a risk to the external environment by modifying a manufacturing process without taking occupational health and safety considerations into account may result in increased risks to the safety of the workplace. Similarly, managing environmental risks involving emergencies typically entails managing health and safety risks at the same time. Sometimes, it is hard to tell whether a risk is "environmental" or "health and safety" or a combination of the two. What, for example, does "process safety management" seek to achieve if not measures of increased safety and environmental protection?

Therefore, an important threshold question is whether the ISO 14001 environmental management system (EMS) also can provide the framework for an integrated EHS management system. You can find the answer in the introduction to ISO 14001:

> "This standard is not intended to address, and does not include requirements for aspects of occupational health and safety management; however it does not seek to discourage an organization from developing integration of such management system elements. Nevertheless the certification/registration process will only be applicable to the environmental management system aspects."

build on what you have
As a practical matter, if your company already has integrated environmental, health, and safety programs, you should continue your integrated approach. The ISO 14001 EMS framework will work very well for an integrated EHS management system. It makes no sense to create a separate ISO 14001 environmental management system on top of existing integrated EHS programs. For purposes of this chapter, you can substitute "EHS" for "environmental" and find that our planning and implementation guidance works just as well for an EHS management system. 📖 (See Part 4 for case studies and other information highlighting management system integration.)

There also is interest in integrating ISO 14001 and ISO 9000 systems. For facilities or sites that are or will be certified to an ISO 9000 quality management system standard, there are clear parallels and similarities between the two standards that will provide important opportunities for integration. For example, system documentation, document control procedures, training systems, system audits, procedures for nonconformance, corrective and preventive action, and management review provide good opportunities for integration. 📖 (See Part 10, Chapter 3 for more information on integration, and *Figures A.1*, *A.2*, and *A3* in Appendix A.)

Transnational Company Strategies

If you operate a large transnational company with facilities in different countries, you will want to take one of two general approaches:

1) allow each facility to decide whether and when to implement ISO 14001; or

2) set a company-wide goal of implementing ISO 14001 at all facilities by a specified date.

Under either approach, your corporate function can play an important role in providing facilities with an internal, company-wide guideline and tools for ISO 14001 planning and implementation.

ISO 14001 provides flexibility
ISO 14001 provides companies with considerable flexibility in implementation. You can decide to use ISO 14001 as an agent of change to integrate EHS management systematically with operations management, to gain high environmental performance improvements,

significant resource productivity enhancements, and to secure other benefits.

Or your company can decide to invest in a less aggressive implementation effort, gain ISO 14001 certification, then continuously improve on its implementation over time. There are obviously variations in between.

clarify limits

Because of the wide latitude of implementation afforded by the ISO 14001 specification, you should clarify your corporate implementation strategy to all facilities at the outset. Facilities often will want to know the degree of ISO 14001 implementation that is expected of them. Moreover, how each facility implements ISO 14001 can influence the expectations of your company's customers and other stakeholders.

Thus, the corporate function can play a valuable role in providing each facility with a more detailed "internal architecture" of ISO 14001 implementation and tools, such as company-wide environmental objectives, a company-wide EMS audit module, and company-wide document management standards. Development of the corporate ISO 14001 implementation strategy, needless to say, should involve executive management, operations and functional managers, as well as environmental and quality professionals.

3.1.3 Facility (or Pilot Plant) Implementation Team and Gap Analysis

form the team

A key step in preparing for ISO 14001 implementation is the formation of an implementation team, with clear authority from the plant/site manager to lead implementation. The implementation team should be led by the facility ISO 14000 (or 9000) "champion" or by an experienced operations/project manager. A small implementation team, with vigorous representation from functions and operations and clearly supported by plant management, provides a superior implementation organization. 📖 (See Part 2, Chapter 2, Section 7 for more insights on forming this team.)

train the team

To ensure that all members of the team understand and communicate ISO 14001 concepts and terms consistently, ISO 14001 training is the first order of business for the implementation team. ISO 14001 course providers offer two- or three-day courses on ISO 14001 implementation and some offer these courses as "in-house" training, customized for the facility's business and operations. Look for ISO 14001 implementation courses whose instructors are experienced in environmental management systems implementation. 📖 (See Part 2, Chapter 4 for more information on training.)

do a gap analysis

Once the team consistently understands ISO 14001 concepts and terms, the next step involves the team undertaking a detailed ISO 14001 "gap analysis" comparing the facility or site's existing management systems with ISO 14001's requirements. Your organization may already have performed a preliminary or paper ISO 14001 gap analysis for the facility or corporate environmental management function as a part of making the decision on ISO 14001. 📖 (See Part 2, Chapter 1 for more insight on making the decision.) However, a paper comparison of your facility's environmental programs with ISO 14001 cannot substitute for the detailed gap analysis that should be conducted at this stage.   📖 (See Part 2, Chapter 2, Section 5 for more information on conducting an initial review/gap analysis and the difference between them.)

Figure 3.2 — Multifunctional team approach is necessary in today's global market.

The detailed gap analysis involves a careful review and comparison of existing facility/site management systems, including human resources, financial, engineering, purchasing, quality, materials resource planning, environment, health, and safety. A key objective of this exercise is to identify opportunities for using parts of non-environmental management systems to fulfill the requirements of ISO 14001, as well as to clarify the gaps.

For example, if your facility is already ISO 9001 or ISO 9002 certified, the detailed "gap analysis" will identify important opportunities to use existing ISO 9000 documentation systems for purposes of ISO 14001. 📖 (See Part 3, Chapter 4 for more information on documentation.)

Similarly, human resource management programs may reveal systems that can be supplemented to fulfill ISO 14001 requirements for defining roles, responsibilities, and authorities in the EMS and for documenting training requirements. And the facility's purchasing management systems may indicate possibilities for meeting ISO 14001's requirement for "establishing and maintaining procedures related to the identifiable significant environmental aspects of goods and services used by the organization."

To avoid creating a separate new ISO 14001 system on top of existing facility management systems, it is important to understand the full range and potential for adapting ISO 14001's requirements to existing management procedures/systems through a detailed facility gap analysis.

Implementation Plan

The output or product of your organization's detailed facility gap analysis is the essential information needed to develop an ISO 14001 planning and implementation plan.

The implementation plan will guide your facility's entire ISO 14001 implementation effort. The plan must identify (based on the detailed gap analysis):

☑ specific ISO 14001 elements requiring development work;

☑ the ISO team member or manager with lead responsibility;

☑ resource requirements;

☑ dependencies/critical interrelationships with other ISO 14001 work items; and

☑ implementation milestones/completion date(s).

See *Figure 3.4* for a simplified version of an implementation plan element covering a specific ISO 14001 requirement relating to training.

Each ISO 14001 work item should be clearly described and backed with a plan or implementation strategy showing how it will be carried out. Critical interrelationships with other ISO 14001 work items should be annotated or cross-referenced. A summary sheet showing all ISO 14001 work items (with horizontal time-lines or other graphics) provides all ISO team members and plant management with a concise means for monitoring progress. 📖 (See Appendix C for sample implementation checklists.)

plan guides
implementation

The implementation plan must be reviewed and approved by the plant management group. Since a management review process is a required component of ISO 14001, you will find it useful to establish the management review process with the initial review and approval of the implementation plan. 📖 (See Part 6, Chapter 4 for more information on management reviews.)

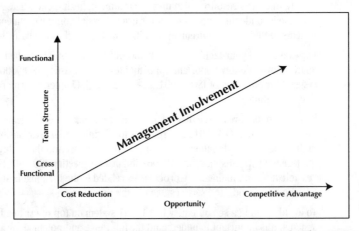

Figure 3.3 — Degree of management involvement rises for structural and competitive gains.

During the implementation phase leading to ISO 14001 certification, the management review process can consist primarily of a review of the implementation plan by the plant management group, implementation issue identification and resolution, and progress monitoring.

Outline of Implementation Plan Using Example of ISO 14001 Work Item					
"Develop a process for training all personnel whose work may create a significant impact on the environment." **(Section 4.3.2**, second sentence)					
ISO 14001 Requirement	**Implementation Actions**	**Resource Requirement**	**Dependencies & Critical Inter-relationships**	**Lead Responsibility**	**Milestones/ Completion**
4.3.2 Training (second sentence)	Identify all employees whose work may create significant environmental impacts.			Mary Crisler	1 September 1996
	Upon completion of "environmental aspects" review and identification of "significant" environmental aspects, identify specific kinds of work associated with "significant' aspects. Identify specific employees whose work is thus affected.		Completion of "environmental aspects" review and identification of "significant" environmental impacts. Availability of up-to-date job descriptions for all employees.		1 July 1996

Figure 3.4 Example implementation plan element.

3.1.4 Identifying Environmental Aspects

Having completed an implementation plan, the work begins in earnest for your ISO 14001 team. A clear understanding of the facility's "environmental aspects" and those that are "significant" is essential to developing or updating your facility's environmental policy, setting environmental objectives and targets, identifying training requirements, establishing operational controls, and developing appropriate monitoring and measurement systems, among other features of the ISO 14001 EMS.

aspects get high priority Assign the highest priority to developing a procedure for identifying environmental aspects of the facility's activities, products, and services.

Generally speaking, environmental aspects can be classified under two broad categories:

1) environmental aspects directly regulated by applicable laws and regulations; and

2) unregulated "environmental aspects."

Regulated Environmental Aspects and Legal Requirements

Because the ISO 14001 environmental management system will need to have a procedure for identifying and gaining access to applicable legal requirements, you might find it useful to combine the legal requirements identification process with the regulated "environmental aspects" identification.

Materials, Process Emissions, Effluents, and Solid/Hazardous Waste

begin with the familiar— regulated aspects

Regulated environmental aspects in the form of regulated chemical and hazardous substances, air and noise emissions, wastewater effluents, and solid/hazardous waste are the familiar territory of facility and site environmental, health, and safety professionals whose job is to help manage compliance. Examples include facility air emissions governed by local, state, and national air pollution control regulations and emission limits, regulated wastewater discharges, and hazardous waste management regulatory requirements, including requirements that govern reporting and remediation of soil and groundwater contamination.

Most industrial facilities already have some method of documenting how environmental, health, and safety regulatory requirements apply to their activities and operations. A typical manufacturing plant may use checklists or even compliance self-assessment tools or protocols to determine if the plant is in compliance.

To illustrate, various water pollution control regulatory requirements may apply to the plant's operations, including general pretreatment standards (e.g. pH and biological oxygen demand (BOD)) and possibly specific pretreatment standards for specific toxic wastewater constituents. Based on the applicable wastewater treatment regulatory requirements, specific regulated contaminants or characteristics in the wastewater stream can be identified and listed as subsets of the wastewater "environmental aspects." Use of regulatory checklists, compliance procedures, and manuals and other tools to determine compliance status, in this sense, is a good starting point to identify and develop an inventory of the regulated environmental aspects of your facility's activities and operations. 📖 (See Part 4, Chapter 3 and Appendix C for sample checklists.)

To the extent that the facility or site does not have checklists or other compliance management tools to identify applicable environmental regulatory requirements, obviously it will need to develop them, not only to reduce compliance exposure but also because ISO 14001 requires the facility or site to have a procedure to identify applicable environmental legal requirements.

challenge: getting specific information

A key challenge in identifying applicable environmental (and health and safety) legal requirements is obtaining specific information about the site operations processes and materials used at your facility or site. Many environmental (and health and safety) regulatory requirements apply to specific chemical or hazardous substances. Unless you know, for example, whether you are using or creating chemical substances that are specifically regulated, you cannot determine if the regulations apply.

Developing a comprehensive set of material safety data sheets (MSDSs) for all hazardous substances used and produced by your facility is a good starting point. Among other things, the MSDS identifies specific chemical substances in materials and products, personal protection and handling instructions, and environmental protection precautions.

use MSDSs

The MSDSs are commonly used in North America and in virtually every European country (except perhaps Eastern Europe), and are increasingly used in the Asia-Pacific region. In many of these countries, an MSDS is required by law to accompany inbound and outbound

Environmental Aspects

Definition of Environmental Aspect:

"Element of an organization's activities, products, and services which can interact with the environment." (ISO 14001)

Plain-language meaning:

An "environmental aspect" signifies the *potential* for an environmental impact. A specific activity, product, or service may already be tightly controlled to prevent environmental impacts. The fact that it has the *potential* for environmental impacts makes it an "environmental aspect" within the meaning of ISO 14001. It does not matter whether the activity, product, or service is regulated to protect the environment. What matters is only whether there is a *potential* for an environmental impact under reasonably foreseeable conditions including absence of voluntary or regulated environmental controls, legal environmental releases of air emissions and wastewater effluents (i.e. below regulated limits), accidents, breakdowns of environmental pollution controls, misuse of products by consumers, or improper end-of-life product disposal by customers.

materials and products containing hazardous substances. The MSDS can be one more tool to help you understand why and how these materials are used, helping you identify appropriately the environmental aspects of the facility or site's products and services, as well as other activities.

In addition, in the U.S. and in some other Organization for Economic Cooperation and Development (OECD) countries, lists are commercially available (in print, in software programs, and in CD-ROM format) showing all regulatory requirements applicable to a specific chemical substance. There are even "lists" of "lists" that will help identify all applicable regulatory requirements once you have a comprehensive understanding of the chemical materials you are using at your site.

The MSDS system, however, will not be too helpful in identifying specific waste substances released from your site processes, such as air contaminants, specific wastewater effluents, and specific types of hazardous wastes.

characterize
waste streams

Therefore, another important step is to characterize your waste streams including air emissions, wastewater, and solid and hazardous wastes to determine the applicability of air and water pollution control and waste management regulatory requirements.

In summary, your regulated "environmental aspects" correlate with many of the environmental regulatory requirements that apply to your facility or site. Using MSDSs and techniques for characterizing your waste streams, you can develop the information to identify applicable regulatory requirements.

Legal requirements also include the administrative requirements to demonstrate compliance, such as:

- permits;
- approvals;
- registrations;
- recordkeeping; and
- reporting requirements.

administrative requirements

Additionally, as a result of government enforcement, your facility or site may be governed by a consent agreement or other legally enforceable agreement, obligating your facility or site to conduct periodic groundwater monitoring or to meet other requirements.

Finally, there are management-system-oriented regulatory requirements such as training employees in chemical safety.

"legal register" may be practical

ISO 14001 does not require that you assemble all the specific applicable environmental requirements in a single document or "legal register." But environmental, health, and safety professionals have found from experience that a regulatory checklist or compliance manual detailing applicable requirements is an important component of effective environmental compliance management.

use audit protocols

An effective way for ensuring that you have identified all applicable environmental regulatory requirements is to conduct an environmental compliance audit using audit protocols that cover all potentially applicable requirements. Compliance auditors are trained to determine whether a specific legal requirement applies to your specific operations processes, materials, or activities. When there is reasonable doubt, an attorney specializing in environmental law can resolve the question.

ISO 14001 Section 4.2.1 — Identification of Environmental Aspects

"The organization shall establish and maintain a procedure to identify the environmental aspects of its activities, products or services that it can control and over which it can be expected to have an influence..."

ISO 14001 Section 4.2.2 — Legal and Other Requirements

The organization shall establish and maintain a procedure to identify and have access to legal and other requirements to which the organization subscribes directly applicable to the environmental aspects of its activities, products and services.

TIP 3.1

> ## Ensuring compliance in small and medium-sized enterprises (SMEs)
>
> Many small and medium industrial and commercial facilities do not have a systematic process for ensuring compliance with applicable environmental regulatory requirements. Good sources of generally free information on applicable environmental regulatory requirements are:
>
> 1) industry associations;
>
> 2) the U.S. EPA and some state regulatory agency programs specifically oriented to help SMEs without compliance penalties; and
>
> 3) suppliers of chemical/hazardous materials and services who have specialized knowledge of applicable regulatory requirements.

Regulated Environmental Aspects of Products and Services

bigger
challenge:
products and
services

Most industrial facilities in the U.S., Canada, and many other industrialized countries already have some kind of documented system for identifying and managing compliance with EHS regulatory requirements applicable to their "activities and operations," such as manufacturing operations (air emissions, wastewater effluents, solid and hazardous waste). But they face a bigger challenge when they begin identifying the regulated environmental aspects associated with the facility or site's *products and services*, particularly if the products are exported to markets in the OECD countries.

"Environmental attribute" product regulations are proliferating in the OECD countries. Just as environmental regulations governing manufacturing operations (e.g., pollution control limits) are a useful source for identifying certain "environmental aspects," so, too, can environmental product-related regulatory requirements help identify "environmental aspects" related to products.

go to
responsible
employees

Where can you locate this information? In the case of transnational companies with engineering, manufacturing, product line, and marketing groups in different countries, keeping track of the numerous product-related environmental requirements often is not the responsibility of the EHS specialists but is assigned, instead, to engineering, product line, or marketing function staff, who also are responsible for product safety regulatory requirements.

identify
product-
related toxic
substance laws

Engineering, product line, and marketing groups may have established systems for monitoring environmental product-related regulatory initiatives to ensure that affected products can be sold legally. In the case of environmental laws governing toxic substances in products, such as the U.S. Toxic Substances Control Act (TSCA) and similar laws in Canada, Europe, and some Asia-Pacific countries, the expertise for managing compliance usually is found in the manufacturing plant. Product-related toxic substances control laws require manufacturers to have systems in place for identifying "new chemical substances" (not already on a list of substances approved for use in commerce), for reporting "new chemical substances" to regulatory agencies, for testing, and for making other kinds of reports.

example:
packaging and
transportation

A final example is laws and regulatory requirements governing packaging and transportation of hazardous materials. A principal objective of these regulatory requirements is to prevent the release of hazardous materials during transportation and, in the event of transportation accidents, to minimize damage to human health and the environment. These hazardous materials transportation requirements apply in some form or other to virtually all industrial and commercial operations involving shipment of chemical materials. Therefore, understanding the way these regulations apply to your logistical operations can be a useful tool for identifying the "environmental aspects" of transportation of chemical materials and products.

The point of this discussion is that companies selling products in large regional or global markets probably already have some kind of systems and documentation of how these requirements affect their products. If they don't have any such systems, developing them should be an important priority — quite apart from ISO 14001 — to avoid business disruptions from noncompliance or inability to meet market requirements.

challenge:
gathering
information
from diverse
sites

For the ISO 14000 team gathering information on these existing systems and documentation, this is not an easy task; the systems and documentation may be located in different parts of the worldwide company, in functional groups such as engineering, purchasing, specific product line management groups, logistics, and marketing. But assembling information on environmentally related product regulatory requirements and standards is a useful way to help identify systematically the environmental aspects of the manufacturing plant's products.

If your company is transnational, you should therefore check with the engineering and marketing functions, as well as manufacturing operations, to gather specific information on "environmental attribute" regulations affecting products your plant manufactures. If you are a manufacturer with a single plant, you already have or should have information on "environmental attribute" regulations affecting your products. Selected examples of environmental product-related regulations are listed in *Figure 3.5*

Aspects of Services

identify
services

So far, we've talked about identifying the regulated environmental aspects and legal requirements applicable to the facility or site's "activities" and its "products." With respect to environmental aspects of the facility or site's "services," existing systems and documentation may not prove too useful. However, the basic information can be developed by understanding the specific "services" offered by the facility/site. For example, if the facility or site provides product maintenance and repair services, you likely will find that chemicals and hazardous materials are used when you provide the service. Again, use your MSDSs as a tool for identifying "environmental aspects" of services.

If your facility has an effective MSDS management system in place, you then have a method that can be used to supplement other methods and procedures for identifying and documenting the environmental aspects of your facility or site's activities, products, and services.

Selected Types of Requirements Relating to Environmental Attributes of Products	
Category	**Examples**
Hazard warning label requirements	• Pesticide labeling • California Proposition 65 • Labels on products containing or manufactured with ozone depleters • Labels on portable batteries
Environmental effects disclosure	• Energy and water usage consumer guides • CAFE standards for U.S. autos • Eco-label programs in many countries
Bans/restrictions covering toxis materials in products	• Phase-out of heavy metals used in packaging materials and certain products • PCBs and asbestos • Pending regulatory initiatives in various OECD countries to restrict specific toxic substances in products
Minimum recycled content, reuse, and government procurement requirements	• Minimum recycled content requirements for packaging and certain other products in Europe and U.S. (states) • Greening of government procurement standards
Ease of dissembley and recycling requirements	• Requirements for coding plastic and other materials for ease of disassembly and recycling • Rechargeable batteries must be "easily removable" from consumer products
Product take-back, recycling, and disposal requirements	• Especially evident in European markets; also to an extent in Japan and some U.S. state markets
Source: Knight & Associates	

Figure 3.5 — Examples of environmental product-related regulations.

TIP 3.2

SMEs: Use the MSDS as a starting point

For small businesses, MSDSs are a good tool to use as a starting point to help identify their "environmental aspects." Your facility or site is required to have MSDS information on file for materials and chemical products containing hazardous substances that are used and produced. For inbound materials, your suppliers are required to provide you with an MSDS for each type of material. If you produce products containing hazardous substances, each such outbound product or chemical material needs an MSDS.

TIP 3.3

> ## Some issues to be considered in establishing and maintaining a process for identifying legal requirements
>
> 1) How does your facility or site access and identify relevant legal requirements?
>
> 2) How does your facility or site keep track of applicable legal requirements?
>
> 3) How does your facility or site keep track of changes to legal requirements?
>
> 4) How does your facility or site communicate relevant information on legal requirement to your employees?
>
> Adapted from **ISO 14004, Section 4.2.3.**

Unregulated Environmental Aspects

Beyond Compliance

look at lower-than-required thresholds

There is an important difference between ISO 14001's approach to environmental management and conventional environmental compliance management. Conventional environmental compliance management focuses on regulated environmental aspects and seeks to ensure full compliance with applicable regulatory requirements. ISO 14001 looks at both regulated and unregulated environmental aspects and seeks to identify opportunities for improving environmental performance of both. Therefore, the process of identifying environmental aspects needs to look beyond regulated environmental aspects to those that are not regulated. (See *Figure 3.6*.)

Unregulated environmental aspects fall into two general categories. There are environmental aspects that are regulated up to specified limits and there are those that are not regulated at all.

example: NOx emissions

An example of an environmental aspect that is regulated to a specified limit is NO_x emissions. Typically, you are allowed by applicable NO_x regulations to release NO_x up to a certain limit based on a prescribed unit of measurement. As long as your NO_x emissions do not exceed the regulatory limits, you are in full compliance. But your NO_x emissions released while in 100 percent compliance nevertheless represent an environmental aspect of your combustion processes. NO_x releases legally below allowable regulatory limits may provide an opportunity for further environmental performance improvements. They may also provide opportunities for cost savings and business opportunities such as marketable NO_x emission units covering the gap between actual emissions and legally allowable releases.

example: public reporting

Another example is the public reporting of environmental releases of specified toxic substances required by the U.S. Emergency Planning and Community Right to Know Act (EPCRA). For manufacturing facilities using materials releasing specified toxic substances, reporting is required for amounts released above the annual threshold limits (typically 10,000 pounds of designated substances used per year). Amounts used and released below the threshold limits do not require reporting. While releases of these toxics below threshold reporting limits are not regulated environmental aspects in this context, they nevertheless present opportunities for environmental performance improvements and cost savings in the form of more efficient use of raw materials.

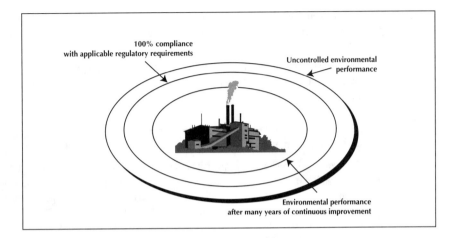

Figure 3.6 — Moving beyond compliance: Where does your company fit?

look at
unregulated
aspects

The second broad category of unregulated environmental aspects are those that are not conventionally regulated at all. The recurring examples of unregulated environmental aspects affecting most industrial operations are:

- water and energy consumption;

- CO_2 releases;

- unregulated (or minimally regulated) wastes such as many forms of non-hazardous solid waste, including office paper waste;

- the still largely unregulated environmental aspects of transportation (e.g., environmental burdens associated with supplying and distributing raw materials, semi-finished materials, parts, components, and business/commuter travel); and

- many types of end-of-life product disposal.

Resource Productivity Approach

What is a useful framework for identifying unregulated environmental aspects of your facility or site's activities, products, and services?

identify
opportunities
in value chain

One general approach is to use practical variations of what Michael E. Porter calls the "resource productivity" framework. The resource productivity approach involves a systematic approach to identifying environmental issues and opportunities in the entire value chain of the enterprise, from suppliers to manufacturing to distribution in commerce to end-of-life product disposition. Needless to say, this should be a long-term effort involving shorter-term, practical goals. ISO 14001 does not require identification of all environmental aspects in the entire "value chain" of the enterprise.

ISO 14001 specifically limits the scope of the environmental aspects identification process to environmental aspects that a facility or site *". . . can control and over which it can be expected to have an influence."* What it requires is a systems approach that is practically oriented and that allows for continual improvement over time. Because many of the environmental aspects identified through this systems approach involve waste, the environmental aspects identification process can lead to very significant opportunities to improve resource productivity.

Practical approaches can be as simple as making an inventory of unused or unusable materials and solid wastes at the facility or site, then examining the opportunity costs of unused and waste materials to rank their significance.

TIP 3.4

Resource productivity

"The concept of resource productivity opens up a new way of looking at both full systems costs and the value associated with any product. Resource inefficiencies are most obvious within a company in the form of incomplete material utilization and poor process controls, which result in unnecessary waste, defects, and stored materials. But there also are many other hidden costs buried in the life cycle of the product. Packaging discarded by distributors or customers, for example, wastes resources and adds costs. Customers bear additional costs when they use products that pollute or waste energy. Resources are lost when products that contain usable materials are discarded and when customers pay — directly or indirectly — for product disposal."

Michael E. Porter and Claas van der Linde, "*Green and Competitive,*" Harvard Business Review, 120, 122 (Sept.- Oct. 1995)

Relationship Between Quality and "Environmental Aspects"

Another important perspective for both large companies and SMEs alike is to understand the tight relationship between the quality of the materials you use and the manufacturing process and their associated environmental aspects.

work with supplier

For example, if you have a good idea of the specifications of the materials you need for producing a high-quality product and are carefully managing your supplier to meet those specifications, then you also have — at the same time — an effective means for understanding the environmental aspects of your materials. By improving your understanding of the environmental aspects of specific chemical or hazardous substances contained in your incoming materials, you are then in a position to work with your supplier to improve the environmental quality of your products and manufacturing processes.

Another example of the relationship between quality and environmental aspects is the correlation between quality defects and environmental aspects. For example, an environmental aspect of your process such as the use of an industrial solvent for cleaning parts used in products may, on closer inspection, indicate a quality process deficiency in parts production that requires a cleaning step. Solving the quality problem may also remove the environmental aspect.

TIP 3.5

> ## Quality and environmental aspects for SMEs
>
> SMEs play a major role in the overall environmental management performance of their manufacturing customers. A durable goods manufacturer using hundreds or thousands of parts and components produced by SMEs sooner or later will put pressure on the SME suppliers to help address the environmental aspects related to parts and components. Environmental aspects management is becoming a supplier "quality" issue. SMEs that have knowledge and insights concerning the chemical/hazardous substances in their materials and products they sell to industrial customers — and are willing to work on these "environmental aspects" — may find that they can win more contracts with their customers.

Materials Identification Approach

work with quality defects

Our brief discussion about the resource productivity perspective and the relationship between quality and environmental aspects indicates the importance of having some kind of methodology for identifying the potentially hazardous as well as reusable or reclaimable materials contained in your incoming raw materials, parts, and components. You should include energy and water consumption in this review. The ultimate objective is to be able to know your materials and their constituent substances in terms of their "environmental aspects" or potential environmental impacts during product manufacturing, distribution, use by customers, and end-of-life disposal.

consider simplified materials identification

Knowing all this information can be a daunting effort that is not expressly required by ISO 14001. For ISO 14001 purposes, you should consider a simplified or rudimentary materials identification process that is aimed over time at improving your facility's manufacturing or other operational use of materials, such as by identifying:

- recycling and reclamation opportunities for used materials;
- opportunities for substituting materials that will produce less waste;
- process modifications that result in a higher percentage of raw materials in the final product;
- opportunities for making products last longer; and
- opportunities for making parts that contain a higher percentage of materials or parts capable of reuse and recycling at the product's end-of-life.

In addition, a materials identification methodology can provide useful information for responding to your customers' concerns about the potential toxic effects of your products on human health and the environment, as well as responding to regulatory requirements, including Material Safety Data Sheets and specific "environmental attribute" product regulations.

TIP 3.6

Materials identification and environmental aspects

For ISO 14001 purposes, begin with a simple process that will capture information on chemical and hazardous substances and specific product-related environmental attributes (e.g., recyclability) based on a survey of key functions or departments in your company or facility. At first, your process or methodology can be simple. Over time, you can gradually improve its accuracy and usefulness consistent with ISO 14001's emphasis on continual improvement.

process industry

Process industry companies such as those in the chemical, glass, metals, paper, textiles, and food industries already have much of the information envisioned in the materials identification approach. From an ISO 14001 perspective, the practical problem they will face is how to pull together voluminous data found in many different parts of their company and organize it as a useful "environmental aspects" identification methodology.

This is another reason why it is essential that the ISO 14000 implementation team adequately represent potential sources of "environmental aspects" information such as R&D, manufacturing, and product line management.

durable product industry

Durable product manufacturers face a different challenge because they may purchase hundreds or thousands of separate parts and components from vendors. MSDSs may not be required for most of these parts and components. Detailed data on the specific environmental attributes of these parts and components thus may only be obtainable by asking for it from their suppliers.

TIP 3.7

Materials identification in manufacturing processes

A more rigorous approach to identifying materials in your manufacturing process is to identify the environmental fate of all the raw materials entering your facility and to quantify how much actually ends up in the manufactured product.

For example, you can use engineering estimating methods, activity-based costing, and a substance "significance" ranking method to identify, quantify, and evaluate what happens to *specific* chemical materials used in each step of a production process (how much goes *into the product* and how much is lost as air emissions, wastewater effluent, and solid/hazardous waste).

After analyzing each step of the production process and aggregating the data, you can enter the resulting data in a currently available software application that will give you a broad range of information, including the environmental costs associated with the materials, opportunities for less costly and environmentally superior process enhancements, and an operations management tool that enables measurements for continual improvement.

Setting practical boundaries defining the scope of the environmental aspects identification effort is acceptable under ISO 14001. For example, setting the boundary at the point where materials come into your facility is an effective strategy for SMEs.

aggregate
data — use
software

But let's assume your facility manufactures durable electronic products and buys many hundreds or thousands of parts and components from a multitude of suppliers. Identifying the environmental aspects based only on the materials entering your facility may not be enough. How far back up the supply chain should you look for environmental aspects of your parts and components? This has to be a matter of sound business judgment based on a competent understanding of the materials contained in the parts and components and the potential for realizing resource productivity increases, cost savings, and environmental performance improvements.

looking back
up the supply
chain

How far back you look at the environmental aspects of your purchased parts and components may also be a function of market requirements. Leading electronic and computer equipment manufacturers in North America and Europe are sending detailed questionnaires to their suppliers seeking data on potentially hazardous or toxic substances and materials contained in the equipment they buy from these suppliers. If you are one of the suppliers, you may not be able to answer the supplier questionnaires without going back to your parts and components vendors for the answers.

Logistics/Transportation Aspects

global
transportation
issues

For many companies, logistics and transportation-related activities and operations may involve important environmental aspects. Factoring in the environmental aspects of transportation-related energy and materials use is a growing area of significance for transnational companies. As global companies shift production of specific parts of their products to low-labor-rate countries, the amount of transportation involved in moving parts or pieces of the product may be a significant aspect of the final product's cost, in terms of traditional financial and environmental aspects accounting.

example:
clothing
manufacturer

If you are a "made in the U.S.A." shoe or clothing manufacturer, how do you account for the environmentally related costs of transporting pieces and parts? If fossil fuel energy prices escalate, what system or process do you have for looking at the transportation-related direct and environmental costs associated with your worldwide distribution system? In the case of a clothing goods manufacturer, if the fabric is manufactured in a distant country, shipped to another country for assembly into a clothing product, then shipped to retailers, and finally shipped next-day air service to the customer, the environmental aspects, such as energy used and wastes generated in this process, may be more significant than those in the initial fabric materials and production processes. Identifying the transportation-related environmental aspects in this case may provide insights pointing to less energy-intensive and more cost-effective production and distribution arrangements.

just-in-time
issues

A simpler example involves an auto parts manufacturer that received daily "just-in-time" truck shipments of copper wire on wood spools from one of its suppliers. After examining the transportation-related environmental aspects of these "just-in-time" raw materials, the auto parts manufacturer determined that the transportation-related environmental aspects (e.g., truck fuel and emissions, disposal of wood spools) could be substantially reduced if it leased its own truck trailer and picked up a larger volume of copper wire once or twice a month. Although this involved backing away from "just-in-time" and increasing on-site inventories, the lower overall costs and improved environmental performance (including returning the wood spools for reuse and avoiding disposal costs) made it worthwhile.

In sum, the logistics/transportation approach to "environmental aspects" identification looks at issues such as:

- energy consumption;

- transportation-related emissions;

- risks and costs of accidental releases of chemicals and hazardous materials during transportation;

- solid and hazardous wastes created during transportation; and

- the potential reuse or recycling of containers and packaging materials used during transportation.

There is no standard approach for identifying transportation-related environmental aspects. The degree of effort applied to this initially should depend in large measure on the extent to which transportation is a significant business issue for your facility or site. Use a simplified approach to identify orders of magnitude. Over time, as quantitative risk assessment and life-cycle assessment tools become more useful in this context, you can improve your methodology.

Product Use and Product End-of-Life Approach

look at end of useful life

Another approach toward environmental aspects identification focuses on the environmental (and health and safety) issues associated with the product during and at the end of its useful life. Understanding and quantifying (where practical) product use and reuse and recycling end-of-life environmental issues provides your company opportunities to add value to the customer while reducing environmental risks.

Several examples illustrate the kinds of "environmental aspects" involved during product use.

example: durable products

Durable products used in industrial and commercial applications require maintenance that may involve the use of chemical and hazardous materials. These "environmental aspects," once clearly identified, may provide you with opportunities to add customer value by reducing or eliminating the need for certain hazardous materials during maintenance. You should ask yourself these questions:

☑ What specific chemical or hazardous materials are used in maintenance service for your products?

☑ How much and what kinds of wastes are created during maintenance?

☑ What are the opportunities for reducing the need for these materials and reducing wastes?

In many cases, these opportunities will require product redesign and may not be practical in the near term. However, by identifying environmental aspects of your product's use, you can develop useful information for your product designers for future improvements providing increased customer value and satisfaction.

example: aerosol products

Aerosol products are another example. These products contain the active ingredients, a propellant, and, frequently, a solvent to make proper release of the active ingredients easier. Although there are various "environmental aspects" in the production process, perhaps the aerosol product's most important environmental aspect is the release of chlorinated solvents such as 1,1,1-trichloroethane (TCA) and methylene chloride during the product's use in industrial, commercial, and consumer applications. Understanding these environmental aspects and developing insights on non-toxic solvent substitutes may lead to increased customer value by reducing or eliminating solvent exposures, easing aerosol container disposal problems, and possibly increasing market share.

Similarly, identifying the environmental aspects related to the disposal of your product at the end of its useful life can yield important benefits. Durable goods, consisting of many parts and components, often contain hazardous materials such as various kinds of heavy metals and toxic substances bound in plastics, glass, or composite materials. Landfill or incineration disposal of these materials may pose long-term environmental impacts on soil and groundwater. Recycling, reclaiming, and reusing certain parts and components after disassembly can provide important economic benefits as well as reduced environmental impacts.

reuse and recycling

Reuse and recycling of parts and components, however, often has product design implications such as designing the product for ease of disassembly, specifying recyclable materials, and minimizing hazardous constituents.

customer satisfaction

The value of identifying the product's end-of-life environmental aspects lies not only in improved environmental performance but also in the potential for improving customer satisfaction, particularly if you can reduce disposal burdens or provide disposition services that reduce long-term environmental impacts and liabilities.

It also may lie in new revenue opportunities in the form of reselling usable parts and components or recycling and reclaiming certain materials. Many manufacturers in the auto, computer, and telecommunications industries, among others, already have launched systematic efforts to identify their product end-of-life environmental aspects and use the information to improve product design, reduce product use costs, and provide environmentally superior disposition options. Similar benefits may come from understanding the environmental aspects of non-durable products, product containers, and packaging materials.

3.1.5 Identifying "Other Requirements"

ISO 14001 requires your facility or site to maintain a process to identify and have access to "other requirements" to which your company or facility subscribes, that are directly applicable to your facility or site. What does ISO 14001 mean by "other requirements?"

These are voluntary codes of conduct such as the chemical industry's Responsible Care® program, the American Petroleum Institute's Strategies for Today's Environmental Partnership (STEP) program, and voluntary environmental performance agreements with government agencies such as the U.S. EPA's Green Lights program, Project XL, and the Environmental Leadership Program. 📖 (See Part 8, Chapter 2, Section 3 for more information on these programs.)

"Other requirements" also include voluntary environmental management principles such as the principles of the World Business Council for Sustainable Development and the Coalition for Environmentally Responsible Economics (CERES) Principles. Examples of other requirements include voluntary partnership agreements with non-profit organizations and communities such as the Natural Resources Defense Council's recycled paper partnership with the Bank of America.

Does ISO 14001 certification require that you track and implement all these "other requirements?" No, not unless your company and/or facility voluntarily subscribes to one or more of them.

But if you are one of many facilities or sites operated by a large company, you will need to know whether your corporate group has signed up to any of these "other requirements" and whether they apply to your facility or site. If any of these "other requirements" do apply to your facility or site, you will need to incorporate their environmental management and performance commitments in your environmental management system.

Many large transnational companies operating in various countries have their own version of "other requirements," such as company-wide internal environmental standards or "internal performance criteria." These are documented environmental management standards, performance criteria, or operating procedures developed by the company to address situations where applicable regulatory requirements do not exist or meet its needs. 📖 (See Part 3, Chapter 2 on **ISO 14004, Section 4.2.4,** for more information on internal performance criteria.)

In planning your facility or site's ISO 14001, it is important to identify directly applicable "other requirements" because they will contain commitments that need to be considered in setting your environmental objectives and targets and in meeting specific ISO 14001 requirements for your environmental management system. ISO 14001 requires that your facility or site translate these "paper" commitments into action.

investigate your company's policies

If your company subscribes to Responsible Care, for example, you will need to implement auditable systems that will enable you to meet your Responsible Care commitments. Many companies have voluntarily subscribed to the 16 Principles of the World Business Council for Sustainable Development without taking formal action to implement the commitments. If your facility is subject to that voluntary commitment, you will now need to develop auditable systems that will carry out the 16 principles. Similarly, SMEs that sign up to a specific industry code of environmental conduct or practice will need to put in place auditable systems that carry out that commitment.

Fortunately, implementing your "other requirements" can be done as an integral part of your ISO 14001 implementation. Finally, "other requirements" also may be important in signaling the importance to your stakeholders or interested parties of the environmental aspects of your activities, products, and processes, thus helping guide your selection of environmental objectives and targets.

Compiling and Presenting Your Facility's Environmental Aspects

practice what you preach

Using the perspectives and approaches discussed above, you have reviewed your facility's activities, products, and services and their potential interaction with the environment. You now need a tool for compiling and presenting this information on your environmental aspects. Outlined below is a simplified method based on ISO 14004.

Step 1: Review

limit the
review

Let's assume you are a manufacturing facility with some on-site product R&D. Review the operations and other activities, products, and services of your facility or site, including off-site operations and activities, post-sale product use and end-of-life, and services. Set boundaries by limiting the review to issues over which you have control or you can be expected to influence.

Step 2: Categorize

categorize by
function or
subject

Place these operations and activities, products, and services in major functional or subject categories such as "materials acquisition," "materials management," "facility maintenance," "process and product R&D," "manufacturing process," "on- or off-site construction," "transportation," and "product use and end-of-life."

Step 3: Identify aspects

identify
interactive
elements

For each operation, activity, product, and service, identify the "environmental aspects," i.e., the specific elements that can interact with the environment. Following the broad approaches discussed above (e.g., materials identification approach), take advantage of the growing body of technical information on "pollution prevention" (much of it freely available from the Internet and from government agencies) to help in the "environmental aspects" identification process.

TIP 3.8

Free technical information to help identify environmental aspects

Internet: There are numerous web pages and files accessible through the Internet on subjects such as "pollution prevention." You may find that a good deal of work has already been done in identifying the "environmental aspects" of materials and operations similar to yours.

Government: The U.S. EPA's Office of Pollution Prevention and Toxics has a wealth of technical information on "environmental aspects" of specific materials and operational processes. Call EPA's Pollution Prevention Information Clearinghouse at +1-202-260-1023.

Many state agencies have similar information and have specific programs geared to SMEs. Call your state environmental agency to see if they have a program that fits your needs. 📖 (See Appendix J for more Internet resources.)

Step 4: Identify impacts

Finally, for each environmental aspect, identify the "environmental impacts." Environmental impacts are defined in the ISO 14001 standard as "any change to the environment, whether adverse or beneficial, wholly or partially resulting from an organization's activities, products or services." This process then can be illustrated in the form of a matrix or comparable graphical tool. (See *Figure 3.7*). 📖 (See Part 4, Chapter 3, Section 2 for more information on environmental aspects.)

Activity	Aspect	Impact
Handling oil or hazardous materials	Potential for accidental spillage Contamination of soil or water	
Product	**Aspect**	**Impact**
Product	Functional eco-efficiency (i.e. amount of material used to achieve functionality), recyclability, reusability	Non-sustainable use of natural resources
Service	**Aspect**	**Impact**
Vehicle maintainance	Release of volatile fuels during refueling	Contamination of air quality

Figure 3.7 — Environmental aspects: practical concepts.

3.1.6 Methods for Identifying Significant Environmental Aspects and Impacts

ISO 14001 requires that your facility or site establish and maintain a procedure to identify the environmental aspects of your activities, products and services *". . . in order to determine those which have or can have significant impacts on the environment."* Being able to identify the significant environmental aspects of your facility or site's activities, products and services is a requirement to meet other ISO 14001 provisions. See *Figure 3.8.*

No standard approaches for determining "significant"

identify impacts

The significance of your facility or site's environmental aspects will depend on a variety of considerations related to your business and its environmental issues. Strictly speaking, ISO 14001 does not require that you use any enumerated criteria in determining significance. It is up to you to apply appropriate criteria and determine the significance in a way that makes sense to your business, the nature of the environmental aspects and impact risks, regulatory and legal liability factors, and the interests of your community and other stakeholders. ISO 14004 lists some of the considerations you might use in determining significance. (See Part 4, Chapter 3, Section 2 for more information on environmental impacts and Appendix A, ISO 14004 environmental concerns/business concerns.)

Develop your own framework for determining significance

grading your environmental aspects

Work with your ISO 14000 team to brainstorm appropriate ways to determine the significant environmental aspects using the criteria in ISO 14004 as a starting point. Decide which criteria are relevant to your activities, products, and services. Then develop a simple rating system to grade your environmental aspects.

An example of this was actually done by a medium-sized auto parts company in Janesville, Wisconsin.

Significant Environmental Aspects and Impacts In an ISO 14001 EMS	
ISO 14001 Element	Specific Provisions Related to *Significant Environmental Aspects or Impacts*
Section 4.2.3 Objectives and Targets	"When establishing and reviewing its objectives and targets an organization shall consider ... its *significant environmental aspects...*"
Section 4.3.2 Training, Awareness, and Competence	"The organization shall ... establish and maintain procedures to make its employees ... at each relevant function and level aware of ... (b) the *significant environmental impacts, actual or potential*, of their work activities..."
Section 4.3.3 Communication	"The organization shall consider processes for external communication on its *significant environmental* aspects and record its decision."
Section 4.3.6 Operational Control	"The organization shall identify those operations and activities that are associated with the identified significant environmental aspects in line with its policy, objectives and targets." "The organization shall plan these activities ... in order to ensure that they are carried out under specified conditions by ... (c) establishing and maintaining procedures related to the *identifiable significant environmental aspects* of goods and services used by the organization..."
Section 4.4.1 Monitoring and Measurement	"The organization shall establish and maintain documented procedures to monitor and measure on a regular basis the key characteristics of its operations and activities that can have a *significant impact on the environment.*"

Figure 3.8 — Identifying environmental aspects and impacts: ISO 14001 requirements.

example: SSI Technologies

Douglas Wall, corporate environmental manager of SSI Technologies, led his EHS management systems team through an open-ended process to identify the "significant (environmental, health, and safety) effects of the company's:

1) operations processes;

2) raw materials and transportation;

3) process waste recycling;

4) packaging; and

5) disposal."

These were the five general categories of environmental aspects that the multifunctional team concluded were the most relevant to their activities, products, and services. 📖 (See Part 4, Chapter 6 for the SSI Technologies case study.)

A breakdown of the specific aspects reviewed by SSI Technologies in these five general categories is shown in *Figure 3.9.*

Specific Operations Processes Reviewed							
Plastic Resin	Lead Dross	Flux / Thinner	Rubber Bands	Clip / Bracket	Oil Soap	Rose Water	Copper Wire
Specific Operations Processes Reviewed							
Magnets	Terminals	O-Rings	Grommets	Protective Coil	Tie	Office Supplies	Electricity
Specific Operations Processes Reviewed							
Water	Compress-ed Air	Humans	Filters	Misc. Chemicals	Compress-ed Gases	PPE	Oil (HT)
Specific Raw Material/Transportation Reviewed							
Trucking	Cardboard Boxes	Pallets	Shrink Wrap	Plastic Bags	Tape	Banding	Wood Spools
Specific Raw Materials/Transportation Reviewed							
Compo-nents	Car usage	Parking					
Specific Process Waste/Recycling Reviewed							
Scrap metal	Lightbulbs	Industrial containers	Plastic runners	Oil/ solvent	Mixed paper	Paper cups	Food
Specific Process Waste/Recycling Reviewed							
Plastic utensils	Bi-metal PC containers	Tables/ chairs	Refriger-ators	Micro-waves			
Specific Packaging Reviewed							
Boxes/ inserts	Labels	Handling equipment					
Specific Disposal Activities Reviewed							
Car shredder	Landfilled defective auto parts	Salvage					

Figure 3.9 — SSI Technologies aspects categories.

The SSI Technologies team then classified each of the identified specific processes, materials, or activities shown in the above tables, using just two criteria for "significance":

1) severity (S); and

2) frequency of occurrence (F),

as applied to potential environmental impacts.

To illustrate the significant effects, SSI Technologies graphed the frequency and severity data from the table *(Figure 3.10)*.

Graphing your significant environmental aspects (using your own metrics) is an extremely useful way to communicate clearly with your facility or site management, as well as with your coworkers, concerning the opportunities for environmental performance improvements and financial benefits. It is also useful in demonstrating your systems and methodology for purposes of ISO 14001 certification and for helping you identify appropriate environmental objectives and targets.

Process	Plastic Resin		Lead Dross		Flux/ Thinner		Rubber Bands		Clip/ Bracket		Oil Soap		Rose Water	
Severity = S Frequency = F	S	F	S	F	S	F	S	F	S	F	S	F	S	F
Energy	5	5	4	5	2	3					2	2		
Resources	5	5	5	5	4	3					3	4		
Air	4	3	4	5	5	4					1	1		
Water	1	5	3	4	2	2					2	2		
Soil	1	1	2	2	2	2					1	1		
Noise	4	4	2	3	1	1					1	1		
Human Beings	3	4	5	5	4	3					4	3		
Climate	4	5	2	4	1	1					1	1		
Ecology	4	5	4	4	3	3					2	2		
Total	31	37	31	37	24	22					17	17		
Rate the activity for severity of EHS effects (S) and the frequency that it occurs (F) according to the following table.														
	Not Applicable		Low		Moderate		High		Highest					
	1		2		3		4		5					

Courtesy of Doug Wall, Corporate Environmental Manager, SSI Technologies Inc.

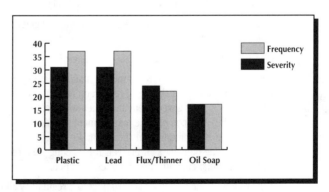

Figures 3.10 and 3.11 — SSI Technologies graphs of frequency and severity data.

3.1.7 Setting Environmental Objectives and Targets

Objectives: Narrowing the Field

Developing environmental objectives and targets is a critical part of the ISO 14001 planning process. In meeting this requirement, you must address the threshold question of what your environmental objectives must cover.

☑ Do you need to establish environmental objectives for the actual or potential significant environmental impacts of all your activities, products, and services?

The ISO 14001 standard does not clearly answer that question.

All that the ISO 14001 standard specifically requires is that, in setting its objectives and targets, your facility or site "consider":

- its legal and other requirements;
- its significant environmental aspects;
- its technological options;
- its financial and business requirements; and
- the views of interested parties.

In addition to taking those factors into account, any objectives and targets established are required to be consistent with your company's and/or your facility's environmental policy and its commitment to prevention of pollution.

Two other specific requirements that must be met are:

1) documenting your environmental objectives and targets; and

2) establishing and maintaining your objectives and targets at each relevant function and level in your facility or site.

As a practical matter, how do you develop appropriate environmental objectives and targets that will meet the ambiguous and open-ended requirements of ISO 14001?

look at compliance

You should start with an objective appraisal of your environmental (and health and safety) compliance posture.

☑ Do you have areas of compliance weakness?

minimum: meet legal obligations

Because your ISO 14001 environmental management system includes a commitment to compliance with applicable legal requirements, and because of the high value placed on compliance by your government and other stakeholders, you should give high priority to strengthening your compliance management systems in the process of setting environmental objectives. At a minimum, your facility or site's regulatory compliance management systems need to include objectives and targets for meeting legal requirements for activities, products, and services that currently are not in compliance.

For example, your facility may be subject to a regulatory consent agreement providing a schedule or timetable for meeting the specific regulatory standard or requirement in question. In such a case, your facility should have an objective and targets tied to meeting the legal requirements by the consent agreement deadline.

beyond
compliance

You should then review the "beyond-compliance" significant environmental aspects of your facility or site's activities, products, and services. Look at these "significant" aspects to see which have the largest opportunities for improving your facility or site's environmental performance while achieving cost savings and new revenues. The right mindset in examining your significant environmental aspects is to think in terms of potential cost-savings and new revenue opportunities, as opposed to new operating costs. You will not always get positive financial results, but you will find a surprising degree of financial benefits through correct identification of opportunities (which we will start calling "environmental objectives"). 📖 (See Appendix A, ISO 14004 for more information on objectives and targets.)

TIP 3.9

Issues to consider in setting environmental objectives and targets

1. How do your environmental objectives and targets reflect your environmental policy and the identified significant environmental impacts of your facility or site's activities, products, and services?

2. How have the views of your customers, your community, and other "interested parties" been considered in setting your environmental objectives?

3. What specific measurement systems and indicators will your facility or site use to measure progress toward your objectives and targets?

Adapted from **ISO 14004, Section 4.2.5.**

Setting Objectives and Targets

✔ Where to invest money?
✔ Compliance
✔ Resource producing improvements
✔ Prevention of pollution
✔ Product and process design innovation
✔ Training
✔ Information technology

Figure 3.12 — Setting objectives and targets.

look at
business
objectives

You should also determine if your company or facility has already established specific "business objectives." You may find that there is a good fit between established business objectives and opportunities to reduce significant environmental impacts.

For example, your company may already have established a business objective of increasing customer satisfaction by 10 percent over a defined period of time. If your facility makes products or provides services, you may find that you can set an environmental objective of reducing a specific significant environmental impact associated with your products or services in a way that adds value for your customers and contributes to increased customer satisfaction.

look at financials As much as practical, you should review your significant environmental aspects and identify the largest opportunities for cost savings and/or new revenues tied directly to environmental performance improvements. Many of these opportunities will be found within the resource productivity framework, particularly in improved raw materials management tied to higher product yields and reduced waste outputs. If you are in the process industries, your environmental objective may be to reduce raw material waste and process environmental releases (not just your Toxic Release Inventory releases, but all releases viewed as lost product). This perspective focuses your management attention on causes of material losses.

As we indicated at the outset, ISO 14001 does not require that you establish an environmental objective for each of your identified significant environmental aspects. You should think realistically about the number of environmental objectives you set. If you establish too many environmental objectives, you may find you lack the organizational capability to carry them out effectively. You may lose focus and drive within your facility or site to make progress on your objectives and this, in turn, can disillusion your employees and management.

set limits As a practical matter, it makes good sense to select a smaller number of environmental objectives you are confident your facility or site can manage to a successful conclusion. Pick environmental objectives that are a realistic stretch for your facility or site, taking into account technological and financial realities.

A critical question to ask is:

☑ Does the environmental objective meet my facility's stakeholder concerns and expectations?

Pick environmental objectives with significant environmental impacts that can yield financial returns. Successful achievement of these objectives, resulting in improved environmental performance and demonstrable financial benefits, will reinforce senior management commitment, stimulate greater support from middle management, and promote greater employee involvement in your ISO 14001 EMS.

TIP 3.10

Keeping track of "significant environmental aspects" for which you have not set environmental objectives and targets.

It is important that you establish a system or process for periodically reviewing and updating all your identified significant environmental aspects. You need to be able to demonstrate to your ISO 14001 registrar/certification body and your EMS auditors that you haven't overlooked some of your significant environmental aspects in setting a smaller, manageable number of environmental objectives. You also need a system for monitoring or tracking those significant environmental aspects for which you are not now setting environmental objectives to help in priority-setting during the EMS management review and to respond to changing circumstances that may raise the importance of a specific significant environmental aspect.

Targets

environmental targets

An environmental target is defined in **ISO 14001 Section 3.10** as a "detailed performance requirement, quantified where practicable, applicable to the organization or parts thereof, that arises from the environmental objectives and that needs to be set and met in order to achieve those objectives."

measurable targets

For each environmental objective, you will need to have at least one measurable target. Try to break down your objectives into specific measurable targets. For example, if energy conservation is one of your environmental objectives, consider setting measurable targets for reducing your energy consumption on the basis of major operations/activities in your facility (such as lighting, compressed air, electric motors, air conditioning/ventilation) and then set measurable targets for each. Or you might divide the energy conservation objective into organizational targets (such as setting energy reduction targets for manufacturing operations, facilities maintenance, etc.). Ask yourself which would be the most effective approach for motivating progress toward the objective. See *Figure 3.13* for an example.

Examples of Possible Objectives With Selected Targets

➻ Reduce waste from materials used in manufacturing and other site activities

Target: Reduce scrap waste by 15 percent by 12/31/97 (from 1996 base).

Target: By 9/1/96, complete analysis of all vendor-supplier bulk containers (pallets, spools, crating, drums etc.) and identify specific opportunities for returning container materials to vendors.

➻ Reduce releases of specific chemical or hazardous materials (or classes of materials) into the air or water

Target: Reduce VOC emissions by 50 percent by 12/31/97 (from 1996 base).

➻ Improve product design to reduce environmental impacts during product use and from end-of-life product disposal

Target: Complete environmental training for design engineers by 9/1/96.

Target: Complete by 12/31/96 technical analysis of end-of-life disposition for products X, Y, Z covering disassembly, feasibility of parts reuse, and feasibility of replacing, reusing,disposing of hazardous materials.

Target: Complete by 6/30/97 technical and financial analysis of product X, Y, Z design changes for improvements based on disposition analysis.

➻ Reduce energy consumption

Target: Reduce energy usage in lighting by 15 percent by 12/31/96 from 1995 base.

Target: Reduce energy usage in compressed air applications by 15% by 12/31/96 from 1995 base.

➻ Extend environmental training to all functional and operations groups

Target: Complete training of purchasing and product engineering groups by 9/1/96.

Target: complete training of manufacturing, logistics, facilities management groups by 11/1/96.

Figure 3.13 — Example of possible objectives and associated targets.

Measurement and Environmental Performance Indicators

documented
procedures
needed

Your environmental objectives and, especially, your environmental targets must be quantifiable where practical. Even if it is not practical to quantify your objectives and targets, ISO 14001 requires that you establish and maintain documented procedures for measuring progress toward your targets and objectives. See *Figure 3.14*.

To measure progress toward your objectives and targets, you will need to develop a consistent measurement system. There are no formal standards to apply in developing your measurement system. Generally speaking, you should consider both qualitative and quantitative measurement approaches.

ISO 14001
Section 4.4.1 Monitoring and Measurement

"This (monitoring and measurement) shall include the recording of information to track performance . . . and conformance with the organization's objectives and targets."

Figure 3.14

qualitative
measurement

A qualitative measurement system applies subjective judgment based on uniform criteria to measure progress.

For example, if your target is to complete environmental training of all your manufacturing and facilities management people by a specific date, you can measure your progress qualitatively by assigning a number on a scale of "1" to "5" ("5" = 100 percent completion) to the status of the effort during periodic reviews. Qualitative measurement is typically applied to the implementation of specific management systems components such as training programs.

quantitative
measurement

Quantitative measurement is the objective measurement of performance results such as quantities of energy or water consumed and amounts of wastes reduced or recycled. Qualitative and quantitative measurement methods also can be combined in specific applications.

environmental
performance
indicator

Qualitative and quantitative measurements can be converted into more useful "environmental performance indicator" (EPI) information.

It is useful to know quantitatively the amounts of solid and hazardous wastes your facility has reduced in one year. It may be even more useful to know the percentage of wastes reduced per unit of production or per unit of "value added" by your facility to the raw materials, part, and components it transforms into commercial products.

Thus, EPIs are ways of making your measurements more meaningful to top management, employees, customers, and other interested parties.

There are no formal standards for determining an appropriate EPI. TC 207 Subcommittee 4 Work Group 4 was developing guidelines on environmental indicators (ISO 14031) that were intended to help organizations develop appropriate EPIs. 📖 (See Part 5, Chapter 2 for more information on EPIs.)

A measurement method and appropriate EPI should be developed at the same time you are establishing your environmental objectives and targets. To measure progress toward your quantifiable objectives and targets, you will need to measure your baseline. By "baseline," we mean the performance level against which you will measure your progress.

For example, if your energy conservation target is a 15 percent reduction by the end of 1996, you will need to know the performance level (such as 1995 annual energy consumption figures) against which you are measuring the 15 percent reduction.

Developing your measurement method and appropriate EPIs along with your objectives and targets has practical importance; you may find that your measurement methods and EPIs will help shape your targets and make it possible to develop a measurement method and EPIs that work *consistently* for many or all of your targets. Trying to impose a measurement method or EPI on your targets after they are established may result in having to use different methods for each target, thus unnecessarily complicating your measurement system.

3.1.8 Environmental Management Programs

environmental management program

ISO 14001 requires that you establish and maintain one or more "environmental management programs" for achieving your environmental objectives and targets.

In developing these programs, it is useful to consider the related ISO 14001 requirement that your environmental objectives and targets must be established "at each relevant function and level" within your facility or site.

relevant function and level

Each relevant function and level in this context means that if a function (e.g., the purchasing function) is organizationally responsible for activities that relate to an environmental objective or target, the objective and target must apply to that function. Similarly, different organizational levels within your facility may be carrying out activities that relate to the objective and targets, so the objective and targets also must apply to them.

Put another way, the requirement for establishing objectives and targets for each relevant function and level in your facility is a requirement that your environmental objectives and targets be integrated with the operations and functions of your facility. The "environmental management programs" are the implementation mechanisms for managing this integration and ensuring that different groups in your facility play a role.

three action features

ISO 14001 also requires your environmental management programs to take into account new developments and new or modified activities, products, or services. For example, your environmental management program covering a toxic emissions release objective (and specific targets) may need to be amended to take into account changes in material inputs, process technologies, new production lines, and other new developments.

1) identification of the person or job position who is responsible for achieving the environmental objectives and targets in each relevant function and level;

2) the means or "action plan" for achieving targets and objectives; and

3) timetables.

The "action plan" is a more detailed implementation plan for an environmental objective and its targets. *Figure 3.15* shows an example of an environmental management plan.

Environmental Management Plan — Outline Example

Environmental Objective: Reduce energy consumption by 20 percent by 12/31/97 (over calendar 1996)

Target: Reduce energy usage in facility lighting by 15 percent by 6/30/97.

Action Plan: Replace lighting with electronic start fluorescents.

Responsibility: Facility manager

Budget: $—

Expected savings (annualized): $—

Completion date: 3/1/96.

Target: Reduce energy usage in compressed air applications by 15 percent by 3/31/97.

Action Plan:

1) Inventory all current compressed air applications and audit current usage rates during 1/1/96 -3/31/96;
   prepare report identifying three largest opportunities and metrics by 5/1/96.

Responsibility: X

2) Analyze opportunities and develop recommended solutions by 6/1/96 for review and approval by
operations, engineering, and facilities managers

Responsibility: Y

3) Adopt compressed air control plan.

Responsibility: Operations/engineering managers.

4) Complete training by 8/1/96.

Responsibility: Z

Target:

Etc.

Note: Achieving the various energy reduction targets will meet or exceed the 20 percent energy reduction
objective by 12/31/97. Total budget for the energy reduction objective is $—. Expected annualized savings
will be $—.

Overall responsibility for implementation: Operations manager.

Figure 3.15 — Example of an environmental management plan.

3.1.9 Developing and Updating Your Environmental Policy

We discuss developing or updating your environmental policy at the conclusion of the ISO 14001 planning process because, as a practical matter, you need to understand your "environmental aspects" and determine which are "significant" before you can prepare an appropriate environmental policy for your facility.

scope of policy

Let's assume that your facility is one of many facilities in a company that has already developed a company-wide environmental policy statement. Will the company environmental policy serve the needs of your facility for purposes of ISO 14001 certification? The answer will depend on the content of the corporate policy and the nature of your facility's activities, products, and services.

You should review the ISO 14001 environmental policy requirements now. 📖 (Turn to Appendix A for text of **ISO 14001 Section 4.1** Environmental Policy.)

If the corporate environmental policy is broadly stated to apply to a variety of different businesses operated by your company, it may not be sufficiently relevant to the nature, scale, and environmental impacts of your facility's activities, products, and services. The corporate environmental policy may also be too abstract to serve as a framework for setting and reviewing your facility's environmental objectives and targets.

example:
four divisions

For example, if your company has four major divisions with substantially different kinds of businesses ranging from manufacturing plastic parts to providing tourism services, you may find that your corporate environmental policy is too diffuse to provide a useful framework for setting your plastics manufacturing facility's environmental objectives and targets.

example:
one product

On the other hand, if your company manufactures only one product — say consumer batteries — in ten different plants, the corporate environmental policy may very well serve the needs of your battery manufacturing facility; the battery design, manufacturing, and distribution processes and their environmental aspects may be very similar in all the plants.

If you decide that your corporate environmental policy is insufficient to provide a framework for setting your facility's environmental objectives and targets (or if your company does not have a corporate environmental policy), you will need to prepare an environmental policy for your facility.

How should you approach the development of an appropriate ISO 14001 environmental policy for your facility?

start with current policy

The starting point for your facility's environmental policy, needless to say, is that it must be fully consistent with your corporate environmental policy (if one exists). Another important starting point is the early involvement of your facility or site manager (the facility's "top management," using the words of ISO 14001). If you begin with your facility's top management support, you will find it easier to get the support and involvement of the operations and functional managers in your facility.

understand implications

Before you and your cross-functional ISO 14000 team begin drafting the environmental policy, you need to review and understand the environmental implications and possibilities of your facility's business.

☑ Who are your customers and other stakeholders and how does your facility or site "add value" to the customer?

☑ If you are processing raw materials and turning them into commodity products, how do you express the value you are adding?

☑ If you are taking parts and components that your company has designed, but are manufactured by suppliers, and are assembling them in a way that makes them useful to customers, how do you articulate the value added by your facility or site?

☑ What are the possibilities of adding greater value in an environmental context to your products and services?

Example: Small Dry Cleaner
Aligning Environmental Objective with Business Objective

Let's assume you operate a small dry cleaning business and that you have identified Perchlorethylene (PERC) as one of your significant environmental aspects. PERC is a volatile organic compound and a listed hazardous air pollutant (tetrachloroethylene) that is now subject to emission standards at the U.S. federal and state levels. Let's also assume you are currently using a "transfer" machine that allows PERC to evaporate when clothes are moved from the cleaning phase to the drying phase.

You have already figured out that you are losing a lot of PERC in the evaporation process and that PERC waste is costing you money. In addition, you realize that an inadvertent PERC spill can cost you dearly in contaminated soil/groundwater cleanup, possible business disruptions, and bad customer relations. To address this issue, you may want to establish an environmental objective of reducing your PERC releases by X percent in two years. The related business objective, in this example, is to reduce your PERC material expenditures by Y percent.

To achieve your environmental objective, you will need to invest in new technologies such as a closed-loop "dry-to-dry" machine that processes fabrics in a single unit and captures virtually all processed PERC for recycling and reuse. You will also want to install secondary containment under the "dry-to-dry" machine to capture PERC spills, as well as install special liners and sealers. In determining the return on your investment, you should consider not only savings in PERC materials but also improved environmental performance, customer and community satisfaction, and greater assurance of complying with applicable state and federal environmental regulations affecting the dry cleaning industry.

☑ If you make durable products, is it possible to make it easier for your customers to dispose of the product in an environmentally responsible way at the end of its useful life?

add value
By simplifying environmentally responsible disposition, you are adding value for the customer. See *Figure 3.16* for a list of other questions you should ask.

example: consumer products
If your facility manufactures consumer products using bulky packaging provided by suppliers, you may find financially rewarding opportunities to add value to the customer through changes in your product and packaging design to reduce packaging waste and simplify end-of-life product disposal. In this example, an environmental policy that is congruent with your business would, among other things, commit you to reducing the environmental burdens associated with your products and packaging.

example: semiconductors
To take another example, if your site is a semiconductor fabrication facility, as much as 80 percent of your incoming materials (including water) go out in some form of waste. Although this issue creates a robust debate, there are significant opportunities to reduce fabrication process waste. By using your facility's environmental policy to focus on waste reduction, you can enlist the support of operations managers to undertake cost-benefit analyses that will identify cost savings as well as environmental performance improvements.

If you can align your environmental policy to address the significant environmental aspects

---

Business Considerations for Your Environmental Policy

☑ What is your facility or site's business?
☑ Who are your customers?
☑ Who are your suppliers?
☑ How can your facility or site add more value
    (in an environmental context) to your customers?

Figure 3.16 — Business consideration questions.

of your business in a way that adds value to customers and other stakeholders and provides you with economic benefits, you will find the "sweet spot" of congruence between your policy and your business. ISO 14001 does not speak of "sweet spots" nor does it require them. But this approach is clearly consistent with ISO 14001 and will make more sense to your top management, the people in your facility, and other "interested parties."

TIP 3.11

Preparing/updating your environmental policy

Don't overlook the specific commitments that ISO 14001 requires your top management to make expressly in the facility or site environmental policy. Required commitments are:

• compliance with applicable environmental law and regulations;

• prevention of pollution (see **ISO 14001, Section 3.13**); and

• continual improvement (of the EMS).

CHAPTER 2
Implementation and Operation

by C. Foster Knight, Managing Director, Knight and Associates and
Robert Ferrone, President, The Ferrone Group

3.2.1 Overview

Having completed the planning process and having developed environmental objectives and targets and an appropriate environmental policy for your plant or facility, you now must consider the formal implementation and operational requirements for your EMS. **ISO 14001 Section 4.3** specifies seven components related to implementation and operation of an EMS. 📖 (See Annex A for more information on implementation.) These seven components are:

Environmental Policy Example: China Light and Power

The following is the China Light and Power Corporate Environmental Policy developed in 1995 that the company will use as the basis for its ISO 14001 environmental management system.

1) CLP will comply with all applicable laws and regulations in the counties and projects in which it operates and participates and will adopt responsible Standards where laws and regulations do not exist. CLP will work with government and industry groups to foster timely development of laws and regulations which are environmentally acceptable and practicable to meet the balanced economic and environmental needs of society.

2) CLP will seek to identify and quantify all emissions and pollutants from our operations, and to understand their environmental pathways and consequences. The Company will continuously monitor international developments in environmental science and policy, and incorporate new standards and technology as appropriate. CLP will also support and encourage relevant research projects on the environmental impacts of the Company operations.

3) CLP will, as a matter of good environmental practice and/or when required by legislation, carry out Environmental Impact Assessments for all major projects and developments so that environmental considerations are incorporated into all of the Company's business decisions.

4) CLP will take suppliers' environmental performance into consideration in its purchasing strategies and require contractors operating on CLP sites to adopt and implement sound environmental policies.

5) CLP will support measures to provide the general public with balanced information on the benefits of electrification and the need for energy conservation. We will encourage responsible energy usage through the promotion of Demand Side Management policies and programmes, and will work with Hong Kong Government Agencies and others relevant bodies to that end.

6) CLP will implement schemes to conserve raw materials and energy and, whenever practicable, will recycle or reduce waste at the source.

7) CLP will encourage concern and respect for the environment amongst its staff, emphasize every employee's responsibility for environmental performance, and adopt appropriate operating practices and training.

8) CLP will adopt high standards of operational integrity to minimize the risk of environmental incidents, and will respond quickly and effectively to minimize their impact if such incidents occur.

9) CLP is committed to the principles of sustainable development as a supporter of the ICC Business Charter and will seek to carry out the Charter's provisions.

10) CLP will play a responsible role in assisting Hong Kong to meet its obligations under relevant international Environmental Treaties, Protocols and Conventions.

1) structure and responsibility;

2) training, awareness, and competence;

3) communication;

4) EMS documentation;

5) document control;

6) operational control; and

7) emergency preparedness and response.

This chapter discusses practical implementation approaches for these seven components. Although we discuss these components in the order that they appear in the ISO 14001 standard, there is no inherent logic in the sequence. You should address specific components out of the sequence if it makes good sense for your facility. In addition, some of these components lend themselves to integration or consolidation. For example, we will discuss EMS documentation and document control together. Another example: Parts of your internal communication procedures can be covered by your environmental awareness training effort.

3.2.2 Organizational Structure, Responsibilities, and Accountability (ISO 14001 Section 4.3.1 and ISO 14004 Section 4.3.2.3)

Traditional facility-based environmental management programs place "environmental management" responsibilities on the environmental (health and safety) specialist, the facilities manager, or even the security manager. While EHS management functions often are integrated at the plant level, they typically exist organizationally apart from operations and other plant management functions.

obstacle: EHS function under-resourced

In some manufacturing plants, the EHS function is integrated at the top. In these cases, the plant's organizational chart will show the plant manager with overall responsibility for EHS compliance. But all too often, the reality is that the plant manager and operations managers consider the EHS manager or specialist to be the person who "owns" plant EHS responsibilities. Typically lacking a budget and operational authority, the EHS manager/specialist must constantly sell, persuade, cajole, and even conjure up imminent compliance sanctions to get the necessary attention and cooperation from plant operations and other functional managers. In such circumstances, EHS managers have little capability to plan and implement most of the requirements of ISO 14001.

higher integration needed

As you prepare for ISO 14001 implementation, your facility or plant therefore needs to develop a different organizational model — a new structure that provides a higher level of integration between environmental (health and safety) and operations management. If you already have formal quality management systems in place, you will find many opportunities to integrate this new EMS organizational model with your quality management organizational structure and process. You also may find opportunities to integrate the new EMS organization with other functional organizational structures such as engineering, purchasing, materials management, operations, human resources, finance, logistics, maintenance, and facilities management.

TIP 3.12

Integrating structure at SMEs

A small manufacturing plant with 50 employees typically will not have separate departments for functions such as purchasing, materials management, logistics, or human resources. Nor will there be an environmental specialist. Often the entire plant is "operations" and the plant manager or owner is the only manager. In such circumstances, integration of environmental management with operations management is actually easier to accomplish.

The EMS for a small plant should be very simple and focused on the highest priorities. The plant manager will need to play an instrumental role in the EMS organizational structure. Key employees should be assigned specific environmental responsibilities and authority to implement the EMS.

EHS manager as consultant

In the new EMS organizational model, the EHS manager or specialist is primarily a consultant to plant and operations management and functional groups supporting the plant. The roles, responsibilities, management authority, and accountability for implementing and maintaining the EMS are defined and documented within operations and other plant functions.

key roles for everyone

Production managers should be assigned key environmental roles and responsibilities. To be met, certain environmental objectives and targets, for example, may require production management operational resources and authority. Employees in other functions, such as purchasing, logistics, engineering, and facilities management will need to play important parts in implementing the EMS. Their roles and responsibilities must be defined and documented.

authority needed

In defining the EMS organizational structure, ISO 14001 specifically requires "top management" (in this context, the plant manager) to appoint a management representative with a defined role, responsibility, and authority for:

a) ensuring that the EMS requirements are established, implemented, and maintained to meet the minimum requirements of ISO 14001; and

b) reporting to the plant manager on the performance of the EMS during management review and identifying opportunities for improvements.

avoid turf battles

The plant manager's designated representative for the EMS should be sufficiently senior and experienced in operations management to provide the necessary clout for ensuring EMS implementation. If your plant or facility is already ISO 9000 certified and you are considering making the ISO 9000 specialist your ISO 14001 EMS "designated representative," be sure that your ISO 9000 specialist has seniority, management experience, and a direct reporting relationship with the plant manager.

Defining environmental roles and responsibilities throughout the plant's operations and functions poses challenges — particularly the challenge of avoiding duplication, overlaps, and potential "turf" battles.

To simplify this process, roles and responsibilities should be considered in the context of the EMS and not in terms of traditional compliance management (although environmental compliance will be a major component of the EMS). You should establish clear reporting channels, authorities, and decision making processes for each element of the EMS. Integration of environmental management with health and safety and with quality will require that you include appropriate roles and responsibilities in the organizational structure. See *Figure 3.17* for example structure.

You can minimize "turf" battles by a combination of:

1) directly involving the plant manager in setting expectations, specifying the EMS information, and reporting requirements;

2) clarifying accountability, performance measurement, and rewards; and

3) integrating key functions by placing greater responsibility on operations and functional managers and emphasizing the "consultant" roles and responsibilities of EHS managers and certain functional managers.

If your plant or facility is considering both ISO 9000 and ISO 14001 certification, you will greatly enhance successful implementation if you integrate these two efforts organizationally at the top, directly under your plant manager's leadership. ▢ (See Part 2, Chapter 2, Section 7 for more information on top management commitment.)

allocate resources

Defining EMS roles, responsibilities, and authorities includes allocating the resources necessary to implement and maintain the EMS. Management allocation of essential resources is a specific requirement of ISO 14001. Resources include human (including specialized skills if necessary), technological, and financial resources. To reinforce the organizational structure, job descriptions should include key EMS roles and responsibilities.

communicate!

Finally, design your EMS roles and responsibilities into an organizational chart and effectively communicate these roles and responsibilities throughout the facility or plant.

Communication is critical. Each employee in the facility must have a clear picture of who is responsible for key elements of the EMS. And each employee needs to be able to relate what he or she is doing with the broader EMS organizational structure.

3.2.3 Training, Awareness, and Competence (ISO 14001 Section 4.3.2 and ISO 14004 Section 4.3.2.5)

training focuses beyond compliance

ISO 14001 contains specific environmental training requirements. Facilities preparing for ISO 14001 will need to look carefully at the ISO 14001 training requirements because they go beyond what is currently being covered by many "best practices" environmental programs. Conventional environmental training tends to focus on environmental (health and safety) compliance training. ISO 14001 training requirements are more broadly aimed at both ensuring compliance and at improving the facility's environmental performance in areas not regulated by law.

ISO 14001's environmental training requirements can be divided into two general categories:

1) competency-based environmental training for employees whose work can cause significant environmental impacts; and

2) awareness training on the importance of the EMS, the importance of an employee's

personal performance, and the importance of compliance with operational and
regulatory requirements.

These two categories of ISO 14001 training overlap to some extent, but we discuss them
separately to simplify implementation approaches.

competency-
based training

A simplified approach to meet ISO 14001's competency-based environmental training
requirements is summarized in the following steps:

Step 1: Environmental Aspects

Identify your facility's "significant" environmental aspects. This step is discussed in the
previous chapter.

Step 2: Environmental Impacts

Identify each employee whose work may cause significant environmental impacts. This step
requires analysis of the work activities that are associated with each of the plant's or facility's
identified "significant" environmental aspects.

Developing an Organizational Structure for Your EMS	
Your EMS organizational structure should cover the following kinds of roles and responsibilities (this is a partial list for illustration purposes with examples of the types of positions for each)	
Role and Responsibility	**Example of Position**
✔ develop and approve environmental policy	— plant manager
✔ designated plant manager representative with overall responsibility for EMS	— senior operations or functional manager (e.g. finance) on plant management staff
✔ assuring compliance with applicable EHS regulatory requirements	— plant manager or senior operations manager
✔ process for identifying legal and other requirements directly applicable to facility	— EHS manager or specialist
✔ process for identifying environmental aspects and those that are "significant"	— EHS manager or specialist
✔ environmental objectives, targets and management programs	— will depend on objective and target (should tie to person with operational responsibility)
✔ operational controls/procedures	— operations managers with technical support from EHS specialist
✔ development and implementation of training requirements	— senior operations or functional manager with technical support from EHS
✔ EMS audit program	— a senior operations or functional manager
✔ EMS management review	— plant manager and senior operations managers

Figure 3.17

example:
wastewater

To illustrate, let's assume you have identified your facility's wastewater effluents as a "significant" environmental aspect. To comply with regulatory requirements, your facility has installed a wastewater treatment unit that is continuously operated by your employees during three work shifts. To identify work activities associated with this "significant" environmental aspect (wastewater effluents), obviously you will want to include the work of the wastewater treatment unit operators during the three shifts.

But you also will need to go "upstream" to include the work activities of the production lines and other processes that are creating the wastewater effluents. Farther "upstream" are the process design engineers whose process design work also can influence process outputs, including byproducts and waste streams. The reason for going "upstream" to the processes creating the wastewater is that specific employee tasks in these processes may cause significant environmental impacts by allowing — by accident or otherwise — significantly higher concentrations of toxic materials in wastewater that exceed the capacity of the treatment unit, thereby causing nonconformance with the wastewater treatment control procedures and regulatory standards. Similarly, process design engineers can influence process optimization to reduce waste streams.

Step 3: Prepare appropriate competency-based training materials

prepare
training
materials

Your facility next should develop the content of training materials to meet the competency-based criteria relating to "significant" environmental impacts that your facility sets for itself. At a minimum, your competency-based criteria must include relevant environmental training required by applicable regulatory requirements.

example:
root-cause
search

For example, local or state government regulations may require that wastewater treatment operators receive specified training and be licensed or certified. For your employees in production or other processes creating wastewater, legally mandated training to minimize wastewater exceedances may not apply, so you will need to establish the level of training you believe is appropriate to minimize releases of contaminants that may be the root cause of overtaxing the facility's wastewater treatment unit and the resulting "significant" environmental impacts.

Similarly, you will need to prepare competency-based environmental training requirements for employees whose work may cause "significant" environmental impacts in areas that you have identified as your facility's "significant" environmental aspects — such as energy and resource conservation, materials management, and product and process design.

Competency-based training requirements can include specified levels of education, professional training, and experience. How you define these requirements for your facility employees, for specified work associated with "significant" environmental impacts, will depend on the circumstances, the existing level of employee skills, and the nature of the "significant" environmental impact risks.

TIP 3.13

> ### Job descriptions
>
> Employees should have job descriptions. Include in their job descriptions their responsibilities for minimizing potential significant environmental impacts associated with their work. Reinforce the importance of competency-based training requirements by including appropriate references in each employee's job description.

Step 4: Plan and Conduct Competency-Based Training of Specific Employees

establish and document training program

Each employee identified in step 2 is required by ISO 14001 to receive appropriate training. It is usually not feasible to train everyone at once. You should prepare a training plan showing when specific employees are scheduled for training and training responsibilities.

ISO 14001 does not explicitly require that you document your training requirements, your plan, and the completed training for each employee. As a practical matter, it will be important to have some method of documenting your training program to meet your own facility's ability to manage this requirement, as well as to simplify demonstration that your facility meets the ISO 14001 training requirements.

Step 5: Develop a System for Measuring Competency

One approach is to include environmental competency evaluation in the employee's annual performance appraisal.

interpretation: training before certification?

An important ISO 14001 interpretation issue may arise as to whether your facility may be registered/certified if all personnel whose work may create significant environmental impacts have not yet received planned competency-based training. To meet the EMS standard, ISO 14001 specifies that your facility "require" that all such employees "have received appropriate training." A conservative interpretation is that you must complete all such training before your facility can be registered or certified. A more liberal interpretation is that your facility may still be registered/certified (even if all mandated training has not been completed) if it has established the training plan identifying each employee's training needs, prepared the training materials, established a training timetable and schedule, and has substantially implemented the training. The accreditation standards for ISO 14001 registrars and the registrars themselves will need to resolve this issue.

Environmental Awareness Training

awareness training

ISO 14001's environmental awareness training requirements apply to all of your facility's employees, including employees whose work may cause significant environmental impacts. The awareness training program should be non-technical and connected as much as possible with your plant's or facility's environmental policy (and its commitments), the purpose and broader goals of the EMS, your environmental objectives and targets, the links between improved environmental performance and business performance, and the importance of each employee's contribution to this effort, including adherence to specific procedures and supporting emergency preparedness and response actions.

Competency-based Environmental Training

**Competency-Based Environmental Training
Related to Significant Environmental Impacts**

ISO 14001 Section 4.3.2 Training, Awareness, and Competence

"The organization shall identify training needs. It shall require that all personnel whose work may create a significant impact upon the environment, have received appropriate training. . . . Personnel performing the tasks which can cause significant environmental impacts shall be competent on the basis of appropriate education, training and/or experience."

Awareness training, to some extent, overlaps competency-based environmental training. For example, both competency-based and awareness training require that employees whose work may cause significant environmental impacts achieve "awareness" of the potential significant environmental impacts of their work activities. Similarly, awareness training may overlap your internal environmental communications effort which is discussed in part 2. 4 below. You should try to consolidate your implementation of these requirements to avoid duplication.

TIP 3.14

Environmental competency-based training for contractors

Do not overlook competency-based training requirements for contractors doing work in or around your plant/facility. Contractors may be engaged in operations or activities with "significant" environmental aspects, including environmental (health and safety) compliance issues. In many locations, regulations require that contractors be trained in specific environmental (health and safety) requirements. In addition, ISO 14001's requirement for operational control procedures requires that your plant/facility establish procedures related to identified "significant" environmental aspects of operations and activities involving contractor services at your plant/facility.

As you develop your environmental awareness training program, strive for a concise, plain-language explanation of what your facility or plant is trying to accomplish with its EMS — the significant environmental aspects, the environmental objectives and targets, the potential financial as well as environmental performance improvement benefits, and the importance of this effort to "interested parties" such as the surrounding community.

keep it short
and to the
point

Awareness training often can be more effectively delivered through short 15 minute segments, through talks, videos, or other media. Avoid long training. Consider developing a series of key messages covering each of your facility's "significant" environmental aspects, briefly discussing what the facility is doing to minimize environmental impacts and how each employee can contribute. You can communicate key messages effectively through electronic message boards, posters, bulletin boards, newsletters, and periodic communication by the plant manager and senior operations and functional managers. It is important to keep these awareness messages simple and not let them become stale.

Environmental Awareness Training

Sec. 4.3.2 Training, Awareness and Competence

"The organization shall ... establish and maintain procedures to make its employees ... at each relevant function and level aware of:

a) the importance of conformance with the environmental policy and procedures and with the requirements of the environmental management system;

b) the significant environmental impacts, actual or potential, of their work activities and the environmental benefits of improved environmental performance;

c) their roles and responsibilities in achieving conformance with the environmental policy and procedures and with the requirements of the environmental management system including emergency preparedness and response requirements."

cascade
training

Another effective approach is to work through your plant management staff by training them first and having these managers cascade the awareness training through their departments and work groups. It is also critically important for the training program leader to get feedback and suggestions from line employees on the usefulness and relevance of the training.

3.2.4 Communication

Internal Communication

formal
communication

The ISO 14001 EMS standard requires that you implement a formal communication component covering internal communications between the various levels and functions of your plant or facility. This is an opportunity to address a systemic problem affecting many manufacturing plants and facilities — confusion over the kinds of environmental (health and safety) data that must be collected and uncertainty over who needs it and to whom it must be reported.

Generally speaking, there are two kinds of internal communication challenges:

1) day-to-day communications between different operational and functional groups (such as design engineering, quality, purchasing, logistics) and environmental (health and safety) managers and specialists within the plant or facility; and

2) environmental (health and safety) data collection and reporting required by regulations, the plant's or facility's internal EMS performance standards, and the company's divisional and corporate EHS groups.

Day-to-Day Communication

Open and honest communication between operations, functional, and environmental (health

informal, honest communication

and safety) professionals is essential to the effective implementation of the EMS. Clearly defined roles, responsibilities, and, especially, accountability, will help promote inter-group communication. Assigning appropriate roles and responsibilities for achieving a specific environmental objective and supporting targets to managers and employees in different operating and functional groups and rewarding a "team" approach will help break down group barriers and facilitate communication. Individuals who do not share their expertise or other valuable information essential to a successful implementation of the EMS must be held accountable.

procedures documentation?

ISO 14001 requires that the plant/facility "establish and maintain procedures for internal communication between the various levels and functions" within the plant or facility. The word "procedures" implies documentation, but ISO 14001 does not explicitly require documentation in this case. Ultimately, the plant manager's ethic concerning the importance of inter-group communications determines the effectiveness of day-to-day communications between the various departments, operational groups, and environmental (health and safety) specialists. This is primarily a plant/facility management policy issue. Because of the enormous variety and unpredictability of the kinds of information that need to be communicated, it is not useful or practical to attempt to document "procedures" for day-to-day environmental communication.

Environmental (Health and Safety) Reporting

official reporting

In selected situations, environmental (health and safety) regulatory requirements applicable to your facility require reporting of specified environmental (health and safety) information to government agencies. In addition, your plant/facility EMS will need to collect specific environmental (health and safety) data relating to the performance of the EMS (and the plant/facility) and ensure data are reported to employees and managers who are responsible and accountable for specific elements or components of the EMS. Examples of regulatory reporting requirements include mandatory reporting to government agencies in the U.S. for spills of "reportable quantities" of hazardous substances, reporting requirements under the Toxic Substances Control Act, the Clean Water Act, and the Emergency Planning and Community Right to Know Act.

resource conservation, waste reduction

An example of a non-regulatory reporting requirement essential to the plant/facility EMS is collecting data concerning implementation of certain plant/facility environmental objectives and targets relating to energy and water conservation and waste reduction — and reporting them to designated employees and managers. Your company's divisional (business unit) and corporate groups may require additional data from your plant/facility for company-wide environmental performance tracking.

data flow

ISO 14001 provides an important opportunity for your plant/facility to establish an environmental (health and safety) information strategy that defines the specific kinds of environmental (health and safety) data that will be collected for:

1) the requirements of your EMS;

2) regulatory compliance and reporting; and

3) the requirements of your company's division and corporate groups.

Visualize the environmental information strategy as a road map for essential environmental data and information flows. The environmental information strategy clarifies who is responsible for collecting the data, who needs to receive it, and how the data is to be used for decision making, for regulatory compliance and reporting, and for monitoring and measuring environmental performance.

example:
incident
reporting

Environmental (health and safety) "incident" reporting is one example of how your environmental (health and safety) information strategy helps reduce confusion and uncertainty in data collection and reporting. U.S. federal and state laws require you to document and report certain EHS "incidents," such as accidental spills of "reportable quantities" of hazardous substances. Many other kinds of EHS "incidents" do not fall under these requirements. Yet appropriate information on EHS "incidents" may be important in tracking your facility's performance and in understanding the root causes of "incidents" so that effective preventive actions can be taken. The problem companies face is that there is no universal, "one size fits all" definition of an EHS "incident."

define terms
and data

Your facility (or company) needs to think through an appropriate definition that is relevant to its "significant" environmental (health and safety) aspects, which include legally reportable "incidents" and corporate requirements, and which can be communicated easily to all employees. Once you have an appropriate definition of an EHS "incident," you can train employees and use positive feedback mechanisms to enhance the accuracy and timeliness of reporting.

example:
information
technologies

Developing an environmental information strategy for your plant/facility provides two significant benefits. First, you will find opportunities to eliminate unnecessary data collection, storage, and reports, saving time and paperwork costs. Second, by clearly defining the environmental data that you need to support your EMS, regulatory requirements, and divisional/corporate requirements, you are in an excellent position to use information technologies to automate data collection, storage/retrieval, communication, and reporting — saving additional costs associated with conventional information management.

Examples of information technologies that effectively address environmental (health and safety) data and information management are:

1) the use of groupware (software) applications such as Lotus Notes™; and

2) data warehouse technologies.

📖 (See Appendix J for more information on resources.)

External Communication

ISO 14001 requires that your plant/facility establish and maintain procedures for

* receiving;

* documenting; and

* responding

to relevant communications from external interested parties regarding its environmental aspects and environmental management system.

"External interested parties" are your plant/facility stakeholders such as the surrounding community, suppliers, customers, shareholders, and environmental groups.

contact point

To implement procedures, your facility should designate a single contact point within the facility (e.g., plant manager or EHS manager) for receiving and responding to letters, telephone calls, or other communications from external stakeholders. A simple system, such as a logbook, needs to be put in place for documenting these communications. Note that ISO 14001 does not require that your plant/facility respond to all external communications — only relevant communications concerning your "environmental aspects" and your EMS.

consider communication options

ISO 14001 also requires that your plant/facility consider options and processes for initiating communications to its external stakeholders and make a decision whether it will or will not institute external communications. Examples of external communication initiatives contemplated by ISO 14001 include a periodic report to the external stakeholders on your plant/facility's environmental performance, the results of its EMS audits, and publication of your plant/facility's environmental policy. Note that ISO 14001 does not require your facility to initiate any form of external communication, but it must record its decision either way.

interested parties

In deciding whether your plant/facility should develop external communication initiatives, consider that external interested parties are a major driving force behind ISO 14001. Some companies will seek ISO 14001 primarily because it may become a customer requirement. Others will be persuaded that ISO 14001 certification is an effective way to demonstrate adherence to a recognized standard of care for the environment. For these companies, credibility with their external stakeholders will be very important. Without some means of communicating their environmental performance, such companies may be hard pressed to gain the credibility they seek.

trend: performance reporting

There is a growing list of companies publishing annual environmental reports on their performance. The early corporate environmental reports tended to be glowing accounts of a company's environmental performance successes. The trend today, however, is toward publishing objective performance information, including incidents of noncompliance, quantities of environmental releases from specific operating units, and performance against environmental goals. This trend is clearly aimed at satisfying external stakeholder requirements and gaining credibility.

Objective environmental performance reporting also anticipates the growing availability of environmental compliance and other performance data obtainable from the public record.

3.2.5 EMS Documentation, Document Control, and Environmental Records

We will briefly discuss three separate but related ISO 14001 document management requirements:

1) documenting the "core elements" of the EMS;

2) document control; and

3) environmental records.

📖 (See Part 3, Chapter 4 for more information on documentation.)

17 core elements

EMS Documentation

ISO 14001 requires that you describe and periodically update the "core elements" of your

EMS and their interaction. You can describe and update the "core elements" either on paper (e.g., an EMS manual) or electronically (e.g., computer-based system). In the ISO 14001 specification standard, "core elements" are not defined. There are, however, 17 numbered elements, the first being the requirement to define the organization's environmental policy. You should consider these 17 elements and any additional elements (e.g., an external communication program if you decide to have one) as your EMS "core elements."

In describing your EMS "core elements" and their interaction, do not feel constrained to describe them in the sequence they appear in the ISO 14001 standard. Many companies already have well-designed EHS manuals at the corporate and plant/facility levels that can be adapted to include a description of their ISO 14001 EMS. 📖 (See Part 4, Chapter 3 for more information on manuals in the SGS Thomson case study.)

example: medical supplier

For example, Becton Dickinson's corporate safety and environmental (S&E) manual, developed before the emergence of the ISO 14001 standard, defines its company-wide safety and environmental management system, including the company's safety and environmental policy, organizational structure, responsibilities, practices, and resources necessary to implement the system. Becton Dickinson is a worldwide manufacturer of medical devices and diagnostic equipment. (See sidebar on page 148 illustrating the manual's components.)

The corporate safety and environmental manual specifies that each Becton Dickinson facility is required to document and implement a facility-based safety and environmental management system, which meets corporate requirements. As you can see, many of the Becton Dickinson S&E management system core elements parallel ISO 14001 requirements. But Becton Dickinson has established additional core elements to meet its requirements. To implement ISO 14001, Becton Dickinson would not need to redesign its S&E Manual to conform to the sequence of the ISO 14001 EMS elements, but only to include any missing elements where they logically fit in its manual.

accessing documentation

In addition to describing the core elements of your EMS and their interaction, ISO 14001 requires that your EMS documentation provide direction or a road map to the location or access point of related documentation. For example, you may want to include a description of your environmental compliance evaluation or audit program as one of the core elements of your EMS, but not include the compliance audit protocols. A reference to the location or means of access to the audit protocols should then be provided in your EMS documentation. Similarly, EMS documentation covering organizational structure and responsibilities and the training core elements should reference the location and means of access to your facility's employee job descriptions to the extent they incorporate environmental performance standards, responsibilities, and competency-based training requirements.

Document Control

document control procedures

ISO 14001 requires that your plant/facility establish and maintain procedures for controlling all documents required by the ISO 14001 standard. ISO 14001's document control requirements are essentially the same as those required by ISO 9000. Document control procedures, among other requirements, must:

*   define responsibilities for the creation and modification of ISO 14001 mandated documents;

- ensure required documents are periodically reviewed, revised as necessary, and approved by authorized personnel;

- ensure that current versions of required documents are available at all locations where they are needed for the effective functioning of the EMS;

- ensure that obsolete documents are promptly removed from all points of issue and points of use.

In developing your document control procedures, consider using a computer-based document management and distribution system that allows access by all employees who need it for carrying out their EMS implementation responsibilities.

Environmental Records

environmental records

Environmental records are documents that contain the performance results of the EMS, such as records of employee training, the results of EMS audits and management reviews, monitoring records, and the results of environmental performance tracking. Environmental records also include documents that demonstrate conformity with the EMS requirements, including environmental permits, registrations, licenses, and other regulatory approvals demonstrating compliance with applicable regulatory requirements.

ISO 14001 requires that your facility establish and maintain an environmental records management system that enables identification, maintenance, retrievability, and disposition of environmental records. The records management system must also specify record retention periods, which must be consistent with applicable legal requirements.

ISO 14001's requirements for EMS documentation, document control, and environmental records closely track the requirements of ISO 9000. There are significant opportunities for integrating your ISO 9000 and 14001 document systems.

📖 (See Part 3, Chapter 4 for more information on documentation.)

3.2.6 Operational Control

identify key activities

ISO 14001's requirements for operational control are somewhat confusingly worded, leaving room for narrow interpretations by skilled legal minds. We do not take the narrow approach in our interpretation.

First, what do we mean by operational controls? Operational controls are essentially procedures for ensuring that operations and activities do not exceed specified conditions or performance standards or violate regulatory compliance limits. Operational control procedures include specific operating criteria or specifications in the case of equipment maintenance, pollution control equipment, and production processes which must be managed within specified parameters to achieve desired optimization (quality yields, waste minimization, pollution prevention).

📖 (See sidebar on pages XX and XX for insights on operational controls.)

To meet ISO 14001's operational control requirements, your plant/facility needs to identify *each operation and activity associated with the plant/facility's identified "significant" environmental aspects* in line with the environmental policy, objectives and targets. 📖

The Becton Dickinson Approach

Core Elements of Each Facility-Based Safety and Environmental Management System

Management and Administration Component

Safety and Environmental Policy Statement (signed by senior facility manager)

Safety and Environmental Performance Standards, including applicable regulatory requirements, tailored to each employee's job description

Annual Safety and Environmental Goals and Objectives

Safety and Environmental Staffing Plan

Safety and Environmental Committees

General Communication procedures for ensuring that specified types of safety and environmental information are regularly communicated among different levels and functions of the facility, which also include safety and environmental promotional activities.

Safety and Environmental Awareness program

Policies and Procedures reflecting the facility's organizational structure and implementation of safety and environmental regulatory issues.

Facility Safety and Environmental Rules and Work Permits

Monitoring and Verification covering regulatory compliance and the Facility's

- Safety and Environmental management system requirements
- reference materials including local safety, health, and environmental documents on hazard assessments as well as the means to verify currency.

Other Required Components for Facility Safety & Environmental Management Systems (bullet subcomponents omitted for brevity)

Orientation and Training

Inspections and Audit

Accident Investigation and Analysis

Task Analysis and Observations

Emergency Preparedness

Environmental Controls

Health Controls

Engineering and Purchasing Controls

Personal Protective Equipment

Courtesy of Thomas Grego, Corporate Safety Manager, Becton Dickinson

Figure 3.18

(See Part 3, Chapter 1, for more on policies, objectives, and targets.) For each identified operation and activity associated with a "significant" environmental aspect, ISO 14001 requires your plant/facility to establish and maintain documented control procedures:

> "covering situations where their absence could lead to deviations from the environmental policy and the objectives and targets."

focus on significant aspects Among other things, your environmental policy commits your plant/facility to prevention of pollution, compliance with regulatory requirements, and continual improvement. Therefore you should focus on ensuring development of operational control procedures covering all operations and activities associated with identified "significant" environmental impacts that need to be controlled to ensure adherence to your plant/facility's commitment to:

- comply with applicable regulatory requirements;

- prevention of pollution;

- continual improvement; and

- achieving its environmental objectives and targets.

unregulated aspects Many facilities already have established operational control procedures for ensuring compliance with environmental (health and safety) regulations. If your plant has not yet done so, this must be your first priority. Developing operational control procedures for *unregulated* "significant" environmental aspects of operations and activities requires some forethought and analysis of how a specific operation or activity is connected to the "significant" environmental aspect.

example: energy usage Let's assume, for example, that your facility has identified energy usage as a "significant" environmental aspect. To address this issue, your plant/facility should not only consider setting an energy usage reduction objective and targets, but also develop appropriate operational control procedures for ensuring that specific operations and activities consuming energy will be sufficiently controlled to meet your objective and targets.

ISO 14001 also requires that your plant/facility establish and maintain operational control procedures:

> "related to the identifiable significant environmental aspects of goods and services used by . . ." your plant/facility.

challenge: methods used in identifying aspects This is an interesting and potentially challenging requirement. It first requires that your plant/facility review the kinds of materials, parts and components, products, and services it uses and identify significant environmental aspects associated with such goods and services. This step is the same step involved in determining which of your overall environmental aspects are "significant." Some of the issues that may be raised in identifying "significant" environmental aspects of goods and services used include toxic constituents of materials, materials reusability and recyclability, and packaging. Services used by your plant/facility with potentially significant environmental aspects might include outsourced manufacturing of parts and components (e.g., printed circuit boards or "toll" manufacturing of chemicals) under a direct contractual relationship involving quality and design specifications.

What kinds of operational control procedures might ISO 14001 contemplate for identifiable significant environmental aspects of goods and services used by your plant/facility? Straightforward examples relating to on-site operations and activities include chemical management procedures (MSDS management and chemical approval systems) and procedures for managing packaging materials and containers to minimize waste.

suppliers

More difficult questions arise in considering operational control procedures that extend to your plant/facility's suppliers. ISO 14001 requires that you *communicate relevant procedures and requirements to suppliers and contractors*. If your plant/facility contractually specifies quality and design details for materials, parts/components, or products it uses, it is in a position to influence reduction of "significant" environmental aspects associated with the manufacture, transportation, and use by your plant/facility of those goods and services.

quality and performance

This is another intersection of quality and environmental performance. Clearly it is in your plant/facility's interest in implementing its EMS to communicate appropriately with suppliers and contractors, to obtain more detailed information on identifiable "significant" environmental aspects of these goods and services. And just as your plant/facility imposes quality requirements on its suppliers, so too it should consider appropriate environmental requirements for goods and services that will help reduce potentially significant environmental impacts and contribute to your plant/facility's EMS. If your plant/facility has no such capability to influence (e.g., the goods are commodities or off-the-shelf products), then operational control procedures oriented to the vendor would not be appropriate.

3.2.7 Emergency Preparedness and Response

required by law

Regulations in OECD countries and many developing nations already require that industrial and commercial sites provide for emergency contingency planning.

ISO 14001's requirements for emergency preparedness and response generally parallel applicable regulatory requirements.

focus on prevention and review

There are several aspects of the ISO 14001 requirements, however, that your plant/facility will need to examine closely:

• Emergency procedures must identify the potential for accidents and emergency situations (identify the reasonably possible accident and emergency scenarios) and make provisions for preventing and mitigating any associated environmental impacts.

• Emergency procedures must be periodically reviewed — particularly after the occurrence of an accident or emergency situation — and revised (when necessary) to incorporate "lessons learned" from experience and new techniques for coping with emergencies.

When practical, emergency procedures must be tested periodically.

ISO 14001 Operational Control and ISO 9000

from International Environmental Systems Update, April 1996

> ## Interpretation: Section 4.3.6 — Operational Control
>
> "The organization shall identify those operations and activities that are associated with the identified significant environmental aspects in line with its policy, objectives, and targets. The organization shall plan these activities, including maintenance, in order to ensure that they are carried out under specified conditions by:
>
> (a) establishing and maintaining documented procedures to cover situations where there absence could lead to deviations from the environmental policy and the objectives and targets . . . ."

❖ **Michael A. Ross,** *CEO and a principal consultant of Ross, Ltd., Quality & Environmental Consulting, suggests correlating ISO 14001's operational control requirement with ISO 9001's process control clause for clarification and integration purposes. He discusses the meaning of Section 4.3.6 below.*

ISO 14001, Section 4.3.6 (a) identifies the requirements for an EMS's "Operational Control." As drafted, this section essentially requires the establishment and maintenance of documented procedures to cover operational "situations" that could potentially lead to deviations from an established EMS policy, objectives, and targets.

ISO 9000 Correlation

This broad and rather vague requirement probably can best be clarified by correlating it to an ISO 9000 quality management system (QMS) clause/requirement. For those readers who are familiar with clause 4.9 of ISO 9001, "Process Control," the requirements of **ISO 14001, Section 4.3.6 (a)** should look somewhat similar and familiar.

To refresh your memories, ISO 9001, clause 4.9, states, in part, that, "The supplier shall identify and plan the production, installation, and servicing processes which directly affect quality and shall ensure that these processes are carried out under controlled conditions. Controlled conditions shall include the following:

a) documented procedures defining the manner of production, installation, and servicing, where the absence of such procedures could adversely affect quality;

b) use of suitable production, installation, and servicing equipment, and suitable working environment;

c) compliance with reference standards/codes, quality plans, and/or documented procedures;

d) monitoring and control of suitable process parameters and product characteristics;

e) the approval of processes and equipment, as appropriate;

f) criteria for workmanship, which shall be stipulated in the clearest practical manner (e.g., written standards, representative samples, or illustrations);

g) suitable maintenance of equipment to ensure continuous process capability."

Take a look at the requirements of **ISO 14001, Section 4.3.6 (a).** Note the similarities in the wording and phrasing. For many companies, ". . . the production, installation, and servicing processes which directly affect quality . . ." will, more often than not, be the same (or at least be related to) ". . . operations and activities that are associated with the identified significant environmental aspects . . ."

Starting Point for Integration

A good starting point in meeting the **ISO 14001, section 4.3.6 (a)** requirement, at least for companies that are already ISO 9000 compliant, is to identify and incorporate the environmental aspects and impacts of your operations, processes, etc., into your existing "process control" documentation. This exercise will get most companies a long way towards meeting the **ISO 14001, 4.3.6 (a)** requirement. It should be remembered that this exercise alone will not capture every operation and activity associated with your identified significant environmental aspects, but it will identify a major portion of them.

This exercise also serves two other purposes. First, it doesn't require you to create a massive new document system to identify operations and activities that have significant environmental aspects associated with them. You already have identified operations and processes that are critical to quality management, and you can build your environmental aspects and impacts from that starting point. Why "reinvent the wheel?"

Second, the majority of corporate America, as part of cost savings and consolidation, will integrate their various management systems as much as possible or practical. Corporations will not have separate and distinct quality management systems, environmental management systems, and occupational health and safety management systems.

Instead, they will have one "management system" that addresses the commonalties of all the various management systems (e.g., management review, document control, records management, internal auditing, training, etc.) with separate annexes or appendices that address distinct issues such as legal and other requirements, objectives and targets, emergency preparedness and response, contract review, purchasing, etc.

Starting from Scratch

As for companies that are starting out from square one with ISO 14001, i.e., they are not ISO 9000 compliant, this requirement may require some significant groundwork.

First, you need to "dissect" the requirement and pick out the key words and/or phrases. For example, ". . .identified significant environmental aspects. . . ," ". . . plan . . . including mainte-nance . . . ," ". . . specified conditions . . . ," ". . . absence could lead to deviation. . . ," etc.

This should lead you to the conclusion that before you even begin to address the requirement itself, you need to establish your environmental policy, objectives, and targets. To properly identify your objectives and targets, you will also have to have identified your environmental aspects and impacts associated with your activities, products, or services.

If you have been thorough in developing your EMS, the environmental aspects of your activities, products, and services that can have significant impacts on the environment have been considered in setting your environmental objectives. Subsequently, your objectives and targets need to be consistent with your environmental policy.

So far, you have ". . . identified significant environmental aspects in line with its policy, objectives and targets. . . ."

Now, you need to identify the operations, processes, and activities that are associated with those "identified significant environmental aspects." For example, if you have identified a byproduct acidic waste as one of your significant environmental aspects, then you need to identify the operations, processes, etc., that contribute to the production or formation of that acidic waste.

Planning

Once those operations and activities associated with the significant environmental aspects have been identified, you need to make sure that those operations and activities are planned and "carried out under specified conditions."

Maintenance (corrective and preventive) activities need to be included in the planning process as well. Using acidic waste, how often is preventive maintenance performed on the interim storage tanks so as to prevent a potential leak? If a leak does occur, are there procedures in place to address the corrective repairs to be performed on the tanks?

This leads us to the next portion of the requirement, ". . . ensure that they are carried out under specified conditions by establishing and maintaining documented procedures to cover situations. . . ". This leads back to the "process control" issue previously identified under ISO 9000.

✔ Do you have documented procedures to address or "cover" normal and abnormal operating conditions, including start-up/shut-down conditions, where a lack of those procedures could lead to deviations from the environmental policy, objectives, and targets?

✔ In the case of our acidic waste, are there documented procedures for proper handling, control, storage, disposal, recycling, etc.?

✔ If these procedures are not in place, could the lack or "absence" of them ". . . lead to deviations from the environmental policy and the objectives and targets. . . ?"

In most cases, the answer to that question is yes.

The documented procedures under part (a) also lead quite nicely into part (b) of clause 4.3.6 which is, "stipulating operating criteria in the procedures." Again, "process control" becomes evident. Part (a) requires you to establish and maintain documented procedures to cover situations where their absence could lead to deviations; part (b) requires you to stipulate the operating criteria in those procedures. They fit together quite nicely.

Handling Deviations

As for deviations themselves, is it ever appropriate to deviate from your stated environmental policy and objectives and targets? You bet it is. While the concept of deviating from your environmental policy and objectives and targets is much like deviating from the quality of your product — you want to keep both to a minimum because they are a form of nonconformance — there are times when you should and must deviate from them.

For example, under "normal operating conditions" deviation should not be a problem. Unfortunately, "normal" is not always the norm. Accident or emergency conditions do occur and, sometimes, they cause you to deviate from your policy or objectives and targets. Hopefully though, accident or emergency conditions occur infrequently. These situations should be addressed as part of your emergency preparedness and response procedure requirements under ISO 14001. Your emergency response and preparedness procedures actually are a good example of documents that illustrate deviation and how to respond to it.

Another, and more common, example of deviation from your environmental policy and objectives and targets is during start-up or shut-down conditions. Usually these are more common and more frequent than your emergency conditions and need to be factored into the "deviation" scenario. It is frequently during the start-up and shut-down phases of an operation that your environmental impacts are potentially the most significant. The key here again is to have documented procedures that address/control the start-up and shut-down of your processes or operations. These procedures/documents also illustrate deviation and how to respond to it.

In conclusion, the "operational control" requirements under clause **ISO 14001 4.3.6 (a) and (b)** of are very similar in nature to the "process control" requirements under clause 4.9 of ISO 9001. If you're not ISO 9000 compliant, the operational control clause will take a little more work, but if you're diligent and methodical, it shouldn't cause you much problem. Just approach it the same way that you'd eat an elephant — "one bite at a time."

Finally, not all deviation is bad. Under certain circumstances, it is not only acceptable, but expected. Just make sure that you have it documented. ISO 14001 is much like ISO 9000 — both boil down to "say what you do, do what you say, and be able to prove it!"

Handling ISO 14001 Operational Control Deviations

from International Environmental Systems Update, May 1996

❖ *Thomas Bartel, a corporate regulatory affairs manager for Unisys Corporation, says it might become appropriate for a company to deviate from its objectives and targets for financial, legal, or quality reasons.*

Most organizations attempt to set cost-effective objectives and targets that are realistic and attainable while meeting the principles outlined in their environmental policies. Deviation from those objectives and targets might become appropriate in circumstances where the financial soundness of your organization could be placed in more jeopardy over the long term than the expected benefit to the environment achieved from accomplishing them would justify.

Your organization must be in a sound financial position to be able to implement programs that sustain the environment in a meaningful way. It would be important, therefore, for your organization to constantly monitor, balance, and revise — if deemed necessary — its original objectives and targets to help minimize any detrimental effects on its financial resources that meeting its original objectives and targets might cause.

Your company also may have various legal requirements, by way of contracts or other agreements, that may cause a conflict or interfere with meeting its proposed objectives and targets. For example, it may have a clause in a revolving loan or line of credit arrangement that requires a certain minimum balance in its cash reserves. This situation might interfere with its ability to provide sufficient resources to meet its proposed objectives and targets.

Another circumstance that might cause deviation from objectives and targets is your organization's commitment to maintain product quality parameters. If it is determined that prescribed objectives and targets interfere with the ability to comply with contractual product quality requirements, then the objectives and targets may have to be revised to meet the contractual obligations.

Samples of Deviations from Objectives and Targets

What are some examples of documents that illustrate deviation?

Within a financial plan, the amount of resources allocated to achieving objectives and targets may be tied directly to an organization fulfilling specifically delineated revenue and income goals. If revenue and income levels did not meet the desired goals, then your organization could decrease its expenditures and attain lower objectives and targets than originally intended.

Similarly, an annual business plan might contain wording either indirectly inferring or specifically permitting deviation from meeting objectives and targets, based upon requirements that your organization satisfies certain operational cost-effective provisions.

Deviation from meeting objectives and targets also might be indirectly triggered by a clause in a financial agreement, which might require meeting minimum cash reserve balances or the need to conserve your financial resources to preclude defaulting on the agreement. This could be particularly conceivable in a situation where your organization is going through a bankruptcy reorganization.

In the last two examples, it should be noted that, although the legal documents do not expressly state that an organization's objectives and targets should be deviated from, it is one obvious area you might investigate to achieve significant cost savings.

A final example would be a contract document executed with another organization to provide products or services that may contain specific language stipulating that a minimum level of quality must be met. Although the contract might not specifically reference that your organization's environmental objectives and targets should be deviated from, it may state that process changes might be necessary during manufacture of the product to satisfy the contractual obligation. The potential loss of business and revenue may influence an organization to modify a process, which, in turn, may result in a deviation from its original objectives and targets.

CHAPTER 3

Tips on Interpretation and Implementation

3.3.1 Overview

As you are learning, the way and depth to which you implement ISO 14001 very much depend on your organization's size, complexity, and driving forces. In this chapter, we offer various perspectives by way of tips and advice to help you hone your approach. We cover general interpretation and application of ISO 14001 and ISO 14004, documentation requirements, help for small and medium-sized enterprises, and relationships to ISO 9000.

This is organized in a clause-by-clause breakdown of the ISO 14001 and ISO 14004 standards, which generally parallel each other. Under each clause, the relevant perspective is marked with an icon for easy reference. Following is the structure of this chapter, with the authors of each section listed. Other parts and chapters in this book address each of these issues as well.

ISO 14001 and ISO 14004 Section References

We recommend that you refer back to Appendix A for the text of the standards referenced in the succeeding tips. Lack of space prohibited us from entirely reiterating the standards in this chapter.

ISO 14001

ISO 14001 Purpose and Interpretation

by Cynthia Neve, ISO Consultant, The Victoria Group;
Michelle Blazek, Environmental Consultant, AT&T Environmental,
Health and Safety Process;
Leilia McAdams, Technical Manager, Environmental Strategic
Planning Department, AT&T (currently with Lucent Technologies)

This section offers insight on the purpose/intent, interpretation/explanation, and implementation tips based on the experience of a team of managers from AT&T Microelectonics who actively helped write the ISO 14000 series of standards. You should note that the annex to ISO 14001 is informative, not normative, meaning it is not intended to be audited against by a third party.

On September 20, 1995, AT&T announced its intention to undergo a reorganization into three companies: AT&T, Lucent Technologies, and NCR. Each of these new companies is reevaluating its environmental, health, and safety goals, and is determining whether and how to pursue ISO 14001.

ISO 14004

ISO 14004 Interpretation

by Marilyn Block, President, MRB Associates and
Phil Marcus, Vice President, ICF Kaiser Inc.

The sections on ISO 14004 were written by two of the most active U.S. participants in developing ISO 14004 itself. You should bear in mind that the ISO 14004 guidance document was written to apply to *any* EMS, not just ISO 14001. Its purpose parallels ISO 9004, the quality management system guidance document. It is not intended for third-party auditing.

The lists it contains are not considered comprehensive, but only illustrative of the sorts of items you should consider. There was concern in the U.S. and elsewhere that this standard, and the informative appendix in ISO 14001, would establish a standard of care. Delegates took great pains to ensure that language made it clear these documents were for private industry use as tools in implementing an EMS, and their contents were purely informative.

Documentation

by Marie Godfrey, Consultant/Project Manager,
Franklin Quest Consulting Group (Formerly Shipley Associates)

One of the most difficult areas of any management system implementation is documentation. Most companies either go too far, or not far enough. Each situation can cause grief. Going too far can stall the entire implementation process or stop it in its tracks, or can bog down the years of maintenance and employee buy-in a good management system requires. Not going far enough can cause nonconformances at audit time when the auditor cannot find evidence that you're doing what you say you do — and can create murkiness in what ought to be a transparent system.

The sections in the standard that require documentation are denoted by the symbol ☞. Those that highly recommend it but do not require it are denoted by the symbol ▲.

Finding "just right" is no easy task, but the sections on documentation were written by an expert in the field of information management systems and their relationship to ISO 14001 and ISO 9001. These sections, and Chapter 4, offer guidance in this swamp.

For Small- and Medium-Sized Enterprises (SMEs)

by Edwin Pinero, Senior Project Manager, EnSafe Inc.;
Leader, ST2 TG4 on Environmental Site Assessments

Large companies logically have more resources to call upon in implementing a holistic system such as ISO 14001. Many can assign a full-time person, or even entire teams, to the task. Small companies rarely have that luxury. Faced with having to get revenue in the door or stop and create a training program, most would opt for the former; this, even though they know the short-term human and financial resource costs of implementation are well worth the long-term gains in management system efficiencies and other benefits. But you don't have to settle for having one or the other when there are ways to ensure solvency *and* an excellent EMS. Note: It is likely you will need to seek external help to implement ISO 14001, but the depth and extent of such help depends on how much effort you are willing to expend on your own behalf.

The sections on SMEs are written by an experienced environmental auditor who was immersed in development of the ISO 14000 auditing standards. His particular area of interest is SMEs.

For ISO 9000 Companies

by Samantha Munn, Manager, Environmental Systems,
Business Development, Inchcape Testing Service/Intertek Services

Companies that are implementing or have become certified to one of the ISO 9000 series of quality management system standards have an advantage over others as they pursue ISO 14001. They have a base of systems understanding and procedures from which to build. The sections on ISO 9000 touch on those areas where you may find some parallels and offer food for thought.

3.3.2 Environmental Policy *(4.1)*

ISO 14001 — 4.1 Environmental Policy

ISO 14001 — A.4.1 Environmental Policy

ISO 14004 — 4.1 How to Start: Commitment and Policy

ISO 14004 — 4.1.1 General

ISO 14004 — 4.1.2 Top Management Commitment and Leadership

ISO 14004 — 4.1.3 Initial Environmental Review

ISO 14004 — 4.1.4 Environmental Policy

ISO 14001

ISO 14001 Interpretation: Environmental Policy

Purpose/Intent

The intent of this element is to ensure that the top management of your organization defines and tangibly commits to an environmental policy that is appropriate for your organization's activities.

Explanation/Interpretation

The ISO 14001 standard is fairly prescriptive about the content of the policy statement. The policy should be documented, implemented, and maintained. It should be relevant to the type of business and associated environmental effects of your organization's activities, products, and services.

Your environmental policy must contain a commitment to three things: continuous improvement, prevention of pollution, and compliance with relevant regulations and other requirements to which your organization subscribes.

An important caveat: Continuous improvement does not imply that at every point there should be continuous improvement. You can choose which factors of the EMS you need to improve. Similarly, a commitment to prevention of pollution does not imply that at every point you must apply the least polluting technology. You can choose which technologies/ approaches provide a satisfactory degree of preventing, avoiding, reducing, or controlling pollution.

U.S. organizations should note that the definition of prevention of pollution in the standard is broader than the U.S. regulatory definition of reducing/eliminating pollution at the source. The standard embodies both upstream and end-of-pipe approaches to preventing pollution including but not limited to work practices, processes, materials substitution, pollution control, recycling, treatment, and conservation of resources.

The commitment to compliance with regulations is no easy feat, particularly in countries with complex legislative/regulatory processes. Note that this is a commitment to compliance and not a "certification" that your organization is indeed in full compliance. Obtaining and maintaining compliance with specific regulations (particularly) may be a credible goal for many organizations.

Your environmental policy also should state and provide a framework for establishing and reviewing your organization's objectives and targets in a way that will provide for continuous improvement.

Your policy must be communicated to all employees. This does not mean that every employee should be able to recite the policy, but employees should have a general aware-ness of how your environmental policy applies to them. For example, a boiler operator may understand that by monitoring and recording the boiler's exhaust temperature, he or she is contributing to the environmental performance of his or her plant and is completing a requirement of a government permit.

Your policy must also be made available to the public. This does not mean that your company should publicly post its policy, but it should not be of a proprietary or confidential nature, and the availability could be handled on an as-requested basis.

Implementation Tips

1) Address the three required "commitments." First, you need to have some understanding of your environmental aspects and of the effects of your activities, and of any prior policy commitments or sets of principles endorsed by your organization. Use that understanding to address the three commitments required in the policy.

2) Decide how broad or narrow, general or detailed, your commitment to continuous improvement will be. Answer the questions: Are we committing to continuous improve-ment:

    • of the EMS (in general terms, with no details identified)?

    • of specific elements of the system?

    • of our environmental performance (in general terms, with no details identified)?

    • of specific environmental performance criteria (stating them clearly)?

    • of some combination of the above?

3) Decide how broad or narrow, general or specific, your commitment to prevention of pollution will be. Answer the question: Are we committing to prevention of pollution:

- in general, unspecified terms, as in "We commit to prevention of pollution"?
- relating to specific activities or operations, with no criteria stated?
- relating to specific activities or operations, with criteria stated?
- in all activities or operations, with no criteria stated?
- in some combination of the above?

4) Decide how to word your statement committing to compliance with relevant environmental legislation and regulations. Here's a possible example:

"We commit to setting up and maintaining programs for compliance with all applicable laws and regulations, at each of our operations."

If you have regulatory and legal experts, you should get their input on this clause, in particular. In addition, if your organization has committed to other requirements (e.g., external principles such as the ICC Business Charter for Sustainable Development), add a statement to explain this "extra" commitment.

5) Add a statement relating to policy implementation, maintenance, and communication to employees. Here again, the degree to which you are specific is up to you. You should consider stating whom the policy applies to, that it will be implemented (and by whom), and that it will be communicated to all employees (at some frequency).

6) Review what you have drafted in your policy statement to make sure it is appropriate to the nature, scale, and environmental impacts of your activities, products, and services. Review the draft internally — get a wide cross-section of management and non-management opinions/comments on it. Revise as necessary to fit your organization's needs.

7) Get your top management to sign off on the environmental policy.

8) Set up and document procedures for deploying your policy. Include explanations of how the policy will be communicated to employees, how it will be available to the public, and how it will be maintained (e.g., who is responsible for disseminating the policy, how it will be reviewed on an annual basis, etc.).

ISO 14004

ISO 14004: Environmental Policy

An environmental policy establishes and validates top management's commitment to the environment. It is clear that the environmental policy places responsibility on top management for implementing the environmental program and reviewing performance against policy. When establishing an environmental policy, organizations should consider not only the requirements found in the 14001 EMS specification document, but also guiding principles developed by other international bodies such as the Business Charter for Sustainable Development of the International Chamber of Commerce and/or the Rio Declaration of the United Nations Conference on Environment and Development, which are printed in the appendix to the guidelines. The environmental policy should be looked on as a firm commitment of the organization to integrating environmental concerns into the daily operations of the firm.

Documentation: Environmental Policy

This clause requires a documented environmental policy. The most likely format for this would be an environmental policy manual or a set of environmental policy statements in another company policy manual. The requirement for communication to all employees and availability to the public suggests additional documentation (although the policy manual could be used for this function also). The specifications do not say, however, that the policy in its entirety must be communicated at one time. So it would be possible to communicate parts of the policy in annual reports, for example, rather than sending a copy of the policy manual to everyone.

☞ The key words in this clause are "top management." This requires not only that a policy be defined but also that top management must be the driving force for seeing that the action occurs. Top management doesn't actually to have write the documents; they must simply ensure they are written.

For SMEs: Environmental Policy

This section should pose no additional concerns for SMEs in that preparing the policy actually is not a cost or manpower-intensive effort. However, the key to success with this section will result from taking a good look at the organization's philosophy and approach to environmental management. This will then need to be integrated into a policy that also reflects the requirements of ISO 14001. The best advice to an SME is to keep it simple, straightforward, and appropriate to the nature and scale of the organization. A valid initial attempt is simply to reiterate the requirements of the standard, worded as a corporate policy commitment. As we shall see below, the greater effort will be in having the infrastructure to support the policy.

For ISO 9000 Companies: Environmental Policy

Akin to the quality policy required by ISO 9001 Clause 4.1.1, the environmental policy must state additional commitments to continual improvement, prevention of pollution, and meeting relevant environmental laws and regulations. The organization needs to ensure that its environmental policy is consistent with the company/site policy and corporate policy and also with legal documentation.

3.3.3 Planning *(4.2)*

ISO 14001 — 4.2 Planning

ISO 14001 — A.4.2 Environmental Planning

ISO 14004 — 4.2 Planning

ISO 14004 — 4.2.1 General.

ISO 14001

ISO 14001 Interpretation: Planning

Purpose/Intent

The intent of the planning section is to ensure a systematic, logical approach in implementing some key "up-front" elements of your EMS (or at least sooner rather than later).

Explanation/Interpretation

This is a general section of the standard that addresses planning as an essential requirement and divides it into four sections — environmental aspects, legal and other requirements, objectives and targets, and environmental management programs. These are the basic requirements of the standard that will ensure your system is well-planned and provides a sound basis and justification for implementing an EMS.

Implementation Tips

Consider the next four sections as a way to build a foundation for your systematic approach to setting priorities and addressing your organization's specific needs. Each successive step should flow logically from the previous step.

ISO 14004

ISO 14004: Planning

EMS Principle 2 requires the formulation of a plan to ensure fulfillment of the commitments contained in the environmental policy.

3.3.4 Environmental Aspects *(4.2.1)*

> *ISO 14001 — 4.2.1 Environmental Aspects*
>
> *ISO 14001 — A.4.2.1 Environmental Aspects*
>
> *ISO 14004 — 4.2.2 Identification of Environmental Aspects and Evaluation of Associated Environmental Impacts*

ISO 14001

ISO 14001 Interpretation: Environmental Aspects

Purpose/intent

The intent of this clause is to ensure that there is a systematic procedure in place to identify your environmental aspects, to evaluate their environmental impacts, to determine which are significant impacts, and to use this information when setting your objectives.

Explanation/Interpretation

Your organization is required to identify the environmental aspects of your "business" and to set up a procedure to do so and maintain this procedure. Put very simply, you are trying to answer the questions, "What is our environmental situation? How does what we do affect the environment?"

Environmental aspects are the elements of a product, activity, or service that have an impact on the environment. Environmental aspects can be considered the sources of environmental impacts. Although there is a connotation that environmental impacts are usually negative, environmental aspects often can be positive. For example, activities such as paper recycling or water conservation may result in positive environmental impacts. In some cases, there may be no clear consensus on whether the aspect is positive or negative, but action on the aspect may be mandated by law.

The standard is looking for an established, documented methodology to identify and review these aspects on an ongoing basis. This methodology can take many forms, including, but not limited to, screening processes, meetings, inspections, analyzing process by process or plant by plant, etc. It does not have to be a complicated system! The standard is not prescriptive about the approach to determining environmental aspects, but it makes sense that the approach be applied systematically throughout your organization and for all identified environmental aspects.

The intent of the methodology is to look at and be aware of those aspects of your business that interact with the air, water, land, natural resources, and other environmental media. Once you have identified these interactions, they can be evaluated as to the extent of their interaction (the "impact") with the environment. Furthermore, consistent criteria should be the basis for determining whether environmental impacts are (or can be) significant.

Significant impacts must be considered when environmental objectives are set. Ideally, your organization would focus its environmental program on those environmental aspects that are the most significant and present priorities. These reviews/evaluations of environmental aspects should also be recorded and maintained as part of the overall EMS system.

Implementation Tips

📖 (See Part 3, Chapter 1, for more information on environmental aspects.)

ISO 14004

ISO 14004: Environmental Aspects

The process of identifying the various environmental aspects associated with an organization's operations provides an opportunity for understanding the absolute and relative environmental impacts that occur in the course of daily activity. Such aspects and impacts may be of the organization's own making or a by-product of purchased goods. Evaluation of environmental impacts enables the organization to establish specific areas for improvement.

Consideration should be given to several issues, including:

- Location of the activity — an activity performed with relatively little environmental harm in a semi-arid region may have significant environmental impact if performed in a semi-tropical location. Therefore, evaluation of environmental impact should be site-specific.

- Frequency — to the extent possible, environmental impact should differentiate between chronic and acute effects.

- Severity — closely related to frequency is the severity of the impact. Organizations will be challenged to evaluate whether a single, severe environmental impact is greater or lesser than an ongoing, mild impact.

Documentation: Environmental Aspects

▲ Although no documentation is required in clause 4.2.1 on establishing and maintaining a procedure to identify environmental aspects, by developing a specific list of environmental aspects and providing (in writing) the basis for their identification, your organization can demonstrate how thoroughly it has investigated its potential impacts on the environment. Reviewing this list periodically (this guideline could be written into the procedure), will help the company stay "on track."

For SMEs: Environmental Aspects

This is one of the few sections where an SME will probably be dependent on outside assistance. The concept of comprehensive environmental aspects, impacts, and significant impacts is not as widespread in industry as is regulatory compliance. An organization will need to look beyond regulatory requirements when evaluating how it interacts with the environment. Typically, this requires some understanding of environmental science of the nature of ecosystems.

Second, it requires looking at processes activities and services more holistically than end of pipe results. Because traditionally SMEs limited resource allocation to regulatory compliance, this expertise and approach is not normally readily available in-house. For example, understanding how the organization interacts with the ecosystem and being able to assess what is a significant impact will be important.

For SMEs, the most cost-effective approach in the long run is to perform a comprehensive review of the organization early, obtaining outside expertise as appropriate. Although this involves initial investment of resources, the through-running implications of accurate assessment of aspects and impacts to the entire EMS warrant such sacrifice.

As will be seen below, all other components of the EMS depend in some form or another on the findings of this section. A way of maximizing the return on this investment would be to develop the process for determining aspects and impacts concurrently with actually doing the assessment. This will provide a process for the organization to use on subsequent assessments, thereby reducing future dependency on outside help.

For ISO 9000 Companies: Environmental Aspects

This clause should be viewed as the primary focus for establishing an EMS. The organization is required to identify those activities over which it has control and influence and determine those of a significant nature, which must then be addressed as a priority of the EMS. It is up to the organization to define what it means by "significant" and set parameters by which to evaluate the impacts of each product, service, or activity. When defining "significant," questions to ask may be whether the activity is regulated, is it currently managed, how is the effect of the activity considered by interested parties? (See *Figure 3.19* for a model.)

Although there is no direct parallel for this clause in ISO 9001, it would be pertinent to consider extending areas such as contract review, purchasing, handling, storage, packaging, preservation, delivery, and servicing, already established within the ISO 9001 system to address these elements within the EMS.

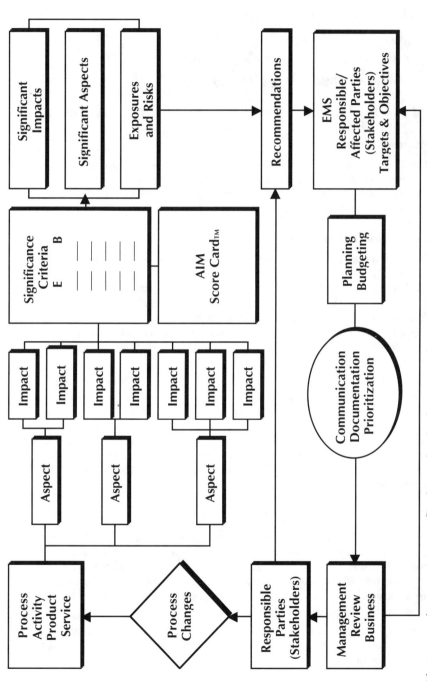

The Aspects and Impacts management flow diagram describes the sequence of management events inherent in the aspects and impacts identification and management process. The process flow displayed includes a double feedback loop mechanism (identified in the lower portion of the chart) that allows for stakeholder input, reinforces management feedback, and refines organizational learning in the EMS process.

The feedback and input loops are key to integrating aspects and impacts with facility planning and management. Improvement in organizational learning is critical to the ultimate success of the continual improvement process.

© 1996 Mick Bilney

Figure 3.19 —Aspects and impacts management model.

3.3.5 Legal and Other Requirements *(4.2.2)*

ISO 14001 — 4.2.2 Legal and Other Requirements

ISO 14001 — A.4.2.2 Legal and Other Requirements

ISO 14004 — 4.2.3 Legal and Other Requirements

ISO 14001

ISO 14001 Interpretation: Legal and Other Requirements

Purpose/Intent

The primary intent of this element is to identify and to have available and/or access to those legal requirements, such as codes, agreements, and regulatory and non-regulatory guidelines, that are applicable to the environmental aspects of your organization, and to set up and maintain a procedure to do so.

Explanation/Interpretation

Put simply, you are setting up a procedure to answer the question, "What are we required to do, given what we do?" Legal requirements may include laws, regulations, permits, contracts, memorandums of agreement, consent orders, etc. In some countries, this process may be complicated by the various levels of regulation (regional, federal, state, and local/municipal) and the complexity of the regulatory system. Other requirements may include voluntary programs like the Coalition for Environmentally Responsible Economies principles or Responsible Care®. If your organization signs up for voluntary initiatives, it should implement the requirements of the programs.

To determine which requirements, legal or otherwise, are applicable to your activities, products, or services, you should understand your environmental aspects and their related (or potential) environmental impacts. Once again, your organization should establish and document a methodology or procedure for this process. Use the procedure/methodology to search out all applicable requirements. The results of this methodology can take many forms, e.g., a listing of requirements, or a list of references to requirements. Document the results — this would be the output and record of proof that the element was addressed and implemented.

ISO 14004

ISO 14004: Legal Requirements

Although ISO 14000 focuses on environmental management, it must be implemented within the context imposed by statutory requirements in whatever jurisdiction the organization resides. Therefore, it is important to develop a procedure that ensures that all affected employees have access to and clearly understand all legal requirements to which the organization is bound. Similar procedures are necessary to ensure implementation of any voluntary code of practice, such those listed in the subsection above.

Identifying existing requirements is only one step in the process. The organization must consider how to keep track of changes in a timely fashion and communicate such changes to affected employees.

For SMEs: Legal and Other Requirements

More often than not, this is an area where an SME has concentrated and has the most complete processes, relative to other EMS requirements. The key to success here will be the completeness of the procedure, and assurance that other requirements are addressed, in addition to regulatory items. An SME may see improvement to this area through the EMS process because the procedure will be more thorough, minimizing oversights and errors. Use of outside databases and access to information in electronic form probably will help address most of this section's expectations.

For ISO 9000 Companies: Legal and Other Requirements

Although not directly related to a specific clause in ISO 9001, legislative, regulatory, and other requirements may be regarded as an extension of the contract review process, incorporated into the customer specification, where the "customer" may be the regulatory body, the community, or an industry association.

3.3.6 Objectives and Targets *(4.2.3)*

ISO 14001 — 4.2.3 Objectives and Targets
ISO 14001 — A.4.2.3 Objectives and Targets
ISO 14004 — 4.2.5 Environmental Objectives and Targets

ISO 14001

ISO 14001 Interpretation: Objectives and Targets

Purpose/Intent

The purpose of this clause is to set out clear overall goals (objectives) and specific, measurable ways of achieving the goals (targets) that are appropriate to your organization.

Explanation/Interpretation

This element takes the policy, environmental aspects, and legal and other requirements and puts them in terms of objectives and targets. It answers the question, "What do you want to accomplish first?"

Your organization should analyze the information from the preceding elements, especially for opportunities for improvement and priorities, and then determine how the priorities/improvements can be measured and tracked. The standard makes the distinction between an objective and a target. An "objective" is a higher-level, overall environmental goal. A "target" is a detailed performance requirement that is a means to achieve the related objective. The target should be measurable and time-bound.

One example is an objective to reduce air pollution in company operations. The target for manufacturing operations might be to reduce emissions of TCE (trichloroethylene) from each manufacturing plant by 10 percent by the year 2000. Also, these objectives and targets should be documented, reviewed, and updated on a periodic basis. Many companies set objectives and targets annually.

Implementation Tips

When deciding on your objectives and targets, there are several factors to consider. First, the targets should be measurable. Like the policy, these are to be realistic kinds of things. The best targets are practical, easy to measure, and obtainable. You should consider available technology, economics, and costs to determine what is feasible and realistic. Making the most of existing information is a good idea. In addition, you should consider the needs of external interested parties (government, communities, etc.) and employees as relevant when determining objectives and targets. Of course, those who are responsible for meeting the targets should agree to them up-front. Some organizations use the "SMART" method to guide them. Wherever possible, targets should be:

- specific;
- measurable;
- agreed-to;
- reasonable; and
- time-bound.

ISO 14004

ISO 14004: Objectives and Targets

The articulation of objectives that reflect the organization's environmental aspects/ impacts, legal requirements, other self-imposed requirements, and internal performance criteria, provide the road map for fulfilling its environmental policy. Measurable targets serve as milestones toward achieving stated objectives.

The organization should develop objectives and targets in concert with those who will be responsible for their successful attainment. Additionally, the views of interested parties, such as regulators or community groups, should be considered. The organization should pursue only those objectives and targets for which it can identify measurable indicators.

Documentation: Objectives and Targets

☞ Objectives and targets are not sufficient for ISO 14001 unless they are documented. Because these must be formulated and documented at each relevant function and level within the organization, the documents containing this information are probably proce- dures-level documentation. In some cases, work instructions and even records may be included under this clause.

For SMEs: Objectives and Targets

An SME needs to be careful not to take on too much through overly aggressive objectives and targets. The SME must remember that the objectives and targets are to be consistent with the scale of the organization and linked back to the policy and significant impacts defined in previous sections. For an SME, close interaction with related groups responsible for financial and resource allocation will further assure success with establishing realistic objectives and targets. On the other hand, the SME may find a need to establish objectives and targets relating to significant impacts not related to traditional end of pipe issues. An example would be packaging material use and energy consumption. An SME should start working on establishing objectives and targets, along with determining the aspects and impacts, to make best use of any outside expertise.

For ISO 9000 Companies: Objectives and Targets

Again, there is no clear comparison with ISO 9001 although the quality policy requires that objectives for quality are defined, and ISO 9001 Clause 4.3 (contract review) is similar in some respects. The commitment to continual improvement and prevention of pollution in ISO 14001 is clear and unequivocal, whereas in ISO 9001, although implied and indeed the intention, a commitment to continual improvement is not specified.

3.3.7 Environmental Management Program *(4.2.4)*

ISO 14001 — 4.2.4 Environmental Management Programs

ISO 14001 — A.4.2.4 Environmental Management Program

ISO 14004 — 4.2.4 Internal Performance Criteria

ISO 14004 — 4.2.6 Environmental Management Program

ISO 14001

ISO 14001 Interpretation: Management Program

Purpose/Intent

The intent of this requirement is to ensure that the next logical follow-on step is taken — the setup and implementation of an environmental management program.

Explanation/Interpretation

This element addresses the individual program(s) that need to be established and implemented to achieve your objectives and targets. For example, if you intend to reduce air emissions by five percent over the next six months, what are you going to do to achieve this goal? You need a program for each stated objective.

Your program(s) should also address certain things. First it should include responsibilities for achieving the objectives and targets. This should be stated for each relevant function and level within an organization to which the program applies. Also, you need to include time frames in which these targets will be achieved. Your program(s) could also be applied to any new or changed processes and/or developments at all stages, from to design to disposal.

Implementation Tips

An environmental program may take the form of an action plan that includes the following information:

- objective;
- target;
- person(s) responsible;

- date of expected completion;
- date of actual completion; and
- description of completed task.

ISO 14004

ISO 14004: Environmental Management Program

Internal Performance Criteria

Establishing organization-specific criteria that go beyond the requirements embodied in regulations, voluntary codes of practice, or ISO 14001 will be of variable importance to various organizations, depending on the nature of their business and the interests of their customers. Organizations should consider whether specific issues, such as product stewardship or property acquisition, require clearly delineated parameters of performance and, if so, to whom such criteria should be communicated.

Management Program

The environmental management program offers a structure for ensuring that responsibilities are assigned and resources allocated to attain the organization's objectives and targets. The program also should specify deadlines by which various activities will be completed.

It is not always necessary to address the environmental management program as a stand-alone effort. Many organizations will benefit by integrating this program with their strategic planning efforts. Regardless of how the environmental management program is implemented, it should be reviewed on a regular basis and revised as necessary.

Documentation: Environmental Management Program

▲ **ISO 14001 Section 4.2.4** describes the environmental management program(s) for achieving objectives and targets, assigning responsibility, and identifying means and time frame.

Documenting the elements of this program seems relatively simple and direct. The only possible objection anyone could have would be potential legal aspects. However, if the elements of the program are not documented, how can your organization be sure everyone involved understands the same set of elements?

For SMEs: Environmental Management Program

This section is also applicable to SMEs but is one where the magnitude is affected by the scale of the organization. The scope and detail of this section are more a function of the nature of the business, rather than only size. You must remember that this section, regardless of its magnitude, must relate back to the standard and direct you to the appropriate procedures. Many SMEs with any type of environmental management efforts normally do not have this "upper level" document that pulls it all together and refers one to lower-level specific procedures. The advantage to an SME of this document is the linkage and integration of the many operating procedures to the overall EMS.

For ISO 9000 Companies: Environmental Management Program

This clause can be broadly related to ISO 9001 Clause 4.3.2 (quality planning), addressing the means by which the requirements for quality will be achieved. ISO 14001 goes a step further, requiring a program not only for meeting the specified requirements for the existing activities, products, or services, but also for meeting those objectives and targets associated with them and for new developments and new or modified activities.

3.3.8 Implementation and Operation *(4.3)*

> *ISO 14001 — 4.3 Implementation and Operation*
>
> *ISO 14001 — A.4.3 Implementation and Operation*
>
> *ISO 14004 — 4.3 Implementation*
>
> *ISO 14004 — 4.3.1 General*

ISO 14001

ISO 14001 Interpretation: Implementation and Operation

Explanation/Interpretation

This general section of the standard addresses the implementation and operations of groups of elements — the heart of an EMS. Following are the sub-elements.

Implementation Tips

For each of your environmental management programs, write a procedure that addresses the sub-elements of this section.

3.3.9 Structure and Responsibility *(4.3.1)*

> *ISO 14001 — 4.3.1 Structure and Responsibility*
>
> *ISO 14001 — A.4.3.1 Structure and Responsibility*
>
> *ISO 14004 — 4.3.2 Ensuring Capability*
>
> *ISO 14004 — 4.3.2.1 Resources — Human, Physical, and Financial*
>
> *ISO 14004 — 4.3.2.2 Environmental Management System Alignment and Integration*
>
> *ISO 14004 — 4.3.2.3 — Accountability and Responsibility*

ISO 14001

ISO 14001 Interpretation: Structure and Responsibility

Purpose/Intent

The main focus of this element is to define the roles, responsibilities, and authorities of everyone involved in the environmental management system.

Explanation/Interpretation

This section is aimed at helping operate your EMS effectively. If people know what they are responsible for and to whom they report, and this is all documented, your organization can eliminate confusion and questions.

Another important aspect of this element is the appointment of a management representative. This person is responsible for the overall implementation, operation, and coordination of the system. The representative should be appointed by the top management of your organization and be responsible for reporting the EMS performance to management for its review.

Your organization's management also is responsible for ensuring that you have adequate resources to implement, control, and maintain the system. These resources include equipment, time, and human resources.

Implementation Tips

There are many ways to accomplish this. Your organization may have job descriptions, organizational charts, a combination of both, or another way that works. Although not specifically called out in the standard, there is an implied sense of accountability. You may want to include a procedure for rewarding good performance and/or issuing disciplinary action for performance that may adversely affect the EMS.

ISO 14004

ISO 14004: Accountability and Responsibility

Clearly, any system is only as effective as an organization allows it to be. The most effective EMSs are those where both responsibility and accountability are assigned to employees at all levels within the organization. This implies that such employees are appropriately trained to fulfill their assigned roles. It is incumbent upon senior management to consider such assignments carefully and, once communicated, to review employee performance.

Documentation: Structure and Responsibility

☛ The environmental policy manual should include information on top management's roles in the environmental management system. Other information would be best defined in the procedures-level documents. The communication required by the specification could be by meetings, videos, etc.; paper documentation is not required.

For SMEs: Structure and Responsibility

This is rather straightforward and applies to an SME in a way similar to a large organization. Key differences with an SME will be the fact that multiple responsibilities may fall on one individual because of limited staff and resources. Secondly, although there will be more of a need for upper management buy-in and support due to limited resources, the SME probably has a lesser number of tiers in the corporate hierarchy, bringing everyone "closer" to the effort. Unlike with some other sections, the SME should not depend on outside help for filling the responsibility roles because it will reduce the feeling of ownership for the program. As a result, buy-in and support will be weakened. It will be critical to identify and support internal "champions."

For ISO 9000 Companies: Structure and Responsibility

This clause broadly corresponds to ISO 9001 Clause 4.1.2, but with particular attention to the resources required to maintain the EMS, including financial and human resources. This clause allows an organization to bring together its core business functions to be considered as an integral part of the organization's overall management system.

3.3.10 Training, Awareness, and Competence *(4.3.2)*

> *ISO 14001 — 4.3.2 Training, Awareness, and Competence*
>
> *ISO 14001 — A.4.3.2 Training, Awareness, and Competence*
>
> *ISO 14004 — 4.3.2.4 Environmental Awareness and Motivation*
>
> *ISO 14004 — 4.3.2.5 Knowledge, Skills, and Training*

ISO 14001

ISO 14001 Interpretation: Training, Awareness, and Competence

Purpose/Intent

The intent here is to ensure that all personnel who may create a significant impact on the environment receive proper, adequate, and appropriate training.

Explanation/Interpretation

Your employees should be made aware of the importance of conformance to the standard as well as compliance to legal requirements. Training is also meant to ensure competency so that jobs are performed as required. Your organization should have a way to ensure that employees can perform competently tasks that affect the environment.

Implementation Tips

The first step is to identify training needs. Your employees should be aware of the environmental impacts associated with their work activities and be fully aware of the implications associated with nonconformance. They should understand their specific roles and responsibilities within the system. In many cases, specific training may be required by law, particularly for those who handle and dispose of chemicals.

Training schedules and procedures should be set up and implemented. Training may take several forms: e.g., formal classes, self-paced courses, or on-the-job group or individual instruction. As with all elements, these requirements should be documented and the records of the training should be maintained for each employee and should indicate the training received.

ISO 14004

ISO 14004: Knowledge, Skills, and Training

Your organization's EMS will flounder if those responsible for its implementation are unable to perform assigned tasks. Your organization should identify the skills necessary for attainment of objectives and targets and ascertain whether assigned personnel possess needed skills. This effort should include subcontractors and temporary employees as well as permanent employees. Training to address identified deficiencies can be obtained through a variety of sources. Your organization must determine whether in-house training programs, customized external training programs, standardized training courses, or other approaches offer the most cost-effective solutions.

Documentation: Training, Awareness, and Competence

▲ Your organization is required to "identify training needs." It seems difficult to do so without some form of documentation. The organization should, for its own sake, document that a needs assessment was done. Also, the clause requires that the organization make its employees or members at each relevant function and level aware of the importance and consequences of the environmental policy and EMS. Although written communication is certainly not the only way, it may be one of the most "permanent" records.

For SMEs: Training, Awareness, and Competence

This is probably one of the most intimidating and difficult sections for an SME to address. More often than not, internal expertise and resources will not be comprehensive enough to address the issues that will be raised by the aspects and impacts assessment. Secondly, the elevated importance of training in ISO 14001, particularly with linkage to supporting areas such as auditing, will be new to many SMEs. Hence this should be an area where an SME should draw on outside expertise, probably integrated with help obtained earlier in the planning sections. The SME will need to develop procedures that assure that training is actually implemented and documented. For auditing, it may be efficient and beneficial to have the appropriate employee obtain auditor training and then provide in-house training for support audit staff. This will limit the need for outside assistance to more of a mentor/consultant role.

For ISO 9000 Companies: Training, Awareness, and Competence

ISO 9001 Clause 4.18 directly parallels the training element in ISO 14001. ISO 14001 does contain additional requirements for developing the employees' awareness of the relevance of their roles and responsibilities within the EMS.

3.3.11 Communications *(4.3.3)*

> *ISO 14001 — 4.3.3 Communication*
>
> *ISO 14001 — A.4.3.3 Communication*
>
> *ISO 14004 — 4.3.3 Support Action*
>
> *ISO 14004 — 4.3.3.1 Communication and Reporting*

ISO 14001

ISO 14001 Interpretation: Communications

Purpose/Intent

A very important aspect of any system is the transfer of information. Communications is meant to ensure that information between internal and external organizations is properly transferred.

Explanation/Interpretation

To comply with this requirement, you should establish communication links denoting who talks to whom internally and the process used to collect and respond to external communications.

Implementation Tips

Keep in mind that the external communication is with customers as well as legal entities and includes responding to inquiries as well as disseminating information. For external parties, records of receipt of requests for information may be useful.

ISO 14004

ISO 14004: Communication and Reporting

The organization should develop communication strategies for several discrete audiences. Internal communication should be more than a top-down distribution of information. Consideration should be given to a process for receiving and responding to employee concerns. A separate strategy should be developed to ensure that data about the EMS (such as progress toward targets, or audit findings) are communicated to senior management.

External interested parties also should be part of a communications loop. The organization should have a means for conveying information to outside groups or individuals and receiving and responding to their concerns.

Documentation: Communication

From Interested Parties

☞ Again, communication doesn't have to be in writing; it could be oral or by some other means. Also, response to relevant communication from external interested parties could be in some form other than writing. But the organization must document relevant communication from interested parties.

External Communication

☞ Although the external communication doesn't have to be in document form, records that processes for external communication have been considered must be recorded. These records might be minutes of meetings, for example.

Response to Communication from External Parties

▲ According to clause 4.3.3, your organization shall document and respond to "relevant communication from external interested parties regarding environmental aspects and the environmental management system."

As part of that documentation, it would seem appropriate to document the responses also. Keeping the original communications (hard copies of electronic transmissions) in the same notebook with the copies of the responses would be best. If the communications need to be used for other purposes in the organization (e.g., tracking the number and type of communications relating to a specific environmental aspect), copies should be used. Content analyses (as for communications to environmental impact statements) can also be made with copies.

For SMEs: Communication

This is a rather straightforward section with no peculiar twists for an SME. Actually, SMEs will probably find this easier than a larger organization because of its smaller staff and simplified hierarchy and administrative infrastructure.

For ISO 9000 Companies: Communication

Sections on external communication are an additional requirement to the overall organizational structure identified in ISO 9001, where emphasis is placed on internal communications.

3.3.12 Environmental Management System Documentation *(4.3.4)*

ISO 14001 — 4.3.4 Environmental Management System Documentation

ISO 14001 — A.4.3.4 Environmental Documentation

ISO 14001

ISO 14001 Interpretation: EMS Documentation

Explanation/Interpretation

This requirement simply states that the core elements of your system should be documented. Documentation can be in paper or electronic form. It should provide direction to the rest of your system. Once again, the amount of documentation required is left up to your organization. The best rule is to have the least amount that works and is effective. More is not necessarily better; in fact, in this case, more can be worse because it is harder to maintain without adding value.

Implementation Tips

📖 (See Part 3, Chapter 4, for more information on documentation.)

ISO 14004

ISO 14004: EMS Documentation

EMS documentation enables your organization to define and communicate its expectations clearly. Documentation should be macro-level and might contain the environmental policy, objectives and targets, and assigned responsibilities and accountability. It also should refer to additional information, such as procedures. Although many organizations think in terms of a written manual, the audience for whom EMS documentation is intended and ease of access should dictate its form.

Documentation: EMS Documentation

"The organization shall establish and maintain information, in paper or electronic form, to: a) describe the core elements of the management system and their interaction; and b) provide direction to related documentation."

☞ This clause is probably the most direct reference to an environmental management system manual. As with the ISO 9001 specifications, the easiest way to fulfill the requirement for documenting the core elements of the management system and their interaction is to design the manual after the clauses of the ISO 14001 specification are identified. By identifying each subclause of Section 4, the manual can also refer to procedures instituted to implement the specifications.

For SMEs: EMS Documentation

This section also is rather straightforward and self-explanatory for an SME. However, the SME will need to make sure its employees understand the importance of the documentation. Our experience shows that this is usually the first area to be neglected due to limited resources. As a matter of fact, most environmental documentation historically has been focused on necessary regulatory-driven documentation. Documentation and document control training similar to that provided in the ISO 9000 arena would be beneficial to allow an SME to get off to a good start.

For ISO 9000 Companies: EMS Documentation

Analogous to ISO 9001 Clause 4.2.1, the experiences gained from developing the ISO 9001 manual will be useful in preparing and integrating the requirements of ISO 14001, both in ensuring appropriate direction to related documentation and in reducing possible areas of duplication.

3.3.13 Document Control *(4.3.5)*

ISO 14001 — 4.3.5 Document Control

ISO 14001 — A.4.3.5 Document Control

ISO 14004 — 4.3.3.2 EMS Documentation

ISO 14001

ISO 14001 Interpretation: Document Control

Purpose/Intent

Although this element somehow causes the most problems, it is really straightforward. Its intent is to ensure that all documentation is controlled and distributed within the environmental management system. It is meant to ensure the correct people have the correct version of the correct documentation.

Explanation/Interpretation

Your organization should ensure that all pertinent documentation can be located by those who need it. All documentation should be reviewed and revised as needed and at regular (documented) intervals. You should also ensure that all documentation is approved and adequate. Also, any obsolete documentation should either be removed or identified — in other words, not used. All documentation should be legible, identifiable, maintained, and retained as specified or required by law.

Implementation Tips

📖 (See Part 3, Chapter 4, for more information on documentation.)

Documentation: Document Control

☛ **ISO 14001 Section 4.3.5** states that: "The organization shall establish and maintain procedures for controlling all documents required by this standard to ensure that:

a) they can be located;

b) they are periodically reviewed, revised as necessary, and approved for adequacy by authorized personnel;

c) the current versions of relevant documents are available at all locations where operations essential to the effective functioning of the system are performed;

d) obsolete documents are promptly removed from all points of issue and points of use or otherwise assured against unintended use; and

e) any obsolete documents retained for legal and/or knowledge preservation purposes are suitably identified.

Documentation shall be legible, dated (with dates of revision) and readily identifiable, maintained in an orderly manner, and retained for a specified period. Procedures and responsibilities shall be established and maintained concerning the creation and modification of the various types of document."

This clause is probably the most specific in telling organizations how to design and manage documents. The wording identifies format, retention, location, etc., but not content. The wording of the list can easily become a checklist to be used by EMS auditors, both internal and external.

Standardization is especially critical in the control of documents. If each page typically includes a revision number and identifies the person responsible for controlling the issue of the document, for example, you will find controlling documents easier.

In determining your company standards, remember that the system you help design will be used for a long time by the whole company. Consider ease of use, storage space, appearance, availability, cost, etc. The best way to consider all eventualities is to get input from as many interested people as possible.

Get the physical design part of the process out of the way rapidly and move on to ensuring consistency of content — that is what auditors look for as evidence of an environmental management system.

For SMEs: Document Control

This section also is rather straightforward and self explanatory for an SME. (Refer to previous section on EMS documentation; comments apply here.)

For ISO 9000 Companies: Document Control

The requirements within this clause are similar to those of ISO 9001 Clause 4.4 (addressing documentation control of design activities) and Clause 4.5 (requiring the control of all documents and data within the quality management system). The established procedures within the quality management system (QMS) can be extended to include the control of environmental documentation.

3.3.14 Operational Control *(4.3.6)*

> *ISO 14001 — 4.3.6 Operational Control*
>
> *ISO 14001 — A.4.3.6 Operational Control (no text intended here)*
>
> *ISO 14004 — 4.3.3.3 Operational Control*

ISO 14001

ISO 14001 Interpretation: Operational Control

Explanation/Interpretation

There are many angles and intents to this element. The temptation is to relegate to this section anything that doesn't fit into other EMS elements. Remember this is the standard section that will probably get you into trouble with auditors if it is misused and/or overused. The general intent is to identify those operations and activities that can impact the environment, fall within the scope of the policy, and affect the objectives and targets. The operational controls are the essential procedures that your organization needs for implementing its policy, objectives, and targets. These key procedures should be documented.

Implementation Tips

One requirement is to plan activities that can or do impact the environment. You must ensure that these activities are carried out under conditions you specify.

Identify situations where the absence of operational controls could lead to deviations from your policy, objectives, and targets. You might do this through audits, reviews, interviews, failure mode analysis, or any other method that works.

You should ensure that operating criteria are stipulated. You should also ensure that all relevant procedures are identified and communicated to suppliers and contractors. This is the only part of the standard that mentions suppliers and contractors.

ISO 14004

ISO 14004: Operational Control

The organization should tie its environmental aspects/impacts to specific activities. This enables it to develop procedures and work instructions that address the aspects/impacts.

The real value in requiring adherence to specific procedures often is one of prevention. The organization should consider potential environmental impacts if procedures are not followed.

Documentation: Operational Control

☛ Although this clause continues to describe some non-document issues, its beginning clearly refers to documented procedures needed to cover critical situations in terms not only of emergencies and unexpected events but also in terms of the organization's objectives and targets. This wording directly links this clause to wording in clause 4.2.3.

For SMEs: Operational Control

Although an apparently straightforward section, the implications for SMEs are deeper. This is an area where outside assistance, preferably in conjunction with developing aspects, impacts, and objectives and targets would be beneficial. Traditionally, SMEs do not look at all operations and activities with the overarching environmental impact perspective. It will require looking at what is done in an additional, different light having an understanding of the linkage to aspects and impacts. As a counterbalance, the SME must remain focused on activities that may lead to significant impacts and not get overwhelmed trying to control every activity and process.

For ISO 9000 Companies: Operational Control

There is no single clause within ISO 9001 that corresponds to this requirement of ISO 14001, but rather a number of clauses relating to production control, including ISO 9001 Clause 4.3 Contract Review; 4.4 Design control; 4.6 Purchasing; 4.7 Control of Customer-Supplied Product; 4.9 Process Control; 4.15 Handling, Storage, Packaging, Preservation, and Delivery; and 4.19 Servicing.

3.3.15 Emergency Preparedness and Response *(4.3.7)*

> *ISO 14001 — 4.3.7 Emergency Preparedness and Response*
>
> *ISO 14001 — A.4.3.7 Emergency Preparedness and Response*
>
> *ISO 14004 — 4.3.3.4 Emergency Preparedness and Response*

ISO 14001

ISO 14001 Interpretation: Emergency Preparedness and Response

Explanation/Interpretation

Your organization should ensure that procedures are in place to respond to potential and/or actual emergencies and accidents. This includes such things as spill control teams, fire control, emergency medical personnel, emergency signs and instructions, and anything else your organization deems necessary for an emergency response.

Implementation Tips

To prepare for this element you might first identify potential emergencies. Next, take preventive measures to avoid their happening. On a regular basis, you may want to test the procedures for adequacy. Last, you might review the test or actual incident and use the response and results to revise the procedures where necessary to prevent reoccurrence. This will provide for some of the continuous improvement that the standard requires.

ISO 14004: Emergency Preparedness and Response

ISO 14004

Many U.S. organizations are required by law to establish and maintain emergency plans. ISO 14004 is less rigorous and so is unlikely to offer additional assistance or insight to regulated organizations.

Documentation: Emergency Preparedness and Response

▲ Whether emergency response procedures are transmitted to employees in writing or orally (or both), these procedures should be documented somewhere. Because the requirements for such procedures are generally a matter of law, rather than of the ISO standard, the requirements of the pertinent laws should be the guiding force here.

For SMEs: Emergency Preparedness and Response

The key effort for SMEs in this section is looking beyond regulatory need for such planning, and ensuring that other potentially significant impacts are covered, even if not regulated. Again, this links back to understanding the aspects and impacts requirements. A second effort for SMEs will be making sure the written plans are actually effective and that appropriate employees understand them. Many times such plans are only paper records to satisfy a regulatory requirement and may not actually be effective. This phenomenon is not unique to SMEs however it is more common in smaller organizations. Regulatory agencies can also be of assistance in preparing such procedures, in addition to private sector outside help.

For ISO 9000 Companies: Emergency Preparedness and Response

Personnel with environmental management experience are a necessary resource when addressing this clause, as knowledge of environmental considerations needs to be integrated into emergency plans.

3.3.16 Checking and Corrective Action *(4.4)*

ISO 14001 — 4.4 Checking and Corrective Action

ISO 14001 — A 4.4 Checking and Corrective Action

ISO 14001

ISO 14001 Interpretation: Checking and Corrective Action

Explanation/Interpretation

Although the entire system is built around the theory of continuous improvement, this is the group of elements that specifically addresses the issue. These include monitoring and measurement, nonconformance and corrective and preventive action, records, and environmental management system audits.

3.3.17 Monitoring and Measurement *(4.4.1)*

ISO 14001 — 4.4.1 Monitoring and Measurement

ISO 14001 — A.4.4.1 Monitoring and Measurement

(no text intended here)

ISO 14004 — 4.4 Measurement and Evaluation

ISO 14004 — 4.4.1 General

ISO 14004 — 4.4.2 Measuring and Monitoring (Ongoing Performance)

ISO 14001

ISO 14001 Interpretation: Monitoring and Measurement

Purpose/Intent

The intent here is that the key characteristics of your operations and activities be monitored and measured on a regular basis.

Explanation/Interpretation

If you know where you are in terms of your EMS, and where you want to be, then this will help you get there.

Some of the requirements are that you record the information to track your performance. You should identify relevant operational controls and decide how to evaluate them. The objectives and targets that you have established should be monitored and measured to ensure completion. Any equipment used to monitor should be calibrated, and records of the calibration should be maintained.

In basic terms, this section means you should monitor and measure compliance with legal and other requirements, whether you've met objectives and targets, and whether and at what levels you are meeting other EMS requirements — all to ensure continuous improvement of the EMS. The standard does not explicitly draw the connection between the EMS and regulatory requirements. But since compliance must be part of the policy and there should be a process to identify regulatory requirements, logically you should have operational controls to implement and measure conformity with these programs.

ISO 14004

ISO 14004: Measuring and Monitoring

ISO 14004 Section 4.4 Measurement and Evaluation

The measurement and evaluation section provides guidelines to realize EMS Principle 4: An organization should measure, monitor, and evaluate its environmental performance. The task of measurement and evaluation represents key activities of an EMS to ensure that the organization's performance is consistent with its stated environmental management program (policy, objectives, targets).

ISO 14004 Section 4.4.2 Measuring and Monitoring (Ongoing Performance)

An implemented and documented system should be in place to measure and monitor performance against environmental objectives and targets, including evaluation of compliance with relevant environmental legislation and regulations. This is a necessity in order to determine areas of success and to identify areas requiring root cause emphasis, corrective action, and improvement activities. The measuring and monitoring activity often uses environmental performance indicators to determine performance; therefore, the emerging ISO 14031 Environmental Performance Evaluation standard will be helpful in identifying objective, relevant, and reproducible indicators of performance.

Documentation: Monitoring and Measurement

"Monitoring equipment shall be calibrated and maintained and **records** of this process shall be retained according to the organization's procedures.

☛ The organization shall establish and maintain a **documented** procedure for periodically evaluating compliance with relevant environmental legislation and regulations."

This clause specifically refers to documented procedures; many other clauses identify procedures but do not specifically require documented procedures. The documents required by this clause would be procedures and records.

For SMEs: Monitoring and Measurement

This is another section that will require relatively more effort by SMEs than by larger organizations. This is because, traditionally, SMEs do not have the resources to monitor their environmental management processes. Instead, monitoring and measurement are focused on actual discharges and effluents. It is likely entire procedures and documentation will need to be created to comply with this section. Discussing and preparing these procedures can be done in conjunction with the other sections mentioned above. On the more positive side, once this is done, implementation will be easier for SMEs because of the reduced tiers of management and simpler administrative infrastructure.

For ISO 9000 Companies: Monitoring and Measurement

The controls and procedures established in the QMS to satisfy the requirements of ISO 9001

Clauses 4.10 Inspection and Testing; 4.11 Control of Inspection, Measuring, and Test Equipment; 4.12 Inspection and Test Status; and 4.20 Statistical Techniques, can be expanded to cover the requirements of ISO 14001.

3.3.18 Nonconformance and Corrective and Preventive Action (4.4.2)

ISO 14001 — 4.4.2 Nonconformance and Corrective and Preventive Action

ISO 14001 — A.4.4.2 Nonconformance and Corrective and Preventive Action

ISO 14004 — 4.4.3 Corrective and Preventive Action

ISO 14001

ISO 14001 Interpretation: Nonconformance and Corrective and Preventive Action

Explanation/Interpretation

The principles of nonconformance and corrective and preventive action are straightforward. First, if a nonconformance exists, identify it. Next, fix it — not just for now but forever. Last, if possible, prevent it from reoccurring.

Implementation Tips

The first thing you should do is identify who is responsible for handling, investigating, and initiating corrective action. You should ensure that corrective and preventive action is appropriate. An appropriate action corrects the nonconformance and, at the same time, is not an overkill. A corrective action involves implementing and recording any changes to procedures resulting from such actions. Next you should look at what you proposed and evaluate it on an ongoing basis to ensure that it works. Simply speaking, first prevent it. If this fails, find it, fix it, change it, evaluate it.

ISO 14004

ISO 14004: Corrective and Preventive Action

It is critical for the continual improvement of the EMS and therefore improvement of the relationship among your organization's activities, products, and services, and the environment that the findings, conclusions, and recommendations reached as a result of monitoring, auditing, and other reviews should be documented and an explicit corrective action program established where warranted. It is a management responsibility to ensure that corrective and preventive actions are implemented as required and there is systematic follow-up to ensure and verify its effectiveness.

Documentation: Nonconformance and Corrective and Preventive Action

Outcomes of Compliance and Management Systems Audits and Associated Corrective and Preventive Actions (Sections 4.4.1 and 4.4.2)

▲ One expert has suggested that the outcomes of audits and associated corrective and preventive actions be documented "to the extent it is not precluded by legal concerns."

While **Section 4.4.1** states that your organization "shall establish and maintain a documented procedure for periodically evaluating compliance with relevant environmental legislation and regulations," it says nothing about recording the results of these evaluations. **Section 4.4.2** refers to nonconformance and corrective and preventive action but, in terms of documentation, only requires the organization to "record any changes in the documented procedures resulting from corrective and preventive action."

The only reason for not documenting the outcomes of audits and evaluations (besides the paperwork, of course) would seem to be legal actions that potentially could develop from recognized deficiencies that go uncorrected. Here, your organization's intention in implementing an EMS would seem to be involved.

If your company intends to "capture" all potential significant impacts on the environment to improve its environmental management, then documentation seems to be a useful tool for tracking. If your company wishes only to avoid potential legal action, then limiting this type of documentation is likely to be the organization's choice. Thus, whether a company chooses to document these outcomes would depend on company policy, in consideration of legal implications.

Section 4.4.2 states: "The organization shall implement and record any changes in the documented procedures resulting from corrective and preventive actions."

☛ Again, records are the required documents.

 ## For SMEs: Nonconformance and Corrective and Preventive Action

The key to SME success with this section is remembering that this applies to addressing nonconformances with the EMS, and not spills or incidents. Appropriate training will be necessary so that applicable personnel thoroughly understand the standard and the EMS to identify these concerns. This deeper understanding will allow root-cause determination and lead to more successful corrective and preventive action.

 ## For ISO 9000 Companies: Nonconformance and Corrective and Preventive Action

The two clauses in ISO 9001 addressing control of nonconforming product (4.13) and corrective and preventive action (4.14) are broad counterparts of the requirements cited within this clause of ISO 14001. Again, established procedures and systems for ISO 14001 can be used here to reduce duplication.

3.3.19 Records *(4.4.3)*

ISO 14001 — *4.4.3 Records*

ISO 14001 — *A.4.4.3 Records*

ISO 14004 — *4.4.4 EMS Records and Information Management*

ISO 14001 Interpretation: Records

ISO 14001

Explanation/Interpretation

Your organization must identify, maintain, and dispose of environmental records. The types of records are identified by your organization or dictated by legal requirements.

First, all records should be legible, identifiable, and traceable to the activity, product, or service involved. This makes sense.

Next, they should be stored for easy retrieval and protected from damage, deterioration, or loss. All common-sense issues once again.

Finally, retention times should be established and are dependent upon your organization or legal requirements. Many times environmental records should be retained indefinitely for explicit legal reasons or to protect from future liability.

ISO 14004

ISO 14004: EMS Records and Information Management

Records are defined broadly within the ISO 14004 guidelines to include legislative and regulatory requirements, permits, documentation of environmental aspects and associated impacts of activities, products and services, training records, inspection, calibration and maintenance records, monitoring data, details of nonconformances and follow-up responses, information regarding suppliers and contractors, environmental audits, and review reports. It is necessary for environmental managers to provide records in an informative way to support management decisions on the environment. This includes reviewing records to identify and track key indicators of performance and any other information required to assure the organization achieves its objectives and targets.

Documentation: Records

☛ This section, as with **Section 4.3.5**, is very specific in terms of details such as legibility and appropriateness of the records. The clause identifies two levels of documentation: procedures and records.

For SMEs: Records

No major concerns unique to SMEs here, other than training in records handling and retention would be helpful. This training can be done in conjunction with the documentation training noted above.

For ISO 9000 Companies: Records

The skills and the system employed to maintain control of quality records (ISO 9001 Clause 4.16) should be sufficient to satisfy the requirements of this section.

3.3.20 Environmental Management System Audit *(4.4.4)*

> ISO 14001 — *4.4.4 Environmental Management System Audit*
> ISO 14001 — *A.4.4.4 Environmental Management System Audit*
> ISO 14004 — *4.4.5 Audits of the Environmental Management System*

ISO 14001

ISO 14001 Interpretation: EMS Audit

Explanation/Interpretation

Your organization should periodically review its environmental management system to ensure continued compliance and improvement. This involves a system of self-audits designed to facilitate continuous improvement. It also enables you to detect and correct any deficiencies before anyone else does, such as environmental agency inspectors.

The requirement here is that you schedule the audits on the basis of importance of the activity involved. They should be based on the results of previous audits. If a certain department is having ongoing problems, then audit the department frequently and initiate corrective action until the problem is solved. Ensure that you cover the audit scope, frequencies, and methodologies. Report results and provide for follow-up activities.

ISO 14004

ISO 14004: Audits of the Environmental Management System

Audits of the EMS are to be conducted periodically to determine whether the EMS as implemented conforms to its planned arrangements. A key requirement for effective auditing is the objectivity and impartiality of those conducting the audit as well as the degree of training they have received. Audit frequency is based on the nature of the operations and potential environmental risks, aspects, and impacts that they pose as well as on results of previous audits. Audit results should be submitted to the appropriate levels of management and incorporated into the corrective and preventive action program.

Documentation: EMS Audit

▲ **Section 4.4.4** pertaining to the EMS audit does not require any documentation. The organization is only required to "establish and maintain a program and procedures for periodic environmental management system audits" to see whether the system is properly implemented and maintained and conforms to the organization's plans and requirements of the ISO 14001 standard.

The word "comprehensive" adds an interesting twist to the interpretation of the clause. "In order to be comprehensive, the audit procedure shall cover the audit scope, frequency, and methodologies, as well as the responsibilities and requirements for conducting audits and reporting results." Thus, your organization has to determine what records it will keep of EMS audits and write that information into its audit procedures.

As with the outcomes of compliance audits, the policy of your organization and its intent in establishing an EMS seem to be key. Legal requirements rarely tell you not to do something, so the risks you must consider are those from not documenting something the law tells you to document or from documenting something that you know is "wrong" and not doing something about it. The clause seems to leave the decision to your organization.

For SMEs: EMS Audit

Traditionally, the SME auditing has been very focused on regulatory issues and the frequency could be too long and inconsistent. As a result, the SME will need to institute audit programs calling for more frequent intervals than in the past. Second, the concept of the EMS will need to be learned; therefore, early on, internal auditors will not have the depth and savvy to audit the EMS efficiently to ISO 14001 expectations.

The procedure to do the EMS audit, including understanding the scope and intent of the audit, will be very important to the SME. Many large organizations have full internal audit teams that understand the management system concept; something not common with SMEs. Outside assistance with auditor training, and possibly with conducting the initial audits, will be key, if not a necessity.

For procedures, ISO 14010, 14011, and 14012 can be used, even if only during the initial years of the EMS to reduce the level of effort expended on preparing audit procedures. It must be remembered that the audit standards, be they ISO, ASTM, or EAR documents, do not teach the science of auditing; but only provide guidance on structuring audit programs. Another advantage of using ISO's audit standards is that they facilitate demonstrating conformance to the ISO 14001 requirement.

For ISO 9000 Companies: EMS Audit

A broadening of the internal audit process under an ISO 9001 system would take into account auditing the EMS. The existing internal quality auditors could be used to train the environmental auditors in auditing techniques, but the environmental auditors must have the additional environmental experience and knowledge to evaluate effectively the organization's practices, processes, and results relating to its activities and environmental aspects.

3.3.21 Management Review *(4.5)*

> *ISO 14001 — 4.5 Management Review*
>
> *ISO 14001 — A.4.5 Management Review*
>
> *ISO 14004 — 4.5 Review and Improvement*
>
> *ISO 14004 — 4.5.1 General*
>
> *ISO 14004 — 4.5.2 Review of the Environmental Management System*

ISO 14001

ISO 14001 Interpretation: Management Review

Explanation/Interpretation

This is the last element of the standard and it stands alone. It is the catcher's mitt of all the information that comes from the EMS and it's the pivot point where that information is used to revise/improve policy and programs. This element is meant to demonstrate management commitment and involvement.

It requires management at the upper levels to review the system to ensure its continuing suitability and effectiveness. You should review and address the need for any changes in policy, objectives, and procedures. The results of internal system audits should be reviewed and evaluated. The results of all this should be recorded.

ISO 14004

ISO 14004: Review and Improvement

The review and improvement element of EMS seeks to achieve EMS Principle 5: An organization should review and continually improve its environmental management systems with the objective of improving its overall environmental performance. At appropriate intervals the top management of the organization should conduct a review of the EMS to ensure its continuing suitability and effectiveness.

When the organization's activities, products, and services change rapidly, some mechanism must be established to check the EMS and its objectives and targets against actual environmental performance. The suitability of the environmental policy and its objectives, targets, and performance should be evaluated in the light of changing legislation, expectations of interested parties, changes in products or services or processes, advances in science and technology, and changing market preferences of buyers.

Documentation: Management Review

☛ The requirement for documentation of the management review implies that the plan for review and the results of the review should both be documented. Although no documented procedure appears to be required, the review itself must be documented.

For ISO 9000 Companies: Management Review

This is a requirement common to both ISO 14001 and ISO 9001. The purpose of the management review of both the QMS and EMS is to ensure the system's continuing suitability and effectiveness. Therefore, it is likely that the approach to the management review will be similar for the quality and environmental management systems, with the additional requirement to review the environmental policy, objectives, and targets to complete the requirements of ISO 14001.

3.3.22 Continual Improvement *(ISO 14004 4.5.3)*

ISO 14004 — 4.5.3 Continual Improvement

ISO 14004

ISO 14004: Continual Improvement

The concept of continual improvement is embedded within all elements of the environmental management system. It is achieved by continually evaluating environmental performance against policies, objectives, and targets at all levels of your organization, and then identifying opportunities for improvement. Elements of the continual improvement process should include a root-cause analysis as appropriate for major nonconformances or deficiencies. A verification process is essential to determine the effectiveness of the corrective and preventative actions selected as is the documentation process for making required changes in operational procedures.

CHAPTER 4
Documentation

by Marie Godfrey, Consultant/Project Manager, Franklin Quest Consulting Group
(Formerly Shipley Associates)

3.4.1 Overview

The 1995 ISO 14001 specification (as revised and issued as a draft international standard) includes a number of situations in which documentation is required. However, to prove to an auditor that you are, in fact, conforming to ISO 14001 requirements, you may have to document additional efforts on your part. Situations calling for both required and recommended documentation were discussed in Chapter 3, where ISO 14001 standard requirements contain references to documentation.

say what you
do and do
what you say

The ISO 14001 environmental management system specification essentially requires your company to say what it does in environmental management and do what it says. Documentation is how your company says what it does. Documents can be written before, during, or after an EMS is developed and implemented.

We continue the discussion of documentation in this chapter, describing:

- dos and don'ts;
- integration with other systems;
- the structure of documentation; and
- creating usable and effective documentation.

3.4.2 How Much Is Too Much? Dos and Don'ts in Documentation

Nearly every section of ISO 14001 describes requirements for documentation. In addition, it would be reasonable to assume that any procedure should be documented in some way so it can be taught to others, for example. Thus, the ISO 14001 specification seems to require fairly extensive documentation. While the previous chapter discussed documentation you should do and might wish to do, this section helps you determine how extensive your documentation will be.

key questions   Whether or not your organization prepares and uses additional documentation may depend on the following:

☑ How large is your organization?

☑ Does your organization operate in more than one geographic location?

☑ How significant are the potential environmental effects of your organization's activities and products?

☑ Does your organization intend to use its "failures" to improve its EMS?

☑ How serious are the potential lapses in the EMS in terms of your organization? If there's a chemical spill, for example, while your organization's trucks are transporting materials from one site to another, what is the potential for liability, bad publicity, etc.? What long-lasting effects can these results have on your organization?

☑ What are the risks vs. benefits of maintaining documented day-to-day transactions, memos, lessons learned, miscommunications?

documentation saves time   In the absence of formal documentation, auditors expect to find clear, consistent descriptions of procedures and internal activities. Interviewing personnel responsible for a variety of operations may take more time, and cost more in an audit, than the audit would take if the auditors could examine existing documentation and build a checklist for examining only specific portions of it.

The document only-where-it-mitigates-risk-or-adds-value approach differs from the approaches in ISO 9000 and BS 7750 (the British national environmental management system standard). Possibly, as certification to ISO 14001 becomes available and common, organizations will be able to refine their degree of documentation by following informal guidelines as they arise.

obstructing operations   When documentation, or the need to create or update it, gets in the way of your organization's most effective operation, you might reasonably assume you have reached the too-much limit. Such a situation is possible if the documentation you create is not effective. If your documentation is effective, then it is being used, and it's not getting in the way.

usability tests   The best way to avoid creating unnecessary documentation is to include ISO 14000 specialists and document users in your documentation planning and prototyping meetings (see the section below on this). To eliminate documents that are not being effectively used, conduct usability tests as part of your EMS audits. If documentation is not being used, eliminate it, fix it, or — better yet — replace it with something more effective.

3.4.3 The Structure of ISO 14000 Documentation

keep it
process-focused

If your company or organization plans its documentation in advance, you can eliminate redundancies and build more useful document systems. When documentation is "process-focused" rather than "regulation- or program-focused," people who need to use documents can do so more efficiently. For example, documents built in modules, on-line systems, and flow-diagrams all help people understand what their jobs are and how their jobs dovetail with the rest of the company.

consider a
facilitator

Your company might consider seeking an outside "facilitator" to help build documents that are really used. Almost anyone within your company can construct an electronic database, but few can construct one that people will actually use. Trained consultants who know documentation can help you focus more clearly on the documentation you need and how to produce and update that documentation in a timely fashion.

There are several key questions to consider:

☑ Will documents solve the problem?

☑ What will the scope and purpose of the documents be?

☑ What kind of documentation do you need?

☑ What will the documents look like?

☑ How will people use them?

☑ How do you fit overlapping material together when not all pieces overlap?

The Four-Tiered System

defining
"documentation"

The term "documentation" has many different interpretations. The term can refer to any or all of the following:

• instructions for doing something;

• records that something was done;

• printed matter that is given or sent to clients, regulatory agencies, customers, the public;

• any electronic copy of the items above; and

• a directory of electronic files.

Although the ISO 14001 specification does not dictate what form documentation must take, how organizations interpret the word "documentation" will depend on their particular experience. For example, a construction company might think in terms of environmental impact statements, construction manuals, blueprints, or even the local newspaper that reports each of its activities on a particularly sensitive building project.

typical tiered
system

The tiered documentation system typical of an ISO 14001 environmental management system consists of four "levels" of documents. The system is typically shown as a pyramid with the environmental management system manual at the top and environmental management system records at the bottom (see *Figure 3.20*).

The pyramid shape was chosen because it illustrates a hierarchy in which the amount of detail, degree of specificity, and number of pages all increase as you progress from the top to the bottom of the figure. Each of the levels has unique characteristics.

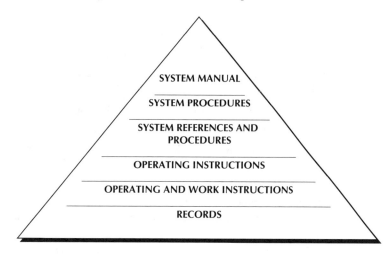

Figure 3.20 Document pyramid.

four types | Four types of documents are needed for an environmental management system. Records are sometimes split from the rest (as they are in this figure) because they are created during work, not before.

This system consists of:

1) the environmental system manual;

2) procedures;

3) work instructions; and

4) forms and records.

This section describes the tiered system in detail and gives examples of the four different levels of documents.

This section is arranged as follows:

- a discussion of the tiered system of documentation;
- suggested ways to standardize documents in an environmental management system while making each level unique; and
- examples demonstrating the content consistency needed in environmental management system documentation.

The EMS Manual

The environmental management system manual is a road map that should not be more than 25 pages long. It provides a map to the environmental management system and serves the following purposes:

- outlines broad company policies and objectives and provides an overview of the environmental management system;
- addresses each of the 20 subclauses in **ISO 14001 Section 4**;
- includes references to procedures; and
- covers the "why" behind organization practices.

In a sense, the environmental management system manual controls all other documentation. It also:

- helps internally in communication, training, and referencing;
- shows customers how the company manages quality; and
- helps auditors structure and define the internal and certification audits.

EMS Procedures

Procedures are process descriptions and flowcharts of activities. They give more detailed descriptions of what activities are, who does them, and where and why they are carried out. They:

- describe processes that occur within the company and between the company and its customers;
- explain interrelationships of organization divisions, departments;
- may require one to five pages each.

EMS Work Instructions

Work instructions:

- provide step-by-step instructions for carrying out a single activity;
- break a procedure into its individual parts;
- typically require a single page each; and
- describe how an activity is done.

These instructions can include step-by-step descriptions for how to carry out a specific task. These instructions are the most detailed.

EMS Records

These records:

- record results of inspections, tests, or other actions;
- allow tracking of individual products or services; and
- are typically completed forms, computer printouts, signed releases, etc., forms used to collect information and record completion of required environmental management system activities.

Sufficient records must be kept to provide objective evidence that the environmental management system activities are being carried out. Several ISO 14001 clauses specifically require records.

3.4.4 Standardizing EMS Documents

visual cues

Organizations typically use visual cues to help personnel and customers recognize their documents as opposed to those from another source. Designers of environmental management system documentation can follow the same principle by using:

- standard logos and other discriminators;
- consistent formatting of documents, pages, and elements on pages; and/or
- consistent terminology.

Your personnel and customers should be able to recognize instantly a document as belonging to your company.

Standardization is especially critical in control of documents. If each page typically includes a revision number and identifies the person responsible for controlling the issue of the document, for example, you will find controlling documents (a requirement of ISO 14001) easier.

contrast to avoid confusion

Be wary of one complication of such standardization: People may confuse one document with another if every document looks the same. You can solve this dilemma by making documents different in a single characteristic; for example, color, size, or binder.

The environmental management system manual could be on glossy paper in a "permanent" binding. Because the manual will be changed only when the company makes a major change in policy, it can be made from more expensive paper than other documents are. Procedures could be in loose-leaf binders of standard size (8.5 inch x 11 inch or A4) or in a vertical format so they could be "hung from a peg" in the proper location. Work instructions could be in a smaller (5 inch x 8 inch) format and be designed to fit easily on a workbench.

form to suit

Nothing in the ISO 14001 specification states what form the documentation must take. For example, it can be paper copy or electronic. Procedures may be especially effective in flow diagram format. Work instructions may be single sheets, easily posted on a bulletin board or at a workstation. Visuals of all types can be very useful.

ensure effectiveness

ISO 14001 does imply one important criterion of all documentation: It must be effective. Employees must use the documentation, and employees are more likely to use documentation they had a part in creating and documentation that takes their specific aspect of the company into consideration.

In addition, most EMS documentation also must be readable by the public. This restriction means that jargon or other specialized language must be avoided. If it can't be avoided, it should be defined. Acronyms should always be defined.

Because of the potential legal ramifications of EMS documentation, wording of some documents can be crucial.

3.4.5 Ensuring Consistency of Content

The pyramid figure does not show one critical aspect of environmental management system documentation: Content must be consistent from one level to another. Or, as quality system auditors say, " Say what you do and do what you say."

example:
training language

If your environmental management system manual says, "The company identifies training needs of all personnel and provides the required training (Procedure AOP-18-01, Training)," then procedure AOP-18-01 should describe how your company identifies training needs and provides required training. Workers should have training manuals or other materials provided to them in training sessions. You should have records of who was trained, on what, when, etc. A worker who is asked if he or she has received training for a particular function should be able to confirm such training.

If a procedure says, "All workers in each area shall only have the current edition of the work instructions specific for their work," and a worker has an old edition of work instructions, an auditor might discover the situation and write a noncompliance report.

The best way to avoid problems of the inconsistency type is to prevent them in the first place. Ensure that each section of a document is consistent with the information in another document and ensure that references are also consistent.

3.4.6 Examples of EMS Documentation

The next pages, which illustrate the concepts discussed here. Each page is an example of a page from an environmental management system manual, a procedures manual, or a work instruction. The name in the header at the top of the page identifies the document type. This material was modified from a quality manual.

These pages are intended only as examples, not as models to be copied. In designing these pages and writing text for them, the following issues were considered:

☑ How specific should the environmental management system manual be?

☑ Must each detail of the ISO 14001 standard be included in the environmental management system manual?

Notes on each page are intended to point out features you may want to include in your documents.

Documentation is an invaluable tool for tracking performance and determining where and when action is required to correct nonconformities. These reports also can help your company design methods to prevent nonconformities.

Environmental Management System
Manufacturing Company EMS Manual

4.13 Control of Nonconforming Product

Company Policy

We ensure that every product not conforming to specified requirements is prevented from unintended use or installation. Our policy is that identifying a conforming product as nonconforming is preferable to allowing a nonconforming product to miss detection. All nonconformities shall be documented, regardless of how insignificant they seem to be or how easily they can be repaired.

Implementation of Policy

This policy is implemented in two steps by two different people:

1. identify and document nonconforming product (one person).

2. evaluate the seriousness of the nonconformity and determine the disposition of the product (other person).

Procedure P-13-01, Control of Nonconforming Product, identifies the personnel involved and outlines the actions they must take.

Repaired or reworked product shall be reinspected in accordance with the applicable inspection and test procedures P-10-01 (receiving), P-10-02 (in-process), or P-10-03 (final).

Environmental Management System
Manufacturing Company EMS Procedures

Procedure P-13-01: Control of Nonconforming Product

1. Purpose

This procedure provides a system for and assigns responsibilities for:

• identifying, segregating, and documenting a nonconforming product; and

• evaluating and disposing of a nonconforming product.

2. Policy

The company's policy is that all nonconformities are documented, regardless of how insignificant they seem or how easily they can be repaired. We ensure that all product not conforming to specifications is prevented from unintended use or installation.

3. Responsibility

All personnel are encouraged to watch for, identify, and segregate nonconforming product. The person who identifies nonconforming product also documents the identification. QC (or EMS) inspectors have the final responsibility for ensuring that nonconforming product is identified and handled in accordance with this procedure.

4. Identification, Segregation, and Documentation

A person who identifies nonconforming product must do the following:

1. Segregate the product from conforming product.

2. Label the product as REJECTED.

3. Complete Part 1 of a Nonconformity Report (Form 13-01-1994) and attach the appropriate portion of the report to the product.

4. Place the nonconforming product in the designated quarantine area.

5. Complete a Nonconformity Evaluation and Disposition

Personnel involved: QC (or EMS) inspector and, when necessary, the QA (or EMS) manager, production manager, or the chief engineer.

Once nonconforming product is segregated from product meeting specifications, the QC (or EMS) inspector shall evaluate and dispose of it, recording disposition information in Part 2 of the Nonconformity Report. The disposition decision depends on the nature of the nonconformity and the risk of an inappropriate decision. The QC (or EMS) inspector shall request assistance from the QA (or EMS) manager, production manager, or chief engineer, as necessary. Disposition may be:

*   accept with or without repair, by concession of customer (see 5.1)

*   rework to meet specifications (see 5.2)

*   regrade for alternative use (see 5.2)

*   reject or scrap (see 5.3)

5.1 Where required by contract, the proposed use of nonconforming or repaired nonconforming product shall be reported for concession to the customer. The description of the nonconformity, and its condition as accepted, shall be recorded.

5.2 Products to be repaired or reworked shall (with their proper identification) be removed to the appropriate location for action. Nonconforming product received as such shall be handled according to Procedure P-10-01. Products repaired or reworked shall be reinspected in accordance with Procedures P-10-02 (In-Process Inspection) or P-10-03 (Final Inspection), as applicable.

5.3 Rejected or scrapped nonconforming products shall be placed in the designated locations until disposal.

5. Reinspection

Repaired or reworked products are reinspected to verify they comply with specifications. Regraded products are clearly marked to identify their new status.

6. Closing Out the Nonconformity Report

If the disposition decision is to accept "as is" or to scrap, the nonconformity report is closed out and filed at that point. Rework or repair decisions require that the reinspection result be entered in Part 3 of the nonconformity report before the report can be closed out. Closed out reports shall be filed with the QA manager.

Environmental Management System
Manufacturing Company EMS Work Instructions

WI-13-01: Identification and Documentation of Nonconforming Product

Personnel: All company personnel.

Purpose: To identify and document nonconforming product.

Policy: All nonconformities shall be documented, regardless of how insignificant they seem or how easily they can be repaired.

Instructions:

When you see a product that does not meet specifications, or that you think will not meet specifications, do the following:

1. Segregate the product from conforming product. If you can do so without neglecting your assigned job, continue with steps 2-5 immediately. If you cannot do so immediately, place the product in your personal quarantine area and complete steps 2-5 as soon as you can.

2. Label the product with a red REJECTED label.

3. Fill out the nonconformity description section (Part 1) of a Nonconformity Report (Form 13-01-1994).

    Note: If you are out of labels or report forms, contact your environmental management system control inspector.

4. Attach the form to the product or to a suitable container holding the product.

5. Place the product and form in the group quarantine area.

Supporting Information

Identifying—and properly labeling—nonconforming product prevents it from being used or installed unintentionally.

Documentation is an invaluable tool for tracking performance and determining where and when action is required to correct nonconformities. These reports can also help the company design methods to prevent nonconformities.

WI-13-02: Evaluation and Disposition of Nonconforming Product

Personnel: Environmental management system control inspector.

Purpose: To evaluate and determine the disposition of product identified as nonconforming.

Policy: All nonconformities shall be documented and evaluated, regardless of how insignificant they seem or how easily they can be repaired.

Instructions:

Following the timing schedule determined by your area supervisor or environmental management system manager, examine the nonconforming products in the group quarantine area. Complete the following steps for each:

1. Determine whether the product is, in fact, nonconforming. If the situation is not obvious, you may need to have the product inspected and/or tested.
2. With the environmental management system manager, area supervisor, and/or chief engineer, determine the disposition of the nonconforming product and complete Part 2 of the Nonconforming Product Report (Form 13-01-1994).

Possible dispositions of nonconforming product:

*   accept with or without repair, by concession of customer (see 2.1).
*   rework to meet specifications (see 2.2).
*   regrade for alternative use (see 2.2).
*   reject or scrap (see 2.3).

2.1 If the product appears flawed in a minor way that should not affect its use, you can request assistance from the environmental management system manager in determining whether a concession to use the product is needed from the customer. Follow Procedure P-13-02 from this point.

2.2 If the product can be repaired or reworked, see that it is delivered to the appropriate location for further action. Leave the Nonconformance Report and REJECTED label with the product so it can be reinspected or retested when it is ready.

2.3 If the product must be rejected or scrapped, place it in the designated location for disposal.

Note: Keep the REJECTED label and Nonconformity Report with the product until necessary action has been completed. The person completing the action closes the report and files it with the environmental management system manager.

Supporting Information

Identifying — and properly labeling — nonconforming product prevents it from being used or installed unintentionally.

3.4.7 Documentation As an Integral Part of Implementation

practice and document concurrently

The tendency in documenting any practice is to define the practice first and then document it. There's a more efficient, more practical way to develop documentation — concurrently. Developing documentation first is even better.

When this concept is introduced, audiences in workshops and clients in conferences typically wonder how documentation can be produced in this manner. The typical ISO edict of "Say what you do and do what you say" begins interestingly enough with "say," or, in our case, "document". There are two important principles involved here:

1) Word-of-mouth information rarely is communicated consistently. Only written information — clearly written — is constant.

A typical auditor's question of "What would happen to your system if X, Y, or Z left your company tomorrow?" indicates the importance of maintaining written procedures and directions for work.

2) Creating documentation helps you critically assess your processes and their quality.

Internal reviewers inevitably will ask, "Is this what we really do?" At that point, and even earlier in prototyping sessions where you must develop consensus about what will be documented and how, you and your employees have a chance to shape company policy and practice. Ironically, if you do first and document later, then you are less likely to present a consistent, clear picture of your company's environmental aspects.

3.4.8 How Can Documentation Be Used to Drive Implementation?

The concepts involved with this are the focus of this section. The steps are as follows:

- ☑ recognize and use the power of frontloading;
- ☑ begin with an internal audit of your system, comparing it to ISO 14001 specifications;
- ☑ develop a plan to create the missing documentation;
- ☑ determine a format for all documents;
- ☑ prototype each document;
- ☑ assign writing tasks;
- ☑ use the prototype to structure reviews;
- ☑ carefully track each document; and
- ☑ establish a permanent document list and "library."

3.4.9 Use Your Documents

1. Recognize and use the power of frontloading.

People typically construct documents ineffectively, by working slowly at the beginning and building to a frenzy before (and often after) the deadline. The effective documentation process, on the other hand, is frontloaded: You work intensely in the beginning and simply tie up loose ends at the end. You complete the work on or before the deadline.

Frontloading includes planning the project, determining the format for all related documents, prototyping each document, and scheduling writing and reviews. If you frontload effectively, the people who know the content are the ones who plan and structure the document; those comfortable with writing do the word processing, editing, and proofreading.

2. Begin with an internal audit of your system, comparing it to ISO 14001 specifications.

Before you dive into your documentation project, find out how deep the water is by auditing your current system — before you begin generating new documentation or establishing goals and objectives, find out what exists and find out whether it works.

Find out what exists.

be thorough There are two goals for your search — to locate everything your company currently has that would be usable in an EMS and to locate materials you can use to begin your EMS implementation and documentation.

Gather copies of all pertinent documents, including the environmental regulations for your company, its products, and its wastes. Most of this information should already exist; part of the difficulty will be locating it and constraining it to a single location. Order two copies of critical documents (depending on their size, of course) — one for your "library" and one for circulation. Many environmental regulations have periodic updates and modifications. Subscribe to a newsletter or other service that can keep your library up to date.

Don't forget to track the written communication that's part of your company's safety and loss prevention program, particularly MSDS and other employee communications. Do you prepare and disseminate community information?

get employee input

Provide a location (e-mail, drop-box at the library, etc.) that can serve as a place for employees to provide copies of news items they see that affect your company and its work. Although a clipping service is more efficient (and probably a good investment depending on your company's size) the effort employees must go through to identify and bring in related information helps involve them in your environmental management system. Don't forget to recognize their contributions.

cross-reference

Collect the documentation for your ISO 9000 system if one exists. A cross-reference sheet of documents and their location (a copy of the listing required for ISO 9001) would be helpful.

Find out whether existing documentation works.

Determine how well the existing documentation meets the ISO 14001 standard and document your findings (you might as well get into the habit immediately).

assess quality

Assess the quality of your documentation by determining whether existing documents meet the needs of their audiences. Documents people cannot use might as well not exist. Conduct a document assessment to determine whether the documents have the following:

- purpose statements;

- clear and logical organization;

- content required for the job to be done as well as for the ISO standard being applied;

- information presented in the most appropriate form (visually whenever possible); and

- messages and supporting information conveyed through good writing techniques.

assess usability

Conduct a usability assessment to determine whether and how your employees use existing documentation. Especially important in such an assessment is objectivity. Be sure employees know the documents are "on trial," not them.

Both document assessments and usability assessments may benefit from the objectivity of outside help.

3. Develop a plan to create the missing documentation.

manual is cornerstone

Once you know what you need, you can develop a plan and a schedule to create the missing documentation. Your plan for documentation should be part of your overall implementation of an EMS. For example, use the de-facto requirement for an EMS manual to schedule a meeting for management to develop or refine its environmental policy. This document and the principles it addresses will be the cornerstone for your EMS.

manage
meetings

Planning meetings are critical jumping-off points for any EMS activity. Invite people critical to success and make implementation and documentation of an EMS concurrent rather than sequential activities. Prepare carefully for the meeting and agree on meeting management guidelines and collaborative techniques for working efficiently.

4. Determine a format for all documents.

plan the format

Before the first prototyping session, plan the format (document and page appearance) for the documents to be created. If a company standard exists, use it. If not, now's your chance to establish one. Consider page size, whether pages are single- or double-sided, what each page looks like in terms of margins, header, footer, type face of text and headings, etc. Include plans for bullet and numbered lists, tables, and even paragraph spacing. Once you have a consistent format for documents, anyone who writes one can simply use the established electronic format and fill in the necessary text. All documents will look like part of an organized, integrated system.

5. Prototype each document.

call on users to
prototype

Prototyping is visualizing the end from the beginning; it is the single most effective way to frontload the documentation process. Who prototypes? The best people to do this are the people who will use the document. Prototyping gives document users the power to develop documents they will actually use (effective documents).

In meetings of representative users, begin prototyping by answering the following questions:

☑ What is the purpose of the document?

☑ Who will use it and how will they use it?

☑ How long should the document be?

☑ What must be included in the document? Which information is most critical?

☑ What is the best arrangement of the information? Will the user read sequentially or randomly?

begin
construction

Now, using sticky notes, large sheets of paper, or any other convenient format, begin constructing the document, one page at a time. At first you simply place the main topics on the number of pages you have set for the document. The pages will look quite empty and you'll be tempted to put one topic on each page. Don't! Allot pages according to the importance of the topic and be sure to plan for a table of contents, index, glossary, etc. This initial prototype should take two to four hours to create. By the time you finish, everyone should understand what the final document will look like and what it will contain.

"Flesh out" the detail of the pages by creating an interim prototype. Determine whether to use drawings, flow diagrams, or other aids to help the user. Add headings and subheadings to create "mock-up" pages of the final document. But do not simply add pages as sections of text "grow"; pare the proposed information to its essential elements.

6. Assign writing tasks.

Now you're ready to assign specific writers to fill in the necessary text. Give writers assignments to fill in text they know best (or are most interested in) and schedule a review of the interim prototype in about a week or two.

Subject matter experts are often the best source of content; they may not always be the best writers. Remember to first focus on capturing the content, then worry about editing, revising, or other techniques that turn rough text into a finished document.

do content
now, edit later

Leave the interim prototype on some visible wall where writers can constantly refer to it. Encourage them to tack notes to the sheets as they have suggestions for improving the prototype.

7. Use the prototype to structure reviews.

focus on
substance

Effective reviews take only a short time when everyone knows ahead of time what they are to review and how they are to review it. When you are the person asking for a review, tell the reviewer exactly what to critique. Early reviews should be for content and organization. Don't waste time on commas and spelling.

Always use the prototype as the basis for review. Incorporate reviewed and corrected material into the prototype, then determine whether the prototype still "works" and identify what is missing.

8. Carefully track each document.

assign single
author

You will probably have a number of documents in progress at one time. Track all documents as they develop, using a consistent numbering system. Include revision number, date, page number, and date/time printed on each document page. Assign one person as the "author" for the electronic copy of each document; only that person authorizes changes and updates revision number and date.

9. Establish a permanent document list and "library."

keep a list

When a document is complete, transfer responsibility to yourself or to a "librarian" who keeps the list of documents, carefully identifying the following:

- the current revision number and date;
- who has copies;
- the name and location of the electronic version of the document;
- who is responsible for updating and when updating should be considered; and
- the document list and library are the key elements of your document control system.

10. Use your documents.

use them!

Effective documents are an essential part of day-to-day work; they are the way of life for your company. Be sure documents are located where they are needed and are being used. If people are not using them, documents are probably not sufficiently effective.

3.4.10 Integration with Other Systems (Quality, Compliance)

Every organization probably already has more documentation than it can handle effectively. How will ISO 14000 add to that? There are a number of possible treatments of the situation:

☑ Ignore existing documentation and just do the documentation needed for the ISO 14000 EMS.

☑ Start from scratch and build an integrated system of documentation for the organization, redoing as much documentation as necessary.

☑ Computerize everything and set up an on-line documentation system.

☑ Tailor the documentation to your organization and its individual needs.

We can consider these options one at a time, including some possible advantages and disadvantages of each.

1. Document the ISO 14001 EMS as its own entity.

Following the implementation patterns described earlier and in other sections of this handbook, your organization could choose to document the EMS as an individual entity. This would mean a four-tiered system with an environmental system manual, environmental system procedures, environmental system work instructions, and environmental system records. The necessary regulatory information would become part of that system.

Advantages

The documentation could be constructed with a clear focus on the environmental aspects of your organization. Other interests or concerns would not interfere. The documentation, and the EMS, would be easy for an auditor (either internal or third-party) to assess. To make the system workable, those in charge of documentation need only make the bindings of EMS documents a color different from those already in use.

Disadvantages

Nothing operates in isolation.

☑ How would the employee know which work instructions to use when?

☑ Would workers' desks be covered with documents that are never used?

☑ How easily could management understand and deal with the interrelationships between quality, loss control, environmental aspects, safety, etc.?

2. Build an integrated system of documentation for the organization.

Ideally, just as the organization is a unified whole, the documentation for that organization is unified. A clearly delineated and integrated system is possible when the organization thinks in terms of objectives and company issues, not in terms of quality management systems or environmental management systems.

A careful examination of existing documentation will probably reveal overlaps, repetition, and unused documents. Even though workers know they are supposed to refer to manuals 1, 2, and Z when they design a new product (for example), they may not be able to do so and maintain their creativity. Using document specialists to build a unified system can make a single, workable system possible.

Advantages

Workers, management, and everyone else will know just how to accomplish any function that routinely occurs. The system will allow for innovation and additions also. Every time some new manual or document is needed, the guidelines will already exist and the writers will know what to do and where to go for information. Some companies already have unified, integrated systems of documentation.

Disadvantages

Building an integrated system will require time and money if the current system is haphazard. Convincing management of the need for such a system could be difficult. Also, when auditors (especially ISO 9000 and ISO 14000) begin an audit, they will have to examine an organization manual that incorporates all systems (and thus covers more than they are interested in). Extensive cross-referencing of materials could require full-time work by a number of people. Updates might be difficult to manage.

3. Set up an on-line documentation system.

The on-line documentation system seems to be an ideal way to maintain a number of separate systems of documentation or a single, integrated one. Many different computer programs (e.g., FrameMaker, MSWord, MSAccess, Interleaf) already exist. Those in charge of documentation simply need to assure that every document exists electronically and then construct the necessary links among them.

Advantages

All necessary information for the company is readily available. The full system requires relatively little space. Updates and control of documents are fairly easy to handle by a single person. Each person has access to the most up-to-date and pertinent information available. Searching for information on a particular topic is easy.

Disadvantages

There are still many people who are not comfortable with computers, either in general or for specific high-powered uses. Everyone in the company would have to be trained to use the system and retraining would be necessary every time the program is modified. Expenditures for computer equipment would depend on the current situation in the company. However, most companies are not standardized in their programs or computers and standardization would be necessary.

4. Tailor the documentation to your organization and its individual needs.

Most likely, no one solution exists for your organization. You will probably have to put together something that meets your needs without over-burdening your budget. The place to start, naturally, is with a detailed analysis of the current situation.

☑ How much already exists and how best can that be extended or infused with information necessary for the EMS?

Consider not only what is an immediate need but what is practical for the company in the long run. A highly integrated, very efficient computerized system is of no value if the company goes bankrupt getting the system in place. On the other hand, continually working with an inefficient system is simply "throwing good money after bad." The following list of questions might help you get started:

☑ Does your business operate in a single location or many?

• A single location is more suitable for an integrated, unified system. Multiple locations may mean multiple solutions to the documentation problem.

☑ What is your current computer capability?

• If everyone in your company travels with a laptop computer and logs in to the home network (for example), your company is closer to on-line documentation systems than a company that has computer operators with varying levels of comfort.

☑ Are the computers relatively new, with all the latest software?

☑ Has your company chosen a single word processing program, database system, etc.?

☑ Is your system reliable?

☑ What security precautions do you need?

• As a computer system becomes larger and can be accessed by more people, the dangers of people accessing and manipulating or destroying information increase. Security can be a critical issue for many companies.

☑ Is recycling part of your company strategy?

Remember, the scope and depth of documentation at your company ultimately depends on how necessary and usable it is. No one wants "big honker binders" gathering dust on their shelves. On the other hand, when that auditor drops by you will want to demonstrate proudly that you are, in fact, doing what you're saying you do.

Different Implementation Approaches

CHAPTER 1
Overview

If you have read this handbook up to this point, it will be clear to you that there are as many ways of implementing ISO 14001 as there are companies doing it. In Part 3, we offered you one method of implementation, based on a business-oriented approach. The authors grounded their advice on years of experience working with company EHS management systems.

Also, we offered you a collection of valuable "tips" on implementing ISO 14001 from a select group of industry and consulting experts.

In part 4, we present to you six additional alternative approaches written with your company's unique circumstances in mind.

Case studies highlighting companies that took different approaches follow. Among them is a look at how SGS-Thomson became the first company in the United States to become certified to ISO/DIS 14001. It became certified to EMAS at the same time.

These case studies first appeared in CEEM Information Services' *International Environmental Systems Update* covering ISO 14000 and EMSs, or *Integrated Management Systems Update*, covering EHS, quality, and financial management systems. They were updated for this handbook, but represent a particular time during the companies' implementation efforts.

We hope you find useful information here, perhaps recognizing similarities with your own company.

CHAPTER 2
Six Alternative Approaches

by Lelia McAdams, Technical Manager, Corporate Environmental Strategic Planning,

AT&T Microelectronics (now with Lucent Technologies)

Let's be honest. No one is a true "expert" about ISO 14001; the standard is too new. Some of us have implemented similar systems, or more often, similar parts of systems. Very few of us have the whole thing in place running smoothly. So do take the following advice on how to implement this standard with a grain of salt. Look around your own organization for similar successful management system approaches and borrow heavily from them.

no "correct"
approach

There has been, and there will continue to be, lots of debate on the "one correct" interpretation of each of the ISO 14001 requirements. There will be no official interpretations of the standard until after it is published in 1996 and the market has some experience with it. Those who were involved in drafting the standard can tell you the legislative history, or what the rationale for the wording in the standard was at the time. The ISO technical committee expects to set up a mechanism for official interpretations of the ISO 14001 document, but this will take some time to put in place.

Since the ISO 14001 specification standard is brief and to the point, it should provide a good basis — and the latitude — for many different organizations to interpret the clauses to fit their situations.

We recommend that you and your organization carefully consider various approaches before you decide how to settle on the "correct" interpretation of the ISO 14001 requirements for your organization. In the end, if an approach works for your organization — if it includes the basic elements in 14001, addresses your significant environmental needs, supports development of a good compliance infrastructure, integrates well with your existing other management structures and systems, fosters continuous improvement, and engages all who should be engaged — then it is the right approach.

4.2.1 Mental Preparation

It may help to understand that you probably will not implement any element just once. This is an iterative process. Expect to redo many parts of your system over time. That's what we mean by "continual improvement." Detailed perfection is not the goal. Rather, a workable and adaptable system is.

Before you get started, you will also need to choose a "scope," or the boundaries of your system. 📖 (See Part 1, Chapter 3, Section 5 for more information on determining the scope.) In addition, if it's not clear where your organization's boundaries are — choose the boundaries that make sense to you and the others that will be responsible for the management system elements. You will want to review all this periodically as you implement ISO 14001 to ensure that your first assumptions are still valid, or to make changes as needed.

Who is this "you" anyway? "You" are the one tasked with getting the ISO 14001 ball rolling. Be mentally prepared to take on multiple roles over time — as a catalyst, coach, trainer, project manager, motivator, team member, assistant, etc. However, do not expect to do all the work — the users of the system should also be the designers of the system. Get them involved from the start and empower them with decisionmaking.

4.2.2 Getting Started

Let's assume you have preliminary management commitment to implement ISO 14001 in your organization. Where do you go from there? After all, there are several pages of requirements in the ISO 14001 standard. Do you start with clause 4.1, go on to 4.2, and so on in chronological order, through clause 4.5? That is an option, but is not likely to make sense in reality. Here are some alternative ways of getting started that you might want to consider.

4.2.3 Method #1 — Fix the Gaps

This method starts by identifying gaps in your existing EMS. You can do this through an initial review, a baseline audit, or a self-readiness test. 📖 (See Part 2, Chapter 2, Section 2 for more information on initial reviews and gap analyses.) Once you have identified which ISO 14001 requirements you are missing or are weak in (your gaps), choose the largest gaps to fix first. There may be some debate about which is your largest gap. If this is so, convene the people who will be most involved in your EMS and let them choose the starting point. Getting started is more important than where you start, since you'll get to all the gaps over time.

It's a good idea to work on one or two gaps first, get them to the workable stage, then fix your third gap, and so on. Each time you fix a gap, review the previous "fixes" and revise your system as needed so that all the sub-parts of your system work well together.

4.2.4 Method #2 — Environmental Aspects

If you have no environmental program or management system at all, start by setting up a procedure to evaluate your environmental aspects, per **Section 4.2.1**. (Others with an EMS can choose to begin here also, or to do this step early in the implementation process. Note that this should never be left to do last.) Implement your procedure and document the results. Next, set up and implement a procedure to identify your legal and other requirements, per **Section 4.2.2** — do it and document the results.

There are several ways you can proceed from here. The following is one approach (follow along with a copy of the standard):

- Do **Section 4.1**, then **4.2.3**, then **4.2.4**. Remember to review your previous work after each new part of the system is added.

- Next do **Sections 4.3.1, 4.3.6, 4.3.7,** and **4.3.2**. Note that Section **4.3.2** covers training needs and procedures, which likely will need to be reviewed and revised and re-implemented repetitively as you add elements to your system.

- Then do **4.3.3, 4.3.4, 4.3.5, 4.4.1, 4.4.2, 4.4.3, 4.4.4,** and **4.5**.

4.2.5 Method #3 — Internal Audits

If you have an established environmental program or management system, but do not do internal audits, by all means start with **Section 4.4** — "checking and corrective action." In particular, set up internal audit procedures to address two areas:

1) evaluating legislative/regulatory compliance — this is part of **Section 4.4.1**; and

2) evaluating the EMS system conformance — this is **Section 4.4.4**.

You can set up one or two sets of procedures to address these jointly or separately.

As you implement your internal auditing, you will be strengthening your management commitment and working on several other elements of your system — documentation, recordkeeping, corrective and preventive action, operational controls, etc. After you have completed two or three cycles of internal auditing (and corrective action and follow-up), you will then have identified your priority system and compliance needs (repetitive items or general trends in audit action items).

Those responsible for the identified areas can proceed to fix them at the working level, which should foster acceptance of the continuous improvement approach. It seems to be a common human trait to want to fix your own mistakes before others see them, so capitalize on this by starting with a solid internal auditing procedure.

4.2.6 Method #4 — Documentation

document as you develop

If you have a fair number of the elements in an EMS in place, but most or all of the procedural knowledge is in one or a few persons' heads, sit down and document what you've got first. Once you start documenting and have decided to what level of detail to document your EMS (when starting, less is better), it will be easier to document procedures as they are developed to meet the other ISO 14001 requirements. If we have learned anything from implementing ISO 9000 standards, it is that we need to "write down what we do, and do what we write down."

4.2.7 Method #5 — The Beginners' Filing System

If you and your organization are relative beginners in applying EMSs, consider using the outline of ISO 14001 sections as your organization/filing system. Develop a basic or skeleton procedure for each ISO 14001 clause. The title of each ISO 14001 clause is the name of your file drawer. The skeleton procedure is what goes in file number one in each file drawer. Implement all of your skeleton procedures. Then, as you gain experience in running your system, go back and revise or add to the appropriate files/file drawers as needed.

4.2.8 Method #6 — Custom-made

This is just a reminder that you are the one implementing your EMS, so feel free to mix and match the above approaches, or to create your own.

4.2.9 Small and Medium-Sized Enterprises

Understanding and establishing this procedure will not be particularly difficult for SMEs. If anything, it should be easier, because of the simpler corporate structure. The key is the upper management commitment to continuous improvement. Your organization's culture must acknowledge the importance of the EMS and listen to feedback and input from the management representatives. Traditionally, because of limited resources, SME management views on environmental issues have been "no news is good news." Hence, they did not get involved as long as operations were in compliance.

CHAPTER 3
SGS-Thomson Case Study — First U.S. Certification

4.3.1 Overview

The SGS-Thomson Microelectronics Inc. facility in San Diego, California, claimed the first certification in the United States to ISO/DIS 14001 on January 3, 1996, and verification to the European Union's Eco-Management and Audit Scheme (EMAS) on December 15, 1995.

SGS-Thomson is a global independent semiconductor company that designs, develops, manufactures, and markets a broad range of semiconductor integrated circuits used in numerous microelectronics applications, including telecommunication systems, computer systems, consumer products, automotive products, and industrial automation and control systems.

Following is the story of how SGS came to receive its certification and verification.

The first section is a reprint of the story as it appeared in the February 1996 issue of CEEM Information Services' *International Environmental Systems Update*, which first reported the accomplishment.

The second section is in SGS-Thomson's own words and goes into detail about three of the major certification tasks it faced: making the decision to go for certification, identifying environmental impacts, and managing the documentation.

4.3.2 First U.S. Facility Certifies to ISO 14001 and EMAS

Adapted from International Environmental Systems Update (IESU), February 1996

The SGS-Thomson Microelectronics semiconductor manufacturing facility in Rancho Bernardo, Calif., has claimed the first certification in the United States to both ISO 14001 and the European Union's Eco-Management and Auditing Scheme (EMAS).

While the Rancho Bernardo site cannot be listed in the official register of EMAS-verified companies in Brussels because it is not located in the European Union, the verification to EMAS shows the site meets all the requirements stipulated under the EMAS regulation.

As part of an overall corporate-wide mandate, all 16 SGS-Thomson facilities located in the U.S., Europe, Southeast Asia, and North Africa will be validated for EMAS and/or certified to ISO 14001 by the end of 1997, the company announced. Several SGS-Thomson facilities also are certified to ISO 9000 quality management systems and receive both corporate and third-party assessment regularly.

The facility's ISO 14001 certificate to the DIS will expire on the date the International Organization for Standardization prints ISO 14001 as an official ISO international standard, expected in October 1996. If no substantive changes are made to the ISO 14001 international standard, the facility's certificate will automatically be updated. However, if any major changes are made, the organization could have to undergo another assessment.

suppliers, contractors eyed

Major suppliers and contractors of SGS may find themselves forced to implement either EMAS or ISO 14001 by 1998 to maintain contractual preference, according to company officials. While SGS does not plan to mandate certification to its suppliers, the company does recognize that environmental performance of its facilities and suppliers relates directly back to the bottom line, explains Fabio Borri, corporate director for environmental strategy and international programs for SGS-Thomson.

"We assign an overall score to our suppliers based on many elements, including quality and environmental performance," he says. "While an EMS alone does not seem that important, it may be the deciding factor when we decide who gets equipment and manufacturing supplier contracts."

He says the company currently implements this scoring system with ISO 9000 certification as a major indicator or factor in the process of granting supplier contracts.

BVQI Was Certification Body

In late 1995, SGS corporate personnel contracted Bureau Veritas Quality International to assess the facility to requirements of both EMAS and ISO 14001 through the accreditation program administered by the United Kingdom Accreditation Service. The Rancho Bernardo site officially received verification of its environmental statement, required by EMAS, December 15, 1995, and certification to the draft ISO 14001 international standard on January 3, 1996.

"This company is positioning itself for the inevitable: that EMAS will become much more than a European regulation," according to John French, director of environmental registration for BVQI. *[Note: French left BVQI in April 1996 to join Environ Corp.]*

French acted as the lead auditor during the Rancho Bernardo audit and says SGS's EMAS and ISO 14001 certifications are further evidence of the company's commitment to pursue the highest standards available and to influence its suppliers and contractors to do the same. He says the company has implemented an EMS that links environmental impacts and aspects with the operational controls of each facility.

EMS is
adaptable

"SGS's environmental management system is highly operable and adaptable to changing situations that occur frequently in the microelectronics manufacturing field," he says. "I expect that this certification will motivate other companies in the industry to stand up and take notice. [BVQI] fully anticipates more companies certifying to ISO 14001 or EMAS very soon."

1,500 Customers

Some of SGS-Thomson's 1,500 customers include Alcatel, Bosch, Ford, Hewlett-Packard, IBM, Sony, Motorola, and Northern Telecom. The SGS-Thomson corporate headquarters is located in Saint Genis, France, and the company is publicly traded on both the New York Stock Exchange and the Bourse de Paris.

In 1994 the company reported a net revenue of more than $2.6 billion and net earnings of more than $362.5 million. The company employs some 25,000 people worldwide with about 300 at the Rancho Bernardo facility.

QMS Came in Handy

Patrick Hoy, the site environmental manager for the Rancho Bernardo facility, acted as the implementation champion for the facility and was responsible for preparing the site for the EMAS verification and ISO 14001 certification audits. Hoy used experience obtained from the company's ISO 9001 quality management system to develop an implementation plan for both EMAS and ISO 14001. He also employed the consulting firm Dames & Moore to help him prepare for the EMAS verification.

Hoy is also a member of the corporate audit team that assesses other facilities within the company. The team consists of an independent environmental consultant who acts as the lead auditor, a member of the corporate strategy department, and two environmental managers from other sites. As a member of the team, Hoy is exposed to different manufacturing conditions within different countries. However, he notes that EMS implementation plans are similar across the company.

Identifying and Ranking Impacts

mechanism to
identify
impacts

Hoy says that the key to any environmental management system is the mechanism employed for identifying aspects and impacts associated with a company's processes, products, and services.

To prepare for the EMAS formal assessment, the Rancho Bernardo facility followed the Failure Mode and Effect Analysis (FEMA) corporate standard developed for assessing the potential significance of each environmental effect identified.

As part of the corporate standard, Hoy and his team conducted a review of all regulations that applied to the facility, any pending environmental legislation, corporate requirements, and all media-specific permitting conditions. He says the group examined potential impacts associated with water, air, hazardous waste, solid waste, soil and groundwater, energy, chemical management, external noise, raw materials, new product processes, product planning, and emergency response planning.

Hoy ranked each impact according to its significance and where it ranked on the corporate list of overall environmental effects. He notes that the facility compiles a list or register of potential environmental impacts and makes it available to the public through its annual environmental statement.

During the assessment, conducted in early 1995, the company identified two potentially significant impacts that, left unattended, could have caused significant negative impact to the environment surrounding the facility.

Hoy explains that the first significant impact involved a small section of single-walled pipe from the facility's acid-waste system that was running "below grade" and that could have an effect on soils during a rupture or leak. He says the facility double-walled the pipe and relocated the section aboveground to solve a potential problem.

"We immediately developed an action plan and allocated resources to fix the problems," Hoy notes.

Noise Pollution Goals

Borri says the Rancho Bernardo facility also identified noise emissions as a significant environmental impact. He says that the city of San Diego prescribes a maximum noise level of 75 dB(A) for any industrial facility but that the company felt it could do better and mandated that "by the end of 1997, no SGS facility should emit more than 60 dB(A)."

The Rancho Bernardo facility is well within the San Diego limit but exceeds the corporate mandate. Because of a planned site expansion, by mid-1997 the Rancho Bernardo team will replace the piece of equipment — a liquid nitrogen plant — responsible for the noise emissions, he says.

"This is a large corporate investment that is consistent with our EMAS commitment to use economically viable best available technology and therefore the replacement has to correspond with other activities at the site," Borri says.

Typical Impacts

water
energy
waste
chemicals

Borri explains that potential environmental aspects associated with microelectronics manufacturers are fairly typical and therefore the facility's use of vast amounts of water, electrical energy, and some chemicals is normal. He also says the facilities generate large amounts of hazardous and solid wastes. But the site's activities can have environmental effects in several ways. These activities are identified in the Rancho Bernardo environmental statement:

- spent acids and the rinse water effluents that are generated to clean the wafers at various points in the production process;
- significant water usage;
- VOC emissions, acidity, and toxic air contaminants;
- chemical spills or leaks that have the potential to contaminate soil, groundwater, or stormwater;

- hazardous and solid waste generation and disposal that could lead to impacts on quality of soil and groundwater as well as impacts on quality of air;

- natural gas and electrical generation that can have an effect on air quality and the global climate; and

- noise emissions beyond the site's perimeter that could lead to a decrease in the quality of life of any person living or working in the vicinity of the site.

Hoy says all the environmental effects of the site are within the regulatory and permit limits that apply and that the above list will be modified as site activities change.

"Before the EMAS verification took place, we hired an independent third party, [Dames & Moore] to perform a compliance audit to ensure we were in compliance with all local and regional requirements," Borri says. "We do this at each facility because as corporate assessors we can't be expected to know all of the environmental laws that pertain to our facilities in the U.S., France, Singapore, and North Africa. Results of the compliance audit was the first documentation the corporate audit team reviewed."

Performance Indicators

Hoy says the Rancho Bernardo facility will use indicators outlined in the EMAS environmental statement to track performance of the company's EMS. He explains that facility personnel will monitor energy usage, recycling and landfill solid waste percentages, and the amount of hazardous waste being recycled vs. the gross amount generated.

"Decalogue"   Also, as part of California's stormwater pollution prevention program, the facility will pull samples twice a year to determine the quality of stormwater.

All performance indicators will be directly tied into the facility's environmental statement and the "SGS-Thomson Decalogue," which is the company's internal commitment for management to set objectives aimed at reducing the impact of industrial activity on the environment. The decalogue is signed and fully supported by CEO of SGS-Thomson Pasquale Pistorio, according to both Hoy and Borri.

As part of the company policy and decalogue, each SGS facility is required to meet all environmental/ecological requirements within the community in which it operates. For example, the facility can track performance by monitoring some of the following decalogue commitments:

- comply with all ecological improvement targets at least one year ahead of official deadlines;

- reduce total energy consumed by manufacturing, buildings, etc., per million dollars sold by at least 5 percent per year, with 25 percent reduction by end 1999;

- for all manufacturing operations, reach a level of 50 percent recycled water by end 1997 and 90 percent by end 1999; and

- include an "environmental awareness" training course in the SGS-Thomson university curriculum, and offer it to suppliers and customers.

Hoy says the Rancho Bernardo facility is implementing a water recycling program that is poised to take the company beyond the corporate goal of 50 percent water reusage by recycling. He notes that the facility is already recycling 60 percent of the water used during the production process.

Overcoming Implementation Hurdles

Borri says that, early on, the company identified that getting employee buy-in for the EMS implementation initiative would be a hurdle. SGS corporate decided to initiate a competition to further employee commitment to EMS implementation and certification.

employee
buy-in

He says the corporate audit team visited each facility and assigned a score point to each element assessed. At the end of the assessment a total score was assigned to each facility based on its competence in identifying aspects and demonstrating EMS knowledge.

"Everyone wants to be the best and, by creating a good competition among the facilities, we were able to motivate all levels of employees," Borri says. "This competition allowed the EMS culture to cascade down from top management to the lower- and middle-level employees throughout the company."

Borri says the company used the same approach to implement ISO 9000 in its facilities and is well-versed in following the total quality management philosophy that suggests using improvement teams to assess and improve overall quality. He says adapting this philosophy for environmental management was "quite easy."

French adds that all SGS-Thomson employees are required to attend eight hours of environmental awareness training that explains environmental impacts, green accounting, and overall environmental management system methodology. He says this further demonstrates SGS-Thomson's strategy of giving its employees ownership of each facility's EMS.

All of the corporate SGS-Thomson training courses are conducted at ST University located outside of Geneva, Switzerland. SGS-Thomson trainers are educated at the university and then sent back to their sites to train employees, contractors, and suppliers.

Documentation Similarities

Hoy says another advantage to having an ISO 9001 system in place is the similarities among the documentation requirements in that standard and those for both EMAS and ISO 14001.

ISO 9001

He says the Rancho Bernardo facility used its ISO 9001 documentation procedures to implement EMAS and ISO 14001 by assigning document control numbers to the EMS manual and EMS procedures. Hoy says this denotes the importance of the documents as "live documents" that are constantly changing. He notes that the EMS manual cross-references the quality manual and vice versa to demonstrate that the two systems are working hand-in-hand.

The Rancho Bernardo site maintains two separate manuals, one for quality and the other for environmental management, but Hoy says the company plans to integrate the two and include health and safety by 2000. This goal corresponds with the corporate vision to have one integrated management system in place in all of the SGS-Thomson facilities, he says.

Corporate Audit Schedule

The Rancho Bernardo facility will be audited by the corporate audit team every 18 months to review the EMS and make appropriate changes. The site will also perform an annual assessment prior to the corporate visit, to prepare for the EMAS statement revalidation audit scheduled for every three years.

pre-certification audits

The corporate audit team will recommend and provide suggestions to facility environmental teams but will not dictate changes. Borri says having at least five audits prior to the official third-party re-verification allows the facility to identify all potential nonconformances and initiate corrective action plans to address the problems.

SGS-Thomson designed its auditing program using ISO 10011 auditing procedures for quality management systems but has started following the three ISO 14000 auditing standards — ISO 14010 auditing principles, ISO 14011/1 auditing procedures, and ISO 14012 auditor requirements.

Hoy is certified by the corporate environmental strategy department and the human resources department as an internal corporate auditor. As part of that internal certification Hoy is required to meet all requirements outlined in ISO 14012.

Implementation/Certification Costs

$100,000

Borri estimates that implementing EMAS in each SGS-Thomson facility costs about $100,000, give or take 10 to 20 percent. He says 95 percent of the work is internal preparation divided equally between the corporate office and each site. Borri declined to put a price tag on the cost of ISO 14001 certification to the Rancho Bernardo facility because he says the cost was "insignificant." Most of the work was already complete for EMAS, and ISO 14001 required little extra.

Borri says the cost of EMAS included external consultants; environmental managers' travel expenses to three worldwide meetings during the implementation process; and the visit by an independent validator.

Rancho Bernardo is the fifth SGS-Thomson site verified to EMAS in 1996 and the first in the U.S. The company verified two sites in France and one site each in Malta and Singapore earlier in 1996 and expects to have two more sites verified to EMAS in France and the U.S., another site in Singapore, and a site in Morocco by the end of 1996.

4.3.3 Tackling Three Areas: The Decision, Impacts, Documentation

by Patrick F. Hoy, Environmental Manager, SGS-Thomson Microelectronics, Inc., and Jennifer L. Kraus, Program Director, Environmental Management Services, Dames & Moore

Based on careful analysis and research regarding the benefits associated with certification, preparation for certification under EMAS and ISO 14001 became a top priority for SGS-Thomson in 1994. One of the first questions we had to ask was, "Why become certified?" *Figure 4.1* presents a simple checklist like the one we used to help us consider certification.

As a corporation, SGS-Thomson's vision is to be environmentally responsible and support sustainable development. Following is the company's vision statement as it is summarized in the environmental policy:

In SGS-Thomson we believe firmly that it is mandatory for a TQM-driven corporation to be at the forefront of ecological commitment, not only for ethical and social reasons, but also for financial return, and the ability to attract the most responsible and best-performing people.

Our "ecological vision" is to become a corporation that closely approaches environmental neutrality.

Will ISO 14000 certification benefit the following elements of my business?	
Business Element	**Yes**
Sales & Marketing	
Product quality	❏
Competitiveness	❏
Market share	❏
Production	
Energy impacts	❏
Waste reduction	❏
Increased efficiency	❏
Financial	
Cost savings	❏
Profitability	❏
Cost avoidance	❏
Shareholder/investor commitments	❏
Distribution	
Packaging	❏
Transportation costs	❏
Public Relations	
Community	❏
Environmental groups	❏
Employees	❏
Personnel	
Motivation and commitment	❏
Participation	
Training and awareness	❏
Compliance	❏
Compliance assistance	❏
Fine avoidance	❏
Documentation	❏

Figure 4.1 — To certify or not to certify — issues to be considered.

This policy naturally led into creation of the "10 environmental commandments" of SGS-Thomson, referred to as the SGS-Thomson *Environmental Decalogue*. The decalogue presents specific objectives within nine specific environmental categories. The text of the decalogue and the 10 objectives appear in the sidebar on page 222.

All performance indicators are directly tied into the facility's environmental statement and the decalogue, which is signed and fully supported by top management.

As noted in the *IESU* story above, each SGS facility is required to meet all environmental/ecological requirements within the community in which it operates.

ladder concept   SGS-Thomson committed to a "ladder concept" (depicted in *Figure 4.2*) for waste management to help meet the company's policy and decalogue.

Level of Preferability	End of Life Treatment	Economic Impact
1	Prevention - avoid waste	+ Saving at source
2	Reuse - use again for original purpose	+ Replacement reduction
3	Recycle - recover for alternative use	+ Material recovery
3a	Recycle - organic conversion (aerobic or anaerobic)	+ Possible compost or methane
4	Combustion - with recovery of energy	+ Energy recovery
5	Incineration - no recovery of energy	– Consumes energy
6	Landfill	– Land consumption and contamination

Figure 4.2 — Ranking waste management by level of preferability to meet corporate policy and decalogue.

In early 1995, the SGS-Thomson facility in San Diego, California, began working to document its environmental management system and prepare for certification. In our minds, there were two essential elements of the entire certification process:

1) identification of the environmental impacts associated with the company's operation;

2) preparing an environmental manual.

Our approach to each of these elements is described in more detail below. We've tried to share with you why we chose the approaches we did and what some of the advantages and disadvantages with each are. The intent is to provide you with useful guidance as you pursue certification.

SGS-Thomson Microelectronics Environmental Decalogue

In SGS-Thomson we believe firmly that it is mandatory for a TQM driven corporation to be at the forefront of ecological commitment, not only for ethical and social reasons, but also for financial return, and the ability to attract the most responsible and performing people. Our "eco-logical vision" is to become a corporation that closely approaches environmental neutrality. To that end, we will meet all local ecological/environmental requirements of those communities in which we operate, but in addition will strive to:

1.0 Regulations

1.1 Meet the most stringent environmental regulations of any country in which we operate, at all of our locations worldwide.

1.2 Comply with all the ecological improvement targets at least one year in advance of official deadlines at all our locations

2.0 Conservation

2.1 *Energy* - Reduce total energy consumed (by our manufacturing, buildings, etc.) per million dollars sold by at least 5% per year with 25% reduction by end 1999.

2.2 *Water* - Reduce water draw-down (per million dollars sold) from local sources (conduits, streams, aquifers) by $\geq$ 10% per year, through conservation.

2.3 *Trees* - Reduce total paper and paper products consumption by 10% per year.

3.0 Recycling

3.1 *Energy* - Utilize alternative energy sources (renewable/co-generation) to a renewable degree. (At least 3 pilot plants by end 1999.)

3.2 *Water* - For all manufacturing operations, reach a level of 50% recycled water by end 1997 and 90% by end 1999.

3.3 *Trees* - Reach a usage level of 90% recycled paper, where we must use paper, by end 1995 and maintain that level.

3.4 *Chemicals* - Recycle the most used chemicals, e.g. for sulfuric acid, recycle $\geq$ 30% by end 1997 and 80% by end 1999.

4.0 Pollution

4.1 *Air Emissions* - Phase out all Class 1 ODS by end 1996. Contribute where we can to the reduction of greenhouse and acid rain generating gases.

4.2 *Water Emissions* - Meet the standards of the most restrictive community in which we operate, at all sites, for wastewater discharge

4.3 *Landfill* - Achieve 100% treatment of waste at level 1 to level 4, of "Ladder Concept" preferability, with a half-life improvement goal of $\leq$ 1 year.

4.4 *Noise* - Meet a "noise to neighbors" standard at any point on our property perimeter $\leq$ 60 dB(A) for all sites, from end 1995.

5.0 Contamination

Handle, store, and dispose of all potential contaminants and hazardous substances at all sites, in a manner to meet or exceed the strictest environmental safety standards of any community in which we operate.

6.0 Waste

6.1 *Manufacturing* - Recycle 80% of manufacturing byproduct waste (metal, plastics, quartz, glassware, etc.) with a 1/2 life for reduction goal of ≤ 1 year.

6.2 *Packing* - Move to > 80% (by weight) recyclable, reused, or biodegradable packing materials (cartons, tubes, reels, bags, trays, padding) with a half-life improvement goal of ≤ 1 year.

7.0 Products and Technologies

Accelerate our efforts to design products for decreased energy consumption, and for enablement of more energy-efficient applications, to reduce energy consumed during operation by a factor of ≥ 10 by the year 2000.

8.0 Proactivity

8.1 Proactively support local initiatives such as "Clean-up the World," "Adopt A Highway," etc. at each site in which we operate, and encourage our employees to participate. Undertake to lead in establishing such initiatives where none exist.

8.2 Sponsor an annual "environment day" at each site in which we operate, involving the local community.

8.3 Encourage our people to lead/participate in environmental committees, symposia, "watch-dog" groups, etc.

8.4 Include an "environmental awareness" training course in the SGS-Thomson University curriculum and offer it to suppliers and customers.

9.0 Measurement

9.1 Develop measurements for, and means of measuring progress/achieve-ment on, above points 1.0 through 7.0 during 1995, using 1994 as a baseline where applicable, and publish annual results in the "environmental report."

9.2 Develop detailed means and goals to realize these policies, and include them in Policy Deployment by the end of 1995.

9.3 Continue the existing Environmental Audit and Improvement program at all sites.

10.0 Validation

Validate to EMAS standard, or equivalent, 50% of sites by end 1996, and 100% by end 1997. (In the event the validating authority is not available, this schedule can be delayed, but only for this reason).

Environmental Impacts Identification

One of the most important elements of SGS-Thomson's environmental management system is how we manage our environmental impacts associated with our operations. The challenge was to come up with a structured methodology to systematically review our operations and to identify the environmental impacts associated with our San Diego operation.

First we consulted our corporate policy. This policy was specific in terms of the issues that had to be considered during the assessment. These issues include the following:

- management systems;
- water use and wastewater discharge;
- air emissions;
- wastes (including radioactive wastes);
- soil and groundwater;
- energy use;
- management of specific materials;
- chemicals management;
- external noise; and
- emergency response planning.

Our next step was to initiate a systematic assessment of our operations within each of these categories. Accordingly, for each of these issues we ascertained impacts from day-to-day normal operations as well as from out-of-the-ordinary situations. We used an assessment checklist, a sample of which is provided in *Figure 4.3*, to get us started asking the right questions.

use documentation at hand

Fortunately for us, SGS-Thomson had quite a bit of documentation on hand from which we were able to draw valuable information with respect to potential environmental impacts. A health risk assessment, phase I and II site assessments, source reduction studies, U.S. Environmental Protection Agency (EPA) reports and databases, and permit conditions provided us with a forum within which to begin identifying environmental impacts.

In accordance with our corporate policy, we addressed the following issues during our assessment with respect to day-to-day operations:

- natural resources used;
- pollutants released;
- listing of corporate, local, state, and federal regulatory standards or limits for either of the above; and
- description of the environmentally important characteristics of the environmental media from which the natural resource is taken or to which the natural resource or pollutant is discharged.

Assessment Checklist						
Issue	**Operating Conditions**			**Activities**		
	Normal	Abnormal	Emergency	Past	Current	Planning
Air Emissions						
Permit limits						
Fugitive releases						
Breakdowns						
Preventive maintenance						
Acute health impacts						
Chronic health impacts						
Emergency Response Planning						
ER team						
Training requirements						
Equipment availability						
Response plan						
Soil and Groundwater						
USTs						
ASTs						
Containment						
Monitoring						
Known contamination						
Historical land use						
Release hazards analysis						
Noise						
Production processes						
New equipment evaluation						
Fenceline survey						
New Products						
Packaging						
Design						
Disposition						
Transportation						
Recyclability						
Suppliers						
Environmental performance						

Remember, if you are unable to complete the sections in this checklist now, it will be important to do so later, in order to ascertain the true potential for environmental impacts.

Figure 4.3 — Assessment checklist of operations within identified categories. Impacts from day-to-day normal operations and from abnormal activities assessed.

Also, in accordance with our corporate policy, we addressed the following elements during our assessment with respect to abnormal or emergency operations:

- description of the possible situations of abnormal operations, or possible incidents, accidents, or potential emergency situations, associated with the topic of the impacts; and

- an evaluation of the potential environmental impacts of such situations.

Two things made this approach unique for identifying environmental aspects. First, we considered any noncompliant item with respect to a local, state, or federal regulatory requirement as an impact. Second, we decided whether the impact was significant or not.

Defining Significance

During our assessment of environmental impacts, one of the biggest challenges we faced was how to determine which were significant. Once again, SGS-Thomson's corporate policy provided guidance for determining whether an impact was significant or not. In general, we were to give top priority to releases or impacts that exceeded regulatory or corporate standards and those that could adversely impact health, safety, and the environment.

significant
impacts

In San Diego, we defined "significant" as it applies to environmental impacts. Our definition is presented below but — in fair warning — it may not be applicable to your industry or particular situation. Therefore, the term *significant impacts* based upon SGS-Thomson's corporate environmental procedures for conducting an assessment refers to the following:

☑ Continuous releases that are above legal limits or ST corporate standards.

☑ Accidental releases with the potential for very serious impacts (greater than an acute health hazard index of 1 for air toxics or releasing result in multiple injuries or death or losses between $100,000 and $1,000,000 AB 2588 and risk screening guidelines) at the property line or on the community and environment and where there is a high probability (a chance of the accidental release occurring each decade (RMPP) criticality guidelines County of San Diego) of such an accident.

☑ The site is the largest or one of the largest (top five) users of natural resources.

☑ Continuous releases close (within five percent) to legal limits or corporate standards.

☑ Continuous releases that cause concern (complaints registered by the public directly through SGS-Thomson or other regulatory agencies) to the surrounding community.

☑ Continuous wastewater releases that are not treated or abated.

When we completed our assessment, we summarized the findings and placed the results in a table similar to the one in *Figure 4.4*. The results composed our *Register of Environmental Impacts*. We presented the assessment and table in our environmental manual (EM).

This exercise allowed us to gain an in-depth understanding of SGS- Thomson's EMS in the context of relevant environmental impacts and regulations.

Once we compiled the register of environmental impacts, we established goals and objectives to reduce, if not eliminate, the impacts listed. Included in our environmental manual were the goals, objectives, and programs for doing this.

The Environmental Manual

An environmental manual is not required by ISO 14001, so we had to consider our rationale for choosing to prepare one. Following is how we developed and implemented the EM, and recommendations (based upon sweat and tears) that we hope will help your EM preparation effort.

Quite simply, we chose to prepare an environmental manual to ensure certification to both EMAS and ISO 14001 by describing and documenting our company's EMS. At the San Diego facility, SGS- Thomson had numerous proactive, aggressive, and multi-media environmental, health, and safety programs in place. The environmental manual provided a tool that anyone could pick up and use to demystify the intricacies of our environmental program with little or no help.

Environmental Assessment Summary and Register of Environmental Impacts					
Subject of Impact	**Limiting Condition**	**Summary of Impact**	**Type of Activity Causing the Impact**	**Significant**	**Reason for Classification**
Water	Water rights	Potential exceedance of water allocation	Planned/normal	No	Water rights are readily available
	Standard operating procedure	Potential large user of raw material	Current/normal	No	The site is not within the top 5 water users in the area
	Corporate Decalogue	Potential not to meet recycling and reduction targets	Planned/normal	No	Site on track to meet reduction and recycling targets

Figure 4.4 — Example of environmental assessment summary as it appears in a register of environmental effects.

first questions

Let's assume you've decided that you are going to prepare your company's EM. Where do you start? The following list of questions can serve as your prerequisite. You'll want to answer all of them before you begin. Remember, this list isn't all-inclusive. The purpose of these questions is to get you thinking about some of the key aspects of preparing an EM before you start.

☑ What is the overall goal of having an EM?

☑ What requirements or standards should the EM meet?

☑ Who will prepare the EM?

☑ What other departments or personnel will contribute to the EM?

☑ How will the EM be maintained and controlled?

☑ How will the EM be structured?

☑ Will other management systems be integrated into the EM?

☑ Will relevant documentation be incorporated by reference?

SGS-Thomson's EM was structured in a way that closely followed Annex I to Council Regulation (EEC) No. 1836/93 because the facility initially sought certification under the Eco-Management and Audit Scheme (EMAS). An abbreviated version of the table of contents from the SGS-Thomson San Diego facility's EM is presented in *Figure 4.5*.

SGS-Thomson Microelectronics Inc. San Diego, California Environmental Manual Table of Contents	
Sec.	**Description**
1)	Purpose
2)	Reference Documents
3)	Definitions and Roadmap
4)	Site Information
5)	Environmental Strategies, Policy, Objectives, and Program
6)	Environmental Management Review
7)	Responsibility, Authority, and Management Representative
8)	Personnel Training
9)	Communication Program
10)	Environmental Review
11)	Operational Controls
12)	Environmental Management Records
13)	Environmental Audit
	Figures
	Tables

Figure 4.5 — SGS-Thomson environmental manual contents.

first steps   We started, therefore, with an outline for the EM that was consistent with the EEC 1836/93. Once we identified our EM objectives, as described above, identifying the major sections and general content was much simpler.

Before we began writing, some additional "first steps" were:

• consolidating and reviewing existing documentation relevant to environmental issues management;

• determining the degree of integration with other company programs such as quality assurance;

• obtaining top management support (this included our site manager, and departmental heads);

• determining whether the manual would serve as a compliance tool. We chose not to have the manual address specific compliance-related issues.

To keep it consistent with SGS-Thomson's document control formatting procedure, we then ascertained the format of our EM. Fortunately, we were able to focus our attention on

EM roadmap

content. Later, we turned over a disk for formatting. The formatting, however, can take significant and laborious effort.

Because the facility was seeking certification under both EMAS and ISO 14001 and, in the near future, to BS 7750 we prepared a roadmap for inclusion in the beginning of the EM. This roadmap served to cross-reference EM sections to the corresponding section of EMAS, ISO 14001, and BS 7750. The roadmap proved to be a useful tool during our verifier assessment. It saved time searching for relevant sections upon questioning. *Figure 4.6* is an example of what our roadmap looked like.

Environmental Manual EMAS and ISO 14001 Roadmap			
Environmental Topic	**Manual Reference**	**ISO 14001 Reference**	**EMAS Reference**
			Annex 1
Environmental Policy	5.2, 5.4, 5.17	4.1	A1, 2, 3,; C; D
Environmental Objectives	5.3, 5.4.1, 5.17.1	4.2.3	A4
Environmental Program	5.3, 5.4.2, 5.17.2	4.2.4	A5
Environmental Review	10	4.4.4	C
Management Review	6	4.5, A4.5	B1
Responsibility and Authority	7.1, 7.2	4.3.1	B2
Management Representative	7.3	4.3.1	B2
Personnel, Communications and Training	8	4.3.2	B2

Figure 4.6 — Cross-referencing standards and environmental manual sections for multi-purpose uses.

purpose section

Your manual should start out with a "purpose" section. This is key because it sets the stage for the rest of the EM contents. Our manual stated specifically that its purpose was to:

- describe the company's EMS;

- serve as a reference for internal and external audits; and

- provide a record of company practices for ensuring consistency and continuous improvement over time with respect to the site's environmental aspects.

The meat of our EM is in the "Environmental Strategies, Policy, Objectives, and Program"

EM is how and what

section. The emphasis here — actually that of your whole manual —should be on the "how" as well as the "what." You not only present your policy and objectives, but you must also have a program that will describe how you will comply with those objectives and policy.

How to Use Your Environmental Manual

stakeholdert

One of the most important aspects of implementing the EM is training stakeholders. ▢ (See Part 2, Chapter 3 for more information on stakeholder perspectives.) The training should include:

- an introduction to the manual;
- its purpose;
- how it should be used; and
- how it is routinely revised and updated.

SGS-Thomson held a one-hour training class for key company representatives during an operations review meeting. The training included the following issues:

☑ introduction to international environmental standards including the company's status with respect to certification (5 min.);

☑ introduction to the EM —this included an overview of the table of contents, how it is structured, its purpose, and who is responsible for its reviews (10 min.);

☑ brief presentation on the corporation's *Environmental Decalogue* and the facility's environmental, health, safety, and security (HSSE) policy and programs (15 min.);

☑ discussion of the facility's environmental aspects and the programs in place to address those significant impacts (15 min.);

☑ identification of business activities that impact HSSE issues (10 min.); and

☑ question and answer session (5 min.).

Tips From Lessons Learned

Don't just adopt, but adapt when developing and implementing your EM. Adapt, but just don't adopt what may have worked for someone else.

Control it. Ensure that the EM becomes a controlled document. This is especially true if your environmental manual combines documentation of other management systems within the facility.

Get multiple authors. Rather than have one individual or department write the manual, consider having multiple departments or disciplines within the company contribute to the manual. The reason for this is to increase stakeholder buy into and accountability for the implementation of the EM.

Integrate. If you are an ISO 9000-certified company, or are considering certification under one of the quality standards, consider integrating your EM with your existing, or soon to be, *Quality Assurance Manual*.

Cross-reference. Make sure that you not only have all of the documents listed in the references section of your EM but that the references are accurate. In addition, you'll want to take the time to review the references to ensure they are adequately referenced and that the content does not conflict with the content of the EM. (Well, you may not want to, but you should.) Trace references from document to document as far back as you can to ensure consistency.

Be prepared. Prior to your third-party audit for certification, make sure that personnel and resources will be available during the audit process. Consider reserving a conference room for the duration of the audit. If practical, have all of your environmental documentation available in one place for review — the conference room would make it easiest. Have all of your eggs in one basket before you present a case to management for pursuing ISO 14000 certification.

For more information, contact U.S. corporate communications department, SGS - Thomson, 55 Old Bedford Rd., Lincoln, MA. 01773.

CHAPTER 4
Westcoast Energy Case Study — On Its Own

Adapted from International Environmental Systems Update (IESU), March 1996

4.4.1 Utility Opts for Corporate EMS vs. ISO 14001

Westcoast Energy, Inc. operates in the North American natural gas industry. Its businesses include gas gathering and processing facilities, transmission pipelines, distribution systems, power generation, gas services, and international energy ventures. It has approximately 6000 employees. Westcoast's Pipeline and Field Services Divisions gather, process, and transport gas to markets within B.C., other parts of western Canada, and the United States Pacific Northwest. The system consists of more than 3400 miles of pipelines and eight processing plants, four of which include sulfur recovery facilities. Its corporate headquarters are in Vancouver, British Colombia. Deborah Bisson, attorney and senior advisor, environmental legislation and risk assessment with Westcoast Energy, developed an M.B.A. thesis on her company's environmental management system and its relationship to ISO 14001.

"Westcoast Energy has a strong commitment to environmental management and is heavily regulated as a utility. Our current environmental management system has already satisfied many of the requirements of the emerging ISO 14000 standards," she says.

4.4.2 EMS Compared with ISO 14001

Since 1991, Westcoast has taken several steps to improve its EMS, many of which bring it in line with the requirements of ISO 14001, Bisson states. The first step involved revamping the environmental policy statement, making it less compliance-oriented and more proactive, focusing on pollution prevention, waste minimization, resource conservation, and sustainable development.

The company also strengthened its policies and procedures, developing a manual that can be used as an auditing tool. It had strong senior management support but wanted to increase environmental awareness at the field level, so the company added environmental coordinators/technicians at all the major sites. The company has a system of performance and critical success indicators that it can act upon as part of the environmental management program and which is incorporated into a success sharing program.

A recently developed environmental management information system continues to expand and could possibly be modified to satisfy ISO document control requirements. And finally, a formal procedure for identifying training needs is underway as is a program to upgrade environmental training.

However, there are several areas of the EMS which would require modification or upgrading if Westcoast were to pursue ISO 14001 registration. For example, according to the standard, a company needs a formal procedure for identifying and documenting environmental aspects. Bisson points out that Westcoast has a system to identify environmental aspects, but probably not in the exact way required by ISO 14001.

According to Bisson, "We've been conducting internal audits and risk assessments of our activities for five years or more. We inherently know what our environmental aspects and impacts are. We've had an environmental department here for 18 years. Therefore, the ISO 14001 environmental aspects review would not be expected to turn up anything new."

Other upgrades which would be required for ISO 14001 certification include:

1) more concerted efforts to research, obtain, and document all applicable environmental industry standards; and

2) better document control.

4.4.3 Level of Certification

Should Westcoast one day decide to pursue certification, Bisson questions the level at which it should be implemented. Because Westcoast's processing plants, pipelines, and compressor stations are organized in a regionalized management structure, It will be difficult to decide the hierarchical level at which the guidelines are applied. These levels might include plant, regional, or corporate.

"Maybe it will be necessary to implement ISO 14001 at three levels, and to have all three interrelated," she suggests. "It might be possible, for instance, to register each plant and each geographical area of pipeline, in addition to the whole corporate entity."

4.4.4 Skepticism About Standard

Bisson is not yet convinced that ISO 14001 is a proposition that adds value to the company. However, Westcoast's top management is deeply committed to good environmental management. For example, she says, on one occasion the president and vice president went out in the field to talk with employees and introduce the environmental policy statement in each facility to increase environmental awareness.

While Bisson says it was difficult to measure the exact effect of the visit on Westcoast employees, when questioned during environmental audits, Westcoast employees can typically identify the location of the policy and tell something about what it contains.

Westcoast's decision not to seek ISO 14001 certification was due in large part to the complex structure and nature of the business. Westcoast does not own the gas. Instead, it gathers it for customers who are the producers, the oil and gas companies who bring it out of the ground, she says.

"We process the gas into marketable quality and transmit it for the customers," she explains. "The company's transmission lines bring gas from the field to processing plants and on to markets in British Columbia, other parts of western Canada, and across the border to the United States."

In turn, Westcoast customers sell gas directly industrial facilities or to local distribution companies (LDCs) that deliver gas to homes.

"Currently, there does not appear to be a trend in the Canadian Gas Industry towards ISO 14001 registration," Bisson explains. "The market is still differentiating primarily on the basis of price."

4.4.5 Pollution Prevention

"We are working with the British Columbia Ministry of Environment, Lands, and Parks along with four other companies in a pollution prevention demonstration project at the Fort Nelson Gas Plant," Bisson explains.

The objective of the joint collaboration is to develop a pollution prevention plan and incorporate it into the regulatory regime. This was our policy statement and commitments of the program include:

- provide greater community involvement;
- reduce the use of polluting substances;
- demonstrate more cost-effective approaches to environmental management;
- demonstrate a more flexible and effective alternative to the conventional permitting process.

In addition, the company uses waste minimization and toxic reduction measures, including a "green" purchasing program, to identify toxic components of products purchased and to target those products as candidates for alternatives. Items targeted include oil-based paints, process water treatment chemicals, steel surface coatings, and products containing ozone-depleting substances.

EMS As Enhanced Pollution Prevention

Pollution prevention is a really "trendy" term now, Bisson comments. She says Westcoast's concept of pollution prevention is a bit broader than just looking at substances.

"What we are actually doing at the Fort Nelson Gas Plant is a really good environmental management plan," she explains. "We may also look at issues that go beyond pollution prevention, such as an on-site drainage ditching program, which has nothing to do with emissions or toxic substances."

The Waste Management Act, British Columbia's principal environmental legislation, focuses on discharges, so that is what the government has to focus on, she says.

"We may want to do things at the site that are good environmental management and have more positive impact in terms of preventing environmental damage." However, the focus of the Waste Management Act diverts resources away from these initiatives toward ever increasing discharge controls that often have limited environmental benefits in proportion to their costs. Bisson explains, "With the pollution prevention pilot project, we're looking for a system that allows us to work with the government to prioritize opportunities for improvement and plan the allocation of resources accordingly.

4.4.6 Training Programs

To address the need to keep employees abreast of environmental issues, Westcoast has set up a training program development team. Members of the team are mostly environmental coordinators from the field and are conducting a needs analysis.

Bruce Kosugi, an environmental coordinator for the Fort Nelson Gas Plant for Westcoast Energy, explains that the plant management posts a monthly bulletin around the plant explaining sections of the company environmental policy, such as air and water quality issues and waste management.

Articles focus on broad issues as well, such as greenhouse climate changes, and how this impacts the gas industry, the operation of the plant, and what Westcoast is doing about it.

Kosugi explains: "We talk about how we operate our plant from a fuel efficiency point of view or explain our concerns about a product we are dealing with, then outline the strategy from the company itself."

Each plant has an occupational health, safety, and environment committee that has typically focused on health and safety issues. These committees are beginning to focus on environmental issues as well.

Some of the environmental awareness classes have included multiple choice tests at the end of the class to see if participants grasp significant concepts of the session, he says.

This feedback gives the instructor an idea of the level of understanding and helps employees become more focused. In addition to teaching about specific topics, the course explains who to contact, for instance, in the case of a spill.

"As employees increase their knowledge about what Westcoast does to protect the environment, their sense of ownership increases," he notes.

For more information, contact Westcoast Energy Inc., 1333 West Georgia Street, Vancouver, BC, V6E 3K9, Canada.

CHAPTER 5
Ontario Hydro Case Study — ISO 14001-Plus

by CEEM Information Services

Ontario Hydro, which is made up of 69 hydroelectric stations, three major nuclear sites with 12 stations, and five large fossil fuel facilities, is very active in environmental management issues in Canada.

Maurice Strong, former chair of Ontario Hydro, an international leader in sustainable development, was responsible for developing Ontario Hydro's environmental management system. Strong was secretary general of the United Nations Conference on Environment and Development (UNCED) — the Earth Summit — in Rio de Janeiro in 1992 and is an advisor to the World Bank.

Don Fraser, manager of auditing, monitoring, and reporting, and Phil Stoesser, senior advisor on the environment for Ontario Hydro, have done extensive research on environmental management systems. They evaluated BS 7750 along with similar EMS models from France, Ireland, the Canadian Standards Association —10 to 12 models in all. In 1994, they created and instituted an environmental management system with five components, not unlike the emergent ISO 14001. Following is a discussion of the company's EMS and the differences between it and ISO 14001. Ontario Hydro has augmented ISO 14001 in several areas.

Ontario Hydro is aligning its environmental management system with ISO 14001 requirements, although it has chosen to change some of the terminology to fit preestablished programs. According to Stoesser, Ontario Hydro will adopt ISO 14001 formally as a minimum standard for environmental management systems after it officially becomes an international standard in mid-1996.

4.5.1 EMS Contents

Ontario Hydro's EMS contains the following sections, many of which parallel the language of ISO 14001. Some sections and terms, however, are specifically germane to Ontario Hydro's operations and appear below.

Leadership and Commitment

- Communication — this section parallels **ISO 14001 Section 4.3.3.**

Planning — Parallels ISO 14001 Section 4.2

- Accountabilities — this term is germane to Ontario Hydro's EMS. Information parallels this section under implementation in **ISO 14001 Section 4.3.1** Structure and Responsibility;

- Issues — germane to Ontario Hydro's EMS. Information parallels this section in **ISO 14001 Section 4.2.1**, which uses the term "environmental aspects;"

- Legislative requirements —germane to Ontario Hydro's EMS. Information parallels this section in **ISO 14001 Section 4.2.2** Legal and Other Requirements;

- Risk assessment — germane to Ontario Hydro's EMS and refers to prioritizing issues. ISO 14001 does *not* specifically mention "risk assessment."

- Objectives and targets — This section parallels **ISO 14001 Section 4.2.3** and sets performance indicators to drive environmental improvements.

- Environmental program/action plans — germane to Ontario Hydro's EMS. When it identifies an issue, Ontario Hydro puts in place an action plan ,complete with its own objectives and targets, to ensure continual environmental performance improvement;

Implementation — Parallels ISO 14001 Section 4.3 Implementation and Operation

- Business plan decisionmaking and resources — germane to Ontario Hydro's EMS. ISO 14001 does *not* address this issue specifically. In Ontario Hydro's EMS, this section discusses where money gets allocated;

- Education and training — germane to Ontario Hydro's EMS and the emphasis is on the need for education in order to create a (corporate) cultural change. This parallels **ISO 14001 Section 4.3.2** Training, Awareness, and Competence;

- Operational procedures — parallels **ISO 14001 Section 4.3.6** Operational Control;

- Emergency preparedness and response — parallels **ISO 14001 Section 4.3.7** Emergency Preparedness and Response;

- EMS documentation — parallels **ISO 14001 Section 4.3.5** Document Control.

Assessment — Parallels ISO 14001 Section 4.4 Checking and Corrective Action;

- Monitoring/self assessment — germane to Ontario Hydro's EMS. Information parallels this section in **ISO 14001 Section 4.4.1** Monitoring and Measurement;

- Records/information management — germane to Ontario Hydro's EMS. Additional information appears in **ISO 14001 Section 4.4.3**;

- Audits — parallels **ISO 14001 Section 4.4.4** Environmental Management System Audit;

- Nonconformance and corrective/preventive action — parallels **ISO 14001 Section 4.4.2**;

- Reporting — this is a separate sub-element in Ontario Hydro's EMS. Addressed in **ISO 14001 Section 4.3.3**, Communication;

- Rewards and recognition — germane to Ontario Hydro's EMS and are not specifically addressed in ISO 14001;

- Management review — parallels **ISO 14001 Section 4.5**.

4.5.2 Leadership and Commitment

Until the environmental management system was instituted at Ontario Hydro, it had historically been difficult to get full commitment to environmental issues. To close this gap, leadership and commitment are addressed up front as the number one component and an integral part of the entire process to functionalize and implement leadership. Don Fraser comments: "If the EMS is promoted and initiated from the bottom up, it will not succeed. It requires an ongoing commitment and leadership from the top."

4.5.3 Communication

Fraser and Stoesser say they have built upon and refined the environmental management systems developed by other organizations to their advantage. In working with their management model and how to make this functional, they say, communication is key and must be constantly stressed, not buried under implementation and operations as it is in ISO 14001. Communication at all levels, at all times, and about everything contributes in large measure to the success of their EMS. It is a large part of making environmental management happen all up and down the line.

4.5.4 Planning

Accountability

They have also brought accountability to planning instead of grouping it under implementation as it appears in the ISO. "If you've got a comprehensive management system, you've effectively got everybody identified and what their roles and responsibilities are from top to bottom in the company," Fraser explains. He wants to address this at the planning stage, not wait until implementation to work out individual responsibilities.

"Issues" vs. "Aspects"

"We also use issues instead of aspects, which allows us to address the management of issues, such as PCBs, CO_2s, electromagnetic fields, and ozone-depleting substances. Issues terminology is an important language distinction for us."

Risk Assessment

Risk assessment is not addressed in the ISO 14000 model. "We do a risk assessment of our environmental issues and prioritize them in terms of how severe their impact is on the environment. We then set objectives and targets at the issues level instead of at the policy level. We have a series of corporate performance measures to drive improvements, but not all issues can be addressed at once, given economic constraints. By prioritizing the issues, we can schedule how to deal with them in a logical sequence."

Environmental Programs/Action Plans

Phil Stoesser speaks of environmental programs and action plans: "When we have an issue that needs to be dealt with, we put an action plan into place. Subsequently, we have enhanced the ISO terminology to meet this need."

4.5.5 Implementation

"In implementation," Stoesser continues, "we have made a few changes to the sub-element which ISO refers to as Structure and Responsibility. We have created a new sub-element, Business Plan Decision-making and Resources, because that is where the money gets allocated for the environmental programs that we are proposing. In other words, programs [that] get funding get done. Although it is a planning function, it happens when you begin implementing program. The ISO EMS makes no mention of a business plan decision-making process, so we put it in with the resourcing aspect of implementation."

4.5.6 Education

"We also added an education section under the training function," Stoesser explains, "because we feel very strongly that you don't have to just train your staff, you have to educate them to know what it means to be an environmental or sustainable leader. ISO does not mention education, but we put it in because we think it's important."

Fraser points out that communication is stressed again in the emergency preparedness and response section, in that the occurrence of spills indicates a deficiency in the system that needs to be communicated to everyone in the corporation. The procedure is not effective if employees on the shop floor do not know it exists.

4.5.7 Assessment

Assessment in the Ontario Hydro document replaces checking and corrective action in the ISO document. "We didn't like that," Stoesser explains. "We've been doing assessments for years, so the term assessment was more appropriate to our business. We've added self-assessments to go with monitoring. We feel fairly strongly that you have to assess yourself constantly on environmental matters. This is where we address continuous improvement and where we are monitoring ourselves to see how we are doing."

Monitoring and Measurement

In **ISO 14001 Section 4.4.1** on monitoring and measurement, Fraser comments, the focus is on calibration and maintenance of equipment. "This is very technical. This is not what we are talking about here necessarily. We're talking about monitoring in a broader sense, too, where we're talking about establishing a set of performance indicators that we want to look at, such as fuel productivity or spills management, or any one of a number of issues like pollution prevention. Some issues get translated into corporate performance measures.

"There are 14 corporate performance measures that cover all kinds of information management issues across the corporation," Fraser continues. "These are very high profile and are part of the contract between our president and our board of directors. Some of these also get used as a part of our senior executives' performance achievement plan. In other words, if you don't satisfy the target, you don't get your bonus. In the context of monitoring and measuring, we have not only done low level technical evaluations, we have elevated these right up through the company to address and reflect on the individual's performance and collectively on the business units and the corporation's performance. I'm not sure whether this view is taken with the ISO document. We view monitoring and measuring issues differently."

Environmental Audits

Ontario Hydro takes a broader approach to the issue of review, he notes. "It focuses on three levels of audits. Compliance audits are conducted to meet regulatory requirements. EMS audits are used to see if all of the pieces of the system are working. A third kind is an environmental audit of a specific issue, such as a spill. In this last case, we'd be auditing for the president to see how the issue of spills is being managed in the company, rather than looking at the whole range of environmental management.

Reporting

"We have also put reporting under assessments because we view it as performance reporting not just operational reporting," Fraser explains. "Operational reporting can be included, but what we are really looking at is how we performed against a series of objectives. We also do internal and external reporting. In fact, we send out about 5,000 copies of a published report globally, talking about our performance. This is not a specific ISO requirement."

Rewards and Recognitions

"We have also added rewards and recognitions. We feel the need to use this to recognize individuals and business units and collectives of people who have done things in a particularly meritorious way. The awards are widely communicated throughout the company. We use this to try to enhance our environmental performance and to get buy-in from the employees."

Of a sense of employee involvement and ownership, Fraser says, "I think it's coming. A lot of what we do in terms of recognizing rewarding people is through the concept of sustainability, not just environmental conformance. However, the concept of sustainability is hard to convey through 20,000 employees, and is hard to understand in a practical sense."

"It takes time." Stoesser agrees. "To communicate this to all the staff throughout the province is quite a mammoth job. We are building an understanding of the concepts of sustainability and the EMS throughout the corporation. It's a big job."

For more information contact Ontario Hydro, 700 University Avenue, Toronto, Ontario, Canada M5G1X6.

CHAPTER 6
SSI Technologies Case Study — ISO/QS 9000 Integration

Adapted from Integrated Management Systems Update (IMSU), May 1996

SSI Technologies, which controls 30 percent of the anti-lock brake sensor market in North America, has committed to pursuing ISO 14001 certification and is integrating it with its occupational health and safety system via ISO/QS-9000, the auto industry's quality management system. The following case study shows how SSI has done this.

The competitive nature of the automotive industry is compelling the anti-lock brake division of SSI Technologies Inc. to implement ISO 14001 with an eye toward certification in 1998 or 1999. In early 1996, SSI also was aggressively integrating ISO 14001 with its health and safety program via ISO/QS-9000.

Many of SSI's customers are direct suppliers to General Motors, Ford, and Chrysler — the U.S.'s Big Three auto manufacturers. SSI also supplies indirectly to KIA, a South Korean corporation that supplies to Hyundai. SSI is working to gain several other contracts in Asia and Europe.

SSI, headquartered in Janesville, Wisconsin, controls about 30 percent of the U.S. anti-lock brake sensor market in North America with approximate annual sales, in 1996, of $78 million, according to Douglas Wall, SSI's corporate environmental manager. The company is the largest independent supplier of ABS wheel-speed sensors in the world, having shipped more than 22 million sensors since 1990 to various markets. In addition, SSI is a world leader in developing future automotive sensor technology.

With about 1,200 employees, SSI considers itself a medium-sized company facing the possibility of certification to ISO 14001 before the turn of the century to remain on the cutting edge, Wall reports.

OHS integration   He says as the company integrates ISO 14001 with its health and safety program, it is also preparing its quality system for certification using the ISO 9000 and QS-9000 quality system requirements. When the ISO quality standards were published, he relates, the automotive industry "got on board," which meant that suppliers like SSI were required to conform. Wall says it is clear to him that the Big Three are likely to support ISO 14001 as well, perhaps by developing a "QS-14001" standard.

Wall explains that the company cannot commit to an ISO 14001 certification until the market benefits are clear. He says recent quotes from certification bodies placed initial certification for his company at $50 to $70 thousand with an estimated cost of $30 thousand every year to keep the certification active.

"SSI has an all-encompassing scope, combining health and safety with environment, whereas others may have a very narrow scope strictly to obtain certification," Wall explains. "This drives the cost of registration through the roof."

EHSMS manual   Wall says that SSI now has a 22-page EHSMS manual, which includes 11 pages of definitions. The actual environment, health, and safety (EHS) programs are much longer, but the 22-page manual describes the vision and operational organization of the system in addition to outlining how environmental impacts are evaluated and objectives and targets are initiated to reduce the effects of these negative impacts — always providing continuous improvement in a common-sense format.

"If the requirements had come down from senior management to get the division ready immediately for ISO 14001 certification, we would never have implemented health and safety," Wall relates. "Instead, we would have implemented a very minimal program with a narrow scope that touched on just a few objectives and targets. As long as all the key elements were in place, SSI would receive certification."

Benefits vs. Cost

Wall says that, by the year 2000, the additional certification of ISO 14001 with QS-9000 registration will provide adequate benefits that will more than outweigh the costs in the automotive industry. However, he stresses that, at this time, justification for ISO 14001 certification cannot be made. He says that the following would be among the driving forces for seeking third-party registration:

- a major customer requests certification;
- a non-domestic facility is involved in an acquisition;

- certification is proven to provide a marketing advantage that sets SSI apart from competitors; or
- there is an opportunity to combine ISO 9000 and ISO 14001 certification in a single audit.

certification   Wall notes that the possibility that major suppliers such as International Telephone, Telegraph, and Automotive (ITTA) or Timken will require ISO 14001 certification may not be far off because of the speed with which ISO 14001 acceptance is progressing. He notes that, at this point, contract negotiations remain focused on the traditional parameters — cost, quality, and delivery.

SSI, using the ABS division as a model, began program development in mid-1995 and began implementing ISO 14001 beginning in 1996, Wall says. SSI also will encourage its recycling and disposal vendors to become certified to ISO 14001 when the standard is published in mid to late 1996, Wall says. This would eliminate the need for second party audits, thus providing cost-reduction benefits for SSI in the search for "safe" disposal and recycling alternatives.

But third-party certification will be market-driven. An appropriate analogy, Wall says, might be to driving a car: "I may be able to drive a car better and safer than anyone else on the road, but may not possess a license. Why should I get a license when I can drive proficiently? But on the other hand, if a license is required by law, then I would obtain one as a necessity to drive."

He says that if or when the Big Three require ISO 14001 officially, SSI will be prepared and will have an effective program ready for third-party certification immediately.

Transitioning

In 1992, SSI started the transition from a reactive company to one with proactive goals and objectives, Wall relates. He admits this transition did not come easily. SSI focused mainly on compliance-type issues and acquired a division in 1992 that required major environmental remediation.

SSI assumed that filing all proper permits and reports for compliance/regulatory issues would guarantee that, at a minimum, the company would pass all Environmental Protection Agency (EPA) and Occupational Safety and Health Administration (OSHA) inspections.

"At that time, SSI was concentrating on a 'drain-to-stack' philosophy," Wall says. "SSI is using the ISO 14001 standard as a tool to evolve to a new understanding of environmental and health and safety aspects [and their] effects on the 'entire' ecosystem, with a 'sincere' concern for the health and safety of all SSI employees."

Proactive Thinking — and Results

When comparing its current EMS system to elements contained in ISO 14001, Wall says the makeup is similar. SSI has an environmental policy in place that uses life-cycle assessment and significant effect evaluation techniques to identify and govern aspects in determining the company's objectives and targets. Wall admits that, previously, SSI had objectives and targets in place but they were assigned reactively and were not well communicated to employees of the company.

savings   Wall explains that SSI is expected to generate nearly $600,000 in savings and revenue in 1996 related to waste minimization and pollution prevention by designing its system with clear and concise objectives and targets that each employee understands.

communication   "An EMS establishes an excellent platform to communicate preparedness plans to all SSI employees," he says. "In addition, it creates a two-way dialogue to enhance communication with:

- production personnel and senior management;

- the community and regulators; and

- lenders and insurers."

He says lenders of the 1990s are very aware of environmental issues and are requiring detailed disclosures of a company's environmental standing prior to approving any type of financial assistance.

objectives and targets   SSI set some aggressive environmental objectives and targets for 1996 and had full management support to achieve all projects submitted under ISO 14001. The following were some objectives and targets SSI worked on in 1995 and others the company is initiating for 1996 and 1997.

1) Objective: Eliminate the landfill disposal of plastic byproducts from manufacturing.

> Target: To establish a plastics regrinding program for resale and/or reuse.

> Completion: Initiated in December 1995; currently operational.

2) Objective: Reduce water usage.

> Target: To establish a closed-loop cooling water recycling system.

> Completion: 1996/1997 capital plan — in progress.

3) Objective: Eliminate landfill disposal of industrial containers.

> Target: Install an aerosol depressurizing unit.

> Target: Install an industrial container processing unit.

> Completion: Initiated in June 1995; currently operational.

"If I can identify a significant effect of a life-cycle assessment, generate an objective and target for it, and show a reasonable payback," Wall says, "upper management will buy in."

Wall says the trick is to get the big moneysavers in first and get them pushed through. Then demonstrate to management "off the bat" what you can generate with financial support and what types of accomplishments can be achieved.

Though the documentation was costly — and probably impossible without a company-wide computer network — SSI has begun to save money in the ISO 14001 objectives and targets area. In addition to grinding up waste products that normally would go to the landfill, SSI has initiated a full-cycle program to return and reuse empty "dunnage," or foldable, plastic boxes and return empty reels to suppliers for reuse.

"There's another job for a truck driver: Someone is needed to transport reusable containers back to the source," Wall relates. "This creates a complete closed loop, or 'use-and-reuse' approach. Cradle-to-grave has evolved to 'cradle to cradle.'"

4.6.1 EHS Integration — First Steps

When discussing the proper place to integrate health and safety into the management system, Wall first considered using QS-9000, but decided that was unrealistic. Where QS-9000 looks for a quality standard, health and safety and environmental issues are more closely tied by regulation. This relationship between environment and health and safety convinced Wall that ISO 14001 would be a better vehicle to integrate these things into every aspect of the company's operation.

"EPA and OSHA regulations overlap in certain areas," he explains. "One example is the 'hazcom' or workers' 'right to know' act and its relationship to EPA's Superfund initiative that requires that all toxic releases exceeding the threshold be reported to the public by EPA."

He says it would not be practical for a company to separate training that employees would receive on material safety data sheets from community right-to-know regulations.

"At SSI, employee health and safety is a very large aspect in the significant effects evaluation process," Wall says.

"Our employees are constantly evaluated on their understanding of environmental, health, and safety issues to ensure individual understanding."

Educating all line employees on environmental impacts associated with their particular tasks has not been difficult, mainly because of the stringent training requirements SSI is required to maintain through QS-9000.

joint training   Joint training is helping. "Once you complete the staggering task of implementing ISO/QS-9000, the rest is easy," Wall says. Most of the training was already in place. Integrating the ISO 14001 system was a cake walk. The ISO/QS-9000 was the conveyance toward that purpose."

Training Challenges

SSI has an entire training section as part of its human resources department, responsible for training employees on different aspects of the job. For example, employees receive comprehensive technical training on soldering techniques. This includes all health and safety as well as environmental issues pertaining to lead.

SSI conducts extensive training that meshes with requirements in ISO 14001, and requires each line employee be trained in the following programs:

- bloodborne pathogens;
- emergency preparedness;
- ergonomics;
- fire prevention;
- lockout/tagout procedures;

- machinery and machine guarding;
- personal protective equipment; and
- workers' right-to-know guidelines.

"Reference copies of all these programs are found at each production line, and employees are encouraged to question any element of these programs that is not clear," Wall says.

middle managers At the start of implementation, Wall says, SSI's challenge lay in training its supervisors and foremen of the production lines on EMS, health, and safety impacts. Both line employees and senior management had a clear understanding of the environmental, health, and safety aspects of the organization, but the same did not appear to be the case with the middle managers.

"This lack of knowledge and understanding was due to the strain felt by supervisors who were responsible for every aspect of quality and production. The strict quality standards associated with manufacturing safety-related components for automobiles, complicated by fierce competition in the automobile industry to meet the ever-fluctuating customer production requirements, was a challenge for supervisors. It was difficult for them to demonstrate the same zeal for EHS issues as they had for quality and production," Wall explains.

kaizen With the addition of production line automation and supervising methods such as "kaizen," production and quality efficiencies were improved, and supervisors were able to develop the skills needed to include EHS issues in their day-to-day operations. The philosophy of "kaizen" best describes a continuous improvement activity — "kai" is Japanese for change; "zen" means to "go with the flow," or conform.

SSI decided that, where EHS training issues were concerned, it would be more logical to train the production line supervisors to provide this training to their production line personnel. This, in itself, has reduced the training gap significantly, Wall says.

Integration Issue: Identifying Aspects

With the ISO 14001-based management system in place, "tracking and traceability of significant environmental aspects" is much easier, Wall says.

With the system in place and with use of ISO verbiage, it makes the job easier for the health and safety specialist, Mark Paulos.

"It gives me more weight to get nonconformance fixed," says Paulos, "and it provides for better tracking. You have a system to provide corrective action. And when the company grows, the program can grow."

example: lead SSI uses lead solder to manufacture parts, says Wall. Since lead can be hazardous, it puts people at risk. SSI determines how significant an aspect lead is by using a scale of 1 to 5 to determine the frequency and severity of its use. For example, if the frequency of lead use is a high 5, its severity (since it can be hazardous to the people using it) would also be a 5. By comparison, cardboard boxes may have a frequency of 5 but a severity of only 1. "You can identify your significant aspects by using this rating system," Wall says.

SSI used a cross-section of employees to help it identify its environmental aspects, says Wall.

This included getting input to the process from staff in the maintenance department, production lines, accounting, and the secretarial pool.

Wall organized four-person teams and challenged them to identify aspects related to the facility, the community, the state, and the world. He divided the facility into function-based categories: raw material transportation, process, disposal, and process waste recycling. Then, with employee feedback, he listed the following "media" as areas for possible aspect identification: energy, resources, air, water, soil, noise, human beings, climate, and ecology.

The human factor in determining aspects must not be overlooked. "Human beings are significant environmental aspects," Wall says. "They are exposed to hazardous materials; they are using them to manufacture the products. Humans and equipment are manufacturing entities."

Joint Audit Preparation

Like many companies, SSI expects that quality system and EMS audits will be combined in the future. Wall is preparing by integrating ISO 14001 requirements into the SSI quality system — QS-9000. By doing this, there will be formal but separate:

- management reviews;
- corrective and preventive action;
- training;
- monitoring of effectiveness; and
- continuous improvement.

consistent language, separate systems
"We will use the same conveyance tools and personnel to conduct training and ensure understanding," Wall explains. "For example, we will have consistent verbiage between our quality system and our environmental management system by using the terms 'corrective action' and 'nonconformity' instead of 'remediation' and 'violation.'"

Wall says this consistent verbiage gears employees toward total quality and away from traditional terms associated with regulatory issues.

SSI chose to design separate systems based on the current versions of ISO 9001, QS-9000, and ISO 14001. Wall says each standard is organized differently and therefore each currently requires a separate audit; for example, Section 4.3 of QS-9001 does not match Section 4.3 of ISO 14001.

However, that does not mean that quality people can't participate in environmental issues and vice versa, he says.

"Our quality manager, David Stumps, supervises QS-9001 implementation along with an SSI quality review committee, and we have a similar committee for environmental issues," Wall notes. "Each team will conduct internal audits on the other team's department to ensure that neither team audits its own programs and systems," he says.

SSI eventually would like to have one system, Wall says. "Business is business. It is based on cost, quality, and delivery. ISO/QS-9000 is so closely related to that reality that it applies to anything you want to sell.

"Another reality is that pollution is waste, waste is inefficiency, and inefficiency is expensive. If you can eliminate the purchase and disposal costs of a certain chemical, you create a better environment, lower operational costs, reduce company liability, and establish a safer work environment for your employees."

For more information contact SSI Technologies Inc., P.O. Box 5011, Janesville, WI 5347-5011.

CHAPTER 7
PPG Industries Case Study — Integration

Adapted from Integrated Management Systems Update (IMSU), April 1996

PPG Industries Inc., a multinational U.S.-based company with manufacturing and process facilities for chemicals, coatings and resins, glass, and fiberglass, is tailoring its company management system to include a variety of industry and international requirements. Paul King, director of environment, health, and safety stewardship for PPG, explained the program.

Using document control and verification processes adapted from ISO 9000 quality management systems, PPG developed and continues to refine its overall management system. The system integrates elements from ISO 14000 environmental management system (EMS) standards, health and safety requirements, the British national EMS standard BS 7750, the Chemical Manufacturers Association's Responsible Care® Program, and the European Union's Eco-Management and Audit-Scheme regulation into an overall management program for the four divisions of the company.

using 30 years of systems

King says the company is convinced that much value lies in the concept of integration and using existing systems that have been in place for almost 30 years to satisfy future industry and regulatory mandates. He explains that officials are integrating elements of ISO 9000 quality management system standards. The company policy reinforces this commitment by combining environment, health, and safety into one policy that is careful not to emphasize one concern over the others.

"We learned years ago that we couldn't continue to roll out new programs with a different emphasis every time a new requirement came down the pike," King says. "We would lose credibility and increase liabilities if field locations perceived a new program as the 'binder of the month.' While we may not be able to quantify the benefits associated with integration on the bottom line, based on interpretations of internal audits, our system appears successful."

4.7.1 A Part of Life

King says PPG's 33,000 employees worldwide live and breathe integration during every business day because training, documentation, and other key activities require employees to have knowledge in each area. He explained that PPG designs its EMS training programs to leverage from existing programs for quality and Responsible Care.

"Employees are able to do some training at their computer workstation as time permits," he says. "For example, a process operator in a plant that has a responsibility to watch the process can pop a compact disc into the computer and answer questions concerning hazard communications or other regulatory programs."

Getting to this point was not easy, admits King. PPG had to overcome certain vocabulary and cultural differences specific to each company unit. Depending on the operating unit, the environmental person was responsible for reporting to different management representatives. Each operating unit had its own EHS organization reporting to manufacturing, human resources, or research and development, etc.

4.7.2 Key System Elements

PPG's management system contains the following key elements, which are part of each business unit's structure and function. The system is based on a prevention process that defines requirements and strives for 100 percent conformance. The PPG management system is designed around ISO 9000 and ISO 14001 with other concepts woven throughout.

based on
prevention

1) Management commitment and leadership — Each and every level of management must be actively involved and committed to the letter and spirit of the EHS policy.

2) Policy — The policy is developed by the company's environmental affairs committee and corporate EHS department, which oversees compliance to the policy.

3) Planning — Each business unit is responsible for planning and implementing activities consistent with the policy.

4) Objectives — EHS corporate and business unit objectives and targets are established and measured for pollution prevention, regulatory compliance, safety and health performance, etc.

5) Implementation — Each business unit is responsible for compliance with applicable laws.

6) Monitoring and Assessment — Business units and the corporate level are responsible for monitoring and assessing operations.

7) Periodic review — The policy is reviewed on a regular basis and updated when appropriate.

8) External affairs and accountability — The company is committed to participating both indirectly and directly in developing effective regulations in EHS areas.

King says several of the company's 120 facilities worldwide provide annual reports to principal stakeholders concerning EHS performance and also foster community advisory panels for guidance.

4.7.3 Don't Ask for More Money

King says each PPG business unit implements initiatives such as Responsible Care and ISO 14001 using existing budgets and can't expect budget increases to cover the costs of these programs. Therefore, he says, PPG had to devise a system for integrating other concerns into the overall company management system to reap a cost benefit from implementing the initiatives.

For example, PPG decided to implement the basic concepts of ISO 14001 beginning in 1995 but will probably not seek third-party certification unless faced with one of the following scenarios:

- a key customer asks for certification;

- there is evidence that certification will increase environmental performance beyond mere implementation; or

- there will be a reduction in regulatory inspections, and certification will mitigate penalties.

long-term
commitment

"It's not worth the cost of certification for our units unless other benefits can be gained at the same time," King notes. "Before we consider any economic benefits, we ask ourselves if implementation will enhance our environmental performance. If the answer is yes, and the project makes long-term economic sense, we will move ahead."

King explains that PPG facilities are encouraged to use Responsible Care as a benchmark for the company's own EHS system. The Responsible Care program asks the unit management to determine where the facility stands in relation to the implementation of a specific principle. Therefore, a facility that has reached an implementation level of "3" on a specific Responsible Care scale can determine its level of PPG guideline implementation at the same time.

"During this assessment process, the unit management is required to develop plans for continuous improvement needed to reach the next level of implementation," he says.

4.7.4 Management Systems Design

PPG's integrated management system was designed to anticipate regulatory obligations and plan strategies to meet regulatory deadlines in an economically viable capacity, according to King. When planning a strategy to comply with upcoming regulatory mandates, he says, the company uses a "stair-step process." Instead of waiting a day before the regulation comes out to devise a compliance strategy, this process builds up to compliance in the four divisions by developing plans that are concurrent with expansions, process changes, or remodeling activities.

For example, a facility may have plans to rebuild a glass tank furnace every six to 10 years on average, but it may be conducive to rebuild sooner if more effective effluent control equipment is developed, he explains. More effective equipment usually means more prescriptive regulations, King notes.

"You have to develop a system that allows you to think in the long term to anticipate regulations and initiatives in the context of everyday operations," King says.

4.7.5 Supplier Plans

While King admits that PPG's EHS commitment does not reach as far down the supplier chain as the company would like, the company is working with suppliers to implement cost-effective EHS programs.

He says each business unit is responsible for educating and training its suppliers in EHS management.

"Our suppliers need to understand that certain process changes are clearly worth the up-front costs," he says. "They have a difficult problem because they have to be cost-conscious and at the same time remain competitive with other suppliers."

For more information, contact PPG Industries Inc., One PPG Place, Pittsburgh, PA 15272.

CHAPTER 8
Integration Roundup — Five Companies Foresee Savings

Adapted from Integrated Management Systems Update (IMSU), April 1996

Five major U.S. companies are taking firm steps toward integrating environment, health, and safety (EHS), and quality programs with one another and into their business plans. Most can point to direct savings from doing so. Documentation and training redundancies have been reduced and waste is now seen as "lost raw materials."

All the companies have aspects that place them in the chemical industry, which may explain their positive approach toward integration. Ashland Chemical, Dow Plastics, Monsanto, and Olin Corporation take part in the Chemical Manufacturers Association's Responsible Care® program, which requires good product stewardship and "systems" thinking versus "product" thinking. J.M. Huber Company has a "rigorous" environmental program that is consistent with Responsible Care and ISO 14000.

sea change

The overwhelming impression left after *IMSU* interviewed EHS officials from these companies is that they are fostering a sea change throughout their companies. No longer can employees think only of the task at hand — every employee is being asked to consider his or her job in light of the impact it has on quality, health, safety, the environment, and, yes, the bottom line.

4.8.1 Business System Integration

Randy Price, director of environment, health, and safety at the J.M. Huber Company, says that integrating EHS issues is a business commitment just like the company's financial commitment. The environmental plan at Huber is a part of the business plan. Huber employs 5,000 people globally.

Huber, a highly diverse company (oil and gas, chemicals, electronics, wood products, and minerals) needs to increase this interdependence, says Price. "The interdependence is there in the big companies. Companies have to integrate to succeed as a world-class company. Environmental and health and safety and technological decisions have to be equal."

R&D
involvement

Price says Huber is "embryonic" in this area but is working toward an interdependence that "maximizes everything." For example, if research and development (R&D) "only worried about yield or operability, they would remain in the old way of thinking. R&D has to think of the end: 'Now, let's put pollution prevention in the front.'"

"When business managers can figure in the environmental costs in dollars, they can project the costs over a period of time. Don't hit them with something late in the business cycle because of a regulation. They don't know how to translate that to dollars." Planning ahead "allows for better business decisionmaking. The more data the business managers get, the better the decisions they can make."

John DiFazio, director of environmental business development at Dow Plastics North America, says that Dow Chemical has already developed successful pilots geared toward the 15 global Dow businesses, which employ 39,500 people. The pilots show each of the companies how to integrate environmental and health and safety issues into the corporate business plan.

DiFazio works with a team of five people who use such resources as eco-efficiency tools, life-cycle analysis (LCA), scenario development, probability analysis, benchmarking, and issue analysis to help companies "see the sense" of integration and relate it back to their businesses.

"This is a new dimension in business management," DiFazio says. "Not only are we doing everything to comply with regulations, but we move on to trying to prioritize external issues on a business." This includes helping companies "develop a mechanism to assess short- and long-term positive and negative financial impacts on their business structure," he notes.

business system integration

"Business management has to be involved," DiFazio says, but he notes that timing and selectivity are very important. The full-time people have to act as catalysts to ease people into integration. Business system integration is a corporate goal at Dow, just as following the CMA's Responsible Care program is. Some resistance is inevitable in any company, he says, but he sees it coming from people who feel pressed for time.

4.8.2 Responsible Care®

Glenn Hammer, vice president of EHS at Ashland Chemical, a division of Ashland Inc., a Fortune 50 company, says his company has had a jump on integration of environmental, health, and safety issues because of its endorsement of Responsible Care, which was a "driver" to help Ashland improve its performance.

Responsible Care requires CMA members to achieve six main objectives through its code of management practices:

1) pollution prevention;

2) worker health and safety;

3) process safety;

4) distribution safety;

5) community awareness and emergency response; and

6) product stewardship.

no resistance

Hammer says that he has not seen resistance to integrating environmental and health issues into the company's business goals. "Most of the divisions in the company have seen the light," he says.

In fact, he says, Ashland is able to use integration as a "competitive advantage" in some ways. For example, companies that have failed to integrate these issues are going to be behind if the ISO 14001 environmental management system standard becomes a market-driven requirement.

William G. McGlasson, corporate director of environment, health, and safety at Olin Corporation, says that the product stewardship code of Responsible Care has brought integration of EHS into Olin's business areas. "We've always been successful in environmental performance," McGlasson says. "We do look at systems to go beyond compliance. Results are very positive."

more opportunities

"There are more opportunities in the company to be on the front end of the business plan," he says. "We're always looking for improvement." He says that if Olin did a gap analysis on where the company is with integration into the business process and where Olin would like to be, there would be a gap, but plans are underway to close the gap.

Olin is a Fortune 500 company that has strengths in chemicals, metals, and ammunition. The company also specializes in microelectronic materials and aerospace and defense products. Olin has 14,000 employees and seven divisions, three of which are chemical products divisions.

Because of the obvious need for the chemical divisions to conform to EHS standards, these divisions proactively pursue "pilot" programs, says McGlasson. The other divisions often share programs with the chemical divisions as those programs fit the needs of the non-chemical divisions in their move toward integration.

4.8.3 Realized Savings

Single-Entry Data

Jeff Felder, a compliance services team leader for Monsanto, says that Monsanto is working toward integration where possible, which includes the company's business plan.

The company has some systems in place to track such things as dollars spent and "overlaps and vacancies" in data, which includes where more than one person records the same information. He says Monsanto is working toward "less paper and more single-entry" of information, which makes integration of the tracking systems more efficient.

long haul

"It's not a problem to be solved overnight," he says. "The real savings come when you make businesses run better. We haven't turned the culture on its head yet, but we're working on it."

Waste Reduction

Hammer says that Ashland has succeeded in tracking dollars in areas such as pollution prevention under Responsible Care. Ashland has realized a million-dollar-a-year savings since it began to reuse a certain "distillate material." A research team found that, by making "minor process changes" to what normally would be waste, the company was able to transform it into a salable low-grade resin product.

product stewardship

Hammer says that product stewardship is a major focus now because Ashland wants to be "a leader in the business" and the company is ingraining Responsible Care in day-to-day work practices.

Ashland tracks financial costs associated with integration on an "as needed" basis, says Hammer, and notes that the industry is struggling with how to set up tracking systems for environmental costs. He anticipates an additional documentation burden with the coming of the ISO 14001 standard.

from compliance capital to voluntary capital

Dow has tracked expenditure of environmental capital over the past 10 years, says DiFazio. This began in the early 1980s with the need to control certain emissions. Dow differentiates "compliance" capital from "voluntary" capital. "Voluntary programs give positive returns," he says. By contrast, negative returns arise from regulations, which are "too prescriptive."

Now, Dow's expenditures for voluntary, continuous improvement are less than costs for compliance with regulations — that is, it is more cost effective for Dow to correct problems and reduce waste than to react to outside regulation. The key is "you've got to reduce waste and show continuous improvement. There are lots of ways to skin a cat," he says.

DiFazio uses the example of CO_2 emissions. "Energy is costly," he says. "If you can reduce energy use, you're more efficient." He says that instead of viewing materials as waste at Dow they are considered "lost raw materials."

Price believes that regulations will always be relevant because no company will ever get out of a "reactive mode. You can cut waste 50 percent, but you'll still have regulations, because there will continue to be waste."

green wall

Price's understanding of the term "green wall" is when a company may say to itself, "It's difficult to quantify the benefits, so why should I do this?" He says that a company has to "see what's coming and plan for it." If a company can "reengineer a process" and change its characteristics, the company can anticipate a coming regulation.

Consulting Consolidation

Price says Huber has saved "observable quantities" on consulting fees since the company began to consolidate the list of consultants called for certain projects. For example, Huber was calling 15 consultants for Title V Clean Air Act work but has narrowed the list to two.

In-House Audits

Huber has also noticed savings by bringing auditing in-house. The company now has a formal environmental auditing program with a two-day training program — both classroom and in the field — which 20 people have completed.

50% savings

Price says that these auditors are trained to audit other businesses within the company. For example, someone from oil and gas might audit the wood products division. Aside from a 50-percent savings in audit costs from using the internal auditing program, Huber now has a single audit format, which allows for better follow-up.

Olin's McGlasson says, "We have realized successful savings, but we haven't measured the savings yet in the reengineering program." He adds that Olin can share success stories across the seven divisions about certain value-added projects, such as a risk assessment, that showed where remediation was not needed at a certain facility.

Olin's environmental safety measures include measuring reduction of metric pounds per year to the air, water, and ground, but McGlasson says that Olin does not have a cost savings associated with that.

Olin has used benchmarking and networking as tools to learn how other companies are attempting to integrate programs. Also, Olin is participating in a "metrics tool" study with other Global Environmental Management Initiative (GEMI) companies.

4.8.4 Quality System Integration

More than a dozen, or at least half of Huber's sites are certified to the ISO 9000 quality management system. The standard requires that everyone understand the impact of his or her work on the quality process, Price says. This includes the engineers who design the plants to the people who run the plants. For example, when oil spills from a drum, "you don't want someone to just say, 'Don't slip.' You want someone to clean it up as well."

total systems, not project-by-project

Huber's goal is to create a total systems approach to operations rather than a project-by-project approach, says Price. This includes managing systems from raw material acquisition through product sales — the entire chain of commerce. "Integration of all aspects will be more efficient. A lot of people are moving in that direction," Price notes.

Dow's DiFazio sees "as a given" the integration of EHS areas into Dow's quality management. He notes that all these systems contain the principle of "continuous improvement." Globally, Dow has 155 sites certified to ISO 9000.

In all systems implementation, the company must balance "cost versus value," he says. "Value in some cases is not easy to define." A company has to understand the systems issues and the alternatives. Companies should see customers and competitors alike as allies in this endeavor. For example, companies should look jointly with customers at emerging environmental issues to see what the best approaches are for product development.

benchmarking

"That's where benchmarking comes in," says DiFazio. "You have to better understand not only others with similar products, but those who have alternatives. Your customers are starting to look at new alternatives. You have got to know where you come from in a performance and cost standpoint."

Ashland's Hammer says his company uses an in-house quality program that predates ISO 9000. It is "a five-step process for solving any type of problem, such as late deliveries or misshipments," he says. He notes, though, that 15 of Ashland Chemical's sites are ISO 9000 certified.

Ashland uses quality tools such as fishbone diagrams — cause and effect diagrams — control charts, Pareto charts, and histograms for analyzing historical performance. "The ISO 14000 initiative will leverage the quality process model even more," he says, "because it's a continuous improvement model."

Olin used the framework of its own total quality management (TQM) program to develop ISO 9000 and expects to use the same method to develop ISO 14001. The program uses a trained group of Olin employees who help different facilities develop and customize programs. Nearly two dozen of Olin's facilities are ISO 9000 certified.

4.8.5 Downsizing vs. Reengineering

Price says downsizing has not had a big effect on Huber, which has always been "lean and mean. We leverage ourselves."

Huber has given sector managers "two hats" to wear: their sector responsibilities and leadership of one of the company's "centers of competence." The centers bring people together to work on common issues, such Title V permitting, waste, audits, air quality, community right to know, and technology.

"The technology person's responsibility is to look for synergy across the business sectors." Price explains. "If [some people are] talking about baghouses, let's all call them baghouses." Huber wants each environmental manager to be "a jack of all trades and a master of one."

Downsizing was not a significant factor for Hammer's department at Ashland, which had been outsourcing some of its work. After undergoing an evaluation by a consulting firm, his department added people. "We didn't start with a number," he says. "We looked at the process."

downsizing piques interest

Felder says that downsizing has made people at Monsanto "more conscious of the need to integrate." For example, "If two plants are running asbestos training, why not bring the people together?" If the two plants are geographically close enough, the classes could be combined, or one instructor could visit both sites.

Olin has performed reengineering as opposed to downsizing in EHS, says McGlasson. At the manufacturing facilities, Olin has combined four parallel programs (environment, Responsible Care, health, and safety) into one, which enables the facilities to benefit from "one-stop shopping" instead of having to work with separate programs.

This combination has also reduced training time for facility employees who can use both classroom training and computer self-teaching programs. EHS is integrated into these programs. There also are centralized locations for training, one of which is a center of excellence.

4.8.6 Documentation and Training

"People time is savings," says Huber's Price. Getting people away from time spent at paperwork is a big potential benefit of integration. This is part of Huber's overall goal of looking for "maximum efficiency with limited resources."

To streamline training resource requirements, Dow avoids the need for each of its 15 global companies to maintain in-house experts by providing what it calls "core resources" at centralized locations where people from within Dow can tap in for the necessary expertise.

new dimension

Documentation adds a new dimension, but not a burdensome one, to the business plan, says DiFazio. "If you don't understand the EHS impacts on your business, then you don't understand your business," he maintains, noting that businesses must respond to the continuous growth of a global society's expectations.

Hammer says that Ashland has a centralized EHS staff that adheres to a regular training schedule. Each facility is responsible for its own training and uses a "training matrix" as a guide.

Although Olin has a strong documentation record (a Responsible Care requirement) the company concentrates more on "performance and metrics" than on documentation, says McGlasson. "We want to show positive measures. Documentation is not as positive as reduction in incidents and development of safety measures."

Olin has its own Responsible Care Council that meets two or three times a year to look at such things as guidelines, priorities, and regulations. Olin publishes an EHS report that is disseminated to all 14,000 employees and keeps people up-to-date on EHS issues.

4.8.7 Toward ISO 14001

All the officials interviewed here say their companies have highly developed systems for EHS on a corporate level, if not on a facility-by-facility level. A common thread for the chemical industry is adherence to the requirements of Responsible Care.

DiFazio comments that the chemical industry does not want to have two standards when ISO 14001 is published. Many companies are looking at ways to include Responsible Care in ISO 14001.

Hammer says Ashland is looking into ISO 14001 but is not sure which direction the company will take.

Some facilities at Monsanto are getting "actively involved" in ISO 14001, and Monsanto is becoming "much more aggressive" generally toward ISO 14001, according to Felder, who sees this as an "operational excellence" issue.

He says Monsanto is waiting to see if ISO 14001 develops the way ISO 9000 did, as "a shift by the industry as a whole" toward adopting the quality standards. The market response to ISO 14001 will affect how Monsanto moves forward. Nevertheless, many of the company's facilities already have environmental systems in place.

Olin is not looking at ISO 14001 certification from a compliance standpoint, says McGlasson. "We are looking for a system that will meet the needs of our external customers. Customers will be the driver." But Olin is keenly interested in the standard, he says. The company sees in it opportunities for improving existing environmental plans. "We're always looking for ways to get to the next plateau," McGlasson says.

Labeling, EPE, and LCA

CHAPTER 1

ISO 14020 Labeling Standards

by CEEM Information Services

The ISO 14000 environmental labeling guidelines are the ones most likely to affect your corporate presence in the retail market. They deal with product marks and their meanings and attempt to harmonize existing third-party labeling programs. The objective is to provide a basis for consumer decisions based on environmental criteria. ISO TC 207 Subcommittee 3 is developing these standards.

One of the most controversial areas regarding these standards involves their implications as potential technical barriers to trade. This topic is discussed in detail in 📖 Part 9 and is not taken up here.

Several of the standards were in committee draft stage or close to it as of March 1996:

- ISO 14020 addresses environmental labeling principles applicable to all environmental labeling activities and programs.

- ISO 14022 on labeling symbols focuses on harmonizing use of the myriad environmental label symbols existing worldwide.

- ISO 14024 addresses labeling programs, operated either by governments or by private organizations, that use a single seal to communicate whether a product is "environmentally preferable" within a given product sector, based on the product's environmental attributes.

One standard in the ISO 14020 series became a Draft International Standard (DIS) in March 1996. ISO 14021 on self-declaration environmental claims establishes general guidelines regarding environmental claims applicable to goods and services. However, ISO did not issue it as an official DIS until more progress was made on the symbols and testing and verification documents (ISO 14023).

5.1.1 ISO 14020: Environmental Labeling — General Principles

Under development within ISO Subcommittee 3, Working Group 3, ISO 14020 describes the goals and principles for all types of eco-labeling. As of early 1996, there was substantial disagreement within SC3 as to whether this document should be a stand-alone guideline or whether its contents should be incorporated in the other environmental labeling guidelines.

ISO 14020 had been somewhat of a challenge for Working Group 3 members. To begin with, two distinct options emerged as goals for this guideline:

1) The goal is to improve the environmental aspects in products.

2) The goal is to create the method for determining and communicating information on the environmental attributes of products.

communicating characteristics vs. improving aspects

The first position was supported by third-party labeling practitioners since they use environmental labeling as an integral part of their overall programs that seek to improve the environmental aspects of products. While that goal was seen as fine for their purpose, it was not seen as the goal of all environmental labeling activities. Critics argued that it should certainly not be the goal of a guideline that only aims to standardize communication terms and symbols.

Other SC3 members supported the second position — creating the methods to provide information to the public regarding relevant product characteristics, such as recyclability, disposability, and emissions — as the standard's main goal. Informing the public about relevant product characteristics could allow consumers to make informed purchasing decisions. Improving the environmental attributes of a product might be a collateral benefit, but product improvement would not be ISO 14020's main goal.

SC3 members were scheduled to make a decision on the status of the ISO 14020 document at the June 1996 TC 207 plenary in Brazil. Whether the content of ISO documents should be limited to principles and methodologies to improve the art of environmental labeling, or whether they should also establish environmental improvement as the end goal of environmental labeling, was under discussion in early 1996.

The ISO 14020 committee draft dated August 21, 1995, which was the version under consideration until the Brazil meeting, states that, though the guideline can be used independently from an environmental management system (EMS), it is one of the tools of an EMS. It notes that:

"Environmental labels/declarations provide information about a product or service in terms of its overall environmental character, a specific environmental attribute, or any number of attributes. Purchasers can use this information in choosing the products or services they desire based on environmental as well as other considerations."

Nine Principles

At the guideline's heart are nine principles that those who develop and use environmental labels and declarations must adhere to:

1) Labels and declarations must be accurate, verifiable, relevant, and nondeceptive.

2) Environmental attributes must be available to purchasers.

3) Labels and declarations must be based on thorough scientific methodology.

4) Criteria for label/declaration must be available to interested parties.

5) Labels and declarations development must take into account the life-cycle of the relevant product or service.

6) The administrative work must be limited to establishing conformance with criteria.

7) Labels and declarations procedures and criteria must not create unfair trade restrictions or discriminate between foreign and domestic products or services.

8) Labels and declarations must not inhibit innovation.

9) Labels and declarations standards and criteria must be developed by consensus.

Perhaps the most controversial — and most important — principle is number seven, relating to unfair trade barriers.

The committee draft listed instances of potentially unfair trade barriers:

- requirements to meet specific national or local legislation, regulations, or standards rather than performance objectives;

- restrictions on testing methods such as the following:

  — requiring national or local procedures rather than an internationally accepted testing or assessment method or an industry/trade test that has been subjected to peer review;

  — restrictions on the recognition of testing facilities that could create an impossible geographic requirement;

  — language requirements related to the transmission of data and performance attributes;

  — inequitable application of costs, fees, charges, or requirements;

  — administrative requirements that limit access by foreign producers to activities or programs related to environmental labels/declarations or their ability to comment on the development of criteria for environmental labels/declarations;

  — requirements to conform with nationally developed technologies or manufacturing processes.

This section of ISO 14020, more than any other, is likely to change as the guidance evolves, but the basic language urging label and declaration developers not to create trade barriers is likely to remain a main focus.

5.1.2 ISO 14021: Environmental Labels and Declarations — Self-Declaration Environmental Claims — Terms and Definitions

This guidance establishes general guidelines regarding environmental claims applicable to goods and services. Like ISO 14020, ISO 14021 has been burdened with a similar product improvement goal that calls on the standard to contribute to a reduction in the environmental burdens and impacts associated with the consumption of goods and services and to harmonize the use of environmental claims. In early 1996, discussions on this point were ongoing. The anticipated benefits include:

- accurate, verifiable, and nondeceptive claims;
- increased potential for market forces to stimulate environmental improvements in products, processes, and service delivery; and
- a reduction of restrictions and barriers to international trade.

ISO 14021 — unofficially known as "Type II" labeling — does not include testing and verification methodologies, the subject of a separate standard that SC3 was to begin work on in 1996.

ISO 14021 is closely aligned with the Federal Trade Commission guidelines interpreting FTC policy, laws, and cases that indicate how the FTC will enforce the law in the area of environmental labeling claims.

Development of this standard is the responsibility of SC3/WG2. It was approved as a committee draft (CD) for ballot and comment in Oslo, Norway, in June 1995. As of early 1996, the date for final adoption was indefinite.

ISO 14021's objectives for manufacturer labels are to ensure:

- the label claims are accurate;
- the label claims are verifiable; and
- the label claims are nondeceptive.

use of LCA   Although an environmental label can be accurate and verifiable, the information it contains may still be deceptive. Labeling claims must not be trivial in the context of the entire product. Accentuating a true but trivial attribute when more serious ones are not addressed may constitute deception. For example, if the manufacturer of a paint-stripping solvent containing methylene chloride claims that it follows "green" practices because its packaging contains only post-consumer recycled paper, one could argue that the claim is deceptive.

Subcommittee 3 was also debating the use of life-cycle methodology in establishing labeling criteria. Opponents argue that, from the standpoints of technical information and cost, using life-cycle assessments (LCAs) to make single labeling claims seems unrealistic.

example:
textile mills

Proponents argue that LCA is the only scientifically sound way to ensure uniformity in the application of labeling criteria. For example, if two textile mills, on two separate rivers, have a water discharge temperature of 15° Celsius, but the ambient temperature of one mill's environment is higher than the discharge, and the other's is lower, then the associated environmental impacts will be different. The problem is that environmental impacts cannot always be determined, and even when they are, it is virtually impossible to make the trade-offs between impacts when there are many different ones.

Among the definitions under discussion in the guidance were:

- recycled content;
- recycled material;
- pre-consumer material;
- post-consumer material;
- reduced resource use;
- recovered energy;
- solid waste reduction;
- energy-efficient/energy-conserving/energy-saving;
- water-efficient/water-conserving/water-saving;
- extended life product;
- reusable/refillable;
- recyclable;
- designed for disassembly;
- compostable; and
- degradable/biodegradable/photodegradable.

5.1.3 ISO 14022: Environmental Labels and Declarations — Self-Declaration Environmental Claims — Symbols

This is intended as a standard to ensure that symbols used to denote such things as recyclability and recycled content are understood to mean the same thing universally. The Möbius loop is one example under consideration.

Figure 5.1 — Möbius loop

Development of this standard is also the responsibility of SC3/WG2. In early 1996, it was in a preliminary stage with further work planned.

5.1.4 ISO 14023: Environmental Labels and Declarations — Self Declaration Environmental Claims — Testing and Verification

This document was scheduled for preliminary work beginning in 1996. SC3 was debating the scope and content of the standard. It was uncertain when it would be adopted as a final standard.

5.1.5 ISO 14024: Environmental Labels and Declarations — Environmental Labeling Type I — Guiding Principles and Procedures

This standard covers labeling programs, operated either by governments or by private organizations, that use a single seal to communicate a judgment that a product is "environmentally preferable" within a given product sector. The judgment is based on an analysis of the product's environmental attributes.

The document is intended to serve as a guide for operating such programs as Germany's Blue Angel, Japan's EcoMark, and the United States' Green Seal. The German and Japanese programs are government sponsored, while Green Seal is a privately operated program.

ISO 14024 lays out principles and practices to use when developing the criteria for product labels. Important elements of the criteria, according to the guidance, include:

- credibility;
- consultation with stakeholders;
- consensus;
- transparency;
- accessibility; and
- avoiding creation of unnecessary obstacles to international trade.

This document was circulated as a committee draft in March 1995. Comments were considered at the November 1995 meeting of SC2 in Seoul, Korea, and a revised CD for comment was being prepared in early 1996. This document was not likely to move to the DIS stage until late 1996.

According to industry experts, the ISO 14024 eco-label standard would help trade and industry because:

- it demands transparency in the label's entire development, e.g., criteria and procedures;
- it requires inclusion of foreign producer interests and characteristics of their systems and consideration for their equivalent regulations;
- it is based on scientific, available information that is repeatable and reproducible;
- it requires the consensus of all international stakeholders;

- the selection of awardees is not based on arbitrary percentage, but on realistic cutoff points — the minimum level of performance necessary to gain a label — to support the claim that those included are environmentally preferable;

- clear and transparent methodologies are used to support evidence of environmental preferability and of equivalent use and performance of the products in a given category;

- it favors a life-cycle approach with clear and transparent information on any departures; and

- application and certification procedures are clear and feasible for all, including foreign producers.

selecting awardees

The issue of selecting awardees was the subject of much debate within SC3. Practitioners argue that smooth cutoff points are not always available or feasible in the context of environmental leadership. For example, if 75 percent of companies seeking an eco-label fall above a break point (a distinct gap between two levels of environmental performance) and 25 percent fall below, then awarding a label to the 75 percent above the break point renders the label meaningless because it does not connote environmental leadership.

Industry argues that cutoff points must occur at statistically significant break points to ensure uniform application of labeling criteria. If, for example, 75 percent of companies meet the aforementioned labeling criteria, then it is the criteria that need changing, not the cutoff point.

detailed procedures

The contents of the CD include detailed procedures for establishing labeling program requirements. The document points out that establishing labeling program requirements is an iterative process, meaning, for example, that initial targets may have to be redefined over time. The following contents are likely to be changed as the CD evolves.

In the CD circulating in early 1996, the labeling program addressed the following:

- consultation with stakeholders;

- selecting product categories;

- selecting and developing product environmental criteria;

- selecting product function characteristics;

- reporting and publishing established product categories, criteria, and characteristics; and

- implementing modifications to the product environmental criteria.

The document included a section on certification procedures, including sections on:

- general rules of the certification program;

- requirements for awarding the label;

- procedures for assessing and demonstrating compliance;

- compliance monitoring; and

- legal protection of the label.

More than 25 independent national labeling programs now exist, and these programs have the potential to create trade barriers throughout the world. However, the draft of the ISO 14024 eco-labeling document reflected many of the acceptable conditions that industry members expect in an ISO standard on this subject.

CHAPTER 2

ISO 14031 Environmental Performance Evaluation Standard

by John E. Master, Consultant, Chemical Manufacturers Association;
Chairman, ST4 on Environmental Performance Evaluation

5.2.1 Overview

ISO 14031 — Environmental Performance Evaluation (EPE) is aimed at doing just what the title says: helping your organization evaluate its environmental performance against established goals and objectives.

EPE is not a substitute for an EMS. An EMS includes the whole concept of planning an organization's environmental performance level, setting objectives and targets, putting into place programs to achieve those objectives and targets, and reviewing performance against those objectives and targets. Specifically, **Section 4.4 of ISO 14001** clearly requires that there be a process in place to monitor and measure environmental performance against goals and objectives set by the organization. The EPE process can fit into this piece of an EMS, but it is not intended that ISO 14031 be the only way to accomplish it, and EPE is not part of the auditable specification system.

EPE as discretionary tool

As part of the ISO 14000 series of environmental management system standards, EPE is a tool your company can use as it sees fit. Auditing is another. So are other ISO 14000 processes, such as labeling and life-cycle assessment. EPE is a process on the operational side of the company rather than on the product side.

The EPE process provides information within which the EMS review can take place and that can be used as a baseline in setting objectives and targets. It also provides information to help your organization understand what its environmental aspects are and determine what its significant environmental impacts may be.

It ought to be a system based on information that can be gathered readily by your organization. For example, the data may be present within existing systems and can simply be presented in a different way to make it compatible with the EMS and your objectives and targets.

The standard has been in the works since 1991, when the Strategic Advisory Group on the Environment (SAGE) was tasked with making recommendations regarding international standards for the environment. SAGE was the predecessor to ISO Technical Committee (TC) 207. 📖 (See Part 1, Chapter 2, Section 4 for more information.) It is being developed by TC 207 Subcommittee 4.

Why is evaluation of environmental performance a component of environmental management?

In the United States especially, environmental performance results are pretty well mandated by command-and-control governmental regulation. Through their reporting to authorities, companies regularly evaluate their performance against regulatory requirements.

need for EPE   So why do we need an additional voluntary standard on evaluating environmental performance in the private sector?

The answer lies in the purpose of ISO 14000 standards and EMSs, and in two old management adages.

First, an environmental management system gives your organization an opportunity and a system to identify and manage all of its environmental aspects, not just those mandated by government. For example, you may want to identify environmental aspects that have business advantages (i.e., for waste, raw material, and cost reductions) apart from those that relate to regulatory requirements.

Second are the old adages: "What gets managed, gets done" and "What gets measured (evaluated) gets managed."

Experience has shown that corporate managers must be able to measure, evaluate, and get feedback on the specific results they are seeking, to really focus on achieving objectives and targets. If your organization cannot measure where its environmental performance is now, it is unlikely to get to where it wants to be. This review loop applies just as strongly to environmental performance as it does to financial performance or to any other function of business.

5.2.2 Definition of EPE

What It Isn't

The ISO EPE standard will not set performance levels — that is the responsibility of the individual organization. It also will not be a specification or certification (registration) standard. Its purpose is not to specify what must be measured nor how measured items should be evaluated.

The EPE guidance document is intended to apply to any type of organization regardless of the kind of business it is in or its size, location, or complexity, or whether it has an EMS in place or not. Public, private, manufacturing, service, process, and governmental organizations have expressed interest in using the standard.

It is not intended to be used to compare one organization's performance with another's. The EPE process can be developed in stages or applied in a narrow scope, even in a large organization. Then, as capability expands and as resources become more available, or as environmental performance improvements spread within the organization, the EPE process can grow with it. For example, your company may simply be interested in measuring and evaluating its environmental performance to establish a baseline or to communicate information to the community.

What It Is

management
tool

According to the fourth working draft of ISO 14031, EPE is a management tool that can provide an organization with reliable, objective, and verifiable information on an ongoing basis to determine if it is meeting the environmental criteria set by management. This information generated by an EPE may also help your organization:

- achieve continual improvement of its environmental performance;
- report and communicate its environmental performance consistent with its policy and needs;
- identify opportunities for prevention of pollution;
- increase efficiency; and
- identify strategic business opportunities.

multi-step
process

In other words, EPE is a process that provides information to organization managers over time, giving them an assessment of actual vs. intended environmental performance. The EPE standards should help your organization develop its own processes to suit its own needs. EPE should be focused on those activities, products, or services that your organization can control and over which it can be expected to have an influence.

Specifically, EPE is a multi-step process that involves:

1) measurement and collection of raw data related to various aspects of environmental performance that are important to your organization;

2) analysis of the raw data to assure their reliability and to convert the raw data into readily understandable environmental performance information;

3) comparison of the environmental performance information to your organization's criteria to assess the actual performance against intentions and to identify strengths and weaknesses in performance; and

4) providing a basis for reporting and communicating environmental performance information and its assessment to management, other internal interested parties, and external interested parties as appropriate.

interested
parties

Because an EPE can produce a great amount of environmental performance data, when you design an EPE process you should consider not only the information needs of your company's management, but also the views of interested parties such as stockholders, environmental groups, neighboring communities, the media, and government agencies. EPE information can be a valuable tool for establishing communication links with these groups.

If you have an EMS in place you should use EPE as a component of the EMS monitoring and measurement requirements. EPE information can also be used to:

- identify and prioritize environmental aspects and impacts;
- determine a baseline from which specific objectives and targets can be established;
- measure progress toward achieving objectives and targets;
- measure the effectiveness of important EMS implementation and operation elements (such as training, internal communications, and operational control);

- provide a basis for determining the need for and extent of corrective actions; and

- provide a basis for evaluating the continuing suitability, adequacy, and effectiveness of your EMS.

If you do not have an environmental management system in place you still may be interested in knowing what your company's environmental performance is. The measurement and analysis steps of EPE are particularly applicable to your organization in this case.

environmental aspects However, some knowledge of your company's environmental aspects is necessary to help you decide what to include in EPE; i.e., what to measure and analyze. ISO 14004, the EMS guidance standard, offers advice on identifying environmental aspects and may be used by organizations without an EMS in planning an EPE. 📖 (See Part 3, Chapter 1, Section 4 for more information about identifying environmental aspects.)

line function To be most effective, EPE should be planned and operated as an integral part of your organization's activities. It should be a "line" function so that workers and managers can see how they are doing at any given time and take immediate corrective action if needed. EPE is not as effective when conducted by uninvolved staff or when it's an external function. In such cases it is often imposed on the line function as a critique that may or may not be accepted willingly. EPE works best when it is an operative part of an EMS.

EPE vs. Auditing

Finally, EPE is not the same as the environmental audit (EA). There are several distinct differences between EPE and EA.

1) EPE works best as an integrated line function. By definition, EA is conducted by independent, objective people. The auditing process, historically and almost as an inherent function, needs to be done by people who are independent of the management system being audited. Those doing the EPE often are responsible for producing the very performance they're evaluating.

2) ISO 14001 requires you to conduct a periodic environmental audit of your EMS. Organizations audit their systems every one to five years, though most do so in a three-year sampling period. EPE is an ongoing process. Your organization could conduct an EPE continuously, monthly, or quarterly. EPE develops information that is consistent over time, allowing you to track your company's performance. It is based on frequent or continuous data collection and use.

3) Auditing is usually based on a sampling of data and documentation rather than on a complete examination of all documentation. It takes place in a slice of time.

4) EPE produces quantified information on your organization's environmental performance. EA produces a verification that your EMS conforms to, or does not conform to, the audit criteria established.

5.2.3 Status of ISO 14031

IS in 1999? ISO 14031 is not as advanced as the standards on environmental management systems and EA. Subcommittee 4 of ISO/TC 207 is responsible for developing the EPE standard. Its work plan envisioned a committee draft for comment in early 1997, an extensive comment and possibly a pilot-testing phase, and a draft international standard in late 1998.

The standard was on a time track relatively consistent with most ISO standards — five to seven years from initiation to publication. In relationship to the fast track EMS and EA standards have taken, ISO 14031's evolution can seem slow.

The ISO/TC 207 subcommittees dealing with EMS and EA had substantial existing standards from which to start work. In contrast, there have been no national or international approved standards on performance evaluation. Although there are many private and public documents generally relating to measuring environmental performance, none of these represent an industry consensus.

Subcommittee 4 started with a blank sheet in defining the objective of an EPE standard, developing a format or table of contents to accomplish the objective, fleshing out the format with words, and refining the words into a consistent, concise description of EPE. In early 1996, SC4 was in the last phase of this process.

5.2.4 ISO 14031 Contents

The fourth working draft of the proposed ISO 14031 EPE standard contains sections that address the following subjects:

- overview of EPE (the major steps in an EPE process);
- planning EPE;
- management considerations;
- environmental aspects and their relationship to EPE;
- selecting appropriate environmental indicators in each of three evaluation areas;
- linkages among the three evaluation areas;
- evaluating environmental performance (doing the planned EPE), including:
- collecting data;
- analyzing data;
- evaluating information; and
- reporting and communicating;
- reviewing and improving EPE; and
- annexes of example environmental indicators.

Although the above represents a rough table of contents of the fourth working draft, as of March 1996 it had not been reviewed by Subcommittee 4. Further evolution of the table of contents was expected as Subcommittee 4 continued its development of the EPE standard.

5.2.5 ISO 14031 Evaluation Areas

Several things can be measured within an EPE process. Bearing in mind that ISO 14031 was still in draft stage at the time of this writing, the standard will probably suggest that evaluation may be conducted in any or all three of these general areas:

- management;
- operations; and
- the environment at large.

Your organization's managers probably decide how your operational processes will function, what resources and training will be available, what the intended level of wastes and releases will be, what controls will be applied, etc. These management decisions, the effectiveness of communicating them, and the degree to which they are carried out in operational processes all impact the loads that are placed on the environment.

Evaluation of Management

You may detect predictive indicators of the environmental performance of your operational processes through measuring performance of management. To measure this performance, for example, you may institute measurable operating requirements and operational controls.

The easiest example to use is the training process where an organization may measure the number of training courses it gives in a year vs. its intention. For example, you would look at the training offering itself, the number of people trained, the number of hours used, some measure of retention of training by the trainees at some period of time after the course, and some measure of the ability of the trainees to apply their training and thereby to change the performance of your organization. These are the kinds of leading indicators or management measures that may help your organization understand whether its environmental performance is being achieved by accident or by measurement.

Evaluation of Operations

A more traditional environmental performance evaluation concept, and one that is more easily understandable, is that of evaluating the performance of the operational processes against waste, emissions, and discharge criteria. The use of purchased materials and energy consumption also may be evaluated if these result in significant environmental impacts.

In many organizations, waste production, amount of emissions and discharges, and consumption of energy and materials are directly related to production rates that vary from period to period. Evaluation of these should be normalized to production rates to provide comparative information over time.

Evaluation of the Environment

One controversial area of debate has been whether and how to measure the environment. Subcommittee 4 recognizes well that most organizations do not have the technical ability to measure and evaluate the environment directly. Also, it is probably impossible for them to isolate their own contributions to changes in the environment.

Changes to the environment are usually complex phenomena resulting from a very large number of individual contributions. In most cases, public bodies or scientific organizations will undertake evaluation of the environment and of changes in it. They have the resources and broad-based incentives to do so.

It is almost impossible for an individual organization to differentiate its own small contribution to changes in the environment from all others. By including "environment" indicators in ISO 14031, drafters sought to offer thought-provoking concepts about the role of organizations on such environmental areas as global warming and ozone depletion.

When most industrial organizations consider factors in evaluating the environment in general, they are simply seeking one guide for evaluating their operational and management evaluation needs.

For instance, if your organization produces or uses substances that contribute to stratospheric ozone depletion, you should probably evaluate your operational contribution of such substances and the management objectives and program you use to control them. If you operate in a high smog area, or a high SO_2 area, you should consider whether you contribute to these local problems and then include these contributions in your EPE.

Indicators of Environmental Performance

The ISO EPE standard will propose that environmental performance information most easily can be presented and understood as simple, concise quantitative indicators. The easiest way to understand the concept of indicators is through examples. An indicator might be:

- tons of SO_2 released per unit of electricity produced;
- pounds of hazardous substance "X" emitted per pound of product;
- percentage reduction in the discharge of a material versus a base year;
- percentage of operational processes for which an operational control manual has been updated within the past two years;
- number of training hours provided vs. the intended training; and
- percentage of corrective actions completed within a specified time.

The most valuable part of the ISO EPE standard for many organizations may well be the annex(es) of illustrative example indicators.

These annexes are not intended to be all-inclusive, nor to list every imaginable indicator. They will be suggestions of the types of indicators that your organization should consider for various types of environmental aspects, objectives, targets, and issues. Perhaps the most appropriate indicator for your EPE application may be in the annex menu. More likely, the menu will help you develop a unique indicator that best suits and expresses your organization's response to its environmental management responsibility.

Environmental Performance Evaluation Training

Those who will be designing an organization's EPE process do not need special training — they need to understand items in the draft document having to do with the information needed to design an EPE process.

The EPI designer should ask the following questions:

1) What are the significant environmental impacts of my organization?

2) How do they relate to and affect the environment?

3) What are my organization's objectives and targets in terms of environmental performance?

4) What do I need to measure to determine whether we are achieving those objectives and targets?

5) What kind of environmental performance information does my organization need to be communicating to its stakeholders? Who are the stakeholders? The local community, environmental interest groups, stockholders?

5.2.6 Getting Started

The first step in beginning the EPE process is understanding what you are trying to accomplish in environmental performance, what your organization's objectives and targets are, and what form measurement will take.

Establishing Management Commitment

As with an EMS, the key to a successful EPE program is gaining and keeping top management commitment.

If top managers in your organization are really committed to being environmentally responsible, then they have inherently committed themselves to managing the organization's environmental performance or its environmental responsibility.

To manage this responsibility, they also have to recognize that they must have some kind of measurement of achievement. That recognition automatically results in a commitment for an EPE process of some sort.

Seeking Outside Help

Whether you seek outside help in establishing and maintaining an EPE process depends on the size, nature, and sophistication of your organization.

Some companies are sophisticated enough to have a lot of existing data management systems and a well-established EMS. The EMS may or may not be compatible and in full conformance with ISO 14001, but any organization that has a good EMS in place also probably has some sort of an EPE in place, and may simply need to fine-tune it, just as it may need to fine-tune its EMS.

These companies probably won't need outside help. But others may not have the resources to put an EPE process into place, just as they probably do not have resources to put an EMS in place. They may need some help in understanding what is required in an EMS or what is suggested by an EPE or in designing a process.

If you believe you may need this kind of help, it should be limited in scope. For example, you may need help to decide what it is you want to measure and what sort of data acquisition or data massaging is needed to get it into a measurable form. But at that point, the EPE process really needs to be internalized. Since EPE is intended to help you determine your actual performance over time, it is properly a function of line management, who have direct understanding and control over performance.

This does not mean that the manager must get the samples and do the laboratory work, but the manager must be responsible for seeing that the information is gathered, reported, and evaluated against objectives and targets.

Mentoring

Both large and small companies can benefit from other companies with experience. For example, numerous companies are sharing information as they implement EMS pilot projects. 📖 (See Part 8, Chapter 2 and Part 10, Chapters 2 and 5 for more information on pilot projects.) In many cases, involved companies are encountering the need for an EPE process of some sort or are streamlining processes to fit an EPE model. The results of these pilot projects will be publicly available in most cases, and companies are already sharing information with interested parties.

Smaller companies may have a leg up on others here. They probably do not have thousands of different emissions, discharges, and waste sources, and probably already know where their environmental impacts are. Establishing an EPE process likely will be a question of writing down information they already have and identifying, modifying, and routinizing existing processes.

Who Decides What to Measure

Deciding what to measure is a management responsibility. Who is considered management depends on your organization's size and what the management infrastructure is. But basically these should be the same people who determine what level of performance your organization should target.

Data Gathering and Analysis

Once you have decided what to measure, you can determine what information is needed to do an EPE. This might depend on where you can get the information most readily, which might depend on your processes and the technology you have in place.

For example, you might measure the concentration of sulfur dioxide (SO_2) in stack gas releases, and then calculate the rate of emission of stack gas so that the amount of SO_2 can be calculated from concentration X. Other organizations may find it easier to measure the generation of SO_2 by measuring the content of sulfur in the fuel burned.

consistency
with current
practices

The EPE process ought to be consistent with existing management systems and procedures, which means data collection for an EPE should be little different from what is being done now. One recipe for failure is to follow advice from a contractor who tells you to focus on something outside the day-to-day operations of your company.

The data analysis piece of the EPE process is driven by technology. The analysis might be done by scientists, engineers, or clerical staff who have been trained to make data calculations. Even a computer, fed the right information, can perform this function.

Who does the analysis is a function of the nature and intent of the analysis and of where it fits within the job descriptions and job performances of staff. Because it is unique to every company, it cannot be established as a specification or as a recommendation even within the ISO 14031 guidance standard.

Identifying Environmental Aspects and Impacts

Environmental performance information can be used as a baseline, but then someone must judge the importance of those data in terms of environmental performance.

None of the ISO 14000 standards can offer a basis for determining what environmmental aspects or impacts are significant because that is a part of each organization's technology, capabilities, and relationship with the environment. What is environmentally important to the company with a desert operation is probably different from one with operations in a tropical rain forest.

Global standards cannot describe what is most significant to each organization just as they cannot determine your customer base or your product portfolio. 📖 (See Part 3, Chapter 1, Section 4 for more information on environmental aspects.)

5.2.7 Related Issues

Usefulness to SMEs and Developing Nations

If SC4 is unable to write a guidance document valuable to developing countries and small and medium-sized enterprises (SMEs), then SC4 will have failed in writing the standard.

There has been debate concerning how much attention should be given to SMEs and developing nations in ISO 14031.

One school of thought is that, to benefit these groups, the document must be concise, short in guidance on EPE, and easy to read.

On the other hand, making it too short without providing any helpful guidance on what ought to be measured and on ways you can measure these things, the guidance document may be of little value to SMEs. The outcome has not been decided, but the final document is likely to contain examples aimed at generating thoughtful implementation solutions.

Value to Environmental Groups

Environmental groups such as the National Wildlife Federation or the Environmental Defense Fund, which have been active participants in the U.S. consensus process relative to the ISO 14000 standards, have interests in environmental performance.

Their interests are first with the compliance system and second with environmental performance. Both are important to them.

Thus, they have a keen interest in information that would come from the EPE process. They are also interested in and understand the relationship between management of responsibility and the ultimate improvement in performance that comes from that management and an EMS.

Internal and External EPE Reporting

The results of EPE should be reported to those in management responsible for your company's environmental performance, and to those who helped set the objectives and targets.

Results of the EPE process also need to be reported internally to employees who are responsible for achieving performance levels. Ideally, employees who see that the performance levels are not in line with your organization's intent might try to do their jobs better and address the problems.

Reporting of EPE results externally is a management decision. To some extent, it depends on your existing relationship with external interested parties or stakeholders. If you have a two-way communication process in place and a set of stakeholders and interested parties who are receptive to information, you may want to handle this as a dialogue. If you have an antagonistic relationship, you will come to a different conclusion concerning how much data and what types of data and information you ought to communicate.

If you want to report externally, the information reported ought to come out of something like an EPE process so it is consistent with the information available internally. The process must be verifiable so there is scientific soundness in the information, so it is consistent over a period of time, and so the trends seen by external interested parties are a true reflection of environmental performance and not a reflection of inconsistencies in the data gathering process.

ISO 14031 will not address this question; it will only state that communications with external stakeholders are totally dependent upon what an organization believes is appropriate.

When EPE — just like an EMS — becomes integral to the job description of everybody in your organization with environmental responsibilities, it will be successfu

CHAPTER 3
ISO 14040 Life-Cycle Assessment Standards

by Dr. Stanley P. Rhodes, President and CEO, Scientific Certification Systems, Inc., and Linda G. Brown, Vice President, Communications, Scientific Certification Systems

5.3.1 Introduction

The ISO 14000 series is the most ambitious international effort ever undertaken to guide global business toward more responsible environmental practices. As currently envisioned, companies will be able to draw upon the ISO 14000 series for assistance in:

1) integrating environmental management systems into overall quality management structures;

2) evaluating current environmental performance and establishing quantitative benchmarks against which to measure improvements; and

3) communicating environmental requirements to suppliers and environmental accomplishments to customers and stakeholders.

But will ISO 14000 live up to its promise? Will it help companies such as yours meet the goals of sustainable environmental and economic development, or will it become a thorn in the side of business, adding a new layer of customer expectations and operational costs without any clear advantages in terms of competitiveness or the environment?

To a large extent, the answer to these questions will be determined by the quality of the implementation tools developed to put flesh on the bones of the ISO 14000 skeleton.

These implementation tools start with life-cycle assessment (LCA). A quick reading of the emerging ISO 14000 standards turns up repeated references to "life-cycle principles," "cradle-to-grave approaches," "systems-based analysis," etc. In many ways, LCA lies at the heart of the ISO 14000 series, in that it is the only assessment methodology to undergo formal ISO standardization.

Once this standardization process is completed, companies should have a much clearer understanding of the scope and quality of information required and the commitment of personnel and resources needed to use this assessment tool effectively in fulfilling environmental management, performance evaluation, auditing, and labeling goals and objectives.

As the LCA standardization process has proceeded, it has become quite clear that the methodology must be thorough to be of lasting value. While there has been much interest in streamlining LCA, the shortcuts typically proposed have been built upon a foundation of assumptions that must in turn be examined and justified before the value of the study conclusions can be determined. In the end, the objective of LCA standardization is to make LCA practical without compromising its scientific credibility and ultimate usefulness.

There have also been some surprising discoveries. For instance, it has become increasingly apparent that historic LCA, as commonly practiced and standardized to date through such institutions as the Society for Environmental Toxicology and Chemistry (SETAC) and various governmental agencies, is not likely to fulfill the full spectrum of environmental assessment objectives envisioned within ISO 14000.

At the same time, a new technical framework has emerged that is capable of extending LCA's ability to fulfill these intended environmental assessment functions. Rather than streamlining the LCA process through a set of arbitrary assumptions, this approach streamlines the process by determining the environmental relevance of data collected before actual data processing begins.

The significance of this new technical framework is that LCA is becoming more adaptable to the needs of its users than ever before, and will be capable of providing increasing support in a wide range of ISO 14000-related applications.

This section is designed to provide you with a short synopsis of each of the ISO LCA standards, as of March 1996, including:

- a review of the standards' scope and contents; 📖 (See Part 5, Chapter 3 for more information on LCA standard status.)

- an overview of the historic development of LCA;

- an examination of LCA practices and the existing technical framework;

- an understanding of some of the key areas of debate surrounding LCA; and

- a description of emerging developments within the TOC 207 Subcommittee 5 on LCA, including the new technical framework and its implications for environmental assessment applications.

Although the issues raised in this section are somewhat technical in nature, it has been written in the belief that LCA will be most effective as an implementation tool if users are well-versed in basic LCA principles and understand its strengths and limitations.

Status of the ISO LCA Standards

The relatively slow pace of progress in completing the LCA standards should come as no surprise, given both their complexity and their implications for the entire spectrum of environmental management activities.

In early 1996, the LCA standards were divided into four sections:

1. Principles and Framework
2. Life-Cycle Inventory Analysis
3. Life-Cycle Impact Assessment, and
4. Interpretation.

The scope and status of each of these standards is summarized in the sidebar. Predictably, work on the standards for general principles and life-cycle inventory have progressed more quickly than standards in the more complex impact assessment and interpretation arenas. This pattern reflects that state of current LCA practice, which has focused heavily on the relatively straightforward mass and energy balancing techniques of life-cycle inventory. It is no wonder, then, that the most interesting debates now taking place in the LCA arena concern the methods for determining the actual environmental significance of this information.

ISO 14040: Environmental Management — Life-Cycle Assessment — Principles and Framework

This document contains a set of guiding principles for undertaking and reporting LCA studies in a responsible, transparent, and consistent manner. It does not describe in detail the life cycle assessment technique.

The experts who developed this guidance understood that LCA practice to date had been largely limited to life-cycle inventories (LCI), the first recognized phase of LCA, and was focused mainly on single, uncomplicated products. There is little experience in practice beyond quantifying inputs and outputs — conducting a life-cycle inventory. Thus, LCA standards other than 14040 and ISO 14041 were still preliminary in early 1996, although work and practice in Life-cycle Impact Assessment were progressing.

A vote was taken in March 1996 during which the committee draft for comment and ballot was elevated to **DIS** status. However, the standard could not become a final ISO standard before progress was made on ISO 14041 *Life-Cycle Assessment — Inventory Analysis*, because it contained normative references to ISO 14041. ISO rules prohibit a document that contains normative references to another document from becoming a final international standard until the second document becomes a **DIS**. Drafters were attempting to tie together the timing of the two documents so this would not be a problem.

ISO 14040 is based on the LCA model developed by SETAC. The standard lists the phases of an LCA but notes that they are interrelated and not linear processes. The standard limits itself to general guidance.

ISO 14040 contains some 27 definitions, including:

- life cycle: "consecutive and inter-linked stages of a product system, from raw material acquisition or generation of natural resources to final disposal;" and

- life-cycle assessment: "compilation and evaluation of the inputs and outputs and the potential environmental impacts of a product system throughout its life cycle."

The standard outlines the key features of the LCA methodology, stating:

- The LCA should systematically and adequately address the environmental aspects of product systems from raw materials acquisition to final disposal.

- The depth of detail and time frame of an LCA study may vary to a large extent according to the goal and scope definition.

- The scope, assumptions, data quality parameters, methodologies, and output of LCAs should be transparent and understandable. LCAs should discuss and document the data sources, and be clearly and appropriately communicated.

- Provisions should be made depending on the intended application of the LCA study to respect confidentiality and proprietary matters.

- LCA methodology should be amenable to the inclusion of new scientific findings and improvements in the state-of-the-art of the methodology.

- Specific requirements are applied to LCA studies that are used to make a comparative assertion that is disclosed to the public.

- There is no scientific basis for reducing results to a single overall score or number since trade-offs and complexities exist for the systems analyzed at different stages of their life-cycles.

- There is no single method for conducting LCAs; organizations should have flexibility to practically implement LCA as established in the standard based on the specific application and the user's need.

The document identifies the phases of an LCA:

1) goal and scope definition;

2) inventory analysis;

3) impact assessment; and

4) interpretation.

It notes that an LCA can help a company identify product development and improvement opportunities, strategic planning, public policy making, and marketing.

In the section on LCA methodology, the standard offers general guidance in the following areas:

- goal and scope definition;
- determining study scope
- function and functional unit specification;
- establishing system boundaries;
- establishing data quality;
- making comparisons between systems;
- verifying the quality of the LCA work conducted through a critical review;
- conducting a life-cycle inventory analysis, including a general description of life-cycle inventory and data collection and calculation procedures;
- life-cycle impact assessment;
- interpretation;
- reporting; and
- conducing a critical review, including different review processes, i.e., internal review, expert review, review by interested parties.

ISO 14041: Environmental Management — Life-Cycle Assessment — Inventory Analysis

The scope of this document is to offer a methodology for performing life-cycle inventory studies and reporting LCI results. There is a great deal of experience in industry on conducting LCIs, so it is not surprising that this standard is among the more lengthy in the ISO 14000 series.

As of March 1996, ISO 14041 was a CD for comment. Comments were expected to be reviewed during meetings in June 1996. Depending on the resolution of the comments, the document would be elevated to CD for ballot. It became an international standard in the fall of 1998.

ISO 14041 includes the following sections:

1. scope;

2. normative references, referring users to ISO 14040;

3. definitions;

4. technical introduction that includes in-depth guidance on the following:

   - product systems;

   - unit processes; and

   - data categories;

5. goal and scope definition, including discussion on:

   - scope of the study

   - function and functional unit;

   - defining the initial system boundaries;

   - data requirements;

   - identifying raw and ancillary material inputs;

   - data quality requirements; and

   - critical review;

6. conducting a life-cycle inventory analysis, including guidance on:

   - preparing for data collection;

   - refining the system boundaries;

   - calculation procedures;

   - validating data;

   - relating data to the unit process;

   - relating data to the functional unit and data aggregation;

   - additional system boundary refinement;

   - the allocation procedures, including recycling;

7. reporting results of the LCI study;

Annex A   example of data collection sheet;

Annex B   checklist of critical aspects of an LCI; and

Annex C   examples of different allocation procedures.

ISO 14042 — Environmental Management — Life-Cycle Impact Assessment

This guidance document provides general principles and procedures to understand and evaluate the magnitude of environmental impacts in life-cycle assessment studies. The document is the responsibility of SC5 working group 4, and was in working draft form. It was expected to reach committee draft form by the end of 1997.

At the working group meeting in Rio de Janeiro (March 1996), agreement was reached on the technical framework for life-cycle impact assessment. Under this agreement, the framework is divided into four areas:

- classification — assignment of LCA inventory data to impact categories;

- characterization — description of the impact categories based on stressor-effects network;

- significance analysis — technical analysis to determine the significance of the LCA results; and

- valuation.

Based on this framework, different approaches for conducting impact assessments are possible, although it was not finally decided whether valuation is to remain within the domain of life-cycle impact assessment (WG4) or to be handled as part of Life-Cycle Interpretation (WG5).

It was agreed that life-cycle inventory data alone does not constitute sufficient data to determine the actual effects of an industrial system. To accurately assess and link environmental effects to specific industrial processes, spatial, temporal, threshold and dose-response characteristics for the inputs and outputs being measured must be included in the analysis, in addition to the relative contribution of the resulting effects. This information is embodied in what has become known as external input/output data and environmental data, which are needed to allow for the determination of the relative contribution of a given stressor to the magnitude of its effects(s). These issues are addressed in Annex 1 to the standard.

A consensus was reached in the March 1996 meeting that the life-cycle inventory and impact assessment draft standards should be considered concurrently, not independently, to ensure the compatibility of data collection guidelines.

ISO 14043: Environmental Management — Life-Cycle Assessment — Interpretation

The scope of SC5 WG5 is to "prepare a generic systematic procedure for interpreting information provided by inventory analysis and/or impact assessment of a system."

The document drafters agreed that the LCA interpretation phase has four elements:

1) synthesis of inventory and impact assessment;

2) comparison to scope and improvement tools;

3) conclusions; and

4) recommendations.

It defined the interpretation phase of an LCA as that "in which a synthesis is drawn from the findings of either the inventory analysis or the impact assessment, or both, in line with the defined goal and scope."

The authors agreed that the document should limit itself to offering guidance on conclusions and recommendations that can be drawn from findings of an LCA study that "could lead to improve the overall environmental performance of the product along with a variety of other applications." They also stated that the findings of this phase "may reflect sensitivity and uncertainty analysis."

However, they also agreed that the document should not address the application of such conclusions in future decision making because subsequent decisions often take into account factors such as performance, economic, and social aspects that lie beyond the scope of the document.

An initial draft and outline was developed, and the first working draft was expected in autumn 1996. However, there remained considerable uncertainty as to whether it would progress as a standard, or be converted into a technical report. The standard was retitled from LCA — Improvement Assessment to clarify its purpose.

5.3.2 Development of the Current Technical Framework

Historic LCA Development

LCA was born during the energy shortages of the early 1970s as a systems-oriented tool for tracking material and energy flows in industrial systems.

Emerging out of the science of throughput analysis, LCA consisted essentially of calculating the inputs and outputs of a given industrial system. Input and output data were collected for each unit process identified within the system, using standard mass and energy balance partitioning and calculation techniques, then aggregated together to generate a sum total of resources used, energy consumed, and environmental emissions released by species. Data from such studies were reported in standard mass and energy units of measurement.

computer models

Several private life-cycle inventory (LCI) computer models were developed in Europe and the United States to conduct the iterative calculations needed to complete the mass/energy balance exercises. Over time, these models were extended to integrate data pertaining to a wider range of environmental releases to air, water, and ground, and to accommodate the growing volume of data for basic upstream processes. By the late 1980s, a variety of LCI models were in operation around the world.

Expanding interest in this methodology has coincided with increased interest among government agencies, industry, institutions, and non-governmental organizations in using LCA for broader environmental assessment purposes than the inventory methodology was initially conceived to address.

For instance, LCA has been viewed as a potential tool for making comparisons of the environmental impacts associated with different production technologies, competing materials, product options, and packaging choices. LCA also has been viewed as a potential basis for communicating the environmental performance profile of products sold in the marketplace via product labeling and other communication strategies.

Current Technical Framework

In an effort to normalize the methodologies and resulting databases of the various models,SETAC began work in the late 1980s on developing a common conceptual technical framework for LCA. This framework was to be hammered out at a series of technical workshops based on the contributions of LCA model developers, practitioners, industry users, and stakeholders.

In 1990, SETAC published the proceedings from its first workshop, in which a technical framework was proposed. Under this framework, LCA was described as having three separate components: inventory, impact assessment, and improvement assessment (*Figure 5.2*) In later workshops, a fourth component — goal-setting and scoping — was added to the framework.

impact
assessment

The inclusion of "impact assessment" as a second, distinct stage within this technical framework represented an effort by workshop participants to encompass formally the expanded environmental assessment objectives of some practitioners and users. At the same time, it represented a departure from actual practice, which continued to revolve around the mass and energy balance inventory stage of the framework.

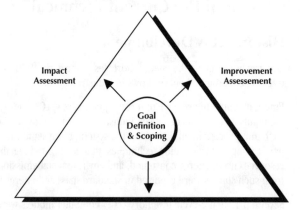

Figure 5.2 — SETAC technical framework for LCA.

Confusion

For LCA to achieve broad environmental assessment objectives and draw meaningful conclusions, it was understood at the outset that dividing the framework into discrete segments should not imply a strict linearity or sequence of assessment, nor suggest that separate segments could be approached entirely independently from one another. SETAC workshop participants were careful to emphasize the iterative and interrelated nature of LCA. For instance, the workshop proceedings stated:

> "It was agreed that conducting an LCA is not a linear process but one that incorporates feedback loops and requires interaction among the LCA components."

not fully understood Despite this intent, the integrated nature of LCA has not been understood fully by either users or practitioners, resulting in considerable confusion in the development of standards, and misapplications in practice. LCI studies have continued to be conducted in accordance with methods originally developed to account for mass and energy flows, yet attempts have been made to interpret these same studies more broadly to address larger environmental questions.

For example, food and beverage packaging studies conducted strictly as inventory exercises have been used as the basis for major government and corporate policy decisions (e.g. European Union, Germany, U.S.) even though no formal efforts were made to link the study findings to actual environmental effects. Nor have any efforts been made to evaluate the packaging burdens in the context of the larger system function, such as delivery of a specified quantity of food or beverage to the consumer.

LCI studies have likewise been cited to compare disposable diapers to cloth diapers, plastic grocery sacks to paper grocery sacks, etc., again without adequate means of assessing the true environmental significance of the LCI findings for each of the systems studied.

Remembering Function

As current LCA practice has shifted toward analyzing specific products as opposed to full systems, some of the basic methodological foundations — defining the function being performed and the system required to perform that function — often have been overlooked or ignored. According to one of the originators of life-cycle methodology, Ian Boustead:

> "Although industry is primarily concerned with products, life cycle analysis is primarily concerned with production systems. This distinction is not trivial and it is the failure to recognize the difference that leads to much of the confusion surrounding the interpretation of the results of LCAs.
>
> Essentially, a system is a collection of operations which when acting together perform some defined function. Specifying the function is crucial to the analysis because not only does it determine what operations go into the system but it also directs the way in which the final results will be normalized."[1]

function before system Without first defining the function, you cannot be certain of adequately defining the system. Product life-cycle inventories (PLCIs), for instance, are typically scoped in terms of the system without first considering function, often leading to an arbitrary establishment of study boundaries. To be most accurately interpreted, PLCIs ideally should be understood in the context of the function they serve. This will provide you with perspective on the relevance of the data being collected.

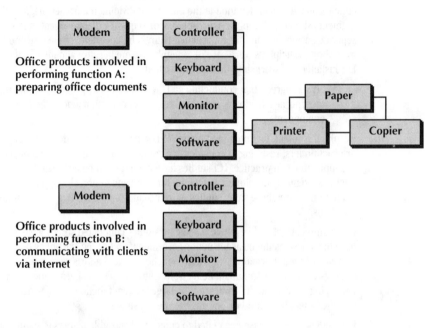

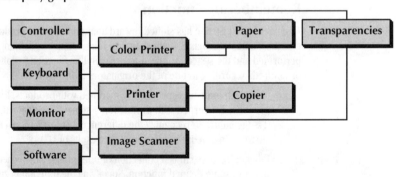

Figure 5.3 — Systems associated with three different office computer-related functions.

example: office computers

Office computers, for example, do not inherently perform a function in and of themselves. Rather, they perform a variety of definable functions in combination with a host of other products. *Figure 5.3* illustrates some of the functions computers help to perform. For each function, the system differs, involving a different configuration of products and a different set of services outside the office. A study of the computer alone will provide the user with no indication of the relative significance of the LCI data associated solely with the use of the computer compared with other aspects of the system, and could easily lead to erroneous interpretations

5.3.3 TC 207's Examination of LCA Practices

ISO 14000 LCA standardization efforts initially were organized to correspond to the SETAC technical framework. However, because the three-stage conceptual framework does not correspond with historic LCA practice, delegates to TOC 207 Subcommittee 5 on LCA have been challenged to reexamine the framework, to determine the strengths and limitations of LCI, and to review the appropriate role of impact assessment in light of the broad environmental assessment needs of environmental management, performance evaluation, and labeling.

mass and
energy balance

In terms of strengths, LCI based on a mass and energy balance approach has proven to be a useful tool for assessing potential material and energy efficiencies on a systemwide basis. By inserting upstream information into the analysis, LCI as currently practiced can help guide industry toward potentially better overall efficiencies from a material and energy throughput standpoint. It also has the potential of indirectly benefiting the environment, especially in identifying energy savings opportunities.

As long as LCI users have confined their goals to match LCI's inherent strengths and recognize its limitations, industry, government, and other stakeholders have found the information useful.

However, an increasing number of users and policy makers are attempting to interpret LCI findings more broadly, assuming that it is automatically valid to link the cumulative treated inventory data obtained from the study to actual environmental effects. This assumption has been made despite the fact that practitioners have long recognized the differences in data required to evaluate environmental impacts. According to the SETAC workshop proceedings, for instance:

> "Because of the expanded nature of some of the data needed to conduct impact assessment, it was recommended that modifications be made, as needed, to the types and extent of data collected in the inventory."

LCI is limited

In reality, LCI is quite limited in its ability to classify and characterize system input and output data collected in an environmentally meaningful way, as the following points illustrate:

• *Uncertainty caused by lack of spatial, temporal, threshold, and dose-response resolutions*

Too little attention has been paid to the relationship of the inventory data to actual environmental effects.

For example, a given point-source emission may be well below the threshold at which an actual measurable environmental effect occurs, and may therefore be of little or no environmental consequence. This threshold consideration, or "resolution," is one of several resolutions that should be used to screen data to determine their environmental relevance.

Other resolutions include:

1) Spatial resolution — determining the geographic scope of the effects of a given environmental release or resource consumption on the environment.

2) Temporal resolution — determining the relevant time period over which a given environmental release or resource use affects the environment.

3) Dose-response resolution — determining the given dose-response curve associated with a given emission or resource consumption with respect to an effect on the environment.

• Uncertainty caused by data aggregation

Common LCI practice involves aggregating input/output data across individual unit processes. While mass and energy input/output data may have relevance for a specific unit process, this relevance can diminish, often dramatically, as data are aggregated across the operations of an entire system.

Cumulative mass calculations for point-source emissions, for example, have little relationship to the actual environmental effects associated with each of the individual point-source emissions, which are generally in different localities. The net effect of arbitrarily and automatically aggregating data from different unit operations is to greatly increase the level of uncertainty with respect to the corresponding environmental effects.

• Uncertainty caused by allocation procedures

Similarly, allocation procedures based strictly on mass inherently do not reflect true relationships between the system inputs/outputs and environmental effects. For example, the steel production system generates both steel and slag, a waste that has found a secondary use market and is now considered a co-product. Traditional mass allocation procedures would accordingly partition 30 percent of all system burdens to slag, based on its proportional mass to the total system. The resulting reduction in burdens assigned to steel (from 100 percent to 70 percent) is clearly arbitrary, and makes little sense given, for instance, that there actually has been no reduction in the amount of iron ore or coke required to make a given amount of steel.

• Uncertainty caused by use of industrial average LCI data

It is quite common within current LCI practice to use published industry average data when site-specific data are unavailable. From a mass and energy perspective, such data may provide a reasonable approximation of actual system inputs/outputs, or may be far off the mark, depending on the range of actual performance within a given industry.

In terms of environmental significance, however, most industry average data are far more problematic because they inherently dilute or even eliminate the spatial, temporal, threshold, and dose-response resolutions required to determine the certainty of relationship between a given measurement and an actual environmental effect. The few notable exceptions are those releases that have a high certainty of effect on a global scale (e.g., global warming gases and ozone depleting gases).

As the above examples illustrate, adherence to a mass and energy data collection and assessment approach does not serve the purpose of LCA as an environmental assessment tool. While traditional LCI is a useful engineering tool for tracking material and energy flows in industrial systems, it generally does not provide the appropriate data sets required to conduct a comprehensive impact assessment — that is, to shed light on the relationship between measurable inputs and outputs and actual environmental effects.

Given what current LCI methodology was actually designed to do in the first place, LCI can be viewed as representing its own complete technical framework — an "engineering" framework — subject to its own level of interpretation that does not depend on impact assessment.

The Critical Role of Life-Cycle Impact Assessment

Whether LCA ultimately can be transformed into an environmental assessment tool beyond the limited scope of the life-cycle inventory "engineering" framework remains to be seen and will depend in large part on the pioneering efforts of the Subcommittee 5 working group on impact assessment (WG4). The working group has been approaching this challenge from two directions.

Inventory interpretation approach

First, it has been exploring an "inventory interpretation" approach, following the model originally conceived within SETAC. In this approach, potential system impacts would be modeled on the basis of input/output data that have been aggregated and partitioned without regard to the applicable spatial, temporal, threshold, and dose-response resolutions.

The purpose of such an approach would be to build directly upon the data generated under the standard LCI in order to provide users with a rough, qualitative profile of potential environmental impacts.

As described in the May 1995 issue of *LCA News,* a Eurpean-based SETAC publication:

> "[The inventory interpretation approach] is a comparative approach which looks at the difference in resource use and emissions between option, rather than any evaluation of likelihood of actual effect or environmental harm. It employs a simplified interpretation of the inventory results, based on a global analysis."

The drawbacks of this approach are substantial.

inventory interpretation drawbacks

By accepting aggregated input/output data without considering the applicable resolutions, such an analysis would be incapable of providing an accurate portrayal of the actual environmental effects associated with the system. From a managerial perspective, it therefore would be difficult, if not impossible, to distinguish those industrial operations responsible for actual environmental effects from those causing no effects, and thereby hamper efforts to use LCA findings to develop targeted improvement strategies.

Equally problematic, the high degree of uncertainty inherent in the predicted impacts would make it exceedingly difficult to compare industrial systems or evaluate competing materials, designs, or production technology options.

Finally, the quantitative reporting of such results could easily suggest a level of precision not achieved by the actual interpretation, leading to potential confusion and misinterpretation by industry users, policy makers, and other stakeholders.

LCSEA technical framework approach

To overcome these hurdles, a second approach is also being developed — one that is oriented toward providing a more accurate profile of an industrial system's actual effects on the environment.

LCSEA: enhance evaluation

The purpose of this approach — referred to as the "Life-Cycle Stressor-Effects Assessment" (LCSEA) — is to enhance the role of LCA as an environmental performance evaluation and management decision tool in line with the objectives of ISO 14000. It is being designed specifically to ensure that the information you collect for analysis is environmentally relevant and accurate and helps you avoid unnecessary data collection and unwarranted disclosure.

Under the new quantitative framework, the magnitude of environmental effects from each unit operation along the life cycle of the industrial system is evaluated, taking into consideration the applicable spatial, temporal, threshold, and dose-response resolutions.

Instead of attempting to graft environmental interpretation onto an existing inventory data collection methodology, the new framework makes stressor-effects assessment the central driving force of the LCA process itself. In other words, you adapt inventory to the needs of impact assessment rather than allow impact assessment to be subordinated to the role of merely interpreting inventory data.

The life-cycle stressor-effects assessment approach is depicted in *Figure 5.4.*

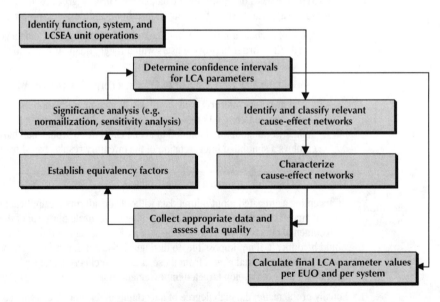

Figure 5.4 — The life-cycle stressor-effects assessment (LCSEA).

Stressor-Effects Networks

key to LCA: interlocking events

At the heart of life-cycle impact assessment lies the concept of "stressor-effects networks". Stressor-effects networks are the interlocking physical, biological, and chemical events that connect a specific cause or "stressor" to an identified environmental effect or effects. Life-cycle impact assessment is concerned with linking those events attributable to a given industrial system (i.e., stressors) to measurable effects on the environment.

To ensure that the data collection process provides meaningful information, potential stressor-effects networks associated with a specific industrial system should be identified as one of the initial steps in the overall LCSEA process. There are cause-effects networks associated with resources, energy, and environmental releases. *Figure 5.5*, for instance, depicts the acid rain cause-effects network linking SO_2 emissions to fish kills.

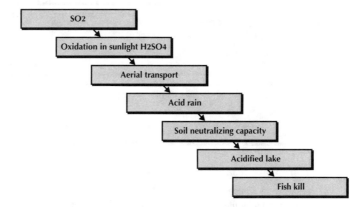

Figure 5.5 — Example of a stressor-effects network.

There are several different types of stressor-effects networks: single networks, parallel networks, serial networks, etc. In parallel cause-effects networks, a single input or output is associated with multiple effects, or alternatively, several inputs or outputs combine to create a single effect. For example, NO_x is a precursor to both smog and acid rain, which are each, in turn, stressors in numerous cause-effects chains.

Life-Cycle Stressor-Effects Model Architecture

Within standard LCI, terms such as "unit operation" and "unit process" are used to refer to an individual physical process or groups of processes within the system that produce a single product or service, and their associated inputs and outputs. Inventory practitioners typically relate the input/output data for a given unit operation back to individual units of production. Additionally, such data are generally averaged over a period of time such as twelve months to account for fluctuations in industrial processes.

Once normalized and averaged in this way, the input and output data for all unit operations comprising the system are aggregated together and allocated to produce an overall mass and energy balance.

LSCEA unit operations

Just as LCI models are designed to link unit operations together, "LCSEA unit operations are the fundamental building blocks of the LCSEA architecture. Each LCSEA unit operation is defined in terms of its relevant stressor-effects networks. Once individual unit operations are defined, they can then be linked to each other not only by process, but also by the significance of the various measurable effects. Together, these unit operations provide an environmental effects profile of the entire system, and make possible the calculation of a corresponding effects profile on a functional unit basis. Because the objective of the LCSEA approach is to assess quantitatively the significance and contribution of a specific industrial system's effects on the environment, the LCSEA unit operation is distinguished from the standard LCI unit operation in several respects.

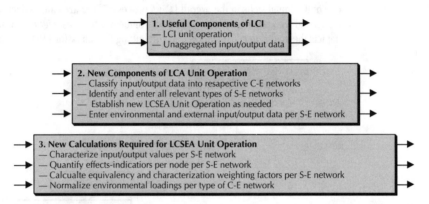

Figure 5.6 — LCSEA unit operation.

As shown in *Figure 5.6*, the physical boundaries of the LCSEA unit operation generally correspond with the boundaries of a standard LCI unit operation. Site-specific input and output data associated with the standard LCI unit operation, when available, provide the initial set of useful data for the LCSEA unit operation. These input/output data are classified into corresponding stressor-effects networks.

However, as reported in the SETAC proceedings, environmental assessment requires the collection of additional types of data beyond the normal input and output data collected under the standard LCI approach.

"Environmental data" are required to quantify accurately the significance and contribution of a unit operation's inputs and outputs to specific, measurable environmental effects. Such data add spatial, temporal, threshold, and/or dose-response dimension to the unaggregated input and output data.

example:
eutophication
For example, in the eutrophication stressor-effects network, environmental data include the baseline percentage of dissolved oxygen (2 percent) in a lake and the reduced percentage (0.2 percent) of dissolved oxygen in that same lake at a later date. These data, in turn, are used to characterize the "effects-indicator" for the LCSEA unit operation — i.e., 90 percent decrease in dissolved oxygen.

While such data are routinely collected within other environmental assessment disciplines, such as environmental impact assessments (EIAs), the LCSEA approach represents the first effort to integrate such data directly into the LCA architecture. It is the inclusion of these new types of data that transforms LCA from a tool used simply to model potential impacts into a tool that assesses the actual effects of a system. Without the perspective that these new data add, inventory data can be misinterpreted easily and potentially can be misused.

Certain stressor-effects networks are not directly revealed by standard input or output data, but can nevertheless be linked back to specific industrial activities in a quantitative manner.

For example, digging and subsequently refilling a mining pit could have significant effects on the local wildlife habitat, even though standard mass and energy LCI would have no mechanism for accounting for this disturbance. Environmental data are again required to quantify the significance and contribution of these activities to defined effects.

The new components of the LCSEA unit operation described above make possible, for the first time, the ability to:

- determine the significance and contribution of each input /output data point;

- identify specific linkages in the cause-effects networks associated with a given unit operation and quantify the magnitudes of their respective effects-indicators;

- establish quantitative equivalency factors with established levels of certainty;

- calculate the "environmental loadings" for each LCSEA unit operation per stressor-effects network on a functional unit basis; and

- calculate the cumulative environmental loadings for the system, product, or service being studied.

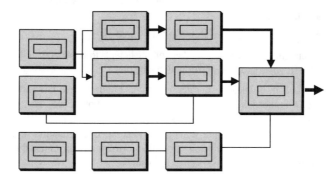

Figure 5.7 — LCSEA unit operations linked by effect and function.

Three concentric rectangles are used to represent an individual LCSEA unit operation, representing:

1) the useful components of standard LCIs;

2) the new components of LCSEA model; and

3) the new calculations required.

As depicted above in *Figure 5.7*, the magnitude of all environmental loadings is cumulative for all relevant stressor-effects networks. In this diagram, the width of the arrows reflects the relative magnitude of the effect.

5.3.4 Applications to ISO 14001

As implementation tools, the "engineering" LCA technical framework (i.e., current life-cycle inventory practice) and the LCSEA approach to life-cycle impact assessment each offer support to ISO 14000-related objectives.

LCA engineering framework

Given the historic role of LCI, this framework may serve as a valuable tool for engineers interested in assessing material and energy efficiencies in specified industrial systems as part of a larger EMS strategy, provided that the framework's strengths and limitations are well understood to avoid misinterpretation.

The LCSEA framework, for its part, has been developed specifically to integrate the resolutions and accuracy requirements needed to support the larger objectives of ISO 14000 in the areas of environmental management systems, environmental performance evaluation, environmental auditing, and environmental labeling. Through this framework, it is possible to construct quantified environmental performance indicators that can serve as an objective basis for a variety of internal and external applications, including:

- measuring current environmental performance in industrial operations;

- establishing environmental improvement goals and monitoring progress toward these goals;

- evaluating product design for environment options;

- enhancing environmental procurement programs by establishing a level playing field for all suppliers;

- educating employees, vendors, and stakeholders; and

- communicating environmental accomplishments to customers and stakeholders via Type III environmental performance labeling.

While LCA is by no means a perfect science, its importance to ISO 14000 must be underscored. Without such a uniform methodology and set of metrics, environmental performance evaluation can only retreat to more subjective criteria, with potentially counterproductive consequences. In the vacuum, a multitude of competing evaluation strategies would most certainly arise, adding confusion rather than clarifying environmental issues, and, most likely, resulting in unnecessary costs to business.

FOOTNOTES

[1]Life-Cycle Inventories: A Qualitative Description, Dr. Ian Boustead, The Open University, March 1992.

Environmental Auditing

The Evolution of Environmental Auditing

© by Jean H. McCreary, Esq., Nixon, Hargrave, Devans & Doyle LLP;
Leader ST2 TG1 on General Principles of Environmental Auditing
Cornelius C. Smith, Jr., Director of Environmental Management Services, ML Strategies Inc.;
Chairman, ST2 on Environmental Auditing,
Elizabeth A. Potts, President, ABS Quality Evaluations and
Raymond W. Kane, Engineer, Environmental Management Consulting

6.1.1 The Birth of Environmental Auditing in the U.S.

The term "**environmental auditing**" unofficially was coined in the United States in the mid-1970s as environmental laws and regulations grew in response to the public's desire for environmental protection.

At about the same time, Europe was undergoing a social shift toward ecologically conscientious management in business and in politics. Fueled largely by environmental disasters of the 1970s and 1980s (Seveso, Bhopal, Basel, and Chernobyl), this social shift, which principally began in Germany, gave rise to the concept of "ecological auditing."

eco-auditing   Environmental auditing and ecological auditing — shortened to "eco-auditing"— are fundamentally distinct. Eco-auditing has its roots in how a company proactively evaluates the impacts of its processes and activities on its external ecology and how management responds to those impacts.

environmental auditing   Environmental auditing was born primarily as a defensive response by U.S. companies to measure themselves against a vast set of federal and state environmental regulations. From 1975 to 1995, federal environmental regulations published in the Code of Federal Regulations grew from about 300 total pages to about 12,500 pages. In addition, state environmental regulations, often more stringent and different from federal laws, added thousands more pages of requirements to the regulated community's burden.

Unlike in Europe, environmental auditing in the United States grew mainly from fear of enforcement, fines, and prison for environmental law violation.

Figure 6.1 shows the recent record of federal enforcement of environmental laws and regulations from 1990-1994. This level of enforcement in the 1970s and 1980s was somewhat less aggressive than what occurred in the first half of the 1990s. From the early 1970s to 1995, government officials have handed out more than 1,000 years of jail time and hundreds of millions of dollars in fines and penalties because of noncompliance with environmental laws and regulations.

	Agents	Cases Initiated	Referrals	Defendants Prosecuted	Sentences*	Fines**
FY 1990	51	112	56	100	75.3	5.5
FY 1991	62	150	81	104	80.3	14.1
FY 1992	72	203	107	150	94.6	37.9
FY 1993	110	410	140	161	74.3	29.7
FY 1994	123	525	220	250	99	36.8

Defandants equal entities and individuals charged in the fiscal year
* Years of incarceration
** Millions of dollars

Figure 6.1 — 1995 EPA record of enforcement.

6.1.2 Securities and Exchange Commission Role

Charged with protecting the investing public against improper financial reporting, the Securities and Exchange Commission (SEC) was the U.S. agency responsible for giving the concept of environmental auditing significant visibility in the late 1970s. The SEC was concerned that companies were not accurately evaluating and reporting their environmentally related expenditures to the public and consequently were over-reporting earnings and financial performance.

The SEC took action against three companies: U.S. Steel in 1977, Allied Chemical in 1979, and Occidental Petroleum in 1980. The SEC consent agreements with these three companies may have been the first time the requirement to conduct environmental auditing was officially used in legal documents. While there were many companies beginning to grapple with how to "audit" their environmental performance prior to this period, the SEC actions in the late 1970s played a key role in establishing environmental auditing as a recognized compliance assurance practice.

6.1.3 Environmental Protection Agency Role

In 1985 the U.S. EPA proposed a draft policy on environmental auditing as interim guidance to the regulated community. After a comment period (which interestingly generated only 13 commenters), EPA published a final policy statement on July 9, 1986. EPA did not make environmental auditing mandatory, but its policy statement was another major influence in the expansion and development of environmental auditing.

EPA's policy statement specifically:

- encourages regulated entities to develop, implement, and upgrade environmental auditing programs;
- discusses when EPA may or may not request audit reports;
- explains how EPA's inspection and enforcement activities may respond to regulated entities' efforts to assure compliance through auditing;
- endorses environmental auditing at federal facilities;
- encourages state and local environmental auditing initiatives; and
- outlines elements of effective audit programs.

On December 22, 1995, EPA announced a final auditing policy, "Incentives for Self-Policing: Discovery, Disclosure, Correction and Prevention of Violations Final Policy Statement." Under the new policy, the agency will greatly reduce civil penalties and limit liability for criminal prosecution for regulated entities that meet the policy's conditions for discovery, disclosure, and correction.

The December 1995 final self-policing policy states:

> "EPA will not seek gravity-based penalties for violations that are discovered through a Corrective Measures Study (CMS) or an environmental audit and that are promptly disclosed and expeditiously corrected, provided other important conditions or safeguards are met.
>
> These entities must take steps to prevent recurrence of the violation and to remediate harm caused by the violation."

The final self-policing policy does not apply to:

- violations that resulted in serious actual harm or may have presented an imminent and substantial endangerment to human health or the environment;
- repeated violations;

- individual criminal acts; or

- corporate criminal acts arising from conscious disregard or

  willful blindness to violations.

Finally, if, in EPA's opinion, a violation does not merit any penalty due to insignificant monetary benefit, it may waive the penalty altogether. 📖 (See Part 8 Chapter 2, Section 3 and Appendix D for more information on the EPA audit policy.)

At about this time in the mid-1980s, the regulated community began to seek one another out to share information on the evolving discipline of environmental auditing. This gave rise to the Environmental Auditing Roundtable (EAR). EAR is considered the most recognized national professional organization dedicated to enhancing the practice of environmental auditing.

In 1996, the EAR had more than 800 members with bylaws, a code of ethics, and an eight-member board of directors. Meetings are held quarterly to share information on a wide spectrum of environmental auditing topics. By the late 1980s, environmental auditing was at a peak and had become a "professional" discipline and management practice.

6.1.4 Department of Justice and U.S. Sentencing Commission Role

In 1991, the U.S. Department of Justice (DOJ) published prosecutorial guidelines that gave DOJ lawyers guidance on prosecuting environmental cases. DOJ's guidelines stated that companies with compliance assurance systems in place were less likely to be prosecuted. To escape prosecution, according to the guidelines, a company needed an environmental audit program with regularly scheduled audits.

Also in 1991, the U.S. Sentencing Commission established its **Organizational Sentencing Guidelines**. Like the DOJ prosecutorial guidelines the organizational guidelines called for implementing monitoring and auditing systems as a way to significantly mitigate criminal penalties.

Both of these guidelines caused a major effect — they encouraged "fence-sitters" to establish environmental auditing programs and procedures. Companies in industrial sectors, not normally known as "polluters," particularly were motivated to start conducting audits as a way of protecting themselves from potential environmental sanctions. 📖 (See Part 8, Chapter 2, Section 3 for more information on the U.S. Sentencing Commission guidelines.)

6.1.5 Voluntary Practices

In the U.S. in the late 1980s, a social and ethical culture change began to affect the way companies viewed responsible environmental management. Compliance with laws and fear of enforcement began to give way to demonstrating conformance with socially acceptable, responsible environmental management principles as a reason why companies conducted environmental audits.

The most notable of these principles are the Coalition for Environmentally Responsible Economies (CERES) Principles. First introduced in 1989 as the Valdez Principles, the CERES

Principles comprise a comprehensive, 10-point environmental code for corporations. These principles were devised to encourage the development of programs to prevent environmental degradation, to help corporations in setting policy, and to enable investors to make informed decisions regarding environmental issues.

One of the 10 principles specifically states that companies should conduct annual self-evaluations of their progress and support the timely creation of generally accepted environmental audit procedures. (Companies signing up to adopt the CERES Principles continues to grow.) More than 100 companies had joined by early 1996, including Fortune 500 companies like GM, Sun, and H.B. Fuller Company.

Other codes of management practice include the Chemical Manufacturers Association (CMA) Responsible Care® program. This program, which emphasizes responsible, proactive environmental management for the chemical process industries, requires, among other things, periodic audits and self-evaluations of environmentally related activities by CMA's 130 member companies. 📖 (See Part 10, Chapter 1, Section 1 for more information on Responsible Care®.)

The International Chamber of Commerce (ICC) Business Principles for Environmental Management, which came out in 1992, is a third example of a nonregulatory code of conduct that encourages environmental auditing.

Principle 16 of ICC's business principles reads:

> "To measure environmental performance; to conduct regular environmental audits and assessments of compliance with company requirements, legal requirements, and these principles; and periodically to provide appropriate information to the Board of Directors, shareholders, employees, the authorities, and the public."

6.1.6 Growth of Environmental Auditing Programs

The 20-year period between 1975 and 1995 saw environmental auditing increase from perhaps fewer than 50 companies in the chemical and heavy manufacturing industries to thousands of companies across all industrial sectors in 1995. Environmental audit surveys published by the Manufacturers Alliance in February 1995 and Price Waterhouse LLP in March 1995 provide the hard evidence. About 85 percent of "manufacturing" companies reported they have formal environmental audit programs, and about 75 percent of all industries said they engage in environmental auditing.

While a small number of environmental auditing programs were started in the early and mid 1970s, the large majority of industries started their audit programs between 1985 and 1995. The median year was 1990 in both surveys, meaning half of the responding companies started their auditing activities prior to 1990 and half started their auditing programs after 1990. This attests to the dramatic growth of auditing in the second five years alone.

6.1.7 Environmental Auditing and EMSs

As noted above, in the early to mid-1980s, most company environmental auditing (EA) programs in the United States focused primarily on compliance with applicable statutory and regulatory requirements. Following are some typical program purpose statements reflecting this legal compliance emphasis:

- avoiding fines, penalties, and loss of image;
- satisfying officer and director fiduciary obligations;
- avoiding manager and employee legal liabilities;
- obtaining comprehensive, accurate, and objective compliance data; and
- providing assurances of future compliance.

In these early years, company environmental compliance auditing programs often were the only identifiable element of a formal or systematic environmental management system. Even where more comprehensive systems were evident, they, like the early EA programs, usually sought only to preserve the status quo by achieving the absence of a negative.

Since the mid-1980s, more and more enlightened corporations have come to realize that sound environmental performance is good business and good environmental management is an essential component of overall business management.

At the same time, industry EA practice has gradually evolved. Companies have increasingly recognized and accepted EA environmental compliance and performance as a line management responsibility, and have established improved business unit monitoring and self-assessment mechanisms. Coincidentally, many corporate EA programs have begun to shift gradually from costly wall-to-wall auditing to increased compliance sampling verification of the implementation and effectiveness of decentralized line management assessments.

An important result of decentralized company EA responsibilities has been that corporate management has increased emphasis on examining the business unit and facility EMSs that drive their environmental performance. These changes reflect an increased awareness that, rather than being a management system in and of itself, the basic function of EA is to serve as an EMS quality control tool.

Most company EA programs have made great strides forward in eliminating the "got-ya" perception of corporate audits. They have accomplished this primarily by increasing the competency, professionalism, and personal attributes and skills of their auditors and program managers.

increased auditor skills

Many companies also contend that their re-engineered EA programs seek to educate and help line management with fulfilling their environmental responsibilities. Although development would appear admirable, it is not without its pitfalls.

While corporate environmental auditors can perform the important function of communicating facility and business best practices to auditees, corporate EA programs must be cautious not to compromise the independence of their auditors, especially when audit teams are called upon to perform root-cause analysis and make corrective action plan recommendations. You can best avoid conflicts of interest in such cases by rotating audit team leadership and membership sufficiently to assure the audit team maintains its independence and integrity.

ISO 14001 implementation and use of the EA guidelines will have a profound effect on many company internal environmental auditing practices. While the great majority of the audit criteria governing historical internal environmental audit programs consisted of applicable legal requirements, a substantial number of future program criteria will be drawn from the ISO 14001 EMS specification and the voluntary commitment requirements identified under **ISO 14001, Section 4.2.2**.

ISO 14001: voluntary commitments wiegh

You should note that ISO 14001 puts those voluntary commitment requirements on an equal plane with legal requirements. Thus, for example, an environmental audit of an ISO 14001 organization will give the same weight to industry code principles (e.g., the ICC Business Charter for Sustainable Redevelopment) as it does to Federal Clean Water Act mandates.

In the name of efficiency, the scope of internal EA program criteria, at least at the corporate or headquarters level, is likely to expand to include not only these voluntary requirements, but also the other EMS requirements of ISO 14001.

ISO 14001 certification body (registrar) audits, unlike their organizational internal audit counterparts, will probably engage in little, if any, traditional environmental legal compliance auditing.

On the contrary, third-party audits will seek to verify that your organization has implemented and maintained a compliance management system consistent with its policy compliance commitment.

internal vs. third-party audits

Hence, the registrar will look at the comprehensiveness and currency of your organization's identified legal and voluntary requirements, related training of managers and employees, the adequacy of compliance related programs and resources, compliance auditing or assessment programs, compliance and enforcement history, corrective action plan adequacy and effectiveness, etc. The distinction between internal and third-party environmental audits will lie primarily in the degree of traditional legal compliance auditing they encompass.

Integration of environmental audits with other types of audits probably will gain popularity in future years. Driven by cost-effectiveness and efficiency, companies will seek to integrate occupational health and safety, quality, and possibly even financial auditing with environmental auditing. The less complex the operations being audited, the greater the opportunity for efficient integration.

As to registrar audits, there is little doubt that, to minimize costs, industry clients will request integrated ISO 9000 and 14000 audits and certifications.

Despite the fact that the environmental auditing guidelines represent international consensus on environmental auditing and auditor criteria best practices, many existing programs of companies with reasonably mature EMSs do not satisfy their criteria in all respects. Hence, as the EA guidelines gain acceptance, internal audit program quality and auditor competence are bound to improve.

Government Use of Audit Standards

Indications are that the EA guidelines will not be translated into federal, state, or local legal requirements in the United States. But, coupled with ISO 14001 certification, they could become important building blocks of industry/government voluntary programs such as the U.S. Environmental Protection Agency's Common Sense Initiative and Environmental Leadership Program. 📖 (See Part 8, Chapter 2, Section 3 for more information on these programs.)

The anticipated outcome of applying these alternatives to the traditional U.S. command-control-punish model will encourage voluntary ISO 14001 implementation and environmental auditing consistent with the EA guidelines by offering valuable benefits such as:

- decreased government inspections,
- reduced reporting requirements,
- fast-track permitting, and
- public recognition.

It is also expected that, at the federal level, EA programs following the EA guidelines will receive positive consideration in government enforcement policies in EPA, in the Department of Justice, and in the U.S. Sentencing Commission guidelines. 📖 (See Part 8, Chapter 2, Section 3 and Annex D for more information on these guidelines.)

The raging debate at both the federal and state levels over the appropriateness of protecting environmental audit findings and documentation by a legislated or judicially recognized legal privilege will most likely continue for years to come.

Historically, the debate has been limited to legal compliance audits. However, as domestic internal environmental audits begin to include EMS audit criteria with increasing frequency, the debate will expand necessarily to cover EMS considerations. Public image and toxic tort liability concerns will probably drive industry to protect the confidentiality of EMS audit findings and documentation in much the same manner as it has sought to shield compliance audit results. 📖 (See Part 8, Chapter 1 for more information on legal aspects of EA and EMSs.)

Client vs. Auditee

The client is the party that requests the audit. The auditee is the party that is being audited. While the client and the auditee may be the same party, this is not always the case. For example, a large manufacturer may request an audit from an external firm for one or more of its suppliers. In this case, the client is the manufacturing firm, and the auditee is the supplier.

The scoping process is one by which the lead auditor, subject to approval of the client, determines the framework within which to achieve the audit. Frequently, agreement on scope of the audit is done after the lead auditor communicates the objectives to your organization (the auditee) and consults with you before the audit **(ISO 14010, Section 5.1; ISO 14011, Section 5.1.1)**.

Once the objectives of the audit are agreed upon, a part of the scoping process should include determining the criteria against which your EMS will be compared, since that will be crucial to determining how to achieve the audit objectives. The criteria should be defined in sufficient detail so that the audit team can collect the requisite audit evidence to be analyzed in the examination and evaluation process of the audit itself to determine whether criteria have been met **(ISO 14010, Section 5.5)**.

The lead auditor and the client need to discuss and agree upon the manner of reporting the results in advance, along with the commitment of resources sufficient to satisfy the intended scope of the audit **(ISO 14011, Section 5.1.1)**.

ISO 14001 and the **ISO 14004** interpretive guidance do not specifically define the EMS audit objectives or scope. These will depend on your organization's EMS, its defined specific objectives, and how the EMS has been implemented. These items can be as varied as organizations themselves. However, the overall criteria against which EMS audit programs will be compared are stated within ISO 14001.

Nevertheless, at the client's request, the objectives (and scope) of the EMS audit could be expanded beyond the minimum established by ISO 14001, to include elements such as corporate performance objectives and identification of potential areas of improvement **(ISO 14011, Section 4.1(e))** or to include corrective action recommendations.

The audit should only be undertaken if, after consultation with the client (and, optionally, the auditee), it is the lead auditor's opinion that:

1) there is sufficient and appropriate information about the subject matter of the audit;

2) there are adequate resources to support the audit process; and

3) there is adequate cooperation from the auditee **(ISO 14010, Section 4)**.

If the lead auditor thoroughly plans the scoping and pre-audit stages, he or she will ensure that the lead auditor is capable of making these determinations.

CHAPTER 2

ISO 14001 EMS Audits

An ISO 14001 environmental management system (EMS) audit is the vehicle through which the environmental aspects of your organization and how they are managed are systematically compared against the requirements of the ISO 14001 specification. (References to specific sections of standards are boldfaced for ease of reference.)

ISO 14001, Section 4.4.4, requires that your organization "shall establish and maintain programs and procedures (including procedures covering the audit scope, frequency, and methodologies, requirements for conducting audits and reporting results) for periodic EMS audits for:

1) "determining whether the EMS conforms to planned arrangements for environmental management, including the requirements of this standard, and has been properly implemented and maintained" and

2) "providing information on the results of audits to management."

According to the standard, your EMS audit program shall be based on "the environmental importance of the activity concerned" and the results of previous audits. These audits are viewed as "internal" to your organization (i.e., commissioned by the organization for its internal purposes) even if conducted using "external" (i.e., consulting) resources.

ISO 14011, Section 3.2 (which closely tracks the definition in **ISO 14001, Section 3.6**), defines an EMS audit as follows:

> "Systematic, documented verification process of objectively obtaining and evaluating audit evidence to determine whether an organization's environmental management system conforms with the environmental management system audit criteria, and communicating the results of this process to the client."

6.2.1 Differing Kinds of Audits

EMS audit is <u>not</u> compliance audit

An EMS audit should not be confused with various other types of audits you might conduct, either as a part of the EMS or otherwise.

For example, an EMS audit is not as limited in scope as a regulatory compliance audit that may be internally performed by your company as a means of ensuring that you comply with all legal and other environmental requirements applicable to your organization (**ISO 14001, Sections 4.2.2 - 4.2.4**).

However, as will be discussed in greater detail, an EMS audit may encompass an evaluation of your internal or external compliance audit program. This is because compliance auditing is likely to be a part of the environmental management system to ensure that you have identified the legal and other requirements applicable to your company and have implemented a systematic means for achieving compliance with them.

The difference is that, although the EMS audit may "spot-check" compliance, the focus will be on whether the system for managing compliance is functional, rather than whether that compliance status can be independently determined.

conformity
assessment

Neither is the EMS audit the same thing as the "conformity assessment process," in which an external auditor, employed by a registrar, compares an organization's implemented ISO 14001 EMS against the requirements of ISO 14001 to determine conformity to that standard and to issue the certificate of registration. ⌸ (See Part 7, Chapters 1 and 2 for more information on the conformity assessment process, and Part 6, Chapter 5 for more information on registration audits.)

Although the mission of the conformity assessment and the EMS audit is the same, the work products are directed at different audiences. In the case of the EMS audit, the audience is the organization's management, so that it can assess how well its EMS is working. In the case of the conformity assessment, the audience is the registrar, so that the registrar can verify that the organization's program functions as described in the program documentation and otherwise conforms to ISO 14001 criteria.

self-declaration

Organizations that implement ISO 14001, but elect to "self-declare" conformity with ISO 14001, may use the internal EMS audit as the basis for the self-declaration. The EMS audit may also be the basis of supplier audit confirmations (SAC, a "hybrid" process falling somewhere between the completely external registration process and the internal "self-declaration" process). ⌸ (See Part 7, Chapter 2 for more information on SACs.)

The following sections describe aspects of EMS audits from the perspective of a moderate- or large-sized organization. Although this discussion also may pertain to small and medium-sized enterprises (SMEs), ⌸ Part 6, Chapter 3 contains a focused discussion of SME interests in the ISO 14001 process.

In addition, there are many U.S. and international standards covering audit programs generally, as well as environmental management systems. ⌸ (These are listed in Appendix F.)

This chapter, however, focuses mainly on the ISO Technical Committee 207's guidelines relating to auditing (**ANSI/ISO 14010**, **14011, and 14012**) as applied to EMS audits. ⌸ The ISO auditing guidelines are also generally discussed in Part 1, Chapter 2, Section 7 .

Existing Environmental Auditing Standards

Following are existing or proposed environmental auditing standards, apart from the ISO standards, you may want to consider as you embark on setting up your environmental auditing program: ⌸ (For more information on obtaining the standards, see relevant organizations Appendix F.)

- American Society for Testing and Materials (ASTM) E-50.04 provisional standard (PS) 12 —*Practice for Environmental Regulatory Compliance Audits*;

- ASTM *Guide for the Study and Evaluation of an Organization's Environmental Management Systems;*

  ASTM E 1529-93 —*Standard Practice for Environmental Site Assessments: Phase I Environmental Site Assessment Process*;

- ASTM E 1529-93 — *Standard Practice for Environmental Site Assessments: Transaction Screen Process*;

- ASTM E-50.02 — *Standard Guide for Environmental Site Assessments: Phase II Environmental Site Assessment Process* [DRAFT];

- Federal Home Loan Bank System — Office of Regulatory Activities Thrift Bulletin 16 — *Environmental Risk and Liability*; Federal Home Loan Bank/Federal Housing Finance Board, 1777 F. Street, NW, Washington, DC 20006; tel: 202-408-2540

- Environmental Auditing Roundtable — *Standards for Design and Implementation of an Environmental Health and Safety Audit Program* (1996); 35888 Mildred Avenue, North Ridgeville, OH 44039

[Not included in this list are various Canadian and European standards, any NSF International provisional standards, various American Society of Civil Engineers and Association of Ground Water Scientists and Engineers (AGWSE) references, and local standards — such as the Consulting Engineers Council of Metropolitan Washington *Guidelines for Environmental Site Assessments.*]

6.2.2 The ISO 14010 Environmental Auditing Standards

The scope of work of ISO TC 207, Subcommittee 2, is development of ISO 14000 standards in the field of environmental auditing and related environmental investigations, such as site assessments and initial reviews.

"shoulds" vs. "shalls"

Unlike the ISO 14001 environmental management systems specification, all of the EA standards developed by Subcommittee 2 are and will be guidelines couched in "should" rather than "shall" language.

In other words, while ISO 14001 criteria are requirements against which a certification body (registrar) will assess conformance, the EA guidelines will function as recommended elements of model environmental auditing programs. As such, they are designed to apply equally to all types of environmental audits, regardless of whether they are conducted by internal or external (e.g., registrar) audit teams.

Environmental Auditing Guidelines

The first three EA guidelines developed by Subcommittee 2 are:

- *ISO 14010 — Guidelines on Environmental Auditing — General Principles on Environmental Auditing*

- *ISO 14011 — Guidelines on Environmental Auditing — Audit Procedures — Auditing of Environmental Management Systems; and*

- *ISO 14012 — Guidelines on Environmental Auditing —Qualification Criteria for Environmental Auditors.*

Like ISO 14001, these environmental auditing guidelines were developed at a rapid pace to respond to the European Union's Eco-Management and Audit Scheme Regulation (EMAS) timetable. Since EMAS has an auditing component as well as an EMS component, the three ISO auditing standards and ISO 14001 should be considered holistically when they are used in meeting EMAS requirements.

Auditing Standards Contents, Terms, and Definitions

Before discussing the main concepts and key requirements of an auditor according to the EA guidelines, a brief understanding of key terms may help you navigate through this section.

Following is the table of contents for each of the three auditing standards. 📖 These are referred to in Chapter 3. The standards themselves may be purchased from several sources. (See Appendix F for more information on purchasing standards.)

ISO 14010 — Guidelines on Environmental Auditing — General Principles on Environmental Auditing

0 Introduction

1 Scope

2 Normative references

3 Definitions

3.1 Audit conclusion: Professional judgement or opinion expressed by an auditor about the subject matter of the audit, based on and limited to reasoning the auditor has applied to audit findings.

3.2 Audit criteria: Policies, practices, procedures, or requirements against which the auditor compares collected audit evidence about the subject matter.

3.3 Audit evidence: Verifiable information, records, or statements of fact.

3.4 Audit findings: Results of the evaluation of the collected audit evidence compared against the agreed audit criteria.

3.5 Audit team: Group of auditors, or a single auditor, designated to perform a given audit; the audit team may also include technical experts and auditors-in-training.

3.6 Auditee: Organization to be audited.

3.7 Auditor: (environmental): Person qualified to perform environmental audits.

3.8 Client: Organization commissioning the audit.

3.9 Environmental audit: Systematic, documented verification process of objectively obtaining and evaluating audit evidence to determine whether specified environmental activities, events, conditions, management systems, or information about these matters conform with audit criteria, and communicating the results of this process to the client.

3.10 Lead auditor (environmental): Person qualified to manage and perform environmental audits.

3.11 Organization: Company, corporation, firm, enterprise, institution, or association, or part thereof, whether incorporated or not, public or private, that has its own function(s) and administration.

3.12 Subject matter: Specified environmental activity, event, condition, management system, and/or information about these matters.

3.13 Technical expert: Person who provides specific knowledge or expertise to the audit team, but who does not participate as an auditor.

4 Requirements for an environmental audit

5 General principles

   5.1 Objectives and scope

   5.2 Objectivity, independence, and competence

   5.3 Due professional care

   5.4 Systematic procedures

   5.5 Audit criteria, evidence, and findings

   5.6 Reliability of audit findings and conclusions

   5.7 Reporting

ISO 14011 — Guidelines on Environmental Auditing —
Audit Procedures — Auditing of Environmental Management Systems

0 Introduction

1 Scope

2 Normative references

3 Definitions

For purposes of ISO 14011, all definitions in ISO 14010 and ISO 14001 apply, plus the following:

   3.1 Environmental management system: That part of the overall management system which includes the organizational structure, planning activities, responsibilities, practices, procedures, processes, and resources for developing, implementing, achieving, reviewing, and maintaining the environmental policy.

   3.2 Environmental management system audit: Systematic, documented verification process of objectively obtaining and evaluating audit evidence to determine whether an organization's environmental management system conforms with the environmental management audit criteria, and communicating the results of this process to the client.

   3.3 Environmental management system audit criteria: Policies, practices, procedures, or requirements, such as covered by ISO 14001 and, if applicable, any additional EMS requirements against which the auditor compares collected audit evidence about the organization's environmental management system.

4 Environmental management system audit objectives, roles, and responsibilities

   4.1 Audit objectives

   4.2.1 Lead auditor

   4.2.2 Auditor

   4.2.3 Audit team

   4.2.4 Client

   4.2.5 Auditee

5 Auditing

5.1 Initiating the audit

5.1.1 Audit scope

5.1.2 Preliminary document review

5.2 Preparing the audit

5.2.1 Audit plan

5.2.2 Audit team assignments

5.2.3 Working documents

5.3 Executing the audit

5.3.1 Opening meeting

5.3.2 Collecting evidence

5.3.3 Audit findings

5.3.4 Closing meeting

5.4 Audit reports and records

5.4.1 Audit report preparation

5.4.2 Report content

5.4.3 Report distribution

5.4.4 Document retention

6 Audit completion

ISO 14012 — Guidelines on Environmental Auditing —
Qualification Criteria for Environmental Auditors

0 Introduction

1 Scope

2 Normative references

3 Definitions

For purposes of ISO 14012, all definitions in ISO 14010 and ISO 14011 apply, plus the following:

3.1 Auditor (environmental): Person qualified to perform environmental audits.

3.2 Lead auditor (environmental): Person qualified to manage and perform environmental audits.

3.3 Degree: Recognized national or international degree, or equivalent qualification, normally obtained after secondary education, through a minimum of three years formal full time, or equivalent part time study.

3.4 Secondary education: That part of the national educational system that comes after the primary or elementary stage, but that is completed immediately prior to entrance to a university or similar establishment.

4 Education and work experience

5 Auditor training

5.1 formal training

5.2 On-the-job training

6 Objective evidence of education, experience, and training

7 Personal attributes and skills

8 Lead auditor

9 Maintenance of competence

10 Due professional care

11 Language

Key Requirements — ISO 14010, ISO 14011

environmental
audit is
verification

The most important concept underlying the **ISO 14010** and **ISO 14011** EA guidelines is that, essentially, an environmental audit is a verification process.

Hence, the environmental auditor's primary role under the guidelines is to determine conformance — and not performance. Unless expressly requested to do so by the client, the environmental auditor should refrain from making performance-related opinions, judgments, or conclusions.

ISO 14010 sets forth several basic principles applicable to all types of environmental audits. It is truly a consensus standard that is generally consistent with previously published standards such as the U.S. Environmental Protection Agency's Environmental Auditing Policy Statement (July 9, 1986, and modified on December 22, 1995), the International Chamber of Commerce Position Paper on Environmental Auditing (March 1989), the U.S. Environmental Auditing Roundtable Standards for Performance of Environmental, Health, and Safety Audits (February 1993), and the European Union's EMAS Regulations (EC Council Reg. No. 1836/93, June 29, 1993).

In a similar vein, while **ISO 14011** expressly applies to procedures for EMS audits, in fact it consists of general environmental auditing procedural best practices that should be applicable to all types of environmental audits. When ISO 14010 and 14011 are updated in accordance with ISO procedures in the future, they probably will be combined into a single generally applicable environmental auditing principles and procedures standard.

Following is a brief explanation of the key requirements in the auditing standards. More detail on conducting the audits according to these standards is presented in the next section of this handbook.

Basic Tasks

auditor's task

The guidelines describe the auditor's basic task as "objectively obtaining and evaluating audit evidence to determine ... conform[ance] with audit criteria..." **(ISO 14010, Section 3.9)**. They recommend that these audit "findings or a summary thereof" be communicated to the client in a "written report."

reporting In addition to this baseline criteria, they allow such matters as the audit's plan, objectives, scope, and criteria to be contained in the report if their inclusion has been agreed upon with the client **(ISO 14010, Section 5.7; ISO 14011, Section 5.4.2)**. Should an audit contract or internal audit program scope so allow, the guidelines also recognize that environmental audits can provide the client with such additional services as root-cause analysis or corrective action recommendations.

evidence The audit evidence, which serves as the foundation of the audit findings, can be qualitative as well as quantitative. Typically, this evidence is obtained by the audit team from interviews, document examinations, and observations **(ISO 14010, Section 3.3)**. It must be sufficient enough that a second audit team would reach similar audit findings from evaluating the audit evidence against the same audit criteria **(ISO 14010, Section 5.5)**.

odjectives, scope, criteria The environmental auditing guidelines provide that, once the audit objectives are defined by the client, the lead auditor in consultation with the client must determine the audit scope, i.e., its extent and boundaries, and the audit criteria. Before the audit begins, the lead auditor should communicate to the auditee what the agreed audit objectives, scope, and criteria are, along with the audit plan approved by the client **(ISO 14010, Sections 5.1 and 5.5; ISO 14011, Section 5.2.1)**.

The audit criteria against which the audit evidence is compared will depend on the type of environmental audit being conducted. For example, if an EMS audit is undertaken, the audit criteria will be the elements of the audited organization's EMS, such as those "covered by ISO 14001 and, if applicable, any additional EMS requirements" to which the organization has made a commitment **(ISO 14011, Section 3.3)**. You should note that ISO 14011 is intended as a procedural guideline for auditing any EMS, and not just one designed to conform to ISO 14001.

client For the purpose of any environmental audit, the client commissioning it "may be the auditee, or any other organization which has the regulatory or contractual right to commission [it] ..." **(ISO 14010, Section 3.8, Note 8)**. Thus, a public interest group or some other stakeholder not having such regulatory or contractual right with respect to the audited organization would not qualify as a "client" under either ISO 14010 or 14011.

Audit Team [1]

team members According to the ISO EA guidelines, an environmental audit team is usually headed by a "lead auditor" "who is properly qualified to manage as well as perform an environmental audit" **(ISO 14010, Section 3.5, Note 6; ISO 14012, Section 3.2)**. Other members of the team may include qualified environmental auditors, auditors in training, and technical experts who provide "specific knowledge and expertise" relevant to the particularities of the given audit but do not function as either an auditor or lead auditor **(ISO 14010, Section 3.13)**. For example, a foreign language translator enlisted to help an American team auditing an organization at a foreign location might serve as team member technical expert but would not function as a team auditor.

objectivity Although **ISO 14012** contains specific recommended minimum auditor and lead auditor qualifications, **ISO 14010, Section 5.2** provides that members of the audit team "should be independent of the activities that are the subject of the audit." This principle, which is designed to ensure the objectivity of the audit process and to avoid conflicts of interest, applies equally to internal and external audits. This section goes on to state that team members should "possess an appropriate combination of knowledge, skills, and experience to carry out audit responsibilities."

due care, disclosure

The general principles guideline **(ISO 14010)** requires that environmental auditors exercise due professional care. It also recommends that quality assurance procedures be followed and emphasizes the confidential nature of audit-related information and documents. It suggests that, unless applicable law requires otherwise, audit information and documents should be disclosed only to a third party when the client and, where appropriate, the auditee, has authorized such disclosure **(ISO 14010, Section 5.3)**.

It also recommends that environmental audits "should be conducted according to documented and well-defined methodologies" to assure consistency and reliability of the audit findings **(ISO 14010, Section 5.4)**. It cautions, however, that all environmental audits inevitably use a sampling methodology because of time and resource limitations. Thus their findings are always subject to some degree of risk.

responsibilities, audit plan

Building on ISO 14010, **ISO 14011, Section 4.2** details the key roles and responsibilities of lead auditors, auditors, clients, and auditees. It addresses audit preparatory activities such as conducting a preliminary document review **(ISO 14011, Section 5.1.2)** and agreements between the parties. It provides a detailed outline of a model audit plan and recommends that it be communicated to the auditors and the auditee for comment. The client is responsible for final review and approval **(ISO 14011, Section 5.2.1)**.

Audit team assignments are briefly discussed in **ISO 14011, Section 5.2.2**, and the nature, confidentiality, and recordkeeping considerations of audit working documents are briefly addressed in **Section 5.2.3**.

Executing the Audit [2]

executing audit

Section 5.3 of ISO 14011 relates to the on-site phase of an environmental audit. It discusses the purposes and scope of the opening meeting **(ISO 14011, Section 5.3.1)**, the evidence collection process **(ISO 14011, Section 5.3.2)**, the determination of audit findings **(ISO 14011, Section 5.3.3)**, and the closing meeting **(ISO 14011, Section 5.3.4)**. It emphasizes the importance of assuring that auditees clearly understand and acknowledge the factual basis of audit findings. It points out, however, that while disagreements should be resolved whenever possible, final responsibility for the audit findings rests with the lead auditor, even where disagreements with the client and the auditee remain.

The reporting section **(ISO 14011, Section 5.4.2)** is generally consistent with its counterpart in **ISO 14040 Section 5.7**. In **ISO 14011, Section 5.4.3**, confidentiality of audit documentation is underlined by the statement that "Audit reports are the sole property of the client...."

Key Qualification Requirements — ISO 14012

ISO 14012 provides guidance on appropriate minimum qualifications for both internal and external environmental auditors and lead auditors, regardless of the type of environmental audit they conduct. Its introduction, however, contains the caveat that, although internal auditors should be as competent as external auditors depending on such factors as the size and complexity of the organization, there may be a sound basis for them not to satisfy all of the guideline's detailed criteria.

education,
experience

ISO 14012 Section 4 of the standard recommends that all environmental auditors have completed at least the equivalent of a secondary education and have appropriate work experience in some or all of the following fields:

- environmental science and technology;
- technical and environmental aspects of facility operations;
- relevant requirements of environmental laws, regulations, and related documents;
- environmental management systems and standards; and
- audit procedures, processes, and techniques.

For auditors with only a secondary education, five years of such work experience is suggested. Four years is suggested for those having the equivalent of a college degree. The standard allows some credit in lieu of work experience if the auditor has completed additional formal education courses addressing the above fields. It is noteworthy that the standard does not address the type of college degree that must be obtained.

Hence, for example, an attorney who majored in English and who has had four years of environmental regulatory experience would appear to meet Section 4's education and work experience criteria.

training

Under **ISO 14012 Section 5**, all environmental auditors should have an unspecified period of formal training in some or all of the five fields identified above.

The auditor also should have completed on-the-job training for the equivalent of 20 workdays of environmental auditing and should have participated in at least four environmental audits. This on-the-job training should have taken place within three consecutive years and should have been under the tutorship of a lead environmental auditor. The guideline also recommends that competence resulting from this formal and on-the-job auditor training be demonstrated by suitable means such as interviews, testing, etc.

According to **ISO 14012, Annex A.3:**

"There should be evidence to show that environmental auditors have acquired and maintained the necessary education, work experience, training, and personal attributes as described in this International Standard. The evaluation process should include some of the following methods:

a) interviews with candidates;

b) written and/or oral assessment or other sustainable means;

c) review of candidates' written work;

d) discussions with former employers, colleagues, etc.;

e) role playing;

f) peer observation under actual audit conditions;

g) reviewing records of education, experience, and training as defined in this International Standard;

h) consideration of professional certifications and qualifications."

attributes, skills   In addition to being properly educated and trained, ISO **14012, Section** 7 of the guideline specifies the following nonexclusive list of personal attributes and skills that an environmental auditor should have:

- competence in clearly expressing concepts and ideas, orally and in writing;

- interpersonal skills conducive to the effective and efficient performance of the audit, such as diplomacy, tact, and the ability to listen;

- the ability to maintain independence and objectivity sufficient to permit the accomplishment of auditor responsibilities;

- skills of personal organization necessary to the effective and efficient performance of the audit;

- the ability to reach sound judgments based on objective evidence; and

- the ability to react with sensitivity to the conventions and culture of the country or region in which the audit is performed.

lead auditor   To qualify as a lead environmental auditor under **Section 8**, a person must either demonstrate to audit program managers or others that:

- he/she has a "thorough understanding and application of those [above-listed] personal attributes and skills necessary to ensure effective and efficient management and leadership of the audit process," or

- otherwise show "thorough understanding and application" and have fifteen additional workdays of environmental auditing for a minimum of three additional complete audits coupled with "acting lead auditor" experience, under a lead auditor for one of those additional audits.

The guideline specifies that these supplementary lead auditor criteria should be met within a period of three consecutive years.

continuing education   **ISO 14012, Section 9** recommends that all environmental auditors take appropriate actions such as refresher courses to maintain the currency of their knowledge and audit execution experience.

Companies Pilot-Testing ISO 14001 Favor Internal Audits

To find out how internal audits are being conducted and what kinds of results companies are getting, CEEM Information Services queried several organizations participating in the NSF International pilot program underway in 1995 and 1996 to test the effectiveness of environmental management system (EMS) draft standards. The following organizations were surveyed:

- Fluke Corporation, a manufacturer of electronic equipment, in Everett, Washington 📖 (See report at end of Part 6, Section 6.6.3);

- Air Products and Chemicals, Inc., in Allentown, Pennsylvania 📖 (See report at end of Part 6, Section 6.3.2);

- Globe Metallurgical, a manufacturer of silicon metal and ferrosilicon products, headquartered in Cleveland, Ohio 📖 (See report and end of Part 6, Section 6.6.2); and

- Rettew Associates, an EMS consulting firm in Lancaster, Pennsylvania 📖 (See report at end of Part 6, Section 6.3.5).

These companies generally follow the Plan-Do-Check-Act loop for conducting internal audits. Audits vary with each company according to company size and complexity, number of facilities, and the characteristics and environmental impact of its products.

Persons questioned responded enthusiastically about the merits of internal versus third-party audits. Most companies say that they are more capable of finding and correcting their own deficiencies than an outside team would be. They believe they are harder on themselves than an outside team would be and that their own people have the knowledge base and training necessary to complete objective audits.

An exception is Globe Metallurgical, whose director of environmental affairs says that a company needs an outsider in addition to the internal audit team to keep the company honest.

In early 1996, some companies were still weighing the costs versus the benefits of pushing toward ISO 14000 certification. They were looking for an indication that certification would be worth the thousands of dollars required to certify each site. Whether or not they seek certification, these companies all have their own management systems in place and will maintain them. They understand the importance of maintaining a preventative, proactive approach to air, water, and waste management. 📖 (See Appendix E for information from ISO 14000 surveys.)

Reports from these companies appear throughout Part 6 of this handbook and are referenced above.

ISO 14000 and the Environmental Audit:
Where do they overlap?

In evaluation areas:

Environmental aspects:

- ✔ Air modeling and testing, release reporting, remediation assessments, community right-to-know evaluations
- ✔ Monitoring and measurement
- ✔ Sampling, monitoring, analysis, inspections, testing (tanks)

In record areas:

Environmental documentation/document control/recordkeeping:

- ✔ Record retention (ODSs, air, waste shipments, training, drinking water, use of chemicals, waste shipments, etc.)
- ✔ Wastewater discharge sampling
- ✔ Plans and updates (stormwater, lab quality control, sampling strategy, etc.
- ✔ Inspections

In business process areas:

Operational controls:

- ✔ IWWT
- ✔ Air abatement Equipment
- ✔ Remediation Activities
- ✔ Emergency Preparedness and response
- ✔ Business support recovery (IWWT, air abatement equipment)
- ✔ Nonconformance, corrective and preventative action
- ✔ Air upsets, spills

In the areas of basic accountability:

Legal and other requirements:

- ✔ Permits and permits management (updating, evaluating data, etc.)
- ✔ Reporting
- ✔ Equipment design requirements
- ✔ Plans and plan updates (stormwater, ODS, SPCC, etc.)
- ✔ Objectives and targets
- ✔ Pollution prevention metrics
- ✔ TRI progress

In human resources issues:

Structure and assignment of owners:

- ✔ Satellite waste areas, chemical container storage areas, pollution prevention, pest
- ✔ Training, awareness, and IWWT
- ✔ Stormwater
- ✔ Air
- ✔ Waste
- ✔ Pest

CHAPTER 3
Conducting the Audit

6.3.1 Who Should Conduct EMS Audits?

Since your EMS audits may be performed with internal resources (your own internal auditors) or using external resources (technical experts and consultants) **(ISO 14004, Section 4.4.5)**, you should address the question of who will conduct the audit early in the planning stages.

auditors

A fundamental principle of the ISO 14000 auditing guidelines is that the auditors performing an EMS audit should be independent, free of bias and conflict, and, by virtue of their training and experience, competent to carry out their responsibilities **(ISO 14010, Section 5.2)**.

internal resources

If you are considering internal resources, you should factor the following questions into your decision:

1) Can the basic independence of the review be established?

2) Do other factors mitigate in favor of an internal or external approach (such as customer and public acceptance, or technical expertise required)?

3) Are the available internal resources sufficient to carry out the audit (a particular consideration for SMEs)?

1) Can you establish the independence of the audit?

To ensure that the results of the EMS audit are reliable as objective and free from the influence of your organization, you may consider turning to external environmental audit consultants.

procedural safeguards

However, you can use internal teams to perform the same functions if appropriate procedural safeguards are established for the audit process so that independence and freedom from bias can be demonstrated.

Examples of such procedural safeguards include ensuring that the internal auditors do not come from the facility, operation, or process being audited; ensuring that the auditors do not report to, are not compensated by, and do not receive performance evaluations from the manager of the facility, operation, or process being audited; placing external resources on the audit team; or having a separate department (such as your legal department) nominally oversee audits.

ISO 14010, Section 5.2 requires that the individuals in your organization who are responsible for day-to-day implementation of an EMS or who compiled the ISO 14001 EMS documentation should not be a part of your EMS audit team. These individuals are not independent of the process or operation that is the subject of the audit and thus cannot be free from bias.

However, although they cannot be a part of your EMS audit team, they are an essential part of the EMS audit process since they must be prepared to explain and demonstrate the EMS components and respond to queries from the audit team.

2) Do other factors mitigate in favor of an internal or external approach?

Internal auditors have the advantage of familiarity with your organization's business processes and thus are arguably better able to comprehend subtle issues requiring detailed process knowledge.

External auditors have the advantage of a broader perspective developed through interactions with multiple clients and processes within your industry sector and across sector lines, enabling them to avoid the "tunnel vision" that can occur within a single organization.

If internal resources are to be used, you should be prepared to demonstrate the assertion of independence. To help you do this, you should consider using one or more external experts as members of the audit team.

3) Are the available internal resources sufficient to carry out your audit?

You will find that determining the adequacy of internal resources to carry out an EMS audit is a complex task. You will have to consider factors such as audit team composition (including need for specialized technical expertise), the scope of the facilities and systems being audited, the scope of the audit itself (including whether analytical data will be collected and the level of detail to which the review will go), and the operating needs of your organization.

Another factor is the scope of the report being prepared. The level of detail encompassed by the report in accordance with management instructions, and the need to interpret any findings and conclusions for management may also divert resources from your operations or require specialized outside expertise.

6.3.2 Audit Team Composition

length of audit

For most large or complex organizations, it will take a team several days to perform an in-depth EMS audit to evaluate conformance with **ISO 14001**, although **ISO 14010, Section 3.5** includes the concept of a single auditor within the definition of the "audit team."

For example, Arthur D. Little recently reported that a company such as Allied Chemical Corporation used, on average, a two-to-four-person team for three to five days to perform its 60-some regular audits each year (**Chemical Engineering** / March 1995, p. 49). While this may not represent the norm in the U.S., experience with EMS verification audits under the Eco-Management and Audit Scheme (EMAS), the European Union's environmental management system regulation, shows that they take approximately 10-15 person-days, according to Roger Brockway, environmental manager of the United Kingdom Accreditation Service.

lead auditor

ISO 14010, 14011, and 14012 provide guidance on defining key terms with respect to your audit team and the responsibilities of the participants on the team. The audit team, whether it contains one or more members, must have a lead auditor to manage the audit and to ensure the efficient and effective conduct and completion of the audit within the audit scope and plan approved by the client (**ISO 14011, Section 4.2** generally and **4.2.1** specifically) .

The lead auditor's tasks are different from those of other members of the audit team, and the lead auditor has overall responsibility for the success of the audit process as a whole.

The client, which may be the auditee or any other organization having the legal authority to commission an audit **(ISO 14010, Section 3.8)**, has final approval over the size and composition of the audit team, which is determined by the lead auditor **(ISO 14011, Section 4.2.1)**.

team size   If your organization is large, has numerous documentation systems, or if there are multiple layers of management and operational personnel to be evaluated during the course of the audit, the circumstances may dictate that the lead auditor designate a larger team. To satisfy these needs, the lead auditor may want additional qualified auditors on the team, auditors having specialized process-related expertise, auditors-in-training, and technical experts such as process specialists **(ISO 14010, Section 3.5)**.

Your organization may want to include someone from a facility, process, or operation that is soon to be audited so that he or she can understand what to expect from the audit process and use the experience as a training tool. This idea also helps you "cross-pollinate" corrective action ideas from one segment of your organization to others.

legal representation   Although there is no requirement that an attorney be a member of the audit team, having an attorney available as a technical expert provides specific safeguards.

Audit findings may be covered by the attorney/client privilege or other legal protections if, for rendering legal advice, an attorney participates or if the internal EMS audit is conducted under the direction of the attorney or the law department.

You should consider including a lawyer when you anticipate having to protect the identity and contents of interviews of specific individuals within your organization, or to protect the process through which compliance with (or violation of) laws or regulations is determined, or when significant enforcement actions (including, potentially, criminal proceedings) are expected.

An attorney, as a technical expert on the team, may also:

- help interpret how management deficiencies uncovered during the EMS audit could interplay with ongoing and future regulatory compliance issues;
- interpret how deficiencies may impact SEC disclosures;
- evaluate whether any legal reporting obligations are triggered by audit findings; and
- help with corrective action procedures.

ISO 9000 role   If you already are implementing an ISO 9000 quality management system, you may get by with a smaller audit team that is familiar with the common areas between ISO 9000 and ISO 14000.

However, before you make a final decision on the size and composition of the audit team, your lead auditor should detail the scope of the EMS audit, with the approval of the client, and then you should briefly revisit the issue of staffing to ensure that the scope can be accomplished with the team as constituted.

Air Products and Chemicals

Allentown, Pennsylvania, United States, January 1996

John Tao, a technical director with Air Products and Chemicals Inc., in Allentown, Pennsylvania, says that his company conducts internal audits according to "the traditional setup." This includes opening meetings, the audit, and closing meetings. Air Products does not have a corporate EMS per se, but various sites have set up their own systems.

Air Products is taking a "wait and see attitude toward ISO 14001 certification because it is not sure of the benefits," says Tao. Most chemical companies are doing the same, he says, because of the tens of thousands of dollars required to certify each site.

In scheduling, Tao says, "Sites are ranked according to where they are and what they do." Sites are normally audited every couple of years or, in some cases, less frequently. Audits are "risk-adjusted" to locations.

Air Products has corporate auditors who visit the plants. Teams are composed of two to five persons who have the specific technical skills necessary, such as safety, industrial hygiene, and environmental (air, water, and waste) backgrounds. "These are corporate people who come from outside the plant," Tao says. He believes that this gives internal audits "some measure of objectivity."

Plant management is used to the audits, Tao says. There are no problems with audits "as long as auditors don't carry a chip on their shoulders."

Tao does not agree with those who say companies must have an outside team for conducting audits. He notes that developing an EMS such as ISO 14001 is voluntary. He says that corporate people have "higher goals" than an outside group might have. He adds that internal auditors are more inclined to protect the company. That is, they are going to do what has to be done to locate and correct any internal problems.

"They have better communication, and they know the people better and what they do," says Tao.

Corrective action is the responsibility of the auditee, Tao says. The auditee generates a correction report, which includes a time schedule. The auditee attaches this to the report and returns it. The corporate team then monitors the corrective action.

This company, interviewed by CEEM Information Services, participated in an NSF International pilot program underway in 1995 and 1996 to test the effectiveness of environmental management system (EMS) draft standards.

6.3.3 Scoping the EMS Audit

📖 (See Appendix C for a compliance questionnaire.)

The audit scope describes the extent and boundaries of the audit in terms of factors such as the physical location and organizational activities to be encompassed by the audit **(ISO 14011, Section 5.1.1)**.

The first steps the audit team and your organization (the auditee) take in scoping an EMS audit are to define and agree upon its objectives and to determine the audit criteria against which your EMS program will be compared.

The objectives of the audit should be defined by the client who may or may not be the auditee **(ISO 14010, Section 5.1)**. 📖 (See box on Page 301.)

6.3.4 Planning an EMS Audit

ISO 14011 requires the lead auditor to develop an audit plan with appropriate consultation with the client, auditee, and audit team members **(ISO 14011, Section 4.2.1 (f))**.

key consideration

The audit plan can include numerous elements, detailed in **Section 5.2.1**, and should be focused on the objectives and scope of the EMS audit. The plan should consider pre-audit activities, such as preliminary document reviews, which might affect the determination of whether you have adequate documentation to carry out the audit, whether you have sufficient commitment of resources for the intended scope and objectives of the audit, and whether audit team assignments need to be adjusted (see, generally, **ISO 14011, Section 5.2**).

protections

Because of the potential for aggressive environmental regulatory enforcement in the U.S., and because many environmental laws can be enforced as criminal offenses, you should consider the following tip:

- the need to establish procedures to protect documents generated during the EMS audit process from disclosure;

- the need to ensure reporting of violations where required by law or voluntarily in response to federal or state audit policies; and

- whether your organization has made a commitment to implement corrective action promptly and completely.

audit protocol

Another part of the EMS audit planning process is to develop an audit protocol or checklist to ensure that, during the audit, all relevant information is systematically collected for later evaluation.

In early 1996, the U.S. TAG to TC 207 was developing generic guidance for use in performing EMS audits. The structure of this document sought to identify the sources of information that an EMS auditor might use in gathering audit evidence, and items in the EMS specification and the EMS guidance that may be applicable. The audit protocol should be made specific to the audit scope and objectives and tailored to your organization.

documentation

Planners also should determine procedures for developing and retaining audit working papers and for drafting and finalizing audit reports, including the structure of the audit report itself. It is good practice to ensure that all documents that were consulted during the audit process are identified, along with all individuals who were interviewed and notes of meetings, so that findings can be verified if needed. The distribution of the audit report should be determined during the planning stage, as well 📖 (See Part 3, Chapter 4 for more information on documentation.)

ISO 14011, Section 5.2.1 recommends that the audit plan be "communicated to the client, the auditors, and you (the auditee)."

setting the tone

Although only the client has the authority to actually approve the plan **(ISO 14011, Sections, 5.2.1 and 4.2.4)**, the audit team members should review the plan to ensure that they clearly understand the nature of the audit evidence they expect to collect during the audit process for comparison against the audit criteria. Often this is accomplished through a team meeting at which primary and secondary assignments can be made. Your participation ensures that the audit plan is practical for your operations, and that approvals can be obtained in advance (if needed) for collection of certain types of evidence, e.g., approvals of photographs or of information concerning proprietary processes.

6.3.5 Executing the EMS Audit

When the planning stages are complete, the on-site portion of an EMS audit usually begins with an "opening meeting." The purpose of the site visit is to evaluate whether the EMS being audited functions as stated in the documentation by comparing its stated objectives and targets with the evidence of their implementation at the site.

1) Opening Meeting

The purposes of the opening meeting are to:

- acquaint the audit team with your representatives and establish communication pathways for their interaction;
- ensure adequate cooperation with the audit team;
- describe the methodologies to be applied during the audit;
- confirm the available resources needed by the audit team;
- review the scope, objectives, and audit plan and agree on the timetable for performance of the EMS audit **(ISO 14011, Section 5.3.1)**.

setting the tone

The opening meeting sets the tone for the audit as a whole and can influence the ultimate success of the EMS audit. No matter how well the pre-site visit planning has gone, and despite all steps taken by you (or the client) to instill a cooperative attitude among your management and staff, there still will be a sense of jeopardy in the minds of your personnel. They will suspect, realistically or otherwise, that the outcome of the EMS audit will be a reflection of how well they, as individuals, are doing their jobs. This concern should be specifically acknowledged and addressed during the opening meeting to foster candor and openness that is vital to the audit process.

Go

The opening meeting is also a key point at which the lead auditor may gather information to make the determination that the requirements for an environmental audit (articulated in

ISO 14010, Section 4) have been met and the audit can go forward; namely that there are adequate information, resources, and cooperation from you (the auditee).

2) Collecting Audit Evidence

To independently verify that your organization's EMS conforms to ISO 14001 and the audit criteria, the audit team must gather evidence, to the extent reasonably consistent within the agreed scope and plan.

what it isn't However, it is important to keep in mind that the EMS audit does **not** consist of a regulatory compliance audit. Nor is it a process of agreeing that an organization has identified all of its environmental aspects or assigned appropriate objectives and targets or prioritized among them.

The objective of the EMS audit is to assess the functionality of the environmental management <u>systems</u> that are in place, such as those designed to achieve regulatory compliance, and to identify and track regulatory requirements applicable to the organization, or to achieve objectives and targets.

Audit evidence is "verifiable information, records, or statements of fact" **(ISO 14010, Section 3.3)**. Audit evidence, whether qualitative or quantitative, is used to determine whether EMS audit criteria are met **(ISO 14010, Section 5.5; ISO 14011, Section 5.3.2)**.

Usually, audit evidence is based on interviews, examination of documents, observations of activities and conditions, and existing results of measurements and tests **(ISO 14010, Section 3.3, Notes 3 and 4)**. The interviews should be verified, where feasible, by supporting independent and objectively verifiable information, or else the unverified statements should be identified as such **(ISO 14011, Section 5.3.2)**.

interviews Care should be given in conducting interviews to ensure that they are non-threatening and designed to elicit candid responses. It is frequently necessary to probe the same subjects repeatedly with interviewees, to dig past the "sales pitch" that might be triggered by an employee feeling defensive during an interview, and to uncover underlying objective facts to support statements made during interviews. Language barriers may be significant in this phase of executing the audit and must be overcome.

The quality and quantity of audit evidence to be collected should be sufficient so that "competent environmental auditors working independently of each other would reach similar audit findings from evaluating the same audit evidence against the same audit criteria" **(ISO 14010, Section 5.5)**. Also, the environmental auditors should endeavor to obtain sufficient audit evidence so that significant individual audit findings and aggregates of less-significant findings are taken into account, since both could impact any audit conclusions **(ISO 14010, Section 5.6)**.

conformances Where the audit evidence indicates nonconformity with the EMS audit criteria, that observation should be recorded by the auditors (at least in the working papers, if not included in the audit report itself) **(ISO 14011, Section 5.3.2)**.

During interviews, it may be helpful to attempt to understand the root cause behind any nonconformities noted, since this information may help you and the client both in determin-

Auditing in an SME

by Edwin Pinero

Special Projects Manager, EnSafe, Inc.;

Leader ST2 TG4 on Environmental Site Assessments

If you operate a small or medium enterprise (SME), stop and take a breather. The biggest challenges an SME must overcome in terms of the auditing standards are the fear of the unknown and a feeling that you must meet every expectation of the standard to the letter. It is important to remember that these standards are voluntary guidance documents. There is flexibility in applying the ISO auditing standards. The auditing standards provide the your SME with a guide or tool to assist in implementing and maintaining an effective EMS. You can apply the standards to a level appropriate to your organization and the goal of the auditing.

As an SME, you may feel that, because of your relatively small scale and possibly less complex nature, you cannot provide the auditing expertise itemized in the standard. The key is to have the expertise to audit at an appropriate level for your EMS. This customization is certainly consistent with the intent of the standards. Keep in mind that the lack of auditing is proportionately offset by a lack of need for such high-level experience. In smaller organizations, auditing is usually less structured and less comprehensive than in larger organizations.

The first order of business is to decide what function the auditing will serve. You should decide if the audit is for internal purposes such as ongoing maintenance and preparation for outside auditors or if the audit is for external purposes such as making self-declarations of conformance with ISO 14001. For most SMEs, auditing is internally driven and will have less stringent requirements.

A key person in the internal auditing procedure is the SME manager. He or she knows the particulars to the operating procedures better than anyone else. At minimum, this person fulfills one of your significant requirements — knowing the operation in question. Keep in mind that, to cut costs, your environmental staff can be trained in EMS needs concerning the auditing procedures.

Another option is to hire a consultant who brings well-rounded expertise. Your consultant can help with routine environmental needs as well as with EMS needs 📖 (See Part 2, Chapter 4 for more information on hiring a consultant.)

Finally, you can call your trade and professional associations. These organizations should be able to provide you with more education — and if it hasn't thought about it, your call might be the catalyst for such training.

Implementing the auditing standards likely will mean investing in additional support through hiring and/or use of consultants, use of training programs, or time spent in self-education. But this probably will be of less magnitude than you expect. You can "retrofit" current activities to meet goals other than those supporting your ISO 14000 initiatives, and make the effort pay for itself in multiple ways.

The frequency of scheduling an audit needs to be consistent with the size of the organization, Pinero says, but companies should audit all components of a management system once a year. A registrar for ISO certification may have a less frequent auditing schedule, but annual internal audits for those companies seeking certification still be done.

Auditing-team composition will differ with companies, but Pinero recommends that every team have the following four areas covered:

1) One or more persons on the auditing team should have general auditing experience. It's a generic science. An experienced auditor does not necessarily have to have experience with environmental audits.

2) Someone on the team needs knowledge of the industry being audited.

3) Someone needs knowledge of the environmental characteristics of the business being audited; that is, how the business interacts with the environment.

4) A team member needs knowledge of environmental regulations, laws, policies, and procedures, and how to apply regulations. Pinero stresses that this person need not be a lawyer, but someone who understands regulatory requirements.

In planning for an audit, there should be a discussion between the auditor and the client or auditee. They need to determine the "scope" of the audit and ask: "Are we going to audit components of the management system in accordance with ISO 14000?"

A management system audit has many more variables than a compliance audit. For example, a warehouse audit would need different people than an audit of a wetland that has been affected by a toxic chemical.

There are two new steps in audits that differ from the traditional audit:

1) the pre-data selection setup; and

2) early discussion on what is going to be required of the auditor.

These are new areas because the traditional audit has been one of compliance regulation.

During the execution of the audit, auditors should work hard on keeping the lines of communication open among themselves, and auditors should periodically check procedures so that they stay in the scope of the audit and not wander off into tangents.

Internal audits offer your company a better working knowledge of the system. It also translates to less cost for small and medium companies because they do not have to import auditors and train them about the companies' procedures.

Regarding "corrective action," auditors are looking for nonconformance to the management system. It's not a spill. Corrective action should focus on the management system and the audit system.

Because an internal audit of an EMS is not focused on regulatory compliance, your difficulties or unexpected findings should be resolved, if possible, through the management review process. Let upper management deal with it; however it was done in the past, let that procedure continue.

ing the appropriate corrective action to be implemented and in understanding whether a nonconformity is systemic or local in nature. For example, a mislabeled drum on a loading dock may be an indication of a localized training issue, or an indication of a failure in the organization's compliance management program.

It is imperative that auditees, auditors, clients, and all users of EMS audits understand that the evidence collected during an EMS audit inevitably only will be a sample of the information available about the subject of the audit. This is partly due to the fact that an environmental audit is conducted necessarily during a limited period of time and with limited resources **(ISO 14010, Section 5.6)**.

3) Developing Audit Findings

The process of comparing the audit evidence against the audit criteria for arriving at audit findings may take place during the site visit, or following the site visit.

review   Because **ISO 14011** guidance recommends reviewing the audit findings with the responsible auditee manager with a view to obtaining acknowledgment of the factual basis of the findings of nonconformity **(ISO 14011, Section 5.3.3)**, this process often occurs during the site visit. Where the issues of nonconformity require detailed research or interpretation, or an analysis and cross-referencing of evidence collected from numerous sources, the audit findings may be developed or finalized following the conclusion of the site visit.

Audit findings are the results of the evaluation of the collected audit evidence compared against the agreed audit criteria, and they serve as the basis for the audit report **(ISO 14010, Section 3.4)**. The audit team should review all of its audit evidence to determine where your organization's EMS does or does not conform to the EMS audit criteria. The audit team should then ensure that any findings of nonconformity are documented in a clear, concise manner and supported by the audit evidence **(ISO 14011, Section 5.3.3)**.

conclusions   Conclusions and recommendations, if desired by the client, may be included in the audit report. These go beyond the factual observations (audit evidence) that will be compared against the defined audit criteria.

These conclusions and recommendations may involve interpretations, legal or technical analysis, and even corrective actions that your organization may be recommended to implement. Your organization (and the client) should have an opportunity to verify the audit evidence of factual observations upon which findings are based, and often this is accomplished during the exit interview or between drafting and finalizing the audit report. It is up to the client to determine what role, if any, your organization (the auditee) and client may play in participating in developing conclusions or recommendations if such are to be encompassed in the scope of the audit process and the report.

4) Conducting the Closing Meeting

The closing meeting (or exit conference) completes the evidence collection phase, and may serve as the vehicle for verification of the factual basis for proposed audit findings **(ISO 14011, Section 5.3.4)**. The closing meeting is also the opportunity to resolve issues and disagreements concerning the audit process and any preliminary findings resulting from the audit, although the final arbiter of what the final audit findings are is the lead auditor (**ISO 14011, Section 5.3.4**).

discussion forum

The closing meeting may also provide a vehicle for identifying and gathering any additional information desirable to the audit process and a forum for discussion (if approved as a part of the audit scope by the client) of recommendations for corrective actions.

Many organizations prefer that the audit report be substantially complete prior to the closing meeting. If this is not the case, provision should be made at the closing meeting for subsequent review of the proposed audit findings and the factual basis supporting the findings.

due care

You should also note that in executing the EMS audit, the auditors should use due professional care. This includes use of the care, skill, diligence, and judgment expected of any auditor in similar circumstances, and the client's entitlement of confidentiality of the fruits of the audit process unless the client has consented to, or the law requires, disclosure (**ISO 14010, Section 5.3**).

6.3.6 Preparing the EMS Audit Report

Your organization's internal EMS audit process must be documented so that the results can be forwarded to management for review, as part of the cycle of continual improvement of the EMS that is required by ISO 14001.

The audit report is the vehicle for communicating to the client the audit findings (or a summary thereof (**ISO 14010, Section 5.7**)). It is not, however, the basis of the conformity assessment or certification process, although the EMS audit report may serve as one of the bases for demonstrating conformity to ISO 14001 to a certification body or by an organization electing to self-declare rather than certify.

objectivity

In the U.S. context, great attention should be given to careful wording of audit reports to ensure that the findings are conveyed in a clear, concise, and factual manner, and are devoid of opinions and value-laden statements.

The audit report, upon agreement with the client, may contain many useful elements besides the audit findings. These are detailed in **ISO 14010, Section 5.7 and ISO 14011, Section 5.4.2**. The report should be prepared in close proximity to performance of the on-site portion of the audit to ensure accurate recall of all necessary information, and significant delays should be communicated to the client and the reasons documented.

documents, confidentiality

Consideration should be given to retention of all working documents, draft and final reports, and analytical information gathered during the audit process in accordance with applicable documentation retention requirements of the organization (**ISO 14011, Section 5.4.4**). Also, the lead auditor should sign the report and distribute it as agreed with the client. The audit report is proprietary to the client, and confidentiality should be respected and safeguarded by all members of the EMS audit team.

Auditing Case Study — Syncrude Canada Ltd.

January 1996

Syncrude Canada Ltd. in Ft. McMurray, Alberta, produces 200,000 barrels a day of synthetic crude oil from oil sands in northern Alberta through the operation of a mine, extraction plant, and refinery. Its 1995 production level was expected to reach 73 million barrels, providing about 12 percent of Canada's ready energy. Most of the synthetic crude oil is refined to Syncrude Sweet Blend. Production is in the $13 to $14 a barrel range. Syncrude employs 3,700 people.

In the early 1980s, Syncrude adopted a loss management program through the Det Norske Veritas/ International Loss Control Institute called the International Safety Rating System (ISRS). This identifies 20 program elements that a loss management system should incorporate, such as inspections, investigations, team meetings, emergency preparedness, and risk analysis.

"In the last four years, we have looked at this and tried to cover a number of our environmental initiatives under this program," explains Keith Fenton, corporate loss management advisor. "When DNV/ILCE introduced the International Environmental Rating System (IERS) in the early 1990s, we worked with them on the development of that particular project." Following is his advice on doing internal audits to an EMS based on this experience.

Compare existing EMS to ISO 14000. Fenton says, "We have taken the activities identified in the environmental rating system and incorporated them into the framework of the safety rating system that we already had in place."

In September 1995, Gary Burns, manager of environmental operations, was comparing the existing EMS to ISO 14001 to see where there might be gaps. The company would like to integrate aspects of ISO 14001 into its own EMS rather than develop yet another separate, parallel program. However, as of January 1996, Syncrude did not know whether it would opt to implement ISO 14001. Burns explains that the company was planning integration of its existing systems, but not necessarily adoption of ISO 14001 exclusively.

Be creative in developing auditing tools. Fenton points out that Syncrude does not audit to IERS since it is doing self-audits to ISRS with IERS components built in. In the future, it plans to develop an audit protocol that will evaluate its management system. This protocol would be specific to Syncrude. "We have identified a number of other initiatives to help manage our program that aren't covered by existing audit programs. We need to customize an audit tool that will meet our needs. It's likely we'll have somebody work with us on developing this tool."

Combine audits for greater efficiency. Past audits at Syncrude had focused on very specific issues, such as safety, security, quality, or the environment. Consequently, its departments had had numerous people who wanted to see how it did business. "We've got some work underway to help streamline that so we can do a more efficient job of it. We won't be duplicating audits." Its strategy centers actually had to deal with about six different audits. It brought the six internal audit teams together and in September 1995 was streamlining a pilot project that could manage all the audits at once.

Coordinate, not consolidate. There are two groups doing audits at Syncrude: the internal audit group and a loss management group. Instead of putting those two groups together, the company was opting for greater coordination of activities the groups were performing when they went into the "strategy center." The strategy centers are departments that appear in each of several aspects of the company's operations, such as mining, extraction, utilities, or upgrading areas. Much of what needs to be coordinated involves scheduling.

Remove duplication from the system. Fenton adds that the company also was making sure that the teams were not duplicating each other's efforts.

Define and document roles. "Our environmental department developed a manual that looks at the legislation we need to be in compliance with. We have identified who has responsibility for certain sections of the manual or for certain activities that need to take place to meet legislation. We have written standards for each of our departments and do compliance audits against these," Fenton reports.

Stay on top of legislation. The same group that writes internal standards tracks emergent legislation and stays on top of new requirements. "It also finds out what we need to do, then rewrites the policy and documents, and works with the departments that need to know this information. "Their standards are on a Local Area Network (LAN) so all departments have access to them. The latest update information can be distributed through LAN, E-mail — which they use extensively — or memos," Fenton says.

CHAPTER 4
Management Review

by John R. Broomfield, President and CEO, Quality Management International, Inc.

Process Overview and Objective

The management review is one of the most important processes of maintaining and growing your environmental management system. The objective of conducting a management review is to improve your company's performance by the top management driving the EMS. Your company's most senior executives periodically evaluate the EMS and decide what actions are required to achieve this objective and "continuing suitability, adequacy, and effectiveness."

The management review process provides executives with the information they need to conduct the evaluation. It is a decision-making process that may sanction further investment, revision, or renewal of the policy or objectives (and targets) and require improvements to the other parts of the EMS.

Who is Involved?

If you operate a small business, your management review may be conducted by the chief executive working alone with the necessary information and without the benefit of a multidisciplined team meeting.

However, environmental policy decisions can be complex even within the context of a fully defined and mature EMS. Larger companies usually assemble a multifunctional team, including the person responsible for maintaining and reporting on the performance of the EMS.

Others may be involved in providing information even though they may not attend the review itself. These include: the community, suppliers (and their suppliers), pressure groups, customers (and perhaps their customers), governmental agencies, advisors, insurers, etc.

Input Information

The scope, policy, objectives, and targets used to drive the EMS determine the information required for a thorough review of its performance. Do not forget to display the specific objective driving the management review process itself. This should appear at the head of the documented procedure for management review.

The following components may be considered essential or useful to the management review process:

EMS audit reports

☑ any compliance audit reports;

☑ other evaluations of EMS effectiveness;

☑ progress reports on earlier management reviews;

☑ changes (actual or planned) to legislation;

☑ new expectations of interested parties;

☑ changes or advances in the designs of processes and products;

☑ advances in science and technology;

☑ planned new projects;

☑ lessons learned from environmental incidents;

☑ market preferences;

☑ education and training needs;

☑ vendor performance records;

☑ continual improvement performance records;

☑ cost-benefit reports and studies; or

☑ other reports, studies, and presentations.

As you design the management review it is important to consider identifying the sources for all the information required. Remember that all review processes will not be identical. You should gather a partial list of standard inputs to be complemented with "special" inputs as the need arises. Your company's management review will be unique to your company's needs.

The agenda

Whether your chief executive plans the management review alone on an afternoon spent in quiet contemplation, in a two hour meeting of managers, or during a weekend retreat for a wider group, in most cases this process evolves in three parts:

1) review of actual performance;

2) proposed improvements; and

3) approval of improvement actions.

Present the raw input information quickly and accurately when you review performance. Accessible and useful information helps everyone's understanding and helps you make reliable decisions.

For example, summarize your EMS audit reports to categorize and show your most common nonconformities. Linking these common nonconformities to root causes and the progress made in corrective actions to prevent recurrence helps management see where their additional requirements of time and money investments.

Managers also must be able to see the justification for recommended changes to the environmental program. These revisions may be linked to changes in the law; processes or products in need of redesign to meet current expectations; or measures to improve profitability by reducing pollution.

justification   EMS policy decisions can be complex and risky, with enormous implications. The tougher decisions demand rigorous analysis and synthesis within the context of your system. For the EMS to serve the business as a decision support system, instead of being seen or kept as an appendage of it, you must integrate it with your management system. Only top management can make this happen.

If your EMS is immature, consider reviewing your system early and frequently. Focus on how well your EMS is supporting the decision making process. For example, if you cannot rely on measurements, then your management review needs to drive those improvements first.

A more mature EMS, if it is driven by senior management, will assist you in making complex and risky environmental policy decisions to fulfill this objective.

Output

Management review is the long stop with a strategic view. Your organization should catch and correct its missed points and communicate them along with a clear vision and plan for the medium-and long-term future.

Budget and fund your corrective actions with milestones and responsibilities allocated for implementation. These outputs may be new programs or updated policy, and they will act as new or refreshed drivers for your EMS.

Communicate the results of your management review with employees and other interested parties. Effective and prompt communication fosters the confidence that management is truly committed to the EMS — it not only "talks the talk" but truly "walks the walk."

Many companies do not fully close out the minutes of their meetings, so consider using the EMS corrective or preventive action procedure to ensure accountability and effective actions. Be certain to verify the effectiveness or measure the progress of these actions to prepare them for the next management review.

Management Review Checklist

by Elizabeth A. Potts, President, ABS Quality Evaluations, Inc.

Management reviews should:

- involve senior management;
- be conducted regularly as scheduled;
- assess the effectiveness of the EMS;
- review the environmental policy and change if necessary;
- review internal audit results;
- set measurable performance objectives;
- evaluate actual performance versus set objectives;
- review progress relative to continual improvement plan;
- review, evaluate, and prioritize all aspects of the business and associated environmental impacts;
- be documented to provide objective evidence;
- be useful in improving and managing the organization; and
- review applicable regulatory requirements and compliance issues to ensure EMS is addressing all requirements.

CHAPTER 5
ISO 14001 Certification

by Elizabeth A. Potts, President, ABS Quality Evaluations

Let's assume that your organization has implemented an environmental management system in accordance with the ISO 14001 standard. Furthermore, your company has elected to go the extra step and pursue formal ISO 14001 certification.

☑ What can and should you expect?

☑ What will be different about a third-party registration audit?

☑ How will it be conducted?

This section will address what your organization can expect during the certification process. The next section will address how to select an appropriate certification body.

certification vs.
registration

First, one item should be cleared up:

☑ What is the difference between "registration" and "certification?"

In the United States, the term "registration" is used interchangeably with "certification" in the context of management system standard conformance and is not relevant to product registration. This can cause confusion. In Europe, environmental management systems **certification** is the usual term. The U.S. legal system denotes a degree of liability with the term "certification" that has been unacceptable to U.S. businesses, and hence the preference for using the term **registration**.

However, since the term "registration" is confusing to companies outside the U.S., it would be prudent for U.S. companies to understand that "certification" is the commonly accepted international term, especially if they seek to have global trading partners. This is the term used throughout this handbook except where noted.

6.5.1 The Certification Process

The certification process typically consists of the following five steps:

1) application or contract;

2) initial or preliminary assessment /document review;

3) certification assessment;

4) certification; and

5) certification maintenance (surveillance)

1) Application or Contract

Most certification bodies will require an application or contract to be completed. This document contains the rights and obligations of the certification body <u>and</u> the audited organization. Some of the areas that should be addressed are:

☑ confidentiality;

☑ appeal and complaint procedures;

☑ certification body access to facilities; and

☑ information on liability issues.

Should termination become necessary, you should be aware of these provisions.

compliance
audit issues

It is appropriate to note that the certification body is not going to conduct a compliance audit. The certification body is there to assess the conformance of the EMS with the requirements of ISO 14001.

Although the organization's compliance management will be one of many subjects the audit will address, the certification body is not there to assess your compliance with individual regulatory documents and requirements. The certification body will assess how your organization ensures that all applicable regulatory requirements are identified and incorporated into the EMS and how well the EMS is functioning.

The emphasis of the compliance-related segment of the audit will focus on the system and how it functions to satisfy the compliance commitment of its policy and compliance objectives and targets it may have defined. The compliance segment of the audit will not focus on whether each and every regulatory requirement is met to full compliance. Any compliance issues noted during the audit will be brought to your organization's attention as a part of the assessment. Regulatory compliance auditing responsibility remains with the organization being audited.

2) Initial Assessment/Document Review

The next step in the certification process is the initial or preliminary assessment and document review. Most certification bodies will wish to conduct this phase of the certification on-site.

The following documents are typically reviewed:

• the EMS manual, if your organization has chosen to develop one;

• analysis of environmental aspects and impacts;

• applicable regulatory requirements;

• audit reports;

• organization charts;

• training programs;

• management review minutes; and

• your organization's continual improvement plans.

While this part of the certification process is used to evaluate the readiness of the organization for a formal certification audit, it also serves to help the certification body in planning the audit.

feedback

The certification body gives you feedback, which should be open and constructive. If the certification body deems that the EMS is not ready to be formally assessed, your organization would be wise to listen and seek help in developing and implementing appropriate responses to the certification body's observations. Proceeding with a formal assessment before your organization is ready usually leads to a frustrating experience and is a waste of time and money.

conflict of
interest

In contrast to internal or second-party audits, the certification body cannot (and should not) provide substantive guidance to your organization on <u>how</u> to achieve conformity with ISO 14001. In other words, the certification body cannot be both a consultant and a certification body, as this clearly constitutes a conflict of interest. The certification body can and should, however, provide your organization interpretive guidance by openly engaging in discussions about these concerns.

3) Certification Assessment

A certification assessment normally follows a successful initial assessment/document review. Usually, the primary difference between this assessment and internal audits will be the "formality" of the assessment. Your organization should expect the same independence, competence, and professionalism of the lead auditor and audit team during a certification assessment as during an internal audit. Details of exactly what will be covered are available elsewhere in this text. (See Part 7, Chapter 4 for more information.)

opening
meeting

You can expect the certification body to conduct the audit based on the criteria of **ISO 14001** and the guidance of **ISO 14010** and **ISO 14011**. When the certification body's auditors arrive on site, an introductory opening meeting will be held and you should be prepared to supply escorts to guide the audit team through the site and provide any necessary assistance. The more knowledgeable your escorts are of the overall EMS, the smoother the assessment will proceed.

interview

To assess whether an EMS is in conformity with ISO 14001 and has been fully implemented and documented in manuals, supporting procedures, and other records, all levels of personnel will be interviewed. Your organization must be able to demonstrate that the EMS is designed (and implemented) to satisfy its policy commitments and the various ISO 14001 criteria. Most certification bodies conduct a daily debriefing with your organization to keep key individuals informed of progress and any apparent deficiencies noted.

report

Generally, at the conclusion of the assessment, a closing meeting session is held and your organization typically will be left with a report. This report will include the assessment team's recommendation regarding certification status and whether the recommendation is binding or open to subsequent review and approval.

4) Certification

Recommendations of approval, conditional approval, or disapproval are typical during the certification phase of the process.

certification
approval

Approval results when your organization's EMS is found to be substantially in conformance with all requirements of ISO 14001 with only minor, non-systemic deficiencies detected.

When all elements of the standard have been addressed but perhaps not fully documented or implemented or when a number of deficiencies (nonconformances) are detected in a

conditional
approval

specific area, revealing a systemic problem, the certification body's recommendation is usually a conditional approval. Your organization will have to submit evidence of completed corrective actions to the certification body before becoming fully certified, and it is the certification body that must evaluate this evidence and accept it or require reevaluation of your site.

If your organization's EMS is not well documented or well implemented disapproval may occur. Disapproval may also result if your organization's EMS is demonstrated to be ineffective in meeting its policy commitments or its defined objectives and targets. Usually a reassessment is required following disapproval.

Once registered, your site receives a certificate, which includes a full description of the scope of the audit. The certification body typically publishes and maintains a listing of registered companies.

5) Surveillance

surveillance

A major difference between third-party ISO 14001 certification and internal EMS audits appears in the final phase of certification: surveillance.

areas of
emphasis

Teams from the certification body will return at prescribed intervals, usually every six months or annually, to assess the continued conformity of your organization's EMS with ISO 14001. Corrections of deficiencies identified by previous assessments or surveillances will be verified, and selected elements of the standard will be reevaluated. During the surveillance phase, emphasis is typically placed on internal EMS audits, management reviews, corrective/preventive action systems, and continual improvement efforts.

Although formal certification can often benefit an organization's marketplace acceptance and enhance its performance, the process has sometimes been associated with copious amounts of documentation and bureaucratic system requirements. Most competent certification bodies subscribe to the position that organizations should keep their EMS as simple as possible and strive for true improvement.

If your certification body appears to focus more on quantity than substance, refer to the next section in this chapter. You may need to select a different certification body!

6.5.2 Choosing a Certification Body (Registrar)

When selecting a certification body, or registrar, the single most important issue your organization needs to remember is that you are the client! This means that your corporate representatives should feel free to ask any and all questions they may have and should expect comprehensive, straightforward answers. These include:

☑ questions regarding legal issues such as confidentiality and liability;

☑ process issues such as the path to certification;

☑ competency of auditors; and

☑ cost issues such as extraneous fees or surveillance charges

partnership | If your certification body isn't responsive to any one of these issues, you should investigate further before you pursue contracting with the certification body for EMS certification services. Certification is a long-term commitment, and your organization should only enter into this commitment with a competent registrar. Essentially, the most desirable certification body is one that can prove it views the relationship with your organization as a partnership.

There are many issues of concern to an organization pursuing certification. These include a potential certification body's:

☑ accreditation

☑ accredited scope

☑ reputation

☑ competence

☑ capacity

☑ cost

☑ philosophy

Although this list is not inclusive, it addresses most of the major concerns your organization should consider when selecting a certification body. Paying attention to these issues will preclude any major pitfalls on the road to certification.

Accreditation

The selected certification body should either be accredited or able to demonstrate it is well on the way to becoming accredited.

Regardless of whether the certification body is recognized by United Kingdom Accreditation Service (UKAS), Raad voor Accreditatie (RvA), Registrar Accreditation Board (RAB), or any other accrediting organization that operates to the EN 45012 requirements, accreditation is a must.

independent review | Accreditation means that the certification body has submitted itself to an independent review by an unbiased third party. It has undergone the rigors of an evaluation to test the quality of its ability to audit to an EMS standard. The technique used to evaluate a certification body's ability to audit is much like the system the certification body uses to audit your organization to see if it complies with a management system standard. An accredited certification body is subject to ongoing surveillance just as your organization would be.

Finally, an accredited organization can provide, in addition to its own certification mark, the backing of its accrediting body by displaying the accrediting body's marks or symbols on the certificate.

Accredited Scope

It is not enough to know that your potential certification body is accredited.

The first question you should ask a potential certification body is:

☑ "Are you accredited to provide services in my organization's specific industrial or service sector?"

If the certification body does not have your type of organization within its accredited scope of operations, it cannot issue you an accredited certificate because it has not been judged competent to assess in your particular area. Particularly if your organization is pursuing accreditation to enhance its marketplace credibility, an unaccredited certificate will do little to demonstrate your organization's commitment to the environment and continual improvement.

Reputation

Your certification body's reputation is crucial to the acceptance of your certificate. Most credible certification bodies are accredited, but even accreditation doesn't fully ensure that the certificate issued will be accepted by your customers or other key stakeholders.

Therefore, selecting a certification body based on interviewing and evaluating a number of certification bodies and inquiring about their philosophies, costs, and approaches to certification is important.

☑ Ask for references!

Of course, the certification body is unlikely to give you bad references, so you must do your homework.

☑ Ask for the complete listing of sites and organizations registered by it and select your own organizations to contact.

The certification body's responsiveness to your needs and its professionalism coupled with a few reference checks is usually a good way to judge the certification body's reputation. A thorough, up-front evaluation of your potential certification body will preclude countless headaches as you proceed toward certification.

Competency

The success of your certification process depends highly on the capabilities of the certification body's auditors.

insurance   ☑ You should feel free to request details on the background and experience of the auditors.

The accreditation process ensures that the certification body has a system to qualify and monitor auditors in place. Your organization, the client, is the ultimate judge of the auditor's competency. The prospective certification body should have a policy regarding customer complaints relative to auditors. You should be assured that, under that policy, your organization can object, with cause, to specific auditors.

Consistency from audit to audit is critical to a long-lasting partnership and a successful certification process.

☑ Ask whether a prospective certification body primarily uses its own employees, all subcontractors, or a mix.

☑ Request information describing actions taken by the certification body to ensure consistent application and interpretation of the standard by its auditors.

The certification process shouldn't be a headache, and there is nothing worse than suffering through learning that specific policies or procedures are acceptable one time but not the next.

Your certification body's involvement in pertinent industry groups like the U.S. Technical Advisory Group (TAG) to ISO/TC 207 and the Environmental Auditing Roundtable (EAR) is further evidence that your certification body is committed to staying current with developments. Participation in these groups also indicates your potential certification body wants to be a player for the long term.

Capacity

The prospective certification body must have the resources available to meet your needs. The certification body can be the most professional, competent organization, but it does you no good if it cannot audit you until 2001! Be aware that the more constraints you place on the certification body relative to auditor qualifications, etc., the more flexible you should be relative to the scheduling of your assessment. On the other hand, the certification body should be able to meet your timing needs in a reasonable period of time.

☑ Ask about available resources.

Costs

There are many costs associated with certification, the first of which is actually developing and implementing an ISO 14001 conforming EMS.

Your organization may elect to use only internal resources to implement the system or may elect to rely completely on the services of an outside consultant. You may also employ a combination of both approaches. No certification body will guarantee that certification will be achieved during the first assessment whether you use a consultant, implement the system internally, or use a combination of the two.

☑ Your organization should assess the costs of the actual certification process in great detail.

When selecting a certification body, it is important that your organization be totally familiar with all costs associated with the program. Your organization should assure itself that it has obtained a price for the following:

- contract review;
- an initial assessment visit/document review;
- the costs of the actual assessment; and
- any costs associated with issuing the certificate and writing the report.

☑ Your organization should know the certification body's policy relative to surveillance visits, including the duration and the cost of those visits.

Also, your organization should know the validity length of the certificate as well as any reassessment or partial reassessment costs that may be required in the future.

☑ Furthermore, your organization should be aware that some certification bodies require application fees, listing fees, and certification fees in addition to those prices normally quoted with the above actions.

Your organization must ask the certification body about all fees to ensure you know, up front, the full cost of the certification process.

Philosophy

A good "fit" is necessary between your organization and its certification body.

☑ You should explore the certification body's philosophies relative to continual improvement, auditing style (positive vs. "gotcha"), and communication.

Certification is an ongoing process, and it requires a certification body that can and is willing to grow with your organization. The certification body's services must remain value-added as your organization evolves and continually improves. Taking time to guarantee a good philosophical "fit" exists is well worth the effort.

In conclusion, remember that your organization is the client when evaluating and selecting a certification body. The certification body cannot (and should not) award certification to an organization that does not fully conform with the criteria of ISO 14001. The certification body can, however, make achievement of certification a low-stress, cost-effective endeavor by its professionalism, appropriate communication, consistent interpretation of requirements, and a true commitment to customer satisfaction.

CHAPTER 6
ISO 14000 and Compliance Auditing

by Dawne Schomer, Corporate ESH Audit and Systems Program Manager,
Texas Instruments Inc; Leader ST2 TG3 on Auditor Qualifications.

6.6.1 Introduction

This chapter is an overview of:

* what environmental compliance auditing is;
* what ISO 14000 is;
* how they compare; and
* what the future holds for the two.

Many changes have occurred in industry and in industrial environmental auditing in the last decade, and the scope of the regulations covered continues to grow. The level of sophistication required of the industry audit program has increased as well as has the use of metrics and trend analysis. A worldwide focus has come more into view as daily business becomes a global endeavor.

Basic-level internal industrial environmental audits have several purposes:

- to assure the stockholders and board of directors of compliance status;
- to assist the manufacturing sites in their environmental efforts; and
- to provide a means for technology transfer and employee education.

The traditional focus of EAs has been as a tool to evaluate compliance status, and its design has largely been in response to a "command-and-control" regulatory environment where laws and regulations are very detailed and specific.

Coming up on the scene internationally is a set of standards that goes beyond a regulatory focus to encompass the wider vision of environmental stewardship.

Among the new ISO 14000 standards you will see in the next few years are the following:

- environmental labeling (EL) of products, that might include certifications or self-declarations of "greenness;"
- environmental performance evaluation (EPE) that may suggest a common approach to metrics and measurements;
- life-cycle assessments (LCAs) of entire manufacturing processes, identifying environmental burdens, determining their impacts, and developing and implementing alternatives;
- auditing standards that address general principles for EAs, guidelines for EMS auditing, and environmental auditor qualifications (due out in mid-1996); and
- the EMS specification standard, ISO 14001 (due out in mid-1996).

6.6.2 Compliance vs. Management System Audits

Environmental Compliance Auditing

"The process of determining whether all or selected levels of an organization are in compliance with regulatory requirements and internal policies and standards..."[1]

"In its most common sense, . . . a methodical examination, involving analyses, tests, and confirmations of local procedures and practices leading to a verification of compliance with legal requirements, internal policies, and/or accepted practices."[2]

1. J. Ladd Greeno, Gilbert S. Hedstrom, and Maryanne DiBerto, **Environmental Auditing Fundamentals and Techniques** (Cambridge: A.D. Little, Inc. Center for Environmental Assurance, 1987) p.3.

2. A.D. Little, Inc. Center for Environmental Assurance, **Current Practices in Environmental Auditing** (Washington, D.C.: U.S. Environmental Protection Agency, 1984; reprinted., Springfield, VA.: U.S. Department of Commerce National Technical Information Service, 1984) p.1.

Globe Metallurgical

Cleveland, Ohio, United States, January 1996

Globe Metallurgical, headquartered in Cleveland, Ohio, manufactures silicon metal and ferrosilicon products. There are four plants, which include locations in Ohio; Niagara Falls, New York; and Selma, Alabama.

Bob Rothwell, director of environmental affairs, says that his company's primary environmental goal is to complete development of a good environmental management system and to integrate it into the existing ISO 9000-certified quality management system. "We won't reinvent the wheel," he says. "We'll plug it into the quality system we have."

Rothwell says that internal auditing for environment issues is "informal," and it works, but it does not have "the built-in checks and balances" of a formal EMS. "We are using the ISO 14000 guidelines as a 'guideline,'" he says, or a "road map. When and if we decide to seek certification," he says, "we'll have the pieces in place."

Currently, Rothwell and the managers of the company's four plants (as well as state inspectors) keep the informal system in operation. When Rothwell visits the plants, personnel there can expect him to take a thorough look at each plant's operation. He depends on the plant managers to follow up once discrepancies are noted.

Once a month, Rothwell gives an environmental report at a meeting at headquarters. It is a rundown on the four plants, he says, and consists of good and bad things that he has seen. He is planning to recommend the delivery of a formal annual report on environmental issues.

Rothwell believes that a company needs both internal auditing and, in an ongoing system, auditing by outside persons to keep the company "honest."

"You need to see yourself as others see you," he says. At the same time, he says, he has not experienced much difficulty with cooperation from plant personnel. "People are anxious to do things right and to find out where their mistakes are."

Once Globe has set up its EMS auditing procedures, teams will consist of at least one environmental person from the plant being audited and persons from the quality management system.

Rothwell says that in February 1995, Globe had just completed a self-assessment with a consultant. The consultant's estimate for a four-year implementation plan for ISO 14000 certification was nearly $400,000. In addition to consultant fees, this included the hours of training required to bring Globe's 400 employees up to speed in environmental matters and paying salaries while people were in training.

This company, interviewed by CEEM Information Services, participated in an NSF International pilot program underway in 1995 and 1996 to test the effectiveness of environmental management system (EMS) draft standards.

Environmental Auditing

- has been a primary means for self-evaluation since the early 1970's
- is an important tool for internal use in industrial environmental management; and
- has historically been compliance-focused

Compliance Audits

The checklists or protocols used by the auditors usually tie directly to prescriptive legal requirements.

The presence or absence of an environmental compliance audit program within industry has been described as either a mitigating factor or an aggravating factor in the U.S. Department of Justice Sentencing Guidelines, so the use of compliance auditing by industry is strongly encouraged by U.S. regulatory agencies.

Management Systems

The European Union (EU) Eco-Management and Audit Regulation (EMAR) went into effect in April 1995. EMAR was used as a key document in the development of ISO 14001. Ninety percent or more of the elements in EMAR are found in ISO 14001, the other 10 percent in ISO 14004. 📖 (See Part 9, Chapter 5 for more information.)

Elements found in ISO 14001 and 14004 are common to several existing environmental quality tools such as the Global Environmental Management Initiative's (GEMI's) Environmental Self-Audit and the National Center for Manufacturing Science's tool for environmental assessment called GreenScore.

Some customer groups have begun to imbed management system requirements into supplier criteria documents such as the National Aerospace Standard NAS 411.

Compliance Auditing is element- or sub-process oriented, whereas management systems audits are geared toward the high-level, process-oriented systems aspects.

To further illustrate the differences, you can look at the typical contents of an environmental (compliance audit) protocol book. It is usually very topic- and media-oriented, and the questions directly align with regulatory compliance requirements. The contents of ISO 14001, on the other hand, are focused on the "big picture" — the macro-processes that drive the system that assures compliance within industry.

6.6.3 Management System Reviews

Policy

The management system review should include each of the following elements:

- be from top management;
- address impacts (activities, products, and services);

Fluke Corporation

Everett, Washington, United States, January 1996

Gwen Blanchard is one of two internal auditors for Fluke Corporation, a manufacturer of electronic measurement and testing equipment headquartered in Everett, Washington. Fluke Corporation also has six service centers located in the U.S. and Canada. In early 1996 Blanchard said that her company was looking into ISO 14001 certification but had not decided how to implement it.

In early 1996, Fluke's EMS was in the developmental stages, according to George Bissonnette, environmental specialist. The company only performed ISO 9000 audits but they were participating in NSF International's pilot project and was expecting continue to develop its EMS program.

Internal audits at Fluke Corporation are executed by department, by element. Blanchard says that it takes 18 months for auditors to cover all areas. The service centers receive a full audit annually.

When the auditors visit an area (once a month) they check up on other facilities within that area. They do that, she says, because "if they don't see you, they go back to what they were doing." The auditing team relies on the knowledge of the company's environmental specialist, according to Bissonnette.

Blanchard says that Fluke Corporation's financial group has an auditing team as well. Her team sometimes invites an auditor from the financial group to be part of the team. To maintain a level of objectivity, her group gets audited by the financial group. Concerning whether or not internal or external audits are more objective, Blanchard says, "I think you're harder on yourself."

Blanchard says that the auditing team prepares a site for audit by sitting down with the auditee to see what areas will be affected, what the standard operating procedures of the area are, and what ISO considerations will be involved. The team tries to give the auditee two or three weeks to prepare for the audit so that the auditee can feel like part of the team. Also, the team sends a copy of the checklist to help prepare the auditee. The team also encourages lots of questions or requests for clarification.

The audit process consists of an opening meeting where more questions are encouraged before the audit takes place. After the audit, there is a closing meeting before the team delivers the preliminary findings. The team then delivers a report to the auditee. The auditors then keep track of the file so that when they are again in the area they can check up on the auditee to ensure that corrections are being made.

Blanchard encourages members of the auditing team to be professional, to be on time, and to watch what they say. She thinks there is still a perception at Fluke Corporation where employees view auditors as the federal Internal Revenue Service. She sometimes hears the auditors being referred to as "them."

This company, interviewed by CEEM Information Services, participated in an NSF International pilot program underway in 1995 and 1996 to test the effectiveness of environmental management system (EMS) draft standards.

- commit to continual improvement and to compliance;
- contain a plan for objectives and targets;
- be documented; and
- be available to the public.

Employees are expected to know about the company's environmental policy and the importance of conforming to it.

Planning

Many manufacturing organizations already do some planning as a part of their management system activities, but it is usually at the sub-process level. Environmental aspects (impacts) ask for a more global evaluation of your company's impact on such environmental factors as air emissions and water pollutant concentrations.

All of these areas of management system concern have several action items in common, such as "identify," "define," "document," "communicate," "evaluate," and "review." The roles and responsibilities need to address human, financial, and technological needs.

Compliance auditing often looks at pollution control processes for operations and maintenance indications. ISO 14001 will require companies to look more routinely at all the operations and activities associated with environmental impacts.

The areas of concern in "checking and corrective action" are similar to those activities addressed at the media-specific, sub-process level inherent in regulatory compliance. A formal strategic plan for addressing nonconformance and corrective and preventative action may not, however, be covered entirely by today's industrial compliance programs. Industry may benefit from ISO 14001 in this area.

Conducting an EMS audit and performing periodic management reviews of the EMS system will be similar to audits and reviews conducted on quality systems.

6.6.4 Overlaps

ISO 14001 and the environmental audit overlap in several key areas including:

- evaluation;
- "records";
- business process;
- basic accountability; and
- human resources issues.

Environmental compliance audits are important, but in some ways, they provide only limited benefits. These audits provide only a "snapshot" of your company's current status and often allow for minimal performance because they focus on an "if you don't meet the regulation then fix it" approach.

In fact, you could argue that compliance audits foster a "get ready for the audit" mentality toward compliance issues. After all, why spend money and resources to exceed regulatory compliance if you don't have to?

6.6.5 Summary

Because compliance audits look at the sub-process level and not the big picture, they typically do not result in a review of the way compliance issues are met.

root-cause
analysis

The focus tends to stay on the symptoms — that is, on compliance or non-compliance. Often a compliance issue is a symptom of an EMS problem, but the compliance program corrective actions may not incorporate root-cause analysis or similar tools that help identify and correct the systems gaps that may be causing regulatory issues to become problems.

There are other limitations inherent to compliance auditing. Often a compliance audit is conducted by an outside party — corporate or a contractor.

This outsider relationship may encourage a lack of site ownership and the resulting "Let's clean up for the auditors" mentality that leads to the approach of "react" and an attitude that we will "address" issues when they are pointed out by someone else. When a site is in this mode, environmental issues are not likely to be considered as an integral part of day-to-day business planning.

ISO 14001 requires a certain level of accountability and communication with the communities surrounding the ISO 14001 manufacturing facility. Establishing productive communications channels with the community will be a new activity for many chemical-use industries.

EMS audits focus on the macro-processes in place to address environmental stewardship and continuous improvement. The results of the EMS audit will be much more definitive and, when used in conjunction with compliance audit information, will provide a clear window into the state of site environmental program development and maturity.

FOOTNOTES

1 Further information on selecting members of the audit team is taken up in Part 6, Section 3.2 entitled "Audit Team Composition."

2 Further information on executing the audit is taken up in Part 6., Section 3.1 entitled, "Executing the Audit."

Conformity Assessment

CHAPTER 1
Overview

by Joel Urman, Program Director of Standards, IBM

The benefits of using standards are widely known and accepted by businesses, governments, and other organizations that use them for products, processes, and services. Most organizations think of them in terms of discreet products or processes, not in terms of systems.

The use of standards saves time and money, which results in lower costs. Technological advances often are incorporated into standards. By using standards, businesses can realize the benefits of advanced technology without investing in expensive design and research that would duplicate what is already available in the standard.

Standardized parts, components, and processes enable economies of scale. Standardized interfaces enhance competition and give users a very large number and variety of choices in their buying decisions.

example: telephones
Telephones, for example, come in an enormous variety of styles, designs, and functions. Since they each use standardized telephone jacks, the buyer can pick any that suits his or her needs and have confidence that it will plug into any telephone outlet. Telephone manufacturers compete based on areas other than the interface to the outlet.

Standards help international commerce by defining common elements that can be accepted worldwide.

Standards also aid the public welfare. Product safety standards, such as electrical codes and public health codes for restaurants, are examples of areas where standards promote the public interest.

Management system standards help guide producers in developing efficient and effective management controls and oversight.

The ISO 9000 Quality Management System (QMS) standards help businesses and organizations develop more effective quality management processes and controls. Similarly, the ISO 14000 EMS standards will guide organizations as they establish procedures, processes, and controls to help them better manage their environmental responsibilities.

7.1.1 Conformity Assessment = Assurance

As important as standards are, their ultimate value depends largely on how well a producer implements them. Conformity assessment is concerned with those activities and procedures that determine if standards are implemented properly. Without conformity assessment, many of the benefits of standards would be lost.

In its most basic sense, conformity assessment is simply confirmation that something does what it is supposed to do.

example: light bulbs

For most things we buy, we do the final assessment ourselves. When we buy a light bulb, for example, we screw it into a socket and turn on the switch. If it lights, we know it works, and conformity is confirmed. Flipping on the switch, however, is not all there is to conformity assessment of the bulb. We haven't confirmed that a 100-watt bulb really uses 100 watts of electricity, or that the stated luminescence is correct. Measuring compliance to those specifications requires more sophistication than demonstrating whether a bulb turns on and off.

In a more specific sense, conformity assessment encompasses the procedures and activities by which products, processes, services, and management systems are assessed, and the degree to which conformance to a particular standard or specification is met.

Conformity assessment focuses on how standards are used and implemented, and how well the supplier's product, processes, service, or management system meets the specifications defined in the standard.

For the EMS standards, then, conformity assessment is all the necessary activity needed to determine if, and to what extent an organization complies with the specifications in the ISO 14000 series of standards.

Suppliers, users, purchasers, and government regulators all need assurance to one degree or another that standards are met.

Suppliers must satisfy themselves that the standards they use, and those that their customers require, are effectively and properly implemented in the products, processes, services, and management systems they produce and use.

Users and purchasers need the assurance that they are getting the benefits of the standards in the product, process, or service they buy.

Government regulators, under a mandate to enforce laws and regulations, must have assurance that the specified standards are implemented and the standards' specifications are met. Assessing conformity for products, processes, and services that affect public heath, safety, and national security is particularly important since lives may be at stake if a required standard or specification is not met.

Conformity Assessment Illustrated

Figure 7.1 illustrates a simplified view of conformity assessment. A product, process, or service must first be tested to determine if it conforms to the specifications in the standard. Tests are usually technical operations that consist of determining specific characteristics of a product, process, or service.

The test results are then evaluated to determine if the standard's specifications are met properly. If they are, a document or certificate may be issued that confirms compliance. In some cases, authorization may be given to display a defined mark of conformity. A mark of conformity is an indication that the item is in conformance with a specific standard, and its use is granted exclusively as a result of the certification process.

Certification is the set of procedures that includes evaluating test results and confirming the product, process, or service actually does conform to specified requirements. Certification also may include issuing a certificate and mark of conformity. The organization or group that does certification is called a certification body.

Management systems do not have a product to test. Instead of a test, a specially trained individual or auditor evaluates whether an organization has implemented properly the specifications in the management system standard. If it has, a specially designated organization called a "registrar" in the U.S. and "certification body" elsewhere issues to the applicant a certificate indicating that his or her organization or site is in compliance with the standard. The certification body also adds the applicant's name to the registration list of those who meet the management standard.

📖 (See Part 7, Chapter 4 for further explanation on certification.)

Process		Output	
Products	Test	Certification	Certificate and/or Mark of Conformity
Management Systems	Audit	Registration	Certificate and Registration List

Figure 7.1 – Simplified view of conformity assessment.

7.1.2 Accreditation

Accreditation is the procedure by which an authoritative body formally recognizes another body or individual and certifies that it is competent to carry out specific tasks. An authoritative body may be a government agency, or a highly respected private organization.

Conformity assessment relies on many bodies and individuals. These must have a high degree of competence and skill to do their job. They need the respect and competence of all relevant parties so there is a high degree of confidence in the conformity assessment results. These bodies and individuals include certification bodies/registrars, test laboratories, and management system auditors.

Accreditation is a formal procedure in which the accreditation or authoritative body inspects, examines, and tests the body or individual to ensure that it is competent. The approved body or individual usually receives a certificate confirming its acceptance. The organization or group that performs accreditation is called an accreditation body.

Many accreditation bodies operate in the United States. For example, ANSI, the American National Standards Institute, is a prominent accreditation body. ANSI works with the Registrar Accreditation Board (RAB), to act as the accreditation body in the U.S. for quality management systems. In early 1996, ANSI and RAB also were working to define an accreditation system for EMS in the U.S. 📖 (See Part 7, Chapter 4 for more information on their efforts.)

In recent years, a new proposal has emerged led by U.S. industry for accrediting a supplier's/organization's own internal auditors to conduct management system audits. This system is called the supplier audit conformation approach. 📖 (See Part 7, Chapter 2 for more information on the supplier audit conformation)

CHAPTER 2

The Conformity Assessment Process

by Jean H. McCreary, Esq.,
Leader ST2 TG1 on Environmental Auditing, General Principles and Initial Reviews
© 1996 Nixon, Hargrave, Devans & Doyle LLP

7.2.1 Conformity Assessment: Definition of Terms

Introduction

To organizations unfamiliar with the concepts of "registration," "accreditation," and "certification" as they are used in ISO 14000 or ISO 9000, these terms can be confusing. They are often misused or used interchangeably, and the different European meanings of the same terms can be attached erroneously. This chapter clarifies these terms and their meanings and scope in the conformity assessment process in the ISO standards arena.

It is not the scope of this section to discuss the specific tasks that would be accomplished during a conformity assessment audit. 📖 (See Part 6 for more information on this topic.)

Defined Terms

Accreditation — Procedure by which an authoritative body gives formal recognition that a body or person is competent to carry out specific tasks. (ISO/IEC Guide 2)

Accreditation body — Body that gives formal recognition that an organization or person is competent to carry out specific tasks.

Audit — A planned, independent, and documented assessment to determine whether agreed-upon requirements are being met. (ASQC Quality Auditing Technical Committee)

Auditor (environmental) — Person qualified to perform environmental audits. (ISO 14010)

Certificate [of conformity] — Document issued under the rules of a certification system, indicating that adequate confidence is provided that a duly identified product, process, or service is in conformity with a specific standard or other normative document. (ISO/IEC Guide 2)

Certification — Procedure by which a third party gives written assurance that a product, process, or service conforms to specified requirements. (ISO/IEC Guide 2)

Certification body — Body that conducts certification of conformity.

Certifier — *See certification body.*

Conformity assessment — Conformity assessment includes all activities that are intended to assure the conformity of products or systems to a set of standards. This can include testing, certification, quality system assessment, and other activities. (ISO 8402)

Recognition agreement — an agreement that is based on the acceptance by one party of results, presented by another party, from the implementation of one or more designated functional elements of a conformity assessment system. (ISO/IEC Guide 2)

Registrar — *See certification body.*

Registration — Procedure by which a body indicates relevant characteristics of a product, process, or service, or particulars of a body or person in an appropriate, publicly available, list. (ISO/IEC Guide 2)

Registration body — *See certification body.*

Verification — Process of authenticating evidence. (ISO 14010) The act of reviewing, inspecting, testing, checking, auditing, or otherwise establishing and documenting whether items, processes, services, or documents conform to specified requirements. (ANSI/ASQC A3)

Editor's note: For the purposes of simplicity, with some exceptions, this book will use "certification" to encompass both certification and registration.

Registration vs. Certification

registration,
registrar
In the United States, "registration" is the process by which your company or organization applies for placement on a publicly available list of entities that conform to a specified standard. In this case, registration would signify that your EMS program conforms to the ISO 14001 specification. A "registrar" is the organization that accepts the registration following an assessment process through which the registrar confirms that your organization's EMS program conforms to ISO 14001 specifications. This is the "conformity assessment."

conformity
assessment

certificate,
certification,
certifier
A registration "certificate" (usually written) is received when the EMS of your organization, location, plant, or process is demonstrated to conform to the ISO 14001 specification and the company has sought to be registered. "Certification" can also be used to describe the process by which individual auditors demonstrate their competence to perform ISO 14001 EMS audits. A "certifier" is the entity that certifies [in writing] that individual auditors have demonstrated the competencies specified by the standard and guidance.

In Europe, the term "certification" has the same meaning that "registration" has in the U.S. The American jurisprudence system attaches liability implications to "certifications," particularly with respect to regulation of professionals, thus leading to the preference, in the U.S., for the term "registration" to apply to the conformity assessment process.

accreditation
"Accreditation" is the procedure by which an authoritative body formally recognizes the competence of a body or person to carry out specified tasks.

In the case of ISO 14001, registrars of companies demonstrating conformity to ISO 14001 may be accredited by domestic or international standard-setting organizations. In addition, certifiers of individual auditors may also be accredited. In the case of training programs, such as ones that would train auditors to perform EMS audits and prepare them for certification as EMS auditors, these may be "approved" by an accrediting organization. 📖 (See Part 6, Chapter 5 for more information on certification.)

7.2.2 Third-Party Certification Process

Organization Certification

In the ISO 14000 context, corporate entities or organizations may elect to become certified to ISO 14001. This is accomplished by application to a "registrar," or "certification body."

The organization functioning as the registrar varies from country to country, and in some countries is a governmental entity. In the U.S., for ISO 14000, various private entities (both domestic and international) will function as registrars.

An organization seeking registration should carefully select a registration body (registrar) according to criteria important to the organization's objectives and business needs. Factors can include the reputation and competence of the registrar (generally, and within specific industry sectors), the ability of the registrar to respond to the organization's specific needs, the backgrounds of specific auditors who will perform the conformity assessment, the reputation of the accrediting bodies that have accredited the registrar, the scope and limitations of any accreditations, cost of registration, and even proximity to facilities being registered. 📖 (See Part 6, Chapter 5 for more information on certification.)

Once an application is filed, the registration body will evaluate an applicant's EMS system against the criteria in ISO 14001. This is called a "conformity assessment."

The evaluation will include an examination of elements of the company's written environmental policies and procedures, its environmental management system components and functionality, its records and documentation, and its internal (compliance) auditing system.

This examination takes place at the applicant's facility and is performed by auditors working for the registration body. Certain record reviews and pre-assessments may be accomplished based on submitted documentation. In most cases, the conformity assessment process includes cycles of deficiencies being noted and corrective action being implemented before the recommendation of acceptance for registration is made by the audit team to the registrar.

A written certificate is given for the scope of the conformity assessment, which can range from applying to a specific process or operation to covering an entire facility or even a multi-facility organization.

surveillance audit — Once received, the registration is listed in a directory (usually published at least annually) and can be publicly displayed as evidence of registration. Registrations are effective for three years in most cases, but most registration bodies perform annual or other periodic "surveillance" audits during the three-year interval before re-registration must be obtained.

registration or "mark" — Registration can also be denied and, in some countries, made conditional on performance of specified corrective actions. Legal action can be taken if a company misuses the registration or "mark." Registration can take from six months to a year to obtain.

Auditor Certification

In many countries, there is a national domestic auditor certification scheme (i.e., one that would apply to ISO 14000 auditors, compliance auditors, site assessors, etc.).

As of January 1996, in the U.S. there was no nationally recognized certification scheme. There were professional organizations that offer environmental auditor-related certifications (such as the Institute of Professional Environmental Practice's very rigorous Qualified Environmental Auditor or Qualified Environmental Professional credential), state-regulated registrations (such as California, which recognizes more than a dozen environmental specialties), and private unaccredited organizations that offer certifications of varying degrees of rigor and respect.

7.2.3 Self-Declaration Process

by Joel Urman, Program Director of Standards, IBM and

Jean H. McCreary, Esq., Nixon, Hargrave, Devans & Doyle;

Leader ST2 TG1 on Environmental Auditing, General Principles and Initial Reviews

As noted at the beginning, conformity assessment applies to products, processes, services, and management systems. Where products are concerned, testing is the likely method of conformity assessment. Where systems are concerned, auditing is the likely method.

Though the scope and manner in which conformity assessment is carried out varies considerably depending on what is being assessed, conformity assessment generally takes two forms:

1) third-party assessment for certification; or

2) self-declaration of conformity.

As *Figure 7.2* illustrates, the difference between the methods is who does the work. For self-declaration, the organization is responsible for performing the test or audit, while for third-party certification, an independent laboratory or specially trained auditor performs these functions.

	Process		Output
Products	**Test**	**Certification**	**Certificate and/or Mark of Conformity**
	Performed by: third-party lab supplier	Performed by: certification body	Issued by: certification body supplier
Management Systems	**Audit**	**Registration**	**Certificate and Registration List**
	Performed by: authorized auditor supplier	Performed by: authorized registrar. Not applicable for supplier's declaration.	Issued by: Authorized registrar. Not applicable for supplier's declaration.

Figure 7.2 – Product vs. management system conformity.

Experience to Date: Self-Declaration Reigns

If you consider experience to date, organizations self-declare their conformity to standards they use in the vast majority of products, processes, and services.

Third-party test laboratories, auditors, and certification bodies are generally more costly than an organization's own resources, and the third-party approach can be more time-consuming. Self-declaration is the method of choice for these reasons. The savings these organizations see often result in lower costs and more timely products for users.

In the light bulb example cited earlier, the bulb's manufacturer attests that the 100-watt bulb actually does use 100 watts of electricity.

relationship between supplier and customer
The degree to which this system of declaration of conformance is adequate depends on the relationship between the supplier and customer. When the customer has confidence in the capability and integrity of the supplier, which is usually the case, the supplier's declaration is satisfactory. For most standards, an organization's declaration of conformity is all that the customer needs to have confidence that what he or she is buying meets the relevant standards.

Sometimes a supplier's declaration is not sufficient to meet market or regulatory requirements and a supplier must use a third party to assess conformity. A customer or government regulator may insist that a supplier obtain a third-party certification. Sometimes a supplier will choose to use a third-party assessment to give added assurance of conformance to his customer, though a third-party assessment may not be formally required.

A supplier's declaration of conformity is usually sufficient to satisfy customers. Having a recognized certificate of approval based on outside laboratory testing and on an unbiased third-party assessment may give the customer additional confidence that the product meets applicable standards. Sometimes, government regulations make third-party certification a mandatory requirement.

Product Conformity

An organization wishing to self-declare conformity to a standard used in its product can test the product in its own facilities or have the testing done by a commercial laboratory. The organization then analyzes the test results and determines if the product passes the test. If it does, the organization declares, usually in writing, the product to be in conformance.

For independent third-party conformity assessment of a product, a third party laboratory must do the testing. Usually this is a laboratory that specializes in specific products or standards testing.

laboratory accreditation
For example, a laboratory may specialize in testing for electronic emanations for compliance with U.S. Federal Communications Commission (FCC) regulations. Testing laboratories require specialized equipment and specially trained personnel. The tests they perform are carefully designed to measure compliance to the standards under consideration. For these reasons, it is often desirable, and sometimes mandated, that organizations use accredited laboratories to conduct the test. Accreditation gives added assurance that the laboratory is competent to conduct the required tests.

type testing,
batch testing,
product testing

The testing can be by type, batch, or for each product. Type testing is used when a single product represents all similar products, and therefore only one has to be tested. Batch testing is used when a representative sample of products is sufficient to determine compliance. All products are tested when it is critical that each individual item is examined.

mark of
conformity

The certification body then evaluates the test results to determine whether the product does pass the test. If it does, then the certification body issues a written statement or official certificate attesting to the product's conformance to that standard. In addition, some certifications also permit the organization to display a mark of conformity on the product. Such marks serve to notify the buyer that the product conforms to a specific standard or standards.

As outlined in *Figure 7.2*, organizations may self-declare their conformance to QMS standards as defined in ISO 9000. The degree to which customers and governments recognize self-declaration to quality management systems is very limited and is not nearly as widespread as recognition of self-declared products. Usually, third-party assessment is required and selected for QMS conformity assessment.

For third-party QMS assessments, a specially trained and accredited auditor inspects an organization's procedures, manuals, documentation, etc., and looks to ensure that the organization is following the ISO 9000 QMS requirements.

If it is determined that the organization's management system conforms to all of the requirements in the standard, the certification body/registrar officially certifies the organization. The certification body keeps a publicly available listing, or register, of those organizations (sites, laboratories, locations, etc.) that have passed the QMS audit.

The Supplier Audit Conformation approach, mentioned earlier and below, would give organizations an additional option, allowing them all the benefits of a third-party audit without the expense and exposure associated with it.

ISO 14000 Self-Declaration

Although certification has been discussed above as a significant component of the conformity assessment process, it is not the only option available to an organization implementing ISO 14001.

ISO 14001, Section 1, Scope, mentions the possibility of self-determining and self-declaring conformance with the ISO 14001 standard, and variations of the self-declaration approach are under discussion in numerous countries.

Self-declaration simply means that an organization that has implemented ISO 14001 publicly asserts that it conforms with the specifications of ISO 14001. The self-declaration, to be credible, should be based upon a conclusion reached after the organization has completed an internal environmental management system audit and determined that its EMS program conforms to the specifications. 📖 (See Part 6, Chapter 2 for more information on what is involved in an audit.)

Making this declaration, which is an option under ISO 9000, may invite public and customer scrutiny of the self-declaring organization's EMS program.

Supplier Audit Conformation Proposal

One of the variations to self-declaration or certification that was under consideration in early 1996 for ISO 9000 and ISO 14001 was the Supplier Audit Conformation proposal.

Under Supplier Audit Conformation, an accredited certification body would accredit an organization's internal management system auditors in the same way they accredit a third-party auditor. The accredited internal auditor would then assess an organization's compliance to management system standards and submit the results to a certification body. If the audit results are satisfactory, the resulting certificate would be identical to one resulting from a third-party audit. This approach would allow the organization to use its own auditors and avoid the time and expense of an outside individual examining an organization's records and internal systems.

The Supplier Audit Conformation proposal would apply to organizations with EMS proposals that, over time, have demonstrated effective performance. This approach could allow the certification body to verify facility-specific EMSs on a spot-check basis without requiring each facility to become certified separately.

The Supplier Audit Conformation approach has been accepted by the International Accreditation Forum (IAF) and ANSI.

Third-Party Verification Option

Another option under informal discussion would enable organizations implementing ISO 14001 to have a third party (but not necessarily a certification body) independently verify and state its agreement with the organization's self-declaration of conformity.

This approach might be attractive to organizations, such as utilities, that would implement ISO 14001 across the organization, but find certifying every single one of several hundred utility transfer stations, maintenance locations, etc., cost-prohibitive.

The third-party verification concept, which likely would include some spot-checking of individual locations and a close evaluation of main facilities, is intended to enhance the credibility of self-declaration. The credibility could be undermined, however, if only the "flagship" locations actually underwent conformity assessment.

There is no formal vehicle for the self-declaration and Supplier Audit Conformation approaches, although market forces and international negotiations may clarify some of these options.

7.2.4 Accreditation Process

Accreditation of Certification Bodies (Registrars)

About half the ISO 9000 registrars operating in the U.S. have been accredited by the RAB, and slightly more than half of all registrations are performed by accredited bodies.

An accredited registrar must have certified auditors performing the conformity assessments. In some cases, the registrar's audit team may be supplemented by experts in a particular field. Auditor certification programs are subject to an equivalent level of scrutiny for their own accreditation as is given to certification bodies who will register companies.

Each nation adopting the ISO 14001 international standard as its domestic standard will develop a scheme for accrediting certification bodies, for the certifiers of individual auditors, and for approval of training programs offered to auditors seeking certification. It is important that such accreditation schemes be sufficiently rigorous to warrant domestic acceptance among stakeholders as well as international recognition.

In the U.S., certification bodies could seek accreditation from the American National Standards Institute (ANSI) or the RAB for ISO 9000.

As of March 1996, the two entities, which accredit ISO 9000 certification bodies in a jointly operated program, were unable to agree on a joint program for ISO 14000, despite a strong preference among U.S. stakeholders for a unified accreditation system in the U.S. While they remained open to operating a joint program, they each were developing separate national accreditation programs for ISO 14000. Both appeared likely to be in place by mid-1996, when the ISO 14000 international standards were to be formally adopted. Most observers agree that the two organizations will reunify on ISO 14000 accreditation because of market pressure to do so.

Mutual Recognition

Ideally, a company certified to ISO 14000 should have its certification recognized anywhere in the world, and auditors certified to ISO 14000 should have their certifications and credentials to perform EMS audits accepted anywhere in the world to avoid costly and multiple certifications.

This mutual recognition of credentials and certification would seem to be, but is not, assured by the participation of more than 100 countries in the development of the ISO 14001 specification and related guidance documents.

Organizations and users have a significant requirement for international recognition of tests, test results, certification, registration, accreditation, and other aspects of conformity assessment. Ideally, they want to test and certify their products, processes, services, and management systems once and have the results recognized throughout the world.

Conformity assessment is a time-consuming and costly activity. These costs escalate when the same product, process, service, or management system must be recertified for each country or region. If each country requires its own conformity assessment, costs grow, and products and services reflect these costs, which are passed along to the users. Obviously, these added costs are undesirable.

In early 1996, while discussion of ISO 14001 mutual recognition was in its infancy, many other efforts to gain international recognition for conformity assessment results were underway.

mutual recognition agreements (MRA)

These included bilateral and multilateral mutual recognition agreements (MRA) negotiated between governments, and between private organizations and laboratories. In the U.S., for example, ANSI had negotiated agreements with similar organizations in other countries. The U.S. government was also negotiating agreements with other countries on a government-to-government level. These agreements directly affect product costs and business competitiveness.

ISO's Committee on Conformity Assessment (CASCO) is taking the lead in developing a system of international recognition for quality system registrations. The system, Quality System Assessment Registration (QSAR), once implemented, will mean that when an organization's quality management system certification is done once, that certification will then be recognized worldwide. The International Accreditation Forum (IAF), a private association of national accreditation bodies, was planning to administer QSAR and was considering expanding the QSAR concept to other management systems, including EMS.

CASCO Guides

The function of CASCO is to study conformity assessment of products, processes, services, and quality systems and develop international guides relating to testing, inspecting, and certifying products, processes, and services, and to assessing quality systems. CASCO is made up delegates from ISO member bodies who meet periodically.

Originally, CASCO was set up in 1970 as the ISO Committee on Certification. The ISO Council changed the name to the ISO Committee on Conformity Assessment.

CASCO has developed a series of guides dealing with all aspects of conformity assessment, and ISO and IEC have published the guides. Governments and private organizations involved with conformity assessment widely use these guides. 📖 (See Appendix F for a list of the key ISO/IEC guides.)

These international guides are important because they provide a common approach for all conformity assessment bodies to follow throughout the world. When all accreditation, certification, and testing bodies follow the same guides and perform conformity assessment based on the same criteria, consistency of the results among similar operations (testing, certification, etc.) is maintained.

Consistent accreditation of test laboratories, for example, helps ensure that all laboratories so accredited operate under the same set of minimum criteria. In addition, these guides aid international recognition of tests, test results, certificates, etc.

As of early 1996, these guides did not specifically mention EMS, nor were there any guides specifically directed at EMS. However, ISO Technical Committee 207 and CASCO were investigating whether new guides for EMS need to be written, or whether CASCO should revise current guides to include EMS elements.

CASCO guide
EMS language
considered

The two ISO/IEC guides they will be reviewing are *ISO/IEC Guide 61 — General Requirements for Assessment and Accreditation of Certification/Registration Bodies*, which was to be adopted as CASCO 226 (Rev. 2), and *ISO/IEC Guide 62 — General Requirements for Bodies Operating Assessment and Certification/ Registration of Quality Systems*.

CASCO is expected to publish the two guides by June1996. While designed for QMS accreditation, they can guide the EMS accreditation process.

For certification of individual auditors, it was likely that guidance also would be taken from the European Union Standard *EN (European Norm) 45013 — General Criteria for Certification Bodies Operating Certification of Personnel* and a draft American Society for Testing and Materials (ASTM) Standard of Practice entitled *Accreditation Criteria to Assess Certification Programs for Environmental Professionals*.

Conclusion

The conformity assessment process provides a mechanism for leveling the field for ISO 14001 implementation worldwide. The lessons learned in the ISO 9000 experience have demonstrated the importance of having mutual recognition of certifications globally. To achieve that objective, it will be necessary to ensure that accreditation bodies apply similar criteria to the entities being accredited.

At the domestic level, the conformity assessment process (whether through certification or self-declaration) should ensure that the customer can have confidence in the organizations implementing ISO 14001.

Conformity assessment is simple in concept but may be complex in its execution. It encompasses many disciplines and uses the skills and experience of many specialists. Significant expense and time may be required to perform conformity assessment activities, and these costs must be weighed against the value to users, organizations, and society in general. However, when done effectively, conformity assessment is a valuable and productive discipline that can significantly benefit organizations, users, and government regulators.

CHAPTER 3
Accreditation Body Perspective

7.3.1 Overview

by Roger Brockway, Environmental Manager, United Kingdom Accreditation Service

Companies that develop ISO 14001 EMSs are encouraged to demonstrate their conformity to the standard. They can do this either by self-determination or by certification (registration). The point of having independent third-party certification is to provide confidence that the environmental management system does, in fact, meet the requirements of the specification.

The added value attached to such confidence will be present only if the bodies that provide certification/registration are seen to be competent and independent.

Accreditation provides such assurance.

Accreditation is defined in the ISO/IEC Guide 2 (1991) as: "[the] procedure by which an authoritative body gives formal recognition that a body or person is competent to carry out specific tasks."

Ideally, accreditation is provided at the national level by a body recognized by government as having the competence to provide the service.

In the U.K., the United Kingdom Accreditation Service (UKAS), formerly the National Accreditation Council for Certification Bodies (NACCB), has such an agreement with the British government. In The Netherlands, Raad voor Accreditatie (formerly Raad voor Certificatie, or RvC) has a similar agreement. Accreditation bodies in most other European countries have one as well.

These national accreditation bodies meet in the European Accreditation of Certification (EAC) to agree on accreditation criteria and to operate a peer review system to ensure that

seeking
agreement
the standards they apply are at the necessary high level of quality. In early 1996, steps were being taken to widen this approach to the global level through the IAF.

European accreditation bodies are developing criteria for accrediting EMS certification bodies through EAC's environmental working group, which has 15 active national member participants.

Some of the accreditation systems, notably UKAS, have experience in certifying EMSs to the British Standard BS 7750. This will be superseded by ISO 14001 when it is published. Attention is therefore now directed to ISO 14001.

Most of the European accreditation bodies are also designated to accredit environmental verifiers for the European Eco-Management and Audit Scheme (EMAS) Regulation. One of the aims in appointing accreditors both for the voluntary standards (ISO 14001) and for this regulation is to bridge the gap between the two as effectively as possible.

The accreditation criteria being developed in EAC are structured on the European standard EN 45012, which sets requirements for management system certification bodies. The organizational requirements of this standard — designed to ensure independence and impartiality — apply for environmental systems to the same extent they apply to quality system certification.

It is in the area of competence that special environmental considerations arise. Here again there is some common ground in the essential requirements for systems auditors.

It is, however, seen as essential that certification bodies accredited in the EMS field have appropriate environmental competence. This must be present at two levels:

1) the management of the certification body must have the competence to understand the environmental aspects of its client's business so as to select the right team of auditors and review their findings; and

2) the auditor must demonstrate similar competence.

The vital ingredients of this competence relate to an understanding of environmental legislation and performance improvement in the industry in question. Auditors are expected to look at the performance results and track them back into the system rather than to let the documentation drive the audit.

Details regarding the mutual recognition effort are given below.

7.3.2 Mutual Recognition

by Peter Goosen, Manager Accreditation, Dutch Council for Accreditation (RvA)

The Dutch Council for Accreditation (RvA)

Raad voor Accreditatie, formerly Raad voor Certificatie (RvC), was established in 1981 as an accreditation body for certification. The initial task of the RvC was to establish a set of consensus-based criteria to which certification bodies could be assessed.

The first set of criteria already contained the four principles upon which accreditation of certification was and is based:

1) Impartiality of third party — The certification body must have impartiality embedded in its structure and must provide the services in a non-discriminatory way.

2) Competence — Evidence must be provided that the body's staff possesses the skills necessary for carrying out the tasks and that these skills are maintained at the required level.

3) Reliability — The body must have documented procedures and must keep them up-to-date. These procedures are part of the body's documented management system and must ensure that the activities are performed in a controlled and auditable manner. The procedures also must be protected against interferences and subjective influences.

4) Acceptability to all parties concerned — The body must have an administrative structure in which all parties concerned are involved, without any single interest predominating. This ensures acceptance of the voluntary certification system in the marketplace.

Based on these criteria the RvC accreditation system became operational in 1983. Initially, accreditation concerned only product certification. After the RvC accredited the first body for quality management certification in 1987, this service grew fast to become worldwide, keeping pace with the development of ISO 9000 quality management systems in industry.

In September 1995, the RvC merged with the Dutch accreditation body for test and calibration laboratories and inspection bodies. Following Dutch economical and political principles, the newly formed Raad voor Accreditatie is a private body recognized by the Dutch government, as was the former RvC. RvA provides a whole range of accreditation services, and, according to an April 1995 ISO publication, in early 1996 RvA was the largest accreditation body, having issued accreditation in twelve countries.

Mutual Recognition Agreements

To facilitate trade, RvA has accredited numerous certification bodies in all regions of the world. RvA accreditation is recognized not only in Europe, but also in the U.S., Brazil, China, and Japan, among other countries. It is the RvA's policy to stimulate accreditation bodies in foreign countries and contribute to the reduction of trade barriers by mutual recognition agreements.

The RvA has signed agreements with (the Registrar Accreditation Board (RAB/ANSI) in the U.S., with the Joint Accreditation System Australia and New Zealand (JAS-ANZ), and with the Japan Accreditation Board (JAB).

Over the past few years, similar accreditation bodies have been established in most European countries. Some are like the RvA, having a formal recognition agreement with national governments (e.g., UKAS, U.K.; TGA, Germany; and COFRAC, France), and others are governmental agencies (e.g., Swedac, Sweden). ▢ (See Appendix G for more information on these organizations.)

In May 1991 European national accreditation bodies established the EAC, whose aim is to create one European accreditation system based on harmonization of accreditation criteria and practices, as well as operation of a peer review system to ensure that accreditation is applied at the high level necessary.

EAC is a member of the European Organisation for Testing and Certification (EOTC).

EOTC is organized by the Comité Europeén de Normalisation (CEN) and Comité Europeén de Normalisation Électrotechnique (CENELEC), the European Union standardization committee, which aims to facilitate mutual recognition. CEN/CENELEC also strives to form an interface between mandatory and voluntary certification.

The EAC has developed harmonized interpretation guidelines to each of the EN 45011, 45012, and 45013 standards. In 1993, initiatives were taken to harmonize EMS certifications. By the end of 1995 nine European countries including The Netherlands had entered the EAC Multi-Lateral Agreement and applied these guidelines. Other countries were expected to follow after a successful peer review assessment.

This regional clustering of effort seems to be a practical manner to achieve confidence in one another's methodologies and to work gradually toward worldwide mutual acceptance. To support this objective the IAF was founded in January 1993. Today, this forum includes world regions such as Asia, Australia, New Zealand, Europe, and North and South America.

goal: build
confidence

The common goal is to cooperate and contribute to mutual understanding and to build confidence in the interest of international trade. However, IAF has not yet taken initiatives to include accreditation of EMS certification.

In September 1995 ISO published the draft ISO/IEC Guide 61 (formerly known as ISO/CASCO 226 rev. 1), *General Requirements for Assessment and Accreditation of Certification/Registration Bodies*.

In Europe, because of the parallel voting process agreed on within CEN/CENELEC, this guide is published as the prEN 45010 standard. This ISO/IEC Guide/EN standard will further promote the mutual recognition of accreditations.

Accreditation Standards for Certification Bodies

After they were published in November 1989, the RvC adopted the European standards (EN 45000 series) endorsed by CEN/CENELEC. For third-party certification these standards concern general rules for the accreditation of certification bodies, in particular:

- EN 45011 for product certification;
- EN 45012 for quality system certification; and
- EN 45013 for certification of personnel.

The EAC established EN 45012 in to harmonize accreditation practices. This standard and its guideline(s) have become the world's standard for accreditation of bodies that perform quality management system certification (e.g., ISO 9000).

Within ISO, ISO/CASCO (Working Group 8) also has revised existing documents concerned with accreditation of certification. These documents have recently been approved by the CASCO membership and will be published soon:

- ISO/CASCO 227 (rev 2): *General requirements for bodies operating assessment and certification/registration of quality systems. This document will be published soon as ISO/CASCO Guide 62* (Draft).

- ISO/CASCO 228 (rev 2): *General requirements for bodies operating product certification systems.*

A revision of the EN 45000 series with CEN/CENELEC was due in 1996, and CEN/CENELEC had decided upon a parallel voting procedure. In the parallel voting procedure, CEN/CENELEC delegates will vote on the same text as ISO delegates but apply their own voting criteria, which is different from ISO's.

ISO Guide 61 and ISO/CASCO 227 (Guide 62) or EN 45010 and the revision of EN 45012 will provide international guidelines for the operation and accreditation of quality management system registration/certification bodies well into the next decade. The RvA was to adopt these standards in 1996.

The standards certainly will have a dominant influence on the criteria applied for certification and accreditation of EMSs. At the June 1995 meeting in Geneva, members of ISO/CASCO and TC 207, ISO/CASCO offered to cooperate with TC 207 in developing conformity assessment standards to environmental specifications. ISO/CASCO's eminent expertise will strengthen the position of ISO 14000 standards.

Accreditation of EMS Certification in Europe

The Netherlands

The first certification body for environmental management systems was accredited in December 1993 by RvC. The Netherlands has always been a front-runner in the development of EMSs within the industry. Where others focused on environmental accountancy, by 1985 the Dutch industry had already taken the initiative to begin developing EMSs. In 1989 this eco/industry initiative was followed by the Dutch government.

EMS pilot studies

Since then numerous pilot studies in a variety of industrial sectors have been completed, raising, among others, the issue of how to approach certifying these management systems. Growing experience has pointed out that much similarity exists in the concepts of environmental management systems and ISO 9000 quality management systems as well as their certification/registration criteria.

Based on its experience certifying accreditation for quality systems, the RvA accepted the challenge of providing certification to the first standard for EMSs, BS 7750 (1992), the British national standard,.

While RvA was developing the accreditation system, the revision of the BS 7750 standard (1994 version) was adopted.

With some reluctance, industry and the Dutch government acknowledged the RvA-accredited BS 7750:1994 certificates. In summer 1995 the Dutch government announced that accredited EMS certificates would lead to reduced legal environmental requirements imposed on particular companies by means of production licenses.

The RvA based its accreditation for EMSs on the sole standard available for accreditation of certification bodies, EN 45012, the standard for certification of quality management systems. The administrative and quality system requirements ensuring independence and *traceability* apply to environmental system certification as they do to quality system certification.

For other criteria — for competence in particular — requirements had to be developed. However, the criteria of the EN standard were interpreted for EMS certification where deemed necessary.

The RvA requirements and guidance interpretations are published in a guideline dated June 1995. *Guidelines for Accreditation of Certification Bodies that Operate Environmental Management System Certification as Well as Verified with Respect to the EMAS Registration (June 1995).* This publicly available guideline gives competence requirements for audit management and environmental auditor qualifications (based on ANSI/ISO 14012 but amended for relevant education and experience) and a specific audit methodology (a two-stage process).

The certification body/registrar must have an understanding of the national environmental legislation and techniques for reduction of environmental effects in the particular industry to be certified/registered.

advice for
auditing any
EMS

The guideline also contains guidance for the certification bodies and auditors on important issues such as evaluation of environmental performance, continuous improvement, and compliance to legal requirements. The guideline is generic and applicable for certification to any EMS standard, e.g., BS 7750, ANSI/ISO 14001, or any other.

Numerous contributions from the Dutch National Committee of Experts established the RvA guideline. The Dutch National Committee of Experts consisted of representatives from industry, consumers, and "green parties," and the Dutch government.

Their task was primarily to develop and maintain the criteria, interpretations, and procedures of the EMS certification scheme.

This certification scheme was originally based on the BS 7750 standard, but attention then was directed to the ANSI/ISO 14001 standard. The general view in The Netherlands was that ANSI/ISO 14001, including the informative interpretations in Annex A, does not show significant differences with BS 7750. Both standards address the capability of the EMS to comply with legal requirements.

Certification assessment to ANSI/ISO 14001, however, would have to include an assessment (on a sampling basis) of the company's performance with regard to environmental aspects and impacts and to continuous improvement. Not only would this assessment occur at the management system level, but also at the level of effects. Given the aforementioned evaluation strategy, the high value and acceptance of the current BS 7750 certificates would thus be maintained for ANSI/ISO 14001 certificates.

Europe and EMAS

On the European scene, Working Group 3 of EAC was developing harmonized criteria for accrediting EMS certification as of early 1996. Fifteen active accreditation bodies were members of this group. The list of accreditation bodies included RvA and UKAS, two bodies with EMS certification accreditation experience who share their documentation practices and experiences.

The first draft of the EAC Guidelines to EN 45012 for EMS certification was agreed on in October 1995 and was subsequently sent out for public comments. In an EOTC workshop in January 1996 the principles were publicly discussed.

Even it its draft form, the EAC guideline was applied by most European accreditation systems for both voluntary EMS certification and within the framework of EMAS verifier accreditation.

The development of these criteria was requested not only by industry and consumers but also by the national governments and the European Commission. The request was made in order to comply with requirements issued by the Council Regulation (EEC) No. 1836/93 (29 June 1993), known as the EMAS Regulation.

The European Commission initiated the EMAS Regulation in order to support continuous improvement of companies' environmental performance. 📖 (See Part 9, Chapter 5 and Part 9, Chapter 6 for more information on EMAS.)

EMAS is voluntary

Participation in the scheme is voluntary for companies. For a specific manufacturing site the company has to implement an EMS (Annex 1 Regulation), perform internal (performance) audits (Annex 2), and publish an environmental statement. An environmental verifier will examine compliance to the requirements of the regulation and, when positive, validate the statement. With this validated statement the site will be registered and the use of the European EMAS logo is granted.

The regulation is addressed to the national governments. Member states shall establish a system for accreditation of independent verifiers and supervision of their activities. Mutual recognition of accredited verifiers is arranged within the regulation itself.

Most of the existing European accreditation bodies are also assigned by their national government to accredit environmental verifiers. This allows them to create a certification "bridge" between the voluntary standards and the EMAS Regulation.

It is intended that the EAC guideline be acceptable to the European Commission for use in EMAS. A certificate to a recognized EMS standard, accredited under the EN 45012 with the harmonized interpretation of the EAC guidelines, would satisfy a major part of a company's compliance to the requirements set in the EMAS Regulation.

However, some requirements in BS 7750 and EMAS are only implicitly within ANSI/ISO 14001 and therefore need explanation or interpretation. In addition, items in the annex of ISO 14001 are only advisory in nature, where EMAS has made them straightforward requirements.

EMAS bridge document

CEN is working on a document designed to bridge the gap between ISO 14001 and EMAS. According to an April 1996 draft of the bridge document, titled *Proposed Text for the Bridging Document Between EMAS and EN ISO 14001, ISO 14010, ISO 14011, and ISO 14012*, there are two purposes for the document:

- identify those areas where EMAS places detailed requirements that are not specifically covered by EN ISO standards (e.g. the requirement for an environmental statement); and

- identify and highlight those areas where the agreement of elements of the EN ISO standards and the requirements of EMAS may not be readily apparent.

The bridge stipulates that a self-declaration of conformance to ISO 14001 will not be accepted for EMAS. Only accredited third-party certifications will be accepted.

CEN was scheduled to publish the bridge document in June 1996.

In addition, the U.S., among others, has raised concerns regarding legal liability that would not only involve the certification body/registrars and the auditors in person, but also the accrediting body. Nevertheless, in Fall 1995, the executive board of the RvA decided to open up its accreditation services for EMS certification in the U.S.

This brings up an important issue: With so many different countries implementing accreditation criteria, it will be particularly important in the coming months and years to pay attention to the development of national interpretations of the ISO 14001 and EMAS standards, and the role these interpretations play in certification/registration.

CHAPTER 4

Certification Body (Registrar) Perspective

by Samantha Munn, Manager, Environmental Management Systems,
Inchape Testing Service/Intertek Services

Top-level managers faced with implementing ISO 14001 are scrutinizing the costs and benefits of third-party certification/registration of their EMSs. (I will use the term "registration" in this section.)

Because the ISO 14001 standard has the potential to become a market requirement through customer pressure, managers have become educated in the certification process and are evaluating the credibility of accreditation criteria. Particularly in the United States, industry players have become involved in developing the ISO 14001 conformity assessment system.

credibility is key

Because the credibility of your company's certificate ultimately rests in the hands of its certification body, registrar credibility is continuously being tested. Every day registrars must respond to a series of "Questions for the Registrar," and the answers are becoming more uniform as registrars work together to bring consistency to the conformity assessment world.

The International Association of Accredited Registrars (IAAR) addresses much of this work. As ISO 14001 neared its release as a final standard, a similar approach was likely to be a priority agenda item for the members.

Registrars have an underlying obligation to industry to objectively and credibly judge management systems (within the confines of a standard's requirements).

Put in the position where clients demand "independent verification," your company has little choice but to place its trust in the registrar. As ISO 14001 certification presses on, management is becoming more knowledgeable and beginning to realize that it has the prerogative to demand a certain level of service from the registrar that it, rightly, deserves.

It is through the conformity assessment system that your organization gains confidence in the registrars.

7.4.1 Registrar Accreditation Process

Registrars achieve their own accreditation in a process similar to that your organization undertakes when seeking certification. Both include:

1)   a documentation review;

2)   interviews;

3)   a formal assessment; and

4)   periodic surveillances.

Registrars must undergo these evaluations to demonstrate that they have the capability and knowledge to perform third-party certification. Generally, an accreditation body has been approved by the government of a country to be the sole provider of accreditation, i.e., the ANSI/RAB in the U.S.; Raad voor Accreditatie in The Netherlands; and the United Kingdom Accreditation Service in the U.K.

EN 45012 is the internationally accepted standard for registrars providing quality system certification. In early 1996, the question was whether there would be a comparable internationally accepted standard for the accreditation of registrars providing environmental system certification.

UKAS was the first to develop formal accreditation criteria for registrars wishing to offer EMS certification against the requirements of BS 7750 (the U.K. equivalent to ISO 14001). Using EN 45012 as its foundation, together with the EAC guidelines, UKAS extended the requirements to include environmental considerations, including environmental auditor qualifications and the methodology for conducting an assessment of your organization's EMS.

auditors judged on knowledge, ability

The registrar develops its management system to comply with the accreditation criteria. The management system is then reviewed for compliance by the accreditation body. The formal assessment consists of a witness assessment and a head-office assessment. The accreditation body assigns an auditor to observe the registrar's environmental auditors as they perform an assessment of an organization's EMS. Auditors are judged on the basis of their:

- knowledge of the standard;

- knowledge of the industry in which they are conducting the assessment;

- knowledge of environmental issues within that industry;

- competence in assessing your organization's EMS by drawing information from documentation and interviews and evaluating this to determine your organization's compliance;

- capability to remain objective;

- professionalism and interpersonal skills; and

- auditing techniques.

During the registrar's head-office assessment, this appraisal subsequently is reviewed to determine how and why the assessors were selected for that particular organization and whether they, indeed, possessed the skills necessary for the assignment.

The head-office management operating the certification program, assigning the auditors and allocating the assessment time, reviewing the assessment reports, and granting the certification also must have the appropriate competence and qualifications to the satisfaction of the accreditation body.

Noncompliances identified by the accreditation body must be addressed by the registrar and cleared up before the accreditation is granted. Maintenance of compliance with the accreditation criteria and to verification of any modifications made within the registrar's management system requires a continuous surveillance.

The scope of the environmental accreditation is primarily determined by the breadth of knowledge and experience of the registrar's auditors.

UKAS, in the development of its accreditation criteria, moved away from the traditional standard industrial codes (SICs) typically used to identify ISO 9000 scopes of accreditation toward defining scopes by industry processes.

industry familiarity is important

The philosophy taken here is that a single process may be common across several industries and have comparable environmental impacts (i.e., a similar chemical process may be employed in the electronics industry, tanning industry, printing industry, and petrochemical industry). An auditor familiar with that process may be competent for all these industry sectors relative to the environmental concerns. However, at least one auditor must still maintain experience specific to the industry in which the assessment is being performed. As of January 1996, it was unclear how the U.S. would approach defining accredited scopes.

For example, in January 1995, Intertek Services Corporation chose UKAS, as a highly reputable accreditation authority, for its accreditation.

Intertek's management system already met EN 45012 for its ISO 9000 services, so the remaining areas of development were the environmental auditor qualification criteria and the competency analysis (or contract review).

The environmental auditor qualification criteria were developed using the guidelines provided in the UKAS criteria and from the requirements set out by the Environmental Auditors Registration Association (EARA) in the U.K. At the time, EARA was the only body registering environmental management system auditors.

auditor qualifications

EARA identified the following areas of expertise as essential components of an auditor's qualifications:

- education and training;

- professional certifications (e.g., registration through the IRCA, RAB, EARA, or equivalent);

- general experience, including environmental and quality management, technical experience, and knowledge of environmental laws and regulations; and

- environmental auditing experience.

The competency analysis is a prerequisite for accepting a contract to ensure that Intertek Services has the capability to provide the service. Intertek has to acquire an initial understanding of the organization, including its:

- size;
- complexity;
- industry type;
- site details and structure of the management system;
- applicable industry codes of practice; and
- identification of significant environmental aspects.

From these, the auditor skills as well as the amount of assessment time that needs to be assigned are determined.

Site or Activity Certification?

Will the EMS certification apply to the whole site or individual activities within the site?

To address this question we need to consider how easily or reliably environmental issues can be isolated within a site.

Two departments or manufacturing lines, for example, may use the same effluent treatment facility or discharge waste into the same sewer, or use the same facility to generate energy, making the environmental effects associated with a particular process difficult to identify and separate out. This is an important distinction between quality management system certification and environmental management system certification, where a broader coverage of people and activities needs to be involved.

ISO 9000 Considerations?

Will the registrar take into consideration an organization's existing ISO 9000 system when allocating time resources to the assessment?

joint audits,
activities

Although it is a requirement of the current accreditation system (through UKAS) to perform the EMS assessment separately from any ISO 9000 activity being conducted, it is possible to perform these activities during the same time period, thus reducing auditor expenses.

Intertek Services has incorporated an approach to further review the adequate time required to assess the organization's EMS by determining the degree of overlap between the ISO 9000 and ISO 14001 systems during the pre-assessment or documentation review (if performed on-site). 📖 (See Part 4, Chapters 3-9 for more information on integrating systems.)

An additional area of consideration is also the degree to which reliance can be placed on the organization's internal auditing system.

Although the UKAS accreditation criteria define much of the methodology for conducting the assessment, the registrars still have to establish a level of consistency between their ISO 14001 certification programs to maintain the standard's credibility. This is the inevitable learning curve that will, through 1997, reach its plateau as experiences are gathered and countries share information and learn from one another.

Business Considerations in Registration

In their paper titled Industry Comments to Develop a Business-Focused Assessment Methodology for ISO 14001 Registration, *six authors make a case to those developing or revising accreditation criteria to consider bottom-line issues affecting industries seeking ISO 14000 certification.*

As of March 1996, the American National Standards Institute and the Registrar Accreditation Board were developing separate but very similar U.S. accreditation schemes.

The paper, published in January 1996, as a propsal for an alternative to the traditional certification process.

Following is an abridged version of the paper written by:

- *Brian Dugan, manager of standards technology, Unisys Corporation;*

- *Stephen Greene, corporate environmental manager, Polaroid Corporation;*

- *Dick Johns, corporate director of environmental safety and industrial hygiene, Motorola Incorporated;*

- *David Ling, corporate ISO 9000 manager, Hewlett-Packard Company;*

- *Dave Rundle, associate director, global standards and approvals, AMP Incorporated; and*

- *Ken Sutherland, environmental manager, Hewlett-Packard Company.*

Objective

The purpose of this paper is to support the development of an ISO 14001 registration infrastructure such that companies may demonstrate sound environmental responsibility at the lowest cost to their customers.

Specifically, we believe that a company that has achieved and demonstrated an effective EMS should be able to obtain and maintain accredited third-party registration to the ISO 14001 management system standard through a business-focused assessment methodology. This business-focused assessment methodology will adhere to the following principles:

- Principle #1. Third-party assessments should focus on the most important system-level elements of an effective EMS and, where practical, leverage from a company's internal audit system.

- Principle #2. [Third-party assessments should] recognize the changing business environment and allow greater flexibility in obtaining and maintaining third-party registration.

- Principle #3. [Third-party assessments should] minimize administrative burdens of third-party conformity assessment (CA) activities, especially those that do not contribute directly to real environmental benefits.

This assessment methodology would provide the benefits of independent third-party assessment of the EMS core elements while placing greater reliance, in controlled situations, upon the company's independent internal assessment processes as verified by a third-party registrar.

It would allow for multi-site or company-level registration that permits:

1) local autonomy;

2) greater flexibility in design and implementation of its EMS; and

3) increased reliance on internal resources.

Although current international standards and norms for accreditation and certification allow for this assessment methodology, the developing ISO 14001 registration community has not clearly supported its use. The intent of this paper is to draw attention to this fact so that the international accreditation system provides adequate support and viability.

Guiding Principles

An "effective" third-party registration infrastructure would motivate industry to take aggressive action on substantiated priority issues and would enable industry to apply resources in creative and flexible ways to address environmental challenges effectively. All stakeholders will gain from this proactive approach. Based on this premise, the guiding principles for an effective third-party registration system are set out as follows:

Principle #1

Third-party assessments should focus on the most important system-level elements of an effective EMS and, where practical, leverage from a company's internal audit system.

Clearly, a company must comply with all the specified requirements of the ISO 14001 standard in order to be issued an accredited third-party registration.

However, there are limitations in proving or disproving a company's conformance. As the resources required increase in pursuit of 100 percent confidence, the value from third-party assessments decreases significantly. A registration body must conduct independent audits, combined with appropriate statistical sampling and records review.

Third-party assessments generally have the most value when they focus on "system-level" requirements such as management responsibility, internal system audits, and corrective action requirements. When third-party resources are diverted to "tactical" requirements at the expense of more important "system-level" requirements, much time can be spent on details without a true determination of the system's overall effectiveness.

In general, the level of confidence required should be commensurate with the severity of the potential nonconformance. Companies that already have established and demonstrated an effective EMS can be better served by leveraging their internal resources subject to independent third-party statistical sampling and verification. With the proper verification and sampling, third-party assessments can focus on the ISO 14001 "system-level" requirements and place more reliance on the company's internal assessment of the "tactical" requirements, thereby reducing duplication and cost.

In addition, greater reliance on internal assessments of "tactical" requirements eases the concerns associated with liability and confidentiality. With a robust set of criteria, practices, and infrastructure supported by the accreditation bodies and registrars, we believe this methodology is a sound basis for achieving third-party accredited registration.

Principle #2

Recognize the changing business environment and allow greater flexibility in obtaining and maintaining third-party registration.

There are two aspects of today's business strategies that third-party registrations do not adequately address. First, multinational companies have increased decentralization and worldwide distribution of business activities to meet the demands of the highly competitive global economy. The result is greater local site and business autonomy. Second, more and more companies define their production or supply chain to include the company's suppliers, subcontractors, value-added resellers, and other non-traditional stakeholders.

Under current registration practice, registrations are issued to a specific site or location. Multi-site registrations are allowed under certain requirements such as prior registration of each site, common management system at each site, and central control of each site. These requirements are incompatible with the business reality of more local autonomy and greater scope of the supply chain.

To provide flexibility, a company should be allowed a business-oriented third-party assessment methodology to obtain ISO 14001 third-party registration. Specifically, a company should be able to choose a methodology for multi-site or company-level registration that allows:

1) local autonomy;

2) greater flexibility in design and implementation of its EMS; and

3) increased reliance on internal resources.

Principle #3

Minimize administrative burdens of third-party conformity assessment activities, especially those that do not contribute directly to real environmental benefits.

The current registration practice is often accompanied by substantial administrative requirements, consisting mostly of documentation and other paperwork solely intended to facilitate third-party audit and recordkeeping.

These burdens affect not only the companies that must devote significant resources in preparation for the third-party audit, but also the customers that will see higher costs in products and services without added value. These bureaucratic burdens generally do not contribute directly to the environmental improvements intended by the EMS and reflect more of an "after-the-fact inspection" mentality instead of a "system effectiveness evaluation" perspective.

Conclusion

An ISO 14001 third-party registration infrastructure that is guided by the above principles has the potential to achieve higher environmental goals. Companies will better see the value of ISO 14001 registration. However, if the above principles are not carefully taken into account, then ISO 14001 registration can easily become unnecessarily costly and bureaucratic.

In the past, business has participated in standards development organizations such as ISO, but for the most part, it has been ambivalent to conformity assessment activities associated with standards.

It is equally important that business proactively and holistically address the ISO 14001 EMS conformity assessment infrastructure in light of the impact it has on business operations.

Industry should continue to recognize companies' commitment in achieving effective environmental management systems instead of a "command-and-control" approach to effectiveness.

Additionally, industry should demand flexible assessment methodologies that take into account the new realities of the global economy. The goal of this paper is to serve as a voice of industry in order to shape the ISO 14001 registration procedures such that they add value to companies, customers, regulators, and society.

This goal is of interest to all stakeholders who want to realize effective environmental responsibility with the least cost and non-value-adding bureaucracy. However, to make this possible, all stakeholders must work in partnership with one another throughout the development process. All stakeholders should accept this challenge.

Recommendations

Current international standards and norms for accreditation and registration allow for this assessment methodology. However, the developing ISO 14001 registration community has yet to clearly support its use.

Several organizations and stakeholders (e.g., ISO Quality System Accreditation Recognition, International Accreditation Forum, ISO CASCO) are addressing similar assessment methodologies for ISO 9000 registration. We believe the same considerations should be given to the developing ISO 14001 registration.

In particular, we strongly encourage the following organizations to provide leadership in applying the principles outlined in this paper for ISO 14001 third-party registration and, where applicable, establish the necessary structure to turn the principles into reality:

- ISO Technical Committee 207;
- ISO Council Committee on Conformity Assessment (ISO CASCO);
- International Accreditation Forum;
- National and regional regulators; and
- National and regional standards and conformity assessment bodies.

We hope that this paper will assist all stakeholders by suggesting the key considerations that ultimately determine the value of ISO 14000 standards and ISO 14001 registration.

CHAPTER 5
Accreditation Criteria

by CEEM Information Services

In January 1996, the 15 member bodies of the European Accreditation for Certification agreed to offer ISO 14001 accreditation services in most of the E.U. As of March 1996 the EAC had not yet published criteria for use in ISO 14001 accreditation.

In the U.S., the Registrar Accreditation Board issued a first draft of accreditation criteria in February 1996. In Australia and New Zealand, the Joint Accreditation System of Australia and New Zealand issued draft criteria in January 1996 and was expected to complete a pilot project in June 1996, at which point participants would be accredited to offer ISO 14001 certification services in both countries.

The United Kingdom Accreditation Service and Raad voor Accreditatie were using BS 7750 criteria until the EAC published its final criteria. The Swiss and French accreditation bodies were using draft criteria adapted from BS 7750 accreditation criteria. All of the E.U. nations' criteria were adapted from EN 45012 — *General Criteria for Certification Bodies Operating Quality Systems Certification*.

While there are local differences, usually with regard to legal issues concerning disclosure and certifier liability, much of the substance of the criteria was drawn from the draft ISO Committee on Conformity Assessment Guide 227 — *General Criteria for Bodies Operating Assessment and Certification/Registration of Suppliers' Quality Systems*.

7.5.1 Basic Requirements

A certification body must administer its services in a non-discriminatory manner and make its services accessible to all interested organizations. However, it may only operate within its scope of accreditation. There must be no undue financial burden placed on organizations seeking certification. It shall have arrangements to cover liabilities arising from its operations and activities.

RAB   RAB's criteria stipulate that the "registrar is responsible for ensuring that all related bodies and all those who perform audits on behalf of the registrar are competent and operate in conformance with [the accreditation criteria]." Auditor certification is seen as one way of assuring conformance.

JAS-ANZ   JAS-ANZ's criteria are more detailed with regard to subcontracted work. In addition to ensuring the competency of the subcontractor, the certification body must enter into a formal agreement covering, among other things, conflict of interest and confidentiality. Furthermore, the certification body must obtain the applicant's consent to use the subcontractor. Final responsibility for all subcontracted work rests with the certification body. JAS-ANZ follows ISO/CASCO Guide 227 verbatim.

UKAS   Under UKAS' and RvA's criteria, subcontractors cannot provide consultancy on the matter in question, e.g. EMS certification. The certification body is responsible for ensuring that the subcontractor's personnel meet any applicable requirements. No formal agreement between the subcontractor and the certification body is necessary.

subcontractors

In all cases, certification bodies are prohibited from providing consulting services to applicants because of a potential conflict of interest. If one part of the certification company provides consulting services, there must be a clear line of demarcation between the consulting and certification.

legal entities

In addition, CASCO guides require that certification bodies be identified legal entities, either private or public. They also must be financially stable and maintain the necessary resources to operate a certification system. The certification body must satisfactorily document its legal standing and means of financial support. If the certification body is part of a larger entity, the links with the larger organization must be clearly described.

impartiality

The certification body is required to be impartial in its judgments. RAB and JAS-ANZ require that the person(s) deciding on whether or not to award the certificate be different from the person(s) who perform the assessment. UKAS and RvA simply state the responsibility for the decision must rest with the person(s) empowered to sign on behalf of the certification body.

In all cases, the certification body must set up an EMS governing or advisory board. No one or more interest(s) must dominate the board membership. RAB allows for a structure wherein all interested parties can participate in formulating a certification system.

In addition, CASCO guides stipulate that permanent personnel under the senior executive responsible to the governing board and the executive must be "free from control by those who have a direct commercial interest in the products or services concerned."

7.5.2 Site Certification

definition of a site

RAB defines a site as: "All land on which the activities under control of a company at a given location are carried out, including any connected or associated storage of raw materials, by-products, intermediate products, end products, and water material, and any equipment or infrastructure involved in the activities, whether or not fixed. Where applicable, the definition of site shall correspond to definitions specified in legal requirements."

UKAS uses the EMAS definition of site for industrial activities falling under the scope of EMAS, which is: "All land on which the industrial activities under the control of a company at a given location are carried out, including any connected or associated storage of raw materials, by-products, intermediate products, end products, and water material, and any equipment or infrastructure involved in the activities, whether or not fixed." For other activities, UKAS states that the site must be defined by demarcation on a map. For service providers, an operational unit may be substituted for a site if appropriate.

If one or more activities take place on a site, the CASCO guides and EN 45012 both state that "an audit that covers the full range of activities is required." If two or more organizations share one site, the organization subject to certification must recognize and manage the interfaces between its site and "all other organizations whose activities are relevant to the environmental effects in question."

Regarding multiple site certification, EN 45012 and UKAS state that a certificate may cover all of the sites, provided that at least one-third of the certified sites have been audited in a three-year period. If the number of sites is so large that the prescribed level of sampling is impractical, certification may be granted on the basis of a smaller sample and a greater demonstration of the applicant's internal audit system. RAB does not specify the size of the sample and must consent to a smaller-than-normal sample size.

Legal and Regulatory Concerns

CHAPTER 1
Legal Issues: Principal Considerations

by David J. Freeman, Esq., Battle Fowler LLP

The success of the ISO standards in gaining widespread acceptance — at least in the United States — may well hinge on legal issues. Companies considering certification will have to decide whether the management, public relations, and commercial benefits of the standards are outweighed by the legal and other risks of implementation.

The key legal issues likely will fall into five general categories:

1) **Privilege/protection afforded to audit documentation**. Will the documentation generated by ISO 14000 requirements be protected from discovery by governmental agencies in enforcement actions or by adverse parties in private litigation?

2) **Establishment of a standard of care**. Will the very existence of ISO 14000 standards cause companies lacking EMS programs to run extra risks of being found negligent if an incident occurs at their facility?

3) **Potential for use in governmental regulatory and enforcement activities**. To

what extent will government agencies be willing or able to use ISO standards as an alternative or supplement to existing "command-and-control" systems? What legal issues are created by such use(s)?

4) **Liability for registrants, registrars, and auditors.** Will companies who are inappropriately registered for conformance with ISO standards, and/or their registrars or auditors, have legal exposure if they receive benefits based on improper or fraudulent registration?

5) **Trade issues.** Will the implementation of the ISO standards be hindered by risks that they will be challenged as constituting impermissible non-tariff barriers to trade?[1]

understand and address legal issues These issues are real, and if you don't understand them in advance and properly address them, they could become serious obstacles to your company's success in implementing the ISO 14000 standards:

- They could discourage your company from being willing to participate in the ISO 14000 implementation process.

- They could interfere with your company's obtaining full benefit of any such participation.

- They could pose an obstacle to governmental agencies' attempts to use ISO 14000 as an alternative to the command-and-control system of regulation.

- And they could result in the public's failing to give your company appropriate credit when you have made the substantial commitment of time, effort, and resources to obtain registration with respect to these standards.

Editor's note: The term "registration" is used throughout this article instead of "certification" because the author of this chapter did not want readers to confuse the latter term with the same term used in the U.S. that has certain legal implications.

8.1.1 Privilege

There are two traditional, common-law privileges that litigants rely on to keep documents confidential: the attorney-client privilege and the attorney work product protection.

attorney-client privilege; work product protection

The attorney-client privilege has as its goal the encouragement of candid communication between client and counsel by protecting the confidentiality of that communication. The underlying components of the privilege are:

1) a confidential communication;

2) to or from an attorney;

3) for the purpose of securing legal advice; and

4) the absence of any action that constitutes a waiver of that privilege;

The goal of the attorney work product protection is to prevent one side in a litigation from unfairly capitalizing on the diligence of the other in preparing its case. The work product protection shields:

1) material prepared by or for an attorney (or his or her agent);

2) in anticipation of litigation; and

3) in the absence of waiver.

Unlike the attorney-client privilege, the work product protection is qualified in certain circumstances by the legitimate need of the other side for information that is otherwise unavailable or unreasonably difficult to obtain.

How ISO 14011 Stacks Up

ISO 14011: little protection

How do ISO 14011 audits stack up against these criteria for legal protection? Not well. In fact, ISO 14011 audits will not possess any of the criteria normally deemed essential for either type of protection.

First, they are generally not performed by or for attorneys but rather by management personnel.

Second, they are generally not performed to obtain legal advice; instead, their impetus comes from a combination of management need and the potential for competitive advantage.

Third, they are not conducted in anticipation of litigation but, instead, are performed routinely on a periodic basis.

Finally, they are generally not kept confidential. In fact, one of the chief benefits of the ISO 14000 process is widespread participation by employees, not only in setting up the system but also in participating in the audits and learning the results. Companies normally want their employees to know the results of the audit so they can see how well they have done and so they can work on addressing whatever shortcomings they discover.

Attorney-client and work product are not the only types of legal protections that are available. Some courts have also found the existence of a "self-evaluative privilege."[2] However, such holdings are not widespread, and even fewer courts have specifically extended this privilege to environmental audits. Those few courts that have done so have defined the privilege rather narrowly.[3]

There is also a growing movement to enact state audit privilege laws. As of April 1996, 17 states had enacted legislation to give at least limited legal protection to environmental audits.[4]

However, each of these laws has significant exceptions, they do not always squarely address systems audits as opposed to compliance audits, and they are not much help without companion federal legislation or federal policies that give such audits protection in the federal courts.

As a result, ISO audit documents — both the reports and the underlying documentation — are at risk of discovery by an adverse party in litigation or by the government in an enforcement action.

Compliance System Issues

Why is this issue important? After all, ISO audits are not compliance audits, so they will not focus on issues of companies' noncompliance with environmental laws. Some believe that as long as regulatory violations are not the target of such audits, they will not contain the type of information that could create legal problems if publicly disclosed.

noncompliance
trail

Such an evaluation may not be realistic. After all, an important element of the environmental management system (EMS) is how well it helps the company achieve its stated goals. One of those goals is compliance with applicable laws.5 In order to evaluate how well your company is achieving that goal, it is virtually inevitable that the ISO audit will look at your company's compliance status. In so doing, it will identify instances of noncompliance and evaluate the effectiveness of the system for detecting, rectifying, and following up once the matter is discovered.6

Second, and even more fundamentally, an ISO audit will identify the effectiveness of your company's management compliance system. That evaluation, in itself, can have critical implications for a corporate liability.

Example: Risks Under Legal Discovery Process

A hypothetical example will illustrate this risk. Suppose your company experiences a break in one of its product lines, and a hazardous substance escapes. Your plant, and perhaps the surrounding area, must be evacuated. People are injured. Nearby businesses are disrupted, causing economic injury as well.

It is likely that such an incident would be the basis of at least one lawsuit. In preparing the inevitable subpoena or document production request, what will the plaintiff's lawyer request?

In the pre-ISO 14000 days, he or she would typically demand production of Material Safety Data Sheet forms, production manuals, and maintenance reports. Also requested would be such documents as memos to the file about the production line, and requests for capital projects. If the plaintiff was lucky, there would be a memo relating to that production line, or a capital request that was turned down because there was not enough money or because your company had other priorities. But the plaintiff's lawyer would be considered lucky if the production request turned up any responsive documents that were helpful to the case.

However, in the world of ISO 14000, a plaintiff's lawyer likely will have much more to work with. First, he or she will ask if your company has implemented an ISO 14001 or similar management system. If the answer is no, you may have a problem of a different sort (see below). If you do have such a system, you will be asked to produce all of the manuals and procedures relating to that production line, as well as all of the systems audits and underlying documentation.

Even worse from your company's point of view would be audits that identify a management system weakness that has not been fully corrected and that can be tied in any way to the incident. Such weaknesses could include inadequate training, poor maintenance, deficient communications between line workers and supervisors, and an inadequate system for correcting and following up identified shortcomings.

Should any of the above weaknesses be reflected in your audit reports, not only can the other side allege negligence for failure to correct the flaw, but it can also ask for punitive damages for reckless disregard of that flaw and, arguably, willfulness in not fixing the problem. One can easily imagine a jury imposing punitive damages to "send the company a lesson" under such circumstances.

The moral is that the availability of these reports, and the lack of confidentiality afforded them, are not trivial issues.

Risk-Control Strategies

But what can be done about them?

There are no easy answers, but a combination of strategies recommended below could give companies at least a fighting chance of preserving the most sensitive parts of the audit.

Pre-Audit

The first strategy is the "pre-audit." The European Eco-Management and Audit Scheme (EMAS) requires an "initial review."[7] This review is part of the EMAS process and therefore is subject to the same disclosure requirements as other EMAS documents. 📖 (See Part 9, Chapter 5 for more information on EMAS.)

Not so with the ISO 14000 process. An initial review is not required by ISO 14001. It is recommended by one of the annexes,[8] but it is not a formal part of the ISO 14011 audit. Accordingly, this audit can be done in whatever manner, and however many times, your company chooses.

The pre-audit is valuable for any number of purposes:

1) it helps to define the scope of the audit;

2) it helps to familiarize those who may be doing the formal audit with your company's facilities and procedures; and

3) it gives your company an idea of the "time and money" costs of the audit process.

From a liability standpoint, however, there is an additional benefit. It gives your company an opportunity to identify any serious legal exposures in advance of the formal audit process.

identify legal exposures early

Such a pre-audit can be protected under the attorney-client privilege. It is legitimately being undertaken to answer a legal question: What are your company's liabilities and risks if it goes forward with an ISO 14011 audit? It therefore should be conducted under the supervision of an attorney, with appropriate documentation created to maximize the likelihood that the audit will be deemed privileged.

The procedure should include and document:

☑ a top management decision to conduct the pre-audit;

☑ a formal request to counsel to conduct the pre-audit in order to provide legal advice;

☑ a request to company officers and employees to extend cooperation to the attorneys and the pre-audit team they are supervising;

☑ a promise of confidentiality;

☑ a report prepared by counsel; and

☑ limited dissemination of that report.

Doing a pre-audit under the supervision of counsel is not a foolproof way to obtain legal protection for all the audit results. It suffers from all the infirmities that standard environmental audits do when attempts are made to protect them from discovery.[9]

But a pre-audit will have greater protection than the typical ISO 14011 audit, and it will give your company an improved chance of protecting the pre-audit findings.

Most important, by the time your company performs a full-fledged 14011 audit, it will have addressed the most serious deficiencies in its processes and management systems.

Bifurcated Audit

A second strategy is the "bifurcated audit."

refer noncompliance to counsel

Let us assume that, when doing an ISO audit, the auditor comes across a noncompliance issue or an issue that could lead to legal liability. As soon as he or she does so, the problem should be referred to legal counsel, and the evaluation and follow-up of that issue should be performed under the supervision of an attorney. The same documentation as noted above should be undertaken to maintain the confidentiality of this evaluation and follow-up process.

While the noncompliance may well have to be noted (even if only briefly) in the ISO 14011 audit, most of the information about the problem, its source, and its correction can be protected by bifurcating those issues from the rest of the audit.

Self-Certification

A third strategy for maximizing the likelihood of ISO 14011 audit protection is self-certification. The confidentiality of ISO 14011 audits is difficult enough to protect even if they are done internally. However, if they are done by a third party, any chance that they could be protected will be compromised by the argument of "waiver." Allowing access to the audit process or documentation to a third party not privy to any confidential relationship or operating under the supervision of counsel may well be fatal to a claim of confidentiality.[10]

Self-certification is a much safer route in this respect. It may well be that your company will choose nonetheless to have outsiders register its compliance — either because of regulatory necessity, business requirements, or the credibility that a third-party audit will give to your company's ISO 14000 efforts. But if confidentiality is a consideration, an outside auditor is something to avoid.

8.1.2 Standard of Care

Let's return to the previous hypothetical situation: a product line break, an evacuation, personal injury, property damage, and business interruption. Among the first questions that a hypothetical plaintiff's lawyer will ask is whether your company has an ISO 14001 or similar environmental management system. If the answer is yes, the lawyer will ask for the types of documents described above.

If the answer is no, your company may be in even worse shape. If the norm in your industry is to have such a system, it will be all too tempting for the lawyer to argue that your company's failure to have implemented an EMS is a direct, or at least contributing, cause of the accident.

lack of EMS can pose risk

It may well be an effective argument. What the lawyer is attempting to have a judge or jury do is to establish a "standard of care," the violation of which is evidence of negligence on the part of your company. Thus, particularly in industries where EMSs are common (and there are more and more such industries these days), the lack of an EMS can in and of itself create a dangerous situation from a liability standpoint.

How likely is this to happen?

There are, obviously, no cases involving ISO 14000 to date. However, there are numerous decisions in which courts have held that violations of customary precautions or good professional practices can be evidence from which a jury can infer negligence.[11]

Under such a theory, a plaintiff's lawyer would need only to show that the establishment of an environmental management system was an accepted or customary good management practice. The judge or jury could then base a finding of negligence on your company's failure to have implemented such a system.

How is one to protect against such a result?

justifiable lack of EMS is defense

The first line of defense is, of course, to have an ISO 14001 or similar system in place.

The next best thing is to have some type of system, accompanied by careful documentation as to why an ISO 14001 system was not thought to be reasonable or necessary under the particular circumstances of your company. The documentation should describe the system (if any) that you do have and the rationale for not having adopted ISO 14001. Of course, any such documentation should be in your company's files <u>before</u> an incident takes place, rather than as an ex post facto rationalization.

As long as you have a reasonable and defensible justification as to why an ISO 14001 system is not necessary, you have a basis for arguing that a judge or jury should not find that your company's lack of such a system establishes, or is evidence of, negligence.

8.1.3 Use by U.S. Government Agencies

For a variety of reasons, both the U.S. Environmental Protection Agency (EPA) and many state regulatory and enforcement agencies are experimenting with ISO 14000 as an alternative to the current "command-and-control" system of regulation. 📖 (See Part 8, Chapter 2 for more information on this topic.)

One major reason is pragmatic. In an era of shrinking budgets, regulatory agencies are looking for ways to get more "bang for the buck" in their enforcement efforts.

Another reason is political. The current trend is to remove the heavy hand of government from industry and to privatize many types of governmental services.

trend toward private sector

Yet a third is programmatic. Even the most ardent environmentalists concede that government regulation can sometimes be counterproductive. Allowing industries to "do it themselves" under governmental supervision might actually yield some environmental (as well as economic) benefits.

U.S. Federal Government

The list of federal governmental regulatory and enforcement programs that are potential candidates for experimentation with ISO 14000 is impressive. It includes the Common Sense Initiative (CSI), the Environmental Leadership Program, Project XL, the EPA audit policy, and the Department of Justice (DOJ) enforcement guidelines.

U.S. Environmental Protection Agency

The Common Sense Initiative, inaugurated in 1994, represents EPA's attempt to customize environmental regulations for all media by specific industry segments. Representatives of selected industries meet with EPA in a "reg-neg" (regulatory negotiation) setting, attempting to reach consensus on alternative ways of achieving a level of environmental protectiveness equivalent (or superior) to that of the current regulatory regime.

The industries for which EPA has established CSI groups include iron and steel, automobile manufacturing, computer, metal finishing and plating, petroleum refining, and printing. Several of these industry groups have suggested the use of ISO standards as one alternative approach for achieving the kind of environmental performance contemplated by the CSI.

The Environmental Leadership Program (ELP) represents EPA's attempt to remove the threat of routine enforcement inspections from companies that are able to demonstrate an alternative means for achieving environmental compliance.

compliance
demonstration

Participants in the ELP have proposed a variety of strategies to demonstrate such compliance. One being proposed with increasing frequency is the establishment of ISO 14001 or ISO 14001-type programs. The acceptability of EMS programs as a qualification for participation in the ELP is likely to grow as ISO 14000 becomes more widely recognized in government and industry circles. (See Part 8, Chapter 2 for more information on ELP.)

Project XL is an even more broadly conceived program to relax not just regulatory inspections, but the entire command-and-control system for individual companies that adopt alternative "environmental excellence" strategies.

To qualify for such treatment, the proposals must be accepted by EPA as yielding at least an equivalent level of environmental performance to that achieved by a compliance-based program.

As of March 1996, EPA had accepted Project XL proposals from 12 companies and governmental units. They were:

- The 3M Corporation;
- The Intel Corporation;
- Merck & Company Inc.;
- State of Minnesota;
- South Coast Air Quality Management District;
- Anheuser-Busch Company;
- HADCO;
- Lucent Technologies Inc. (formerly AT&T Microelectronics);
- Pennsylvania Electric Company (PENELEC);
- Union Carbide Corporation;
- IBM Corporation; and
- Weyerhaueser.

A number of them rely on an EMS approach. One proposal in particular, from Lucent Technologies, basically adopts ISO 14001 as its alternative system. 📖 (See Part 8, Chapter 2 for more information about Project XL.)

If this pilot project is successful, EPA may be willing to broaden the program to allow other companies to opt for EMSs as an alternative to standard government regulatory approaches.

civil penalty reduction

The EPA's policy on environmental audits, promulgated on December 18, 1995, permits reductions in civil penalties for regulated entities if violations found in audits are voluntarily corrected and reported to EPA, and if certain other conditions are met. EPA also will decline to refer criminal violations to the Department of Justice for prosecution if certain additional conditions apply.

The EPA policy does not, however, provide a "privilege" for the results of environmental audits. EPA's policy explicitly allows problems uncovered by management systems audits, as well as compliance audits, to qualify for this favorable treatment.

U.S. Department of Justice

The DOJ guidance document on policies for environmental criminal prosecutions[12] also encourages self-audits of environmental violations. The guidance contains a "non-definitive list" of factors that will warrant lenient treatment of violations of environmental laws. Among those factors are the existence and scope of any "regular, intensive, and comprehensive environmental compliance program." An ISO 14001 system and related audit protocol would clearly qualify a company for leniency.

Other factors cited by DOJ as relevant to leniency are an internal disciplinary system within the company to address environmental noncompliance, and the ongoing efforts to remedy such noncompliance. Both of these factors also are likely to be part of ISO standards programs.[13]

In a December 15, 1995, letter written by Lois J. Schiffer, assistant attorney general, environment and natural resources division, the Department of Justice expressed reservations about ISO 14001 because the standard is not performance-based and provides no assurance of improved environmental performance. DOJ acknowledged, however, that ISO 14001 can be a valuable internal tool for companies that desire to maintain a consistent system for managing their environmental impacts and ensuring compliance.

Despite DOJ's reluctance to voice public support for ISO 14001, the department will continue to monitor closely development and implementation of the ISO standards, with particular attention to ISO 14001. According to Schiffer's letter, analysis of the environmental performance of ISO 14001 certified companies is the key to determining whether or not registration has any regulatory or enforcement application.

State Government

Even more significant, perhaps, are the attitudes of state governments. At a U.S. Technical Advisory Group meeting in September 1995, James Seif, director of the Pennsylvania Department of Environmental Protection, envisioned a day when companies that were properly certified to ISO 14001 would "never see an [environmental department] inspector again." The attitude of other state administrators, while perhaps not as far-reaching, is reportedly similar.

Government Procurement

Another key area of potential governmental favoritism toward ISO 14001 registered companies is in the area of governmental purchases.

The U.S. government is the largest single consumer of goods and services in the world. Its purchases account for approximately two percent of the U.S. gross national product. Were the federal government to favor ISO 14001 registered companies in its purchasing decisions, the popularity of such registrations would receive an immediate and powerful boost.

heading
toward
preferability

And the government seems to be heading in that direction.

Last year, President Bill Clinton convened a meeting of governmental agencies aimed at finding ways to improve their environmental performance by, among other things, purchasing environmentally preferable products.

It takes no stretch of the imagination to anticipate an executive order on ISO 14001 comparable to Executive Order 12873 (which promotes the use of recyclable materials by governmental agencies) and Executive Order 12169 (which requires governmental agencies to purchase from companies in full compliance with toxic release reporting requirements).

The legal issues created by government's favoring ISO-registered companies in regulatory enforcement and purchasing decisions do not relate to whether agencies have the power to extend such treatment.[14] Rather, the major legal issue presented by such treatment is the one discussed in the next section: What happens to companies that obtain such treatment on false pretenses, by improperly self-certifying or being registered to the ISO standards when they do not, in fact, qualify for such registration?

8.1.4 Liability for Registrants, Registrars, and Auditors

As discussed above, a variety of government programs potentially favors companies that are registered to the ISO 14001 EMS standard.

But favored treatment by government is not the only kind of favoritism that ISO 14001 registered companies may expect. Particularly with respect to purchasing decisions, many companies have indicated that they will either favor or insist upon suppliers who are ISO 14000 registered. Such a development, if it occurs, would mirror the experience to date with the ISO 9000 quality management standards.

Whether this governmental and private company favoritism toward ISO-registered companies creates a non-tariff barrier to trade is dealt with in Part 9 — Global Status.

But there is another legal issue lurking here. Suppose a company is registered improperly or even fraudulently to the ISO standard and receives one or more of the above benefits. Does it have legal exposure for having done so?

Example: Improper Registration

Again, a hypothetical example may help clarify the issues. Suppose a company registers as adhering to the ISO standards, thereby obtaining a benefit either from the government or from another company. Later, there is an incident at that company's plant (alternatively, the precipitating event could be a failed regulatory inspection, or a disgruntled whistle-blower).

There is an investigation that indicates some irregularity in the registration process. Perhaps corners were cut. A problem was overlooked, or auditors were given or withheld benefits in order to induce registration. Maybe the third-party registrar was not appropriately accredited. In any event, it is later determined that the registration was in some way improper.

The potential sanctions against the improperly registering company would appear most serious in the case of a government contract.

canceling contracts

First of all, it is more likely than not that the government will be able to cancel the contract for cause.[15]

Second, even though the government may not have suffered financial damages, there exists the potential for automatic penalties under the False Claims Act.[16] Because the registration was improper, each invoice submitted to the governmental agencies is arguably a "false claim."

false claims

Under the act, there is a mandatory $5,000 to $10,000 fine per false claim, even if there is no government financial loss. If there is such a loss, the government's damages are trebled. Moreover, there is a "bounty hunter" provision whereby those who assist the government in prosecuting such claims receive between 15-30 percent of the total recovery. The recent Accudyne case,[17] in which the defendant agreed to pay a $12 million fine ($2.6 million of which went to a citizens' group), is stark testimony to the potential exposure of companies in a false claims situation where the company knew or should have known of the falsity of the representation.

criminal penalties

Finally, although this is a bit of a long shot, there is also the possibility of criminal penalties. The knowing submission of a false document to the federal government is punishable by fines and imprisonment under 18 U.S.C. §1001. A document falsely stating that a company was properly registered to ISO 14001 would certainly seem to fit within the parameters of a submission punishable by that statute.[18]

In a private contractual context, the potential exposure is not so Draconian, but it exists nonetheless. The company to whom a false registration was provided is certainly entitled to cancel the contract. There certainly exists a potential suit for breach of contract, particularly if the other company suffered any kind of financial loss.

Even more likely is a suit for interference with actual or prospective contractual relationships by a competitor of the allegedly registered company. After all, it is the competitor (which may itself be properly registered to ISO 14001) that may be the truly aggrieved party, since it was presumably deprived of the benefit of the contract because of the false or improper registration. This type of cause of action is recognized in many states.[19]

Example: False Advertising

There is another type of potential sanction for false or improper registration as well — a false advertising or labeling proceeding brought by the Federal Trade Commission (FTC) or a state agency. The FTC may seek an injunction and monetary penalties under Section 5 of the Federal Trade Commission Act.[20] Moreover, in an extreme case, the FTC can order corrective advertising.[21]

You don't want to be the one to tell your CEO that your company will have to spend $1 million on corrective advertising because of an impression in the public's mind that the company was properly registered to ISO 14001, when in fact it was not.

The bottom line is that, if registration results in obtaining commercial or regulatory advantages, companies must be careful in claiming registration. Registrars must be careful when they register other companies, and accreditors must be careful that they properly accredit companies that are performing registration functions.

In addition, all such companies must carefully document their activities in this regard should they be unfortunate enough to become defendants in a suit based on the legitimacy of registration.

8.1.5 Conclusion

food for thought

Are the above legal issues the only ones presented by the ISO 14000 series of standards? Probably not. Insofar as the standards were not yet official in most countries, and implementation was just beginning, other issues were bound to arise.

As should be obvious from the preceding discussion, none of these issues is necessarily a "show-stopper" in terms of seriously interfering with implementation of the ISO standards.

However, they will take thoughtful planning to address, and they should be dealt with before a company finds itself in trouble. In that context, the legal issues are very much like many other issues presented by ISO: If you think through the problem ahead of time and do your homework, your implementation process will not be as likely to be marred by unpleasant surprises.

CHAPTER 2
Regulatory Issues: Principal Considerations

by Brian P. Riedel, Special Counsel, EPA Office of Planning and Policy Analysis

8.2.1 Introduction

ISO 14001 is a systematic approach to identifying and managing environmental obligations. These international and voluntary industry standards were developed primarily to avoid non-tariff barriers to trade.

As a systems tool, ISO 14001 has the potential for becoming a very effective tool for lifting and leveling environmental performance above and beyond regulatory compliance. However, conformance with ISO 14001 will not in itself guarantee optimal environmental outcomes. Whether an ISO 14001 registered organization meets regulatory obligations depends upon many factors, including its level of commitment to compliance.

level of compliance commitment is key

Applicants to the U.S. Environmental Protection Agency's Project XL and potential ISO certifying organizations believe that EPA should provide regulatory benefits — such as reduced enforcement response, reduced monitoring and reporting requirements, fewer inspections, streamlined permitting — to encourage conformance with the ISO standards.

The extent to which an ISO-certified organization is entitled to reduced enforcement response (reduced penalties) likely will depend on the extent to which it meets the factors in applicable enforcement policies. Under criminal enforcement policies, the presence of a sound EMS is a factor considered in exercising criminal investigative and prosecutorial discretion and in sentencing convicted corporations. Another important factor is voluntary and prompt disclosure and correction. 📖 (See Part 8, Chapter 1 above for more information on legal issues.)

Under the 1995 final self-policing policy, ISO 14001 certified organizations likely will be required to meet the listed safeguards in the policy — e.g., prompt disclosure, expeditious correction, no serious harm or imminent and substantial endangerment, remediation of any harm, measures to prevent recurrence, no repeat violations, etc. — in order to obtain mitigation of gravity-based penalties and a criminal safe harbor. Given the potential for effective environmental management under ISO 14001, ISO 14001 certified organizations should have an advantage in meeting these self-policing policy conditions.

ISO 14001 alone is unlikey to offer big regulatory benefits

It is unlikely that EPA will provide other significant regulatory benefits, such as fewer inspections, by virtue of ISO 14001 certification alone because certification does not guarantee any specific level of environmental performance — including achievement of regulatory compliance.

However, ISO 14001 certified organizations that have demonstrated their increased potential to achieve high and consistent environmental performance through a significant history of compliance or superior performance should be candidates for increased regulatory benefits.

ISO 14001 provides the foundation for a systems-based regulatory analogue featuring environmental performance beyond compliance levels. It has the potential to relieve some of the strain upon the limited government resources devoted to inspecting facilities, reviewing reporting data, processing permits, and engaging in enforcement action.

environmental performance is key

Several important issues must be resolved to make such a systems-based regulatory analogue possible. These issues include measurement of the environmental performance flowing from ISO-certified organizations to assure that health and the environment are being adequately protected. Another issue is accountability and the disclosure of environmental performance results to the government and/or the public, including disclosure to and involvement of communities.

Nonetheless, there are many opportunities within the existing regulatory structure to achieve greater environmental efficiencies in conjunction with ISO 14001. For example, the ISO structure is conducive to consolidating monitoring and reporting requirements and to developing flexible, multi-media permitting programs.

U.S. Regulatory System

The development of international standards for environmental management has the potential to change the way EPA carries out its mission. As the time approaches when organizations will begin certifying to the ISO 14001 standards, the following question is increasingly being raised: What role will ISO 14001 play in the U.S. regulatory system?

A review of the background and development of the ISO 14001 standards would be instructive in understanding how these standards may be used in a regulatory context.

EPA: protect
health and
environment

In 1970, EPA was created with a mission to protect human health and the environment. Through the years Congress granted EPA powerful tools to address pressing environmental problems. These tools generally consisted of authority to set and enforce health- and technology-based environmental standards. For years, the premise was that adverse environmental impacts arising from human activity were inevitable and that it was government's role to strike the appropriate balance between social and economic costs and benefits.

Many of the standards and methods prescribed to control pollutants were often quite rigid. Nonetheless, most of the laws and regulations have been very successful in solving or alleviating many of the problems associated with uncontrolled releases, emissions, and discharges into the environment.

By the late 1980s, as many of the most blatant environmental problems were being solved or alleviated, a new set of environmental problems or challenges emerged.

macro-level
problems arise

Scientists began to identify macro-level environmental problems involving dispersion of toxics and pollutants, depletion of natural resources and raw materials, and accumulation of heat attributed to human activity. Specific examples of such problems include global climate change, sustainable development, acid rain, ozone depletion, biodiversity, and desertification.

In addition, the universe of entities regulated under the profusion of federal, state, and local environmental regulations has grown exponentially. There are now more smaller entities that are less able or unable to cope adequately with all of the environmental requirements.

Moreover, despite the great increase in the number of regulated entities, there has been no commensurate increase in government resources. These new problems required new solutions. Government, industry, and public interest groups began to develop more flexible and efficient mechanisms for protecting health and the environment.

For example, the Clean Air Act Amendments of 1990 set forth a framework of market-based incentives for controlling sulphur dioxide emissions.[22] Stakeholders are developing and refining pollution prevention approaches, tools, and programs such as Design for the Environment (DFE), the 33/50 program, and Green Lights.

In general, there was a growing recognition that "command-and-control" regulation might not be the most effective and efficient means of setting and achieving a desirable level of environmental performance in all situations.

EPA Administrator Carol Browner has emphasized the need for the agency to develop and use an array of regulatory tools to provide more flexibility in the way it accomplishes its mission. As one example, the new Office of Enforcement and Compliance Assurance (OECA)[23] has augmented its traditional enforcement tools of compliance inspections and enforcement actions with voluntary compliance incentive policies and programs.

8.2.2 ISO 14001 and Environmental Performance

ISO 14001 contains only provisions that can be objectively audited against by third parties or for self-declaration.[24]

As with the ISO 9000 standard series for quality management, ISO 14000 certification does not certify a certain quality of output from the system. As the introduction to ISO 14001 states, "[A]doption of this specification will not in itself guarantee optimal environmental outcomes."

In other words, ISO 14000 addresses systems and continuous improvement tools, *i.e.*, *processes,* not environmental performance. It is critical to recognize that conformance to ISO 14001 does not guarantee any particular level of environmental performance, yet it is potentially a powerful instrument for improving environmental performance.

In discussing the U.S. government regulatory issues related to ISO 14001, it is worthwhile recapping what ISO 14001 requires. 📖 (See Part 2, Chapter 2 and Part 3, Chapters 1 and 2 and for more information on ISO 14001 requirements.)

ISO 14001 legal and regulatory requirements

It is a systematic approach for identifying and managing environmental obligations. The ISO 14001 standard requires your organization to:

- identify its significant impacts on the environment;

- establish objectives and targets;

- define operational procedures on how to meet the objectives and targets;

- assign responsibility for carrying them out;

- establish procedures for measuring environmental performance;

- develop procedures for handling nonconformance with the EMS requirements and taking corrective actions; and

- review and take appropriate measures to improve the EMS.

Under the ISO 14001 EMS standard, the EMS is "[t]hat part of the overall management system which includes organizational structure, planning activities, responsibilities, practices, procedures, processes, and resources for developing, implementing, achieving, reviewing, and maintaining the environmental policy." **(ISO 14001 Section 3.5)**

policy

The "environmental policy" must include a "commitment" to regulatory compliance, to prevention of pollution, and to continual improvement of the EMS. The environmental policy also provides the framework for your organization to set and review its environmental "objectives and targets." **(ISO 14001 Section 3.9)**

objectives and targets; environmental aspects

In setting objectives and targets, you must "consider" your organization's "relevant legal and other requirements," "significant environmental aspects and impacts," and views of interested parties. You must have a procedure to identify "legal and other requirements to which it subscribes"[25] that are directly applicable to its "environmental aspects." You must develop a procedure for identifying the "environmental aspects" of your company's activities, products, and services in order to determine which have or can have "significant impacts" on the environment. **(ISO 14001 Section 4.2.2)**

You might want to re-familiarize yourself with the other ISO 14001 requirements for this discussion. 📖 (See Part 3, Chapters 1 and 3 and Part 4, Chapter 3 for more information on identifying environmental aspects.)

Many organizations will seek third-party registration to demonstrate conformance[26] to the

ISO 14001 standard because customers may require it, they see competitive advantages, or to help improve environmental performance.

"Lifting and Leveling" Environmental Performance

As mentioned earlier, ISO 14001 has the potential to "lift and level" your organization's environmental performance significantly above and beyond compliance levels.

The "caliber" or quality of your organization's environmental performance under ISO 14001 will depend upon a myriad of factors including the objectives your organization sets for itself and its level of commitment to regulatory compliance, prevention of pollution, and continual improvement.

EMS must mature in market   As an illustration, an organization with a strong commitment to prevention of pollution, an ambitious but realistic set of associated objectives, and the resources to carry them out will likely yield a high level of environmental performance. Note that an EMS must have time for maturity and for policies and procedures to become inculcated in the workforce before improved environmental performance can be expected.

ISO 14001 benefits   Conformance with the ISO EMS standards should have the following other ancillary effects:

1) ISO certification should result in a positive culture change in your organization, with more employees able to identify and respond to regulated and unregulated problems.

   Environmental responsibility will rest with all employees, not just with an individual or group of environmental engineers or coordinators. All employees "whose work may create a significant impact upon the environment" **(ISO 14001 Section 4.3.2)** must be trained to be made aware of the significant environmental impacts of their work activities, the environmental benefits of improved personal performance, and their roles with respect to conformance with policies, procedures, and EMS requirements. This training should result in the dispersion of environmental awareness and responsibility throughout your entire organization. Many employees want to do the right thing with respect to the environment — the ISO standard provides a framework for them to do so.

2) ISO 14001 operates on a holistic multi-media basis that more accurately reflects the impacts of human activity on the environment and the dynamics of environmental ecosystems than a media-by-media approach.

3) The ISO standard addresses all "significant environmental aspects and impacts," not just regulated ones. This identification and control of a more expansive set of environmental impacts may result in the reduction of substantial unregulated risks. Moreover, an organization must identify all significant aspects and impacts resulting from its "products and services" in addition to its "activities."

8.2.3 The Regulatory Context

Applicants for EPA's Project XL and organizations that are contemplating ISO certification have indicated that EPA should encourage ISO certification by providing regulatory incentives such as reduced enforcement response (penalties), reduced monitoring and reporting, fewer inspections, streamlined permitting, etc.

Whether your organization, certified or not, is in regulatory compliance depends upon many factors, including the nature of its business and its regulatory responsibilities, and its level of commitment to compliance-related objectives in light of the many other business decisions it faces.

ISO 14001 was designed to offer a flexible means of structuring environmental management. This flexibility allows organizations to set their own objectives and determine the appropriate level of resources needed to carry them out, based on a variety of considerations. Consistent with this flexible approach to environmental management, ISO 14001 states that an organization must "consider" legal and other requirements in establishing its objectives and must make a "commitment" to regulatory compliance. The ISO 14001 standard does not prescribe what level of priority or commitment should be accorded compliance-related goals.

ISO 14001 certification does not guarantee any specific level of environmental performance, including regulatory compliance. Since a high level of environmental performance is the desired behavior, and ISO 14001 is a means to that end, ISO 14001 certification should not be the sole basis for providing regulatory benefits.

better position with EMS

While ISO 14001 certification will not provide a "talisman for compliance," the ISO framework — setting objectives, procedures, measures, and reviewing and improving the framework — should better position your organization to meet or exceed regulatory requirements. You are more likely to detect and correct violations if your company has a workable system for doing so.

In light of ISO 14001's requirements for monitoring, measuring, and reviewing, ISO 14001 certified organizations generally should be in a position to prevent environmental violations from becoming serious, e.g., catastrophic environmental disasters such as major spills.

A regulatory structure that can incorporate ISO 14001 certification while assuring protection of human health and the environment can greatly relieve government's strained resources devoted to inspecting facilities, reviewing reporting data, processing permits, and engaging in enforcement action. However, before ISO 14001 can serve as the foundation for a "systems-based regulatory analogue," several issues, such as measurement and disclosure of environmental performance, must be addressed.

The following discussion of regulatory benefits for ISO 14001 certified organizations will begin with the end of the regulatory process — after a violation has been committed. Existing enforcement policies provide the likely "reduced enforcement response" potentially accorded an ISO 14001 certified organization. The government has not set up a program for reduced enforcement response. What the government has set up are enforcement policies that are defined in a way that allows them to address ISO 14001 certified companies.

Enforcement Response and Penalty Mitigation

Would your organization be eligible for reduced enforcement response by virtue of its ISO 14001 certification? In one respect, violations committed by a certified company may be symptoms of an EMS that has been ineffective in preventing violations. However, no EMS will prevent all noncompliance, particularly those for sophisticated operations or highly regulated activities.

Regulators have recognized the value of a "systems approach" to managing environmental requirements and have fashioned enforcement policies to encourage the adoption and implementation of systems to prevent, detect, disclose, and correct environmental violations.

EPA Criminal Investigative Discretion

In determining whether a matter is worthy of criminal investigation, a 1994 EPA memorandum on criminal investigative discretion[27] states that EPA will consider:

1) actual and threatened harm to human health or the environment; and

2) culpable conduct that may be indicated by, for example, evidence of criminal intent or an organization's compliance history.

With respect to determining corporate culpability, the memorandum states,

> "[A] violation that is voluntarily revealed and fully and promptly remedied as part of a corporation's systematic and comprehensive self-evaluation program generally will not be a candidate for the expenditure of scarce criminal investigative resources."

DOJ Criminal Prosecutorial Discretion

A 1991 DOJ memorandum sets forth the factors it will consider in determining whether to prosecute an environmental violation involving significant voluntary compliance or disclosure efforts.[28]

These factors include:

- voluntary disclosure;
- cooperation;
- preventive measures and compliance programs;
- pervasiveness of noncompliance;
- internal disciplinary action; and
- subsequent compliance efforts.

With respect to preventive measures and compliance programs, the DOJ policy identified numerous factors, including the existence of a compliance management system and commitment to regulatory compliance.[29] (See Footnote 29 for a verbatim text of relevant portions.)

Corporate Criminal Sentencing Guidelines

Finally, the 1991 U.S. Sentencing Commission guidelines state that the existence of "an effective program to prevent and detect violations of law" will provide the basis for substantial reductions in criminal sentences for convicted corporations.[30] 📖 (See Appendix D for verbatim text of these guidelines.)

The guidelines state, "The hallmark of an effective program to prevent and detect violations of law is that the organization exercised due diligence in seeking to prevent and detect criminal conduct by its employees and other agents." In defining "due diligence," the

Sentencing Commission set forth what has become the generally accepted core components of a compliance management system. These include:

- development of standards and procedures to prevent noncompliant behavior;

- allocation of responsibility to oversee conformance to these standards and procedures;

- training to communicate the standards, procedures, and roles;

- use of appropriate disciplinary mechanisms to encourage consistent enforcement of the standards;

- execution of steps such as monitoring and auditing systems to implement the standards; and

- steps to correct the noncompliance and prevent future noncompliance.31

three guidelines = enormous impact

These three sets of guidances — the DOJ guidelines, the EPA audit policy, and the U.S. Sentencing Commission Guidelines — have had an enormous impact in encouraging the development and implementation of compliance management systems in the U.S.

EPA Audit and Self-Policing Policies

EPA's 1986 auditing policy strongly encourages organizations to use environmental auditing to help achieve and maintain regulatory compliance. Toward that end, the 1986 policy set forth the basic elements of effective environmental auditing programs. 📖 (See Appendix D for text of 1986 auditing policy.)

On December 22, 1995, EPA announced the "Incentives for Self-Policing: Discovery, Disclosure, Correction, and Prevention of Violations Final Policy Statement" (final self-policing policy). Under the new policy, the agency will reduce civil penalties greatly and limit liability for criminal prosecution for regulated entities that meet the policy's conditions for discovery, disclosure, and correction. 📖 (See Appendix D for text of 1995 policy.)

Specifically, EPA will not seek gravity-based civil penalties32 for violations that are discovered through a compliance management system or an environmental audit33 and that are promptly disclosed and expeditiously corrected, provided other important conditions or safeguards are met.

prevent recurrence, remediate

These safeguards require entities to take steps to prevent recurrence of the violation and to remediate any harm caused by the violation. In addition, the policy does not apply to violations that resulted in serious actual harm or that may have presented an imminent and substantial endangerment to human health or the environment.

Moreover, repeated violations are not eligible for relief under the policy. The policy does not apply to individual criminal acts or corporate criminal acts arising from conscious disregard or willful blindness to violations.

collect economic benefit

Finally, EPA retains its discretion to collect any economic benefit gained from noncompliance in order to preserve a "level playing field" for entities that invest in timely compliance.34

With respect to discovery through a compliance management system, the policy states that the violation must have been discovered through an "objective, documented, systematic procedure or practice reflecting the regulated entity's due diligence in preventing, detecting, and correcting violations."

due diligence

"Due diligence" is defined in terms of criteria based on the 1991 Sentencing Guidelines and generally recognized as these fundamental elements of a sound compliance management system:

- the development of compliance policies, standards, and procedures to meet regulatory requirements;

- allocation of responsibility to oversee conformance with these policies, standards, and procedures;

- mechanisms including monitoring and auditing of compliance and the compliance management system to assure the policies, standards, and procedures are being carried out;

- training to communicate the standards and procedures;

- incentives for managers and employees to perform in accordance with the compliance policies, standards, and procedures, including consistent enforcement through appropriate disciplinary mechanisms; and

- procedures for the prompt and appropriate correction of violations including program modifications needed to prevent future violations.

In addition to full mitigation of gravity-based penalties for satisfaction of all of these conditions, EPA generally will not recommend criminal prosecution against the organization if the violation results from the unauthorized criminal conduct of an employee.

Finally, where the violation is not discovered through a compliance management system or audit, but where all the other conditions are met, EPA will reduce gravity-based penalties by 75 percent.35

Analysis

Criminal Enforcement Policy Documents

The fact that a violator has a sound EMS (certified or not) will be one of the many factors a criminal investigator, prosecutor, or judge will consider in applying the appropriate criminal policy documents.

But to obtain maximum benefit under these policies, a violator must actually accomplish many of the tasks for which the ISO EMS has established procedures. One example is correction of the violation.

ISO 14001 requires your organization to "establish and maintain procedures . . . for initiating and completing corrective and preventive action." All three policy documents indicate that prompt correction of the violation is a very important factor.

prompt
disclosure

Prompt disclosure of the violation is another important factor considered under the policy documents. Disclosure is not a featured component of ISO 14001.

Other examples are as follows. ISO 14001 requires your organization:

- to consider regulatory requirements in setting its objectives and targets;

- to have a procedure for tracking conformance with those objectives and targets; and

- to have a management review that addresses the possible need to change the EMS.

In contrast, factors in the DOJ memorandum include:

- whether "environmental compliance was a standard by which employee and corporate departmental performance was judged;" and

- whether "the [EMS/compliance] auditor's recommendations [were] implemented in a timely fashion."

sound EMS = unlikely investigation

Practically speaking, an organization that vigorously implements a sound EMS is not likely to be the subject of a criminal investigation, or to be criminally prosecuted or convicted. The requisite level of intent for criminal liability under most environmental statutes — knowing or intentional — involves behavior that is antithetical to behavior required to implement an EMS effectively.

In addition, the systematic management of environmental activity, commitment to compliance, procedures for emergency preparedness and response, and procedures for employee accountability, among other things, would tend to prevent a violation from resulting in serious harm, a factor under the three policy documents.

Final Self-Policing Policy

The prerequisite conditions for significant reductions in civil penalties and for other relief under the final self-policing policy are consistent with many of the factors featured in the criminal policy documents. The conditions in the final self-policing policy represent safeguards to deter irresponsible behavior and protect health and the environment.

certification = no EPA assurance, necessarily

ISO 14001 certification does not assure EPA and the public that these important safeguards will be met.

For example:

☑ Certification does not mean that your organization's violations will not result in serious harm or imminent and substantial endangerment to the public or the environment.

☑ Certification does not confirm that you will promptly disclose, expeditiously correct, or remediate harm caused by the violation.

☑ Certification does not guarantee that you will take measures to prevent recurrence of the violation or that the same violation had not occurred many times recently.

EPA has determined that it would be inappropriate to provide significant penalty mitigation or a criminal safe harbor unless those safeguards are met.

EPA's enforcement response toward certified organizations likely will be consistent with existing enforcement response policies. Specifically:

☑ Full mitigation of gravity-based civil penalties likely will require your organization to meet the conditions or safeguards in the final self-policing policy.

☑ Consistent with the self-policing policy, complete penalty amnesty — including waiver of significant economic benefit gained from noncompliance — will probably not be available.

☑ It is highly unlikely that EPA would refrain from pursuing injunctive relief by virtue of the fact that the threat at issue involves a certified organization.36

Advantages of Certification

Nonetheless, certified organizations may have substantial advantages over non-certified organizations with respect to application of EPA's final self-policing policy.

First, ISO-registered companies may be more likely to satisfy the condition involving discovery of the violation through a system reflecting "due diligence" or a compliance management system. The "due diligence" criteria in the final self-policing policy are similar to many requirements in the ISO EMS standards. Theoretically, this makes sense because ISO 14001 EMS standards include and subsume the generally accepted elements of a compliance management or compliance assurance system.

However, there are important differences between the "due diligence" criteria and ISO 14001.

ISO 14001and
EPA audit
policy:
differences

☑ First and most significantly, the "due diligence" criteria generally focus on compliance with regulatory requirements whereas the EMS standard focuses on selected "objectives and targets" that may include regulatory compliance. (**ISO 14001 Section 4.2.3.**) In addition, the "due diligence" criteria require "appropriate incentives" (including disciplinary mechanisms) to encourage performance in accordance with compliance policies, standards, and procedures. In contrast, ISO 14001 merely requires training on the "potential consequences of departing from specific operating procedures," without stating what those consequences might be.(**ISO 14001 Section 4.3.2.**)

Note that whether your certified organization meets the "due diligence" criteria also rests upon the integrity and credibility of the program and process for accrediting registrars and auditor certifiers, for approving training providers, and for certifying auditors and registering companies.37

☑ Second, as discussed above, a mature and effective ISO EMS should make it less likely that violations will occur in the first place, and where they do, procedures should be in place to correct the violation promptly and take appropriate action to remediate the harm.

☑ Third, as discussed above, violations that do occur should not rise to the level of actual serious harm or imminent and substantial endangerment.

☑ Fourth, the mandate for continuous improvement of the EMS and management review sets forth the processes by which your organization can meet the condition to agree to take steps to prevent recurrence of the violation.

☑ Finally, these same processes should make it unlikely that the violation at hand was a "repeat violation" as defined under the final audit policy.

☑ The remaining conditions for penalty mitigation under the final audit policy are "full and prompt disclosure" and "cooperation," both of which are not addressed in the ISO EMS standard. Many of the legal issues related to disclosure are considered in the previous chapter.

Determining Extent of Benefits

Reliable Indicator Needed

Since ISO 14001 certification does not guarantee any specific level of environmental performance, regulatory benefits should not be provided by virtue of certification alone.

environmental
performance
indicator

In determining the extent to which regulatory benefits are appropriate for certified organizations, the central question is whether certification will be a reliable indicator of a minimum level of environmental performance. Given EPA's mission to protect human health and the environment, this minimum level of performance would provide at least the level of protection under the current regulatory structure.

Since certification does not guarantee any particular level of environmental performance including compliance with regulatory requirements, regulators will probably not be willing to provide any significant regulatory benefits for ISO 14001 certification in and of itself.

ISO 14001 can be likened to a "tapestry board" that may be used to weave a splendid or a shoddy tapestry, depending on the quality of the threads used and the craftsmanship of the weaver. A customer would not be likely to order a tapestry simply on the basis of information about the tapestry board without having knowledge of the weaver's skill, threads woven, or quality of tapestries woven in the past.

History of Compliance Needed

ISO 14001 certification combined with a history of compliance or superior performance would be a likely candidate for additional regulatory benefits.

If a history of good performance is combined with an objective "certification" of sound environmental management, regulators would be much more likely to provide meaningful regulatory benefits. Regulators may be willing to provide additional regulatory benefits to certified organizations if the results of the ISO 14001 system have yielded a significant history of compliance or a history of superior performance.

In other words, if the same weaver using the same "tapestry board" has woven many high quality tapestries in the past, it is likely that the weaver will weave high-quality tapestries in the future.

EPA is evaluating proposals to provide regulatory benefits to organizations — ISO 14001 certified or not — that have a history of compliance or a history of superior performance levels above compliance.38

Performance Measures Needed

Development of performance measures for certified organizations would promote regulatory reliance on ISO 14001 certification.

The primary value of ISO 14001 from a regulatory standpoint will be its effect on improving environmental performance.

Your certified company may use many performance measures that are designed to serve its needs according to its selected objectives. Improvement of the EMS and environmental performance requires monitoring and measurement of performance.

multimedia performance measures

Since the EMS addresses the significant environmental impacts of your company's activities, services, and products across all media, many of these performance measures must be multi-media based. In addition, many of these performance measures may not directly relate to current regulatory measures of compliance, yet they are still valuable in characterizing your organization's impact on the environment.

For example, the amount of a raw material such as water used per unit of production is not a measurement employed in the current regulatory system, but nonetheless it is useful information from the perspective of developing mechanisms for addressing problems involving depletion of natural resources, sustainable development, and desertification.

challenge = consistent measures

Thus, the challenge is to develop measures of environmental performance that are consistent or fungible with measures of performance used within an ISO 14001 certified EMS. This requires a definition of "environmental performance" that captures activity beyond the range of regulated activity.

The work of ISO TC 207 on environmental performance evaluation (EPE) should provide some insight into development of useful measures of performance. (See Part 5, Chapter 2 for more information on EPE.)

EPE will be used to help organizations measure their performance vis-à-vis their selected objectives and targets.39 One component of this task is to identify indicators of environmental performance and/or the state of the environment.40 Indicators can reflect the total amount of toxics released, or can be information scaled to another parameter such as production, or can be characterized in other ways.41 Some of the information that is required for regulatory compliance purposes, such as toxic release data and emissions and discharge monitoring data, could be measured as part of an EPE.

In addition, activities relating to assessment of the "life cycle" of a product or service could prove very useful in developing performance measures. The TC 207 subcommittee on Life-Cycle Analysis (SC5) could provide valuable input. (See Part 5, Chapter 3 for more information on LCA.)

As noted above, the levels of performance flowing from an EMS in an "ISO regulatory scheme" should be adequate to protect the public and environment. It is therefore important to develop performance measures that are capable of being used in setting standards for protecting the health and the environment. Such standards should be flexible and multi-media based wherever possible.

pollution-control flexiblity needed

For example, a flexible multi-media approach may be taken in setting overall permit limits with respect to a pollutant or class of pollutants for an entire facility, group of facilities, or even an entire industry sector or geographical region. Sector-based standards, including those that rely upon relative indicators of environmental performance involving materials used or waste generated per unit of product, have particular promise. Your facility should have sufficient flexibility to develop and use the method of controlling or reducing pollutants that makes the most sense from your perspective; government should not prescribe the technology.

Accountability and Disclosure Needed

Regulatory recognition of ISO 14001 certified organizations would require accountability for and disclosure of environmental performance.

Without disclosure of environmental performance, the public and government will not know whether your organization is operating in a manner consistent with the environmental goals society has set for itself.

The external communication requirements of the EMS standard are weak in this regard: "The organization shall consider processes for external communication on its significant environmental aspects and record its decision," and must make its environmental policy publicly available.

EMAS requires
environmental
statement

Countries or blocs may integrate their own disclosure schemes in conjunction with the ISO standard. For example, the EMAS requires companies to prepare and publish a validated site-specific environmental statement that sets forth the significant environmental issues and data on performance. In addition, the company must publish its policies, programs, and a description of its EMS system. 📖 (See Part 9, Chapter 5 for more information on EMAS.)

If regulatory benefits are provided for certification and such benefits rely upon your organization's environmental performance, there must be a means of verifying performance. This must involve some degree of disclosur to the government or the public in order to ensure that the public and environment are being adequately protected.

pressure for
information

There is greater and greater pressure for companies to provide communities with performance information and to consider the perspectives of community stakeholders in making decisions that affect these stakeholders. As a condition of providing regulatory benefits for ISO 14001 certified organizations, the government should require disclosure to and involvement of local communities.

Incentives for increased levels of performance may be provided through public and market pressures that in turn require dissemination of information about your organization's environmental performance information. Examples include public pressure in response to information voluntarily or involuntarily provided by your organization through the government and/or press. In addition, there are myriad market incentives that exert themselves through preference toward suppliers, reduced insurance premiums, and other risk-based benefits manifested through financial, lender, and investment markets. In general, there is greater pressure — public and market — toward greater disclosure of environmental performance.

Specific Regulatory Benefits for Certification

Reduced Reporting and Monitoring Requirements

demonstrate
compliance
history

Self-monitoring and self-reporting requirements have been an absolutely essential part of determining whether applicable permit limits are being met. It is unlikely that EPA would reduce the amount of substantive information that a certified organization must report by virtue of its certification. However, if a certified company can demonstrate significant compliance history or superior performance, less information would need to be reported or reported less frequently to verify its performance.

With respect to organizations that achieve "superior" environmental performance, an alternative model could be developed that involves identification of performance measures that can be used to determine whether the public and environment are being adequately protected. Consistent with the ISO EMS standards, these performance measures should be multi-media and flexible. Your organization still must report or "disclose" a certain level of information, but it could be much less burdensome and more easily integrated into its own management system.

Consolidated Reporting and Monitoring Requirements

Under the ISO EMS standard, identification of significant environmental aspects and impacts, development of objectives, and measurement of key characteristics of operations and activities all have a multi-media focus. From the perspective of a certified organization, regulatory requirements for monitoring, reporting, and recordkeeping should (optimally) be consistent with this multi-media focus. From a regulatory perspective, a multi-media characterization of impacts on the environment is generally more accurate than is a media-specific focus. In addition, multi-media regulation generally provides more effective controls over environmental effects than media-specific controls.

streamline
information
submissions

The implementation of ISO 14001 presents the regulated community and regulators with an opportunity to streamline information submissions. Consolidation and simplification of reporting, monitoring, and recordkeeping requirements are occurring under the auspices of EPA's "one-stop reporting" initiative.

Information Required for Permitting; Streamlined Permitting

Flexibility regarding permitting procedures may be possible for certified organizations where environmental performance is measured, meets a minimum level protecting the public and environment, and is disclosed. Much of the information required for permit applications already will be collected through operation of the ISO EMS information collection functions.

EPA may require permit application information in a form that is consistent with information generated through its EMS. This re-characterization of information also may eliminate much of the process associated with modifying a specific permit. As discussed, permit standards should be flexible (at least facility-wide) and multimedia focused.

Reduced Inspections

narrow scope
of inspections

Given the substantial resources that are expended by government and industry in preparing for and conducting EPA compliance inspections and the perceived environmental benefits associated with ISO 14001 certification, it has been suggested that certified companies might be subject to fewer EPA inspections and/or inspections that are narrower in scope.

Whether a facility or group of facilities within an industry sector are inspected depends upon many factors, including the Toxic Release Inventory (TRI) data with toxicological weights, demographic information, compliance history, and productivity of the facility.42

Conformance with ISO 14001 has a great potential to improve environmental performance both in preventing serious violations and ultimately decreasing the number of violations overall. A demonstrated direct correlation between certification and significantly higher rates of compliance would be valuable information to EPA for purposes of targeting inspections. This may be a potential area for a sector-based pilot project.

reduced inspection = exceptions

Nonetheless, compliance rates and seriousness of violations would not address factors relating to demographics and exposure of substances to humans or the environment. For example, a certified organization with a facility that handles hazardous waste in a heavily populated area may be inspected regardless of a facility's performance history.

Accreditation and Registration

The above analysis of the possible impact of ISO 14001 on regulatory enforcement and compliance is contingent upon use of an ISO 14001 certification mechanism that is credible. The credibility of the certification depends upon the credibility of the entire program for accrediting certification bodies and for approving training providers and programs. EPA has indicated that a credible accreditation program should include a single dedicated body with environmental expertise and an open and inclusive process for developing criteria and accrediting qualified entities. 📖 (See Part 7 for more information on the conformity assessment process and related issues.)

Voluntary Programs Involving ISO 14001

EPA is considering several proposals involving ISO 14001 under its compliance incentive programs. They have been summarized below.

Project XL involves the granting of regulatory flexibility in exchange for a commitment by a regulated entity to achieve better environmental results than would have been attained through full compliance with regulations. As of January 1996, EPA had received two Project XL proposals that specifically involve ISO 14001: the AT&T-Microelectronics proposal and the Anheuser-Busch Companies proposal.

EPA projects well underway

In response to the administration call for a reduction in reporting requirements by at least 25 percent, in early 1996 the Office of Water was developing a program that may involve reducing monitoring and reporting requirements for National Pollution Discharge Elimination System (NPDES) permit holders that demonstrate superior compliance history or superior control performance. This program may involve greater burden reductions for organizations that are ISO-registered and satisfy other requirements.

The ELP was developed to recognize facilities that have shown leadership and innovation in complying with environmental requirements. As part of ELP's pilot program, in May 1995 EPA received two proposals that involve ISO 14001: the Gillette Company proposal and the Salt River Project proposal.

Finally, EPA's Sustainable Industry Project (SIP) is designed to improve the efficiency of environmental activities to facilitate international competitiveness of U.S. companies. In early 1996, the SIP Best Management Practices (BMP) work group was working on a project with Union Carbide involving ISO 14001.

As of March 1996, EPA was in the preliminary stages of determining what role ISO 14001 may play in each of these initiatives. EPA has indicated that it welcomes working with the states, regulated community, public interest groups, and other important stakeholders in exploring this exciting area.

CHAPTER 3

Beyond Compliance: Escape from Command-and-Control

by Ira R. Feldman, President, gt stratagies + solutions

When Joseph Cascio, chairman of the U.S. Technical Advisory Group (TAG) to TC 207, announced the arrival of James Seif, secretary of the Pennsylvania Department of Environmental Protection, at the TAG's September 14, 1995, meeting in Philadelphia, many in attendance were pleasantly surprised that the Pennsylvania environmental secretary would take note of the group's ongoing activities related to the ISO 14000 series of voluntary environmental management system standards.

Pennsylvania's chief environmental regulator then surprised the TAG membership again. In his opinion, he announced, soon would come the day that a company certified to ISO 14001 would never again need to see an inspector from his agency.

While it is unlikely that ISO 14001 certification by itself will ever be sufficient to allow a company or individual facility to "de-regulate" itself, Seif is on the right track in acknowledging the powerful potential of the voluntary ISO 14000 framework to complement environmental regulation.

As Pennsylvania and other states begin to explore options in moving toward more flexible and less adversarial regulatory systems, they will increasingly recognize useful linkages to the ISO 14000 series. Some state and federal programs are already looking at the possible role of ISO 14001 certification in certain existing regulatory programs.

Even more intriguing is the prospect of using the ISO 14000 framework as a basic building block in creating an alternative or parallel regulatory pathway, one based on a more flexible management system approach to improving environmental performance.

Implementation Drivers

The conventional wisdom in the U.S. has been that the ISO 14000 series will be widely embraced only if accepted by the marketplace. Initially, it is quite likely that competitive and commercial pressures — in the form of contractual provisions, procurement guidelines, and the like — will drive implementation of the EMS specification. However, many companies are rapidly realizing that customer and supplier demand is only one element of the implementation equation for the ISO 14000 series.

The determinative factor for many organizations may, in fact, be the internal use of the EMS as a vehicle for improving environmental performance and achieving greater cost efficiencies.

determining
factor: internal
benefits

Organizations also will consider the role of ISO 14001 certification (or self-declaration) in improving their communication of environmental performance to a range of stakeholders — consumers, lenders, the neighboring community to name but a few. In time, however, the strongest driver for the successful implementation of the ISO 14000 series may prove to be its regulatory applications.

The regulatory driver for ISO 14000 implementation largely has been overlooked in the U.S. It is important to state clearly that it would be inappropriate to convert ISO 14001, designed as a voluntary consensus standard, directly into a regulatory requirement. But, as an adjunct to regulation, an ISO 14000 series linkage would serve both as a basis for "beyond compliance" incentives for industry and as a mechanism for conserving increasingly scarce regulatory agency resources.

Will the ISO 14000 series be the key to unlocking the "command and control" box? There is good reason for both industry and regulators to be optimistic.

In the search for an alternative scheme that is more flexible and less prescriptive, yet at the same time addresses the regulatory goals and stakeholder concerns, the ISO 14001 management systems approach provides a compelling framework.

ISO 14001: Holistic Framework

ISO 14001 is multimedia and comprehensive, so it encourages companies to take a holistic rather than media-specific approach to environmental performance.

The documentation and communication requirements of the ISO 14001 EMS specification provide a basis for integrated monitoring and recordkeeping, and could provide the impetus for establishing a consolidated reporting mechanism.

less reliance on
end-of-pipe

A commitment to ISO 14001 comes with a requirement to aim for a "prevention of pollution" goal, so increased attention will be paid to pollution prevention opportunities with less reliance on "end-of-pipe" solutions.

Under ISO 14001, an EMS must include not only a commitment to compliance, but also to document conformance with voluntary obligations. Thus, ISO 14001 provides a basis for building voluntary programs like EPA's 33/50 program or industry-specific initiatives like the Chemical Manufacturers Association's Responsible Care® program together into a coherent framework.

Finally, ISO 14001 is verifiable. While self-declaration may be available, third-party verification will provide a comfort level to stakeholders and could form the basis for privatizing inspections for a subset of the regulated community. Regulators would then focus attention on bad actors or divert resources to compliance assurance activities for small and medium-sized businesses.

Specific Regulatory Proposals

Some specific proposals for the regulatory application of ISO 14001 have also begun to appear. Most notably, in July 1995 EPA's Office of Wastewater Management developed a "strawman" proposal that would encourage the use of ISO 14001 or similar EMS principles in the NPDES permit program.

The NPDES proposal is linked to the U.S. federal administration's "reinventing" mandate to cut reporting and recordkeeping requirements. Thus, the rationale here would be to allow more flexible monitoring and less frequent reporting requirements for facilities that have both good performance records and an EMS certified to an accepted standard such as ISO 14001.

This type of single-media regulatory application of ISO 14000 is an important first step, but only a beginning.

true potential: cross-media programs

The true potential of ISO 14000 will emerge in its application to cross-media programs. EPA and the administration have sent other signals of their interest in exploring the potential interrelationship of voluntary initiatives like ISO 14000 and the broader regulatory system.

EPA's Environmental Leadership Program recognized the importance of an EMS approach and built such considerations into its "environmental excellence" criteria. The ELP solicitation required pilot project applicants to address EMS issues and encouraged proposals that were linked to ISO 14000. One of the first of the ELP pilots selected, the Gillette Company proposal, relies on third-party verification of compliance and EMS.

Model Programs

The Gillette project is seen as such a promising model that it has, in turn, spawned a new round of regional ELP pilots in EPA-New England, Region 1. One of the new regional initiatives, known as "3PC," intends to establish a process for third-party verification of a company's environmental performance, specifically focusing on EMSs, compliance audit programs, and pollution prevention programs.

Region representatives have stated that "participating companies will be expected to develop EMSs appropriate to their operations, modeled largely after the developing ISO 14000 standards."

project XL

One of the U.S. administration's key building blocks for reinventing environmental regulation is Project XL, a series of projects that will "provide a limited number of responsible companies the opportunity to demonstrate excellence and leadership."

alternative strategies

While the definition of a "responsible company" is not specified, proposed projects or "alternative strategies" must meet the following conditions. To be eligible, the alternative strategy must:

☑ produce environmental performance superior to that which would be achieved by full compliance with current laws and regulations;

☑ be "transparent" so that citizens can examine assumptions and track progress toward meeting promised results;

☑ not create worker safety or environmental justice problems;

☑ enjoy the support of the community surrounding the facility; and

☑ be enforceable.

Several of the project proposals submitted by September 1995, explore the regulatory linkages with ISO 14000.

For example, the XL application submitted by AT&T-Microelectronics (now Lucent Technologies) notes that "the comprehensive approach of ISO 14001, if linked to meaningful regulatory flexibility, would allow AT&T-ME to meet its commercial competition while at the same time more flexibly and effectively meet its environmental obligations."

AT&T adds that, "since ISO 14001 establishes a defined protocol for documenting the existence and performance of an EMS . . . it offers a reliable, predictable, and verifiable basis for the exercise of enforcement discretion and penalty mitigation." 📖 (See Part 3, Chapter 3 for clause-by-clause implementation tips form AT&T on implementation.)

The ELP and XL pilots likely will demonstrate that a management system approach offers an opportunity to establish a new regime — an alternative regulatory pathway that would help companies making a commitment to enhanced environmental management activities opt out of the traditional command-and-control model.

Indeed, since early 1995 there has been much creative energy devoted to such "outside-the-box" thinking on alternative or parallel pathways by such groups as the Eco-Efficiency Task Force of the President's Council on Sustainable Development, several of the Common Sense Initiative sectors, the Aspen Institute series on environmental regulation, and the Green Track initiative.

Complementing Regulations

Perhaps most notably, the National Environmental Policy Institute (NEPI) in its Phase One report, *Reinventing the Vehicle for Environmental Management*, released in August 1995, recommended the creation of an alternative regulatory track based on "environmental excellence."

The report states: "Regulated entities that commit to environmental excellence principles, implement comprehensive management systems, and strive to continuously improve their performance should be able to opt out of the command-and-control system into a more flexible, consistent regulatory scheme.

This alternative track would not replace or revamp the current system, nor would it relax any standards or performance requirements stipulated by existing regulations. Instead, it would offer regulated entities a choice: operate under command-and-control, or strive to reach the alternative track, which would be built on emerging environmental management trends and would be a more flexible, consistent, and lower-cost system.

The NEPI report is careful to recognize that the proposed two-track system does not mean eliminating all mandatory aspects of environmental regulation — "command-and-control" mechanisms necessarily must continue to exist as one of the components of the two-track system.

The two-track approach protects environmental gains made over the last decades while providing a strong incentive for business to pursue alternative approaches. It still will be necessary, in the NEPI vision, for Congress and the EPA to set national minimal environmental goals and standards mandated across all the states.

One of the most interesting aspects of the NEPI proposal is that this alternative track could lay the foundation for the development and passage of a unified environmental statute. Such a statute would address all media, establish a set of goals, establish a common metric for risk, embrace a powerful set of environmental management tools, and institute a sensible system of decisionmaking at appropriate local, state, and national levels.

The guts of the NEPI two-track proposal, as well as of the Green Track initiative, rely on the separation, or "filtering," of the regulated community based on environmental excellence criteria, as opposed to arbitrary indicators such as compliance history, Toxic Release Inventory releases, or the Standard Industrial Code.

Clearly, while ISO 14001 certification itself is not evidence of environmental excellence, in combination with other proactive corporate environmental commitments like auditing, benchmarking, mentoring, and external voluntary reporting, an excellence program begins to take shape.

The NEPI (and Green Track) excellence approach provides an important comfort level to stakeholders. Regulators, financial and insurance institutions, environmental groups, local communities, and other interested parties will know with a high degree of certainty that entities that take the alternative track take their environmental obligations seriously, have comprehensive systems in place to deal with the range of issues they face, and, in fact, deserve more flexible, consistent treatment.

Not insignificantly, under these proposals, ISO 14001 remains strictly voluntary, as intended, available to those organizations wanting to "opt out" of command and control.

The time has arrived to begin the shift away from prescriptive regulation to a greater reliance on an EMS approach to environmental policy.

The U.S. environmental regulatory system should build upon the many emerging non-regulatory trends that emphasize regulatory flexibility and enhance global competitiveness. ISO 14001 may be the key to unlock the old box.

FOOTNOTES

1 The legal and other issues presented by the intersection of ISO 14000 and trade rules are covered in Part 9 of the Handbook.

2 See, e.g., *Kansas Gas & Elec. v. Eye*, 789 P.2d 1161 (Kan.1990).

3 *Reichhold Chemicals, Inc. v. Textron, Inc.*, 157 F.R.D. 522(N.D. Fla. 1994).

4 These states are Arkansas, Colorado, Idaho, Illinois, Indiana, Kansas, Kentucky, Michigan, Minnesota, Mississippi, New Hampshire, Oregon, South Dakota, Texas, Utah, Virginia, and Wyoming.

5 ISO 14001.0 requires "commitment . . . to compliance with applicable legislation and regulations."

6 See ISO 14001.4.4.2.

7 See *Council Regulation No. 1836/93* [establishing EMAS], Article 3(b).

8 See ISO 14001, Annex A, § A.4.2.1.

9   See David J. Freeman and Carolyn C. Cunningham, "The Environmental Audit: Management Tool or Government Weapon?," *New York Law Journal*, Dec. 30, 1991, at 1, col. 2.

10 See, e.g., *United States v. Cote*, 456 F.2d 142 (8th Cir. 1972).

11 See, e.g., *Loehr v. Offshore Logistics, Inc.*, 691 F.2d 758 (5th Cir. 1982); *Thropp v. Bache Halsey Stuart Shields, Inc.*, 650 F.2d 817 (6th Cir. 1981).

12 "Factors in Decisions on Criminal Prosecutions for Environmental Violations in the Context of Significant Voluntary Compliance or Disclosure Efforts by the Violator," July 1, 1991.

13 See ISO 14001.4.4.2.

14 Excluded from this generalization, of course, are issues that would be presented by arbitrary or discriminatory extension of such benefits (which could be challenged in the same way as any other arbitrary or discriminatory government action); by making ISO programs mandatory under certain regulatory programs (an idea that has not been seriously suggested); or by treatment that constitutes a non-tariff barrier to trade (See Part 9).

15 See *United States v. Mississippi Valley Generating Co.*, 364 U.S. 520 (1961).

16 31 U.S.C. §§ 3729-33.

17 United States *ex rel. Fallon v. Accudyne Corp.*, 880 F. Supp. 636 (W.D. Wis. 1995).

18 See, e.g., *United States v. Yermian*, 468 U.S. 63 (1984).

19 See, e.g., *Guard-Life Corp. v. S. Parker Manufacturing Corp.*, 50 N.Y.2d 183 (1980).

20 15 U.S.C. § 45.

21 *Warner-Lambert Co. v. Federal Trade Commission*, 562 F.2d 749 (D.C. Cir.), cert. denied, 435 U.S. 950 (1978).

22 Note, however, as part of the same 1990 amendments, Congress prescribed the use of technology-based Most Achievable Control Technology (MACT) standards in controlling air toxic emissions.

23 In 1993, EPA amalgamated the enforcement and the media-specific compliance offices to create the new Office of Enforcement and Compliance Assurance.

24 See Part 7 on the conformity assessment process for information about third-party "registration" or "certification."

25 Under the ISO 14001 annex, "other requirements to which [an organization] subscribes" include industry codes of practices, agreements with public authorities, and nonregulatory guidelines. This would include responsibilities agreed to under voluntary programs such as the 33/50 and Responsible Care® programs.

26 See Part 7 for a discussion of conformity assessment.

27 Memorandum from Earl E. Devaney, Director, EPA Office of Criminal Enforcement, regarding The Exercise of Investigative Discretion," January 12, 1994.

28 *U.S. Department of Justice, Factors in Decisions on Criminal Prosecutions for Environmental Violations in the Context of Significant Voluntary Compliance or Disclosure Efforts by the Violator,* July 1, 1991.

29 The DOJ policy states: "The attorney for the Department should consider the existence and scope of any regularized, intensive, and comprehensive environmental compliance program. . . . Compliance programs may vary but the following questions should be asked in evaluating any program: Was there a strong institutional policy to comply with all environmental requirements? Had safeguards beyond those required by existing law been developed and implemented to prevent noncompliance from occurring? Were there regular procedures, including internal or external compliance and management audits, to evaluate, detect, and prevent and remedy circumstances like those that led to the noncompliance? Were there procedures and safeguards to ensure the integrity of any audit conducted? Did the audit evaluate all sources of pollution (i.e., all media), including the possibility of cross-media transfers of pollutants? Were the auditor's recommendations implemented in a timely fashion? Were adequate resources committed to the auditing program and to implementing its recommendations? Was environmental compliance a standard by which employee and corporate departmental performance was judged?"

30 United States Sentencing Commission Guidelines Manual, Chapter 8 - Sentencing of Organizations, Part A-General Application Principles (effective November 1, 1991).

31 The Sentencing Guidelines state: "Due diligence requires at a minimum that the organization must have taken the following types of steps:

(1) The organization must have established compliance standards and procedures to be followed by its employees and other agents that are reasonably capable of reducing the prospect of criminal conduct.

(2) Specific individual(s) within high-level personnel of the organization must have been assigned overall responsibility to oversee compliance with such standards and procedures.

(3) The organization must have used due care not to delegate substantial discretionary authority to individuals whom the organization knew, or should have known through the exercise of due diligence, had a propensity to engage in illegal activities.

(4) The organization must have taken steps to communicate effectively its standards and procedures to all employees and other agents, e.g., by requiring participation in training programs or by disseminating publications that explain in a practical manner what is required.

(5) The organization must have taken reasonable steps to achieve compliance with its standards, e.g., by utilizing monitoring and auditing systems reasonably designed to detect

criminal conduct by its employees and other agents and by having in place and publicizing a reporting system whereby employees and other agents could report criminal conduct by others within the organization without fear of retribution.

(6) The standards must have been consistently enforced through appropriate disciplinary mechanisms, including, as appropriate, discipline of individuals responsible for the failure to detect an offense. Adequate discipline of individuals responsible for an offense is a necessary component of enforcement; however, the form of discipline that will be appropriate will be case specific.

(7) After an offense has been detected, the organization must have taken all reasonable steps to respond appropriately to the offense and to prevent further similar offenses — including any necessary modifications to its program to prevent and detect violations of law."

32 The "gravity" component of a penalty represents the "seriousness" or "punitive" portion of penalties. The other major part of a penalty, the economic benefit component, represents the economic advantage a violator gains through its noncompliance.

33 An environmental audit has the definition given to it under EPA's 1986 auditing policy, i.e., "a systematic, documented, periodic and objective review by regulated entities of facility operations and practices related to meeting environmental requirements."

34 Under the final self-policing policy, EPA may waive the entire penalty for violations that, in EPA's opinion, do not merit any penalty due to the insignificant amount of any economic benefit.

Under some environmental statutes, EPA is required to consider the economic benefit a violator gains from noncompliance in assessing penalties. See, e.g., CWA §309(g), CAA §113(e), and SDWA §1423(c). EPA's longstanding policy has been to collect significant economic benefit gained from noncompliance. See A Framework for Statute-Specific Approaches to [Civil] Penalty Assessments, EPA General Enforcement Policy #GM-22, February 16, 1984; see also the approximately 24 EPA media and program-specific penalty and enforcement response policies. The reason for collecting economic benefit is to preserve a level playing field for entities that make the timely investment in compliance. Recovery of economic benefit can be likened to the IRS requirement of paying interest or fees on taxes paid late.

35 For a more detailed discussion of EPA's final self-policing policy, see this author's chapter in *The Environmental Audits Book*, 7th Edition, Government Institutes, 1995.

36 Note that the minimum conditions of the self-policing policy — disclosure, correction, no repeat violations, no criminal acts, no serious actual or threat of harm, recovery of economic benefit, etc. — are also part of the enforcement response agreed to by EPA and Environmental Leadership Program pilot participants in exchange for no enforcement action if violations are corrected within 90 days.

37 See also discussion of the ISO 14001 conformity assessment process in Part 7.

38 See, e.g., the draft document describing the NPDES "Program of Performance-Based Reporting and Monitoring," June 14, 1995.

39 The ISO 14031 working draft 4 *Evaluation of the Environmental Performance of the Management System and its Relationship to the Environment* defines EPE as a process to "measure, analyze, assess, and describe an organization's environmental performance against agreed criteria for appropriate management purposes."

40 The SC4 working draft defines environmental indicator as an "expression that is used to provide information about environmental performance or the condition of the environment. NOTE: the expression can be relative or absolute."

41 The working draft provides the following examples of ways to characterize EPIs:

- absolute (e.g., total emissions of SO_2);

- relative (e.g., SO_2 emissions per ton of primary product);

- indexes (baseline year at 100 percent or weighing of equivalents to consolidate data, e.g., total greenhouse gas releases expressed as CO_2);

- aggregated (combining from various sites or assigning data to a category of environmental effect, e.g., SO_2 emissions aggregated from 20 plants or amount of hazardous waste generated per site);

- and weighted (weighing of noncomparable effects, involves making value judgments).

42 *Final FY 96/97 OECA Memorandum of Agreement Guidance,* June 22, 1995.

9

Global Status

CHAPTER 1
Trade Barriers, GATT, and ISO 14000

by Marissa A. Perrone, President, ECO-TRADE Consulting

9.1.1 Overview

This section will discuss the relationship between the ISO 14000 standards and existing international trade rules under the General Agreement on Tariffs and Trade (GATT). The ultimate question is whether and how the ISO 14000 standards will create technical barriers to trade.

labeling and EMS concerns Since early 1995, there has been an increased level of concern that the ISO 14000 standards will pose a barrier to trade, particularly for small- and medium-sized enterprises (SMEs) and for companies from developing countries. Many trade issues have been raised concerning the ISO 14001 standard on environmental management systems (EMSs) and trade issues regarding the ISO 14024 standards on labeling. 📖 (See Part 5, Chapter 1 for more information on labeling.)

three trade issues This analysis will discuss three trade issues relevant to the EMS standards and several issues relevant to the labeling standards:

1) There is significant concern that the ISO 14001 standards will be adopted as a mandatory requirement in some countries, and consequently will pose a barrier to trade.

2) There is the prospect that numerous countries will adopt/maintain national laws more environmentally stringent than the ISO 14001 standard — thereby undermining the international harmonization effort and affecting global trade.

3) There is a concern that government procurement practices will favor suppliers with ISO 14001 certification.

Similarly, trade issues have been raised regarding eco-labeling and self-declaration programs. The final section of this analysis addresses the trade implications of labeling programs that label products based on how the product was made, also known as the product's production process methods (PPMs).

production
process
methods
(PPMs)

Admittedly, these trade issues regarding the EMS labeling standards represent only some of the many concerns raised throughout the negotiations of the ISO 14000 standards.

9.1.2 GATT, WTO, and ISO 14000

To understand the context of these trade concerns, we should discuss how the ISO 14000 standards fit into the international trade arena.

One might argue that GATT is the preeminent international trade regime of our day. Since its inception in 1947, GATT has undergone numerous rounds of negotiations to reduce tariff and non-tariff barriers. Most recently, the Uruguay Round of GATT concluded in 1993 after seven years of negotiations. The Uruguay Round resulted in the 1994 agreement to establish a new World Trade Organization (WTO), which replaces the existing GATT institution. Consequently, GATT is referred to as the WTO agreement. There are more than 100 government WTO agreement signatories, referred to as WTO members.

technical
barriers to
trade

The WTO agreement contains numerous individual agreements that address various areas relevant to trade in goods and services (e.g., textiles, intellectual property). One area particularly relevant to the ISO 14000 standards is the Agreement on Technical Barriers to Trade (TBT agreement).

The TBT agreement governs technical regulations and standards, including environmental regulations and standards. It establishes rules and procedures for the development and application of voluntary standards and mandatory regulations as well as procedures to determine if standards are met (conformity assessment). 📖 (See Part 7 for more information on conformity assessment.) When a WTO member prepares, adopts, or implements a voluntary standard or a mandatory regulation for environmental protection purposes, its actions must be consistent with all GATT obligations and, in particular, with the provisions set forth in the TBT agreement.

use of
international
standards

One of the cornerstone provisions in the TBT agreement that clearly carves out a role for the ISO 14000 standards is the provision regarding the use of international standards. The TBT states that, with respect to mandatory regulations and voluntary standards, where relevant international standards exist or their completion is imminent they shall be used as a basis of the technical regulation or standard. Based on this TBT provision, the ISO 14000 standards are likely to be considered among the most important international standards guiding industry behavior in the area of environmental protection.

WTO's Committee on Trade and the Environment

The GATT agreement of 1994 is one of the first multilateral trade agreements to address environmental concerns as part of the agreement. In fact, the agreement contains several provisions meant to ensure that WTO members may adopt national and regional environmental laws appropriate to their desired level of environmental protection. The agreement also contains provisions meant to ensure that WTO members do not adopt environmental laws that unfairly affect international trade.

While the many environment-related provisions in the GATT agreement are a useful step forward in the trade and environment debate, they fall short of expectations from many in the international environmental and business communities.

trade committee established — Consequently, the GATT accord established the WTO Committee on Trade and the Environment (CTE) to discuss trade and environment issues further. Several of the trade issues discussed below are under review by the CTE. For example, one of the work items on the agenda for the CTE is eco-labeling, including PPM-based labeling. The outcome of the CTE's work is likely to affect implementation of the ISO 14000 standards. For that reason, the CTE's work should be followed closely by the ISO 14000 standards negotiators.

interpretation only by WTO governments — Also, many individuals have attempted to interpret the meaning of certain GATT and TBT provisions as they relate to the ISO 14000 standards. It may be useful to note that definitive interpretation of GATT and TBT provisions can only be made by WTO member governments via formal clarifications or by WTO panel decisions arising from disputes. Here we discuss several TBT provisions and provide possible interpretations that are made solely by us.

We'll lay out only some of the trade issues that may be relevant to implementing the ISO 14000 standards. How the ISO 14000 standards are adopted and implemented at a national level will tell the U.S. whether or how the standards will impact trade. Future interpretation of several important GATT and TBT provisions also will affect the potential trade impact of the ISO 14000 standards.

9.1.3 Implications of Government-Mandated ISO 14001 Compliance

ISO Technical Committee 207 delegations have raised trade concerns that the ISO 14001 EMS standard will be adopted as a mandatory requirement in certain countries. Specifically, they are concerned that, if the voluntary ISO 14001 standard becomes a mandatory requirement at the national level, it will evolve into another trade obstacle for developing countries.

Many developing countries already fear that the ISO 14001 standard in its current form as a voluntary tool will become a de facto requirement for doing business in developed countries. There is mounting concern that the standards not only will become extremely popular, but that the standards will be an absolute mandatory requirement.

national law
does not mean
barrier

In response to this concern, we can argue that a national law mandating compliance with the ISO 14001 standard need not pose any more of a trade barrier than in its form as a voluntary standard. There are several reasons to support this position.

First, the TBT agreement contains provisions to ensure that neither mandatory regulations nor voluntary standards are developed, adopted, or implemented in a manner that restricts trade. In fact, there are numerous important TBT and GATT requirements that are applicable both to regulations and to standards (discussed below).

Second, there are several additional requirements that govern regulations more strictly than standards. In particular, mandatory regulations must meet the "Least Trade Restrictive" test as well as rigorous dispute settlement provisions (discussed below).

Mandatory vs. Voluntary

To understand the trade implications of a mandatory EMS law, we should discuss the relationship between mandatory regulations, voluntary standards, and the TBT agreement.

conformance is
voluntary

The TBT agreement makes a distinction that regulations are generally set by governments and that compliance with regulations is mandatory. In contrast, standards are generally set by industry (through standards organizations) and *conformance* with standards is voluntary. As a result of the mandatory nature of regulations, they are subject to a more stringent set of provisions in the TBT agreement to ensure that regulations do not unfairly affect trade.

Voluntary standards are thought to be comparatively less trade-distorting than regulations since they are market-based programs set primarily by industry. Consequently, voluntary standards are not governed as strictly as mandatory regulations are.

Applicable TBT Provisions for Both Regulations and Standards

When a WTO member prepares, adopts, or applies an environmental regulation or standard it is obligated to adhere to certain TBT provisions. These provisions, along with other GATT obligations, are designed to reduce the chances that *neither* a regulation nor a standard becomes a non-tariff trade barrier. Below is a description of some of the key TBT provisions that apply to both mandatory regulations and to voluntary standards (the list is not exhaustive).

☑ **Meet national treatment requirement** — Imported products from any GATT member "shall be accorded treatment no less favorable than that accorded to like products of national origin." In other words, imported products shall not be subject to taxation, charges, or regulations that are more stringent than those applied to domestic products.

☑ **Meet most-favored-nation requirement** — Any privileges or immunity granted by a WTO member to any country must be granted to like products of all other WTO members.

☑ **Do not create unnecessary obstacles to trade** — Regulations and standards shall not create "unnecessary obstacles to international trade."

☑ **Use international standards** — WTO members and standards organizations shall use relevant international standards if they exist or are nearly complete as a basis for national regulations and standards, respectively.

☑ **Participate in harmonization of regulations** — WTO members shall participate in international efforts to harmonize standards for products "for which they either have adopted, or expect to adopt, technical regulations."

Applicable TBT Provisions for Regulations

least trade
restrictive LTR
provision

To prevent mandatory regulations from becoming non-tariff trade barriers, the regulations are subject to several additional provisions. In particular, the "least trade restrictive" (LTR) provision in the TBT agreement (see below) is applicable to mandatory regulations but not to voluntary standards.

Further, there are several distinctions between dispute settlement procedures that govern mandatory regulations, and voluntary standards. The provisions appear to subject mandatory regulations to a more rigorous set of dispute settlement procedures. Below is a brief discussion of both the LTR and the dispute settlement provisions.

☑ **Regulations must meet the least-trade-restrictive test** — While both regulations and standards must not create "unnecessary obstacles to international trade," mandatory regulations must meet the least-trade-restrictive test. Specifically, the TBT agreement requires that regulations "shall not be more trade-restrictive than necessary to fulfill a legitimate objective, taking account of the risks non-fulfillment would create."

LTR seen as
unfair

When this TBT language was under negotiation, the environmental community around the world was, and many members continue to be, opposed to the LTR test. Environmentalists have argued that the LTR test unfairly pits environmental objectives against trade objectives.

Many mandatory environmental laws contain measures chosen specifically to restrict trade to achieve an environmental objective (e.g., a law banning the import of hazardous materials). In contrast, industry generally argues that without an LTR provision mandatory environmental regulations will be used as a tool to unfairly protect industries and to distort international trade.

national law
subject to LTR

Therefore, if a country adopts a national law mandating compliance with the ISO 14001 standard, the law will become subject to this LTR test. In contrast, if a country maintains the ISO 14001 standard as a voluntary standard, the standard need not meet this LTR requirement set out in the TBT agreement.

☑ **Dispute-settlement provisions are more rigorous** — Dispute-settlement procedures set out in the TBT agreement are more rigorous for disputes involving mandatory regulations than for disputes involving voluntary standards.

For example, disputes involving mandatory laws must go through a formal dispute settlement process through a TBT committee and are resolved by WTO government bodies. In contrast, the dispute settlement process for disputes involving voluntary standards is informal and is to be resolved by standards organizations. Theoretically, in the future as in the past, governments will involve themselves minimally in disputes regarding voluntary standards.

The net effect of these differences in dispute settlement procedures is that if a company or a government believes that another's mandatory regulation is unfairly affecting trade it may formally bring the matter before the TBT committee and, if desired, before a WTO dispute settlement panel to arbitrate. It is highly unlikely that the same formal procedures will be followed if a dispute arises regarding a voluntary standard. Disputes involving voluntary standards are likely to get less attention and scrutiny by WTO governments since the matters are supposed to be resolved by standards organizations.

Conclusion

The provisions subjecting mandatory regulations to the stringent least-trade-restrictive test as well as to rigorous dispute settlement procedures, along with other TBT provisions, are likely to help ensure that mandatory regulations do not create barriers to international trade.

standards in
law scrutinized

Consequently, if the ISO 14001 standard is embodied in a national law mandating its compliance, the national law will become the object of greater scrutiny by the trade community as well as subject to more restrictions. As a result, a national mandatory EMS law may not necessarily pose any greater trade barrier than a national voluntary EMS standard. A mandatory regulation is not deemed to be an automatic trade barrier; rather, such a determination will depend upon how the regulation is prepared, adopted, and implemented.

9.1.4 Implications of Government-Adopted EMS Rules

Trade concerns have been raised surrounding the prospect that numerous countries will adopt/maintain national laws that are more environmentally stringent than the ISO 14001 standard is, and that, by doing so, the national law will undermine international harmonization efforts and create a barrier to trade.

This scenario illustrates one of the central issues in trade and environment debates regarding such multilateral trade agreements as the North American Free Trade Agreement (NAFTA) and GATT. 📖 (See Part 9, Chapter 2 for more information on NAFTA.) At issue is the balance between preserving the sovereign right of a country to set national environmental protection laws and preserving the trade objective of national environmental laws not creating barriers to international trade.

Consider the following scenario.

example:
country G

Country G decides that the ISO 14001 standards are not rigorous enough to be used as national tools in achieving its desired level of environmental protection. Consequently, country G adopts a regulation establishing a national EMS standard more environmentally stringent than the ISO 14001 standard. Over time, country G's national EMS is effectively promoted as the true "green" standard for industry. As a result, market demand for certification under the national EMS standard appears to be greater than for certification under the ISO 14001 standard. Trading partners complain that country G's national EMS law is creating a barrier to trading in their market.

How realistic is this scenario? Well, consider the situation in the European Union (E.U.) in which the E.U. adopted a regional EMS regulation in 1993 that is arguably "greener" than the ISO 14001 standard — the Eco-Management and Audit Regulation (EMAR).

📖 (See Part 9 , Chapter 5, Section 1, for more information on EMAR. See Part 9, Chapter 6, Section 9 oncontrasting U.S. view.)

For example, the E.U. regulation requires companies to commit to continually improving the environmental performance of their industrial operations. In contrast, the ISO 14001 standards delineate a commitment merely to continual improvement of the environmental management system (which may incidentally lead to improvement of your company's environmental performance). Numerous other examples exist that illustrate the different approaches (from an environmental perspective) between the E.U. EMS regulation and the ISO 14001 standard.

Since the potential exists for other countries and regions to adopt national EMS laws that are more stringent than the 14001 standard, you might wonder how such laws will affect international trade.

diverging laws create conflicts

It is fair to speculate that diverging national EMS laws may create the very trade conflicts that the ISO 14000 standards series seek to avoid. If countries choose to ignore the ISO 14001 EMS standard and establish their own programs that contain substantially different require- ments, industry likely will be faced with a potential trade problem. Different EMS require- ments in several countries will demand extensive resources to understand and fulfill the individual requirements. Such a resource burden could impede the ability of companies, particularly SMEs and companies from developing countries, to enter certain markets freely.

In response to this potential trade conflict, the TBT agreement contains several provisions meant to encourage countries to use international standards when setting a national law or standard.

One TBT provision specifically speaks to the issue of using international standards, while another provision discusses preferential dispute settlement treatment in disputes involving laws that were in fact based on an international standard.

However, it is critical to note that the TBT agreement does not prohibit or preclude the ability of WTO members to set national laws that are more stringent than international standards. In fact, the agreement provides for an exception to using international standards as a basis for national laws.

Below is a brief discussion of these relevant TBT provisions.

☑ **International standards use encouraged** — The TBT agreement clearly encourages WTO members to use international standards as a basis for national and regional regulations and standards. Specifically, WTO members and standards organizations are encouraged to use relevant international standards if they exist or are nearly complete.

single standard helps trade

The underlying trade concept behind this provision is the notion that international trade will be helped if industry is expected to meet one set of standards — preferably international standards — rather than meeting a series of different regional or national standards.

Although the TBT agreement encourages development and use of international standards to avoid trade conflicts, the agreement does contain an important exception.

In particular, international standards need not be used if their use would be "ineffective or inappropriate" for several reasons, including "an insufficient level of protection." The definitive interpretation of this TBT language has not been clear. However, one interpretation may be that the provision allows countries to adopt national environmental regulations that are more stringent than an international standard when the international standard does not provide a sufficient level of environmental protection for that country.

settlements
favor standards

☑ **Dispute settlement favors international standards** — The TBT agreement contains specific dispute settlement provisions that appear to treat preferentially regulations and standards that are based on international standards. One implication may be that national laws based on international standards are less likely to be challenged successfully under the WTO, as compared to laws that are not based on international standards.

For example, the TBT agreement states that regulations based on a legitimate objective and on relevant international standards "shall be rebuttably presumed not to create an unnecessary obstacle to international trade." Therefore, if a country challenges another member's regulation as a trade barrier, and the regulation in question is based on an international standard, then the burden of proof appears to be on the country bringing the challenge.

In contrast, the TBT agreement is unclear as to which party will have the burden of proof if a challenge is brought against a WTO member's regulation and the regulation is not based on an international standard.

Conclusion

What, then, are the trade implications if a country adopts or maintains a national law that is more environmentally stringent than the ISO 14001 standard?

The answer is likely to lie somewhere in the interpretation of the TBT provisions discussed in this section. The agreement clearly encourages WTO members to use international standards when setting national (environmental) laws and standards. However, one might wonder where the line will be drawn in determining how much of an international standard must be used when setting a national law.

☑ For example, how will the WTO characterize a national law that is substantially based on the ISO 14001 standard but is more stringent in merely two areas (e.g., continual improvement; internal vs. external auditing)?

☑ What type of treatment will that law receive according to the provisions in the TBT agreement?

☑ Will the law be viewed as one that is based, or not based, on an international standard?

These types of questions are not easily answered and are likely to be debated within the context of the WTO's Committee on Trade and the Environment. One side of the debate argues that the WTO agreement should preserve the trade goal that an individual environmental law, such as a stringent EMS law, should not create a barrier to international trade. The other side of the debate argues that the WTO agreement should preserve the environmental objective that a country has a sovereign right to set national environmental protection laws.

9.1.5 Implications of ISO 14001 in Government Procurement

There is growing concern that government procurement contracts will be awarded preferentially to suppliers who are ISO 14001 certified. Delegations representing the interests of developing countries and SMEs argue that this type of situation will create an unfair barrier to international trade.

It appears likely that certification with the ISO 14001 EMS standards may, in fact, become a significant component in government procurement practices in some countries. The interesting question is to what extent ISO 14001 certification will be involved in government procurement and to what degree such a situation will affect international trade.

ISO 14001 certification may play a role in government procurement in one of two ways.

EMS likely government component

First, it is very possible that EMS certification will become another component used by government procurement officials to differentiate and evaluate goods and services — just as they use traditional components such as price, quality, service, etc.

Second, EMS certification may become another tool in evaluating whether a supplier is technically qualified to supply a good or service to a government entity.

In either case, several GATT principles must guide the behavior of government procurement practices (some of the key principles are discussed below). These principles are laid out in the GATT Agreement on Government Procurement.

National Treatment and Non-Discrimination

Perhaps one of the most fundamental principles guiding procurement practices is that of national treatment and non-discrimination. Essentially the GATT indicates that government procurement practices and procedures must treat domestic and foreign suppliers equally. Any favor extended or requirement demanded of a domestic supplier also must be extended and demanded of a foreign supplier.

Notification of Supplier Qualifications

Government procurement officials must publish and notify qualification requirements so that all interested suppliers, both domestic and foreign, have ample opportunity to initiate and complete qualification procedures.

It is unclear whether certification with the ISO 14001 standard can or will become a valid qualification required by government procurement entities.

Conclusion

look at GATT procurement provisions

When considering government procurement's role in international trade, we must look to several GATT principles and provisions that govern government procurement practices.

As identified above, the national treatment provision is defined to prevent government procurement practices from discriminating against foreign suppliers as a means to protect and favor domestic suppliers. The implication of this provision may be that preferential treatment to government suppliers who are ISO 14001 certified might be acceptable as long as the preferential treatment is extended to domestic and foreign suppliers alike.

Similarly, GATT disciplines on publication and notification are designed to make government procurement practices understandable and accessible to suppliers. If ISO 14001 certification evolves into a technical qualification of suppliers in certain government contracts, then the qualification must be published and notified in a timely manner.

9.1.6 Implications of PPM-Based Eco-Labeling / Self-Declaration Programs

Several TC 207 delegations have raised trade concerns regarding eco-labeling or self-declaration programs where products are labeled based on how the product was made — also known as the product's production process method (PPM). As of early 1996, there were more than 25 labeling programs worldwide.

In general, the concern is that PPM-based labeling/declaration programs will favor nationally developed technologies and manufacturing processes. Also, there is concern that these types of programs may establish environmental criteria that are specific to a country's geographic location or societal values.

Consequently, some argue that these labeling programs may place foreign suppliers at a competitive disadvantage, especially small- and medium-sized companies and companies from developing countries. Further, some argue that any PPM labeling is not consistent with GATT. For these reasons, it has been suggested that any reference to PPM-related labeling be omitted from the final ISO 14024 standards on labeling. 📖 (See Part 5, Chapter 1 for more information on labeling.)

PPM issues

To understand the context of the PPM issue, it may be useful to address three questions:

1) Does the TBT agreement allow PPM labeling and self declaration programs?

2) If so, how might PPM labeling/declaration programs create trade problems?

3) What TBT provisions exist that might help to reduce the chances that such programs will create trade barriers?

PPMs in the TBT Agreement

The first question surrounding the PPM issue is critical to address properly. Namely, does the new TBT agreement cover, or allow, PPM labeling? The answer is yes.

In fact, the TBT agreement clearly states that a regulation or a standard may set "product characteristics or their related processes and production methods." To further clarify, the agreement states that a regulation or a standard may deal exclusively with "terminology, symbols, packaging, marking, or labeling requirements as they apply to a product, process, or production method." These provisions clearly allow regulations or standards to be based on related PPM characteristics. What remains unclear is the definitive meaning of the term "related PPMs."

example: dolphin-safe tuna

For example, tuna manufacturers use the term "dolphin safe." This claim refers to the harvesting process of tuna fish in which tuna are caught in a manner resulting in minimal death/harm to dolphins (dolphins swim above certain types of tuna and are killed by tuna fishing nets). Industry argues that a dolphin-safe label does not reflect a PPM characteristic related to the final tuna fish product. In contrast, environmental groups emphatically maintain that the "dolphin-safe" claim is a PPM characteristic related to the harvesting of the tuna product.

PPM terms examined

The WTO's CTE is expected to examine the terms "related PPMs" and "unrelated PPMs" with respect to eco-labeling programs. These terms may be clarified as a result of this work, or as a result of any WTO ruling in a dispute involving a country's PPM labeling program. Any work involving these terms is likely to have a significant impact in determining what types of PPM labeling programs are acceptable from the perspective of the WTO agreement.

It should also be noted that the mere fact that the TBT agreement covers or recognizes PPM labeling does not exempt such programs from meeting numerous TBT and GATT disciplines (e.g., most favored nation (MFN) or national treatment requirement) to ensure that the programs do not create trade barriers. In other words, all PPM labeling/declaration programs are not automatically considered consistent with GATT. Such a determination will depend upon how the programs are developed, adopted, and implemented.

PPM Labeling Programs and Trade

One of the primary trade concerns regarding PPM labeling is that such programs will award labels to companies that use a certain type of manufacturing process or technology that has been developed in the country administering the labeling program.

example: paper company

For instance, consider a self-declaration claim made by the U.S.-based paper company, Marcal. On numerous Marcal paper products (e.g., tissue paper and napkins) the company makes an environmental claim based on how the product was made, namely that the product is "Paper from Paper Not from Trees." This declaration is meant to inform consumers that Marcal's paper products were produced by using recycled paper instead of using virgin pulp from trees. Marcal's manufacturing process may involve costly technology or equipment that SMEs and companies from developing countries may not be able to access or afford.

Another trade concern surrounding PPM labeling/declaration programs is the prospect that such programs will award labels based on environmental issues specific to a country's locale or societal values.

example: animal testing

One example of this situation is a voluntary labeling program administered by the U.S.-based People for the Ethical Treatment of Animals (PETA). Its labeling program grants the use of PETA's "Not Tested on Animals" label. The PETA labeling program seeks to inform consumers that a product was manufactured in a manner that did not include the use of animals to test its safety. While this labeling program may reflect the concern for animal rights in the U.S., the same societal value may not be true in a developing country that might be more concerned with other issues (e.g., hunger, population, etc.).

label transparency

The TBT agreement addresses, to some extent, some of these concerns regarding the potential trade effect of PPM-based labeling programs. In particular, the TBT contains numerous provisions applicable to the transparency of labeling programs as well as provisions regarding mutual recognition and equivalency. These TBT provisions are discussed below and respond to the third question raised earlier.

Relevant TBT Provisions

☑ **Transparency** — The TBT agreement contains numerous provisions designed to ensure that both regulations and standards are prepared, adopted, and implemented in a transparent manner that helps dialogue between interested parties, both domestic and foreign. Below is a brief overview of some transparency provisions relevant to labeling programs.

In general, WTO members and standards organizations are expected to do the following:

* notify trading partners of proposed regulations and standards under development;

* provide copies of the proposed regulation/standard;

* accept comments and take comments into consideration;

* resolve potential trade concerns that have been raised during the comment period; and

* publish the regulation/standard once adopted.

Also, WTO members must establish inquiry points to answer questions regarding regulations and standards under development and those that are published.

If these and other transparency provisions are followed when new labeling programs are under development, perhaps governments and industry bodies from developing countries will have ample opportunity to raise and resolve trade concerns relevant to a labeling program.

In the past, however, government bodies did not sufficiently notify GATT in advance of finalizing a regulation or standard (called "ex-ante notification"). More often, notification to GATT would occur after the regulation/standard was finalized and published (called "ex-post notification"). There are no formal sanctions for countries that do not notify and publish in a timely manner. This shortcoming in the TBT agreement should and may be addressed in future discussions surrounding the TBT agreement.

Additionally, you may note that representatives from developing countries have suggested that special transparency provisions should be considered with respect to labeling programs. One suggestion is for foreign producers and other stakeholders to be invited to participate in developing product criteria used in labeling programs for products supplied largely by developing countries. This suggestion has been raised in forums sponsored by the United Nations Conference on Trade and the Environment (UNCTAD), as well as within forums of the ISO TC 207 standards negotiations.

☑ **Equivalency and Mutual Recognition** — The TBT also contains provisions on equivalency and mutual recognition that may help mitigate potential trade problems caused by PPM-based labeling programs. In general, the agreement encourages members to consider accepting as equivalent the regulations of other countries that fulfill the same objective as their own regulations.

The ISO TC 207 subcommittee on labeling may incorporate these concepts of equivalency and mutual recognition into the ISO standards on labeling. For example, in early 1996 the subcommittee was considering language that suggested that domestic labeling programs recognize the environmental improvement in different countries as "potentially equivalent," as well as develop mutual recognition among label/declaration programs based on equivalency of "procedure, criteria, and objectives."

example:
paper products

To illustrate these concepts, consider two different labeling programs in countries X and Y that award labels to paper products based on several PPM-related criteria.

The labeling program in country X awards a label to paper manufactured in a manner that reduces pollutants into the water, while the program in country Y awards a label to paper manufactured in a manner that reduces pollutants into the air. Each labeling program sets its own criteria based on the environmental conditions and objectives in each country. Reducing water pollution is a primary goal of country X, while reducing air pollution is a primary goal of country Y — and each labeling program reflects these different objectives.

If the concepts of equivalency and mutual recognition are applied to this scenario, then it may be possible for a paper product to be awarded a label in both country X and country Y — even if the product meets the criteria of only one country.

Conclusion

The propensity of PPM programs to affect international trade is not fully known, since many of these programs are emerging. However, as consumers become increasingly sophisticated in their concern for domestic/global environmental issues, their ability to purchase products bearing PPM-based labels preferentially should not be underestimated. Therefore, it is crucial for governments, industry, and environmentalists to examine extensively the issues surrounding PPM labeling programs.

They might begin with a discussion of the meaning and scope of the term "related PPM," and go on to review existing transparency provisions in the TBT agreement. They might consider how to improve the level of compliance with current transparency provisions as well as consider whether additional provisions would be constructive. And finally, they might explore the concepts of equivalency and mutual recognition.

Trade Role of ISO 14024 on Labeling

Many of the issues raised in this section pertaining to PPM-based labeling are likely to be addressed by the WTO's Committee on Trade and the Environment. The CTE's work on this agenda item is expected to continue through 1997.

A relevant question, then, is whether and how the ISO standards on labeling should address the PPM issue. In early 1996, it appeared that the ISO labeling standards might avoid any direct references to PPM-based labeling in the final standards.

labeling trade
problems
mitigated

However, the final labeling standards are likely to contain several important provisions that may help mitigate potential trade problems envisioned or actually engendered by PPM-based labeling programs.

The January 1996 drafts of the ISO labeling standards, particularly ISO 14024, contained draft language speaking to the issues of transparency, non-discrimination, and participation in labeling programs. The standards were expected to promote the concept that labeling programs should be open and accessible to all interested parties, as well as the principle that labeling programs should not discriminate against foreign suppliers. In addition, the standards were likely to include the concept that stakeholders should be involved in various stages of a labeling program, such as in setting product criteria.

If these and other important principles are included in the final labeling standards — and followed by labeling practitioners — perhaps several concerns regarding PPM-based labeling will be addressed and resolved. The standards are expected to be final in 1997. 📖 (See Part 5, Chapter 1 for more information about the labeling standards.)

CHAPTER 2
NAFTA and ISO 14000

by John J. Audley, Assistant Professor, Environmental Policy and Political Economy
Purdue University

9.2.1 Overview

conformance is voluntary

Most of the debate on the intersection of trade and environmental policies arising out of NAFTA has been related to whether NAFTA would exacerbate environmental degradation in Mexico by attracting U.S. and other firms to take advantage of weaker environmental enforcement.

weaker enforcement

Another important issue in the NAFTA environmental debate concerns whether harmonizing environmental requirements promoted by NAFTA would tend to force down higher Canadian and U.S. environmental standards.

Conflicts centering on the environmental consequences of non-tariff trade barriers (NTBs) are now beginning to shift away from trade negotiations and onto the less glamorous but equally important area of industry standards and certification. This chapter explores the relationship between NTBs and ISO 14001 within the framework of NAFTA's environmental provisions.

Environmental NTBs occur when governments use domestic policies that indirectly create obstacles to trade between countries. Although not as obvious as quantitative trade restrictions, NTBs such as procurement policies or product standards often are equally trade-distorting because they increase the price of an imported product or actually prohibit it from sale.

example: metal in skis

To illustrate, assume that a country issues a product standard calling for a specific kind of metal for use in manufacturing snow skis because of the unique characteristics of snow peculiar to that country. If foreign ski manufacturers don't normally use this kind of metal (but domestic producers do), then the product standard has the effect of creating a monopoly market for domestic ski producers. It is an "illegal" trade barrier if it cannot be scientifically shown that "local" snow has such unique characteristics.

Recent studies have shown that the use of NTBs has generally risen in the past two decades, a fact prompting trade negotiators to try and restrict government use of this kind of policy. Multilateral rules that impose constraints on governments' use of NTBs are generally found in trade agreements such as NAFTA or GATT. 📖 (See Part 9, Chapter 1 for a discussion of

GATT.) The assumption of both trade agreements is that NTBs are a violation of trade rules because they distort trade patterns and often provide unfair advantages to domestic producers.

Under certain circumstances, parties to GATT or NAFTA can use NTBs, provided they abide by internationally accepted standards, or they can produce adequate scientific evidence to support their restrictive claim.

NAFTA language is designed to restrict governments from legislating future trade-distorting policies. Leading trade experts have given this language high marks because it creates specific criteria for evaluating product and food safety standards, improves the level of communication between parties when standards are created, and creates multilateral committees to harmonize these standards.

The nature of NTBs is important to efforts to create international environmental standards because NTBs and the certification process behind ISO 14001 share some key characteristics. Both NTBs and ISO 14001 guidelines involve establishing and implementing environmental product or process standards. A product standard specifies certain qualities of a finished product (tensile strength, for example), while process standards focus on the way a product is made.

For example, as illustrated in the previous section, laws prohibiting the presence of certain levels of metals (such as mercury) in fish are examples of product standards because they address the qualities of the final product. Portions of the United States Marine Mammal Protection Act (MMPA) that restrict the number of incidental dolphin deaths occurring while catching tuna is a process standard because it affects the way in which tuna is caught.

If the MMPA restrictions are considered "GATT-inconsistent," will the same thing happen to ISO 14001?

The answer to this question is, "It depends." In the situation just described, a GATT panel ruled that MMPA *is* inconsistent with trade rules because it involves unjustifiable process standards imposed by a government. But steps taken by a private ISO 14001 certified organization to reduce incidental dolphin kills would probably not be a violation.

standards can have NTB role

However, private organizations acting in their own self-interest in ways that indirectly restrict trade flows for environmental reasons are not entirely free from NTB implications.

Areas of Conflict

Generally speaking, the greater the linkages between a national government and ISO 14001, either through the certification process or through the use of standards as part of a government's own policies and regulations, the greater the potential for conflict between ISO 14001 and NTB restrictions in NAFTA.

two conflict areas

There are two possible instances where the potential for conflict arises, and these are:

1) The potential for conflict increases when national governments use ISO 14001 as a vehicle to extend the effectiveness of their own regulatory programs, or as part of their own procurement practices.

2) Conflict between ISO 14001 and NAFTA is likely to occur in the area of product labeling. Environmental labeling certification inherently recognizes a good or service's

environmental product and process qualities. If specific product qualities or production processes become part of the criteria for ISO 14000 certified labels, the standardization risks challenges from countries that do not share the same policies, unless the standard reflects internationally recognized principles.

Below, we will highlight the potential conflicts between government policies and ISO 14001, and their implication in trade. We'll also take a look at labeling certification and NTB, exploring the implications created by this potential conflict.

If NAFTA sanctions threaten ISO standards because the standards are tied to government action, businesses will tend to distance themselves from working with governments to focus market mechanisms on environmental problems, and some businesses might externalize environmental costs with little concern for consequences. This would be unfortunate because governments play important roles establishing and enforcing the rules governing both trade and the environment.

However, it makes sense to anticipate collaboration between industries and governments as they look for ways to reduce the costs of compliance with, and the enforcement of, national environmental laws.

collaboration increasing This is happening in numerous areas: governments establish and enforce performance standards, environmental regulations, and other "guidelines" that influence business behavior. Private organizations need governing institutions to establish and enforce trade rules and protect property rights. Governments increasingly seek ways to achieve national environmental objectives in more economically efficient ways that are less intrusive to the market.

By the same token, as these collaborative efforts increase, so does the risk of a violation of trade and NTBs.

9.2.2 When Do Voluntary Actions Become NTBs?

ISO 14001 certification requires two things:

1) You must establish and maintain an EMS consistent with ISO 14001 guidelines.

2) You must be able to prove your organization's conformance with these guidelines before it can become certified.

The voluntary nature of adopting and maintaining ISO 14001 guidelines is critical to understanding its potential as a non-tariff barrier to trade. Although an ISO 14001-certified EMS must contain a commitment to compliance with applicable laws and regulations, your organization could receive ISO 14001 certification and still not be in compliance with environmental legal requirements. This is because the ISO 14001 certification process audits the underlying EMS, not your legal compliance.

You are only obliged to commit to compliance and to continual improvement of your EMS. Up to this point, actions taken by your organization to earn certification cannot be construed as an NTB, because yours is a private organization that cannot be party to international trade agreement. The actions are voluntarily implemented and are not in response to particular mandates by national governments.

But voluntary actions taken by private organizations can and do have tremendous environmental implications on trade and NTBs. For example, when a manufacturer requires an EMS from its suppliers, that decision may indeed have tremendous trade implications

To understand where the lines of NTB demarcation are drawn, the first issue to explore is the interaction among private organizations, governments, and ISO 14000 standards.

Certification and NTBs

An important point of interaction between ISO 14000 standards and national environmental standards involves the certification process. To be recognized as ISO 14001 certified, your organization must submit to an audit and certification by a recognized certification body. In turn, certification bodies must be accredited by an accreditation body. 📖 (See Part 6, Chapter 5 for more information on the certification process.)

In many countries, such as the U.K., Germany, and France, the national government is involved to a greater or lesser extent in accrediting certification bodies because the accreditation body is a government agency. In most developing countries the national government acts as the certifying agency.[1]

For example, in the United Kingdom, the British government recognizes the United Kingdom Accreditation Service (UKAS) and charges it with auditing organizations seeking ISO 9000 and ISO 14001 certification.

In the United States, the Registrar Accreditation Board (RAB) and the American National Standards Institute (ANSI) are private-sector accreditation bodies. While U.S. Environmental Protection Agency officials are involved unofficially in providing input into the process, RAB and ANSI are not "recognized" by the U.S. government as official bodies.

ISO-government links

ISO member organizations are standards bodies that have varying official government links. The different relationships between certifying organizations and national governments underscore the possibility that national environmental policies and ISO 14001 certification may overlap. For example, ISO recognizes that:

1) to motivate organizations to adopt the standards, the standards must somehow help them comply with applicable environmental laws. ISO 14001 does not test an organization's compliance with environmental regulations, but it does test underlying compliance management systems and the organization's commitment to compliance.

2) each country establishes its own procedure for ISO standard certification, which increase the likelihood that an EMS satisfies national environmental standards.

NAFTA recognizes that its signatories use nongovernmental organizations (NGOs) to set and maintain standards. While it recognizes that such relationships are necessary, it assumes that any independent organization working on behalf of a party to NAFTA does so in a manner consistent with national laws and regulations.

Parties are asked to rely on relevant international standards, guidelines, or recommendations when setting standards. However, in the absence of international standards, or when governments take it upon themselves to set different (and presumably higher) standards than those recognized by other nations, national environmental standards may not uniformly address environmental issues.

unique
national
standards

A potential conflict arises if the unique characteristics of national standards become part of the criteria used to certify organizations. If the accrediting body is a governmental agency, or a private organization empowered by the government to certify organizations, there may be an increased likelihood that the certification criteria may reflect national environmental standards as opposed to uniform environmental standards.

stricter national
criteria

On the other hand, if the certifying agency uses an international environmental standard such as ISO 14001 as a base and then adds stricter national environmental criteria on top of the international standard for entities operating in that nation's jurisdiction, the additional stricter national environmental criteria would not constitute an NTB.

A standard might be construed as an NTB only to the extent that it is made applicable to products manufactured by entities operating outside that country. This approach can be extended to a regional trade area such as NAFTA without creating an NTB.

Thus, Canada, Mexico, and the United States might agree to use ISO 14001 plus certain additional, stricter environmental criteria uniformly applied to entities operating in the NAFTA market as the basis for a voluntary NAFTA environmental management system standard aimed at "upward harmonization" of environmental management system performance within the NAFTA market. So long as the stricter environmental criteria are not applied to entities operating outside the NAFTA market that are seeking to sell their products in the NAFTA market, the additional stricter environmental criteria would not pose NTB issues.

At this stage there is no evidence to evaluate the potential relationship between national standards and ISO 14001. However, a number of possible scenarios bear exploration.

Process Standards and NTBs

example:
pesticides

A particularly thorny situation involves process standards. Like other trade agreements, NAFTA focuses on circumstances when product-related NTBs conflict with trade rules. Importing fruit with pesticide residue in violation of product standards for human health and safety is acceptable under NAFTA, provided the scientific evidence offered in defense of the residue standard meets a battery of challenges.

However, if the pesticide standard addresses the use of pesticides, even when there is no detectable residue, then the standard is "process-oriented" — that is, it relates to the way in which a product is made rather than the qualities of the final product itself.

product/
process
dilemma

NAFTA Technical Barriers and Sanitary and Phytosanitary Chapters recognize the legitimate right of NAFTA parties to restrict market access for process-related reasons better than most trade agreements do, but it does not resolve the "product/process" dilemma created by the trade and environment debate.

Returning to the pesticide example, if ISO 14001 certification by U.S.-accredited bodies required private organizations to consider systematically the implications of using pesticides that contaminate soil or groundwater, and if those pesticides do not leave any measurable residue on the fruit scientifically shown to be harmful to human health, then the certification itself could be in violation of NTB rules.

This kind of situation is unlikely, especially during a period when governments increasingly rely on voluntary guidelines in their environmental programs.

NO$_x$ emissions

A good example is provided in U.S. regulations for clean air or water. To achieve 1990 Clean Air standards to reduce nitrogen oxide by 30 to 50 percent, U.S. Environmental Protection Agency regulations authorized by the Clinton Administration now require certain coal-burning technologies. The program does not set specific standards but instead allows companies to comply with applicable NOx emission standards by purchasing pollution allowances from other companies whose NOx releases are lower than allowable limits.

Since the ISO 14001 standard in this context would require these companies to make continual improvements to their ISO 14001 certified environmental management systems (and indirectly, to a continual improvement of their NO$_x$ release performance), EPA's voluntary emissions trading program probably would not be construed as an NTB.

As of early 1996, EPA was promoting at least 16 such voluntary programs designed to encourage business and industry to use market forces to reduce their negative impact on the environment. 📖 (See Part 8, Chapter 2 for more information on these programs.) But because there is no direct linkage between organization compliance with national laws and ISO 14001 certification, will market forces be adequate to compel industries to high standards for environmental quality when doing so may reduce profits? The history of voluntary industry standards suggests that market forces will not have this effect unless governments are able to compel industries to internalize the costs of higher environmental quality.

Understanding this, all the EPA's voluntary programs use incentives to encourage industries to seek ways to reduce the level of pollution voluntarily. As long as adopting these measures does not become a requirement for ISO 14001 certification in the United States, even though they may have NTB implications, it is difficult to make the case that they violate NAFTA trade rules.

E.U. may pose conflict

However, to the extent that EPA was to become involved in the ISO 14001 certification/ registration process (e.g., by issuing ISO 14001 certifications or by inspecting ISO 14001 certified facilities for adherence to ISO 14001), there is a potential for the ISO 14001 certification/registration process in the United States to be construed as an NTB. This latter scenario is less realistic as an issue in the U.S., where EPA is quite unlikely to be involved in ISO 14001 certification. Within the European Union, however, the closer relationship between governments and EMS certification bodies makes this a more plausible NTB issue.

Government Procurement and NTBs

discrimination

Another possible conflict between ISO 14001 and NTB restrictions occurs when governments begin to require ISO 14001 certification from their own suppliers. NAFTA parties may not establish government procurement policies that either directly or indirectly discriminate between private suppliers within the NAFTA countries. However, procurement policies that require ISO 14001 certification may be in conflict with NTB rules if:

- governments seek their own environmental goals through purchasing practices; and
- those goals are not strictly based upon international environmental guidelines.

As with the example involving Clean Air requirements, the scenario just described would not be a likely result because the U.S. government is not the formal accrediting body. However, if a government is the formal accrediting body, then the likelihood of conflict again increases, because it is more difficult to differentiate between the particular regulatory policies of a government and the standards by which they interpret the ISO 14001 guidelines.

In each situation, the most important question is whether or not certifying bodies have any relationship with NAFTA signatories.

As NAFTA parties determine the nature of the certification process for ISO 14001, they would be wise to consider two things:

1) The implications for NTB conflicts between ISO 14001 and trade rules increase when linkages between certification guidelines and the unique characteristics of national environmental policies are strong.

2) The implication for linkages between national standards and certification guidelines are enhanced when governmental agencies or private organizations directly authorized by governments act as certifying agents.

However, as governments increasingly rely upon broad guidelines or voluntary standards to encourage industry compliance with national environmental regulations, the likelihood for conflicts continues to diminish.

9.2.3 Labeling As an NTB

Labeling is perhaps the clearest example of an ISO 14000 standard's potential for violating NTB restrictions. The very nature of any labeling/declaration scheme focuses attention on the environmental qualities of a given product, be they associated with the use or consumption of the product or its production.

The principles for environmental labeling outlined by ISO Technical Committee 207 require that "the development of environmental labels/declarations should, wherever appropriate, take into consideration the life cycle of the product or service," a clear reference to both product and process standards that create non-tariff barriers.

harnessing market forces

Most labeling schemes aim at identifying the full environmental implications of a product because they try to harness market forces to put pressure on manufacturers to be more environmentally sensitive during all phases of a product's life cycle. The dilemma regarding labeling occurs because no international standard for labeling exists, and the criteria used by the numerous labeling regimes are normally shaped by the unique environmental objectives of a given country, region, or trading area.

The draft language of ISO 14020 *Environmental Labeling — General Principles* goes to great lengths to distance labeling certification from imposing negative effects on trade. Draft principle 7 specifically states that "Procedures and criteria for environmental labels/ declarations shall not create unfair trade restrictions, nor discriminate in the treatment of domestic and foreign products and services." Its goal instead is to provide accurate, verifiably relevant, and non-deceptive information for consumers to help make informed choices.

terms and
definitions

To improve accuracy and reduce deception, ISO 14020 and ISO 14021 guidelines provide detailed definitions of all terms relevant to labeling. For example, the term "recycled content" has a universal meaning for all ISO 14020 and ISO 14021 *Environmental Labels and Declarations — Self-Declaration Environmental Claims — Terms and Definitions* uses as do the terms "reusable/refillable," "designed for disassembly," and "compostable." In all, 16 definitions of terms related to environmental labeling are provided.

Specifying the meaning of these terms is an important step toward establishing uniform standards for environmental labeling. Whether a product uses "recycled-content paper" or is "reusable/refillable" or "recyclable" now has meaning outside the context of a specific labeling scheme. Universal terms describing a product's inherent qualities enable parties to trade agreements to discriminate between products on scientific evidence.

Terms such as these do not directly address issues involving process issues, however. It seems clear that the standards' negotiators were aware of the potential conflict surrounding process issues as they tried to avoid any references to specific process measures in the selection of their terms.

As was discussed in the pesticide example, NAFTA prohibits parties from using NTBs that restrict market access for product-related reasons. If ISO labeling guidelines allow organizations to make claims regarding the full range of product life-cycle issues, and if the guidelines become de facto government policy in some countries without the accompanying international environmental agreement, then the label certification risks violation of NTB rules.

Differences of opinion regarding labeling schemes and the absence of international norms make ISO 14020 and ISO 14021 controversial documents as they relate to NTBs. Until international standards for labeling exist, efforts by standards-setting bodies to use environmental labeling programs to harness market forces and compel industries to act in an environmentally sensitive fashion will continue to meet international resistance from countries whose environmental standards are not as fully developed, or because of their different environmental priorities.

9.2.4 Implications of ISO 14000 Standards and NTBs

The implications of the relationship between ISO 14000 standards and NTBs suggest two things.

conflicts:
greater links
with
government

First, a great deal of care should be given when linkages between parties to trade agreements and ISO certification are established. The greater the linkages, the greater the likelihood for conflicts arising from efforts to constrain governments from employing environmental NTBs as artificial barriers to trade.

A conflict may arise when government efforts seek to expand environmental protection while working with private organizations to reduce the regulatory effects on economic activity. Government programs increasingly rely on voluntary programs (such as the Green Light program) to achieve environmental objectives, in part because traditional policy tools (such as performance mandates) may be illegal NTBs. This constraint may hinder collaborative efforts between domestic industries and governments from developing creative solutions to environmental problems, because trade policies may restrict them from choosing anything that may appear to be an NTB.

The second implication is that the ISO labeling guidelines should continue to be based on an international consensus effort (including both trade and environmental policy) if they are to withstand trade law scrutiny.

Incentives Are Necessary

collaborate anyway

Having said this, private parties or governments seeking to make use of ISO 14000 standards would be unwise to base a course of action on these implications. Governments play an important part in the efforts to harness market forces for environmental goals in two ways.

procurement incentives

First, through their own purchasing practices they set an example for other private organizations to follow. Purchasing policies that require recycled content papers or energy-saving light bulbs or ask suppliers to consider the environmental implications of their waste streams encourage suppliers to think environmentally to capture portions of the very large government market. Procurement policies and even environmental regulations themselves act as incentives for business entrepreneurs to think of environmental waste in economic terms.

minimizing litigation risks

Second, while de-coupling the ISO 14000 series from governmental interests reduces the risk of NTB violation, it also decreases the incentive for organizations to use ISO 14000 standards to internalize environmental costs. Companies are not likely to devote resources to ever-better environmental performance if doing so does not minimize litigation risks associated with regulatory noncompliance offers — even if certification increases the potential for capturing consumer demand for environmentally sensitive products.

There are many opportunities for the NAFTA parties to promote ISO 14001 within the NAFTA market without creating NTB issues. Consistent with NAFTA's provisions for "upward harmonization" of environmental standards, the NAFTA parties can use the environmental regulatory incentives to promote voluntary ISO 14001 certification by companies operating in the NAFTA market. The NAFTA signatories also can couple certification with additional environmental performance criteria that are applicable only to companies operating within NAFTA countries, but not to non-NAFTA companies selling products in the NAFTA market.

CHAPTER 3
Developed Nations and ISO 14000

by Turner T. Smith, Jr. Esq., Hunton & Williams

9.3.1 Overview

Industries and governments from developed nations have expressed several concerns about the trade implications of the ISO 14000 series of standards. Their concerns are different from those of developing nations and depend upon whether the ISO 14001 EMS or the ISO 14020 and ISO 14021 environmental product labeling standards are involved. The latter two have more substantive product-oriented criteria that cause special alarm.

labeling and
EMS concerns

Among their concerns with ISO 14001 is how these standards are likely to be used in the future:

☑ Will the ISO 14001 standards remain voluntary, both de facto in the global marketplace and de jure in various jurisdictions?

☑ To the extent that they become a regulatory or marketplace necessity, will self-declaration rather than certification remain a viable option?

☑ To what extent will the E.U.'s Environmental Management and Audit Scheme (EMAS) regulation be different from ISO 14001? How will any gaps be bridged? How will EMAS be adopted by governments or incorporated by the marketplace outside the E.U.?

☑ What role will BS 7750 play in the picture, given that it has become an auditable EMS standard and is more like EMAS than ISO 14001?

The governments of developed nations and their industries do not all have the same perspective. For example, the U.S. on one hand and E.U. member countries on the other have widely different views. E.U. members differ among themselves. Other developed nations, such as Japan, Canada, or Australia, also may have both differing interests and different views from those of either the U.S. or the E.U.

multiple
markets,
jurisdictions

At the same time, many companies from developed countries have similar interests without regard to their nationality, at least when operating outside their home jurisdictions. U.S. multinational companies, for example, operate in effect as local companies when they manufacture and sell in Europe, and vice versa with European multinationals. Such multinationals are subject simultaneously to the requirements of multiple markets and multiple jurisdictions. Generally, their nationality is only relevant when operating in their home market and jurisdiction, where some element of favoritism is likely.

SMEs

The concept of a company's nationality may be more relevant when speaking about a small or medium-sized local company, either competing with foreign companies in its home market or jurisdiction, or attempting to market or manufacture elsewhere. Even here, many of the most important consequences of ISO 14001 are due to such a company's small size and lack of international sophistication, not its nationality per se.

United States vs. European Union Members

The U.S. and the E.U. countries, chief protagonists in the development of ISO 14001, have views shaped mainly by the history of U.S. environmental auditing and the E.U.'s EMAS regulation — as well as by the regulatory and litigation context in both locations. 📖 (See Part 9, Chapter 5 for more information on EMAS and 📖Part 6 for more information on auditing.)

environmental
auditing

Environmental auditing had its origins in the U.S. and developed into an internal company management tool, designed primarily to ensure legal compliance to avoid the severe U.S. sanctions for noncompliance. Auditing also was strongly influenced by the need for caution and confidentiality in creating written records that could be used during discovery in civil or criminal litigation in the U.S.

U.S. avoids
top-heaviness

Thus, U.S. companies have tried to avoid a top-heavy, paperwork-intensive management system standard that would undermine the effective, frequently decentralized, performance-based environmental management systems already in place at most major U.S. companies. Further, they have been concerned about such matters as:

1) avoiding the creation of new substantive standards (and possible associated standards of care or newly assumed duties to others); and

2) maintaining confidentiality of management and audit records.

E.U. promotes performance

The E.U., on the other hand, faced with varying and frequently inadequate implementation and enforcement of E.U. environmental law by member states, turned in the late 1980s to promoting "voluntary" use by European industry of environmental auditing. Initially it looked to the U.S. experience for guidance.

U.S.-style compliance auditing went through a transformation in Europe, however, and the EMAS regulation became very different from its original version. That regulation evolved into, in effect, a government regulatory tool with considerable substantive content. The content is designed to achieve environmental improvement by bypassing ineffective implementation by member states' environmental regulatory bureaucracies. Its independently verified public environmental statements were designed to spur those bureaucracies to more effective implementation of already existing E.U. environmental laws, once environmental problems were highlighted and disclosed. Its context anticipates its use in a much more relaxed and forgiving regulatory and litigatory context than prevails in the U.S.

European Union

E.U. member states reacted in two predictable ways. Some, like The Netherlands (source of the EMAS focus on documented compliance with environmental management systems, which were modeled on those developed by Dutch consultants), moved to reshape EMAS to their national mold as it went through the E.U. legislative process. Other states, like the U.K., undertook immediate development of their own national environmental standards to preempt EMAS and the ISO process, or at least to occupy the field first.

It was clear from the time of its adoption that the EMAS regulation needed further elaboration to be effectively implemented both by the private sector and by governments — a task that the European commission assigned to the European standards organization, Comité Européen de Normalisation (CEN). 📖 (See Part 9, Chapter 5 for more information on E.U. structure.)

When the ISO environmental series began to take shape, CEN agreed to defer to the ISO process, and the E.U. and European companies took an early leading role in drafting ISO 14001 using the EMAS model. Their chief objective was to ensure that qualifying under ISO 14001 would constitute qualifying under EMAS.

E.U. motive: export EMAS

An unspoken but likely further E.U. objective from the outset has been to use the ISO standards as vehicles to export EMAS worldwide, to the advantage of European manufacturing companies, products, and consulting firms. While ISO 14001 has now been written so that it does not incorporate all of the EMAS requirements, the ease with which other countries can adopt the additional EMAS provisions likely to be incorporated in a CEN supplement or an implementing E.U. decision may result in their having accomplished this objective as well in the long run.

E.U. motive: regulatory tool

Thus, EMAS from the outset has been regarded by the E.U. Commission as a regulatory tool — albeit an indirect one, and one that is in theory voluntary (although indications are that it clearly will be made mandatory if it is not voluntarily adopted by industry).

Because some member states maneuvered for competitive advantage as the regulation was developed, others and the E.U. Commission have had a keen interest in "harmonizing" E.U. environmental management standards (that is, developing one E.U.-level management standard that would replace all national standards).

Finally, because CEN decided to work through ISO, the Europeans have seen the international standards process as a vehicle for accomplishing their various intra-Europe objectives, as well as probably for projecting their own European environmental management standards onto the world stage, to the competitive advantage of their own companies.

Early in the ISO 14000 development process, the U.S. government and U.S. industry had already become worried about the possible impact of the EMAS rule as a trade barrier for non-European firms when doing business in Europe. With the development of an ISO standard, their chief objective was to avoid having EMAS requirements imported into the U.S. regulatory and litigation context through the ISO process. The final ISO 14001 standards reflect the resulting U.S./European debate, which dominated their development.

9.3.2 Multinational Company Concerns

Multinational companies will approach ISO 14001 from a strategic perspective. Their analysis of when, where, and how to participate will be driven by their analysis of likely competitive advantages and disadvantages. While certain core concerns are outlined below, companies of different nationalities, in different industries, and with differing markets, market presence, types of environmental management systems, and levels of environmental performance will react differently. There is unlikely to be lock-step acceptance or rejection.

Further, companies' strategic analyses will be affected by the lack of satisfactory remedies should adverse trade impacts develop. As discussed earlier in Part 9, Chapter 1, formal trade sanctions normally can be applied only against government or quasi-government sponsored or mandated acts, and even then it is the government that must take up the cudgels.

anti-
competition
laws

Informal but amorphous remedies such as those available through the voluntary standards process are neither straightforward nor certain. Private remedies should exist, in theory, under national laws governing market competition among private-sector organizations. But real relief will depend on the strength of the relevant anti-competition laws, and in many cases on the extent of the extraterritorial reach of the stronger laws.

Thus, multinational companies primarily will look to their own strategic foresight and to self-help for dealing with the types of concerns outlined below and with other trade barriers or impacts arising from ISO 14001 or other elements of the ISO 14000 series.

Multiple Standards, Multiple Approvals

proliferation of
standards

multiple
certification
requirements

Perhaps the most important concern multinational companies of any nationality have is avoiding a proliferation of different standards, particularly if they become mandatory de facto or de jure. Likewise, they would like to avoid multiple certification requirements in various national jurisdictions, even if identical standards are involved. 📖 (See Part 7, Chapter 2, Section 4 for more information on conformity assessment and mutual recognition of certifications.)

organization

Both issues are important, because the ISO 14001 standards, as written, cut across borders. They apply on their face to all "activities, products, and services" of an "organization," with no mention whatsoever of national boundaries. The scope of the "organization" to be covered is up to the company implementing the standards. It is easy to foresee, however, that the process of external conformity assessment, whether de facto in the marketplace or de jure by governments, may influence and dictate the implementing company's choice. The key point is that the "organization" selected as the ISO unit (or required as a practical or legal matter by the market, procurement policy, or regulation) may extend across national borders. To the extent that it does, logically the activities, products, and services covered do so as well.

In short, ISO 14001 appears by its terms not to be limited to one national jurisdiction. Thus it potentially calls for extraterritorial application as necessary to reach all "activities, products, and services," and by each jurisdiction engaging in conformity assessment.

Environmental product labeling standards, of course, also would have transboundary implications, since presumably they would apply to all products sold within the implementing jurisdiction, no matter where they were produced. The key concern here would be whether product PPM requirements were stated in eco-label criteria and applied to imported products.

multiple standards

As for the first concern — multiple standards — it is already clear that the E.U. will go its own way with EMAS and eco-label requirements, and may end up with multiple versions of both within the E.U. As for the second — multiple approvals — it remains to be seen what progress will be made in the area of reciprocity in conformity assessment.

Lower Standards for Interpretations, Applications

A second important multinational company concern, felt by companies that must meet stringent national regulatory requirements in their home jurisdictions, is that companies from countries with less-well-implemented or -enforced regulatory systems (and with lower environmental performance records) will gain unwarranted credibility in the marketplace by adoption of the largely non-substantive ISO 14001 standards.

A related concern is that the ISO 14001 requirements will be read more literally and will be more stringently applied in some countries than in others. This is a particular concern for U.S. companies vis-à-vis European ones.

Discoverability

A third concern, although not really a trade issue, is that companies of any nationality operating in the U.S. will want to ensure that ISO 14001 compliance (particularly if the EMAS supplement is involved) does not lead to obligations or production of records reachable by the U.S. legal process of discovery (i.e., including those outside the U.S.), which could cause adverse liability consequences in U.S. courts.

Onerous Documentation

A fourth concern is the impact of ISO 14001's documentation requirements. Adoption of this standard's paperwork structure is costly — particularly for a smaller company, or one that otherwise does not have the same experience in implementing such a system as do competitors. In fact, such a system may be counterproductive where a company already has a streamlined, highly decentralized "empowerment"-based environmental management system. 📖 (See Part 3, Chapter 4 for more information on documentation.)

Indeed, it is now clear that it is much easier and less costly for a company that already has undertaken the paperwork burden of the ISO 9000 quality management system standards to comply with the ISO 14000 series, than it is for those that have not. This alone may give a competitive advantage to European companies generally vis-à-vis U.S. companies, since they have tended to sign on to the ISO 9000 series in larger numbers than their U.S. counterparts. These problems will be aggravated for U.S., Japanese, Canadian, Australian and other companies doing business in Europe because of the likely effect of the EMAS add-on.

Favoritism

Fifth, to the extent that any form of certification is involved, conducted by a governmental body or by persons appointed, certified, or approved by the government, there is a real possibility for "home cooking" — a disguised intent to favor local companies over their foreign competitors. It remains to be seen whether reciprocity provisions will evolve to undermine such effects.

Trade Issues

Finally, to the extent that one country requires ISO 14001 of manufacturing facilities or products manufactured in another, questions of GATT compatibility arise. 📖 (See Part 9, Chapter 1 for more information on GATT.) Issues of differing interpretations of the ISO standards also may surface. To the extent that the "other country" is the U.S., the special U.S. concerns outlined above will arise, particularly if the version of the ISO standards so applied involves the EMAS add-on provisions.

To the extent that the other country is a third-world country, any requirement for use of ISO 14001 standards there, especially if the EMAS add-ons were required, could result in competitive disadvantages in those countries for the companies concerned, particularly vis-à-vis local competitors.

9.3.3 E.U. Company Concerns — EMAS

Concerns about ISO 14000 among developed nations in Europe are driven by the fact that they likely will have to comply with the more extensive EMAS regulations. Thus, their first concern is to ensure that they do not need to have two separate showings of conformance. In early 1996 it was clear that the ISO standards would not be the functional equivalent of EMAS in every way, and an annex to the ISO standards (or a CEN supplement) was being discussed that would contain the additional provisions for full compliance with EMAS.

EMAS annex   While Europeans wanted this annex to be "normative," so that it would be an obligatory part of the standard, it was likely only to be made "informative" at the ISO level. An E.U. decision would be needed to make conformance to this "informative" section effective for showing EMAS compliance in E.U. countries.

The E.U.'s largest environmental lobby group, the European Environmental Bureau (EEB), urged European governments to vote against ISO 14001, arguing that it is not sufficiently strict. Further, EEB wanted the planned "bridging document" covering differences between ISO 14001 and EMAS to be adopted as a formal European standard, and not simply as a nonbinding guidance document.

In the interim, the British, Spanish, and Irish environmental management system standards have been formally recognized by the European Commission as fulfilling corresponding requirements (but not all) of the E.U.'s EMAS regulation. Formal recognition means that companies wanting to register under EMAS may use these national standards as a starting point. National standards will have to be withdrawn, however, once the European version of the draft international management standard, ISO 14001, takes effect.

All three national standards are deemed to correspond to parts of EMAS's requirements relating to participation in the scheme (Article 3 of EMAS); environmental policies, programs, and management systems (Annex I); and environmental auditing (Annex II). The British and Spanish standards also are deemed to correspond to part of EMAS's auditing and validation requirements (Article 4).

100 sites registered

In a press statement announcing recognition of the standards, the Commission said that more than 100 industrial sites and over 41 verifiers had been registered under EMAS as of February 2, 1996. Sites had been registered in nine countries — Belgium, Ireland, Britain, Germany, Denmark, The Netherlands, France, Sweden, and Norway (although Norway is not an E.U. member state, it is subject to E.U. law through European Economic Area Agreement). The registration tallies per state were: Germany, 84; U.K., 7; France, 3; Denmark, 3; The Netherlands, 2; Belgium, 2; Ireland, 1; Sweden, 1; Norway, 1. "It is anticipated that the numbers will grow rapidly over the coming months now that verifiers are in place," the Commission said.

harmonization

The E.U. and most E.U. companies (but not necessarily all of the E.U.'s member states) will be driven by a desire to "harmonize" E.U. law — that is, to make EMAS (and ISO 14001 and the EMAS Annex) standard in Europe and to replace the various national standards that have grown up over the years. Some British or other companies that have already qualified under BS 7750, or other national environmental management standards, also will want to see those standards made acceptable for EMAS compliance purposes.

Finally, it is noteworthy that Scandinavian companies have been early to comply with various of the developing environmental management standards, possibly as a method of becoming better known in the increasingly "green" European markets into which they are venturing.

9.3.4 Small and Medium-Sized Company Concerns

Small or medium-sized U.S. companies (SMEs) have special problems with the ISO 14001 standards because of the paperwork and administrative superstructure requirements. The drafters have attempted to avoid or at least minimize this problem, and it is not unique to U.S. companies. However, the standard could end up introducing a systemic market- or government-driven bias against small or medium-sized companies, a bias that would be aggravated to the extent that such companies attempted to operate internationally.

The trade-off is that having multiple, differing national standards could be even worse. 📖 (See Part 3, Chapter 3 for more information on SMEs.)

9.3.5 United Kingdom Company Concerns

As for some individual country perspectives, the U.K. has sought mainly to develop and implement a competing standard, BS 7750, which it did speedily. By so doing, it sought to achieve two main ends — first, to ensure that a non-substantive, systems-only template was laid down early, and second, to ensure a head start for its environmental consultants and companies. As noted above, the British have succeeded in having the BS 7750 standards recognized as fulfilling the requirements of some portions of EMAS. Thus, some of the same concerns companies have with use and acceptance of EMAS among governments and organizations may also arise with BS 7750.

9.3.6 German Company Concerns

The Germans have had other objectives. A constant theme of German environmental policy at the E.U. level on all matters is to require industry elsewhere in Europe to incur the same costs as their own (and, incidentally, to have to purchase the sophisticated control technologies that German industry has had to develop).

compliance

They have thus argued for more substantive and compliance-oriented audit provisions, concerned (like the U.S.) that the relatively poorer currency of management standards alone would devalue the costly efforts of their own industry in meeting the stringent substantive environmental standards in Germany.

Further, to the extent that even governments will not see the distinction between the hard work of ensuring actual effective environmental regulation and the less taxing method (and in some cases only the useful public facade) of promoting good corporate environmental management, the Germans may be concerned that, again, the coin of lesser value will drive out that of better value, and the market for their sophisticated control technologies will suffer. The Germans are now developing their own national good management practices standards system, albeit belatedly, to supplement their comprehensive technical standards.

9.3.7 French Company Concerns

The French have a habit of standing back and letting others pay the price of initial experience, and then developing centralized, bureaucracy-driven programs. They are developing their own management standards, Association Française de Normalization (AFNOR)x30-200. While they have not played the same leading role in the debates as the U.S., the U.K., and Germany have done, French companies have the same concerns other E.U. companies do with ISO 14001.

9.3.8 Will ISO 14001 Remain a Voluntary, Self-Declaration Standard?

It seems unlikely that compliance with ISO 14001 will remain voluntary in the long run, and to the extent that it does not, self-declaration is likely to lose out to a requirement for certification.

Flanders, Belgium has adopted a decree (1) requiring, as of January 4, 1996, certain substantial "Class 1" industrial facilities to designate an "environmental coordinator," and (2) authorizing the government to require environmental audits and reporting for particular facilities.

Environmental coordinators, as in Germany, will be required to oversee monitoring and compliance, and to supervise preparation of waste reports and registers. They will also submit opinions on all environmentally "significant" investments. Environmental coordinators are required for Class 1 facilities, but the government may exempt particular Class 1 facilities or specifically include other facilities.

Belgian decree

The decree enables the government to require annual or periodic environmental audits (essentially the same scope as EMAS), the results of which must be verified by third parties. It authorizes the government to require facilities to (1) provide emissions reports, (2) monitor groundwater quality, (3) maintain hazardous waste registers, and (4) produce energy and natural resource balance sheets. The government is also empowered to require annual environmental reports on emissions, waste generation, energy use, and to impose accident and release reporting requirements.

While regulations requiring environmental reporting and audits had not been issued as of early 1996 in Flanders, the authorizing law may be a harbinger of similar mandatory auditing and reporting requirements in other European countries.

1) Market Demand

First, certain portions of the commercial marketplace may demand ISO certification, at least in the first flush of enthusiasm, in Europe (where companies are subject in any case to the "voluntary" EMAS Regulation), and in the consumer-product industries. It is hard to predict whether and how the ISO standards will become, de facto, required for doing business internationally, although some conclusions can already be drawn.

German auto suppliers

Taking market pressure alone, companies selling directly to the retail consumer are likely to feel pressure early to convert. In early 1996, German automakers were already implementing EMAS internally, and intended to certify all sites during the course of 1996. By 1998, these manufacturers reportedly are intending to deal only with EMAS-certified suppliers. Companies selling to retailers who sell directly to the consumer likely will be pressured to conform, particularly when faced with large, monopsonist buyers in concentrated retail markets who, for example, can use access to shelf space as a coercive tool. At some point bulk suppliers of chemicals or specialty suppliers of hazardous products or components may find that their customers are trying to legitimize their use of the products or components by pressuring them to manufacture in ISO 14001 qualified plants.

Finally, one can say that companies already using the ISO 9000 series are more likely to adopt the ISO 14001 standard, at least partially out of habit, and to expect that suppliers or others that have adopted the former will be willing to, and should, adopt the latter.

2) Banking and Insurance Demands

Second, even if the commercial marketplace for goods and services does not require use of ISO 14001, the financial and insurance markets may do so. Conditioning loans or insurance coverage on ISO 14001 compliance would only reach certain segments of industry, but could be a significant motivator when used.

3) Government Procurement

Third, European governments are tightening their procurement policies to limit access to "green" suppliers and may begin to use EMAS and ISO certification as a public procurement requirement. At an industry consultation meeting in February, the commission announced plans to draft "green" public procurement guidelines for use by the commissions and national governments when making purchasing decisions. The policy document is to provide guidance to government purchasing agents on how to evaluate, for example, whether suppliers participate in environmental management schemes, whether products have eco-labels, whether suppliers offer product take-back schemes, and whether products include hazardous substances. Further, similar developments may take place at multilateral institutions. Imposed on products, this type of requirement will affect some companies manufacturing outside the boundaries of the country in question.

The Netherlands

Sweden

U.K.

Denmark

Germany

Switzerland

France

Norway

An informal survey conducted in 1995 of procurement policies in The Netherlands, Sweden, U.K., Denmark, Germany, Switzerland, and France found that none of these countries were demanding EMAS or ISO certifications outright as a requirement under public tenders. The U.K. typically asked whether companies had complied with EMAS or BS 7750. By contrast, the Dutch, Swedes, Danes, and Germans tended not to ask if a company had an EMS system, but rather how they implemented environmental rules and for proof of compliance.

Notwithstanding this study, there are many new developments in the field of "green" public procurement. At the international level, the Norwegian government has proposed a work program on "Sustainable Production and Consumption" within the framework of the UN Commission on Sustainable Development, calling for integration of environmental costs in the price of products, "producer responsibility," energy efficiency, minimized pollution and waste, and "green" public procurement. The program urges industry to integrate environmental criteria into supplier and purchasing policies, supply product information on environmental parameters, design for reduced energy and material consumption, and increase product recovery and recycling. At the July 1995 summit, G-7 environment ministers specifically supported "green" government procurement strategies to encourage manufacturers to adopt more rigorous pollution prevention standards.

education program

At the national level, Norway intended by 1996 to revise its public procurement policy to incorporate environmental criteria. An education program also was planned for government "buyers" to inform them of environmental effects of products. Although as of early 1996 no concrete proposals existed, the Environment Ministry envisioned that product criteria would rely on the E.U. and Nordic Council eco-labeling schemes, and that vendors would have to be in compliance with the EMAS Regulation or ISO 14000 management systems.

Dutch Environment Minister Margaretha de Boer was urging companies operating in The Netherlands to adopt integrated management systems. De Boer has stated that this is necessary to achieve the goals of a clean environment and a sustainable society — goals that form core elements of Dutch environmental policy. The Dutch management system requirements were to be revised to conform to those of the E.U. EMAS Regulation. Legislation scheduled for 1996 would further encourage manufacturers to adopt environmental management systems, obliging industry to prepare environmental reports. The Dutch system is based on the notion of continuous improvement — that is, once a company's management system is certified, the company is expected to continue improving its environmental performance.

Denmark   The Danish government was considering legislation obliging industry to make environmental reports with information on emissions, waste production, energy use, raw material input, and water use. The report was to be made publicly available. EMAS-certified companies would be exempt for the first three years but would have to fulfill the reporting obligations thereafter. Insurers, creditors, and industrial clients had indicated that they would use the reports when assessing a company's environmental performance and in procurement bids.

Sweden   With a view to promoting "green procurement," the Swedish Environmental Protection Agency (EPA) was pressing industry to develop product "ecoprofiles." The ecoprofiles would accompany eco-labels to provide detailed environmental information on product life-cycle, emissions data, and energy consumption to industrial and government customers. By early 1996, the Swedish EPA had presented draft "blueprints" for ecoprofiles for product groups including refrigerators. Sweden was pressing forward with its own requirements rather than seeking multilateral solutions through the E.U. or ISO. The Swedish EPA had also issued a policy paper calling for electronic take-back legislation that would also increase "green" public procurement, and eco-labels for electronics products to help consumers choose "green" products.

4) EMAS Imposition for Facility Licensing

Fourth, several European countries are already beginning to impose EMAS requirements in permits as plant facilities are licensed. Under the highly discretionary administrative structure in Europe, where there is little recourse in court, these administrative extractions, even if unauthorized, are difficult to oppose successfully. Given that many central and eastern European countries desire to join the E.U. and are already conforming their environmental regulatory system to that of the union, this and other E.U. tendencies or difficulties are likely to spread to neighboring countries.

5) EMAS As Mandatory

Directorate   Fifth, in 1995 the E.U. Commission's Directorate General 11 (DG XI, responsible for
General 11   environmental matters) had already made it clear that EMAS will be made mandatory if not voluntarily taken up by industry in Europe. Representatives of the E.U.'s DG XI have noted that they were coming under increasing pressure from national governments and from

companies intending to certify under EMAS to render the scheme mandatory. Flanders, in Belgium, has in effect already done so. These representatives speculated that this pressure would only mount in the future and that EMAS likely would be made mandatory following the required 1998 review by the commission. When EMAS is made mandatory for certain E.U. industries, neighboring countries are likely to follow suit.

6) Eco-Label Usage

Sixth, EMAS or ISO certification is likely at some point to become part of eco-label criteria for various products. The Norwegian efforts noted above may lead the way.

7) Use As Prosecutorial Factor

Finally, any government that "encourages" ISO 14001 by making compliance either a defense to prosecution of the corporate entity or of its officers or directors individually, or a significant factor in mitigation of a violation in either case, may make ISO 14001 a de facto requirement for prudent companies independent of other factors.

While these things will not all happen immediately nor apply to all situations, it seems unlikely that the ISO 14001 requirements will stay truly voluntary over the long term. Further, those insisting on their use, whether through the market or through some form of government intervention, probably will prefer some form of more credible independent certification to self-declaration. This will take some of the discretion out of the hands of the implementing companies regarding the scope and nature of application of these standards.

9.3.9 Will ISO 14001 Remain Separate from EMAS?

European companies as well as foreign companies manufacturing in Europe must meet EMAS requirements to the extent that they become mandatory, de facto or de jure. This may also apply to companies selling into Europe, depending on whether EMAS becomes a product-related requirement through government procurement provisions or by incorporation into eco-label criteria. Further, the same may be true for companies associated with neighboring countries that wish to join the E.U. For such companies, ISO 14001 plus a "bridge" document is in reality more relevant than ISO 14001 alone, and is a greater trade threat to non-E.U. companies.

EMAS bridge | The key issue is the extent to which the mere existence of an appendage to the ISO 14001 standards incorporating the additional elements from EMAS (in whatever form is finally used) will result in other non-European countries adopting both ISO 14001 and the appendage, leading to proliferation of the more problematic EMAS provisions around the world. While we must await these developments, the trade impact will be more significant, and the concerns of non-European countries heightened, by any such development.

The ISO 14001 standard likely will spread around the world as a voluntary national standard and may have a useful impact on the overall level of environmental care taken by many companies. Developed nations and their industries will be watching closely — some attempting to use these standards offensively as a vehicle for gaining competitive advantage and others acting defensively to avoid being put at a competitive disadvantage.

CHAPTER 4
Developing Nations and ISO 14000

by Laura B. Campbell2, Senior Legal Officer
United Nations Environment Programme, North America

9.4.1 Overview

While ISO encouraged developing-country representatives to participate in the ISO 14000 environmental management standards development process, many of them found participation difficult or impossible because they lacked technical and financial resources to do so. At the same time, industry and governments in developing countries are anxious about the relationship between access to export markets and their ability to understand and comply with the ISO environmental management standards.

Perhaps most important, developing nations are extremely concerned with the impact that these international standards will have, especially since they were developed outside the normal intergovernmental negotiating process and are not governed by the principles of the Stockholm and Rio Declarations.3 📖 (See Annex A, ISO 14004 for text of Rio Declarations.)

condition of trade
In particular, developing nations fear that the effect of the ISO 14000 standards will be to apply industrialized nations' environmental standards extraterritorially as a condition of trade. On the issues of international standards, Principle 23 of the Stockholm Declaration states:

> "Without prejudice to such criteria as may be developed by the international community, or to standards which will have to be determined nationally, it will be essential in all cases to consider the systems of values prevailing in each country, and the extent of the application of standards which are valid for the most advanced countries but which may be inappropriate and of unwarranted social cost for the developing countries."

lack of information
Even though the ISO EMSs are designed to encourage compliance with local environmental standards and not those of the export market, many developing country governments and companies have not been well informed about the standards and remain anxious about their application.4

This chapter discusses some of the problems encountered by developing country manufacturers who would like to comply with ISO 14000 EMS standards and suggests some ways these problems could be mitigated using the mechanisms contained in the 1994 Technical Barriers to Trade Agreement.

Specifically the main concerns among developing nations about the ISO 14001 are:

- the lack of developing country participation in the development of the standards;

- the level of environmental protection that will be required by the standards; and

- the potential impact of their application on international trade.

These problems could be alleviated by use of provisions in the 1994 Technical Barriers to Trade Agreement such as those relating to transparency and technical and financial assistance.

9.4.2 Conforming to ISO 14001

In understanding developing country concerns about ISO 14001, it is helpful to consider the situation of a local manufacturer in a developing country.

example: supplier certification — The company has just received notice from its largest customer that soon it will begin to require all of its suppliers to provide certification of their conformance to ISO 14001.

Anxious to retain its contract, the manufacturer immediately calls its local industry association to find out what the ISO 14000 EMS standards are and what needs to be done to meet them. Unfortunately, no representatives of the association participated in the ISO standards development process and the association does not have copies of the standards or information on how to achieve conformance.

The manufacturer then contacts government officials in the Ministries of Trade and Environment. Again, no detailed information is available and the company is told that ISO is not an inter-governmental organization, no funding is available for participation in the ISO standards development process, and governmental representatives did not attend ISO meetings.

Upon inquiring about the procedure for obtaining certification of compliance with ISO 14001, the government officials inform the company that there is currently no body or organization in the country that can certify conformance nor any plan to establish such a certification authority.

bigger implementation curve — In addition to the difficulties of obtaining either information on the ISO 14000 standards or certification of conformance, a company in a developing country may have to do more to comply with the standards than a similar company in an industrialized country. Because industrialized countries tend to have more stringent national and local environmental regulations and tougher enforcement programs, many companies have already established internal environmental auditing and management plans to monitor their compliance with these regulations. In countries with less stringent standards and enforcement, a company is less likely to have established the type of internal procedures required by an EMS.

For subsidiaries of multinational companies or joint venture operations with an industrialized country partner, the expertise of the parent or partner can help. For locally owned companies in developing countries, financial and technical difficulties in obtaining access to information and receiving certification may make compliance more difficult.

9.4.3 The 1994 Agreement on Technical Barriers to Trade

In 1994, GATT, a multilateral trade regime, was substantially amended following a lengthy series of negotiations known as the Uruguay Round (GATT 1994).5 📖 (See Part 9, Chapter 1 for more information on GATT.) The 1994 GATT covers areas not even envisioned in the post-World War II economy in which the original GATT was negotiated. By 1994, the original focus of multilateral trade negotiations — reduction of tariffs — had expanded to include technical barriers to trade, intellectual property rights, trade in services, food safety, and environmental subsidies.

Why was GATT expanded to include so many new areas? In essence, the success of earlier GATT negotiations and agreements in reducing tariffs on imports resulted in increased concern over less direct impediments to free trade such as technical standards. All countries, but particularly developing countries, were concerned that the liberalization of trade would be threatened by the use of so-called "non-tariff trade barriers" such as technical standards, constraining export competitiveness, and access to markets on a global basis.

ensuring
transparency
The 1994 TBT agreement, signed as part of the Uruguay Round, was designed to ensure transparency and openness in the development and application of technical standards and conformity assessment procedures. The provisions of the TBT agreement distinguish between technical requirements that are meant to achieve legitimate objectives from those that are disguised barriers to trade.

As noted earlier in Part 9, under the TBT agreement national or international technical standards that have an impact on trade are permitted only to the extent that they are the "least trade-restrictive" measure necessary to fulfill a "legitimate objective." A legitimate objective is defined to include the "the protection of human health or safety, animal or plant life or health, or the environment."

The TBT agreement creates a strong preference for the use of international standards whenever available. There are two primary reasons for this preference. One reason is that the process of developing international standards is generally more open and transparent than that of national standards and more countries have an opportunity to participate in their development. As a result, international standards are more likely to reflect the interests and priorities of many countries rather than only those of the importing country, as national standards often do. Another benefit is that it is much easier to comply with a single international standard than with numerous national standards, thus making export to global markets easier.

The TBT also shows a preference for using international standards as the basis for national standards where relevant international standards exist. Article 2.4 of TBT provides:

> "Where technical regulations are required and relevant international standards exist or their completion is imminent, Members shall use them, as a basis for their technical regulations."

If a national technical standard is created to fulfill one of the legitimate objectives listed in the TBT agreement and is based on an international standard, under the TBT agreement it is presumed to be in compliance with the trade disciplines of GATT, i.e., it is not viewed as a non-tariff trade barrier.

The preamble of the TBT recognizes the important contribution that international standards and conformity assessment systems can make in furthering the objectives of trade liberalization by improving efficiency of production and facilitating the conduct of international trade.

ISO already notifies the World Trade Organization about adoption of its standards to ensure that its initiatives do not create unintentional trade barriers. Clearly the ISO 14000 standards are designed to fulfill a legitimate purpose under the TBT agreement — the protection of human health and the environment. Other provisions of the TBT agreement concerning special and differential treatment for developing countries, transparency, and financial and technical assistance for developing countries also should be considered in implementing the ISO standards.

9.4.4 Benefits of a Single International Standard

While there are potential difficulties for developing nations in complying with ISO 14001, the TBT agreement recognizes the benefits of applying a single set of international environmental management standards rather than national standards. When properly applied, the standards should help avoid multiple or conflicting inspection, certification, and labeling schemes.

A proliferation of unilateral schemes would impose additional burdens on developing countries in obtaining information and meeting the costs of compliance. In addition, conformity assessment and certification could be required on a country-by-country basis from each importing country. ISO 14000 can play a valuable role in reducing proliferation of such unilateral schemes.

9.4.5 National Environmental Standards

While developing countries are concerned about the use of the ISO 14000 EMS standards to indirectly impose industrialized countries' environmental standards extraterritorially, the ISO standards are procedural and descriptive in nature and do not create normative require-ments.

The ISO standards do not specify environmental performance criteria such as emission limitations, environmental performance levels, or production standards. To date, ISO has not developed test methods for monitoring pollutants. However, ISO 14001 does require an organization to formulate a policy and objectives taking into account national legislative requirements and information about significant environmental impacts.

lower
national
levels
The overall purpose of ISO 14001 — to help organizations in implementing environmental management systems by providing guidance and methodologies for doing this — can benefit companies in both developed and developing countries. However, in most cases, developing country companies will face a greater burden in implementing ISO 14001 than their counterparts will in an industrialized country. This is caused, at least partially, by differences in the existing national regulatory frameworks in countries at different stages of develop-ment.

9.4.6 Process of Standards Development

Countries at different stages of economic development tend to have different environmental priorities, objectives, and methods of achieving them. Development of international standards based on international consensus, therefore, is likely to be more effective and achieve greater acceptance among producers and consumers than those based on national or regional priorities.

To ensure that the views of all nations are heard during standards development, provisions such as those contained in the *Codes of Good Practice for the Preparation, Adoption and Application of Standards* of the TBT agreement should be applied, including those relating to transparency and notification.

Transparency and notification are important means of ensuring credibility of the standards development process. Only when the criteria-setting process is transparent and provides at least indirect access for all interested parties can it generate confidence in the final outcome. Information on the structure of the scheme and its operation should be readily available to all interested parties.

more
transparency
needed

An important aspect of transparency in the context of international trade is the notification of draft criteria with a view to providing trading partners with an opportunity to comment.

Taking account of the interests of developing countries in the implementation of ISO 14001 requires improved transparency. Early notification, information, and communication about ISO 14000 standards should be provided.

9.4.7 Financial and Technical Assistance

The preamble to the TBT agreement recognizes the contribution that international standardization can make to the transfer of technology from developed to developing countries. Under Article 11 of the TBT agreement, World Trade Organization members are required, when requested, to grant technical assistance to developing countries establishing national bodies for assessing conformity with standards and participation in the activities of international standardizing bodies.

more help
needed

To ensure that companies in developing countries that want to implement the ISO 14000 standards are able to do so, support is needed for:

- identifying and accommodating developing country standardization needs;
- creating awareness about ISO 14000;
- setting up certification bodies;
- preparing and publishing standards development manuals;
- providing training; and
- participating in ISO committee meetings and the further development of international standards.

9.4.8 Conclusion

In conclusion, while developing countries can benefit from international standards rather than facing a proliferation of national standards applied to imports, concerns remain about developing country participation in the standards development process, the relationship between industrialized country environmental standards and ISO 14000, and the potential effect of the standards as a non-tariff trade barrier.

In many cases, developing countries will need technical support to adjust to ISO 14001 as well as better information about conformance to the standard. It is also critical that companies in developing countries have access to certification bodies that can provide services at a reasonable cost and in a timely manner.

CHAPTER 5
E.U. Eco-Management and Audit Regulation

*by Rozell Hunter, Esq. Hunton & Williams*6

Based on an article originally published by International Environment Reporter, *Vol. 17, No. 3, pp. 142-149 (Feb. 9, 1994). Copyright 1994 by The Bureau of National Affairs, Inc. (800-372-1033). Reprinted with permission.*

9.5.1 Overview

The E.U. *Regulation 1836/93 Allowing Voluntary Participation in an Eco-Management and Audit Scheme*, O.J. L. 168/1 (July 10, 1993) (EMAS Regulation), establishes an environmental management and auditing system for industrial facilities. Participation in this program entitles a company to register a participating site on an E.U.-authorized list of participating sites, and to use an E.U.-approved statement of participation and graphics to publicize participation in the program.

The hope is that industrial companies will participate in this scheme voluntarily to avoid being placed at a competitive disadvantage. As of early 1996, many large manufacturers were planning to participate. Others may find they have no choice, as customers and retailers demand proof of the companies' "environmental probity."

In drafting the EMAS Regulation, the European Commission was inspired by U.S. corporate experience with environmental management systems and by the model of ISO 9000 quality management systems. The commission also has been motivated by its inability to ensure adequate compliance with E.U. law.

The result of the commission's labors is something entirely different from either inspiration.

EMAS/ISO 9000 differences

Where ISO 9000 involves principally auditing process and performance vis-à-vis goals a company sets for itself, the EMAS regulation requires auditing for, among other things, legal compliance and environmental contamination. Where U.S. corporate environmental management systems are flexible and confidential tools used by management to control liability risks, the EMAS regulation prescribes auditing scope and procedure, and requires publication of statements covering "significant" environmental issues after validation by external auditors.

The commission hopes that disclosure will induce companies not just to achieve compliance with law, but to go well beyond the law. It also hopes that the disclosure will result in public pressure on national authorities to enforce more aggressively E.U. and national environmental law, and provide environmental groups with the information necessary to bring their own enforcement and clean-up actions, where allowed under national law (e.g., Belgium).

EMAR is enforcement tool

Thus, while the two principal inspirations for the EMAS Regulation may have been management tools, the regulation is, at bottom, an enforcement tool.

While the EMAS regulation has been in force since April 1995, in early 1996 important work concerning the EMAS system was still underway and should be of interest even to manufacturers with no E.U. sites. The commission was working on a "code of practice" defining the role of the external auditors or "verifiers" who will vet public environmental statements. Standardization bodies are working on standards elaborating the detail of the environmental management and auditing systems envisaged by the regulation. The commission has delegated this rule-making task to Comité Europeén de Normalisation (CEN), the pan-European standardization body constituted of national standardization bodies in E.U. and European Free Trade Association (EFTA) countries. CEN has been working through and with ISO to develop these standards.

This chapter examines the EMAS regulation and comments on its implications. The first part describes the background and context of the regulation. The second focuses on the regulation itself. The third briefly discusses related work afoot at various standardization bodies. The fourth highlights issues to be considered in deciding whether and how to participate.

9.5.2 Antecedents and Context

U.S. Precedents

The origins of elaborate environmental management systems, including environmental auditing, can be traced to the 1970s in the United States, when the United States began erecting its rigorous environmental regulatory and liability framework in earnest. This environmental legislation created significant criminal, civil, and administrative liability risks for companies and their officers and directors. Management of companies in the chemical and other high-risk industries sought to control these liability risks through environmental management systems, typically with a heavy emphasis on assuring legal compliance. These management systems have since proliferated throughout American industry and beyond.

codifying EMSs   The U.S. Environmental Protection Agency sought to codify in regulations these environmental management and auditing systems but was rebuffed by adamant industry opposition. Industrial spokesmen argued that environmental management systems are useful management tools precisely because they are voluntary, flexible, and above all confidential. If environmental management systems were to become formalized, and were to be used for generating public information, their effectiveness would be undermined. Rather than using audits to uncover and address problems early on, companies might grow timorous in their self-evaluation for fear of public disclosure of audit results, and attendant public and official attention. 📖 (See Part 6 for more information on auditing and Part 6, Chapter 1 on the history of EMSs.)

DOJ guidelines   Environmental management systems have received an impetus from other quarters. The U.S. Department of Justice (DOJ) has stated that the existence of an environmental compliance program will be considered in deciding whether to prosecute a company for environmental violations. 📖 (See Part 8, Chapters 1 and 2 for more information on the DOJ guidelines.)

Perhaps more importantly, the U.S. Sentencing Guidelines, which seek to achieve greater

sentencing
guidelines

consistency in sentencing convicted defendants, provide courts with sentencing formula under which sanctions may be increased or decreased in light of aggravating or mitigating factors. Under the Sentencing Guidelines' chapter on organizations (corporations, partnerships, associations), the fact that the convicted corporate defendant had an "effective program to prevent and detect violations of law" may be a mitigating factor (revised draft guidelines for organizational environmental crimes were circulated in November 1993). 📖 (See Part 8, Chapter 2 for more information on the Sentencing Commission guidelines, and Appendix D for verbatim text.)

The sentencing guidelines explain that an effective compliance program is one that is "reasonably designed, implemented, and enforced so that it generally will be effective in preventing and detecting criminal conduct." The guidelines go on to trace the outlines of an effective compliance program and mention in particular (1) compliance standards, (2) definition of organizational responsibility, (3) training, (4) monitoring and auditing, and (5) response to legal violations and failures of the program. They recognize that the specific actions necessary for a particular company will depend on its size, the likelihood of offenses given the nature of its business, and prior history of violations.

These compliance programs do not result in public environmental statements of the sort envisaged by the E.U. EMAS regulation. These programs of course often uncover information requiring self-reporting (e.g., discovery of reportable releases), as well the EMAS regulation. However, companies tailor these programs to their own particular circumstances and typically design them with a view to maintaining, where possible, the confidentiality of generated information and reports.

European Union Structure, Organizations, and Documents

The relationship between the E.U. and its 15 member nations is comparable to the U.S. federal government's relationship with state governments and their legislative, executive, and regulatory bodies. E.U. members vest the E.U. with certain authority and have agreed to abide by its regulations, directives, and decisions. As with U.S. states, E.U. nations may not make laws more lenient than E.U.'s laws.

One critical difference, however, is that the balance of power lies firmly with E.U. member states. In fact, not all member bodies, including the U.K., fully endorse the extension of the E.U. as a strong federal government structure, and are concerned with giving up sovereignty. In addition, the E.U. has no defense considerations, no constitution, and no head of state.

The following is a guide to E.U. legislative terminology:

Rulemakers, Advisors

The Maastricht Treaty of 1992 substantially changed the balance of powers among E.U. bodies, and refined the framework for member state integration. The ultimate goal is to create a European constitution.

- **European Commission** — The E.U.'s executive branch, made up of 20 appointed members who serve five-year terms. The only E.U. institution able to propose new legislation, does so from E.U. perspective. Carries out Treaty of Rome provisions. Submits proposals to Council of Ministers after consulting the E.U.'s advisory board, the Economic and Social Committee, and the European Parliament. Also consults national government experts and interest groups. Loosely analogous to the U.S. executive branch.

- **European Council** — Made up of all E.U. heads of government. Approves strategies and resolves legislative blockages.

- **Council of Ministers** — Made up of representatives of each member state. Only body able to adopt legislation, which members review from national perspectives. Council meets frequently, based on topic of European regulation, directive, or decision at hand. Loosely analogous to U.S. Senate.

- **European Parliament** — Has 567 elected members who have power to amend legislative proposals from Council of Ministers. Functions as E.U.'s public forum. Loosely analogous to the U.S. House of Representatives.

- **Economic and Social Committee (ESC)** — Consists of 189 members representing economic and social sectors. Generally acts by simple majority vote. Acts as an advisory group to Commission.

- **Committee of the Regions** — Has 189 members representing regional and local bodies. Acts as a consulting group as well.

- **European Court of Justice** — Has judges from each member state and a president. Ensures that policy proposals and implementation adhere to E.U. law. Superior to national courts on E.U. legal matters, including disputes involving member states and others. Has power to impose fines or penalties.

- **European Environmental Agency** — Provides technical and scientific support to E.U. and member states, and coordinates information network.

Documents

Before passage, the following documents must be approved by the European Commission, the European Parliament, and the European Council, which makes the final decision. In addition, an ESC committee must be consulted.

- **Regulations** — Binding laws in all member countries. Analogous to national laws. Stronger than directives and binding on all E.U. member states.

- **Directives** — Binding laws for affected states, but countries have discretion on how desired results will be achieved.

- **Decisions** — Binding on state, organization, or individual to whom they are addressed.

- **Recommendations and Opinions** — Are not binding but are expected to be taken into account when decisions are made on relevant issue.

- **Resolutions** — Non-binding statements by Council of Ministers on a political commitment to an objective.

The vigorous enforcement practices, combined with the guidelines by the Department of Justice and the U.S. Sentencing Commission that consider effective compliance programs, have resulted in fairly systematic use by U.S. industry of these confidential environmental management programs. While these programs involve various degrees of process and bureaucracy, they typically place a heavy emphasis on compliance with law.

European Context

Why did the E.U. take, with the EMAS regulation, such a different approach to environmental management systems?

The regulation's rationale is best understood in the larger context of E.U. environmental law. The European Commission frequently encounters difficulty in trying to induce the Council of Ministers to adopt rigorous environmental legislation — the council, the E.U.'s real legislature, is, after all, the member states whose discretion would be constrained by detailed E.U. legislation. 📖 (See sidebar for information on the E.U. structure.) The commission faces even more obdurate impediments in seeking the consistent enforcement of E.U. environmental law, once adopted.

lack of teeth

The commission has neither the staff nor the legal power to enforce directly against individuals violating environmental law. Its enforcement powers are confined to cumbersome, time-consuming actions before the Court of Justice against member states for failure to implement E.U. law. Such cases are necessarily reserved for the most flagrant instances of national delinquency.

Confronted with these obstacles, the commission has begun exploring other means of achieving its environmental objectives. The commission is increasingly designing legislation that harnesses public participation and bypasses national authorities. The common theme is the generation of more public information on industrial activities in hopes that environmental groups and others will use this information in demanding from industry and enforcement authorities more effective application of environmental law and policy.

Examples of these public participation initiatives include the Directive on Freedom of Information on the Environment, the Eco-Labeling Regulation, and above all the EMAS Regulation. In this context, it becomes apparent that the EMAS regulation's purpose has less to do with assisting companies in developing a helpful environmental management tool, and more with creating a new enforcement tool.

9.5.3 The EMAS Regulation

The EMAS Regulation provides for corporate participation on a site-specific basis. To participate, a company must implement several key requirements.

- *Environmental policy*, including a commitment to legal compliance, and to "continuous improvement of environmental performance."
- *Environmental management system* covering the particular site and including:
    — definition of management responsibilities;
    — preparation of an environmental effects register;

— establishment of organizational structures, and operating and record-keeping procedures; and

— periodic audits.

- Verification by an *external auditor* (the *"verifier"*) of

  — the company's environmental management system, and

  — a *public environmental statement* noting "significant environmental issues," including an emissions register.

Participation is voluntary in theory, though member states are free to make the scheme mandatory for particular industrial sectors, and the commission is to reconsider the regime (including whether it should remain voluntary) by July 1998.

Environmental Policy and Program

Participating companies must adopt an environmental policy "in accordance with" the regulation. The policy is critical, as it is the principal vehicle by which substantive standards are incorporated in the EMAS system. As discussed in more detail below, the policy must:

1) provide for "compliance with all relevant regulatory requirements regarding the environment";

2) make "commitments aimed at the continuous improvement of environmental performance"; and

3) be based on "good management practices."

The regulation goes on to require that the policy must address some 12 broadly cast issues, including:

1) assessment, control, and reduction of environmental impact;

2) energy and raw material management;

3) waste management;

4) production process changes;

5) "[p]roduct planning design, packaging, transportation, use, and disposal"; and

6) "[e]nvironmental performance and practices of contractors, subcontractors, and suppliers."

company   The environmental policy must be adopted at the "company" level. It is not at all clear whether the policy can be limited to a multinational corporation's participating sites, or even to its E.U. sites. The regulation defines "company" as "the organization which has overall management control over activities at a given site." Depending on its corporate structure and where "overall management control" is deemed to lie, a multinational corporation could find that it must adopt a policy "in accordance with" the regulation for its worldwide operations as the price of qualifying one E.U. site under the EMAS regulation.

The company-level policy is to be reduced to an "environmental programme" for the particular participating site. The program shall include the company's "specific objectives and activities to ensure greater protection of the environment at a given site, including a description of the measures . . . envisaged to achieve such objectives and where appropriate the deadlines set for implementation . . . ."

In drafting site-specific environmental programs, companies may find themselves navigating narrow straits. The program is to set quantifiable objectives and deadlines, where possible, for the various matters discussed in the company policy.

audits against
objectives

It will be safer for companies to write their programs in vague and aspiring terms, for companies ultimately will be audited against undertakings in programs. Nonetheless, companies may be tempted to set ambitious, detailed objectives in their programs as a means of stimulating "continuous improvement." More to the point, auditors and verifiers may demand that objectives be set out in detail, with numbers and dates.

Failure to meet these objectives may then result in unflattering comments in the public environmental statement. Accordingly, companies will need to pay close attention to drafting policies and programs to ensure they are comprehensive and specific enough to satisfy the regulation (and verifiers), yet not cast so as to put companies at risk of negative comment in the statement for having failed to achieve the program's objectives. This will require the input of the company's environmental managers and engineers, but also the review of that professional Cassandra, the company's counsel.

Environmental Management System

The environmental management system is defined as "that part of the overall management system which includes the organizational structure, responsibilities[,] practices, procedures, processes, and resources for determining and implementing the environmental policy." The environmental management system must meet a series of requirements set out in the regulation's annexes and covering, among other things, organization and training, preparation of registers on environmental effects and on environmental law, and record-keeping. This management system must then be complemented by periodic auditing.

Organization and Training

The company must define and document "responsibility, authority, and interrelations of key personnel who manage, perform, and monitor work affecting the environment." It must appoint a "management representative" with "authority and responsibility for ensuring the management system is implemented and maintained." It must train workers and set up internal and external communication procedures.

liability

These designations of who is responsible for environmental management may well have implications for the liability of particular managers. Environmental law is typically enforced in Europe through administrative and criminal sanctions.

There is now a trend in a number of member states to seek criminal sanctions against responsible managers. Indeed, in Germany, only natural persons, and hence not companies, may be criminally sanctioned, a circumstance that has not surprisingly heightened the interest of prosecutors in focusing their attention on managers. In such cases, questions of which manager is responsible for a particular subject matter inevitably arise. The designations under the regulation, particularly with regard to the "management representative," may make the answer fairly clear.

Registers

The company must examine the environmental effects of its activities and compile a register of effects identified as "significant." In preparing that register, the company must consider:

1) "controlled and uncontrolled" releases to air and water;

2) solid and hazardous wastes;

3) "contamination of land";

4) natural resource use; and

5) "discharge of thermal energy, noise, odor, dust, vibration, and visual impact."

The company is also to consider, with some repetition, effects arising from:

1) normal and abnormal operating conditions;

2) incidents, accidents, and emergencies; and

3) "past activities, current activities, and planned activities."

These provisions effectively require the company to investigate all releases, waste management, and contamination related to its activities, and record those that are "significant." The company must investigate whether there is contamination on its site, arguably regardless of whether contamination was caused by its own activities or those of neighbors or predecessors.

The company apparently also would need to investigate its off-site effects — e.g., off-site waste disposal — arising from current as well as past activities. After searching out these legacies from the past and present, the company must record in the register those deemed "significant" — an undefined term over which there inevitably will be debate. Of course, even if contamination is not deemed "significant" for these purposes, its mere discovery may well trigger national law obligations to notify authorities, or to disclose to a would-be purchaser.

The company is to possess a second register, which is to include all legal and policy requirements applicable to its activities, products, and services. The preparation of a register including E.U., national, and local requirements for activities at a site may be fairly straightforward. Consulting firms have been selling such lists of applicable requirements for several years, though the thoroughness and usefulness of such canned documents are doubtful.

inclusive register The obligation that the register include all requirements applicable to products may be more problematic.

In the first instance, one may wonder whether many such requirements are relevant at the plant level rather than at corporate headquarters or in the marketing department where product decisions are made.

scope unclear Second, the scope of the requirement is not clear. Must this register include product requirements for the locality of production? Or, must the register include any product requirements applicable anywhere the products from that site are sold or are otherwise put into commerce? In any event, if this requirement is taken seriously, it will be no easy task to keep such a register up-to-date given the proliferation of product-related environmental regulatory requirements.

Documentation and Recordkeeping

A participating company must establish records "to demonstrate compliance with the requirements of the environmental management system," and the extent that the company's environmental objectives are obtained.

The recordkeeping and documentation procedures may prove to be an important, and sensitive, element of the EMAS system. The recordkeeping procedures could be particularly significant in the event the company or its management sought to rely on the presence of an effective environmental management program in a defense to a prosecution. Also, companies will want to be careful that their document-retention programs appropriately cover documents generated under the regulation. Lastly, they will want to consider:

☑ the nature and contents of collected documentation;

☑ the extent of any legal privileges (probably pretty limited); and

☑ the likelihood of ultimate disclosure.

📖 (See Part 3, Chapter 4 for more information on documentation.)

Reviews and Audits

review   At the outset, a company must conduct for a participating site an initial audit or "review," which is defined as the "initial comprehensive analysis of the environmental issues, impact, and performances related to activities at a site." The information generated by the review is then to be used in developing the details of the environmental management system and in preparing the site's first environmental statement.

The company must then periodically conduct an audit, which is defined as a "management tool comprising a systematic, documented, periodic, and objective evaluation of the performance of the organization, management system, and processes designed to protect the environment with the aim of assessing compliance with company environmental policies." These reviews and audits may be conducted by either in-house personnel or external auditors. Frequency of audits is to be determined on the basis of guidelines drawn up by the commission, but at least every three years.

Audits are to assess the management system and determine conformity with the environmental policy and site program. Audits are to include an "assessment of the factual data necessary to evaluate performance." They are to cover:

☑ control of the activities' environmental impact;

☑ energy and raw material management;

☑ waste management;

☑ noise;

☑ new products and processes;

☑ environmental performance of suppliers; and

☑ accident planning and prevention.

Assessing compliance with the law and with company policies and site programs is conceptually straightforward, as is the requirement that the audit involve "assessment of the factual data necessary to evaluate performance." It is less clear how these audits are to cover "new products and processes" given the absence of standards against which to audit. Audits seem unrelated in that context.

The requirement that the "environmental performance of suppliers" be audited is potentially problematic. The apparent intention is to force a proliferation of the EMAS system up the production chain, with each manufacturer demanding proof of his suppliers' "environmental probity," and with the ultimate proof being participation in the EMAS system.

The reality may be more complicated. To take the example of the ISO 9000 quality systems, some companies that have tried to verify that all of their suppliers meet the same quality standards have found it a daunting if not impossible task.

legal compliance

The regulation incorporates through the "environmental policy" the substantive standards against which auditors and their verifiers evaluate participating companies. The environmental policy must:

☑ provide for "compliance with all relevant regulatory requirements regarding the environment";

☑ include "commitments aimed at reasonable continuous improvement of environmental performance, with a view to reducing environmental impacts to levels not exceeding those corresponding to economically viable application of best available technology; and

☑ be based on "good management practices."

second-guessing

The reference to legal requirements includes compliance with *all* applicable law — not just what appears on the face of permits. This will require review of compliance not only with local, regional, and national environmental law, but also with E.U. environmental law. This subtlety might matter, as the member states are not always rigorous in their application of E.U. environmental law and there are instances where national and E.U. laws are in direct conflict.

At first glance, the obligation to make commitments aimed at "reasonable continuous improvement" seems insignificant. Such commitments will, by their nature, be vague and aspiring, and require in effect only that the company be able to show that it has gone through the motions of at least thinking of ways to improve performance (but see the comments above regarding the difficulties in drafting policies and programs).

On the other hand, the reference to "reducing environmental impacts to levels not exceeding those corresponding to economically viable application of best available technology," may provide auditors and then verifiers a standard on the basis of which they may second-guess management.

The requirement that policies be based on "good management practices" may turn out to have more practical import. "Good management practices" are defined to include:

☑ assessment in advance of the environmental impact of "all new activities, products, and processes";

☑ assessment and monitoring of environmental impacts of current activities;

☑ execution of "measures necessary to . . . reduce pollutant emissions and waste generation to the minimum and to conserve resources . . . taking account of possible clean technologies";

☑ implementation "measures necessary to prevent accidental emissions of materials or energy";

☑ establishment of "[m]onitoring procedures ... to check compliance with the environmental policy and, where these procedures require measurement and testing, [establishment] of records of results"; and

☑ provision of information to the public and "[a]ppropriate advice" to customers on "relevant environmental aspects of the handling, use, and disposal of the products made by the company."

Auditing against these "good management practices" appears to give the auditor and hence the verifier broad powers to question a company's operating procedures and decisions. For example, the auditor — and again, later, the verifier — may be able to question whether a participating company, which is in compliance with law, has taken all "measures necessary to . . . reduce pollutant emissions and waste generation . . . taking account of possible clean technologies." Auditors and verifiers may well have their own views on what the "possible" clean technologies are in a particular sector.

Also, it is at best odd that an audit focusing on a particular site would include a review of whether the company provides customers with "appropriate advice" on "relevant environmental aspects of the handling, use, and disposal of the products made by the *company*." (Emphasis added.) Such product-related requirements do not belong in a plant-focused auditing system. And one might question the capacity of auditors and verifiers to opine on such matters.

The auditor must prepare a written audit report. The report must "provide management with information on the state of compliance with the company's environmental policy and the environmental progress at the site," and "demonstrate the need for corrective action, where appropriate." These reports may turn out to be sensitive documents, and how they are prepared will be important to the audited companies, particularly in the event of litigation.

The regulation provides a means for companies, following the ISO 9000 model, to have these environmental management and auditing systems certified.

First, the European Commission may recognize national, European (i.e., CEN), or international (i.e., ISO) standards on environmental management systems and auditing, if those standards include all of the corresponding elements of the EMAS regulation.

Then, a company whose environmental management and auditing systems have been certified by an accredited body pursuant to recognized standards "shall be considered as meeting the corresponding requirements of this Regulation."

The arrangement does not relieve the company of obligations under the EMAS regulation. It merely allows for a certification of the management and auditing systems, though it may, as is discussed below, simplify the verification process. Nonetheless, the substantive standards still apply, as do the validation requirements for the environmental statements, to which we may now turn.

Environmental Statements and Validation

The key to effectiveness of the EMAS system as an enforcement tool is the public environmental statement validated by the external auditor, the verifier.

Environmental Statement

annual
statement

The regulation provides for full and simplified statements. A full statement is to be prepared after the initial review and each subsequent audit. A simplified statement, which is verified at the end of the audit cycle, is generally prepared annually in intervening years and includes a summary of figures on raw material, energy and water consumption, and noise.

A full statement shall include, in addition to a description of activities:

☑ an "assessment of all the significant environmental issues of relevance to the activities concerned";

☑ a "summary of the figures on pollutant emissions, waste generation, consumption of raw material, energy and water, noise and other significant environmental aspects"; and

☑ "their factors regarding environmental performance."

The first bullet requires the inclusion of "significant environmental issues," and thus presumably disclosure of the "significant" items noted in the environmental effects register, such as soil and groundwater contamination, as well as instances of noncompliance. Clearly there will be questions of thresholds — whether an isolated violation rises to the level "significant" and thus merits disclosure, or whether only persistent noncompliance problems need be disclosed.

compliance
not easy to see

At least one of the companies that piloted the regulation's EMAS found that compliance was not necessarily easy to determine. The company operated a small facility in the United Kingdom, which was subject to permitting under the Environmental Protection Act 1990. The facility's terms of operation were prescribed in a guidance note issued by Her Majesty's Inspectorate of Pollution (HMIP). That note set an emission limit for a particular substance but did not specify a measuring time.

The company ran a batch process and hence had no emissions of the regulated substances, except for during several limited periods, during which its emissions exceeded the emission limit by half again. Were a 24-hour measuring time used, the facility's emissions would be well within legal limits. In the absence of a prescribed measuring time, however, it would appear that the company was obliged to meet the emission limit at all times. The regulatory authority was sympathetic and had no intention of enforcing. Nonetheless, the company was obliged to note in its statement its actual emission levels and the legal limits.

This type of problem is not unique, since European national environmental legislation frequently fails to provide such necessary regulatory detail and permitting officials do not always have authority to supply that detail. Also, as the commission hopes, this kind of information will provide the means for environmental groups to play an active role in ensuring enforcement, even where national enforcement authorities might prefer not to take action.

The second bullet is, in effect, an emissions register on a plant basis. Thus, although the commission's efforts to adopt a toxic emissions register modeled on the U.S. Toxic Release Inventory attracted much criticism from industry, a potentially broader emissions register (applicable to "pollutant," not just "toxic," emissions) is already incorporated in the EMAS regulation.

register scope
unclear

As of early 1996, the scope of this "pollutant emissions" register remained unclear. Would it include figures on permitted emissions only, or others as well? Would it include only point-source emissions, or fugitive emissions too? If fugitive emissions are included, how would they be calculated? Here again, it seems that verifiers will have broad discretion in determining how much information will need to be supplied.

The third bullet — "other factors regarding environmental performance" — is a catchall. In contrast to the first bullet, there is no requirement that matters be "significant." This heading will enable verifiers to go beyond matters that needed to be recorded in the effects register and to require disclosure of anything the verifier deems noteworthy.

Verification and Validation

The verifier's role is the most controversial and least understood aspect of the EMAS regulation. It is probably the most important, as well.

The nub is how precise and thorough is the verifier to be? Will he or she, as some in industry hope, merely carry out a process audit — that is, merely check whether the company has the right systems in place? Or, will he or she, following the financial accounting model, examine the underlying data? Further, how much latitude will the verifier have in imposing his or her own views of substantive standards? A clue to the answers lies in the regulation's description of his tasks.

verifiers verify
audit

Verifiers must check compliance with the regulation of environmental policies, programs, management systems, audit procedures, and environmental statements. The verifier must "investigate in a sound professional manner, the technical validity of the environmental review or audit or other procedures carried out by the company, without unnecessarily duplicating those procedures." He or she must also check whether the information in the environmental statement is "reliable" and whether the statement "adequately covers all the significant environmental issues" regarding the site.

The verifier must then prepare a report for management, in which he or she must specify:

1) cases of noncompliance with the regulation;

2) technical defects in the environmental management system, auditing, etc.; and

3) points of disagreement with the draft statement and amendments.

Only once he or she is satisfied that the environmental management and auditing systems comply with the regulation and the statement adequately reflects all significant issues, may he or she validate the environmental statement, thereby allowing the company's participation in the EMAS system with regard to the site.

verifier
guidance

The commission is working on a guidance document elaborating in more detail the verifier's role. A draft of the guidance for verifiers document, seeks to describe the verifier's responsibilities. The draft guidance document essentially restates the contents of the EMAS regulation when it states that "the aim of the verification is not to substitute, repeat, or complement the company's environmental audit assessment or any internal monitoring procedures, but rather, to confirm their validity."

The draft guidance document opines that the verifier's function should be limited to:

1) checking compliance with EMAS requirements;

2) verifying data found in the environmental statement; and

3) ensuring that the statement covers all significant environmental issues.

In prognosticating on the way verifiers fulfill their tasks, it is also worth considering the prior experience of the firms that will act as verifiers, and the specter of liability for verifiers. It is worth keeping in mind that the financial accounting firms are among the group of consultants who aspire to operate as verifiers. Indeed, the chairman of the ISO working group on environmental auditing standards was an employee of one of the big accounting firms. These consultants likely will bring to the environmental area their financial accounting methodology and mindset.

liability   Prudent verifiers likely also will be influenced by potential liability exposure. Take a company that succeeds in getting a verifier to validate its environmental statement, even though the statement does not note extensive soil and groundwater contamination that would have been revealed had the verifier investigated the statement's assertions in a "sound professional manner." Assume that another company buys the equity of the first company and, in making its bid, relies on the clean bill of environmental health validated by the verifier. When the clean-up costs or the penalties come home to roost, the verifier may find the second company seeking compensation for the financial harm it suffered in relying on his or her validation of the statement.

These liability risks could be all the greater for verifiers where validated statements are relied on by insurers or lenders. Self-serving language inserted by verifiers that third parties should not rely on their work may well provide verifiers little protection, especially given that the purpose of the EMAS system is to provide such third parties with information on the "environmental performance" of participating companies.

Some in industry argue that if a company has certified management and auditing systems, the verifier's role is reduced to little more than checking that the systems are indeed certified and that the statement's assertions appear plausible. The argument runs as follows: The regulation provides that a company that has certified management and auditing systems in place "shall be considered as meeting the corresponding requirements of this Regulation."

The verifier is to check:

1) compliance with the regulation of the environmental management system;

2) the auditing system's technical validity, "without unnecessarily duplicating those procedures"; and

3) the reliability of the environmental statement's information.

Thus, the mere fact that the company's management and auditing systems are certified tells U.S. that those parts of the regulation have been satisfied. Extensive checks of the auditing system would "unnecessarily" duplicate the certified auditing and other procedures, and information generated by certified systems is presumptively "reliable."

statement validation

While that line of argument may have its attractions, verifiers may be reluctant to validate statements — and assume liability risks — without first satisfying themselves as to the adequacy of the statements through checking underlying data. Besides, certification of management and auditing systems establishes presumptively only that those elements of the regulation are satisfied. The verifier must in any event check whether the environmental statement is "reliable" and "adequately covers all the significant environmental issues."

verifier can be fired

There are, however, some rather practical limitations on the power of verifiers. If a company finds a verifier overbearing, it can fire him. The verifier is engaged by the company and has a confidentiality obligation independent of continued employment (see below). But if the company still wants to participate in the EMAS system, it will need to go through the process with another verifier.

The greatest constraint on a verifier may well be more subtle than the threat of his or her own severance. The large accounting and environmental consulting firms that aspire to act as verifiers sell other, more lucrative services to the companies they will vet — e.g., tax advice, management, and environmental consulting advice. The verifiers in these large consultancies may find themselves under pressure from colleagues not to "spoil the relationship" with the client.

Confidentiality

Confidentiality issues will be delicate for participating companies, as well as for external auditors and verifiers. The regulation provides that external auditors and verifiers shall "not divulge, without authorization from the company management, any information or data obtained in the course of their auditing or verification activities."

This provision has been taken by some as comfort that information generated by EMAS need not be made public. That seems overly optimistic. True, E.U. law is supreme (though sometimes national authorities overlook that nicely). But the confidentiality provision is quite limited — it extends only to external auditors and verifiers. It does not relieve the participating company, nor its officers, directors, and employees, of their disclosure or notification obligations under national law. So, if an external auditor of a facility in France discovers an "incident" posing a risk for water quality, he or she would not have to report that incident to the authorities. He or she would have to report the incident to the company's management, who in turn would have to report to the authorities under French water law. Moreover, the verifier arguably would not be able to validate the environmental statement unless the authorities were so notified.

Moreover, a participating company will not necessarily be able to count on materials and notes remaining confidential in the event of litigation. Depending on the rules of procedure in the particular member state, such documentation may be discoverable by public prosecutors and plaintiffs.

9.5.4 Standardization Activities

As noted, the regulation provides for the recognition of national, CEN, and ISO standards on environmental management systems and auditing. The commission hopes to rely on such standardization bodies for the elaboration of requirements that are already set out in detail in the regulation and its annexes.

In early 1996, The E.U. recognized the British BS 7750 standard, the Irish IS 310 standard, and the Spanish UNE 77 801(2)-94 standard as a means of becoming EMAS-certified. Even if recognized under EMAS, these national standards may well be replaced by a CEN standard once it is approved.

Should You Participate?

Does it make sense to participate in EMAS? Given the cost implications of implementing such a labor- and documentation-intensive scheme and the legal issues concerning managing sensitive, confidential information, you should carefully weigh the costs and benefits of EMAS participation.

regulatory
market forces

Regulatory and market forces may create significant pressure to participate in EMAS. Companies with operations in Europe may find that the "voluntary" EMAS may well become mandatory in several years. More immediately, commercial pressure may make EMAS registration (or ISO 14001 certification) a condition for doing business. Both government procurement tenders and industrial customers (particularly those who are themselves EMAS participants) may discriminate in their purchases in favor of suppliers participating in the scheme. Retailers may give prime shelf space to products coming from participating sites.

usefulness

Quite apart from market considerations, European manufacturers may find it useful for liability reasons to participate in the EMAS scheme, or at least to follow national or international environmental management and auditing standards. Such an environmental management program could be a useful device for minimizing the occurrence of environmental violations, and hence a company's and management's ultimate exposure to prosecution. A properly operated environmental management and legal compliance program might also be useful in a defense to a prosecution, and perhaps in persuading prosecutors not to begin legal action.

surrender
control

In deciding to participate in the EMAS regulation's system, you should be mindful that your company surrenders control over the scope of auditing, accepts a good deal of bureaucracy, and embarks on a process of public disclosure you do not control. For example, as noted before, under the regulation's scheme you will have to investigate contamination. Independent of the regulation's public environmental statement disclosure obligations, a company that finds contamination may find that (1) under the environmental laws, it must notify authorities of the contamination, and (2) under the accounting rules, it must comment in its financial statements on the contingent liabilities associated with the contamination.

Legal Implications

Given the legal implications of such environmental management systems, corporate counsel should be intimately involved in their design, installation and supervision.

Liability risks

First, mere participation in the EMAS system might not be very persuasive to enforcement authorities contemplating prosecution, nor adequate to ensure a legal defense (e.g., to show that a U.K. manager is not guilty of "consent," "connivance," or "neglect" in the occurrence of a violation of his or her company, and hence not personally criminally liable under the U.K. Environmental Protection Act 1990).

To minimize liability risks, the environmental management system will have to focus on ensuring compliance and should not be allowed to degrade into a checklist-ticking exercise. The system will have to ensure compliance with *all* applicable (including local) environmental laws, not just those provisions appearing in the permits. It will need to ensure that instances of noncompliance are resolved immediately — given the costs that can involve, that demands unflinching support by top management.

Documentation trail

Second, as with the U.S. Sentencing Guidelines, the E.U. EMAS regulation places an emphasis on documentation. Thorough documentation could be important in the event that the effectiveness of a compliance program is at issue in a legal proceeding.

For this reason, it will be advisable to have legal counsel participate in organizing and maintaining that documentation. If your company and its officers and directors ever have to "prove their case," it will be critical to show that the program is "real" and that the policies and procedures established by your company reflect a genuine concern of upper management with legal compliance. Credible testimony buttressed by thorough documentation may well provide the best demonstration of the effectiveness of the company's compliance efforts.

Disclosure

Third, you should keep in mind that, despite any protection afforded by legal professional privilege, the environmental management and auditing systems information may ultimately be disclosed in many instances, whether inadvertently, intentionally, or under compulsion. All documentation should be prepared with that eventuality clearly in mind.

You should pay attention to the type of information solicited by questionnaires and protocols. Those completing the forms — whether in-house staff or outside consultants — should be counseled on the implications of particular language in their answers, and on document management. They should submit their reports in draft to your company's in-house or outside counsel, and counsel should review those drafts for ambiguous, misleading, and conclusory phrasing. The object is not to "whitewash," but to ensure sensitivity to the fact that imprecision or carelessness can come back to haunt your company and its management.

Reporting

Fourth, the involvement of legal counsel is essential given that effective audits almost invariably will uncover situations posing delicate legal questions concerning compliance and notification obligations. For example, national law often requires that operators notify environmental authorities immediately on discovery of certain regulatory violations. Similarly, discovery of contamination can — depending on the specific terms of applicable legislation — require prompt notification of environmental authorities. Accordingly, companies will need to involve their counsel in evaluating specific compliance issues and whether, how, and when particular events or discoveries should be reported.

9.5.5 Conclusions

The E.U. EMAS Regulation is a clever ploy on the part of the commission to achieve more effective enforcement and to induce industry to go beyond compliance. The EMAS regulation will result in more public information on particular facilities and likely will excite more interest in compliance at the local and national levels. Even where national enforcement authorities might not otherwise be inclined to take action, environmental groups may find it easier to drum up public support, leaving enforcement authorities with no choice.

Further, in some European countries, environmental groups have powers to bring enforcement and cleanup actions (e.g., Belgium). Information on noncompliance and contamination at EMAS participating sites certainly will make such actions easier to mount.

But the regulation's effects will be selective, and the regulation is a poor substitute for effective environmental law consistently applied.

pressure for
larger
companies

It will be principally larger companies with important brand names that will be under the heaviest pressure to participate in the EMAS system. While the regulation suggests that efforts should be made to draw in small and medium- sized enterprises, little success is likely. A local dry cleaner simply will not be subject to the same pressure as a multinational consumer goods company. Also, the regulation envisions experiments with public services, but it remains highly unlikely that, for example, publicly owned utilities will find participation under the EMAS regulation worth the nuisance.

Industry may look on the EMAS regulation with a bit more ambivalence. Companies, at least in some sectors, may find that they have little choice but to join. These companies may find some benefits, for example, in minimizing legal violations and in establishing a defense in the event of a prosecution against management (though these benefits could be obtained through less cumbersome environmental management systems outside the EMAS system).

On the other hand, the costs of the EMAS system will likely be significant. ISO 9000 experience has already demonstrated that such standardized and certified management and auditing systems can be costly. In the environmental context, the costs and complications likely will be more grave, given the legal implications and the disclosure consequences.

CHAPTER 6
Acceptance in Countries

9.6.1 Overview

This section discusses how a variety of countries view ISO 14001 and how the standard is expected to be used. This information was compiled in late 1995 and early 1996, and was likely to evolve over time. In certain countries, governments are taking a more active role in making use of ISO 14001 and other ISO 14000 standards than are other governments. In some countries, industry is beginning to seize a competitive advantage by proactively pursuing both implementation and certification.

While we tried to gain as complete information as possible about the status of ISO 14001 in these countries, absence of information does not construe absence of a particular aspect of the standard in that country. For example, while we may not have discussed formal accreditation procedures in a country, that country may have such procedures in place. 📖 (See Appendix G for a list of accreditation bodies.)

9.6.2 Asia Roundup

by CEEM Information Services

Pilots, Workshops, Seminars, Mandates: Asia is Rife with ISO 14000 Interest

In early 1996, *International Environmental Systems Update* queried management consulting firms that have business ties with Asian countries to see how ISO 14000 was taking hold in Asia. The following report on activities in Asian countries was drawn from interviews with key consultants who have had extensive experience doing EMS work in Asia. They were:

- John Kinsella, vice president of SCS Engineers, an international environmental consulting firm based in Bellevue, Washington;

- Edwin Pinero, a Lancaster, Pennsylvania-based senior project manager with EnSafe Inc., an environmental consulting firm;

- John J. Mapes, a consultant to the United States–Asia Environmental Partnership (US–AEP), part of Agency for International Development, from John J. Mapes & Associates in Oakland, California.; and

- Larry Taylor, managing principal of the Creighton Group in Los Angeles, California.

China

growing interest

The Chinese State Bureau of Technical Supervision, the national standards body, is a member of ISO. Chinese delegations have participated in TC 207 committee meetings.

Mapes said that many companies with operations in China had attended ISO 14000 workshops and seminars in Hong Kong, and that the Norwegian Agency for International Development in early 1996 proposed to conduct an ISO 14000 training project with companies and potential auditors in China. 📖 (See China Power and Light story in section on China below; its environmental policy appears in Part 3.)

Hong Kong

The Hong Kong Productivity Council has collaborated with the Canadian Standards Association to develop a pilot "self-help" program to help companies implement or tailor existing environmental management systems (EMSs) to conform to the ISO 14000 draft standards.

government
incentives?

The government of Hong Kong has disallowed companies that lack ISO 9000 certification from bidding on projects that exceed $1.25 million (U.S.). Also, said Mapes, the government was contemplating decreasing government scrutiny of companies that self-regulate via an EMS that is certified to ISO 14000 standards. 📖 (See more on Hong Kong below.)

India

certification
with help

In November 1995 the first Indian company in India gained BS 7750 certification with the help of the Environmental Management Division of the Confederation of Indian Industries (CII). Twelve other companies were receiving CII assistance for BS 7750 certification. The Bureau of Indian Standards also had its own national environmental standard (based on BS 7750) since 1993.

Mapes said that many leading Indian companies are ISO 9000 certified and noted that these companies "whether intended by the ISO standards or not, see certification as a statement of product quality as much as quality assurance."

Japan

"We will see more rapid acceptance of ISO 14000 in Japan than in the U.S.," Kinsella said, and the larger industries in Japan are "moving ahead under voluntary suggestions" with the Japanese Ministry of International Trade and Industry. 📖 (See more on Japan below.)

embracing ISO
14001 for trade

Japan, an export-oriented country where ISO 9000 has been widely accepted, has embraced ISO 14001 as another part of doing business internationally. This contrasts the Japanese vision with that of the U.S., which has been compliance-driven. In Japan, where population density and limited usable land are major operating factors for businesses, cooperation with government agencies is not unusual.

Japan has been ahead in its acceptance of ISO 14000, according to Pinero. Japan-based companies dictate that they will be ISO 14000 compliant, if not certified. Japan was seen as an early leader in getting beyond its own borders, with its major companies even seeking ISO 14000 compliance in overseas facilities, such as in the U.S.

Korea

larger
industries
implementing

Pinero said that Korea may be ahead of the U.S. in its acceptance of ISO 14001, but perhaps not from a technical standpoint. The very large industries were planning to implement ISO 14001, and there was a liaison between industry and government on how to implement the standard.

legislation

Samsung, Korea, gained BS 7750 certification in 1994, said Mapes. In 1995, the South Korean Ministry of Trade, Industry, and Energy introduced legislation defining an "industrial environment vision" and proposing to assist companies in preparation for ISO 14000. He added that South Korean representatives were very active in the TC 207 committee meetings.

Malaysia

In late 1995, Pinero attended a corporate environmental excellence conference in Malaysia that was sponsored by the Association of Southeast Asian Nations. He said that the conference themes often covered environmental issues and noted the progress made by a Malaysian palm oil processing industry to be "in line" with ISO 14001.

active interest/
particpation

Mapes met with a group of 15 Malaysians who had been hosted by electronics companies in the Silicon Valley. He said that the group spent a couple of weeks at Stanford doing executive training courses and then were "farmed out" to observe the EHS departments of different electronics companies. The group's intention was to return to Malaysia to write the health and safety laws and regulations. Malaysia sent some 13 delegates to the 1995 TC 207 meeting in Oslo, Norway, among the highest from developing nations.

Singapore

workshops,
training

Singapore has an Environmental Management Technical Committee consisting of representatives from government ministries (environment, health, labor), Trade Development Board, Economic Development Board, Singapore Manufacturers Association, Singapore Chemical Industry Council, the Packaging Council of Singapore, the Oil Industry Steering Committee, and the Association of Electronic Industry in Singapore.

Many industry associations have held workshops and seminars on ISO 14000.

Thailand

Taylor said that there was substantial interest in ISO 14000 in Thailand. "The first to show interest were the large multinational oil companies. Now, [in early 1996], all industries are actively seeking education and training. The British and Swiss seem to have made the most significant in-road at this point."

Taylor said that,among the projects his company in Bankgok completed was Doi Suthep Temple environmental impact study and an ISO 14000 workshop, which were both "widely covered" in the press.

accreditation
council

He added that the Thailand Industrial Standards Institute was seeking to establish the country's National Accreditation Council (NAC), seeking help from accreditation bodies such as the American National Standards Institute and the Registrar Accreditation Board in the U.S. Several developing countries from other parts of the world were asking for similar assistance, he said.

The Thai NAC is striving to be an internationally recognized full service accreditation body that offers registrar, auditor, and course certification services. Taylor expected to see the NAC fully established by the fall of 1996, but he did not know how the NAC would be accepted in the international community.

Taiwan

The Industrial Research and Technology Institute, a quasi-public technical arm of the government of Taiwan, has been tasked with developing a national ISO 14000 implementation plan, according to Mapes. This includes "a certification/accreditation scheme, the development of tools and implementation technology, the conduct of promotional efforts, and the pursuit of international cooperation and recognition."

The high-technology industry of Taiwan formed a Green Computer Association to help members meet environmental requirements of international markets. The association was aiming to increase assistance to members on management systems, to include ISO 14000 requirements.

Taiwan, perhaps more than any other Asian country, has acknowledged environmental requirements as a strategic factor in its international competitiveness, Mapes related. In an effort to be competitive, the country identified about 10 industries to promote becauuse of thr lower levels of pollution.

The downside for Taiwan in deciding to "clean up its island" has been to force all the "dirty businesses" off the island, Mapes said. Taiwan has invested about $30 billion in China and is the largest investor in the Philippines. He suggested that Taiwan is "shipping off" the polluting and low-skilled industries, but is positioning itself to be competitive.

Summary

Mapes said that Asian companies were looking at ISO 14001 "as a way to maintain access to international markets and gain competitive advantage." He added that U.S. companies that compete with Asian companies as suppliers and as exporters to international markets should consider pursuing ISO 14001 certification as a competitive strategy.

Asian companies realize that they must get on board with products that are produced according to international specifications and world-class standards or risk getting "sidelined" in the international market, according to Mapes.

In some areas of Asia, though, environmental progress has been far behind. Mapes said that the rivers in Indonesia are so polluted that the water has to be cleaned up before it can be used by businesses in their processes. "The intake water is dirtier than discharge water in other countries after other countries have used it," Mapes said. "They've taken water treatment and put it on the front end of the manufacturing process. And they'll discharge back into the rivers without treating because [the water] is still cleaner than what they've gotten."

The positive side of ISO awareness can be seen in countries such as Thailand, where Mapes said he saw "ISO 9000" spray-painted on factory walls that line the freeway to the airport in Bangkok.

9.6.3 Canada

Pilot Project, Audit Group, Indicate Strong Support for ISO 14001

from International Evironmental Systems Update, January 1995

Canadian industries involved in an ISO 14000-based pilot project found top-down commitment, training, and financial support essential for successfully implementing the standard's provisions. According to participants, the pilot effort also highlighted gaps in the companies' existing environmental management systems (EMSs).

The Canadian Standards Association (CSA) said the pilot project had two purposes: to help gain field experience so that Canada could return to TC 207 meetings with better information, and to help Canadian organizations prepare for the ISO 14001 document when it is published.

The pilot project was implemented by the CSA, Canada's largest integrated standards development and conformity assessment organization. Launched in May 1994, the project involved the ISO 14001 draft specification standard and the ISO 14004 guideline. Both were expected to be final by October 1996.

Canada was the second country after the United Kingdom to implement an EMS pilot program. Canada, the international ministry for TC 176, which developed the ISO 9000 quality system standards, was also entrusted with the ministry of TC 207. NSF International launched a similar pilot in the U.S. in the fall of 1994.

Broad Support

According to CSA pilot project manager R. Keith MacEachern, the pilot project had the support of a large section of Canadian industry, federal, provincial, and municipal governments, environmental interest groups; labor; and other organizations. CSA initially accommodated about 20 companies.

Several industries that could not be included desired another pilot, so CSA started a second pilot group of industry organizations. Interest eventually grew to form a third group.

The three pilot groups total about 55 organizations, which included: Ontario Hydro, Bell Canada, Domtar Inc., Syncrude Canada Ltd., Pitney Bowes, C N North America, and West Coast Energy Inc. According to MacEachern, the companies participating in the pilot have been mainly large companies from the natural resources and utilities industries.

Originally, the pilot held meetings in Toronto, but the groups were separated into three geographic units: Western, Central, and Eastern Canada.

CSA expected that the results of the two-phase pilot, which was scheduled to run until the ISO 14001 and ISO 14004 standards were final, would interest organizations in other nations willing to adopt the international standard. CSA planned to prepare a concluding report. The first phase was an introduction providing background on the standards and an overview of the international status of EMSs. The second implementation phase consisted of working groups helping participating organizations implement the standard.

Lessons

big benefit:
sharing ideas

In the early months, the participants agreed that the ISO 14000 documents had provided them with the methodology to effectively initiate, improve, and sustain an EMS. Companies especially liked sharing improvement ideas with their peers in a workshop format.

Syncrude environmental services manager Gary Burns said that his company already had an environmental policy and that the pilot had helped Syncrude to be a little more specific. Burns expected that Syncrude would have to make a few changes in its policy.

Paul Tessier, environmental coordinator at Domtar Inc., related that risk assessment and defining accountability were more relevant to his company than any of the other issues, concerns, and solutions discussed at the implementation meetings.

Dennis Durrant, special adviser at the National Office of Pollution Control in Canada, said the implementation process showed that senior management commitment, training, and financial support were among the important issues necessary for the successful implementation of an EMS.

A majority of the participants contacted stressed that they had senior management commitment; otherwise, they would not have been part of the pilot.

Tessier said his company was seeking ways to provide sufficient resources — financial, human, etc. — to meet its environmental commitments under ISO 14000. He added, though, that environmental commitments were not strictly related to ISO certification but were the results of a variety of incentives — market, compliance, finance, and public image. He also admitted that the pilot showed that his company needed to review and improve its EMS to improve environmental performance, which meant taking a more systematic approach.

But the manager of a Vancouver-based energy company found that, while participation in the pilot project did not change the company's action plan, it did show that the company was headed in the right direction, and it gave the company a good target to shoot for. Participants praised the practical suggestions in ISO 14004 on how to get started on an EMS.

Audits

not enough on
audits

Unlike the draft specification document (ISO 14001), which is written in prescriptive language and contains those system elements that may be objectively audited, the ISO 14004 draft guideline merely touches upon the necessity of audits and how to go about them. MacEachern said that the pilot also skirted the issue. Auditors had not yet been accredited since the ISO documents were still in the development stages. Several participants were non-committal on whether they supported third-party audits. They also were not in favor of any public disclosure requirement nor of the prescriptive approach contained in EMAS. Tessier asserted that the certification process should remain confidential.

Small Companies Left Out

Another issue the pilot highlighted was that small companies perceived the EMS standard as too costly to implement, or not applicable to their systems. Of the 55 companies involved in the pilot, most were large companies.

Durrant said that the results from the pilot and the increased awareness of the CSA/ISO documents would encourage and assist other organizations in implementing the EMS. He added, however, that more work needed to be done to encourage small and even micro enterprises to participate.

SME task force

To do this, Durrant said, his office had plans to formulate a national task force involving a partnership of associations, industry, and business groups to build awareness and promotion and adoption of EMSs among micro organizations.

Canadian Auditing Association Plans For Auditor Certification Program

from International Evironmental Systems Update, March 1996

In early 1996, the Canadian Environmental Auditing Association (CEAA) was establishing an environmental auditor certification program for ISO 14001 and expected to have the program certified by the Standards Council of Canada (SCC) by June 1, 1996. The association was determined to have a certified program in place by the time ISO published the ISO 14001 standard, expected by October 1996.

certification task force

CEAA established a certification task force in December 1995 and was beginning to work on documents for qualifications criteria, examinations, application processes, grandparenting (based on experience and/or standing in the association), and discipline.

CEAA was developing the program in response to the Canadian Institute of Chartered Accountants (CICA), which identified CEAA as the premier organization in the country to assume responsibility for certifying environmental auditors. CEAA has an active membership of 300 to 400 professionals in the accounting, environmental management, engineering, science, legal, banking, insurance, and utility fields.

Mutual recognition pacts between the SCC and other accreditation bodies such as the United States Registrar Accreditation Board and the American National Standards Institute should provide the opportunity for CEAA-registered auditors to conduct accredited audits for companies worldwide.

Program Structure

Kim Shikaze, executive director of the CEAA, explained that CEAA members were invited to participate in developing the criteria for the program through five working groups that were set up to address specific aspects of the certification program.

five working groups

The CEAA established working groups in the following areas:

- qualifications criteria working group: establishes qualification criteria, syllabus designations, training specification,s and ongoing certification maintenance requirements;

- examination group: examines design and administration;

- application process group: focuses on administrative appeals and the registry;

- grandparenting group: determines and executes a process for approving the exam and will act as the association's board of examiners and application approval mechanism; and

- discipline group: will confirm and publicize a code of ethics and design a process for handling questions and complaints, as well as recommend disciplinary actions.

Mutual Recognition

mutual
recognition
with EAR

Shikaze said CEAA has had a good working relationship with the U.S.-based Environmental Auditing Roundtable (EAR) and therefore expected the United States accreditation program to recognize CEAA-registered auditors in the U.S. Also, he said that through SCC's use of ISO's Committee on Conformity Assessment guides, mutual recognition in other countries should not be an obstacle.

CEAA also was discussing accreditation approval with a newly formed Canadian Environmental Accreditation and Certification Board, but the association did not expect that another accreditation body would be necessary.

Shikaze said the development and implementation of the certification program would be expensive and beyond the capability of CEAA to initiate independently. CICA would need financial and volunteer support for the program. CEAA met with government officials in January 1996 to discuss financial assistance. Shikaze said the government agreed to fund a percentage of the program.

For more information on the CEAA environmental auditor program, contact Kim Shikaze, CEAA, 6519B Mississauga, Ontario, Canada L5N1A6; tel: 905-567-4705; fax: 905-567-7191.

9.6.4 Hong Kong

Business Council Encourages ISO 14001
from International Evironmental Systems Update, March 1996

Is Government Requirement Far Behind?

HONG KONG

The Hong Kong Productivity Council (HKPC), a branch of the Hong Kong government, was launching an ISO 14001 pilot in mid-May 1996 for small- and medium-sized enterprises using resources from larger Hong Kong companies to help fund the project. The project was to last six to nine months.

focus on SMEs

Leveraging from the larger companies' resources, HKPC was seeking between 10 and 12 non-manufacturing SMEs to participate in developing an EMS modeled after ISO 14001. Motorola, Canon, Canadian Airlines, Rank Xerox, Cathay Pacific, China Light and Power, and the Kowloon Canton Railway Corporation had all agreed to cosponsor the program.

According to Thomas Chapman, principal consultant with the environmental management division of the council, Hong Kong government officials mandated that all consulting firms and contractors conducting business with the government totaling a minimum of $1.25 million have ISO 9001 or ISO 9002 certification by April 1, 1996, and October 1, 1996, respectively.

ISO 9000
mandates =
ISO 14001?

Chapman said multinational corporations as well as Hong Kong-based companies were fearful that ISO 14001 certification would not be far behind. While the ISO 9000 mandates likely would affect several SMEs immediately, he said that most smaller companies operating in Hong Kong were not prepared for ISO 14001.

suppliers

ISO 14001 certification was expected to be a reality for larger companies doing global business because of their experiences with ISO 9000 certification. Some large companies were already beginning to query their suppliers on whether they had elements of an EMS in place. Some of these queries included questions about a supplier's environmenal policy, objectives, and targets, and the responsible person appointed to address environmental issues.

The First Step

Motorola and Philips Hong Kong Ltd. environmental personnel sent out questionnaires in early 1996 asking suppliers for a list of hazardous materials used during the production process, Chapman said. The questionnaire also asked when suppliers planned to phase out the hazardous material and replace it with something environmentally preferable.

It was too early to tell whether these companies would give preference to suppliers with an EMS in place, according to Chapman.

The SME program was to follow much the same format as HKPC's EMS pilot program for larger companies that began in November 1995.

11 companies

Eleven companies were participating in the first pilot, which was being conducted in association with the Canadian Standards Association, representing both the manufacturing and service sectors of the Hong Kong economy. The following companies were all taking part in HKPC ISO 14001 lectures, workshops, and assessments:

> Shell Greater China; Mobil Oil Hong Kong Ltd.; the Island Shangri-La Hotel; Philips Hong Kong Ltd.; China Light and Power; Elec and Eltek Co. Ltd.; Green Valley Landfill Ltd.; Lee Construction; Shui Wing Steel; Sylva Industries Ltd; and Electrical and Mechanical Services of the Hong Kong government

Chapman says that the HKPC was visiting each site to identify and understand the environmental considerations that the companies must manage, and the HKPC was giving the companies advice on how to use a checklist for system assessment purposes.

The SME project was to be similar in nature but would focus more on smaller companies' limited knowledge of environmental impacts and availability of resources. HKPC was planning to facilitate frequent meetings with the companies and conduct more workshops and demonstrations than called for with larger companies.

Auditing Training

HKPC was expecting to begin offering a five-day EMS advanced auditing course approved by the U.K.-based Environmental Auditors egistration Association (EARA) for Hong Kong company representatives beginning in May 1996. HKPC also offers a basic EARA-approved course that teaches participants knowledge of compliance, supplier, and EMS audits. HKPC was planning to launch another SME program for manufacturing facilities in late 1996, but was awaiting word on government-funded grants for the project.

For more information, contact Thomas Chapman, principal consultant with the environmental management division of the HKPC, HKPC Building, 78 Tat Chee Avenue, Kowloon, Hong Kong; tel: +852-2788-5638; fax: 852-2788-5608.

Airline, Power Companies in Hong Kong Value Implementation

from International Environmental Systems Update, August 1995

Seeking to enhance current market share and gain a competitive advantage, two Hong Kong companies were moving rapidly toward implementing the ISO 14001 environmental management system (EMS) in August 1995, and both were already perceiving many internal and external benefits.

Cathay Pacific Airways Ltd., a large Hong Kong-based airline, was planning first to seek third-party certification of its own facilities and then require its suppliers and contractors to have a certificate, according to Fred Luk, environmental services manager with Cathay. He said requiring certification of suppliers was the next logical step after the company saw the benefits an EMS can provide.

China Light & Power (CLP), one of the largest power producers in Asia, was implementing an EMS, but had no plans to register to any EMS standard.

Cathay Strategies

budget
problems

Luk explained that Cathay was discussing implementation strategies with its consultant and initially wanted to begin implementing the standard in June 1995, but encountered budget problems.

He said evidence showed that an ISO 14001 EMS would minimize wastes; increase staff morale; provide a better indoor environment for staff; decrease costs; help the company's public image; and help increase market share.

"We have just started initial implementation, but we will be prepared to register to the ISO 14001 specification soon," he said.

Certification Benefit Questioned

Unlike Cathay, CLP saw no benefit from certification and no justification for incurring its costs, said Richard Jack, corporate environmental manager for CLP. "Our aim is to have an EMS which could be certified if necessary without major additional work," he said.

In April 1995, the company began introducing employees to the concept of an EMS, and subsequently drafted a corporate environmental statement, making it available to the public.

Jack said each department of the company was charged with drafting initial targets for its own use. Each department was responsible for:

- drawing up a register of environmental effects;
- formulating an improvement plan that includes specific targets; and
- introducing any local management systems needed to implement the corporate EMS.

"Our corporate target is to ensure that all of the above are done, after which we shall review the improvement plans and consider targets and objectives for the future," he said.

Internal Value

"It is possible that we shall save money, e.g., reducing wastes, but this is something that we should be doing as good management anyway," Jack said. "I suggest that some of the companies who make extravagant claims of savings from an EMS in one forum will attribute the same benefits to the CEO's cost-cutting initiative in another forum."

different
benefits

Rather than attributing any bottom-line savings to the EMS, Jack identified slightly different benefits of implementing it than did Cathay, including:

- commitment to continuous improvement;
- introduction of a formal management process to ensure delivery of improvements;
- a clear statement of environmental commitment and positioning;
- a clear understanding of who was responsible for what; and
- putting the company in the position to run its environmental affairs rather than being reactive to external changes.

Jack said some major external benefits of an EMS were:

- credibility in the marketplace and public-relations value;
- potential competitive edge when bidding for overseas projects; and
- reduced opposition to development proposals in Hong Kong.

Problems Identified

CLP encountered some minor problems as it began to conduct strategy meetings to address implementation, Jack explained, including:

- positioning problems with respect to how far the company was willing to go: "very green, just green, not quite green";
- writing the corporate environmental statement to reflect the company's positioning accurately and still satisfy demands for a good public-relations image;
- persuading senior management that the company could legitimately include environmental considerations in purchasing decisions; and
- convincing non-operational departments (finance, personnel) they had a focus in environmental issues.

"Some senior people wanted to claim to be greener than they were prepared to pay for in practice," Jack remarked.

6.5 Japan

Trade Ministry Asks Firms to Prepare for ISO 14000
from International Environmental Systems Update, January 1996

Beginning in early 1996, the Japanese Ministry of International Trade and Industry (MITI) was expected to ask companies to prepare new environmental management plans that conform with requirements contained in the ISO 14001 environmental management system standard by the end of 1996.

While it was unclear how Japanese companies would respond, several experts speculated that MITI was using the ISO 14001 process to raise the floor on Japanese companies' environmental performance.

MITI is a Japanese government department that formulates industrial policy and assists organizations with managing trade issues to better their position in the global marketplace. MITI encourages Japanese companies to develop contacts overseas and participate in technology transfer and information-sharing initiatives.

The standards department of MITI promulgates national standards established by the Japanese Industrial Standards (JIS) Committee and nationalizes international standards.

MITI was planning to use ISO 14001 to build upon companies' existing environmental plans, which include provisions that direct companies on how to prevent air, water, and noise pollution, according to the Japanese Agency of Industrial Science and Technology (AIST).

Experts speculated that MITI's request was based upon the realization that environmental problems extend across borders and are no longer an isolated concern. With that understanding, many Japanese companies have recognized the need to implement a system for identifying and managing their environmental responsibilities.

national
standards

Tomosaburo Yano, deputy director of the Standards Planning Office, AIST within MITI, said JIS was scheduled to adopt the ISO 14001 specification, ISO 14004 guidance, and the ISO 14000 auditing standards in July 1996 to coincide with the ISO timeline. He also said the Japanese Accreditation Board would establish certification and accreditation schemes during the same time frame.

certification
and
accreditation
schemes

"This is a voluntary plan based on companies' decision whether or not to do it," Yano stressed. "We are introducing the ISO 14000 series to companies to illustrate the importance of ISO activities to environmental management systems in industry."

Most of the environmental management programs that were being implemented by Japanese companies conformed with ISO 14001, despite the fact that ISO 14000 did not exist when Japanese companies began implementing EMSs in the early 1980s, according to Kazutomo Ohtake, professor and chairman of the Department of Ecological Engineering at Toyohashi University of Technology in Tokyo.

strong
company
programs exist

Ohtake said several Japanese companies with strong environmental management programs included Sony, Honda, Asahi Chemicals, Itoh Yohkado Super Market, Ebara Corporation, Tokyo Electric Power Company, Tokyo Gas Company, Inforest Company, Tamanohada Soap Company, and Kinzoku Metal Research Company.

"These environmental management programs meet the severest Japanese environmental regulations. However, small- and medium-sized companies must now be encouraged to willingly participate," he said. "Existing environmental laws are well-considered, detailed, and powerful, and it would be difficult to measure the degree of ISO 14000 attainment of other countries, as each country has its own culture."

Support Evident

bottom-line benefits sought

Ohtake, a delegate working on the environmental performance evaluation (EPE) standard being developed by TC 207 Subcommittee 4, said most Japanese companies would be eager to embrace a system if they could be shown that it increases their performance and at the same time provides them a clear advantage in the marketplace. He noted that several symposia, study meetings, and panel discussions promoting ISO 14000 were being presented throughout Japan with strong support from the industrial community.

land limitations foster stewardship

He said several major Japanese companies were beginning to realize the importance of preserving the country for future generations. Japan's land area is almost equal to the state of California, yet due to mountainous terrain, people are only able to live on 14 percent of the total land. "In addition, the population of Japan is almost half that of the U.S., which has 30 times more land," Ohtake noted. "If our companies do not find a way to manage their environmental impacts, we may not have anywhere to live."

Groundwater Concern

John Kinsella, vice president of SCS Engineers, an international environmental consulting firm in the U.S., said his company completed a cleanup project in 1995 on a U.S. military base in Japan.

He said Japan is very concerned about solvents in groundwater, particularly trichlorethylene (TCE), a universal solvent used in the electronics industry. For example, TCE is a chlorinated solvent used as a degreaser in washing electronics parts during manufacture.

"It's an extremely good solvent but it is very soluble in water and is a carcinogen and doesn't break down easily," Kinsella explained. "Once it gets into the groundwater system, it spreads rapidly and can contaminate a very large area of water."

He said that, unfortunately, all of Japan's population is on the coastal plain, with everyone living and manufacturing in this narrow strip of land. The rest of the country is mountains or earthquake-prone.

"The groundwater is shallow, and as a consequence, it is being contaminated," Kinsella explained. "For this reason, they are very concerned about solvents, PCBs, and mercury because of their deleterious effects on the food chain. They have very strict regulations about these."

property transfer regulation

The issues that the U.S. focuses on, such as underground storage tanks and petroleum, are not the biggest concerns in Japan. The country has begun a regulation on property transfer that is similar to the U.S.'s, said Kinsella. However, unlike in the U.S., a Japanese owner selling land must make sure it is clean and is responsible for cleaning it up.

Industry Perspective

industry is preparing

Hideki Kobayashi, staff general manager of the Environmental Control and Energy Department for Kawasaki Steel Corporation, explained that his company was considering changes in its EMS in accordance with ISO 14001. He said this will help the company be prepared to respond as soon as possible to the future requests from customers about third-party certification.

Kobayashi added that Kawasaki's existing environmental management systems comply with the most stringent environmental regulations in Japan and therefore have most of the elements of ISO 14001 already in place.

MITI announcement downplayed

Kobayashi downplayed the MITI announcement because its impact is unclear to industry. As to how Kawasaki's environmental management systems may change, Kobayashi says that it plans to apply some of the concrete examples described in ISO 14004 guidelines.

"I do not think that the decision of MITI will have a major impact on the Japanese companies that have their own environmental management systems to comply with the regulations, although they may have to do a little modification of their systems," he noted. But ISO 14000 series will have a more direct impact on Japanese companies than the ISO 9000 series of quality management system standards, because of the wide range of stakeholders involved with EMS, he said.

Measuring Results

obtaining measurement results

Ohtake said Nippon Electric and Electronics Company (NEC) has a method for obtaining measurable results of its environmental management system. Several other companies had adopted this method and planned to integrate it into their current systems.

"They have had [an] EMS for more than 20 years," he said. "They give points for the level of attainment for each item and use this point system as a basis for refining the system and creating more tools to attain their goals."

Further, they had applied this method not only to their EMS, but also to reduction of production material, labor time, and production costs, Ohtake said. "Their emission levels are far under the regulation requirements."

Other Key Environmental Issues

"For production companies, pollution protection of water and soil is the most important issue," Ohtake said. He added that pollution-prevention from factories had almost been completed and that automobile emissions were the current hot topic.

carbon dioxide is key concern

"Carbon dioxide is being discussed in the industries in which much fuel is consumed, such as electric power companies and the iron and steel industries," he explained.

Although Japan did not have a major ozone depletion area (ODA), as does the U.S., Ohtake anticipated a steep increase in carbon dioxide concentration, and was promoting the development of systems and installations to attain higher thermal efficiencies for production activities in industry.

"I expect that Japan will transfer its emission-controlling technologies to Asian countries by means of ODA activities," he explained. "This means that Japan knows that environmental protection is not just a problem for one country, but is one that needs to be solved by international linkage and cooperation among countries."

Ohtake said ISO 14001's strict requirements for documenting procedures may not be implemented by Japanese companies. He said most companies operate more smoothly by oral commands with simple written materials, rather than by formal and detailed documents.

For more information, contact Tomosaburo Yano, Standards Planning Office, AIST, MITI, 1-3-1, Kasumigaseki, Chiyoda-ku, Tokyo 100, Japan; tel: 81-3-3501-9295; fax: 81-3-3580-1418; e-mail: ytaa3398@miti.go.jp

9.6.6 Mexico

by C. Foster Knight, Managing Director, Knight and Associates

Mexico's Participation in ISO TC 207

MEXICO
In June 1995, Mexico began participating in TC 207 by sending a representative, Leonardo Cárdenas from the Instituto Technológico y de Estudios Superiores de Monterrey (ITESM), to the TC 207 plenary meeting in Oslo, Norway. At that time, there were only a handful of people in Mexico familiar with the ISO 14000 series standards.

initial participation low
During the summer of 1995, Mexico formally established a technical advisory group to TC 207, coordinated by the Mexican Institute for Standardization and Certification (IMNC). Mexico's TC 207 technical advisory group, the National Technical Committee for Environmental Management Systems Standards (COTENNSAM), is chaired by Raul Tornel, director of production for the Compañía Hulera Tornel and chairman of the Ecology Committee for the National Council of Industry Associations (CONCAMIN).

COTENNSAM parallels the TC 207 structure and organization, except that in early 1996 it only had active working groups for SC1 (ISO 14001 and 14004), SC2 (auditing), SC 4 (environmental performance evaluation), and SC6 (terms and definitions). COTENNSAM may become active in SC3 (labeling) and SC 4 (life-cycle assessment) at a later date.

80 organizations participate
Within the time span of one year (May 1995–May 1996) Mexico's participation in the ISO 14000 series of standards increased substantially. By March 1996, more than 80 private Mexican companies and industry groups, including leading member companies in Mexico's national Chemical Industries Association (ANIQ), the National Council of Industrial Ecologists (CONIECO), and Iniciativa GEMI, actively participated on COTENNSAM. Other participants included representatives from the National Ecology Institute (INE), the federal Environmental Attorney General's Office (PROFEPA), and the Instituto Technológico y de Estudios Superiores de Monterrey.

COTENNSAM had produced draft (Mexican) Spanish versions of ISO 14001 and 14004, which were circulating for review and comment in early 1996. The Spanish translations were to become the official Mexican ISO 14001 and 14004 standards after ISO 14001 and ISO 14004 become final.

Issues and Opportunities

NAFTA
pressure

The environmental debate leading up to the NAFTA treaty focused on significant disparities between Mexico's environmental regulatory standards and enforcement, leading to political pressures for increased environmental enforcement — particularly along the U.S.– Mexico border — and for large environmental infrastructure projects for improving waste management, water quality, and wastewater treatment.

Coming shortly after NAFTA's ratification, Mexico's peso devaluation in December 1994 and the ensuing economic crisis could not have come at a worst time. Mexico's economic woes during 1994 and 1995 severely strained government and industry capacity to make progress on critical environmental quality issues. Government budgets for environmental programs were slashed, and Mexican industry was forced to cope with serious capital and foreign exchange scarcity in addition to soaring interest rates.

despite
challenges,
environmental
protection
sought

Despite these challenges, Mexico was continuing to give priority to environmental protection and improvement through an interesting blend of "command-and-control" and voluntary environmental initiatives.

Mexico's Ministry for the Environment, Natural Resources, and Fisheries (SEMARNAP), elevated to cabinet level by the newly inaugurated President Zedillo in December 1994, generally held the line with continuing environmental enforcement through its enforcement arm, the federal Environmental Attorney General's Office (PROFEPA). PROFEPA was given expanded enforcement priorities in natural resources protection in addition to its focus on hazardous waste management. The environmental regulatory arm of SEMARNAP, the National Institute of Ecology, continued to promulgate increasing numbers of specific "command-and-control" environmental regulations — the official Mexican standards, or normas officiales de Mexico (NOMs).

voluntary
programs

As Mexico continued to develop traditional "command-and-control" environmental regulation and enforcement mechanisms, it also put an increasingly significant effort on market-based voluntary incentives. Among these voluntary environmental improvement initiatives were:

* The environmental protection and industrial competitiveness agreement (Industrial Cooperation Agreement) signed by the National Council of Industry Associations, the federal environmental attorney general, and the National Institute of Ecology.

   The purpose of this initiative was to simplify and increase industry compliance, promote improved environmental technologies through a new information network, and promote market-based environmental performance incentives.

* Greater sensitivity to and renewed governmental support for small and medium industry environmental improvements based on redeploying scarce technical expertise from end-of-pipe control approaches toward pollution prevention possibilities that yield improved "eco-efficiencies," savings, and better environmental results.

* Promoting greater use of Mexico's unique voluntary environmental, health, and safety (EHS) audit program.

EHS
improvements

The voluntary environmental audits are supervised by PROFEPA under a contract with the industrial site. The audits evaluate not only EHS compliance but also opportunities for improving EHS performance "beyond compliance" and strengthening the sites' EHS management systems. Audited sites gain a partial safe harbor from enforcement for EHS violations discovered during the audit, but must commit to correct deficiencies by deadlines set through negotiation, including:

- privatization and greater use of voluntary environmental standards (the normas Mexicanas voluntarias or NMX series) in areas such as energy efficiency and material reuse/recycling; and

- greater recognition of the role of formal environmental management systems such as ISO 14001 for coordinating and implementing voluntary environmental improvement initiatives.

beyond compliance

The Instituto Nacional de Ecología and the federal environmental attorney general were discussing with industry opportunities for linking "beyond compliance" environmental performance improvements with greater regulatory and enforcement flexibility.

In this respect, Part E (Environmental Management Programs) of PROFEPA's Terms of Reference for Conducting Voluntary Environmental Audits closely parallels the ISO 14001 EMS standard in many respects. The Mexican Congress was considering amendments to the Ley General del Equilibrio Ecológico y Protección al Ambiente (LGEEPA) clarifying SEMARNAP's authority to conduct voluntary environmental audits and promote voluntary environmental regulatory standards that are stricter than the official "command-and-control" environmental standards, the NOMs.

SME concerns

The fact that over 90 percent of all Mexican companies are small and medium (and micro) enterprises that lack basic resources and environmental awareness hobbles Mexican progress with voluntary environmental performance initiatives. Moreover, SEMARNAP has had mixed feelings about the value of ISO 14001 environmental management systems, primarily because it may be inaccessible to small and medium enterprises. If ISO 14001 certification becomes widespread among large companies and a "requirement" pushed down on suppliers, there was some fear that small companies would get frozen out of the market.

Accreditation and Certification

same as ISO 9000

The formalities for accreditation of ISO 14001 certification bodies and for the certification process as not scheduled be adopted until the ISO 14001 standard became final in late 1996. Certification body accreditation and Mexico's certification process was expected to follow the same process in effect for the ISO 9000 quality standards, with the exception that Mexico's Ministry for the Environment, Natural Resources, and Fisheries was to be involved in the ISO 14001 Registrar accreditation process.

private entities develop standards

The Mexican government's Ministry for Trade and Industrial Development (SECOFI) is responsible by federal law for managing Mexico's national standards process. Prior to 1992, the government had exclusive jurisdiction over standards-setting. The revised federal law on metrology standards of 1992 opened up the process to allow private entities to participate in the development of voluntary standards and in the certification of conformity with voluntary standards.

Private entities participating in voluntary standard-setting and in certification must meet specific legal requirements and be accredited. Within SECOFI, Dirección General de Normas (DGN), the standards department, is responsible for accrediting and authorizing private entities to issue voluntary standards for commerce and industry. In the case of ISO 9000, DGN had accredited the Mexican Institute for Standards and Certification (IMNC) to issue Mexico's ISO 9000 standards. As the issuer of Mexico's ISO 9000 quality standards, the IMNC is like ANSI in the U.S. SECOFI's DGN is also responsible for administering the accreditation of ISO 9000 certification bodies. In this respect, DGN functions like the RAB in the U.S. In early 1996, only the IMNC and another non-governmental entity, Calmecac, are accredited by DGN as Mexico-based certification bodies for ISO 9000.

*market decides
mutual
recognition*

ISO 9000 registrars and trainers who are accredited by the duly constituted body in their country of origin may provide commercial services in Mexico without first obtaining DGN accreditation. For example, Underwriter's Laboratories is accredited as an ISO 9000 registrar by the RAB in the United States and may provide commercial ISO 9000 certification services to companies in Mexico. Thus, Mexico's market decides whether to seek certification by a Mexico-based accredited certification body like the IMNC or a foreign-based certification body accredited in its country of origin.

According to Leonardo Cárdenas, Mexico's first delegate to the TC 207 plenary meeting in Oslo and now an environmental management consultant based in Monterrey, DGN has opened its doors for both Mexican and foreign registrars to compete in the Mexican market. "The DGN is accessible to business right now," Cárdenas said. "Large certifying companies are going through the (DGN accreditation) process." Cárdenas pointed out that the increasing acceptance of the NMX — Mexico's voluntary standards for industrial and commercial products and processes — promotes demand for independent third-party certification and greater competition among certification providers.

*training
needed*

Cárdenas was concerned that Mexican industry and ISO 9000 certifiers do not understand the implicit differences between ISO 9000 and ISO 14001. "I believe there should be an intense training program for ISO 9000 certifiers who wish to become ISO 14001 certifiers," he said. "Without a good understanding of environmental performance issues and environmental management, there is danger that companies seeking ISO 14001 certification will end up with excessive procedures and documentation and not enough environmental performance improvement."

*exporters seek
certification*

Foreign-based ISO 9000 certification bodies may have an initial advantage over the IMNC and Calmecac. Companies in Mexico seeking ISO 9000 certification mainly do so because they are exporters, and their customers in foreign markets value the ISO 9000 certification. Registrars accredited in those foreign markets who are offering certification services in Mexico will have greater name recognition and credibility with the foreign customers, so they may be more attractive to Mexican companies and subsidiaries of foreign-based transnationals for this reason.

*government
procurement*

Jorge Govea Villaseñor, a director of the IMNC, points out, however, that if the Mexican government moves to specify ISO 9000 (and ISO 14001) certification in government procurement, including procurement by parastatal enterprises such as the petroleum organization PEMEX, only DGN-accredited certification bodies such as the IMNC will be eligible to provide the certification. "This would put pressure on foreign-based registrars to become DGN-accredited in Mexico," he said.

With respect to ISO 14001 certification, Mexico's Ministry for the Environment, Natural Resources, and Fisheries was expected to play a key role in reviewing and approving the environmental technical competence of the ISO 14001 registrar before action by SECOFI's DGN on accreditation.

The Future

large
companies
taking lead

By early 1996, Mexico was actively engaged in the ISO 14000 standardization process. Leaders from large Mexican companies and subsidiaries of U.S., Canadian, European, and Japanese transnationals operating in Mexico had taken the reins in developing a broader Mexican constituency supporting ISO 14000. But only the large Mexican exporting companies, environmental leader industrialists, and subsidiaries of transnationals operating in Mexico were considering conforming their environmental programs to the ISO 14001 standard. The vast majority of Mexican companies, the SMEs, had not heard of ISO 14001.

According to Richard Wells, president of the Lexington Group environmental management consultants, and a U.S. Technical Advisory Group to TC 207 expert on environmental performance evaluation, "ISO 14001 will be particularly important to Mexican companies in the coming years." Wells, who is working with Mexican companies on environmental management systems and ISO 14001, said there were three reasons why Mexican companies should take a hard look at ISO 14001:

1) Mexico has an opportunity to avoid the complex and costly environmental "command-and-control" regulatory system of the U.S., and increase its competitiveness through a systems approach to environmental management that can achieve better environmental performance at lower cost. ISO 14000 presents an unprecedented opportunity for Mexican industry to seek an alternative to expensive "command-and-control" requirements focused on the end-of-the-pipe.

2) ISO 14001 provides Mexican industry with a much-needed model for environmental management systems. This will have practical importance in Mexico because there were relatively few environmental professionals and not many opportunities for networking and sharing management practices. Mexican companies have an opportunity to implement the ISO 14001 without complex documentation and an environmental bureaucracy, by integrating their EMS directly with operations and other functional management.

3) External market requirements may be even a more important factor for Mexican industry than they are for U.S. companies. An ISO 14001 EMS will provide an internationally accepted reference against which Mexican companies can demonstrate their environmental responsibility, and help overcome negative environmental performance stereotypes in European and North American markets. Moreover, for some Mexican exporting companies, ISO 14001 certification may become a customer requirement.

For more information, contact Mercedes Irueste and Jorge Govea Villaseñor, Instituto Mexicano de Normalización y Certificación (IMNC), Mexico City, tel: +525-546-4546; Ing. Raul Tornel, chairman of COTENNSAM and CONCAMIN's Ecology Committee, Mexico

City, tel: +525-703-2591; Ing. Leonardo Cárdenas, director, Environmental Quality Consultants, Monterrey, Mexico, tel: +528-357-9949; Richard Wells, president, the Lexington Group, Environmental Management Consultants, Lexington, MA. tel: 1-617-674-7306, fax: 1-617-674-2851.

9.6.7 European Union

by CEEM Information Services

Several European Union states have officially adopted ISO 14001 in its draft form for use as a tool to satisfy the E.U.'s voluntary Environmental Management and Auditing Regulation. Austria, Switzerland, and Turkey were among the first to adopt the standard with Germany, France, Ireland, The Netherlands, Denmark, and Norway following closely behind.

Motivated by the success of ISO 9000 quality management system standards, E.U. state representatives were convinced that a systematic management approach to the environment would lessen an organization's impact on the environment. At the same time, European officials were banking that ISO 14001 combined with other ISO 14000 documents would improve organizations' environmental performance and lead to widespread pollution-prevention activities.

Following the July 1995 TC 207 plenary, several European delegations believed they could convince their local governments that ISO 14001 indeed could be interpreted as a performance standard. When the following ISO 14001 terms and concepts were tied directly to the company's environmental policy, Europeans believed they could effectively accomplish this:

- continual improvement;
- environmental management system;
- environmental performance;
- aspects and impacts; and
- prevention of pollution.

Austria

regulatory flexibility

Austria adopted the standard when it was still in the draft committee stage and sanctioned the certification of Philips Components Lebring, a division of the multinational firm Philips Electronics. Early in the 1990s, the Austrian government informed native companies that EMS standards would have to contain an environmental performance element for any regulatory flexibility to be granted them. Other European delegates to ISO TC 207 indicated the same preference from their government officials.

Switzerland

Following the July 1995 vote to elevate ISO 14001 to draft international standard status, Switzerland adopted the DIS version. By mid-July 1995, the Swiss Association for Standardization had developed an accreditation program for ISO 14001 by accrediting

SGS International Certification Services to offer certificates to the DIS version of the standard. Immediately following its accreditation, SGS auditors certified Castelletti Luciano, a small Swiss plumbing installation firm, to the draft standard.

France

As of March 1996, the French accreditation body, Comité Française d'Accreditation, had accredited five certification organizations to issue French certificates for ISO 14001:

- The Association Française pour l'Assurance;
- Bureau Veritas Quality International;
- Lloyd's Register Quality Assurance;
- Ascert International; and
- Det Norske Veritas.

While certification bodies were prepared to certify companies from a variety of industry sectors, all reported that when it came to ISO 14001 implementation and certification, electronics manufacturers were well ahead.

EMAS pilot

Beginning in May 1993, the French Environmental Ministry conducted a two-phase EMAS pilot plan involving both large and small- to medium-sized companies.

The first pilot centered on 14 large sites, with most having ISO 9000 certification. The second pilot, conducted between March 1994 and March 1995, covered 29 SMEs on 34 sites. Some of the industry sectors involved were chemicals, refining, steel, paper, electronics, and hazardous materials transporting.

Included in the pilot conclusions were the need to stress environmental factors without an excessive increase in management workload; and that the qualities of auditors should be ranked first by expertise in industrial environmental issues, then by technical knowledge of the activity concerned, and finally by management knowledge and audit capacity.

The Netherlands

pledge among 10,000

Companies in The Netherlands were embracing EMS standards as a means of eliminating redundant permits that were not cost-effective. The Netherlands, along with the U.K., was among the first countries to use BS 7750 for EMS certification. In early 1995, 10,000 of the largest Dutch companies obligated themselves to having a comprehensive EMS in place before year's end, and several were eyeing ISO 14001 or BS 7750 as a means to satisfy this pledge. The companies were bound by emission-reduction covenants forged among business sectors, government bodies, and licensing facilities.

industry association requirement

Several companies in The Netherlands have been preparing for ISO 14001 publication since 1993, and fully expected to implement the standard as the 1990s wind-down. Printing and packaging, base metals, chemicals, dairy, metal products, textiles, abattoirs, meat, and paper products companies must implement an EMS in the form of ISO 14001 to maintain industry association membership. Additionally, manufacturers of leather goods, rubber and plastic products, concrete and cement products, and bricks and tiles were negotiating covenants with licensing agencies for 1996.

Among the things Mexico is importing from the United States is a heavy reliance on acronyms.

Following is a list of acronyms used in this section for ease of reference.

ANIQ — Chemical Industries Association

CONCAMIN — National Council of Industry Associations

CONIECO — National Council of Industrial Ecologists

COTENNSAM — National Technical Committee for Environmental Management Systems Standards

DGN — Within SECOFI, Dirección General de Normas, or the standards department

IMNC — Mexican Institute for Standardization and Certification, Mexico's TC 207 technical advisory group

INE — National Ecology Institute

Iniciativa GEMI — Global Environmental Management Initiative

ITESM — Instituto Technológico y de Estudios Superiores de Monterrey

LGEEPA — Ley General del Equilibrio Ecológico y Protección al Ambiente

NAFTA — North American Free Trade Association

NMX series — Normas Mexicanas voluntarias or voluntary Mexican standards

NOMs — Normas Officiales de Mexico

PROFEPA — Environmental Attorney General's Office

SECOFI — Ministry for Trade and Industrial Development

SEMARNAP — Ministry for the Environment, Natural Resources, and Fisheries

Raad voor Accreditatie (RvA), the Dutch accreditation body, had accredited six organizations to offer ISO 14001 and/or BS 7750 as of April 1996. RvA personnel were working closely with other members of the European Union through the European Accreditation Council to ensure mutual recognition of accreditation criteria. The list of companies having received an accredited EMS certificate from RvA included auto repair, sanitation, chemical, electronics, and transportation facilities. The Dutch Environmental Ministry also had certified organizations to EMAS in various industry sectors.

Germany

Germany, a country many considered to be lagging behind in EMS registrations, surprised the world when 43 German companies reportedly certified to ISO/DIS 14001 in 1995 and 1996. The certifications were done on the state level among several company sectors, including automotive, chemical processing, electronics, and metal fabricators.

The Deutsche Akkreditierungs und Zulassungsgesellschaft für Umweltgutachter mbh developed accreditation criteria for EMS using Annex III of the EMAS regulation, *Requirements Concerning the Accreditation of Environmental Verifiers and the Function of the Verifier*.

The German system is different from most E.U. state accreditation systems because other European countries are using the European Accreditation Council's EN45012, which provides guidance on setting up an accreditation system. This deviation has caused some experts to question whether German certifications will be recognized under multilateral agreements with other accreditation bodies.

For more information, contact Michel Jeanson, technical officer, European Committee for Standardization, Rue de Stassart, 36 B-1050 Brussels, Belgium, tel: +32 2 519 69 51, fax: +32 2 519 68 19 x400.

9.6.8 United Kingdom

by CEEM Information Services

The United Kingdom exploded upon the environmental management system scene with the publication of BS 7750 in March 1992. Following on the heals of BS 5750 and ISO 9000 quality management system standards, U.K. stakeholders comprised of industry, government, environmentalists, registration bodies, consultants, and others began developing an EMS specification document in the early 1990s through the British Standards Institution; this standard became BS 7750.

Publication of BS 7750 provided companies in the U.K. with a marked advantage over companies in the rest of the world. For the first time U.K. companies had at their disposal a list of elements that composed the "ideal" or preferred system for managing environmental concerns.

BS 7750 is viewed by experts as a more stringent standard requiring companies to make more information available to the third-party auditor and the public. Some important requirements of BS 7750 include:

BS 7750 more stringent?

- The organization must develop a full environmental plan that specifically details the objectives and targets of the EMS and the means that will be used to achieve them.

- The organization must compile a register of all environmental regulation, legislation, and industry codes of practice that affect its business.

- A full review of the environmental impact of the organization's operations, including site assessment, must be performed.

- The organization must assign environmental management responsibilities to staff employees, defining exactly who will manage the EMS.

- Personal environmental targets for individual employees must be assigned.

- The organization must train its employees to understand the potential problems that may arise if they stray from the defined EMS.

- Proof of continuous improvement in environmental performance is required.

- Specific procedures must have environmental targets that must be met over time or be reviewed and changed.

- Records regarding the achievement of objectives and targets, including the disposal of waste materials, must be kept.

- A statement of objectives must be made public (a significant requirement not in ISO 14001).

- Internal audits must be conducted.

- The organization must periodically review its EMS and its compliance with the standard.

In the informative annex, which is not audited, it is suggested that the organization's EMS should "be capable of evolution to suit changing circumstances."

public register of environmental effects

While BS 7750 and ISO 14001 appear almost identical in structure, a closer examination reveals that BS 7750 requires more information be revealed to both the third-party auditor and the general public. For example, companies wanting certification to BS 7750 are required to show the auditor a comprehensive register of environmental aspects and explain how each aspect is considered in the organization's EMS. Also, any interested party should be able to obtain information relating to an organization's EMS objectives and targets and what steps are being taken to reach those objectives and targets.

In early 1995, the United Kingdom Accreditation Service (UKAS), formally known as the National Accreditation Council for Certification Bodies (NACCB), accredited eight registration organizations to offer BS 7750 certification following an extensive pilot program with the organizations. During the year-long pilot, NACCB officials observed audits conducted by the organizations and approved procedures for operation. The following organizations obtained BS 7750 accreditation in March 1995, and in early 1996 offered ISO 14001 certification services under the UKAS accreditation criteria as well:

- Aspects Certification Services Ltd.;

- British Standards Institution;

- Bureau Veritas Quality International Ltd.;

- Det Norske Veritas Quality Assurance Ltd.;

- Lloyd's Register Quality Assurance Ltd.;

- Professional Environmental & Caring Services (QA) Ltd.;

- SGS Yarsley International Certification Services Ltd.; and

- Trada Certification Ltd.

UKAS actively accredits other organizations to offer ISO 14001 certification on a rolling basis, and as of March 1996 granted accreditation to 12 registration bodies in and outside of the U.K.

Chemical, electronic, and metal fabrication companies were leading the charge toward EMS certification in the U.K. with almost 50 EMS certificates being issued for either BS 7750, ISO 14001, or the European Union's Eco-Management Audit Scheme. Until early 1996, U.K. officials were pushing for the European Commission to recognize BS 7750 as a standard that

European companies could use to meet the requirements of the E.U.'s Eco-Management and Audit Regulation.

BS 7750 phase-out?

However, once it became clear that ISO 14001 would become an international EMS standard in late 1995, companies began preparing to phase out BS 7750 in place of ISO 14001. 📖 (See Part 9, Chapter 5, for more information on EMAS.)

defense procurement

Officials in the U.K.'s Ministry of Defense were indicating that companies with a certification to BS 7750 and ISO 14001 could receive preferential treatment with MOD contracts. Other departments within the U.K. government are reportedly considering the same approach but are declining public comment on the issue.

mutual recognition

The Environmental Auditors Registration Association (EARA) is based in the U.K. but establishes environmental auditor and course-provider criteria for several regions of the world, including Europe, Asia, and the U.S. In early 1996, EARA was engaged in prolonged discussions with representatives from the American National Standards Institution and the U.K.'s Institute of Quality Assurance/International Register of Certified Auditors, the U.K.'s ISO 9000 course accreditation organization. Without mutual agreements between the organizations, auditors could be faced with multiple systems for certification.

EMS course provider organizations, too, could be squeezed by non-mutual recognition, thereby causing providers to apply to individual accreditation bodies in each country of the world in which they would like to develop an EMS course. Besides a U.K.-specific syllabus, EARA also developed a U.S. syllabus for advanced EMS auditing in early 1996. EARA officials also considered a syllabus for Japan, but decided to alter existing syllabi according to the legal structure of the country in question. For example, the Japanese syllabus will closely resemble the U.K. version as opposed to the U.S., which has a more regulation-intensive atmosphere.

EARA leadership planned to accredit several course providers for both the U.K. and U.S. syllabi by the end of 1996 depending upon the interest. EARA was viewed by several experts as the premier organization in the world for environmental auditors, considering the organization had a program well ahead of any other auditor registration organization in the world.

Environmental Management Services International and Excel Partnership Inc. were accredited by EARA to offer EMS courses based on U.K. laws and regulations in late 1995. Also, EARA issued accreditation to Quality System Development Inc. in January 1996 to offer EMS courses based on U.S. laws and regulations. Others are likely to follow.

For more information, contact Roger Brockway, environmental manager, United Kingdom Accreditation Service (UKAS), Audley House, 13 Palace Street, London SW1E 5HS, England, tel: +44-0-171-233-7111, fax: +44-0-171-233-5115.

9.6.9 United States

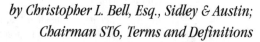

U.S.A.

by Christopher L. Bell, Esq., Sidley & Austin;
Chairman ST6, Terms and Definitions

This article was adapted from one originally published in the December 1995 issue of Business and the Environment's ISO 14000 Update *and as a special supplement to the 1 December 1995 issue of* Environment Watch: Western Europe*. Both newsletters are published by Cutter Information Corporation, 37 Broadway, Suite 1, Arlington, MA 02174, USA. Tel: +1 617 641-5125; Fax: +1 617 648-1950; E-mail: dcrowley@cutter.com; Web: http:// www.cutter.com. Reprinted with permission.*

ISO 14001 has as its goal protecting human health and the environment by applying systematic management principles to environmental issues. Flexible, practical, and consistent with existing EMS standards, ISO 14001 is likely to be widely implemented and therefore to enhance the likelihood of improved environmental performance. The worldwide acceptance of ISO 14001 is consistent with one of the primary missions of ISO: to harmonize regional and national standards to avoid creating barriers to international trade. Accordingly, industry in the U.S. and around the world is focusing on the ISO 14001. This commentary provides a view from the U.S. regarding these developments.

Overview

The U.S. views on ISO 14001 are based on decades of very practical experience designing and implementing EMSs. To fully understand the U.S. EMS experience, one must be aware of two critical elements of the environmental situation in the U.S.: first, the complexity of environmental obligations and the seriousness with which they are taken; and second, the degree of public involvement in environmental issues.

Environmental Regulation in the U.S.

The U.S. has issued tens of thousands of pages of statutes and regulations on environmental issues in the past 30 years, creating a comprehensive command-and-control system that is implemented through detailed numeric standards, documentation and reporting requirements, and strict enforcement policies. Most of the environmental laws in the U.S. operate on a strict liability basis: Good-faith efforts to comply or a record of improved environmental performance typically are not defenses. Further, it is very difficult, if not impossible, to obtain variances from the published regulations.

The consequences of noncompliance are severe. For example, in 1993, the federal government alone collected more than $140 million in fines and obtained 135 criminal convictions. These figures do not include the penalties obtained through state and citizen enforcement actions. Enforcement activity in the U.S. is not reserved for cases in which there is demonstrated injury to the environment; companies have received significant penalties primarily for failure to comply with the extensive and detailed reporting and documentation requirements. 📖 (See Part 8, Chapter 2 for more information on enforcement trends.)

Editor's note: According to the EPA's FY 1994 Enforcement and Compliance Assurance Accomplishments Report, ". . . [In FY 1994,] the Agency brought a record 2,246 enforcement actions with sanctions, including 220 criminal cases, 1,596 administrative penalty actions, 403 new civil referrals to the Department of Justice, and 27 additional civil referrals to enforce existing consent decrees."

In addition to enforcement consequences, companies that pollute the environment in the U.S. must pay cleanup costs as well as compensation for damages to the environment, property, and human health. This includes costs associated with past disposal activities, even if those activities were legal at the time of disposal. Consequently, facilities operating in the U.S. must take the full range of environmental obligations very seriously, which has encouraged the development of EMS to manage these obligations.

Public Involvement in Environmental Issues

public
reporting
The impact of public involvement in environmental issues in the U.S. cannot be overestimated. Most U.S. companies must by law regularly publish detailed reports on releases of chemicals to the environment, the generation of wastes, and recycling activities. These reports identify specific facilities, chemicals, and volumes of releases in accordance with specific requirements, and are not simply summaries or aggregations of data.

These reports are made available to the public in user-friendly form, and the government conducts training sessions for citizens groups and the media on how to interpret these data. With these data, citizens can often accurately characterize the environmental outputs from local facilities. Facilities have been subjected to severe enforcement actions by both government and citizens for failure to submit reports or for submitting inaccurate data. Every permit application, in all of its details, whether for air, water, or waste, is also available for public inspection and comment. The public also has the right, which is frequently exercised, to challenge in court the issuance of permits.

note penalties
Once permits are issued, the public has full access to all regular permit monitoring reports. In addition to the legally required communications obligations, many U.S. companies also voluntarily make environmental performance information available through periodic reports, using models such as those developed by the Public Environmental Reporting Initiative.

This information is a powerful tool for public involvement. Public availability of environmental information has become a powerful motivator for companies to engage in voluntary pollution-prevention activities. Further, private citizens have the authority — independent of government authority — to enforce most legal requirements, including permit requirements, by taking companies to court to seek penalties for violations of the law. Penalties obtained by citizen suits go to the government; this is not a mechanism intended to enrich private citizens. This independent citizen enforcement authority is regularly exercised in the U.S. Citizens may also, and regularly and successfully do, take the U.S. government to court if they believe that regulations issued by the government are not stringent enough.

Citizens in the U.S. have a very large quantity of environmental data available to them, have the right to be involved in key issues, such as permitting and rulemaking, and have the independent authority to make companies comply with the law. Accordingly, most facilities operating in the U.S. find it prudent to consider carefully the views of the public regarding environmental issues.

Environmental Management Systems in the U.S.

compliance

The compliance and public scrutiny situation in the U.S. has encouraged companies to manage their environmental obligations in a systematic manner. Failure to do so increases a company's exposure to significant penalties, public pressure, potential criminal action, or burdensome cleanup costs. Therefore, many U.S. companies have had environmental management systems in place for many years. Initially, these systems were not based on any formal standards or requirements. Rather, companies applied normal management practices to environmental issues and thereby developed EMSs that were integrated into and consistent with their existing management systems.

The U.S. government also recognizes the relationship between EMSs and compliance. The result has been several policies outlining what the U.S. government believes the key elements of a legal compliance assurance program should be, the first being an audit policy document published in 1986 (updated in 1995), followed by more detailed policies published in the late 1980s and early 1990s. 📖 (See Appendix D for a copy of the EPA Auditing Document.)

The most recent of these policies, published by the U.S. Department of Justice (the U.S. government's primary enforcement agency) and the U.S. Sentencing Commission (a governmental body that sets guidelines for criminal penalties), describe the core elements of compliance assurance systems. If a company has implemented an effective compliance assurance and auditing system, the U.S. government may take less severe enforcement action, and the resulting penalties may be lower.

The primary elements of the compliance assurance programs set forth in the U.S. policies are consistent with ISO 14001, though not as detailed. These policies also call for the disclosure of violations to the government as well as full cooperation with the government in investigating violations. Companies seeking to benefit from these policies must be able to demonstrate to the government that the systems have been implemented, a process that is typically more stressful than undergoing third-party registration to a standard. For several years many companies in the U.S. have been implementing EMSs that are modeled on these policies.

beyond compliance

U.S. regulations also are increasingly reflecting a systems approach. For example, many facilities in the U.S. are subject to detailed process safety management and accidental-release prevention regulations intended to reduce the likelihood of chemical accidents and releases.

The U.S. Environmental Protection Agency (EPA) also has been encouraging companies to think outside the traditional command-and-control context, and to look beyond the traditional end-of-pipe control technology approach to pollution-prevention strategies that include raw materials substitution, energy efficiency, and process and product redesign. For example, hundreds of U.S. companies have committed to a voluntary EPA program to significantly reduce emissions of a group of high-priority chemicals, beyond what would be required by law. Since these strategies typically require attention to product and process functions, their implementation usually demands a more systematic and integrated approach to environmental issues. 📖 (See Part 8, Chapter 2 for more information EPA initiatives.)

EPA has also been encouraging EMSs through a variety of pilot programs, in which it is selecting leading companies to participate in innovative EMS projects. In addition to the government activities, recent years have seen the development of private industry initiatives in the U.S. These include the Chemical Manufacturers Association's "Responsible Care®" program and guidance documents produced by such organizations as the Global Environmental Management Initiative. 📖 (See Part 10, Chapter 1 for more on Responsible Care®.)

Many companies and industrial sectors have realized that an EMS is beneficial not only for legal compliance, but also from the perspectives of overall environmental performance and community relations. A survey of Standard & Poor's 500 companies in the U.S. conducted in 1992 by the Investor Responsibility Research Center revealed the following:

- 83 percent of the companies had written environmental policies;

- More than 50 percent of the companies were applying total quality management approaches to environmental issues;

- 33 percent subscribe to corporate codes of conduct;

- More than 60 percent have a board of directors committee responsible for addressing environmental issues;

- The senior executive responsible for environmental affairs was a vice president at 44 percent of the companies, and an executive vice president at 22 percent; and

- 80 percent of the companies had environmental auditing programs in place, with 72 percent stating that their U.S. facilities had been audited in the past two years.

A 1995 Price Waterhouse survey that was broader in scope indicated that approximately three-quarters of companies in the U.S. have environmental auditing programs in place. 📖 (See Appendix E for a synopsis of several such surveys.)

practical EMS experience
The conclusion that can be drawn is that companies operating in the U.S. have had decades of very practical experience in designing and implementing EMSs in a very rigorous environment, where the requirements are extensive and detailed, the margin for error is very small, and the consequences of mistakes are very large. Therefore, environmental professionals in the U.S. take EMSs and the development of EMS standards extremely seriously and bring considerable practical experience to the ISO negotiating table.

U.S. Positions on EMSs and ISO 14001

U.S. position: practicality
The fundamental position of the U.S. delegation to ISO Technical Committee 207 was that ISO should create a practical and cost-effective standard that will assist companies in the systematic identification and management of their environmental obligations in order to operate in a manner that protects human health and the environment.

It is not the function of ISO, a voluntary non-governmental organization, to attempt to establish what the substantive performance obligations of facilities around the world should be. These are set by the countries or regions within which particular facilities operate. Not only is TC 207, which is drafting the ISO 14000 standards, barred by its mandate from setting such obligations, but it would also be an unacceptable intrusion on national sovereignty to do so.

systems, not performance standard
ISO 14001 is a systems standard that does not itself create substantive obligations. That is why, read in a vacuum, ISO 14001 is viewed by some as "empty." However, ISO 14001 obtains its content from the environmental obligations and requirements that are imposed by the sovereign national or regional authorities where facilities operate. ISO 14001 helps organizations identify and manage those obligations, as well as support voluntary initiatives to go beyond those obligations.

ISO 14001 not a panacea
ISO 14001 will not by itself guarantee improved environmental protection or performance. There is a legitimate concern that relying on local, national, or regional requirements may not be a sufficient basis for environmental protection in regions where environmental protection may not be such a high priority.

However, the problem in such regions is typically not the absence of adequate requirements, but the failure of the authorities to enforce them. Most countries — whatever their stage of development — have environmental laws on the books, often based on the laws of highly developed countries. The number of countries without significant environmental laws in place is steadily decreasing. The real problem is that, for a variety of reasons, these requirements are sometimes not adhered to as strictly as one might hope. 📖 (See Part 9, Chapter 3 for more information on developing nations.)

Conforming to ISO 14001 should provide a positive influence on compliance and performance in these situations because, from a standards perspective (and particularly a registrar's), local enforcement practices are not a relevant factor in determining whether an organization is meeting its commitment under ISO 14001 to comply with the law. ISO 14001 does not say organizations should be committed to comply with the law except in countries where this is not necessary. While ISO 14001 is, of course, not an absolute guarantee of compliance with requirements that provide adequate protection to the environment in regions with a tradition of lax compliance, the standard certainly puts pressure on organizations to perform.

national sovereignty
One must also recognize the legitimate prerogatives of national sovereignty and the limits of what can be attained with voluntary standards issued by a nongovernmental organization. (See note 1.) Neither ISO 14001 nor any other standard can by itself solve the world's environmental problems; other avenues of international discourse involving governments must be the basis for reaching an agreement on substantive environmental requirements. (See note 2.) What an EMS standard does is supply the framework for implementing such requirements.

no one way to implement
One key lesson learned from the extensive EMS experience in the U.S. is that there is no "one way" to design or implement an EMS, and that different companies in different industries or regions may have different, but equally legitimate, approaches to EMSs. There are many different ways to run a business, and the standard must be flexible enough to be useful in a wide variety of contexts. ISO must recognize these differences and not demand that companies change their entire way of doing business simply to fit someone's theory of the ideal EMS.

This diversity grows considerably when the different business practices around the world are taken into account. Different countries have different approaches to environmental protection that must be respected. Not only is this a matter of national sovereignty, it is also a very practical matter for business. If ISO 14001 is to be of any use at all to business, and therefore meet the objective of improving environmental protection, it must be capable of practical implementation throughout the world.

universal
elements
sought Therefore, the U.S. delegation opposed the inclusion of requirements in the ISO standards that reflected only regional concerns and were not compatible with international application. Deviations from specific regional approaches to achieve flexibility have sometimes been criticized as leading to the creation of a "weaker" document. Nothing could be further from the truth. Recognizing that there is more than one way to design and implement an EMS is the first step toward creating a practical standard that is likely to be effectively implemented. A narrow standard suitable only to certain regions will not achieve its stated goal of worldwide environmental improvement.

The U.S. did not seek a "less stringent" EMS standard. Because of their extensive experience with EMS, U.S. companies are better situated than those of most other countries to conform to any EMS standard. U.S. companies will not derive a competitive advantage from a "weaker" standard, and may perhaps give up an opportunity to create such an advantage through a more stringent international standard. Given the strict environmental regulatory context in the U.S., and the amount of money and resources devoted to environmental issues in the U.S., it could be argued that a "more stringent" EMS standard would level the playing field for U.S. companies by forcing competitors to devote similar resources to environmental protection.

However, the U.S. delegation did not attempt to use the ISO process to export stringent U.S. requirements, such as those regarding public disclosure and the unique elements of the U.S. compliance systems policy documents; nor has it sought to include tough U.S. liability concepts in the ISO standard. The U.S. positions on EMSs have been based on a desire to create a standard that will be practical and enhance organizations' ability to protect human health and the environment, rather than on a mechanical reliance on what any particular document states. ISO should not be used as a forum to put an international stamp on national or regional views.

It is also important to understand that concerns about the propensity to resolve disputes through litigation in the U.S. have not been the primary factor in the development of the U.S. ISO positions. The focus of the U.S. delegation was to avoid requirements in ISO 14001 that experience has taught business would not work, were not universal elements that would always be applicable to all organizations worldwide, or would incur unnecessary costs in relation to the environmental benefit derived.

ISO 14001, EMAS, and BS 7750

There has been considerable discussion and debate regarding the consistency of ISO 14001 with two other prominent standards: the European Union's Eco-Management and Audit Scheme (EMAS) and the British Standards Institution's BS 7750. (See note 3.)

stringency
debate Unfortunately, this discussion has sometimes deteriorated into debates about which standard is more "stringent" rather than what will provide organizations with the best assistance in protecting the environment. Indeed, the more flexible approach of ISO has led some to mistakenly conclude that the ISO standard is "weaker" than EMAS or BS 7750. To the contrary, a flexible standard that is more suitable for worldwide implementation, and hence worldwide improvement of environmental protection, is hardly weaker.

Continual Improvement

Perhaps the most fundamental dispute during the development of ISO 14001 was the concept of "continual improvement." EMAS calls for companies to commit to continual improvement, which is defined as the continual improvement of environmental performance to a level established by economically viable best available technology (EVABAT).

ISO 14001's definition focuses on the EMS itself: A participating organization must commit to the continual improvement of the system, with the overall objective of improving environmental performance. The U.S. believes that the intended objective of the two approaches is the same: protection of human health and the environment.

However, using improved environmental performance as the primary measure of an EMS is too narrow of an approach. The more fundamental goal is adequate protection of human health and the environment.

must protect health

Improved environmental performance is not synonymous with adequate performance. A facility may have an admirable record of improvement yet still have a relatively poor performance. On the other hand, a facility that has excellent performance may find it very difficult to obtain further improvements.

Without an underlying concept of protecting human health and the environment, improving performance is by itself a relatively empty notion. What constitutes adequate protection of human health and the environment is established by sovereign governments or through international agreements between governments.

Since ISO 14001 is an EMS standard, its focus should be on continually improving the EMS. As discussed above, actual performance standards are established outside of the ISO EMS standards-writing context. However, unless one discounts the value of EMSs entirely, improvements in the EMS will lead to improved performance. To believe otherwise is to reject EMSs. ISO 14001, which emphasizes a commitment to continually improving the EMS, prevention of pollution, and compliance with the law, achieves the same objectives intended in EMAS.

Best Available Technology

EVABAT only one option

EMAS demands a commitment to improve performance to a level set by EVABAT. ISO 14001 does not demand a similar commitment to technology. Instead, it describes EVABAT as one of many available technological options and also demands a commitment to the more general concept of the prevention of pollution.

The ISO approach provides more flexibility to meet the same objective. The U.S. position is based on decades of extensive (and billions of dollars worth) experience with various approaches to best available technology. For years, best available technology has been an integral component of the U.S. requirements under the clean water, clean air, and waste management laws. EVABAT is only one of many legitimate approaches to protecting the environment. In some cases, it may be the best approach.

However, there are many situations where other approaches will be more effective from either cost or environmental perspectives. A pure technology-based approach can lead to "treatment for treatment's sake." If good science can demonstrate that a particular concentration of pollutant is low enough to not pose a risk to human health or the environment, it does not make environmental or economic sense to treat to below those levels simply because the technology is available. There is increasing concern that a purely technology-based approach sometimes leads to very expensive solutions that do not always produce the best environmental result.

pollution prevention

There are a variety of approaches to protecting the environment, not all of which involve best available technology. That is why the U.S. delegation introduced the concept of prevention of pollution as an important element of an EMS. Significant gains in environmental protection may be achieved via implementing a number of pollution-prevention approaches, such as materials substitution, energy efficiency, water efficiency, recycling, changes in production processes, product design, etc. Placing too much emphasis on best available technology often leads regulators and organizations to focus their attention primarily on end-of-pipe solutions.

In addition, the relatively low cost of many pollution-prevention strategies makes them more appropriate for smaller companies and developing economies, two important constituencies of the ISO documents.

Identifying Significant Environmental Obligations

EMAS and BS 7750 require organizations to review their activities to identify significant environmental impacts or effects. ISO 14001 requires organizations to identify their significant environmental "aspects." The scope of ISO 14001 is broader than EMAS, because it is not limited to specific industrial sectors and unambiguously includes services and products as well as facilities. However, there are differences in how the three standards implement this function.

use of terms debated

The U.S. and other delegations were concerned about the use of the terms "impacts" and "effects" because they imply that organizations typically can measure the actual environmental impacts associated with their activities. Most organizations are capable of measuring their inputs (e.g., energy and water use, raw materials, etc.) and outputs (e.g., air emissions, water discharges, waste disposal, etc.). However, it is very difficult for most organizations to determine with any degree of certainty the actual impact on the environment of those environmental outputs and inputs. Even if the science exists — and in most cases it does not — most companies do not have the financial or technical resources to conduct full risk assessments.

Therefore, ISO 14001 focuses on environmental "aspects," which are environmental inputs and outputs, rather than environmental impacts. Of course, information about environmental impacts will be relevant in understanding environmental aspects. For example, even though an organization typically cannot determine with precision its contribution to global warming, it could use scientific information about which chemical releases are linked to global warming and determine whether it emits any of those chemicals. The approach developed by the ISO experts better reflects what can practically be done.

EMAS and BS 7750 also contain lengthy lists identifying precisely what environmental issues organizations should consider. ISO takes a more flexible approach, defining the term "environment" in an all-inclusive manner and then specifying that organizations should review their activities and products and identify significant environmental aspects. The annex to the ISO standard provides additional guidance on what environmental issues an organization might consider, guidance that is similar to what is contained in EMAS and BS 7750.

Given that different organizations in different circumstances will have different environmental issues, it does not make environmental or economic sense to demand that all organizations conform to the identical "cookbook" approach to identifying environmental issues. Therefore, while all of the standards require organizations to address key environmental issues, ISO 14001 provides organizations more flexibility in how this should be done.

U.S. opposed
initial review

The U.S. also opposed including in ISO the "initial review" requirement of EMAS. The initial review requirement presumes that all organizations that seek to conform to the standard, or implement EMS, are beginning with nothing. This assumption does not reflect reality. Many organizations around the world have already implemented EMS with various degrees of sophistication. All organizations do not begin from the same place. Therefore, the standard should set forth the basic requirement: identification of significant environmental aspects and legal obligations. If an organization has never done this before, then the first time it does so is obviously an "initial review." For companies that are at a more advanced stage of EMS, this process may be a simple confirmation of what the organization has already done. This point is made in the annex of ISO 14001. Therefore, ISO 14001 allows for an initial review but does not mandate it for all organizations.

Registers and Documentation

EMAS and BS 7750 require qualifying facilities to create "registers" of environmental effects and legal and other obligations. ISO 14001 does not. ISO 14001 requires organizations to identify the significant environmental aspects associated with their activities and products, and also identify their legal obligations, as well as any nonlegal obligations to which the organization voluntarily subscribes. EMAS, BS 7750, and ISO agree on the fundamental principle that an organization should identify its key environmental issues and obligations. However, the U.S. delegation opposed specifying the form in which this information should be collected and maintained.

All environmental professionals agree that the appropriate people in organizations should have the correct information at the right time. However, different organizations may use different but equally legitimate ways of collecting, managing, and maintaining that information.

Organizations in the U.S. already collect detailed information on both environmental performance and legal obligations, but do so in a variety of ways. Some organizations maintain documents that would conform to the concept of "registers." Other organizations might organize the data by different environmental media, and create one set of documents for water issues, another for waste, and so on. Individuals responsible for those particular areas might maintain and review these separately but never collect them into a single book. Other organizations have this information available on a variety of computer databases. In addition, organizations are already required by law to create and maintain many documents in a certain format.

Therefore, many companies in the U.S. believe that requiring creation of distinct environmental aspects or legal registers would be an unnecessary and expensive paperwork exercise that would not improve the performance of their EMS. The U.S. delegation has opposed approaches to EMS that put too much emphasis on documentation requirements rather than on the underlying functions of the system. It has been the experience of U.S. industry that excessive emphasis on documentation can be very expensive and distract companies from the true goal: environmental protection.

This conclusion is based on decades of experience with an environmental regulatory system that stresses, in great detail, documentation and recordkeeping requirements. Organizations may begin to make the serious mistake of believing that good documentation is the equivalent of a properly functioning EMS.

registrar is not stakeholder

The primary goal of documentation is to help the company in implementing its EMS, not to create an elegant paperwork package for the benefit of third-party auditors. Registrars are not one of the primary stakeholders in writing ISO 14001; it is not the environmental performance of registrars that ISO 14001 is concerned with. The highest priority of the U.S. was to create a standard useful to implementing organizations — and only secondarily to address the demands of registrars. Particularly in an age when companies around the world are attempting to become more efficient and less bureaucratic, it would be highly inappropriate for ISO to establish a standard that creates more, not less, red tape.

Public Participation

One of the core elements of EMAS is the verified public environmental statement that summarizes key aspects of an organization's EMS and environmental performance. ISO 14001 does not contain such a requirement, instead providing only that an organization must have a procedure for dealing with the public.

The U.S. strongly believes in the importance of public participation in environmental issues. Indeed, probably no other country in the world provides its citizens with this kind of volume and quality of detailed information on the environmental performance of industry, combined with the unique power to participate in environmental decisionmaking and to independently enforce environmental requirements.

existing mechanisms

The U.S. achieves this level of information-sharing and public power through a number of mechanisms, most of them legally required and some of them voluntary, including annual environmental statements. What the U.S. opposes is choosing only one of the various methods of communicating with the public and enshrining it as the primary method for international application. The verified public environmental statement is not necessarily the best method of ensuring public involvement in environmental affairs in all situations. In fact, some environmental groups in the U.S. are suspicious of such summary statements, viewing them as primarily publicity tools. These groups often prefer to have access to the raw technical data from facilities to reassure themselves that claims about environmental performance are indeed true.

Conclusion

The ISO process, bringing together experts from around the world, has produced an EMS standard that improves on existing environmental standards, whether from the U.S., the E.U., or elsewhere. The in-depth ISO negotiations revealed a number of areas where the approaches of particular countries and regions could be improved. ISO 14001 is more flexible and practical, and less bureaucratic than existing standards, while sharing the same fundamental goal of protecting human health and the environment through the application of systematic management principles to environmental issues. It would be a mistake to confuse this flexibility and practicality with a "weak" document.

ISO 14001 is at the same time consistent with existing EMS standards. Accordingly, it is more likely to be widely implemented and therefore achieve the desired improvement in environmental conditions.

harmonization   Lastly, one of the fundamental purposes of ISO is to harmonize national and regional standards. This simplifies conforming activities by industry and decreases the likelihood of trade barriers being erected through the inappropriate application of national standards. ISO 14001 has created an "international vocabulary" for EMS that will improve international communication on environmental issues. Accordingly, the U.S. believes very strongly that companies seeking to improve their environmental performance by implementing EMSs with reference to standards should look to ISO 14001 for guidance, and not to individual national or regional standards.

9.6.9 NOTES

1) Other prominent documents, such as EMAS and BS 7750, do not handle this difficult issue any differently than ISO 14001. The only arguably substantive requirement in EMAS is a commitment to improve performance to a level that can be reached by economically viable best available technology, an approach which, as is discussed above, has its own limitations.

2) For example, the Basel Convention governing the transboundary movement of hazardous waste, or the Montreal Protocol on the manufacture and use of ozone-depleting substances.

3) Though it is popular to compare EMAS with ISO 14001, it is important to remember that, while ISO 14001 is a voluntary standard developed by an international NGO, EMAS is a regulation promulgated by the European Union. ISO cannot be expected to conform directly with a regulation developed by the E.U. any more than it could be expected to adopt any particular environmental regulation or scheme issued by the U.S. government.

FOOTNOTES

1 Information obtained through direct questionnaire to ISO member organizations, November 8, 1995. John Audley, "Environmental Policy Implications of the ISO 14000 Environmental Management System," paper presented at the Western Political Science Association Meeting, March 1995.

2These are the personal views of the author and do not represent any official position of the United Nations Environment Programme.

3 While the principles contained in the Stockholm Declaration, signed at the 1972 United Nations Conference on the Human Environment, and the Rio Declaration, signed at the 1992 United Nations Conference on Environment and Development, are not legally binding treaty law, they have been widely incorporated in environmental agreements negotiated since the Stockholm Conference.

4 Discussions with J. Casio, November 19, 1995, concerning possible activities to provide developing countries with information about ISO 14000.

5 The General Agreement on Tariffs and Trade (GATT) is a contract between 123 governments which together account for around 90 percent of world merchandise trade. The most recent round of GATT negotiations, the Uruguay Round, was concluded in April 1994. The challenge of GATT 1994 is to stimulate worldwide economic growth and to provide a more secure and predictable multilateral trading system. GATT 1994 also provided for the creation of the World Trade Organization (WTO), bringing all trade agreements of the Uruguay Round under one institutional umbrella and facilitating the implementation of the agreements.

6Mr. Hunter is a Brussels-based environmental lawyer with Hunton & Williams.

10

Related Initiatives

CHAPTER 1
Chemical Manufacturers Association — Responsible Care®

by John E. Master, Consultant, Chemical Manufacturers Association; Chairman ST4 on Environmental Performance Evaluation

Responsible Care® is an initiative of the chemical industry. It grew out of a response in the late 1980s to growing public concerns about health and safety related to the chemical industry. Its focus was to provide a common commitment and action to continually improve the performance of the chemical industry in the areas of health, safety, and environmental responsibility and be responsible to public concern about the management of chemicals.

global acceptance; local features

In practice, Responsible Care takes many forms throughout the world. The chemical industry association's 39 countries have each adopted versions of Responsible Care that have some basic similarities, but also respond to unique characteristics, issues, and social, economic, and cultural factors of the country and its people. One of the features of the U.S. version of Responsible Care is its six codes of management practices. In other countries, different code structures have been adopted to address differing perceptions of the most important issues; indeed, some countries have not found it necessary to adopt any codes of management practices.

The comments in this chapter relating an EMS to Responsible Care are based upon the U.S. practice of Responsible Care as adopted by the U.S. Chemical Manufacturers Association (CMA). These comments may apply in broad concepts to other versions of Responsible Care, but certainly not in detail.

CMA membership responsibility

In the U.S., Responsible Care is a condition of membership in CMA. All companies belonging to CMA are required to commit to and implement Responsible Care. Its purpose and objective is to improve the performance of the chemical industry in response to public concerns about the impact of chemicals on health, safety, and environmental quality. Membership in CMA comprises approximately 190 companies, representing nearly 90 percent of the chemical manufacturing and production in the U.S.

10.1.1 Responsible Care Elements

There are 10 primary elements of Responsible Care:

1) 10 Guiding Principles;

2) six Codes of Management Practices;

3) a public advisory panel providing for public input to the initiative and advisory evaluation of its implementation;

4) member company self-evaluations of their progress toward full implementation of each of the codes;

5) a series of geographic regional executive leadership (senior company management) groups providing opportunities to evaluate progress and to share experiences;

6) a commitment to Responsible Care as an obligation of membership;

7) performance measures;

8) mutual assistance networks;

9) partnership program; and

10) management system verification.

10 Guiding Principles

The 10 Guiding Principles, in summary form, address:

1) response to community concerns about chemicals;

2) production of chemicals that can be handled safely;

3) consideration of health, safety, and environmental protection among the highest priorities of the company;

4) prompt reporting of hazards;

5) counseling customers in the safe handling of chemicals;

6) safe facility operation;

7) extension of knowledge of chemicals through research;

8) program toward resolution of past problems;

9) participation in public policy development; and

10) sharing experiences.

Six Codes of Management Practice

The six Codes of Management Practices address:

1) pollution prevention;

2) worker health and safety;

3) process safety;

4) distribution;

5) product stewardship; and

6) community awareness and emergency response.

As an example of Responsible Care code of management practices, the Pollution Prevention code's purpose is to promote environmental protection via reduced waste and emissions and sound management of residues. Among the 14 elements of the code are the following concepts:

- development of an inventory of wastes and releases at each facility;

- development of priorities, goals, and plans for reduction of wastes and releases;

- priority of source reduction as a methodology;

- role of technology (research and design) in reduction;

- use of process and administrative controls to achieve reduction.

comparison with EMS
In comparison to these major elements of Responsible Care, an EMS as described by ISO 14001 or ISO 14004 comprises five major elements:

1) an environmental policy describing what the organization is committed to as its environmental responsibility;

2) development of a plan, taking into account the organization's environmental aspects, its legal requirements, the views of interested parties, and other factors in determining its environmental performance objectives and targets, to achieve its environmental policy;

3) implementation and operation of a program to achieve its objectives and targets;

4) a monitoring and measurement system to evaluate its environmental performance and its conformance to its EMS requirements; and

5) a management review process to evaluate whether its EMS continues to be suitable and adequate.

Note that these elements of an EMS are formulated in the chemical total-quality-management (TQM) "plan-do-check-act" cycle.

10.1.2 Similarities and Differences

Now that the major elements of Responsible Care and of an EMS have been described, you can see that they are really two different things — totally compatible and with similar goals, but entirely different.

An EMS is a means of determining what the organization wants to accomplish in managing its environmental responsibility, and then putting in place a management system capable of accomplishing the management goals. Responsible Care is a statement by the chemical industry of what it wants to achieve in managing not only its environmental responsibility, but also its health and safety responsibilities.

management process needed

Responsible Care has thus already developed and stated some of the things to be accomplished for environmental responsibility management by its member companies. Each member company needs some sort of a management process to accomplish Responsible Care. That management process could be ISO 14001, ISO 14004, or any other management process system the organization wishes to use. CMA takes no position on whether a member company uses the ISO 14000 series as its EMS; that is an individual company's decision and responsibility.

series of objectives

Put very simply, Responsible Care can be viewed as a series of objectives that a CMA member company has committed to achieving. An EMS (ISO 14001 or otherwise) is a management system capable of managing the achievement of those objectives, as well as any others established by the organization.

management system verification

In fact, CMA has recognized the desirability of a management system. One of the recently adopted enhancements to the Responsible Care initiative is a concept referred to as management system verification (MSV). Although the specific program has not yet been approved, the concepts of MSV have been pilot-tested and refined based upon those experiences and other input. Approval is expected in April 1996.

MSV is a voluntary component of Responsible Care. Just like use of ISO 14001, or certification to it, a CMA member company may or may not seek verification of its Responsible Care management system. Those that do will see a great deal of similarity between the MSV process, ISO 14001, and the ISO 14001 certification criteria.

Some CMA member companies and their facilities will see value added only in use of ISO 14001 or ISO 14004 as guidance in establishing or enhancing their own EMS. Some will be confident with their existing management system and will not be interested in either ISO 14001 certification or in Responsible Care MSV. Others will see value in certification/verification in one or both.

harmonizing MSV

In developing and pilot-testing the proposed MSV component, it became obvious that structuring it around ISO 14001 made a lot of sense. Obviously, a lot of thought had already gone into the international process of agreement on the most important elements of an EMS. Also, harmonizing MSV with ISO 14001 was extremely important to&Lhose companies that believe they will seek certification/verification to both. Thus, the proposed MSV process and protocol contain the same five major elements of a management system as does ISO 14001.

Differences

However, there are some major differences and issues between Responsible Care and ISO 14001 that had to be taken into account.

EMS+   One obvious difference is that ISO 14001 only addresses environmental management. The introduction to ISO 14001 states that it is not intended to address and does not include requirements for elements of occupational, health, and safety management. Also, it states that the certification process will only be applicable to the environmental management system elements. Responsible Care not only addresses occupational health and safety, it also addresses public concerns via the process safety, distribution, product stewardship, and community awareness codes. The MSV process has to be broader than the ISO 14001 certification process to account for the broader scope of Responsible Care.

documentation   On the other hand, ISO 14001 requires considerable documentation to provide an auditable trail for certification. Requirements for documented determination of environmental aspects, documented procedures, recordkeeping, EMS audit, and periodic management review are not inherent in Responsible Care. Although the five major elements of ISO 14001 EMS are built into MSV, they are handled in a process that is based much more on dialogue and demonstration than on documented audit.

mutual assistance   Unlike an ISO 14001 audit, MSV is conducted by industry peers from other CMA member companies who are intimately familiar with implementing Responsible Care. Along with the dialogue framework, this provides an opportunity for mutual assistance and suggestion for management system improvement based on the verifier's own experiences. The ISO 14001 certification process is based on third-party assessment and identification of nonconformities to ISO 14001; it does not allow for a mutual assistance component.

public participation   A final significant difference between Responsible Care MSV and ISO 14001 certification is the participation by a representative of the public in MSV. The ISO 14001 certification process is conducted by certified professional auditors who should meet qualification criteria in **ISO 14012**. Responsible Care was established in response to public concerns and includes requirements for establishing and monitoring a dialogue with the public. It is believed that public participation in MSV is a key component toward improving the image of the chemical industry. Pilot-testing public participation in MSV has been positive from the perspectives of both the public participants and chemical industry participation.

In summary, the chemical industry has not seen anything incompatible among Responsible Care, the concepts of EMS, and ISO 14001 specifically. EMS is a valuable tool in achieving Responsible Care. Both share improved environmental responsibility management as a goal. Although each has its unique characteristics and requirements, together they form a powerful means to achieve the Responsible Care commitment.

More detailed information on Responsible Care® is available from: Chemical ManufacturerAssociation, 1300 Wilson Blvd., Arlington, VA 22209; tel: 703-741-5000; fax: 703-741-6094.

CHAPTER 2
American Petroleum Institute — STEP

The American Petroleum Institute (API) has developed "preferred modes of operation" that relate to environment, health, and safety practices and at the same time can be used in unison with ISO 14001. While API's Strategies for Today's Environmental Partnership (STEP) program is not a complete EMS, it does provide direction to companies in the petroleum and natural gas industries on managing their environmental aspects.

overlaps
Several elements of the ISO 14001 and STEP programs overlap since both are designed to help companies improve performance through a systems management approach. The API program preceded ISO 14001 and was created to offset some of the negative public perception of the industry.

auditing criteria
API would like to see some of the auditing criteria be the same for the two standards. Companies that already are implementing the STEP program have most of the elements for ISO 14001 certification in place — it is just a matter of having those elements certified by a third party.

The U.S. petroleum industry is not asking ISO to create an industry-specific standard for the petroleum industry because such a standard would not be appropriate on the international level. However, it would approve of individual industries creating such a standard on the national level.

CHAPTER 3
Occupational Health and Safety Administration — VPP

by Richard Quick, Senior Industrial Hygienist, AT&T
(now with Lucent Technologies)

Even as companies begin getting used to quality and environmental management systems, the International Organization for Standardization has been considering whether to develop a similar management system standard for occupational health and safety. 📖 (See Part 10, Chapter 6, for more information on a potential new standard.)

Many U.S. companies have already realized the benefits of participating in a formal safety and health management system known as the Occupational Safety and Health Administration's (OSHA) Voluntary Protection Program (VPP).

complimentary programs
ISO 14001 and the OSHA VPP are complimentary programs based on "total quality management" principles that will allow your organization's environment, health, and safety program to be incorporated into a single management process.

Developed by OSHA in 1982 to recognize and promote effective safety and health management systems and programs, more than 90 companies participated in the VPP as of

November 1995. There were some 225 sites in the program, ranging in size from fewer than 50 employees to more than 10,000 employees. Participants in the OSHA VPP are from diversified industries such as telecommunications, chemical, textile, food processing, and wood products. Many corporations, including AT&T and Monsanto Corporation, have made corporate commitments for participation in the OSHA VPP.

benefits

Participants in the OSHA VPP have identified numerous benefits of participating in the program. VPP sites generally report injury incident rates on the average of 60 to 80 percent below their industry averages. The reduction of injury rates correlates to lower costs associated with on-the-job injuries, including workers' compensation costs and insurance premiums.

OHSA Star: increased productivity

A safety and health management system, or lack thereof, can have a major impact on a facility's ability to comply with governmental safety and health regulations. At AT&T, for example, the six OSHA VPP Star sites perform very well on the safety and health compliance audits performed by both corporate staff and outside consultants. Because VPP participation requires employee involvement and "empowerment" in the safety and health program, VPP participants have reported an improvement in employee morale, leading to an increase in quality and productivity. VPP participants often cite improvement or development of a cooperative relationship between local management and labor as well as with OSHA as a benefit of program participation. They also see as a benefit that both the community and the business view the company as a "safe place to work."

10.3.1 Three Participation Categories

There are three categories of participation in the OSHA VPP:

1) Star;

2) Merit; and

3) Demonstration.

Star participants have developed safety and health programs that operate at a high level of effectiveness. Star participants meet all VPP requirements and have injury incidence rates at or below the national average for their industry.

Merit participants do not initially meet all VPP requirements, but they demonstrate a willingness and commitment to meet all program requirements in a specified period of time (usually one or two years). The Demonstration program is reserved for those industries involved in unusual situations or that have developed alternative methods for worker protection that may differ from current Star requirements.

10.3.2 On-Site Review

The OSHA VPP requires that applicants complete and submit an application to OSHA. If the application appears to demonstrate that the site has implemented a safety and health program that meets VPP requirements, OSHA will schedule an on-site verification review. The on-site review team normally will include three to four safety and health professionals who spend approximately one week at the site. The on-site review consists of both an opening and closing conference, documentation review, facility walk-through, and employee interviews.

opening conference

The opening conference is an opportunity to introduce site and OSHA personnel, discuss on-site review team member roles and responsibilities, plan schedules, etc. Site management and labor personnel who are responsible for meeting VPP requirements or who could assist the on-site review team should be in attendance.

documentation & walkthrough

Documentation is an important and critical element of the OSHA VPP. The on-site review team will review safety and health documentation to ensure that the program is operating effectively. All safety and health programs and processes must be adequately documented. The facility walk-through of the site provides OSHA with further verification that the safety and health program is being implemented as described in the application.

Because a cooperative relationship between OSHA and management is essential to VPP participation, safety and health violations identified by the on-site review team are expected to be abated and will not result in OSHA enforcement action.

interviews

OSHA also will conduct both informal and formal interviews with randomly selected employees to determine the level of employee involvement and awareness of the safety and health program. Informal interviews are short in duration (usually 5-10 minutes) and take place at the employee workstation during the walk-through inspection. Formal interviews, which can normally last 30 minutes, are performed in private rooms. The total number of employee interviews performed by OSHA will usually depend on the size of the facility. It is not uncommon for OSHA to conduct at least 20-50 employee interviews during the on-site review.

closing conference

At the closing conference, the OSHA on-site review team will make a recommendation as to whether or not the facility meets VPP requirements and the category of participation that is applicable (i.e., Star, Merit, Demonstration). Facilities recommended for the Star program often will be provided with a list of "contingency" items that must be corrected within a specified period of time (usually 90 days). Contingency items represent "minor" safety and health program deficiencies. Facilities recommended for the Merit program will often receive contingency items and "merit goals." Merit goals are more significant safety and health program deficiencies that must be corrected in a longer period of time (usually one or two years) in order to qualify for Star status.

report

OSHA will prepare a report on the on-site visit and provide a copy to site personnel. After any contingency items have been addressed to the satisfaction of the OSHA on-site review team, the report will be sent to the assistant secretary of labor for occupational safety and health at OSHA for approval.

approval

If the facility is approved, a ceremony is often held to celebrate the significant achievement. OSHA will perform an on-site reevaluation of Star participants every three years and every year for Merit and Demonstration participants. This process ensures that VPP sites continue to meet the rigorous program requirements.

continual improvement

As more corporations have begun to implement total quality management principles to manage all aspects of their business, they have discovered that the OSHA VPP, like ISO

14001, supports and complements a management system of continual improvement. The program elements of the OSHA VPP are merely the "blueprint" used by corporations to define the safety and health program elements that are essential to an effective management system. It is not surprising that program elements of the OSHA VPP are very similar to those of ISO 14001. Listed below are the program elements of the OSHA VPP.

10.3.3 OSHA Voluntary Protection Program Elements

Management Leadership and Employee Involvement

- commitment (includes policy, goals, and objectives)
- organization
- responsibility
- accountability
- resources
- planning
- contract workers
- employee involvement (includes safety and health committees)
- annual safety and health program evaluation
- employee notification
- site plan

Worksite Analysis

- pre-use analysis
- comprehensive surveys
- self-inspections
- routine hazard analysis
- employee reports of hazards
- accident investigations
- pattern analysis

Hazard Prevention and Control

- professional expertise
- safety and health rules
- personal protective equipment
- emergency preparedness
- preventative maintenance
- medical program

Safety and Health Training — Statement of Commitment

• labor union statement (if applicable)

• management statement

10.3.4 VPP and ISO 14001

evident
similarities

Although the structure of the OSHA VPP requirements are organized differently than those of ISO 14001 (environmental policy, planning, implementation and operation, checking and corrective action, and management review), the similarities between the two management systems are quite evident. Many of the program requirements of the OSHA VPP and ISO 14001 are identical. The policy, goals and objectives, accountability, responsibility, organization, resources, professional expertise, training, emergency response, and management review requirements are components of both programs that are presented using similar category classifications. (See Appendix A for more information in ISO 14001)

The "self-inspection" and "accident investigation" requirements of the VPP are synonymous with ISO 14001's requirement for "checking and corrective action." Other OSHA VPP requirements, including "safety and health rules, personal protective equipment, preventative maintenance, and contract workers," are simply examples of ISO 14001's "operational controls."

Differences

There are some differences between the two management systems.

policy
statement

ISO 14001, for example, includes specific requirements regarding the elements of the policy statement. The OSHA VPP does not include specific requirements for the policy statement, but OSHA on-site review team members will verify its existence and adequacy.

environmental
aspects

One element of ISO 14001 is the requirement to identify "environmental aspects," which does not match directly with an element of the OSHA VPP. (See Part 3, Chapter 1, Section 4 for more information on identifying "environmental aspects".)

employee
involvement

Employee involvement, which is a significant element of the OSHA VPP, is not specifically referenced in ISO 14001. OSHA VPP participants must ensure that employees can make a meaningful contribution and have a significant impact on the administration of the safety and health program. Employee involvement in ISO 14004 may be implied in the section on "environmental awareness and motivation," but does not appear to be given the same significance it is in the OSHA VPP.

document
control

The ISO element of "document control" is not a specific program element of the OSHA VPP. Documentation of all safety and health programs is required and will be evaluated by the OSHA on-site review team. However, "ISO-type" document control requirements are not a prerequisite for participation in the OSHA VPP.

legal
requirements

The "legal and other requirements" element of ISO 14001 also is not specifically included in the OSHA VPP, but compliance with safety and health regulations is expected and is evaluated during the on-site review.

The fact that minor differences exist between the two management systems does not detract from the benefits of establishing and implementing an environment and safety management system. The OSHA VPP concept of government, management, and labor engaged in a cooperative effort to improve employee safety and health has a proven track record of success. Applying the quality principles of ISO 9000 to environmental management systems will duplicate the success that the standard has had on quality performance. Sites that participate in the OSHA VPP have established the internal discipline needed to meet the requirements of ISO 14001.

Achieving ISO 14001 certification for these facilities will require additional effort, but the "framework" of the OSHA VPP will make the task considerably easier than if a management system had never been implemented at all. Combining a safety and health and environmental management system into a single management system is a logical progression that should be the goal of every corporation that desires to be "world class" in environment, health, and safety leadership. Environment, health, and safety can and should be managed as a single process.

10.3.5 Combining ISO 14001 and VPP Requirements

Following is an example of how the requirements of ISO 14001 and the OSHA VPP can be combined into a single list of elements for an environmental, health, and safety management system:

Management Commitment and Policy

- policy
- responsibility
- accountability

Planning

- significant E&S effects analysis
- new process/operation hazard review
- environmental and safety objectives and targets
- environmental and safety planning
- legal requirements
- comprehensive surveys
- medical program
- pattern analysis

Implementation

- organization
- resources

- professional experience
- communications
- environmental and safety training
- employee involvement
- safety and health committee
- employee reporting of safety and health concerns
- records
- operational control
  — safety and health rules
  — personal protective equipment
  — preventative maintenance
  — permits
  — contract workers
- documentation
- document control
- emergency preparedness

Monitoring and Corrective Action

- monitoring and measurement
- nonconformance and corrective and preventive action
- self-inspections
- accident/incident/spill investigations
- E&S management system audit

E&S Management Review— Statement of Commitment

- management statement

CHAPTER 4
American Society for Testing and Materials — PS 11 and PS 12 Standards

In early 1996, the American Society for Testing and Materials (ASTM) was developing two standards that could be seen as complementing or competing with ISO 14001, depending on whose view is taken. Expected to be published by ASTM Subcommittee E-50.04 by mid-1996, these two provisional standards could provide U.S. companies with more than one EMS standard to choose from when developing an environmental management program.

U.S. focus Representatives from industry and government had been working on Proposed Standard (PS) 11, *Practice for Environmental Compliance Audits,* and PS 12, *Guide for the Study and Evaluation of an Organization's Environmental Management System*, both of which are guidance standards, since 1992. According to the standards' authors, ASTM is committed to publishing standards that best address U.S. companies' specific needs for environmental management.

10.4.1 PS 11 — Practice for Environmental Compliance Audits

compliance standard Proponents of the American Society for Testing Materials (ASTM) standards have claimed that PS 11 is a compliance-based standard that does not contradict ISO 14001. Aimed at state, local, and federal agencies, judicial systems, industry managers, consultants, and other interested parties, PS 11 offers a description of accepted practices, procedures, and policies associated with environmental regulatory compliance audits. The main goal of the standard is to help organizations understand whether they are in compliance with U.S. legal requirements.

The ISO 14000 standards, however, are not designed for use in determining whether a company is in regulatory compliance, since they are aimed for use worldwide and such a task is viewed as inappropriate for an international standard. However, ASTM delegates working on PS 11 contend it's important that companies implementing an environmental management system (EMS) be aware of subjects such as auditor liability and constantly changing state laws involving environmental auditing.

Thus, according to a draft dated November 1995, PS 11 on compliance audits:

* documents minimum requirements for audits;

* identifies some legal issues associated with audits;

* presents minimum criteria for auditor qualifications; and

* explains how compliance audits are different from other types of environmental audits.

PS 11 includes an appendix that offers legal citation information for unique U.S. concerns, such as Environmental Protection Agency regulations and Department of Justice guidelines.

10.4.2 PS 12 — Guide for the Study and Evaluation of an Organization's Environmental Management System

According to its scope, PS 12 on EMS auditing:

- defines guidance for the study and evaluation of environmental management systems;

- governs the conduct of environmental audits of environmental management systems; and

- identifies elements for evaluating an organization's environmental management system.

specific to U.S. companies

ASTM contends that PS 12 is specific to U.S. companies and does not infringe upon the ISO 14001 scope. ASTM delegates developed the PS 12 standard to help U.S. companies bridge what is seen as a gap between the international focus of ISO 14001 and application of that standard in a U.S. market by U.S. industry. Because ASTM PS 12 was developed solely with U.S. marketplace concerns in mind, it reflects U.S. industry practices more accurately, according to its authors.

Delegates developing the ISO 14000 series have disagreed with ASTM's position and have claimed that PS 12 essentially describes the elements of an EMS. They said this description interprets what elements must be contained in an EMS, making it contrary to the flexibility inherent in ISO 14001.

PS 12 is designed for industry members to evaluate whether they have an EMS such as ISO 14001 in place and essentially is a guide on auditing an environmental management system. As with PS 11, it is based on current U.S. regulations, state programs, and newly created Environmental Protection Agency programs such as the Environmental Leadership Program.

The Institute for Environmental Auditing originally developed PS 12 in the early 1980s. In 1992, ASTM was given permission to borrow and revise the standard to be used as a national standard.

The ASTM standard advises users that PS 12 is consistent with principles and procedures found in ISO 14011 and can be used to reach the same results.

different EMS definitions

An environmental management system, as defined in PS 12, differs from the definition found in ISO standards. PS 12 defines EMSs as "those policies, procedures, and activities effected by the entity's board of directors, management, and other personnel, that are designed to provide reasonable assurance that environmental objectives are being achieved."

ISO 14001 defines an EMS as "that part of the overall management system which includes organizational structure, planning activities, responsibilities, practices, procedures, processes, and resources for developing, implementing, achieving, reviewing, and maintaining the environmental policy."

Representatives from ASTM have stated that they expect the marketplace to decide whether the ASTM standards will be useful.

📖 (See Appendix F, for information on getting copies of these standards.)

CHAPTER 5
NSF International — Pilot Project

by Craig Diamond, Project Coordinator, NSF International, and CEEM Information Services

NSF International — a not-for-profit organization specializing in voluntary, consensus standards development and public health and environmental certification — launched a pilot project in March 1995 to demonstrate EMS implementation using various EMS standards.

NSF 110 vs. ISO 14001

Initially, the EMS Demonstration Project focused on NSF 110: *Environmental Management Systems—Guiding Principles and Generic Requirements*, NSF's proposed national, voluntary EMS specification standard. NSF International first began developing an EMS standard in 1993 to increase understanding and awareness of environmental management in the U.S. Its goal was to provide a standard from the U.S. perspective in the event ISO 14001, the draft international EMS standard, did not meet U.S. needs.

Essentially, NSF 110 mirrors ISO 14001. Both cover policy, environmental impact assessment, objectives and targets, implementation, emergency planning, control procedures, monitoring, auditing, corrective action, documentation, and communications. One main difference is that ISO 14001 requires that "prevention of pollution" be considered in policy development and in setting objectives and targets, while NSF 110 does not.

In the initial launch stage of the NSF International pilot project, NSF 110 was used as the working standard because ISO 14001 was still in an early draft stage and NSF 110 was nearing completion. The project later began focusing more on ISO 14001 since progress on that standard had been rapid and was nearing a final ballot. Ultimately, in February 1995, NSF withdrew its NSF 110 submittal to the American National Standards Institute.

10.5.1 NSF International Project Structure and Goals

The Environmental Protection Agency (EPA) funded the EMS Demonstration Project through a cooperative agreement in which the EPA participated in the project's planning and implementation.

NSF kicked off the project on March 1, 1995, with an initial meeting of the 18 participating organizations. Among those participating were two government entities as well as companies representing the chemical, electronics, and utilities industries. The participants' objective, to operate in an environmentally proactive manner, was clearly evident by the desire of many to act as a role model for environmental leadership and continuous environmental improvement in their respective areas. The project gave these organizations the opportunity to demonstrate their commitment to improving environmental performance while preparing for certification to an EMS standard.

At the March meeting, NSF provided participants with guidance documents on EMS development and tools for EMS self-assessment, such as checklists and EMS resource lists.

The training included comparisons among all the EMS standards — including NSF 110, BS 7750, and ISO 14001 — to assess the organizations' current EMS status. NSF gave the participants the opportunity to choose which elements from each standard would be useful for EMS implementation in their respective organization. Participants expressed concerns regarding implementation, including costs, documentation, assessing specific objectives and targets, and uncertainty about EMS benefits.

Additional EMS Workshops/Training

Two mid-course meetings were held in August and December 1995 to address implementation concerns, to discuss initial assessment results, and to develop problem-solving strategies. The workshops covered:

- environmental effects and performance evaluation;
- guidance on setting objectives and targets;
- an overview of the links between ISO 14001 and ISO 9000 quality management system standards;
- advice on how to integrate environmental considerations into every aspect of an organization; and
- EMS benefits and costs.

The December meeting of NSF personnel, EPA representatives, and pilot participants included updates from all the participants regarding implementation progress. Joel Charm, chairman of SubTAG 1 on EMS, and Jean McCreary, president of the Environmental Auditing Roundtable, discussed interpretation of ISO 14001 and developments in selecting an accreditor as well as EMS auditor training and certification.

The last scheduled meeting of the pilot project will be in June 1996. At its conclusion, NSF will prepare a summary for the EPA, detailing the participants' EMS experiences. Assessment results of each organization will remain anonymous.

In the meantime, NSF International launched another project called the ISO 14000 Assessment and Training Program in February 1996. It is very similar to the EMS demonstration project except that it is focusing solely on ISO 14001 and is funded through participation fees and not the EPA. NSF chose participants for the second phase from applications it received through January 1996 on a first-come basis.

EMS Demonstration Project Participating Organizations

- 3M Corporation, EE&PC, Building 2-3-09, P.O. Box 33331, St. Paul, MN 55133-3331
- Allergan Inc., 2525 Dupont Drive, Irvine, CA 92715
- Commodore Environmental Services, 1487 Delashnut Avenue, Columbus, OH 43212
- Fluke Corporation, P.O. Box 9090, Mail Stop 203A, Everett, WA 98206-9090
- Globe Metallurgical, P.O. Box 348, Selma, AL 36702-0348
- Hach Company, P.O. Box 907, Ames, IA 50010

- K.J. Quinn & Co., 135 Folly Mill Road, Seabrook, NH 03874

- Loral Federal Systems-Manassas, 9500 Godwin Drive, Mail Stop 115/015, Manassas, VA 22110

- Madison Gas & Electric, P.O. Box 1231, Madison, WI 53701

- Milan Screw Products, 640 Ash Street, Milan, MI 48160

- NEO Industries Ltd., 1775 Willowcreek Road, Portage, IN 46368

- NIBCO Incorporated, 500 Simpson Avenue, Elkhart, IN 46526

- Pacific Gas & Electric, P.O. Box 7640, San Francisco, CA 94120

- Pitney Bowes, 1 Emcroft Road, Stamford, CT 06926

- Prime Tanning Company Inc., P.O. Box 713, Berwick, ME 03901

- TRINOVA Corporation, 3000 Strayer, Maumee, OH 43537

- U.S. Postal Service, Washington, DC (Contact: Christopher Werle, LMI, 2000 Corporate Ridge, McLean, VA 22102-7805)

- Washtenaw County Government, Ann Arbor, MI (Contact: Barry Johnson, Environment & Infrastructure Services, P.O. Box 8645, Ann Arbor, MI 48107)

CHAPTER 6
International OHS Standard

There has been some interest expressed, both in the U.S. and internationally, in having ISO develop international voluntary standards on occupational health and safety management systems (OHSMS). This issue came up in the context of both ISO Technical Committee 176 (TC 176), which developed and is continuing to enhance the ISO 9000 series of standards on quality management systems, and TC 207, which is developing the ISO 14000 series of standards on environmental management systems.

The ISO Technical Management Board (TMB), which determines whether a proposed standard will add value to the international community, initially determined there was too little information to decide whether an OHSMS standard would have any merit.

It formed an ad hoc committee and in June 1995, it met in Geneva, Switzerland, to review existing requirements for potential content of an OHSMS program that would ensure coherence and consistency with existing management systems.

As a result, ISO scheduled an international workshop on the OHSMS issue to be held September 5-6, 1996, in Geneva, Switzerland. To prepare to participate effectively in the ISO workshop, the American National Standards Institute (ANSI) planned a national workshop on May 7-8, 1996, to which the various stakeholders were invited. ANSI is recognized as the U.S. member of ISO and it is through the ANSI workshop that U.S. opinions can be channeled to the ISO workshop.

Discussion Leading to Workshop

At the June 1995 working group meeting, several countries were represented by their ISO member bodies at the meeting in Switzerland, along with representatives from the International Labor Organization (ILO) and the World Health Organization (WHO). Countries in attendance were France, China, Germany, Japan, Australia, Canada, Sweden, Switzerland, the U.S., and the United Kingdom.

The ad hoc committee determined that most organizations have to comply with OHS regulations, but may or may not need ISO management standards to fulfill their obligations. Representatives from the ILO and WHO stressed that a safe working environment should involve a good management system.

They advocated that regulatory and voluntary approaches have to support each other and that the availability of international OHS management standards may help to avoid repetition of mistakes in national policy development.

A long discussion culminated in the following possible justifications for ISO standards on OHS management:

- there is a wide range of views among numerous stakeholders; and
- voluntary OHS standards may contribute to increasing awareness in organizations of the importance of implementing an effective OHS management policy.

Others said there was no need for ISO management standards in this already highly regulated field, and that the existence of OHS management standards may lead to third-party certification that would force companies to incur more cost.

In discussions on the possible content of an ISO-sponsored OHS workshop, they determined that key issues were the distinction among regulations, ILO or WHO recommendations, and the role of ISO voluntary standards.

"Borderlines between voluntary standardization and regulations would have to be carefully explained in the first keynote address, as well as the method of reference to standards in legislation," according to notes from the ad hoc committee.

The proposed workshop, limiting itself to management standards, would define key aspects of OHS but would not deal with detailed technical standards on specific aspects such as air, water, soil quality, noise, vibration limits, or prescriptions of performance. The workshop was aimed at establishing:

- who the stakeholders are;
- what stakeholder needs are;
- the value of OHS management standards for society, and their ethical value;
- the value of OHS standards in terms of business performance;
- the value of OHS standards for large, medium, and small businesses; and
- the differences in perception between countries with high and low levels of OHS regulation.

The scheduled workshop would also examine existing national and regional examples of

OHS management standards and strive to avoid duplication. The workshop would pay particular attention to the relationship between OHS management standards and other ISO management standards and guides. A cost/benefit analysis on the issue of conformity assessment and auditing of OHS systems was also planned.

10.6.1 ANSI Response to OHS Standardization Issue

The following text is an issues paper prepared by a task group of the American National Standards Institute (ANSI) Board of Directors' International Advisory Committee. It addresses some of the issues concerning proposed standardization of occupational health and safety management systems. The paper was to be presented in a U.S. workshop sponsored by ANSI in May 1996. It has been modified slightly for this handbook.

For more information on the workshop or the issues paper, please contact ANSI Director of Public Relations, American National Standards Institute, 11 West 42nd St., New York, NY 10036; tel: 800-417-0348 or 212-642-4900; fax: 212-3908-0023.

International Standardization of Occupational Health And Safety Management Systems — Is There a Need?

Introduction

The purpose of this paper is to explore some of the key issues associated with the potential involvement of ISO in the area of OHSMS, as well as to provide some background information on the standards system process and on how an OHSMS standard might be developed by ISO. This document is part of ANSI's effort to raise awareness and initiate discussion on this issue in the U.S.

Since the ISO forum on OHSMS standards will not be held until September 1996, the ISO Technical Management Board (TMB) is unlikely to make a decision regarding whether to proceed until late 1996 or early 1997. It will be important for the U.S. to develop clear opinions on the issues so that it can, through ANSI, participate effectively in these deliberations.

Is There a Need for an ISO Occupational Health and Safety Management Systems Standard?

This is the question on which ISO seeks to gain information through its upcoming forum, and on which ANSI will also be seeking input in the U.S. over the next several months. This involves a consideration of who the primary stakeholders are in this process. The obvious stakeholders whose views need to be assessed are those who are the subject of an OHSMS standard: employees and their employers. Other relevant stakeholders include health and safety professionals, insurers, and interested government officials. An open question is how do we assess the views of the various stakeholders in determining the demand for an OHSMS standard.

Is This a Topic That is Ready and Suitable for International Standardization?

ISO's historical function has been to harmonize existing national and regional standards to facilitate international commerce. This is reflected in the standardization process itself. Experts from around the world bring their practical experience with national and regional standards to the table to identify the core elements appropriate to an international standard. Accordingly, one of the most important questions that must be addressed when considering whether to proceed with a new ISO standard is the international experience with respect to the topic at hand. This will be one of the tasks that ISO and ANSI will be exploring within each respective workshop. However, a few initial observations can be made.

There appears to be a considerable body of expertise already developed on OHS issues. Occupational health and safety has been regulated in most industrialized countries for more than a century. Considerable attention has been given to the topic of employee health and safety by industry, labor, insurers, and government. Therefore, it is likely that there are many OHS experts among a number of the ISO member countries who could be brought together under the auspices of ISO to develop an international standard.

It is important to note that an ISO OHSMS standard would focus on systems issues, and some of these systems extend beyond the occupational health and safety arena. For example, the standard may address issues such as the degree to which employers should communicate with employees regarding OHSMS issues, or the extent to which the views of employees should be taken into account. Discussions on matters such as these imply a broad range of employer-employee issues that would likely call for expertise and input from stakeholders in addition to the OHSMS professionals.

It should also be noted that despite the existence of widespread expertise on OHSMS issues, there are no approved, consensus national or regional standards on OHSMS. Three countries — Australia, the U.K., and Norway — have proposed such national standards, but they have not been completed. In the U.S., industry and professional groups, in addition to individual companies, have developed or are developing private sector standards or guidelines addressing OHSMS. The U.S. Occupational Safety and Health Administration (OSHA), through its Voluntary Protection Program, plus a recent safety and health program standard initiative, has endeavored to address certain management systems issues. Certain states have also endeavored to address these issues.

Given this current state of affairs, a question arises as to what ISO can contribute in the area of OHSMS. One of the purposes of ISO is to facilitate international commerce by harmonizing different, and potentially conflicting, national and regional standards that might impede trade. It is not clear whether an ISO OHSMS standard will facilitate commerce. While there are no competing national or regional consensus standards in this area, there are differing practices, standards, and regulations. It is commonly believed that differences in manufacturing practices and working conditions in different regions of the world provide some economies with competitive advantages. However, the international disputes about trade and labor issues typically focus on wages, length of the working day, and the nature of employees (e.g., child or prison labor). ISO is not likely to be the appropriate forum for addressing these issues.

ISO's development of an OHSMS standard could minimize the potential for future conflicts in the ongoing development of OHSMS standards. In addition, apart from any trade considerations, there may be value to ISO developing an internationally accepted standard that could promote health and safety management practices.

Implementation of an ISO OHSMS standard may conflict with U.S. laws and regulations. For example, in the U.S., the employer-employee relationship is subject to almost a century of case-law and over fifty years of statutory, regulatory, and administrative law. To the extent that an ISO standard includes provisions on employer-employee communication/cooperation, these may conflict with such legal standards. This could be particularly problematic for organizations that may face commercial pressure to conform to the ISO standard while at the same time having to comply with U.S. labor law, and perhaps even with legally binding collective bargaining agreements that cover OHSMS issues.

Application of ISO Standards

ISO standards are voluntary. However, they sometimes are transformed into legal requirements, such as requirements that certain types of products conform to specific ISO standards, or as a condition of government procurement.

In the U.S., for example, the Food and Drug Administration has revised its good manufacturing practice regulations for medical devices to incorporate ISO 9000. Though ISO 14001 is still at the draft international standard stage, the U.S. Environmental Protection Agency (EPA) has been considering the potential use of the standard, including enforcement discretion, penalty mitigation, and regulatory flexibility. There can also be commercial pressure to conform to ISO standards; customers may demand that suppliers demonstrate conformance to a particular ISO standard. This has been the primary pressure pushing conformance to ISO 9000. Some organizations may seek conformance to ISO standards for their own reasons, such as improved performance, competitive advantages, or publicity.

One type of conformance to ISO standards deserves special attention: third-party registration. An organization achieves registration to a standard through an accredited registrar that audits the organization against the desired standard. The registrar is accredited by a national "competent body" that is established for that purpose. For example, in the U.S., ISO 9000 registrars are accredited through the American National Accreditation Program for Registrars of Quality Systems, a joint effort of ANSI and the Registrar Accreditation Board.

However, third-party registration is not the norm for ISO standards. Most organizations that conform to the hundreds of ISO technical standards do not obtain registration to those standards; they simply self-declare their conformance to such standards. Registration is a recent phenomenon associated primarily with the ISO 9000 quality management systems standards series. The actual ISO standards, such as the ISO 9000 series and the draft ISO 14001, do not require registration; the pressure to seek registration is external to ISO itself. It should be noted that BS 8750, the British Standards Institution's draft OHS management systems standard, states explicitly that it is intended for guidance only and is not for use as a specification for third-party registration purposes.

These are a few of the important considerations in developing a view on whether ISO should develop an OHSMS standard.

Potential Advantages

- A standard encouraging a systematic approach to OHSMS may improve performance in the employee health and safety area;

- An international standard would provide a baseline and vocabulary for OHSMS, which may assist companies in establishing a common platform for addressing and communicating OHS issues;

- A standard could assist companies in managing risk and liability associated with OHSMS issues;

- A standard might become a vehicle for cost-savings in the OHSMS area, for example, preventing injury and illness and thereby reducing worker compensation costs;

- A standard may be a framework for exploring opportunities for more flexible regulatory approaches to OHSMS issues in the U.S.; and

- An OHSMS standard consistent with ISO 9000 and ISO 14000 could promote an integrated approach to quality, environmental, and health and safety management systems issues.

Potential Disadvantages

- A new standard will require the commitment of resources to the development of another ISO management standard;

- A new standard may require additional costs, including the costs of development and implementation of a system conforming to this standard, and the costs of third-party registration;

- It may be difficult to address in the ISO context sensitive issues related to the labor-management relationship that are addressed in very different ways in various economic, cultural, and political contexts. ISO might become a forum for various stakeholders to advocate particular cultural, socio-economic, or political views regarding responsibility for OHSMS issues;

- An ISO OHSMS standard may conflict with existing laws and regulations impacting on employers and employees in the U.S.;

- There is uncertainty regarding the potential scope of the work of an ISO OHSMS standard;

- It may be difficult to achieve international consensus based on different systems of labor relations and management worldwide, and competing and widely divergent goals of stakeholders even within nations; and

- An ISO OHSMS standard might change the legal standards of care on OHSMS issues.

CHAPTER 7
Sustainable Forest Management Standard

Standards for sustainable forest management (SFM) became a controversial issue in ISO TC 207 when the Canadian and Australian delegations proposed a new work item in May 1995. The proposal called for an auditable standard that companies can use to certify SFM programs. It was withdrawn at the 1995 TC 207 plenary session in Oslo, Norway, in July 1995 for further review outside the scope of TC 207.

opposition

Among the leaders in opposition to the proposed standard was the U.S. Technical Advisory Group to TC 207, which subsequently passed a resolution against development of sector-specific standards. Such a standard, the TAG contended, would open the door for other industries, such as the electronics and chemical industries, to propose sector-specific standards for themselves, thereby diluting the universal applicability of ISO 14001.

Another major source of opposition has been environmental groups. They argue that any forestry standard must be performance-based and not allow ecologically destructive practices. One activist noted that a certification mark would be misleading because consumers could make the interpretation that marked lumber came from companies that do not practice forest degradation, which would not necessarily be true.

Following the withdrawal of the new work item proposal, Standards New Zealand convened the International Study Group on Sustainable Forest Management to study SFM and the possible role of ISO in developing standards for SFM. The study group has met only on an informal basis and has not been under ISO's jurisdiction. However, it has used ISO's protocols, membership designations, and participatory levels. Non-governmental organizations (NGOs) have complained that use of the ISO rules unnecessarily limits their participation in the study group. Consequently, several major NGOs dropped out of the group.

U.S. group

A similar group was formed in the U.S., made up of representatives from industry, trade associations, and public interest groups, but is not affiliated with the New Zealand Group. According to a paper prepared in early 1996 by the U.S. group, the group was planning to study:

- initiatives being considered by governmental and non-governmental organizations;
- the extent to which there are additional SFM needs; and
- whether the tools ISO develops could be used to meet those needs.

The group formed a drafting committee to develop a proposal to TC 207 in accordance with agreements reached by the study group. In addition, the committee was developing the outline for a "bridging document" to outline additional requirements, above and beyond ISO 14001, for SFM certification.

The group was expected to report to TC 207 at the June 1996 plenary meeting in Rio de Janeiro, Brazil.

CHAPTER 7
Offshore Oil and Gas Standard

A standard for environmental, health, and safety management designed for offshore oil and natural gas platforms will be delayed until at least 1998. Early in January 1996, ISO TC 67 mustered enough votes to elevate ISO *14690 Petroleum and Natural Gas Industries — Health, Safety, and Environmental Management Systems* to official draft international standard (DIS) stage despite apparent opposition.

In June 1996 the ISO TMB was expected to decide if the document should be elevated to final draft standard status or be delayed indefinitely. Despite being a DIS document, the ISO TMB could declare an overriding interest in the document and halt all work on the standard.

Delegates from TC 67 were expected to debate the fate of ISO 14690 at the plenary meeting in Milan, Italy, in September 1996. Delegates would discuss the possibility of removing ISO 14690 from the technical committee's work plan or rewriting the standard without environmental elements and only developing an occupational health and safety management standard.

Critics of ISO 14690 have charged that sector-specific standards for EMSs could set an unacceptable precedent for other industries considering similar initiatives, including the forest industry. They also claimed that TC 67 was violating a directive from the ISO Technical Management Board that work on occupational health and safety standards should not begin until ISO evaluates the appropriateness of such standards.

Some delegates to TC 207 on EMSs have said TC 67's proposed standard threatens the scope of TC 207's work. Both technical committees have contended that the standard falls under their scope.

TC 67 is charged with creating standards for materials, equipment, and offshore structures for the petroleum and natural gas industries. Its work has primarily covered product-related standards. ISO 14690 is the TC's first venture into the realm of management system standards.

ANSI/ISO 14001-1996 and ANSI/ISO 14004-1996

SECTION 1
ANSI/ISO 14001 — Environmental Management Systems — Specification with Guidance for Use

Approved as a American National Standard by:
American Society for Quality Control
American Society for Testing and Materials
NSF International

An American National Standard Approved on September 23, 1996

American National Standards: *An American National Standard implies a consensus of those substantially concerned with its scope and provisions. An American National Standard is intended as a guide to aid the manufacturer, the consumer, and the general public. The existence of an American National Standard does not in any respect preclude anyone, whether he or she has approved the standard or not, from manufacturing, purchasing, or using products, processes, or procedures not conforming to the standard. American National Standards are subject to periodic review and users are cautioned to obtain the latest edition.*

Caution Notice: *This American National Standard may be revised or withdrawn at any time. The procedures of the American National Standards Institute require that action be taken to reaffirm, revise, or withdraw this standard no later than five years from the date of publication. Purchasers of American National Standards may receive current information on all standards by calling or writing the American National Standards Institute.*

© *1996 ISO.*

ANSI/ISO 14001

Foreword

ISO (the International Organization for Standardization) is a worldwide federation of national standards bodies (ISO member bodies). The work of preparing International Standards is normally carried out through ISO technical committees. Each member body interested in a subject for which a technical committee has been established has the right to be represented on that committee. International organizations, governmental and nongovernmental, in liaison with ISO, also take part in the work. ISO collaborates closely with the International Electrotechnical Commission (IEC) on all matters of electrotechnical standardization.

Draft International Standards adopted by the technical committees are circulated to the member bodies for voting. Publication as an International Standard requires approval by at least 75% of the member bodies casting a vote.

International Standard ISO 14001 was prepared by Technical Committee ISO/TC 207, Environmental management, Subcommittee SC 1, Environmental management systems.

Annexes A, B and C of this International Standard are for information only.

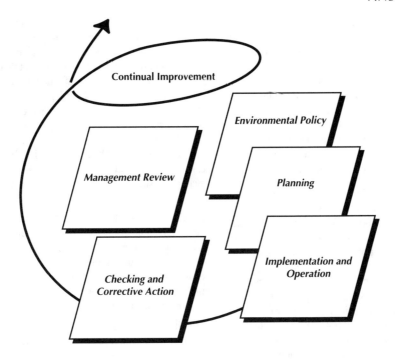

Figure 1 Environmental management system model for this International Standard

Introduction

Organizations of all kinds are increasingly concerned to achieve and demonstrate sound environmental performance by controlling the impact of their activities, products or services on the environment, taking into account their environmental policy and objectives. They do so in the context of increasingly stringent legislation, the development of economic policies and other measures to foster environmental protection, and a general growth of concern from interested parties about environmental matters including sustainable development.

Many organizations have undertaken environmental "reviews" or "audits" to assess their environmental performance. On their own, however, these "reviews" and "audits" may not be sufficient to provide an organization with the assurance that its performance not only meets, but will continue to meet, its legal and policy requirements. To be effective, they need to be

conducted within a structured management system and integrated with overall management activity.

International Standards covering environmental management are intended to provide organizations with the elements of an effective environmental management system which can be integrated with other management requirements, to assist organizations to achieve environmental and economic goals. These Standards, like other International Standards, are not intended to be used to create non-tariff trade barriers or to increase or change an organization's legal obligations.

This International Standard specifies the requirements of such an environmental management system. It has been written to be applicable to all types and sizes of organizations and to accommodate diverse geographical, cultural and social conditions. The basis of the approach is shown in figure 1. The success of the system depends on commitment from all levels and functions, especially from top management. A system of this kind enables an organization to establish, and assess the effectiveness of, procedures to set an environmental policy and objectives, achieve conformance with them, and demonstrate such conformance to others. The overall aim of this International Standard is to support environmental protection and prevention of pollution in balance with socioeconomic needs. It should be noted that many of the requirements may be addressed concurrently or revisited at any time.

There is an important distinction between this specification which describes the requirements for certification/registration and/or self-declaration of an organization's environmental management system and a non-certifiable guideline intended to provide generic assistance to an organization for implementing or improving an environmental management system. Environmental management encompasses a full range of issues including those with strategic and competitive implications. Demonstration of successful implementation of this International Standard can be used by an organization to assure interested parties that an appropriate environmental management system is in place.

Guidance on supporting environmental management techniques will be contained in other International Standards.

This International Standard contains only those requirements that may be objectively audited for certification/registration purposes and/or self-declaration purposes. Those organizations requiring more general guidance on a broad range of environmental management system issues should refer to ISO 14004:1996, Environmental management systems—General guidelines on principles, systems and supporting techniques.

It should be noted that this International Standard does not establish absolute requirements for environmental performance beyond commitment, in the policy, to compliance with applicable legislation and regulations and to continual improvement. Thus, two organizations carrying out similar activities but having different environmental performance may both comply with its requirements.

The adoption and implementation of a range of environmental management techniques in a systematic manner can contribute to optimal outcomes for all interested parties. However, adoption of this International Standard will not in itself guarantee optimal environmental outcomes. In order to achieve environmental objectives, the environmental management system should encourage organizations to consider implementation of the best available technology, where appropriate and where economically viable. In addition, the cost effectiveness of such technology should be fully taken into account.

This International Standard is not intended to address, and does not include requirements for, aspects of occupational health and safety management; however, it does not seek to discourage an organization from developing integration of such management system elements. Nevertheless, the certification/registration process will only be applicable to aspects of the environmental management system.

This International Standard shares common management system principles with the ISO 9000 series of quality system Standards. Organizations may elect to use an existing management system consistent with the ISO 9000 series as a basis for its environmental management system. It should be understood, however, that the application of various elements of the management system may differ due to different purposes and different interested parties. While quality management systems deal with customer needs, environmental management systems address the needs of a broad range of interested parties and the evolving needs of society for environmental protection.

The environmental management system requirements specified in this International Standard do not need to be established independently of existing management system elements. In some cases, it will be possible to comply with the requirements by adapting existing management system elements.

1 Scope

This International Standard specifies requirements for an environmental management system, to enable an organization to formulate a policy and objectives taking into account legislative requirements and information about significant environmental impacts. It applies to those environmental aspects which the organization can control and over which it can be expected to have an influence. It does not itself state specific environmental performance criteria.

This International Standard is applicable to any organization that wishes to

a) implement, maintain and improve an environmental management system;

b) assure itself of its conformance with its stated environmental policy;

c) demonstrate such conformance to others;

d) seek certification/registration of its environmental management system by an external organization;

e) make a self-determination and self-declaration of conformance with this International Standard.

All the requirements in this International Standard are intended to be incorporated into any environmental management system. The extent of the application will depend on such factors as the environmental policy of the organization, the nature of its activities and the conditions in which it operates. This International Standard also provides, in annex A, informative guidance on the use of the specification.

The scope of any application of this International Standard must be clearly identified.

NOTE—For ease of use, the subclause of the specification and annex A have related numbers; thus, for example, 4.3.3. and A.3.3 both deal with environmental objectives and targets, and 4.5.4 and A.5.4 both deal with environmental management system audit.

2 Normative references

There are no normative references at present.

3 Definitions

For the purposes of this International Standard, the following definitions apply.

3.1
continual improvement
Process of enhancing the environmental management system to achieve improvements in overall environmental performance in line with the organization's environmental policy.

NOTE—The process need not take place in all areas of activity simultaneously.

3.2
environment
Surroundings in which an organization operates, including air, water, land, natural resources, flora, fauna, humans, and their interrelation.

NOTE—Surroundings in this context extend from within an organization to the global system.

3.3
environmental aspect
Element of an organization's activities, products or services that can interact with the environment.

NOTE—A significant environmental aspect is an environmental aspect that has or can have a significant environmental impact.

3.4
environmental impact
Any change to the environment, whether adverse or beneficial, wholly or partially resulting from an organization's activities, products or services.

3.5
environmental management system
The part of the overall management system that includes organizational structure, planning activities, responsibilities, practices, procedures, processes and resources for developing, implementing, achieving, reviewing and maintaining the environmental policy.

3.6
environmental management system audit
A systematic and documented verification process of objectively obtaining and evaluating evidence to determine whether an organization's environmental

ANSI/ISO 14001

management system conforms to the environmental management system audit criteria set by the organization, and for communication of the results of this process to management.

3.7
environmental objective
Overall environmental goal, arising from the environmental policy, that an organization sets itself to achieve, and which is quantified where practicable.

3.8
environmental performance
Measurable results of the environmental management system, related to an organization's control of its environmental aspects, based on its environmental policy, objectives and targets.

3.9
environmental policy
Statement by the organization of its intentions and principles in relation to its overall environmental performance which provides a framework for action and for the setting of its environmental objectives and targets.

3.10
environmental target
Detailed performance requirement, quantified where practicable, applicable to the organization or parts thereof, that arises from the environmental objectives and that needs to be set and met in order to achieve those objectives.

3.11
interested party
Individual or group concerned with or affected by the environmental performance of an organization.

3.12
organization
Company, corporation, firm, enterprise, authority or institution, or part or combination thereof, whether incorporated or not, public or private, that has its own functions and administration.

NOTE—For organizations with more than one operating unit, a single operating unit may be defined as an organization.

3.13
prevention of pollution
Use of processes, practices, materials or products that avoid, reduce or control pollution, which may include recycling, treatment, process changes, control mechanisms, efficient use of resources and material substitution.

NOTE—The potential benefits of prevention of pollution include the reduction of adverse environmental impacts, improved efficiency and reduced costs.

4 Environmental Management System Requirements

4.1 General requirements

The organization shall establish and maintain an environmental management system, the requirements of which are described in the whole of clause 4.

4.2 Environmental policy

Top management shall define the organization's environmental policy and ensure that it

a) is appropriate to the nature, scale and environmental impacts of its activities, products or services;

b) includes a commitment to continual improvement and prevention of pollution;

c) includes a commitment to comply with relevant environmental legislation and regulations, and with other requirements to which the organization subscribes;

d) provides the framework for setting and reviewing environmental objectives and targets;

e) is documented, implemented and maintained and communicated to all employees;

f) is available to the public.

4.3 4 (b)

ASK JEFFS. ON NEW PROJECT
START UP. HOW/WHAT/ CHEL CUST.

4.3 Planning

4.3.1 Environmental aspects

The organization shall establish and maintain (a) procedure(s) to identify the environmental aspects of its activities, products or services that it can control and over which it can be expected to have an influence, in order to determine those which have or can have significant impacts on the environment. The organization shall ensure that the aspects related to these significant impacts are considered in setting its environmental objectives.

The organization shall keep this information up-to-date.

4.3.2 Legal and other requirements

The organization shall establish and maintain a procedure to identify and have access to legal and other requirements to which the organization subscribes, that are applicable to the environmental aspects of its activities, products or services.

4.3.3 Objectives and targets — Look AT pg.559 LAYOUT.

The organization shall establish and maintain documented environmental objectives and targets, at each relevant function and level within the organization.

When establishing and reviewing its objectives, an organization shall consider the legal and other requirements, its significant environmental aspects, its technological options and its financial, operational and business requirements, and the views of interested parties.

 The objectives and targets shall be consistent with the environmental policy, including the commitment to prevention of pollution.

4.3.4 Environmental management programme(s)

The organization shall establish and maintain (a) programme(s) for achieving its objectives and targets. It shall include

a) designation of responsibility for achieving objectives and targets at each relevant function and level of the organization;

b) the means and time-frame by which they are to be achieved.

If a project relates to new developments and new or modified activities, products or services, programme(s) shall be amended where relevant to ensure that environmental management applies to such projects.

4.4 Implementation and operation

4.4.1 Structure and responsibility

Roles, responsibility and authorities shall be defined, documented and communicated in order to facilitate effective environmental management.

Management shall provide resources essential to the implementation and control of the environmental management system. Resources include human resources and specialized skills, technology and financial resources.

The organization's top management shall appoint (a) specific management representative(s) who, irrespective of other responsibilities, shall have defined roles, responsibilities and authority for

a) ensuring that environmental management system requirements are established, implemented and maintained in accordance with this International Standard;

b) reporting on the performance of the environmental management system to top management for review and as a basis for improvement of the environmental management system.

4.4.2 Training, awareness and competence — Look AT pg.563

The organization shall identify training needs. It shall require that all personnel whose work may create a significant impact upon the environment, have received appropriate training.

It shall establish and maintain procedures to make its employees or members at each relevant function and level aware of

a) the importance of conformance with the environmental policy and procedures and with the requirements of the environmental management system;

b) the significant environmental impacts, actual or potential, of their work activities and the environmental benefits of improved personal performance;

c) their roles and responsibilities in achieving conformance with the environmental policy and procedures and with the requirements of the environmental management system, including emergency preparedness and response requirements;

d) the potential consequences of departure from specified operating procedures.

Personnel performing the tasks which can cause significant environmental impacts shall be competent on the basis of appropriate education, training and/or experience.

4.4.3 Communication

With regard to its environmental aspects and environmental management system, the organization shall establish and maintain procedures for

a) internal communication between the various levels and functions of the organization;

b) receiving, documenting and responding to relevant communication from external interested parties.

The organization shall consider processes for external communication on its significant environmental aspects and record its decision.

4.4.4 Environmental management system documentation

The organization shall establish and maintain information, in paper or electronic form, to

a) describe the core elements of the management system and their interaction;

b) provide direction to related documentation.

4.4.5 Document control

The organization shall establish and maintain procedures for controlling all documents required by this International Standard to ensure that

a) they can be located;

b) they are periodically reviewed, revised as necessary and approved for adequacy by authorized personnel;

c) the current versions of relevant documents are available at all locations where operations essential to the effective functioning of the environmental management system are performed;

d) obsolete documents are promptly removed from all points of issue and points of use, or otherwise assured against unintended use;

e) any obsolete documents retained for legal and/or knowledge preservation purposes are suitably identified.

Documentation shall be legible, dated (with dates of revision) and readily identifiable, maintained in an orderly manner and retained for a specified period. Procedures and responsibilities shall be established and maintained concerning the creation and modification of the various types of document.

4.4.6 Operational control

The organization shall identify those operations and activities that are associated with the identified significant environmental aspects in line with its policy, objectives and targets. The organization shall plan these activities, including maintenance, in order to ensure that they are carried out under specified conditions by

a) establishing and maintaining documented procedures to cover situations where their absence could lead to deviations from the environmental policy and the objectives and targets;

b) stipulating operating criteria in the procedures;

c) establishing and maintaining procedures related to the identifiable significant environmental aspects of goods and services used by the organization and communicating relevant procedures and requirements to suppliers and contractors.

4.4.7 Emergency preparedness and response

The organization shall establish and maintain procedures to identify potential for and respond to accidents and emergency situations, and for preventing and mitigating the environmental impacts that may be associated with them.

The organization shall review and revise, where necessary, its emergency preparedness and response procedures, in particular, after the occurrence of accidents or emergency situations.

The organization shall also periodically test such procedures where practicable.

4.5 Checking and corrective action

4.5.1 Monitoring and measurement

The organization shall establish and maintain documented procedures to monitor and measure, on a regular basis, the key characteristics of its operations and activities that can have a significant impact on the environment. This shall include the recording of information to track performance, relevant operational controls and conformance with the organization's environmental objectives and targets.

Monitoring equipment shall be calibrated and maintained and records of this process shall be retained according to the organization's procedures.

The organization shall establish and maintain a documented procedure for periodically evaluating compliance with relevant environmental legislation and regulations.

4.5.2 Nonconformance and corrective and preventive action

The organization shall establish and maintain procedures for defining responsibility and authority for handling and investigating nonconformance, taking action to mitigate any impacts caused and for initiating and completing corrective and preventive action.

Any corrective or preventive action taken to eliminate the causes of actual and potential nonconformances shall be appropriate to the magnitude of problems and commensurate with the environmental impact encountered.

The organization shall implement and record any changes in the documented procedures resulting from corrective and preventive action.

4.5.3 Records

The organization shall establish and maintain procedures for the identification, maintenance and disposition of environmental records. These records shall include training records and the results of audits and reviews.

Environmental records shall be legible, identifiable and traceable to the activity, product or service involved. Environmental records shall be stored and maintained in such a way that they are readily retrievable and protected against damage, deterioration or loss. Their retention times shall be established and recorded.

Records shall be maintained, as appropriate to the system and to the organization, to demonstrate conformance to the requirements of this International Standard.

4.5.4 Environmental management system audit

The organization shall establish and maintain (a) programme(s) and procedures for periodic environmental management system audits to be carried out, in order to

a) determine whether or not the environmental management system

   1) conforms to planned arrangements for environmental management including the requirements of this International Standard; and

   2) has been properly implemented and maintained; and

b) provide information on the results of audits to management.

The organization's audit programme, including any schedule, shall be based on the environmental importance of the activity concerned and the results of previous audits. In order to be comprehensive, the audit procedures shall cover the audit scope, frequency and methodologies, as well as the responsibilities and requirements for conducting audits and reporting results.

4.6 Management review

The organization's top management shall, at intervals that it determines, review the environmental management system, to ensure its continuing suitability, adequacy and effectiveness. The management review process shall ensure that the necessary information is collected to allow management to carry out this evaluation. This review shall be documented.

The management review shall address the possible need for changes to policy, objectives and other elements of the environmental management system, in the light of environmental management system audit results, changing circumstances and the commitment to continual improvement.

Annex A

(informative)

This annex gives additional information on the requirements and is intended to avoid misinterpretation of the specification. This annex only addresses the environmental management system requirements contained in clause 4.

A.1 General requirements

It is intended that the implementation of an environmental management system described by the specification will result in improved environmental performance. The specification is based on the concept that the organization will periodically review and evaluate its environmental management system in order to identify opportunities for improvement and their implementation. Improvements in its environmental management system are intended to result in additional improvements in environmental performance.

The environmental management system provides a structured process for the achievement of continual improvement, the rate and extent of which will be determined by the organization in the light of economic and other circumstances. Although some improvement in environmental performance can be expected due to the adoption of a systematic approach, it should be understood that the environmental management system is a tool which enables the organization to achieve and systematically control the level of environmental performance that it sets itself. The establishment and operation of an environmental management system will not, in itself, necessarily result in an immediate reduction of adverse environmental impact.

An organization has the freedom and flexibility to define its boundaries and may choose to implement this International Standard with respect to the entire organization, or to specific operating units or activities of the organization. If this International Standard is implemented for a specific operating unit or activity, policies and procedures developed by other parts of the organization can be used to meet the requirements of this International Standard, provided that they are applicable to the specific operating unit or activity that will be subject to it. The level of detail and complexity of the environmental management system, the extent of documentation and the resources devoted to it will be dependent on the size of an organization and the nature of its activities. This may be the case in particular for small and medium-sized enterprises. Integration of environmental matters with the overall management system can contribute to the effective implementation of the environmental management system, as well as to efficiency and to clarity of roles.

This International Standard contains management system requirements, based on the dynamic cyclical process of "plan, implement, check and review".

The system should enable an organization to

a) establish an environmental policy appropriate to itself;

b) identify the environmental aspects arising from the organization's past, existing or planned activities, products or services, to determine the environmental impacts of significance;

c) identify the relevant legislative and regulatory requirements;

d) identify priorities and set appropriate environmental objectives and targets;

e) establish a structure and (a) programme(s) to implement the policy and achieve objectives and targets;

f) facilitate planning, control, monitoring, corrective action, auditing and review activities to ensure both that the policy is complied with and that the environmental management system remains appropriate;

g) be capable of adapting to changing circumstances.

A.2 Environmental policy

The environmental policy is the driver for implementing and improving the organization's environmental management system so that it can maintain and potentially improve its environmental performance. The policy should therefore reflect the commitment of top management to compliance with applicable laws and continual improvement. The policy forms the basis upon which the organization sets its objectives and targets. The policy should be sufficiently clear to be capable of being understood by internal and external interested parties and should be periodically reviewed and revised to reflect changing conditions and information. Its area of application should be clearly identifiable.

The organization's top management should define and document its environmental policy within the context of the environmental policy of any broader corporate body of which it is a part and with the endorsement of that body, if there is one.

NOTE—Top management may consist of an individual or group of individuals with executive responsibility for the organization.

A.3 Planning

A.3.1 Environmental aspects

Subclause 4.3.1 is intended to provide a process for an organization to identify significant environmental aspects that should be addressed as a priority by the organization's environmental management system. This process should take into account the cost and time of undertaking the analysis and the availability of reliable data. Information already developed for regulatory or other purposes may be used in this process. Organizations may also take into account the degree of practical control they may have over the environmental aspects being considered. Organizations should determine what their environmental aspects are, taking into account the inputs and outputs associated with their current and relevant past activities, products and/or services.

An organization with no existing environmental management system should, initially, establish its current position with regard to the environment by

means of a review. The aim should be to consider all environmental aspects of the organization as a basis for establishing the environmental management system.

Those organizations with operating environmental management systems do not have to undertake such a review.

The review should cover four key areas:

a) legislative and regulatory requirements;

b) an identification of significant environmental aspects;

c) an examination of all existing environmental management practices and procedures;

d) an evaluation of feedback from the investigation of previous incidents.

In all cases, consideration should be given to normal and abnormal operations within the organization, and to potential emergency conditions.

A suitable approach to the review may include checklists, interviews, direct inspection and measurement, results of previous audits or other reviews depending on the nature of the activities.

The process to identify the significant environmental aspects associated with the activities at operating units should, where relevant, consider

a) emissions to air;

b) releases to water;

c) waste management;

d) contamination of land;

e) use of raw materials and natural resources;

f) other local environmental and community issues.

This process should consider normal operating conditions, shut-down and start-up conditions, as well as the realistic potential significant impacts associated with reasonably foreseeable or emergency situations.

The process is intended to identify significant environmental aspects associated with activities, products or services, and is not intended to require a detailed life cycle assessment. Organizations do not have to evaluate each product, component or raw material input. They may select categories of activities, products or services to identify those aspects most likely to have a significant impact.

The control and influence over the environmental aspects of products vary significantly, depending on the market situation of the organization. A contractor or supplier to the organization may have comparatively little control, while the organization responsible for product design can alter the aspects significantly by changing, for example, a single input material. Whilst recognizing that organizations may have limited control over the use and disposal of their products, they should consider, where practical, proper handling and disposal mechanisms. This provision is not intended to change or increase an organization's legal obligations.

A.3.2 Legal and other requirements

Examples of other requirements to which the organization may subscribe are

a) industry codes of practice;

b) agreements with public authorities;

c) non-regulatory guidelines.

A.3.3 Objectives and targets

The objectives should be specific and targets should be measurable wherever practicable, and where appropriate take preventative measures into account.

When considering their technological options, an organization may consider the use of the best available technology where economically viable, cost-effective and judged appropriate.

The reference to the financial requirements of the organization is not intended to imply that organizations are obliged to use environmental cost-accounting methodologies.

A.3.4 Environmental management programme(s)

The creation and use of one or more programmes is a key element to the successful implementation of an environmental management system. The programme should describe how the organization's

objectives and targets will be achieved, including time-scales and personnel responsible for implementing the organization's environmental policy. This programme may be subdivided to address specific elements of the organization's operations. The programme should include an environmental review for new activities.

The programme may include, where appropriate and practical, consideration of planning, design, production, marketing and disposal stages. This may be undertaken for both current and new activities, products or services. For products this may address design, materials, production processes, use and ultimate disposal. For installations or significant modifications of processes this may address planning, design, construction, commissioning, operation and, at the appropriate time determined by the organization, decommissioning.

A.4 Implementation and operation

A.4.1 Structure and responsibility

The successful implementation of an environmental management system calls for the commitment of all employees of the organization. Environmental responsibilities therefore should not be seen as confined to the environmental function, but may also include other areas of an organization, such as operational management or staff functions other than environmental.

This commitment should begin at the highest levels of management. Accordingly, top management should establish the organization's environmental policy and ensure that the environmental management system is implemented. As part of this commitment, the top management should designate (a) specific management representative(s) with defined responsibility and authority for implementing the environmental management system. In large or complex organizations there may be more than one designated representative. In small or medium sized enterprises, these responsibilities may be undertaken by one individual. Top management should also ensure that appropriate resources are provided to ensure that the environmental management system is implemented and maintained. It is also important that the key environmental management system responsibilities are well defined and communicated to the relevant personnel.

A.4.2 Training, awareness and competence

The organization should establish and maintain procedures for identifying training needs. The organization should also require that contractors working on its behalf are able to demonstrate that their employees have the requisite training.

Management should determine the level of experience, competence and training necessary to ensure the capability of personnel, especially those carrying out specialized environmental management functions.

A.4.3 Communication

Organizations should implement a procedure for receiving, documenting and responding to relevant information and requests from interested parties. This procedure may include a dialogue with interested parties and consideration of their relevant concerns. In some circumstances, responses to interested parties' concerns may include relevant information about the environmental impacts associated with the organization's operations. These procedures should also address necessary communications with public authorities regarding emergency planning and other relevant issues.

A.4.4 Environmental management system documentation

The level of detail of the documentation should be sufficient to describe the core elements of the environmental management system and their interaction and provide direction on where to obtain more detailed information on the operation of specific parts of the environmental management system. This documentation may be integrated with documentation of other systems implemented by the organization. It does not have to be in the form of a single manual.

Related documentation may include

a) process information;

b) organizational charts;

c) internal standards and operational procedures;

d) site emergency plans.

A.4.5 Document control

The intent of 4.4.5 is to ensure that organizations create and maintain documents in a manner sufficient to implement the environmental management system. However, the primary focus of organizations should be on the effective implementation of the environmental management system and on environmental performance and not on a complex documentation control system.

A.4.6 Operational control

Text may be included here in a future revision.

A.4.7 Emergency preparedness and response

Text may be included here in a future revision.

A.5 Checking and corrective action

A.5.1 Monitoring and measurement

Text may be included here in a future revision.

A.5.2 Nonconformance and corrective and preventive action

In establishing and maintaining procedures for investigating and correcting nonconformance, the organization should include these basic elements:

a) identifying the cause of the nonconformance;

b) identifying and implementing the necessary corrective action;

c) implementing or modifying controls necessary to avoid repetition of the nonconformance;

d) recording any changes in written procedures resulting from the corrective action.

Depending on the situation, this may be accomplished rapidly and with a minimum of formal planning or it may be a more complex and long-term activity. The associated documentation should be appropriate to the level of corrective action.

A.5.3 Records

Procedures for identification, maintenance and disposition of records should focus on those records needed for the implementation and operation of the environmental management system and for recording the extent to which planned objectives and targets have been met.

Environmental records may include

a) information on applicable environmental laws or other requirements;

b) complaint records;

c) training records;

d) process information;

e) product information;

f) inspection, maintenance and calibration records;

g) pertinent contractor and supplier information;

h) incident reports;

i) information on emergency preparedness and response;

j) information on significant environmental aspects;

k) audit results;

l) management reviews.

Proper account should be taken of confidential business information.

A.5.4 Environmental management system audit

The audit programme and procedures should cover

a) the activities and areas to be considered in audits;

b) the frequency of audits;

c) the responsibilities associated with managing and conducting audits;

d) the communication of audit results;

e) auditor competence;

f) how audits will be conducted.

Audits may be performed by personnel from within the organization and/or by external persons selected by the organization. In either case, the persons conducting the audit should be in a position to do so impartially and objectively.

A.6 Management review

In order to maintain continual improvement, suitability and effectiveness of the environmental management system, and thereby its performance, the organization's management should review and evaluate the environmental management system at defined intervals. The scope of the review should be comprehensive, though not all elements of an environmental management system need to be reviewed at once and the review process may take place over a period of time.

The review of the policy, objectives and procedures should be carried out by the level of management that defined them.

Reviews should include

a) results from audits;

b) the extent to which objectives and targets have been met;

c) the continuing suitability of the environmental management system in relation to changing conditions and information;

d) concerns amongst relevant interested parties.

Observations, conclusions and recommendations should be documented for necessary action.

Annex B
(informative)

Links between ISO 14001 and ISO 9001

Tables B.1 and B.2 identify links and broad technical correspondences between ISO 14001 and ISO 9001 and vice versa.

The objective of the comparison is to demonstrate the combinability of both systems to those organizations already operating one of these International Standards and which may wish to operate both.

A direct link between subclauses of the two International Standards has only been established if the two subclauses are largely congruent in requirements. Beyond that, many detailed cross-connections of minor relevance exist which could not be shown here.

Annex C
(informative)

Bibliography

[1]   ISO 9000-1:1994, *Quality management and quality assurance standards—Part 1: Guidelines for selection and use.*

[2]   ISO 9000-2:1993, *Quality management and quality assurance standards—Part 2: Generic guidelines for the application of ISO 9001, ISO 9002 and ISO 9003.*

[3]   ISO 9000-3:1991, *Quality management and quality assurance standards—Part 3: Guidelines for the application of ISO 9001 to the development, supply and maintenance of software.*

[4]   ISO 9000-4:1993, *Quality management and quality assurance standards—Part 4: Guide to dependability programme management.*

[5]   ISO 9001:1994, *Quality systems—Model for quality assurance in design, development, production, installation and servicing.*

[6]   ISO 14004:1996, *Environmental management systems—General guidelines on principles, systems and supporting techniques.*

[7]   ISO 14010:1996, *Guidelines for environmental auditing—General principles.*

[8]   ISO 14011:1996, *Guidelines for environmental auditing—Audit procedures—Auditing of environmental management systems.*

[9]   ISO 14012:1996, *Guidelines for environmental auditing—Qualification criteria for environmental auditors.*

ANSI/ISO 14001

ISO 14001:1996		ISO 9001:1994	
General requirements	4.1	4.2.1 1st sentence	General
Environmental Policy	4.2	4.1.1	Quality policy
Planning			
Environmental aspects	4.3.1	— 1)	
Legal and other requirements	4.3.2	— 2)	
Objectives and targets	4.3.3		
Environmental management programme(s)	4.3.4	4.2.3	Quality planning
Implementation and Operation			
Structure and responsibility	4.4.1	4.1.2	Organization
Training, awareness and competence	4.4.2	4.18	Training
Communication	4.4.3	—	
Environmental management system documentation	4.4.4	4.2.1 without 1st sentence	General
Document control	4.4.5	4.5	Document and data control
Operational control	4.4.6	4.2.2	Quality system procedures
	4.4.6	4.3 3)	Contract Review
	4.4.6	4.4	Design control
	4.4.6	4.6	Purchasing
	4.4.6	4.7	Control of customer-supplied product
	4.4.6	4.9	Process control
	4.4.6	4.15	Handling, storage, packaging, preservation & delivery
	4.4.6	4.19	Servicing
	4.4.6	4.8	Product identification and traceability
Emergency preparedness and response	4.4.7	—	
Checking and Corrective Action			
Monitoring and measurement	4.5.1 1st & 3rd paragraphs	4.10	Inspection and testing
		4.12	Inspection and test status
		4.20	Statistical techniques
Monitoring and measurement	4.5.1 2nd paragraph	4.11	Control of inspection, measurement and test equipment
Non-conformance and corrective and preventive action	4.5.2 1st part of 1st sentence	4.13	Control of non-conforming product
Non-conformance and corrective and preventive action	4.5.2 w/o 1st part of 1st sentence	4.14	Corrective and preventive action
Records	4.5.3	4.16	Control of quality records
Environmental management system audit	4.5.4	4.17	Internal quality audits
Management Review	4.6	4.1.3	Management review

1) Legal requirements addressed in ISO 9001, 4.4.4.
2) Objectives addressed in ISO 9001, 4.1.1
3) Communication with the quality stakeholders (customers).

Table B.1 Correspondence Between ISO 14001 and ISO 9001.

ISO 9001: 1994		ISO 14001: 1996	
Management responsibility			
Quality policy	4.1.1	4.2	Environmental policy
	—1)	4.3.1	Environmental aspects
	—2)	4.3.2	Legal and other requirements
	—	4.3.3	Objectives and targets
	—	4.3.4	Environmental management programme(s)
Organization	4.1.2	4.4.1	Structure and responsibility
Management review	4.1.3	4.6	Management review
Quality system			
General	4.2.1 1st sentence	4.1	General requirements
	4.2.1 w/o 1st sentence	4.4.4	Environmental management system documentation
Quality system procedures	4.2.2	4.4.6	Operational control
Quality planning	4.2.3	—	
Contract review	4.3,3)	4.4.6	Operational control
Design control	4.4	4.4.6	Operational control
Document and data control	4.5	4.4.5	Document control
Purchasing	4.6	4.4.6	Operational control
Control of customer-supplied product	4.7	4.4.6	Operational control
Product identification and traceability	4.8	—	
Process control	4.9	4.4.6	Operational control
Inspection and testing	4.10	4.5.1 1st and 3rd paragraph	Monitoring and measurement
Control of inspection, measuring, and test equipment	4.11	4.5.1 2nd paragraph	Monitoring and measurement
Inspection and test status	4.12	—	
Control of non-conforming product	4.13	4.5.2 1st pt. of 1st sentence	Non-conformance and corrective and preventive action
Corrective and preventive action	4.14	4.5.2 w/o 1st pt. of 1st sen.	Non-conformance and corrective and preventive action
	—	4.4.7	Emergency preparedness and response
Handling, storage, packaging, preservation and delivery	4.15	4.4.6	Operational control
Control of quality records	4.16	4.5.3	Records
Internal quality audits	4.17	4.5.4	Environmental management system audit
Training	4.18	4.4.2	Training, awareness, and competence
Servicing	4.19	4.4.6	Operational control
Statistical techniques	4.20	—	
	—	4.4.3	Communication

1) Legal requirements addressed in ISO 9001, 4.4.4.
2) Objectives addressed in ISO 9001, 4.1.1
3) Communication with the quality stakeholders (customers)

Table B.2 Correspondence Between ISO 9001 and ISO 14001

SECTION 2
ANSI/ISO 14004 — Environmental Management Systems — General Guidelines on Principles, Systems and Supporting Techniques

Approved as a American National Standard by:
American Society for Quality
American Society for Testing and Materials
NSF International

An American National Standard Approved on September 23, 1996

American National Standards: *An American National Standard implies a consensus of those substantially concerned with its scope and provisions. An American National Standard is intended as a guide to aid the manufacturer, the consumer, and the general public. The existence of an American National Standard does not in any respect preclude anyone, whether he or she has approved the standard or not, from manufacturing, purchasing, or using products, processes, or procedures not conforming to the standard. American National Standards are subject to periodic review and users are cautioned to obtain the latest edition.*

Caution Notice: *This American National Standard may be revised or withdrawn at any time. The procedures of the American National Standards Institute require that action be taken to reaffirm, revise, or withdraw this standard no later than five years from the date of publication. Purchasers of American National Standards may receive current information on all standards by calling or writing the American National Standards Institute.*

© *1996 ISO.*

These Materials are subject to copyright claims of ISO, ANSI, and ASQC. Not for resale. No part of this publication may be reproduced in any form, including an electronic retrieval system, without the prior written permission of ASQC. All requests pertaining to the ANSI/ISO 14000 Series Standards should be submitted to ASQC.

Note: As used in this document, the term "International Standard" refers to the American National adoption of this and other International Standards.

ASQC Mission: *To facilitate continuous improvement and increase customer satisfaction by identifying, communicating, and promoting the use of quality principles, concepts, and technologies; and thereby be recognized throughout the world as the leading authority on, and champion for, quality.*

10 9 8 7 6 5 4 3 2 1

Foreword

ISO (the International Organization for Standardization) is a worldwide federation of national standards bodies (ISO member bodies). The work of preparing International Standards is normally carried out through ISO technical committees. Each member body interested in a subject for which a technical committee has been established has the right to be represented on that committee. International organizations, governmental and non-governmental, in liaison with ISO, also take part in the work. ISO collaborates closely with the International Electrotechnical Commission (IEC) on all matters of electrotechnical standardization.

Draft International Standards adopted by the technical committees are circulated to the member bodies for voting. Publication as an International Standard requires approval by at least 75% of the member bodies casting a vote.

International Standard ISO 14004 was prepared by Technical Committee ISO/TC 207, *Environmental management*, Subcommittee SC 1, *Environmental management systems*.

Annexes A and B of this International Standard are for information only.

Introduction

0.1 Overview

As concern grows for maintaining and improving the quality of the environment and protecting human health, organizations of all sizes are increasingly turning their attention to the potential environmental impacts of their activities, products or services. The environmental performance of an organization is of increasing importance to internal and external interested parties. Achieving sound environmental performance requires organizational commitment to a systematic approach and to continual improvement of the environmental management system (EMS).

The general purpose of this International Standard is to provide assistance to organizations implementing or improving an EMS. It is consistent with the concept of sustainable development and is compatible with diverse cultural, social and organizational frameworks.

It should be noted that only ISO 14001 contains requirements that may be objectively audited for certification/registration purposes or for self-declaration purposes. Alternatively, this International Standard includes examples, descriptions and options that aid both in the implementation of an EMS and in strengthening its relation to the overall management of the organization.

An EMS provides order and consistency for organizations to address environmental concerns through the allocation of resources, assignment of responsibilities, and ongoing evaluation of practices, procedures and processes.

This International Standard considers the elements of an EMS and provides practical advice on implementing or enhancing such a system. It also provides organizations with advice on how to effectively initiate, improve or sustain an environmental management system. Such a system is essential to an organization's ability to anticipate and meet its environmental objectives and to ensure ongoing compliance with national and/or international requirements.

Environmental management is an integral part of an organization's overall management system. The design of an EMS is an ongoing and interactive process. The structure, responsibilities, practices, procedures, processes and resources for implementing environmental policies, objectives and targets can be coordinated with existing efforts in other areas (e.g. operations, finance, quality, occupational health and safety).

Key principles for managers implementing or enhancing an environmental management system include, but are not limited to, the following.

- Recognize that environmental management is among the highest corporate priorities.

- Establish and maintain communication with internal and external interested parties.

- Determine the legislative requirements and environmental aspects associated with the organization's activities, products or services.

- Develop management and employee commitment to the protection of the environment, with clear assignment of accountability and responsibility.

- Encourage environmental planning throughout the product or process life cycle.

- Establish a process for achieving targeted performance levels.

- Provide appropriate and sufficient resources, including training, to achieve targeted performance levels on an ongoing basis.

- Evaluate environmental performance against the organization's environmental policy, objectives and targets and seek improvement where appropriate.

- Establish a management process to audit and review the EMS and to identify opportunities for improvement of the system and resulting environmental performance.

- Encourage contractors and suppliers to establish an EMS.

Organizations can consider the following different uses of the EMS International Standards.

- Using ISO 14001:1996, *Environmental management systems—Specification with guidance for use* to achieve third-party certification/registration, or self-declaration of an organization's EMS.

- Using this International Standard, or parts of it, to initiate and/or improve its EMS. It is not intended for certification/registration purposes.

- Using this International Standard as a guideline or ISO 14001 as a specification for second-party recognition between contracting parties, which may be suitable for some business relationships.

- Using related ISO documents.

The choice will depend on factors such as:

- organization policy;

- level of maturity of the organization: whether systematic management that can facilitate the introduction of systematic environmental management is already in place;

- possible advantages and disadvantages, influenced by such things as market position, existing reputation and external relations;

- size of the organization.

This International Standard can be used by organizations of any size. Nonetheless, the importance of small and medium-sized enterprises (SMEs) is being increasingly recognized by governments and business. This International Standard acknowledges and accommodates the needs of SMEs.

0.2 Benefits of having an environmental management system

An organization should implement an effective environmental management system in order to help protect human health and the environment from the potential impacts of its activities, products or services; and to assist in maintaining and improving the quality of the environment.

Having an EMS can help an organization provide confidence to its interested parties that

- a management commitment exists to meet the provisions of its policy, objectives, and targets;

- emphasis is placed on prevention rather than corrective action;

- evidence of reasonable care and regulatory compliance can be provided; and

- the systems design incorporates the process of continual improvement.

An organization whose management system incorporates an EMS has a framework to balance and integrate economic and environmental interests. An organization that has implemented an EMS can achieve significant competitive advantages.

Economic benefits can be gained from implementing an environmental management system. These should be identified in order to demonstrate to interested parties, especially shareholders, the value to the organization of good environmental management. It also provides the organization with the opportunity to link environmental objectives and targets with specific financial outcomes and thus to ensure that resources are made available where they provide the most benefit in both financial and environmental terms.

The potential benefits associated with an effective EMS include

- assuring customers of commitment to demonstrable environmental management;

- maintaining good public/community relations;

- satisfying investor criteria and improving access to capital;

- obtaining insurance at reasonable cost;

- enhancing image and market share;

- meeting vendor certification criteria;

- improving cost control;

- reducing incidents that result in liability;

- demonstrating reasonable care;

- conserving input materials and energy;

- facilitating the attainment of permits and authorizations;

- fostering development and sharing environmental solutions;

- improving industry-government relations.

Environmental management systems—General guidelines on principles, systems and supporting techniques

1 Scope

This International Standard provides guidance on the development and implementation of environmental management systems and principles, and their coordination with other management systems.

The guidelines in this International Standard are applicable to any organization, regardless of size, type, or level of maturity, that is interested in developing, implementing and/or improving an environmental management system.

The guidelines are intended for use as a voluntary, internal management tool and are not intended to be used as EMS certification/registration criteria.

2 Normative references

There are no normative references at present.

3 Definitions

For the purposes of this International Standard, the following definitions apply.

3.1
continual improvement
process of enhancing the environmental management system to achieve improvements in overall environmental performance in line with the organization's environmental policy

NOTE—The process need not take place in all areas of activity simultaneously.

3.2
environment
surroundings in which an organization operates, including air, water, land, natural resources, flora, fauna, humans, and their interrelation

NOTE—Surroundings in this context extend from within an organization to the global system.

3.3
environmental aspect
element of an organization's activities, products or services that can interact with the environment

NOTE—A significant environmental aspect is an environmental aspect that has or can have a significant environmental impact.

3.4
environmental impact
any change to the environment, whether adverse or beneficial, wholly or partially resulting from an organization's activities, products or services

3.5
environmental management system
that part of the overall management system that includes organizational structure, planning activities, responsibilities, practices, procedures, processes and resources for developing, implementing, achieving, reviewing and maintaining the environmental policy

3.6
environmental management system audit
systematic and documented verification process of objectively obtaining and evaluating evidence to determine whether an organization's environmental management system conforms to the environmental management system audit criteria set by the organization, and for communication of the results of this process to management

3.7
environmental objective
overall environmental goal, arising from the environmental policy, that an organization sets itself to achieve, and which is quantified where practicable

3.8
environmental performance
measurable results of the environmental management system, related to an organization's control of its environmental aspects, based on its environmental policy, objectives and targets

3.9
environmental policy
statement by the organization of its intentions and principles in relation to its overall environmental performance which provides a framework for action and for the setting of its environmental objectives and targets

3.10
environmental target
detailed performance requirement, quantified where practicable, applicable to the organization or parts thereof, that arises from the environmental objectives and that needs to be set and met in order to achieve those objectives

3.11
interested party
individual or group concerned with or affected by the environmental performance of an organization

3.12
organization
company, corporation, firm, enterprise, authority or institution, or part or combination thereof, whether incorporated or not, public or private, that has its own functions and administration

NOTE—For organizations with more than one operating unit, a single operating unit may be defined as an organization.

3.13
prevention of pollution
use of processes, practices, materials or products that avoid, reduce or control pollution, which may include recycling, treatment, process changes, control mechanisms, efficient use of resources and material substitution

NOTE—The potential benefits of prevention of pollution include the reduction of adverse environmental impacts, improved efficiency and reduced costs.

4 Environmental management system (EMS) principles and elements

The EMS model (see figure 1) follows the basic view of an organization which subscribes to the following principles.

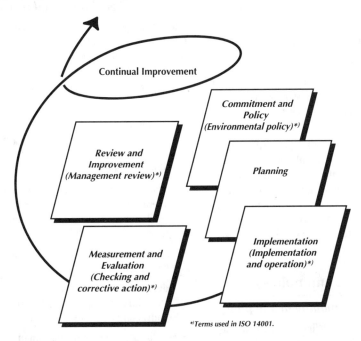

Figure 1 Environmental management system model for this International Standard

ANSI/ISO 14004

Principle 1—Commitment and policy

An organization should define its environmental policy and ensure commitment to its EMS.

Principle 2—Planning

An organization should formulate a plan to fulfil its environmental policy.

Principle 3—Implementation

For effective implementation, an organization should develop the capabilities and support mechanisms necessary to achieve its environmental policy, objectives and targets.

Principle 4—Measurement and evaluation

An organization should measure, monitor and evaluate its environmental performance.

Principle 5—Review and improvement

An organization should review and continually improve its environmental management system, with the objective of improving its overall environmental performance.

With this in mind, the EMS is best viewed as an organizing framework that should be continually monitored and periodically reviewed to provide effective direction for an organization's environmental activities in response to changing internal and external factors. Every individual in an organization should accept responsibility for environmental improvements.

4.1 Commitment and policy

> ### Principle 1 — Commitment and policy
> An organization should define its environmental policy and ensure commitment to its EMS.

4.1.1 General

The organization should begin where there is obvious benefit, for example, by focusing on regulatory compliance, by limiting sources of liability or by making more efficient use of materials.

As the organization grows in experience, and its EMS starts to take shape, procedures, pro-grammes and technologies can be put in place to further improve environmental performance. Then, as the EMS matures, environmental considerations can be integrated into all business decisions.

4.1.2 Top management commitment and leadership

To ensure success, an early step in developing or improving an EMS involves obtaining commitment from the top management of the organization to improve the environmental management of its activities, products or services. The ongoing commitment and leadership of the top management are crucial.

4.1.3 Initial environmental review

The current position of an organization with regard to the environment can be established by means of an initial environmental review. The initial review can cover the following:

- identification of legislative and regulatory requirements;

- identification of environmental aspects of its activities, products or services so as to determine those that have or can have significant environmental impacts and liabilities;

- evaluation of performance compared with relevant internal criteria, external standards, regulations, codes of practice and sets of principles and guidelines;

- existing environmental management practices and procedures;

- identification of the existing policies and procedures dealing with procurement and contracting activities;

- feedback from the investigation of previous incidents of non-compliance;

- opportunities for competitive advantage;
- the views of interested parties;
- functions or activities of other organizational systems that can enable or impede environmental performance.

In all cases, consideration should be given to the full range of operating conditions, including possible incidents and emergency situations.

The process and results of the initial environmental review should be documented and opportunities for EMS development should be identified.

Practical help — Initial environmental review

An important first step is to develop the list of areas to be reviewed. This can include organization activities, specific operations or a specific site.

Some common techniques for conducting a review include

- *questionnaires,*
- *interviews,*
- *checklists,*
- *direct inspection and measurement,*
- *record review,*
- *benchmarking* [1].

Organizations, including SMEs, can consult a number of outside sources such as:

- *government agencies in relation to laws and permits;*
- *local or regional libraries or databases;*
- *other organizations for exchange of information;*
- *industry associations;*
- *larger customer organizations;*
- *manufacturers of equipment in use;*

---

1) Benchmarking is a technique for studying best practice, whether within the organization, in a competitor's organization or in a different industry, to enable the organization to adopt or improve on it.

- *business relations (e.g. with those who transport and dispose of waste);*
- *professional help.*

4.1.4 Environmental policy

An environmental policy establishes an overall sense of direction and sets the principles of action for an organization. It sets the goal as to the level of environmental responsibility and performance required of the organization, against which all subsequent actions will be judged.

A growing number of international organizations including government, industry associations and citizens' groups have developed guiding principles (see annex A for two examples). Such guiding principles have helped organizations define the overall scope of their commitment to the environment. They also help to give different organizations a common set of values. Guiding principles such as these can assist the organization in developing its policy, which can be as individual as the organization for which it is written.

The responsibility for setting environmental policy normally rests with the organization's top management. The organization's management is responsible for implementing the policy and for providing input to the formulation and modification of the policy.

An environmental policy should consider the following:

- the organization's mission, vision, core values and beliefs
- requirements of and communication with interested parties;
- continual improvement;
- prevention of pollution;
- guiding principles;
- coordination with other organizational policies (e.g. quality, occupational health and safety);
- specific local or regional conditions;
- compliance with relevant environmental regulations, laws and other criteria to which the organization subscribes.

Some issues to be considered in environmental policy

1   *Does the organization have an environmental policy that is relevant to its activities, products and services?*

2   *Does the policy reflect the organization's values and guiding principles?*

3   *Has the environmental policy been approved by top management and has someone been identified and given the authority to oversee and implement the policy?*

4   *Does the policy guide the setting of environmental objectives and targets?*

5   *Does the policy guide the organization towards monitoring appropriate technology and management practices?*

6   *What commitments are embodied in the environmental policy, for example, support for continual improvement, support for the prevention of pollution, monitoring, meeting or exceeding legal requirements, and consideration of the expectations of interested parties?*

Practical help — Environmental policy

All activities, products or services can cause impacts on the environment. The environmental policy should recognize this.

A detailed review of the guiding principles in annex A can help in drafting an appropriate policy. The issues addressed in the policy depend on the nature of the organization. In addition to compliance with environmental regulations, the policy can state commitments to

• *minimize any significant adverse environmental impacts of new developments through the use of the integrated environmental management procedures and planning;*

• *development of environmental performance evaluation procedures and associated indicators;*

• *embody life cycle thinking;*

• *design products in such a way as to minimize their environmental impacts in production, use and disposal;*

• *prevent pollution, reduce waste and the consumption of resources (materials, fuel and energy), and commit to recovery and recycling, as opposed to disposal where feasible;*

• *education and training;*

• *sharing environmental experience;*

• *involvement of and communication with interested parties;*

• *work towards sustainable development;*

• *encourage the use of EMS by suppliers and contractors.*

4.2 Planning

Principle 2 — Planning

An organization should formulate a plan to fulfil its environmental policy.

4.2.1 General

The environmental management system elements relating to planning include

• identification of environmental aspects and evaluation of associated environmental impacts;

• legal requirements;

• environmental policy;

• internal performance criteria;

• environmental objectives and targets;

• environmental plans and management programme.

4.2.2 Identification of environmental aspects and evaluation of associated environmental impacts

An organization's policy, objectives and targets should be based on knowledge about the environmental aspects and significant environmental impacts associated with its activities, products or services. This can ensure that the significant environmental impacts associated with these aspects are taken into account in setting the environmental objectives.

The identification of the environmental aspects is an ongoing process that determines the past, current and potential impact (positive or negative) of an organization's activities on the environment. This process also includes the identification of the potential regulatory, legal and business exposure affecting the organization. It can also include identification of health and safety impacts, and environmental risk assessment.

Some issues to be considered in identification of environmental aspects and evaluation of environmental impacts

1   *What are the environmental aspects of the organization's activities, products and services?*

2   *Do the organization's activities, products or services create any significant adverse environmental impacts?*

3   *Does the organization have a procedure for evaluating the environmental impacts of new projects?*

4   *Does the location of the organization require special environmental consideration, for example sensitive environmental areas?*

5   *How will any intended changes or additions to activities, products or services affect the environmental aspects and their associated impacts?*

6   *How significant or severe are the potential environmental impacts should a process failure occur?*

7   *How frequently will the situation arise that could lead to the impact?*

8   *What are the significant environmental aspects; considering impacts, likelihood, severity and frequency?*

9   *Are the significant environmental impacts local, regional or global in scope?*

Practical help — Identification of environmental aspects and evaluation of associated environmental impacts

The relationship between environmental aspects and environmental impacts is one of cause and effect.

An environmental aspect refers to an element of an organization's activity, product or service which can have a beneficial or adverse impact on the environment. For example, it could involve a discharge, an emission, consumption or reuse of a material, or noise.

An environmental impact refers to the change which takes place in the environment as a result of the aspect. Examples of impacts might include pollution or contamination of water or depletion of a natural resource.

The identification of environmental aspects and the evaluation of associated environmental impacts is a process that can be dealt with in four steps.

Step 1 — Select an activity, a product or service

The selected activity, product or service should be large enough for meaningful examination and small enough to be sufficiently understood.

Step 2 — Identify environmental aspects of the activity, product or service

Identify as many environmental aspects as possible associated with the selected activity, product or service.

Step 3 — Identify environmental impacts

Identify as many actual and potential, positive and negative, environmental impacts as possible associated with each identified aspect.

Examples from the three steps above are shown in the following table.

Step 4 — Evaluate significance of impacts

The significance of each of the identified environmental impacts can be different for each organization. Quantification can aid judgement.

Activity, product or service	Aspect	Impact
Activity —Handling of hazardous materials	*Potential for accidental spillage*	*Contamination of soil or water*
Product —Product refinement	*Reformulation of the product to reduce its volume*	*Conservation of natural resources*
Service —Vehicle maintenance	*Exhaust emissions*	*Reduction of air emissions*

Practical help — Identification of environmental aspects and evaluation of associated environmental impacts

Evaluation can be facilitated by considering the following.

Environmental concerns:

- *the scale of the impact;*
- *the severity of the impact;*
- *probability of occurrence;*
- *duration of impact.*

Business concerns:

- *potential regulatory and legal exposure;*
- *difficulty of changing the impact;*
- *cost of changing the impact;*
- *effect of change on other activities and processes;*
- *concerns of interested parties;*
- *effect on the public image of the organization.*

4.2.3 Legal and other requirements

The organization should establish and maintain procedures to identify, have access to and understand all legal and other requirements to which it subscribes, directly attributable to the environmental aspects of its activities, products or services.

Some issues to be considered in legal and other requirements

1 *How does the organization access and identify relevant legal and other requirements*

2 *How does the organization keep track of legal and other requirements?*

3 *How does the organization keep track of changes to legal and other requirements?*

4 *How does the organization communicate relevant information on legal and other requirements to employees?*

Practical help — Legal and other requirements

To maintain regulatory compliance, an organization should identify and understand regulatory requirements applicable to its activities, products or services. Regulations can exist in several forms:

- *those specific to the activity (e.g. site operating permits);*
- *those specific to the organization's products or services;*
- *those specific to the organization's industry;*
- *general environmental laws;*
- *authorizations, licenses and permits.*

Several sources can be used to identify environmental regulations and ongoing changes, including

- *all levels of government;*
- *industry associations or groups;*
- *commercial databases;*
- *professional services.*

To facilitate keeping track of legal requirements, an organization can establish and maintain a list of all laws and regulations pertaining to its activities, products or services.

- *water management (e.g. waste, storm, ground);*
- *air quality management;*
- *energy management;*
- *transportation.*

4.2.4 Internal performance criteria

Internal priorities and criteria should be developed and implemented where external standards do not meet the needs of the organization or are non-existent. Internal performance criteria, together with external standards, assist the organization in developing its own objectives and targets.

Practical help — Internal performance criteria

Examples of areas where an organization can have internal performance criteria might include

- *management systems;*
- *employee responsibilities;*
- *acquisition, property management and divestiture;*
- *suppliers;*
- *contractors;*
- *product stewardship;*
- *environmental communications;*
- *regulatory relationships;*
- *environmental incident response and preparedness;*
- *environmental awareness and training;*
- *environmental measurement and improvement;*
- *process risk reduction;*
- *prevention of pollution and resource conservation;*
- *capital projects;*
- *process change;*
- *hazardous material management;*
- *waste management;*

4.2.5 Environmental objectives and targets

Objectives should be established to meet the organization's environmental policy. These objectives are the overall goals for environmental performance identified in the environmental policy. When establishing its objectives, an organization should also take into account the relevant findings from environmental reviews, and the identified environmental aspects and associated environmental impacts.

Environmental targets can then be set to achieve these objectives within a specified time-frame. The targets should be specific and measurable.

When the objectives and targets are set, the organization should consider establishing measurable environmental performance indicators. These indicators can be used as the basis for an environmental performance evaluation system and can provide information on both the environmental management and the operational systems.

Objectives and targets can apply broadly across an organization or more narrowly to site-specific or individual activities. Appropriate levels of management should define the objectives and targets. Objectives and targets should be periodically reviewed and revised, and should take into consideration the views of interested parties.

Some issues to be considered in environmental objectives and targets

1 *How do environmental objectives and targets reflect both the environmental policy and significant environmental impacts associated with the organization's activities, products or services?*

2 *How have the employees responsible for achieving the objectives and targets had input into their development?*

3 *How have the views of interested parties been considered?*

4 *What specific measurable indicators have been established for objectives and targets?*

5 *How are objectives and targets regularly reviewed and revised to reflect desired improvements in environmental performance?*

Practical help—Objectives and targets

Objectives can include commitments to

- *reduce waste and the depletion of resources;*
- *reduce or eliminate the release of pollutants into the environment;*
- *design products to minimize their environmental impact in production, use and disposal;*
- *control the environmental impact of sources of raw material;*
- *minimize any significant adverse environmental impact of new developments;*
- *promote environmental awareness among employees and the community.*

Progress towards an objective can generally be measured using environmental performance indicators such as:

- *quantity of raw material or energy used;*
- *quantity of emissions such as CO_2;*
- *waste produced per quantity of finished product;*
- *efficiency of material and energy use;*
- *number of environmental incidents (e.g. excursions above limits);*
- *number of environmental accidents (e.g. unplanned releases);*
- *percentage waste recycled;*
- *percentage recycled material used in packaging;*
- *number of vehicle kilometres per unit of production;*
- *specific pollutant quantities, e.g. NO_x, SO_2 CO, HC, Pb, CFCs;*

- *investment in environmental protection;*
- *number of prosecutions;*
- *land area set aside for wildlife habitat.*

An integrated example

Objective: reduce energy required in manufacturing operations.

Target: achieve ten percent reduction of energy consumption compared to the previous year.

Indicator: quantity of fuels and electricity per unit of production.

4.2.6 Environmental management programme(s)

Within the general planning of activities, an organization should establish an environmental management programme that addresses all of its environmental objectives. To be most effective, environmental management planning should be integrated into the organization's strategic plan. Environmental management programmes should address schedules, resources and responsibilities for achieving the organization's environmental objectives and targets.

Within the framework provided by the environmental management planning, an environmental management programme identifies specific actions in order of their priority to the organization. These actions may deal with individual processes, projects, products, services, sites or facilities within a site.

Environmental management programmes help the organization to improve its environmental performance. They should be dynamic and revised regularly to reflect changes in organizational objectives and targets.

Some issues to be considered in environmental management programme(s)

1 *What is the organization's process for developing environmental management programmes?*

2 *Does the environmental management planning process involve all responsible parties?*

3 Is there a process for periodic reviews of the programme?

4 How do these programmes address the issues of resources, responsibility, timing and priority?

5 How are the environmental management programmes responsive to the environmental policy and general planning activities?

6 How are the environmental management programmes monitored and revised?

Practical help — Environmental management programme

Below is an example of a process for developing an environmental management programme.

4.3 Implementation

> ### Principle 3 — Implementation
>
> For effective implementation, an organization should develop the capabilities and support mechanisms necessary to achieve its environmental policy, objectives and targets.

4.3.1 General

The capabilities and support required by the organization constantly evolve in response to the changing requirements of interested parties, a dynamic business environment, and the process of continual improvement. To achieve its environmental objectives an organization should focus and align its people, systems, strategy, resources and structure.

For many organizations, implementing environmental management can be approached in stages and should be based on the level of awareness of environmental

Practical help — Environmental management programme

Commitment and policy	Planning	Example
Environmental policy commitment 1[1)]		*Conserve natural resources*
	Objective 1	*Minimize water use wherever technically and commercially practical*
	Target 1	*Reduce water consumption at selected sites by fifteen percent of present levels within one year*
	Environmental programme 1	*Water reuse*
	Action 1	*Install equipment to recycle water used for rinsing in Process A for reuse in Process B*

1) This iterative process should be repeated for all policy commitments, objectives and targets.

requirements, aspects, expectations and benefits, and the availability of resources.

4.3.2 Ensuring capability

4.3.2.1 Resources — Human, physical and financial

The appropriate human, physical (e.g. facilities, equipment), and financial resources essential to the implementation of an organization's environmental policies and the achievement of its objectives should be defined and made available. In allocating resources, organizations can develop procedures to track the benefits as well as the costs of their environmentally or related activities. Issues such as the cost of pollution control, wastes and disposal can be included.

Some issues to be considered in human, physical and financial resources

1 How does the organization identify and allocate the human, technical and financial resources necessary to meet its environmental objectives and targets, including those for new projects?

2 How does the organization track the costs and benefits of environmental activities?

Practical help — Human, physical and financial resources

The resource base and the organization structure of the small or medium enterprise (SME) can impose certain limitations on implementation. In order to manage these constraints the SME should, wherever possible, consider cooperative strategies with

- *larger client organizations to share technology and know-how;*

- *other SMEs on a supply chain or local basis to define and address common issues, to share know-how, to facilitate technical development, to use facilities jointly, to establish a way to study the EMS, to collectively engage consultants;*

- *standardization organizations, SME associations, Chambers of Commerce, for training and awareness programmes;*

- *universities and other research centres to support production and innovation.*

4.3.2.2 EMS alignment and integration

To effectively manage environmental concerns, the EMS elements should be designed or revised so that they are effectively aligned and integrated with existing management system elements.

Management system elements that can benefit from integration include

- organization policies;

- resource allocation;

- operational controls and documentation;

- information and support systems;

- training and development;

- organization and accountability structure;

- reward and appraisal systems;

- measuring and monitoring systems;

- communication and reporting.

Some issues to be considered in organizational alignment and integration

1 How has the environmental management system been integrated into the overall business management process ?

2 What is the process for balancing and resolving conflicts between environmental and other business objectives and priorities?

4.3.2.3 Accountability and responsibility

Responsibility for the overall effectiveness of the EMS should be assigned to (a) senior person(s) or function(s) with sufficient authority, competence and resources.

Operational managers should clearly define the responsibilities of relevant personnel and be responsible and accountable for effective implementation of the EMS and environmental performance. Employees at all levels should be accountable, within the scope of their responsibilities, for environmental performance in support of the overall environmental management system.

Some issues to be considered in accountability and responsibility

1 *What are the responsibilities and accountability of personnel who manage, perform and verify work affecting the environment, and are these defined and documented?*

2 *What is the relationship between environmental responsibility and individual performance and is this periodically reviewed ?*

3 *How do the responsible and accountable personnel*

- *obtain sufficient training, resources and personnel for implementation?*

- *initiate action to ensure compliance with environmental policy?*

- *anticipate, identify and record any environmental problems?*

- *initiate, recommend, or provide solutions to those problems?*

- *verify the implementation of such solutions?*

- *control further activities until any environmental deficiency or unsatisfactory condition has been corrected ?*

- *obtain appropriate training to act in emergency situations?*

- *gain an understanding of the consequences of non-compliance?*

- *gain an understanding of the accountability that applies to them?*

- *encourage voluntary action and initiatives?*

Practical help — Accountability and responsibility

To ensure effective development and implementation of an EMS, it is necessary to assign appropriate responsibilities. One possible approach for developing environmental responsibilities is indicated below. It should be recognized that companies and institutions

have different organizational structures, and need to understand and define environmental responsibilities based upon their own work processes.

A sample model of environmental responsibilities is shown on the following page

4.3.2.4 Environmental awareness and motivation

Top management has a key role to play in building awareness and motivating employees by explaining the organization's environmental values and communicating its commitment to the environmental policy. It is the commitment of the individual people, in the context of shared environmental values, that transforms an environmental management system from paperwork into an effective process.

All members of the organization should understand and be encouraged to accept the importance of achieving the environmental objectives and targets for which they are responsible and/or accountable. They in turn should encourage, where necessary, the other members of their organization to respond in a similar manner.

Motivation to continually improve can be enhanced when employees are recognized for achieving environmental objectives and targets and encouraged to make suggestions that can lead to improved environmental performance.

Some issues to be considered in environmental awareness and motivation

1 *How has top management established, reinforced and communicated organizational commitment to the environmental policy?*

2 *To what extent do employees understand, accept and share the environmental values of the organization?*

3 *To what extent do shared environmental values serve to motivate environmentally responsible action?*

4 *How does the organization recognize employees' environmental achievements?*

ANSI/ISO 14004

Sample environmental responsibilities	Typical person(s) responsible
Establish overall direction	*President, chief executive officer (CEO), board of directors*
Develop environmental policy	*President, CEO, chief environmental manager*
Develop environmental objectives, targets and programmes	*Relevant managers*
Monitor overall EMS performance	*Chief environmental manager*
Assure regulatory compliance	*Senior operating manager*
Ensure continual improvement	*All managers*
Identify customers' expectations	*Sales and marketing staff*
Identify suppliers' expectations	*Purchasers, buyers*
Develop and maintain accounting procedures	*Finance/accounting managers*
Comply with defined procedures	*All staff*
NOTE —In the case of SMEs the person responsible can be the owner.	

Practical help — Accountability and responsibility

4.3.2.5 Knowledge, skills and training

The knowledge and skills necessary to achieve environmental objectives should be identified. These should be considered in personnel selection, recruitment, training, development of skills and ongoing education.

Appropriate training relevant to the achievement of environmental policies, objectives and targets should be provided to all personnel within an organization. Employees should have an appropriate knowledge base, which includes training in the methods and skills required to perform their tasks in an efficient and competent fashion and knowledge of the impact their activities can have on the environment if performed incorrectly.

The organization should also ensure that contractors working at the site provide evidence that they have the requisite knowledge and skills to perform the work in an "environmentally responsible manner".

Education and training is needed to ensure that employees have appropriate and current knowledge of regulatory requirements, internal standards and the organization's policies and objectives. The level and detail of training may vary according to the task.

Training programmes typically have the following elements:

* identification of employee training needs;

- development of a training plan to address defined needs;
- verification of conformance of training programme to regulatory or organizational requirements;
- training of target employee groups;
- documentation of training received;
- evaluation of training received.

Some issues to be considered in knowledge, skills and training

1 *How does the organization identify environmental training needs?*

2 *How are the training needs of specific job functions analysed ?*

3 *Is training developed and reviewed and modified as needed?*

4 *How is the training documented and tracked?*

Practical help — Knowledge, skills and training

Examples of the types of environmental training which can be provided by the organization are shown below.

4.3.3 Support action

4.3.3.1 Communication and reporting

Communication includes establishing processes to report internally and, where desired, externally on the environmental activities of the organization in order to

- demonstrate management commitment to the environment;

 Practical help — Knowledge, skills and training

Type of training	*Audience*	*Purpose*
Raising awareness of the strategic importance of environmental management	*Senior management*	*To gain commitment and alignment to the organization's environmental policy*
Raising general environmental awareness	*All employees*	*To gain commitment to the environmental policy, objectives and targets of the organization; and instil a sense of individual responsibility*
Skills enhancement	*Employees with environmental responsibilities*	*To improve performance in specific areas of the organization, e.g. operations, research and development, and engineering*
Compliance	*Employees whose actions can affect compliance*	*To ensure regulatory and internal requirements for training are met*

ANSI/ISO 14004

- deal with concerns and questions about the environmental aspects of the organization's activities, products or services;

- raise awareness of the organization's environmental policies, objectives, targets and programmes;

- inform internal or external interested parties about the organization's environmental management system and performance as appropriate.

Results from EMS monitoring, audit and management review should be communicated to those within the organization who are responsible for performance.

The provision of appropriate information to the organization's employees and other interested parties serves to motivate employees and encourage public understanding and acceptance of the organization's efforts to improve its environmental performance.

Some issues to be considered in communication and reporting

1 What is the process for receiving and responding to employee concerns?

2 What is the process for receiving and considering the concerns of other interested parties?

3 What is the process for communicating the organization's environmental policy and performance?

4 How are the results from EMS audits and reviews communicated to all appropriate people in the organization?

5 What is the process for making the environmental policy available to the public?

6 Is internal communication adequate to support continual improvement around environmental issues?

Practical help — Communication and reporting

a) Items that can be included in reports:

- *organization's profile;*

- *environmental policy, objectives and targets;*

- *environmental management processes (including interested party involvement and employee recognition);*

- *environmental performance evaluation (including releases, resource conservation, compliance, product stewardship and risk);*

- *opportunities for improvement;*

- *supplementary information, such as glossaries;*

- *independent verification of the contents.*

b) It is important to remember for both internal and external environmental communication and reporting:

- *two-way communication should be encouraged;*

- *information should be understandable and adequately explained;*

- *information should be verifiable;*

- *the organization should present an accurate picture of its performance;*

- *information should be presented in a consistent form (e.g. similar units of measurement to allow for comparison between one period and another).*

c) An organization can communicate environmental information in a variety of ways:

- *externally, through an annual report, regulatory submissions, public government records, industry association publications, the media, and paid advertising;*

- *organization of open days, the publication of telephone numbers where complaints and questions can be directed;*

- *internally, through bulletin board postings, internal newspapers, meetings and electronic mail messages.*

4.3.3.2 EMS documentation

Operational processes and procedures should be defined and appropriately documented and updated as necessary. The organization should clearly define the various types of documents which establish and specify effective operational procedures and control.

The existence of EMS documentation supports employee awareness of what is required to achieve the organization's environmental objectives and enables the evaluation of the system and environmental performance.

The nature of the documentation can vary depending on the size and complexity of the organization. Where elements of the EMS are integrated with an organization's overall management system, the environmental documentation should be integrated into existing documentation. For ease of use, the organization can consider organizing and maintaining a summary of the documentation to

- collate the environmental policy, objectives and targets;

- describe the means of achieving environmental objectives and targets;

- document the key roles, responsibilities and procedures;

- provide direction to related documentation and describe other elements of the organization's management system, where appropriate;

- demonstrate that the environmental management system elements which are appropriate for the organization are implemented.

Such a summary document can serve as a reference to the implementation and maintenance of the organization's environmental management system.

Some issues to be considered in EMS documentation

1 *How are environmental management procedures identified, documented, communicated and revised ?*

2 *Does the organization have a process for developing and maintaining EMS documentation?*

3 *How is EMS documentation integrated with existing documentation where appropriate?*

4 *How do employees access EMS documentation needed to conduct their job activities?*

Practical help — EMS documentation

Documents can be in any medium and should be useful and easily understood.

All documentation should be dated (with dates of revision), readily identifiable, organized, and retained for a specified period. The organization should ensure that

- *documents can be identified with the appropriate organization, division, function, activity, and/or contact person;*

- *documents are periodically reviewed, revised as necessary and approved by authorized personnel prior to issue;*

- *the current versions of relevant documents are available at all locations where operations essential to the effective functioning of the system are performed;*

- *obsolete documents are promptly removed from all points of issue and points of use.*

4.3.3.3 Operational control

Implementation is accomplished through the establishment and maintenance of operational procedures and controls to ensure that the organization's environmental policy, objectives and targets can be met.

Practical help — Operational control

The organization should consider the different operations and activities contributing to its significant environmental impacts when developing or modifying operational controls and procedures. Such operations and activities may include

- *research and development design and engineering;*
- *purchasing;*
- *contracting;*
- *handling and storage of raw materials;*
- *production and maintenance processes;*
- *laboratories;*
- *storage of products;*
- *transportation;*
- *marketing, advertising;*
- *customer service;*
- *acquisition, construction or modification of property and facilities.*

Activities can be divided into three categories:

- *activities to prevent pollution and conserve resources in new capital projects, process changes and resources management, property (acquisitions, divestitures and property management), and new products and packaging;*
- *daily management activities to assure conformance to internal and external organizational requirements, and to ensure their efficiency and effectiveness;*
- *strategic management activities to anticipate and respond to changing environmental requirements.*

4.3.3.4 Emergency preparedness and response

Emergency plans and procedures should be established to ensure that there will be an appropriate response to unexpected or accidental incidents.

The organization should define and maintain procedures for dealing with environmental incidents and potential emergency situations. The operating procedures and controls should include, where appropriate, consideration of

- accidental emissions to the atmosphere;
- accidental discharges to water and land;
- specific environment and ecosystem effects from accidental releases.

The procedures should take into account incidents arising, or likely to arise, as consequences of

- abnormal operating conditions;
- accidents and potential emergency situations.

Practical help — Emergency preparedness and response

Emergency plans can include

- *emergency organization and responsibilities;*
- *a list of key personnel;*
- *details of emergency services (e.g. fire department, spill clean-up services);*
- *internal and external communication plans;*
- *actions taken in the event of different types of emergencies;*
- *information on hazardous materials, including each material's potential impact on the environment, and measures to be taken in the event of accidental release;*
- *training plans and testing for effectiveness.*

4.4 Measurement and evaluation

Principle 4 — Measurement and evaluation

An organization should measure, monitor and evaluate its environmental performance.

4.4.1 General

Measuring, monitoring and evaluating are key activities of an environmental management system which ensure that the organization is performing in accordance with the stated environmental management programme.

4.4.2 Measuring and monitoring (ongoing performance)

There should be a system in place for measuring and monitoring actual performance against the organization's environmental objectives and targets in the areas of management systems and operational processes. This includes evaluation of compliance with relevant environmental legislation and regulations. The results should be analysed and used to determine areas of success and to identify activities requiring corrective action and improvement.

Appropriate processes should be in place to ensure the reliability of data, such as calibration of instruments, test equipment, and software and hardware sampling.

Identifying appropriate environmental performance indicators for the organization should be an ongoing process. Such indicators should be objective, verifiable and reproducible. They should be relevant to the organization's activities, consistent with its environmental policy, practical, cost-effective, and technologically feasible.

NOTE — Examples of environmental performance indicators are shown in "Practical help — Objectives and targets" (4.2.5).

Some issues to be considered in measuring and monitoring

1 How is environmental performance regularly monitored ?

2 How have specific environmental performance indicators been established which relate to the organization's objectives and targets and what are they?

3 What control processes are in place to regularly calibrate and sample measuring and monitoring equipment and systems?

4 What is the process to periodically evaluate compliance with relevant legal and other compliance?

4.4.3 Corrective and preventive action

The findings, conclusions, and recommendations reached as a result of measuring, monitoring, audits and other reviews of the environmental management

system should be documented, and the necessary corrective and preventive actions identified. Management should ensure that these corrective and preventive actions have been implemented and that there is systematic follow-up to ensure their effectiveness.

4.4.4 EMS records and information management

Records are evidence of the ongoing operation of the EMS and should cover

- legislative and regulatory requirements;
- permits;
- environmental aspects and their associated impacts;
- environmental training activity;
- inspection, calibration and maintenance activity;
- monitoring data;
- details of non-conformance: incidents, complaints and follow-up action;
- product identification: composition and property data;
- supplier and contractor information;
- environmental audits and management reviews.

A complex range of information can result. The effective management of these records is essential to the successful implementation of the EMS. The key features of good environmental information management include means of identification, collection, indexing, filing, storage, maintenance, retrieval, retention and disposition of pertinent EMS documentation and records.

Some issues to be considered in EMS records and information management

1 What environmental information does the organization need to manage effectively?

2 What capability does the organization have to identify and track key indicators of performance and other data necessary to achieve its objectives?

3 How does the organization's record/information management system make information available to the employees who need it when they need it?

4.4.5 Audits of the environmental management system

Audits of the EMS should be conducted on a periodic basis to determine whether the system conforms to planned arrangements and has been properly implemented and maintained.

Audits of the EMS can be carried out by organization personnel, and/or by external parties selected by the organization. In any case, the person(s) conducting the audit should be in a position to do so objectively and impartially and should be properly trained.

The frequency of audits should be guided by the nature of the operation in terms of its environmental aspects and potential impacts. Also, the results of previous audits should be considered in determining frequency.

The EMS audit report should be submitted in accordance with the audit plan.

4.5 Review and improvement

> ### Principle 5 — Review and improvement
>
> An organization should review and continually improve its environmental management system, with the objective of improving its overall environmental performance.

4.5.1 General

A continual improvement process should be applied to an environmental management system to achieve overall improvement in environmental performance.

4.5.2 Review of the environmental management system

The organization's management should, at appropriate intervals, conduct a review of the EMS to ensure its continuing suitability and effectiveness.

The review of the EMS should be broad enough in scope to address the environmental dimensions of all activities, products or services of the organization, including their impact on financial performance and possibly competitive position.

The review of the EMS should include

- a review of environmental objectives, targets and environmental performance;

- findings of the EMS audits;

- an evaluation of its effectiveness;

- an evaluation of the suitability of the environmental policy and the need for changes in the light of

    - changing legislation,

    - changing expectations and requirements of interested parties,

    - changes in the products or activities of the organization,

    - advances in science and technology,

    - lessons learned from environmental incidents,

    - market preferences,

    - reporting and communication.

Some issues to be considered in the review of the EMS

1   How is the EMS periodically reviewed ?

2   How are the appropriate employees involved in the review of the EMS and follow-up?

3   How are the views of interested parties taken into account in the EMS review?

4.5.3 Continual improvement

The concept of continual improvement is embodied in the EMS. It is achieved by continually evaluating the environmental performance of the EMS against its environmental policies, objectives and targets for the purpose of identifying opportunities for improvement (see figure A.4).

The continual improvement process should

- identify areas of opportunity for improvement of the environmental management system which lead to improved environmental performance;

- determine the root cause or causes of nonconformances or deficiencies;

- develop and implement (a) plan(s) of corrective and preventive action to address root cause(s);

- verify the effectiveness of the corrective and preventive actions;

- document any changes in procedures resulting from process improvement;

- make comparisons with objectives and targets.

Some issues to be considered in corrective and preventive action and continual improvement

1 *What process does the organization have to identify corrective and preventive action and improvement?*

2 *How does the organization verify that corrective and preventive actions and improvements are effective and timely?*

Annex A

(informative)

Examples of international environmental guiding principles

Guiding principles are formal declarations that express the basis on which an environmental policy can be built and which provide a foundation for action.

A.1 The Rio Declaration on Environment and Development

The United Nations Conference on Environment and Development, having met at Rio de Janeiro from 3 to 14 June 1992, reaffirming the Declaration of the United Nations Conference on the Human Environment, adopted at Stockholm on 16 June 1972, and seeking to build upon it, with the goal of establishing a new and equitable global partnership through the creation of new levels of co-operation among States, key sectors of societies and people, working towards international agreements which respect the interests of all and protect the integrity of the global environmental and developmental system, recognizing the integral and interdependent nature of the Earth, our home proclaims that:

Principle 1

Human beings are at the centre of concerns for sustainable development. They are entitled to a healthy and productive life in harmony with nature.

Principle 2

States have, in accordance with the Charter of the United Nations and the principles of international law, the sovereign right to exploit their own resources pursuant to their own environmental and developmental policies, and the responsibility to ensure that activities within their jurisdiction or control do not cause damage to the environment of other States or of areas beyond the limits of national jurisdiction.

Principle 3

The right to development must be fulfilled so as to equitably meet developmental and environmental needs of present and future generations.

Principle 4

In order to achieve sustainable development, environmental protection shall constitute an integral part of the development process and cannot be considered in isolation from it.

Principle 5

All States and people shall co-operate in the essential task of eradicating poverty as an indispensable requirement for sustainable development, in order to decrease the disparities in standards of living and better meet the needs of the majority of the people of the world.

Principle 6

The special situation and needs of developing countries, particularly the least developed and those most environmentally vulnerable, shall be given special priority. International actions in the field of environment and development should also address the interests and needs of all countries.

Principle 7

States shall co-operate in a spirit of global partnership to conserve, protect and restore the health and integrity of the Earth's ecosystem. In view of the different contributions to global environmental degradation, States have common but differentiated responsibilities. The developed countries acknowledge the responsibility that they bear in the international pursuit of sustainable development in view of the pressures their societies place on the global environment and of the technologies and financial resources they command.

Principle 8

To achieve sustainable development and a higher quality of life for all people, States should reduce and eliminate unsustainable patterns of production and consumption and promote appropriate demographic policies.

Principle 9

States should co-operate to strengthen endogenous capacity-building for sustainable development by improving scientific understanding through exchanges of scientific and technological knowledge, and by enhancing the development, adaptation, diffusion and transfer of technologies, including new and innovative technologies.

Principle 10

Environmental issues are best handled with the participation of all concerned citizens, at the relevant level. At the national level, each individual shall have appropriate access to information concerning the environment that is held by public authorities, including information on hazardous materials and activities in their communities, and the opportunity to participate in decision-making processes. States shall facilitate and encourage public awareness and participation by making information widely available. Effective access to judicial and administrative proceedings, including redress and remedy, shall be provided.

Principle 11

States shall enact effective environmental legislation. Environmental standards, management objectives and priorities should reflect the environmental and developmental context to which they apply. Standards applied by some countries can be inappropriate and of unwarranted economic and social cost to other countries, in particular developing countries.

Principle 12

States should co-operate to promote a supportive and open international economic system that would lead to economic growth and sustainable development in all countries, to better address the problems of environmental degradation. Trade policy measures for environmental purposes should not constitute a means of arbitrary or unjustifiable discrimination or a disguised restriction on international trade. Unilateral actions to deal with environmental challenges outside the jurisdiction of the importing country should be avoided. Environmental measures addressing transboundary or global environmental problems should, as far as possible, be based on an international consensus.

Principle 13

States shall develop national law regarding liability and compensation for the victims of pollution and other environmental damage. States shall also co-operate in an expeditious and more determined manner to develop further international law regarding liability and compensation for adverse effects of environmental damage caused by activities within their jurisdiction or control to areas beyond their jurisdiction.

Principle 14

States should effectively co-operate to discourage or prevent the relocation and transfer to other States of any activities and substances that cause severe environmental degradation or are found to be harmful to human health.

Principle 15

In order to protect the environment, the precautionary approach shall be widely applied by States according to their capabilities. Where there are threats of serious or irreversible damage, lack of full scientific certainty shall not be used as a reason for postponing cost-effective measures to prevent environmental degradation.

Principle 16

National authorities should endeavour to promote the internalization of environmental costs and the use of economic instruments, taking into account the approach that the polluter should, in principle, bear the cost of pollution, with due regard to the public interest and without distorting international trade and investment.

Principle 17

Environmental impact assessment, as a national instrument, shall be undertaken for proposed activities that are likely to have a significant adverse impact on the environment and are subject to a decision of a competent national authority.

Principle 18

States shall immediately notify other States of any natural disasters or other emergencies that are likely to produce sudden harmful effects on the environment of those States. Every effort shall be made by the international community to help States so afflicted.

Principle 19

States shall provide prior and timely notification and relevant information to potentially affected States on activities that can have a significant adverse transboundary environmental effect and shall consult with those States at an early stage and in good faith.

Principle 20

Women have a vital role in environmental management and development. Their full participation is therefore essential to achieve sustainable development.

Principle 21

The creativity, ideals and courage of the youth of the world should be mobilized to forge a global partnership in order to achieve sustainable development and ensure a better future for all.

Principle 22

Indigenous people and their communities, and other local communities, have a vital role in environmental management and development because of their knowledge and traditional practices. States should recognize and duly support their identity, culture and interest and enable their effective participation in the achievement of sustainable development.

Principle 23

The environment and natural resources of people under oppression, domination and occupation shall be protected.

Principle 24

Warfare is inherently destructive of sustainable development. States shall therefore respect international law providing protection for the environment in times of armed conflict and co-operate in its further development, as necessary.

Principle 25

Peace, development and environmental protection are interdependent and indivisible.

Principle 26

States shall resolve all their environmental disputes peacefully and by appropriate means in accordance with the Charter of the United Nations.

Principle 27

States and people shall co-operate in good faith and in a spirit of partnership in the fulfilment of the principles embodied in this Declaration and in the further development of international law in the field of sustainable development.

A.2 International Chamber of Commerce (ICC) Business Charter for Sustainable Development

1. Corporate Priority

To recognize environmental management as among the highest corporate priorities and as a key determinant to sustainable development; to establish policies, programs and practices for conducting operations in an environmentally sound manner.

2. Integrated Management

To integrate these policies, programs and practices fully into each business as an essential element of management in all its functions.

3. Process of Improvement

To continue to improve policies, programs and environmental performance, taking into account technical developments, scientific understanding, consumer needs and community expectations, with legal regulations as starting point; and to apply the same environmental criteria internationally.

4. Employee Education

To educate, train and motivate employees to conduct their activities in an environmentally responsible manner.

5. Prior Assessment

To assess environmental impacts before starting a new activity or project and before decommissioning a facility or leaving a site.

6. Products or services

To develop and provide products or services that have no undue environmental impact and are safe in their intended use, that are efficient in their consumption of energy and natural resources, and that can be recycled, reused, or disposed of safely.

7. Customer Advice

To advise, and where relevant educate, customers, distributors, and the public in the safe use, transportation, storage and disposal of products provided; and to apply similar considerations to the provisions of services.

8. Facilities and Operations

To develop, design and operate facilities and conduct activities taking into consideration the efficient use of energy and materials, the sustainable use of renewable resources, the minimization of adverse environmental impact and waste generation, and the safe and responsible disposal of residual wastes.

9. Research

To conduct or support research on the environmental impacts of raw materials, products, processes, emissions, and wastes associated with the enterprise and on the means of minimizing such adverse impacts.

10. Precautionary Approach

To modify the manufacture, marketing, or use of products or services or the conduct of activities, consistent with scientific and technical understanding, to prevent serious or irreversible environmental degradation.

11. Contractors and Suppliers

To promote the adoption of these principles by contractors acting on behalf of the enterprise, encouraging and, where appropriate, requiring improvements in their practices to make them consistent with those of the enterprise; and to encourage the wider adoption of these principles by suppliers.

12. Emergency Preparedness

To develop and maintain, where significant hazards exist, emergency preparedness plans in conjunction with the emergency services, relevant authorities and the local community, recognizing potential transboundary impacts.

13. Transfer of Technology

To contribute to the transfer of environmentally sound technology and management methods throughout the industrial and public sectors.

14. Contributing to the Common Effect

To contribute to the development of public policy and to business, governmental and intergovernmental programs and educational initiatives that will enhance environmental awareness and protection.

15. Openness to Concerns

To foster openness and dialogue with employees and the public, anticipating and responding to their concerns about potential hazards and impacts of operations, products, wastes or services, including those of transboundary or global significance.

16. Compliance and Reporting

To measure environmental performance; to conduct regular environmental audits and assessments of compliance with company requirements, legal requirements and these principles; and periodically to provide appropriate information to the Board of Directors, shareholders, employees, the authorities and the public.

Annex B
(informative)

Bibliography

[1] ISO 14001:1996, *Environmental management systems—Specification with guidance for use.*

[2] ISO 14010:1996, *Guidelines for environmental auditing—General principles.*

[3] ISO 14011 :1996, *Guidelines for environmental auditing—Audit procedures—Auditing of environmental management systems.*

[4] ISO 14012:1996, *Guidelines for environmental auditing—Qualification criteria for environmental auditors.*

ISO & IEC Member Bodies

International Organization for Standardization (ISO) Member Bodies

As of March 1996. Source: ISO

ISO Members

Albania (DSC)

Drejtoria e Standardizimit dhe Cilesise
Rruga Mine Peza
Tirana
Tel: +355 42 2 6255
Fax: +355 42 2 6255
Telegrams:standardi tirana

*Algeria (INAPI)

Institut Algérien de Normalisation et de
Propriété Industrielle
5, rue Abou Hamou Moussa

B.P. 1021 - Centre de tri
Alger
Tel: +213 2 63 9642
Fax: +213 2 61 0971
Telex: 6 64 09 inapi dz
Telegrams: inapi-alger

◆Argentina (IRAM)

Instituto Argentino de Racionalización de
Materiales
Chile 1192
1098 Buenos Aires
Tel: +54 1 383 3751
Fax: +54 1 383 8463
Internet: postmaster@iram.org.ar

*u = TC 207 Participating Member * = TC 207 Observer Member*

◆Australia (SAA)

Standards Australia
1 The Crescent
Homebush - N.S.W. 2140
Postal: P.O. Box 1055
Strathfield - N.S.W. 2135
Tel: +61 2 746 4700
Fax: +61 2 746 8450
Telex: 2 65 14 astan aa
Internet: intsect@saa.sa.telememo.au
X.400:s=intsect; o=saa; p=sa; a=telememo;
c=au

◆Austria (ON)

Österreichisches Normungsinstitut
Heinestrasse 38
Postfach 130
A-1021 Wien
Tel: +43 1 213 00
Fax: +43 1 21 30 0650
Telegrams: austrianorm
Internet: iro@tbxa.telecom.at
X.400:c=at; a=ada; p=telebox; o=on; s=iro

Bangladesh (BSTI)

Bangladesh Standards and Testing Institution
116-A, Tejgaon Industrial Area
Dhaka 1208
Tel: +880 2 88 1462
Telegrams: besteye

Belarus (BELST)

Committee for Standardization, Metrology and
Certification
Starovilensky Trakt 93
Minsk 220053
Tel: +375 172 37 5213
Fax: +375 172 37 2588
Telex: 25 21 70 shkala
Internet: belst@mcsm.belpak.minsk.by

◆Belgium (IBN)

Institut Belge de Normalisation
Av. de la Brabançonne 29
B-1040 Bruxelles
Tel: +32 2 738 0111
Fax: +32 2 733 4264

Bosnia and Herzegovina (BASMP)

Institute for Standardization, Metrology and
Patents (BASMP)
c/o Permanent Mission of Bosnia and
Herzegovina
22 bis, rue Lamartine
CH-1203 Genève
Tel: +387 71 67 0655
Fax: +387 71 67 0656

◆Brazil (ABNT)

Associaçao Brasileira de Normas Técnicas
Av. 13 de Maio, no 13, 27o andar
Caixa Postal 1680
20003-900 - Rio de Janeiro RJ
Tel: +55 21 210 3122
Fax: +55 21 532 2143
Telex: 213 43 33 abnt br
Telegrams: normatécnica rio

Bulgaria (BDS)

Committee for Standardization and Metrology at
the Council of Ministers
21, 6th September Str.
1000 Sofia
Tel: +359 2 85 91
Fax: +359 2 80 14 02
Telex: 2 25 70 dks bg

◆Canada (SCC)

Standards Council of Canada
45 O'Connor Street, Suite 1200
Ottawa, Ontario K1P 6N7
Tel: +1 613 238 3222
Fax: +1 613 995 4564
Internet: info@scc.ca

◆ = TC 207 Participating Member   * = TC 207 Observer Member

◆Chile (INN)

Instituto Nacional de Normalización
Matías Cousiño 64 - 6o piso
Casilla 995 - Correo Central
Santiago
Tel: +56 2 696 81 44
Fax: +56 2 696 02 47
Telegrams: inn

◆China (CSBTS)

China State Bureau of Technical Supervision
4, Zhi Chun Road
Haidian District
P.O. Box 8010
Beijing 100088
Tel: +86 10 203 24 24
Fax: +86 10 203 10 10
Telegrams: 1918 beijing

◆Colombia (ICONTEC)

Instituto Colombiano de Normas Técnicas
Carrera 37 52-95
Edificio ICONTEC
P.O. Box 14237
Santafé de Bogotá
Tel: +57 91 315 03 77
Fax: +57 91 222 14 35
Telex: 4 25 00 icont co
Telegrams: icontec
Internet: sicontec@itecs5.telecom-co.net

Costa Rica (INTECO)

Instituto de Normas Técnicas de Costa Rica
Barrio González Flores
Ciudad Científica
San Pedro de Montes de Oca
San José
Postal: P.O. Box 6189-1000
San José
Tel: +506 283 45 22
Fax: +506 283 45 22
Internet: inteco@sol.racsa.co.cr

*Croatia (DZNM)

State Office for Standardization and Metrology
Ulica grada Vukovara 78
10000 Zagreb
Tel: +385 1 53 99 34
Fax: +385 1 53 65 98

◆Cuba (NC)

Oficina Nacional de Normalización
Calle E No. 261 entre 11 y 13
Vedado, La Habana 10400
Tel: +53 7 30 00 22
Fax: +53 7 33 80 48
Telex: 51 22 45 cen cu

Cyprus (CYS)

Cyprus Organization for Standards and Control
of Quality
Ministry of Commerce, Industry and Tourism
Nicosia 1421
Tel: +357 2 37 50 53
Fax: +357 2 37 51 20
Telex: 22 83 mincomind cy
Telegrams: mincomind nicosia

◆Czech Republic (COSMT)

Czech Office for Standards, Metrology and
Testing
Biskupsky dvur 5
113 47 Praha 1
Tel: +42 2 232 44 30
Fax: +42 2 232 43 73
Telex: 12 19 48 unm c
Telegrams: normalizace praha

◆Denmark (DS)

Dansk Standard
Baunegaardsvej 73
DK-2900 Hellerup
Tel: +45 39 77 01 01
Fax: +45 39 77 02 02
Telex: 11 92 03 ds stand
Telegrams: danskstandard

◆Ecuador (INEN)

Instituto Ecuatoriano de Normalización
Baquerizo Moreno 454 y Av. 6 de Diciembre
Casilla 17-01-3999
Quito
Tel: +593 2 56 56 26
Fax: +593 2 56 78 15
Internet: inen1@inen.gov.ec

*Egypt (EOS)

Egyptian Organization for Standardization and
Quality Control
2 Latin America Street
Garden City
Cairo
Tel: +20 2 354 97 20
Fax: +20 2 355 78 41
Telex: 9 32 96 eos un
Telegrams: tawhid

Ethiopia (ESA)

Ethiopian Authority for Standardization
P.O. Box 2310
Addis Ababa
Tel: +251 1 61 01 11
Fax: +251 1 61 31 77
Telex: 21725 ethsaeth
Telegrams: ethiostan

◆Finland (SFS)

Finnish Standards Association SFS
P.O. Box 116
FIN-00241 Helsinki
Tel: +358 0 149 93 31
Fax: +358 0 146 49 25
Internet: sfs@sfs.fi
X.400:g=[givenname]; s=[surname]; o=sfs;
p=inet; a=mailnet; c=fi

◆France (AFNOR)

Association française de normalisation
Tour Europe
F-92049 Paris La Défense Cedex
Tel: +33 1 42 91 55 55

Fax: +33 1 42 91 56 56
Telex: 61 19 74 afnor f
Telegrams: afnor courbevoie

◆Germany (DIN)

Deutsches Institut für Normung
Burggrafenstrasse 6
D-10787 Berlin
Postal: D-10772 Berlin
Tel: +49 30 26 01 23 44
Fax: +49 30 26 01 12 31
Telex: 18 42 73 din d
Telegrams: deutschnormen berlin
Internet: postmaster@din.de
X.400:c=de; a=d400; p=din; s=postmaster

Ghana (GSB)

Ghana Standards Board
P.O. Box M 245
Accra
Tel: +233 21 50 00 65
Fax: +233 21 50 00 92

Greece (ELOT)

Hellenic Organization for Standardization
313, Acharnon Street
GR-111 45 Athens
Tel: +30 1 201 50 25
Fax: +30 1 202 07 76
Telex: 21 96 70 elot gr
Telegrams: elotyp-athens

Hungary (MSZT)

Magyar Szabványügyi Testület
Üllöi út 25; Pf. 24.
H-1450 Budapest 9
Tel: +36 1 218 30 11
Fax: +36 1 218 51 25
Telex: 22 57 23 norm h
Telegrams: normhungaria budapest

*Iceland (STRI)

Icelandic Council for Standardization
Keldnaholt
IS-112 Reykjavik
Tel: +354 587 70 00
Fax: +354 587 74 09
Internet: stri@iti.is

◆India (BIS)

Bureau of Indian Standards
Manak Bhavan
9 Bahadur Shah Zafar Marg
New Delhi 110002
Tel: +91 11 331 79 91
Fax: +91 11 331 40 62
Telex: 316 58 70 bis in
Telegrams: manaksanstha

◆Indonesia (DSN)

Dewan Standardisasi Nasional - DSN
(Standardization Council of Indonesia)
c/o Pusat Standardisasi - LIPI
Jalan Jend. Gatot Subroto 10
Jakarta 12710
Tel: +62 21 522 16 86
Fax: +62 21 520 65 74
Telex: 6 28 75 pdii ia
Telegrams: lipi jakarta

Iran, Islamic Republic of (ISIRI)

Institute of Standards and Industrial Research
of Iran
P.O. Box 31585-163
Karaj
Tel: +98 261 22 60 31
Fax: +98 261 22 50 15
Telex: 21 54 42 stan ir
Telegrams: standinst

◆Ireland (NSAI)

National Standards Authority of Ireland
Glasnevin
Dublin-9

Tel: +353 1 837 01 01
Fax: +353 1 836 98 21
Telex: 3 25 01 olas ei
Telegrams: research, dublin

◆Israel (SII)

Standards Institution of Israel
42 Chaim Levanon Street
Tel Aviv 69977
Tel: +972 3 646 51 54
Fax: +972 3 641 96 83
Telegrams: standardis
Internet: standard@netvision.net.il

◆Italy (UNI)

Ente Nazionale Italiano di Unificazione
Via Battistotti Sassi 11/b
I-20133 Milano
Tel: +39 2 70 02 41
Fax: +39 2 70 10 61 06
Telegrams: unificazione
Internet: webmaster@uni.unicei.it

◆Jamaica (JBS)

Jamaica Bureau of Standards
6 Winchester Road
P.O. Box 113
Kingston 10
Tel: +1 809 926 31 40 6
Fax: +1 809 929 47 36
Telex: 22 91 stanbur ja
Telegrams: stanbureau

◆Japan (JISC)

Japanese Industrial Standards Committee
c/o Standards Department
Ministry of International Trade and Industry
1-3-1, Kasumigaseki, Chiyoda-ku
Tokyo 100
Tel: +81 3 35 01 92 95
Fax: +81 3 35 80 14 18
Telex: 02 42 42 45 jsatyo j
Telegrams: mitijisc tokyo

◆ = *TC 207 Participating Member* * = *TC 207 Observer Member*

Kazakhstan (KAZMEMST)

Committee for Standardization, Metrology and
Certification
pr. Altynsarina 83
480035 Almaty
Tel: +7 327 2 21 08 08
Fax: +7 327 2 28 68 22
Telegrams: gostandart almata 35

◆Kenya (KEBS)

Kenya Bureau of Standards
Off Mombasa Road
Behind Belle Vue Cinema
P.O. Box 54974
Nairobi
Tel: +254 2 50 22 10/19
Fax: +254 2 50 32 93
Telex: 2 52 52 viwango
Telegrams: kenstand
Internet: kebs@arso.gn.apc.org

Korea, Dem. P. Rep. of (CSK)

Committee for Standardization of the Demo-
cratic People's Republic of Korea
Zung Gu Yok Seungli-Street
Pyongyang
Tel: +85 02 57 15 76
Telex: 59 72 tech kp
Telegrams: standard

◆Korea, Republic of (KIAA)

Industrial Advancement Administration (KIAA)
2, Chungang-dong, Kwachon-city
Kyonggi-do 427-010
Tel: +82 2 503 79 38
Fax: +82 2 503 79 41
Telex: 2 84 56 fincen k
Telegrams: koreaiaa

*Libyan Arab Jamahiriya (LNCSM)

Libyan National Centre for Standardization and
Metrology

Industrial Research, Centre Building
P.O. Box 5178
Tripoli
Tel: +218 21 499 49
Fax: +218 21 69 00 28
Telex: 2 05 49 ncsm

The former Yugoslav Republic of Macedonia (ZSM)

Zavod za standardizacija i metrologija (ZSM)
Ministry of Economy
Samoilova 10
91000 Skopje
Tel: +389 91 22 47 74

Fax: +389 91 23 19 02

◆Malaysia (SIRIM)

Standards and Industrial Research Institute of
Malaysia
Persiaran Dato' Menteri, Section 2
P.O. Box 7035, 40911 Shah Alam
Selangor Darul Ehsan
Tel: +60 3 559 26 01
Fax: +60 3 550 80 95
Telex: ma 3 86 72
Telegrams: sirimsec shah alam

◆Mauritius (MSB)

Mauritius Standards Bureau
Reduit
Tel: +230 454 19 33
Fax: +230 464 11 44

◆Mexico (DGN)

Dirección General de Normas
Calle Puente de Tecamachalco No 6
Lomas de Tecamachalco
Sección Fuentes
Naucalpan de Juárez
53 950 Mexico
Tel: +52 5 729 93 00
Fax: +52 5 729 94 84
Telex: 177 58 40 imceme
Telegrams: secofi/147

◆Mongolia (MNISM)

Mongolian National Institute for Standardization
and Metrology
Ulaanbaatar-51
Tel: +976 1 35 83 49
Fax: +976 1 35 80 32
Telex: 7 93 40 it co mh
Telegrams: ulaanbaatar 51 mnism

Morocco (SNIMA)

Service de normalisation industrielle marocaine
Ministère du commerce, de l'industrie et
l'artisanat
Quartier administratif
Rabat Chellah
Tel: +212 7 76 37 33
Fax: +212 7 76 62 96
Telex: 36 872

◆Netherlands (NNI)

Nederlands Normalisatie-instituut
Kalfjeslaan 2
P.O. Box 5059
NL-2600 GB Delft
Tel: +31 15 2 69 03 90
Fax: +31 15 2 69 01 90
Telex: 3 81 44 nni nl
Telegrams: normalisatie delft
X.400:c=nl; a=400net; p=nni; o=nni;
s=[surname]

◆New Zealand (SNZ)

Standards New Zealand
Standards House
155 The Terrace
Wellington 6001
Postal: Private Bag 2439
Wellington 6020
Tel: +64 4 498 59 90
Fax: +64 4 498 59 94

Nigeria (SON)

Standards Organisation of Nigeria
Federal Secretariat
Phase 1, 9th Floor
Ikoyi
LAGOS
Tel: +234 1 68 26 15
Fax: +234 1 68 18 20

◆Norway (NSF)

Norges Standardiseringsforbund
Hegdehaugsveien 31
Postboks 7020 Homansbyen
N-0306 Oslo 3
Tel: +47 22 46 60 94
Fax: +47 22 46 44 57
Telegrams: standardisering
X.400:s=firmapost; o=norsk-standard;
p=msmail; a=telemax; c=no

Pakistan (PSI)

Pakistan Standards Institution
39 Garden Road, Saddar
Karachi-74400
Tel: +92 21 772 95 27
Fax: +92 21 772 81 24
Telegrams: peyasai

Panama (COPANIT)

Comisión Panameña de Normas Industriales y
Técnicas
Ministerio de Comercio e Industrias
Apartado Postal 9658
Panama, Zona 4
Tel: +507 2 27 47 49
Fax: +507 2 25 78 53

◆ = *TC 207 Participating Member* * = *TC 207 Observer Member*

◆Philippines (BPS)

Bureau of Product Standards
Department of Trade and Industry
361 Sen. Gil J. Puyat Avenue
Makati
Metro Manila 1200
Tel: +63 2 890 51 29
Fax: +63 2 890 49 26
Telex: 1 48 30 mti ps
Telegrams: philstand

*Poland (PKN)

Polish Committee for Standardization
ul. Elektoralna 2
P.O. Box 411
00-950 Warszawa
Tel: +48 22 620 54 34
Fax: +48 22 620 07 41

*Portugal (IPQ)

Instituto Português da Qualidade
Rua C à Avenida dos Três Vales
P-2825 Monte de Caparica
Tel: +351 1 294 81 00
Fax: +351 1 294 81 01
X.400:c=pt; a=mailpac; p=gtw-ms; o=ipq;
ou1=ipqm; s=nor

◆Romania (IRS)

Institutul Român de Standardizare
Str. Jean-Louis Calderon Nr. 13
Cod 70201
Bucuresti 2
Tel: +40 1 211 32 96
Fax: +40 1 210 08 33

◆Russian Federation (GOST R)

Committee of the Russian Federation for
Standardization, Metrology and Certification
Leninsky Prospekt 9
Moskva 117049
Tel: +7 095 236 40 44
Fax: +7 095 237 60 32
Telex: 41 13 78 gost su
Telegrams: moskva standart

Saudi Arabia (SASO)

Saudi Arabian Standards Organization
Imam Saud Bin Abdul Aziz Bin Mohammed
Road (West End)
P.O. Box 3437
Riyadh 11471
Tel: +966 1 452 00 00
Fax: +966 1 452 00 86
Telex: 40 16 10 saso sj
Telegrams: giasy

◆Singapore (SISIR)

Singapore Institute of Standards and Industrial
Research (SISIR)
1 Science Park Drive
Singapore 118221
Tel: +65 778 77 77
Fax: +65 778 00 86

*Slovakia (UNMS)

Slovak Office of Standards, Metrology and Testing
Stefanovicova 3
814 39 Bratislava
Tel: +42 7 49 10 85
Fax: +42 7 49 10 50

*Slovenia (SMIS)

Standards and Metrology Institute
Ministry of Science and Technology
Kotnikova 6
SI-61000 Ljubljana
Tel: +386 61 131 23 22
Fax: +386 61 31 48 82
Internet: ic@usm.mzt.si
X.400:s=ic; u=usm; o=mzt; p=ac; a=mail;
c=si

*◆ = TC 207 Participating Member   * = TC 207 Observer Member*

◆South Africa (SABS)

South African Bureau of Standards
1 Dr Lategan Rd, Groenkloof
Private Bag X191
Pretoria 0001
Tel: +27 12 428 79 11
Fax: +27 12 344 15 68
Telex: 32 13 08 sa
Telegrams: comparator
X.400:c=za; a=telekom 400; o=south african
bureau of standards; s=sabs

◆Spain (AENOR)

Asociación Española de Normalización y
Certificación
Fernández de la Hoz, 52
E-28010 Madrid
Tel: +34 1 432 60 00
Fax: +34 1 310 49 76
Telegrams: aenor

*Sri Lanka (SLSI)

Sri Lanka Standards Institution
53 Dharmapala Mawatha
P.O. Box 17
Colombo 3
Tel: +94 1 32 60 51
Fax: +94 1 44 60 18
Telegrams: pramika

◆Sweden (SIS)

Standardiseringen i Sverige
St Eriksgatan 115
Box 6455
S-113 82 Stockholm
Tel: +46 8 610 30 00
Fax: +46 8 30 77 57
Telegrams: standardis
Internet: info@sis.se

◆Switzerland (SNV)

Swiss Association for Standardization
Mühlebachstrasse 54
CH-8008 Zurich
Tel: +41 1 254 54 54
Fax: +41 1 254 54 74
Telegrams: normbureau

Syrian Arab Republic (SASMO)

Syrian Arab Organization for Standardization
and Metrology
P.O. Box 11836
Damascus
Tel: +963 11 445 05 38
Fax: +963 11 441 39 13
Telex: 41 19 99 sasmo
Telegrams: systand

◆Tanzania, United Rep. of (TBS)

Tanzania Bureau of Standards
Ubungo Area
Morogoro Road/Sam Nujoma Road
Dar es Salaam
Postal: P.O. Box 9524
Dar es Salaam
Tel: +255 51 4 32 98
Fax: +255 51 4 32 98
Telex: 4 16 67 tbs tz
Telegrams: standards

◆Thailand (TISI)

Thai Industrial Standards Institute
Ministry of Industry
Rama VI Street
Bangkok 10400
Tel: +66 2 245 78 02
Fax: +66 2 247 87 41
Telex: 8 43 75 minidus th (attention tisi)
Telegrams: thastan
Internet: thaistandl.tisi.go.th

◆Trinidad and Tobago (TTBS)

Trinidad and Tobago Bureau of Standards
#2 Century Drive
Trincity Industrial Estate
Tunapuna
Postal: P.O. Box 467
Port of Spain
Tel: +1 809 662 88 27
Fax: +1 809 663 43 35
Telegrams: qualassure
Internet: ttbs@opus-networx.com

Tunisia (INNORPI)

Institut national de la normalisation et de la
propriété industrielle
B.P. 23
1012 Tunis-Belvédère
Tel: +216 1 78 59 22
Fax: +216 1 78 15 63

◆Turkey (TSE)

Türk Standardlari Enstitüsü
Necatibey Cad. 112
Bakanliklar
06100 Ankara
Tel: +90 312 417 83 30
Fax: +90 312 425 43 99
Telex: 4 20 47 tse-tr
Telegrams: standard
Internet: tse-d@servis.net.tr

◆United States of America (ANSI)

American National Standards Institute
11 West 42nd Street
13th floor
New York, N.Y. 10036
Tel: +1 212 642 49 00
Fax: +1 212 398 00 23
Internet: smazza@ansi.org

◆Ukraine (DSTU)

State Committee of Ukraine for Standardization,
Metrology and Certification
174 Gorky Street

GSP, Kiev-6, 252650
Tel: +380 44 226 29 71
Fax: +380 44 226 29 70

◆United Kingdom (BSI)

British Standards Institution
389 Chiswick High Road
GB-London W4 4AL
Tel: +44 181 996 90 00
Fax: +44 181 996 74 00
X.400:c=gb; a=gold 400; p=bsi; o=bsi;
s=surname; g=first name;

◆Uruguay (UNIT)

Instituto Uruguayo de Normas Técnicas
San José 1031 P.7
Galeria Elysée
Montevideo
Tel: +598 2 91 20 48
Fax: +598 2 92 16 81
Telex: 2 31 68 ancap uy

Uzbekistan (UZGOST)

Uzbek State Centre for Standardization,
Metrology and Certification
Ulitsa Farobi, 333-A
700049 Tachkent
Tel: +7 371 2 46 17 10
Fax: +7 371 2 46 17 11
Telex: 11 63 82 fasad

◆Venezuela (COVENIN)

Comisión Venezolana de Normas Industriales
Avda. Andrés Bello-Edf. Torre Fondo Común
Piso 12
Caracas 1050
Tel: +58 2 575 22 98
Fax: +58 2 574 13 12
Telex: 2 42 35 minfo vc
Telegrams: covenindus
Internet: covenin@dino.conicit.ve

◆ = *TC 207 Participating Member*   * = *TC 207 Observer Memberr*

*Viet Nam (TCVN)

Directorate for Standards and Quality
70, Tran Hung Dao Street
Hanoi
Tel: +84 4 26 62 20
Fax: +84 4 26 74 18
Telex: 41 22 87 ukkn vt
Telegrams: vinastand

*Yugoslavia (SZS)

Savezni zavod za standardizaciju
Kneza Milosa 20
Post Pregr. 933
YU-11000 Beograd
Tel: +381 11 64 35 57
Fax: +381 11 68 23 82
Telex: 1 20 89 jus yu
Telegrams: standardizacija
Internet: etanasko@ubbg.etf.bg.ac.yu
X.400:s=jusszs; g=veroljub; prmd=public;
admd=beograd400; c=yu

*Zimbabwe (SAZ)

Standards Association of Zimbabwe
P.O. Box 2259
Harare
Tel: +263 4 88 34 46
Fax: +263 4 88 20 20
Telegrams: saca

ISO Correspondent Members

Armenia (SARM)

Department for Standardization, Metrology and
Certification
Komitas Avenue 49/2
375051 Yerevan
Tel: +374 2 23 56 00
Fax: +374 2 28 56 20
Internet: sarm@arminco.com

Bahrain

Directorate of Standards and Metrology
Ministry of Commerce
P.O. Box 5479
Bahrain
Tel: +973 53 01 00
Fax: +973 53 07 30
Telex: 91 71 tejara bn

*Barbados (BNSI)

Barbados National Standards Institution
Flodden Culloden Road, St. Michael
Tel: +1 809 426 38 70
Fax: +1 809 436 14 95
Telex: barstand, barbados

Brunei Darussalam

Construction Planning and Research Unit
Ministry of Development
Negara Brunei Darussalam
Tel: +673 2 24 20 33
Fax: +673 2 24 22 67
Telex: 27 22 midev bu
Telegrams: midevbrunei

*Estonia (EVS)

National Standards Board of Estonia
Aru 10
EE-0003 Tallinn
Tel: +372 2 49 35 72
Fax: +372 654 13 30
Internet: @evs.ee

*Hong Kong

Industry Department
36/F., Immigration Tower
7 Gloucester Road
Wan Chai
Hong Kong
Tel: +852 28 29 48 24
Fax: +852 28 24 13 02
Telex: 5 01 51 indhk hx

Jordan (JISM)

Jordanian Institution for Standards and
Metrology
P.O. Box 941287
Amman 11194
Tel: +962 6 68 01 39
Fax: +962 6 68 10 99

Kuwait

Ministry of Commerce and Industry
Standards and Metrology Affairs
Post Box 2944 Safat
13030 Kuwait
Tel: +965 246 51 03
Fax: +965 243 66 38
Telex: 2 26 82 commind kt

Kyrgyzstan (KYRGYZST)

State Inspection for Standardization and
Metrology (KYRGYZST)
197 Panfilova str.
720040 Bishkek
Tel: +7 331 2 26 48 62
Fax: +7 331 2 26 47 08
Internet: kmc@infotel.bishkek.su

Latvia (LVS)

Latvian National Center of Standardization and
Metrology (LVS)
157, Kr. Valdemara Street
1013 Riga
Tel: +371 2 37 81 65
Fax: +371 2 36 28 05

Lebanon (LIBNOR)

Lebanese Standards Institution
Industry Institute Building
Next to Riviera Hotel, Beirut Corniche
Beirut
Postal: P.O. Box 14-6473
Beirut
Tel: +961 1 34 82 19
Fax: +961 1 42 70 04

Lithuania (LST)

Lithuanian Standards Board
A. Jaksto g. 1/25
2600 Vilnius
Tel: +370 2 22 69 62
Fax: +370 2 22 62 52

Malawi (MBS Malawi)

Malawi Bureau of Standards
P.O. Box 946
Blantyre
Tel: +265 67 04 88
Fax: +265 67 07 56
Telex: 4 43 25
Telegrams: standards

Malta (MBS Malta)

Malta Board of Standards
Department of Industry
Triq il-Kukkanja
Santa Venera CMR 02
Tel: +356 44 62 50
Fax: +356 44 62 57

Mozambique (INNOQ)

National Institute of Standardization and Quality
C.P. 2983
Maputo
Tel: +258 1 42 14 09
Fax: +258 1 42 45 85
Telex: 69 33 innoq mo

Nepal (NBSM)

Nepal Bureau of Standards and Metrology
(NBSM)
P.O. Box 985
Sundhara
Kathmandu
Tel: +977 1 27 26 89
Fax: +977 1 27 26 89
Telegrams: gunis

Oman

Directorate General for Specifications and
Measurements
Ministry of Commerce and Industry
P.O. Box 550 - Postal code No. 113
Muscat
Tel: +968 70 32 38
Fax: +968 79 59 92
Telex: 36 65 wizara on
Telegrams: wizara

Papua New Guinea (NISIT)

National Institute of Standards and Industrial
Technology
P.O. Box 3042
National Capital District
Boroko
Tel: +675 27 21 02
Fax: +675 25 87 93

Peru (INDECOPI)

Instituto Nacional de Defensa de la
Competencia y de la Protección de la Propiedad
Intelectual
Calle La Prosa 138
San Borja
Lima 41
Tel: +51 1 224 78 00
Fax: +51 1 224 03 48
Internet: postmast@indecopi.gob.pe

Qatar

Department of Standards, Measurements and
Consumer Protection
Ministry of Finance, Economy and Commerce
P.O. Box 1968
Doha
Tel: +974 40 85 55
Fax: +974 42 54 49
Telex: 44 88 ecom dh

Turkmenistan (MSIT)

Major State Inspection of Turkmenistan
Seydi, 14

744000 Ashgabat
Tel: +7 363 2 51 14 94
Fax: +7 363 2 51 04 98
Telex: 22 81 37

Uganda (UNBS)

Uganda National Bureau of Standards
P.O. Box 6329
Kampala
Tel: +256 41 22 23 69
Internet: unbs@mukla.gn.apc.org

United Arab Emirates (SSUAE)

Directorate of Standardization and Metrology
Ministry of Finance and Industry
El Falah Street
P.O. Box 433
Abu Dhabi
Tel: +971 2 72 60 00
Fax: +971 2 77 97 71
Telex: 2 29 37 fedfin em

Yemen (YSMO)

Yemen Standardization, Metrology and Quality
Control Organization
P.O. Box 19213
Sana'a
Tel: +967 1 20 22 49
Fax: +967 1 20 22 49

ISO Subscriber Members

Antigua and Barbuda (ABBS)

Antigua and Barbuda Bureau of Standards
P.O. Box 1550
Redcliffe Street
St. John's
Tel: +1 809 462 15 32
Fax: +1 809 462 16 25

◆ = *TC 207 Participating Member*   * = *TC 207 Observer Member*

Bolivia (IBNORCA)

Instituto Boliviano de Normalización y Calidad
Av. Camacho No 1488
Casilla 8680-5034
La Paz
Tel: +591 2 37 20 45
Fax: +591 2 37 09 81

Burundi (BBN)

Bureau burundais de normalisation et de
contrôle de la qualité
25, rue de la Victoire
B.P. 3535
Bujumbura
Tel: +257 22 15 77
Fax: +257 22 18 15

Cambodia

Ministry of Industry, Mines and Energy
Technical Department
45, Blvd Norodom
Phnom Penh
Tel: +855 23 278 40
Fax: +855 23 278 40

Fiji

Fiji Trade Standards and Quality Control Office
Ministry of Commerce, Industry and Tourism
Nabati House, Government Buildings
P.O. Box 2118
Suva
Tel: +679 30 54 11
Fax: +679 30 26 17

Grenada (GDBS)

Grenada Bureau of Standards
H.A. Blaize Street
St. George's
Tel: +1 809 440 58 86
Fax: +1 809 440 41 15
Telex: 34 23 grenex ga

Guyana (GNBS)

Guyana National Bureau of Standards

Sophia Exhibition Centre
Sophia Complex
P.O. Box 10926
Georgetown
Tel: +592 2 590 41
Fax: +592 2 574 55
Telegrams: guystand

Paraguay (INTN)

Instituto Nacional de Tecnología y
Normalización (INTN)
Casilla de Correo 967
Asunción
Tel: +595 21 29 01 60
Fax: +595 21 29 08 73

Saint Lucia (SLBS)

Saint Lucia Bureau of Standards
Government Buildings
Block B, 4th floor
John Campton Highway
Castries
Tel: +1 809 453 00 49
Fax: +1 809 453 73 47
Telex: 63 94 foraff Australia

SECTION 2
International Electrotechnical Commission (IEC) Member Bodies

As of March 1996. Source: IEC

Australia

Australian National Committee of IEC
Standards Australia
PO Box 1055
Strathfield NSW 2135
Tel: +61 2 746 4700
Fax: +61 2 746 8450
Secretary: Mr. W.A. Miller
Vice President: Mr. P.N. Walsh

Austria

Austrian Electrotechnical Committee
c/o Oesterreichischer Verband für
Elecktrotechnik
Eschenbachgasse 9
1010 Wein
Tel: +43 1 587 6373
Fax: +43 1 586 7408
General Secretary: Dipl.-Ing. Dr. H. Staerker
Executive Secretary: Mr. Peter Rausch

Belarus

Belarus National Committee of the IEC
Belstandart
Starovilensky Trakt, 93
220053 Minsk
Tel: +375 0172 37 5213
Fax: +375 0172 37 2588
Secretary: Mrs. I. Nikolaeva
Vice President: Mr. V. Savitch

Belgium

Comite Electrotechnique Belge
9A Av. Frans Van Kalken
Boite 2
1070 Bruxelles
Tel: +32 2 556 0110

Fax: +32 2 556 0120
Secrétaire Général: Monsieur J. Papier
Président d'Honneur: Monsieur L. de Backer

Brazil

Brazil National Committee of the IEC
COBEI
Rua Libero Dadaro, 496-10° andar
01008.000 Sao-Paulo-SP
Tel: +55 11 239 1155
Fax: +55 11 604 0192
Executive Secretary: Eng. Antonio Sartorio

Bulgaria

Bulgarian National Committee of the IEC
Committee for Standardization and Metrology
21, 6th September Street
1000 Sofia

Tel: +359 2 85 91
Fax: +359 2 801 402
Secretary: Mr. S. Simeonov
Vice President: Mr. G. Rashev

Canada

Canadian National Committee of the IEC
Standards Council of Canada
International Standardization Division
45 O'Connor Street, Suite 1200
Ottawa, ONT K1P 6N7
Tel: +1 613 238 3222
Fax: +1 613 995 4564
Secretary: Mr. Charles S. Ender

China

Chinese National Committee of the IEC
4 Zhi Chun Rd.
Haidian District, PO Box 8010
Beijing 100088

Tel: +86 10 202 5835
Fax: +86 10 203 1010
Secretary General: Mr. Guang Jin

Croatia

State Office for Standardization and Metrology
Ulica Grada Vukovara 78
41000 Zagreb
Tel: +385 1 63 3444
Fax: +385 1 53 6688
Director General: Mr. Jaksa Topic

Cyprus (Associate Member)

IEC National Committee of Cyprus
Cyprus Organization for Standards & Control of
Quality
Ministry of Commerce, Industry & Tourism
1421 Nicosia
Tel: +357 2 30 0192; +357 2 37 5053
Fax: +357 2 37 5120
Secretary: Mr. A. Ioannou
Director: Dr. Ioannis G. Karis

Czech Republic

Czech National Committee of the IEC
Czech Office for Standards, Metrology and
Testing (COSMT)
Biskupsky dvur 5
113 47 Praha 1
Tel: +42 2 232 4430/4373
Fax: +42 2 232 4373/4560
Secretary: Mrs. M. Dobrotova
Vice President: Mrs. V. Horakuva

Denmark

Dansk Standard
Electrotechnical Sector
Baunegardsvej 73
2800 Hellrup
Tel: +45 39 77 0101
Fax: +45 39 77 0202
Secretary: Mr. J. Roed
Vice President: Mr. H. Hougs
Managing Director: Mr. J.E. Holmblad

Egypt

The Egyptian National Committee
Ministry of Electricity & Energy
Abbassia Post Office
Cairo
Tel: +20 2 83 0641
Fax: +20 2 261 6512
Admin. & Financial Director: Mr. M. El
Shabrawy
Rapporteur: Mr. M.S. Ali
President: Mr. M.T. Safty

Estonia (Associate Member)

Estonian National Committee of the IEC
Estonian Electrotechnical Committee for
Standardization (EEK)
Kopli 82
0004 Tallinn
Tel: +372 2 493 497
Fax: +372 6 541 276
Director: Dr. O. Tapupere
Vice President: Mr. A. Toomsoo

Finland

Finnish Electrotechnical Standards Association
(SESKO)
PO Box 134
00211 Helsinki
Tel: +358 0 696 391
Fax: +358 0 677 059
Vice President: Mr. O. Kuusisto
Director: Mr. T. Ilomaki

France

Comite Electrotechnique Francais
UTE
Immeuble Lavoisier
92052 Paris la Defense Cedex
Tel: +33 1 46 91 1111
Fax: +33 1 47 89 4775
Secrétaire: Monsieur J. Benoist
Fax: +33 1 46 91 1265
Secrétaire Adjoint: Madame M.C. Bansse
Fax: +33 1 46 911160

Germany

Deutsches Komitee Der IEC
Deutsche Elektrotechnische Kommission in DIN
und VDE (DKE)
Stresemannallee 15
60596 Frankfurt Am Main 70
Tel: +49 69 630 80
Fax: +49 69 96 31 5218
Secretary: Dipl.-Ing. K. Orth
Vice Presidents: Dipl.-Ing. G. Seip; Prof. K.H.
Schneider

Greece

Hellenic Organization for Standardization
(ELOT)
313, Acharnon St.
111 45 Athens
Tel: +30 1 201 5025
Fax: +30 1 202 0776
Secretary: Mrs. I. Frangopoulou

Hungary

Hungarian National Committee of the IEC
Magyar Szabvanyugyi Iitvatal
Ulloi ut 25; Pf. 24
1450 Budapest 9
Tel: +36 1 218 3011
Fax: +36 1 218 5125
Acting President of Menb: Mr. I. Kerenyi;
Head of Electrotechnical dpt. in MSZH
Tel: +36 1 217 4306

India

Bureau of Indian Standards
Manak Bhavan
9, Bahadur Shah Zafar Marg
New Delhi 110 002
Tel: +91 11 323 0131
Fax: +91 11 323 4062
Director General: Mr. N.S. Choudhary
Director (International Relations): Mr. V.S.
Mathur
Fax: +91 11 323 9399

Indonesia

Dewan Standardisasi Nasional-DSN
Sasana Widya Grahn-LIPI 5th Floor
PO Box 3132, Jin. Jend. Gatot Subroto 10
Jakarta 12710
Tel: +62 21 520 6574
Fax: +62 21 520 6574
Secretary for IEC Activities: Mr. Sjarif Husen
Secretary of Executive Council: Mr. Bambang H.
Hadiwiardjo

Ireland

Electro-Technical Council of Ireland
Ballymun Road
Dublin
Tel: +353 1 83 76 773
Fax: +353 1 83 69 821
Head of Secretariat: Mr. B. Cunningham

Israel

The Standards Institution of Israel
42 Chaim Levanon Street
Tel Aviv 69977
Tel: +972 3 64 65 154
Fax: +972 3 641 96 83
Director General: Mr. E. Iladar

Italy

Comitato Elettrotecnico Italiano
Viale Monza, 259
20126 Milano
Tel: +39 2 25 77 31
Fax: +39 2 257 73 210
Secretaire General: Dr. Ing. E. Camagni

Japan

Japanese Industrial Standards Committee
Agency of Industrial Science and Technology
(MITI)
1-3-1, Kasumigaseki, Chiyoda-ku
Tokyo 100
Tel: +81 3 3501 5725
Fax: +81 3 3580 8631
Secretary General: Mr. M. Tanaka

Korea, Dem. People's Rep. of

Electrotechnical Committee of the D.P.R. of Korea
Zung Gu Yok Seungli-Street
Pyongyang (Coree Du Nord)
Tel: +850 37 428
Secretary: Mr. Hong Rin Taek

Korea, Republic of

Korean National Committee of IEC
Industrial Advancement Administration
2, Chungang-dong, Kwachon-city
Kyonggi-Do 427-010 (Coree Du Sud)
Tel: +82 2 503 79 38
Fax: +82 2 503 79 41
Secretary: Mr. Soo-Hyun Paik
Tel: +82 2 860 12 10

Latvia (Associate Member)

Latvian National Committee of the IEC
Latvian Electrotechnical Commission (LEC)
1, Ganibu Dambis 12
Riga
Tel: +371 2 328 219
Fax: +371 2 328 880
Vice-Chairman: Mr. Maris A. Gerke

Luxembourg

Comite National Cei De Luxembourg
Service de l'Energie de l'Etat
B.P.N. 10
2010 Luxembourg
Tel: +352 46 97 461
Fax: +352 22 25 24
Directeur: Monsieur Jean-Paul Hoffmann

Malaysia

Malaysia National Committee of the IEC
SIRIM
Persiaran Dato' Menteri, Section 2
PO Box 7035
40911 Shah Alam/Selangor Darul Ehsan
Tel: +60 3 559 2601
Fax: +60 3 550 8095
Secretary: Mr. Tok Poie Goh

Mexico

Comite Electrotecnico Mexicano
Direccion General de Normas
Direccion de Normalizacion
Calle Puente de Tecamachalco No. 6
53 950 Naucaplan De Juarez
Tel: +52 5 729 9480
Fax: +52 5 729 9484
President: Mr. Ricardo Gonzalez Aguilar

Netherlands

Netherlands National Committee of the IEC
Kalfjeslaan 2
Post Box 5059
2600 GB Delft
Tel: +31 15 2 690 390
Fax: +31 15 2690 190
Vice Presidents: Mr. C. Ch. Smit, Mr. C.A.J.
Simons
Tel: +31 40 273 2800
Fax: +31 40 273 4269
Director: Mr. T.D. Roodbergen

New Zealand

New Zealand Electrontechnical Committee
Standards House
155 The Terrace
Private Bag 2439
Wellington 6020
Tel: +64 4 498 5990
Fax: +64 4 498 5994
Secretary: Mr. A.B. Scott-Hill

Norway

Norsk Elektroteknisk Komite
Norwegian Standards Association (NSF)
PO 353 Skoyen
0212 Oslo
Tel: +47 22 04 92 00
Fax: +47 22 04 92 11
Director: Mr. B.I. Odegard
Norsk Elektroteknisk Komite
Harbitzalléen 2A
Postboks 280 Skoyen
0212 Oslo

Tel: +47 22 52 6950
Fax: +47 22 52 6961
Director: Mr. B.I. Odegard

Pakistan

Pakistan National Committee of the IEC
EDC
Pakistan Standards Institution
39, Garden Road, Saddar
Karachi 3
Tel: +92 21 772 6501
Fax: +92 21 772 8124
Secretary: Engr. Tasfir Ahmed Khan

Poland

Polish National Committee of the IEC
Polish Committee for Standardization
Ul. Elektoraina 2
PO Box 411
00 950 Warszawa
Tel: +48 22 620 5434
Fax: +48 22 620 5434 or +48 22 620 0741

Portugal

Portugese National Committee of the IEC
Instituto Portugues Da Qualidade
Rua C à Avenida dos Très Vales
2825 Monte Da Caparica
Tel: +351 1 294 8100/02
Fax: +351 1 294 8101
President: Mr. Cândido dos Santos

Romania

Romanian National Committee for the IEC
ICPE
313, Splaiul Unirü
74204 Bucharest 3
Tel: +40 1 323 6016
Fax: +40 1 322 2748
Secretary: Mr. V. Ciofu; Fax: +40 1 321 3769
Vice President: Mr. M. Ciocodeica; Tel: +40 1
211 3296; Fax: +40 1 210 0833

Russian Federation

Russian Federation Committee for the IEC
Russian Federation for Standards
Leninsky pr.9
1170049 Moscow M-49
Tel: +7 095 236 4044
Fax: +7 095 237 6032
Secretary: Mr. I.M. Youtskovski
Vice Presidents: Dr. V.N. Otrukhou; Dr. V.V.
Shildin

Singapore

Singapore National Committee of the IEC
c/o Singapore Institute of Standards &
Industrial Research
1 Science Park Drive
Singapore 0511
Tel: +65 778 7777
Fax: +65 776 1280
Secretary: Mrs. Guat Hiong Chan-Leow
Vice President: Mr. Soh Siew Cheong

Slovakia

Slovensky Elektrotrechnicky Vybor (SEV)
Slovak Office of Standards, Metrology and
Testing (UNMS)
Stefanovicova 3
814 39 Bratislava
Tel: +42 7 494 728
Fax: +42 7 491 050
Secretary of SEV: Mr. A. Svatik
Tel: +42 7 493 522

Slovenia

Slovenian IEC National Committee
Ministrstvo Za Znanost In Tehnologijo
Standards & Metrology Institute
Kotnikova 6
61 000 Ljubljana
Tel: +386 61 1312 322
Fax: +386 61 314 882
General Secretary: Mr. E. Sersen

South Africa

South African National Committee of the IEC
South African Bureau of Standards
Private Bag X191
Pretoria 0001
Tel: +27 12 428 7911
Fax: +27 12 344 1568
Secretary: Mr. I.P. Kruger

Spain

Comite Nacional Espanol de la Cei
Aenor
Fernandez de la Hoz, 52
28010 Madrid
Tel: +34 1 432 6000
Fax: +34 1 310 4596
Deputy Secretary: Mrs. Elena Santiago
Director General: Mr. Ramon Naz

Sweden

Svenska Elektriska Kommissionen
Box 1284
16428 Kista-Stockholm
Tel: +46 8 111 1400
Fax: +46 8 444 1430
Vice Presidents: Mr. L. Ljung; Tel: +46 8 453
9714; Fax: +46 8 453 9710
Mr. G. Sandquist; Tel: +46 120 11800
Director: Mr. H.E. Rundqvist

Switzerland

Swiss Electrotechnical Committee (CES)
Swiss Electrotechnical Association
Luppmenstrasse 1
8320 Fehraltorf
Tel: +41 1 956 1170
Fax: +41 1 956 1190
Secretary General: El. Ing. HTL R.E. Spaar

Thailand

Thai Industrial Standards Institute (TISI)
Ministry of Industry
Rama VI Street
Bankok 10400
Tel: +66 2 245 7802
Fax: +66 2 247 8741
Secretary: Miss K. Sinsakul
Assistant Secretary: Miss S. Sunthrarak

Turkey

Turkish National Committee of the IEC
Türk Standardlari Enstitüsü
Necatibey Caddesi, 112
Bakanliklar/Ankara
Tel: +90 312 417 8330
Fax: +90 312 425 4399
General Secretary: Mr. R. Aksoy

Ukraine

Ukrainian National Committee of the IEC
State Committee of Standardization, Metrology
& Certification
Gorki St. 174, 252006 Kiev 006
Tel: +380 44 226 2971
Fax: +380 44 226 2970
Technical Secretary: Mr. Alexandre Belov

United Kingdom

British Electrotechnical Committee
British Standards Institution
389 Chiswick High Road, London W4 4AL
Tel: +44 181 996 9000
Fax: +44 181 996 7799
Secretary: Mr. M.H. Lockton; Tel: +44 181 996
7459; Fax: +44 181 996 7460
President: Mr. N.J.A. Holland; Tel: +44 1703
270 605; Fax: +44 1703 270 605

United States of America

U.S. National Committee of the IEC
American National Standards Institute (ANSI)
11 West 42nd Street, 13th Floor
New York, New York 10036
Tel: +1 212 642 4900
Fax: +1 212 398 0023
Secretary: Mr. Charles T. Zegers; Tel: +1 212
642 4965; Fax: +1 212 398 0023

Yugoslavia

Federal Institution for Standardization
Electrotechnical Coordinating Commission
Kneza Milosa 20; p.p. 933, 11000 Beograd
Tel: +381 11 688 999/173
Fax: +381 11 682 382
General Secretary: Dipl.-Ing. Dj. Lisica

Checklists

SECTION 1
An EMS Project Checklist

by John R. Broomfield, President and CEO, Quality Management International

Hundreds of firms have developed this checklist to become a well-proven methodology over the past decade of designing and developing management systems. This approach works for all organizations that have tried it.

This methodology appears on the World Wide Web for free use across the world by organizations structuring their approach to environmental management and risk or loss prevention. For the latest edition, please aim your browser at URL:
http://www.stoller.com/isofiles/qmiinc.html (See Appendix J for more information on Internet resources.)

Whatever your organization's maturity, all firms can quickly benefit by comparing what they are doing with the actions described below.

1 — Become convinced and appoint a champion.

Assess the cost of not using a well-defined EMS. Study the case for upgrading your system to meet ISO 14001. If you are not convinced, it will not happen. If convinced, appoint a champion with a direct reporting relationship to the top to facilitate upgrading, use, and audit of the EMS and report on its performance. Train the champion to substantially raise understanding of environmental issues, management systems, and expertise in auditing to the relevant system standard.

2 — Appoint a task force.

The task force is selected from a cross-section of grades and functions and is led by the champion with clear objectives. Consider the need/role of an adviser and publish a charter for the task force so the EMS is built to ensure ownership by those who must make it work. Agree on the schedule of progress meetings to appear on the action plan (see 4 below).

3 — Analyze gaps in existing system.

Conduct an audit of the existing system using ANSI/ISO 14001 guided by ANSI/ISO 14004. Use a very experienced registered lead system auditor to elicit facts without upsetting people. The report identifies adequacy of as-is procedures and the need for new procedures. Respect existing methods even if they are not the best they can be; they never will be. Improvement is always possible, but the completed EMS is to be used for this.

4 — Publish goals and plan of action.

Policy and objectives incorporate the vision and strategy to become part of the EMS and aid the setting of targets. Deploy the environmental and business plans into the policy and objectives for implementation or realization by the EMS itself. An EMS manager who drafts a policy for the boss who then signs it has a problem. The policy must be from the heart of the person in charge and not from his or her adviser.

5 — Enable leaders to involve the team.

Leaders must sustain employee interest in upgrading their EMS by explaining the logic and benefits of systems to the entire team, groups and individuals. Conduct workshops so leaders create awareness materials to inspire employee enthusiasm for the EMS. This can make leaders visible in their commitment. Do not use consultants to make employees aware of the importance of this for the company. Employees need to see the involvement and determination of their leaders. Do not waste money on teaching everyone about the detail of the standard. It is unnecessary and indicates lack of senior management commitment to take responsibility for the need of a management system instead of "blaming it" on a new standard.

6 — Define organizational relationships.

Organization, responsibilities, and authorities are defined in formal documents so they can help identify training needs and inform the team of roles and changes. Learn how to define organization, authority, responsibility, and accountability without duplication in the EMS to avoid updating and control problems. Detailed job descriptions are not necessary in a system containing well-defined processes. This may be a problem for the organizations that keep detailed job descriptions for performance appraisal and other outmoded reasons.

7 — Involve everyone.

Involve all employees in upgrading their system by awareness sessions, flowcharting sessions, team reviews and experience feedback, and whatever works. Assess the extent and depth of employee involvement in system thinking, building, and action, also auditing to ensure the involvement is effective in meeting agreed objectives. Consider also using a formal suggested improvement request (SIR) to feed into the work of the task force and later to drive corrective action as part of the EMS. This can relieve the tension felt if the employees are not used to working exactly as agreed in procedures.

8 — Enable control of documents and data.

Develop a document coding procedure to ensure reliable delivery of the correct and required information to the workplace. Use proven document coding design principles to give the system structure, indicate ownership, and eliminate document and data control problems. Also use this to deploy responsibility for environmental performance away from the system manager (or champion) to the people making the decisions, planning and doing the work. Consider document control software to maintain registers, history, and distribution. Dates are not necessary but master lists always are. Use the coding procedure from the beginning to control draft EMS documents, too. Put well-maintained form stations within easy reach to dissuade users from keeping their private supply of (out-of-control) blank forms in hard-copy systems.

9 — Identify and define key work processes.

Identify, analyze, and define key processes from the core processes and then the support processes. Conduct training in this to enable EMS builders to create effective procedures using well-proven techniques to improve communication, process control, and system thinking. Remember core processes are how a firm converts customer needs into cash in the bank. Support processes are vital to direct, sustain, verify, correct, and improve core processes. Only key processes need be documented to be sure of meeting objectives. Define objectives for the work (or process), not for the paper defining the process.

10 — Code and simplify blank forms.

Ensure every form (old and new, external and internal) belongs to a process, thereby identifying possibly redundant forms. Redesign and simplify forms (paper and electronic) and make them available so they cause systemic action to meet EMS objectives. Design the form so users do not have to read a separate procedure to complete it.

11 — Link forms to processes.

Correlate all forms to flowcharts to check if any key processes have been missed and see if more flowcharting is required. Review flowcharts against the objectives and targets for each process. Consider putting the flowchart on the back of the form to reduce paper by removing the need for a separate textual procedure or instruction.

12 — Build a practical system.

Review flowcharts of existing (as-is) processes for accuracy to prevent the EMS from becoming a work of fiction in describing the way objectives are met. Mini-audits can ensure accuracy of flowcharts and guard against impractical procedures becoming part of the EMS. Remember, every new procedure requires an investment in training and the cash may not be available until the system has been running for a while.

13 — Integrate the EMS into the business system.

Keep key process flowcharts to one page. Drill down (flowcharting software with hyperlink is great for this) to a separate one-page flowchart for each complex activity. Keep drilling down until the work is defined well enough to control the process. Do not create a separate EMS process if one exists that could be improved within the business system. Tie the EMS and business process flowcharts into each other (use the logic of the coding procedure) to show the flow of information, material, or subassembly. Meet user needs by being creative in the ease of accessibility, format, and graphics.

14 — Formally issue as-is procedures.

Encouraged by the task force, teams review their procedures, reconcile comments, approve and issue as-is procedures. Approval by process owners further empowers them. Do not wait to issue these documents, since employees have been told they are important for the future of the business. Encourage early issue of procedures so they can be continually improved based on experience. No procedure is ever finished, even after a decade of use.

15 — Design and implement new processes.

Limit new processes to those required to render the EMS effective. New processes require investment in design and training for effective implementation. New processes may include:

- designing for the environment (DFE);
- environmental planning;
- EMS auditing;
- corrective and preventive action;
- emergency action; and
- management review.

Deliver accredited (or credible) training where available to add value for the people who are essential for making the EMS work by professional application of these new skills.

16 — Issue new procedures.

Approve and issue new procedures and the environmental program to start the EMS cycles of continued improvement: plan>do>check>act>plan etc. Ensure the planning process quickly becomes thoroughly integrated and properly deploys the EMS to ensure specific policy, objectives, targets, and other stakeholder needs are met.

17 — Publish the EMS manual.

Publish the policies and describe the EMS in a slim manual for stakeholders to see, for every employee to keep, and to encourage vendors and subcontractors. Keep it simple to update and easy to read and use. Too many organizations write their manual to specify the EMS instead of describing what employees have built for themselves to use and improve.

18 — Launch it!

Have a party. You deserve it! Launch the EMS complete with internal audits (see 19 below) and respond very quickly and publicly to revision requests to show employees and other stakeholders how responsive and useful it is. Expect and quickly solve problems in immature systems during the first three to six months to avoid loss of confidence in the EMS.

19 — Target improvements continually.

Audit to improve the EMS so it makes processes more and more effective at preventing pollution. Watch carefully the intensity and style of the audit program so auditing is well accepted and integrated with the business strategy as a systems-thinking and knowledge-creating organization for continuous improvement. Ensure this is driven more by the management review process than audit to protect the impartiality of auditors.

20 — Consider the registration/certification option (may become a market necessity).

You may wish to mark the fact that your EMS meets national and international standards for environmental management systems by obtaining accredited registration. The registrar should enhance and protect the reputation of the business. Check this out before appointing the registrar. Conduct an independent assessment of your EMS using a registered lead systems auditor to be sure of readiness before any loss of registrar impartiality.

21 — Ongoing improvements.

Registration or declarations of compliance with ANSI/ISO 14001 are not the end. This merely marks the beginning of using the EMS to achieve never-ending improvements in environmental performance to create a sustainable business.

These actions take from six to 18 months depending on the extent of formalized system, the skills base, workload, and the degree of management commitment.

Companies successfully operating ISO 9000 quality management systems can more easily upgrade these "teamwork" systems to also meet the EMS standard.

SECTION 2

Example of a Pre-Audit Questionnaire

by Raymond Kane, Engineer, Environmental Management Consulting

General Information Data Sheet

Plant Name:
Address:
Contact Person(s):
Date:

❑ Major products currently manufactured at site:

❑ List the 10 most-used raw materials (include solids, liquids, gases):

❑ Have there been any changes in either the products manufactured or processes used in the past 10 years? If yes, please describe:

❑ Is the plant property owned or leased?

❑ When was the property first acquired or leased?

❑ Describe the dates, ownership, and use(s) of the property as far back as possible, prior to the date of acquisition or lease:

❑ Please describe the nature of other industries located within a radius of three miles (light, medium, heavy industrial; refineries; steel mills; etc.):

Air Emissions Data Sheet

Plant Name:
Address:
Contact Person(s):
Date:

❑ Number of stacks at location:

❑ Sources being vented by stacks:

    ❑ 1. Heating

    ❑ 2. Manufacturing-related air pollutants

    ❑ 3. Other: _____

❑ Nature of air emissions (check all that apply):

    ❑ Toxic gases and vapors

    ❑ Malodorous gases and vapors

    ❑ Aerosols

    ❑ Irritant gases

- ❑ Asphyxiants
- ❑ Dust and ash
- ❑ Other: _____
❑ Air permits:
- ❑ Name _____
- ❑ Permit Number _____
❑ Check specific emissions that are regulated by permit:
- ❑ Volatile organic compounds
- ❑ Carbon monoxide
- ❑ Nitrogen oxides
- ❑ Total suspended particulates
- ❑ Sulfur dioxide
- ❑ Lead
❑ List of control equipment:

Devices:
- ❑ Filters
- ❑ Scrubbers
- ❑ Backwashes
- ❑ Baghouse
- ❑ Incinerator

Other:
- ❑ _____
- ❑ _____

❑ Regulatory contact (please provide the name, title, affiliation, and telephone number of local, state, or federal officials who are regularly involved in air quality issues at the plant):

❑ Has the facility been cited for any violations of air pollution control regulations in the past three years? If yes, please describe:

Wastewater Data Sheet

Plant Name:
Address:
Contact Person(s):
Date:

❑ Type of permitted discharge and volume

❑ Check type of discharge at plant and list volume:

    ❑ Sanitary discharge

        ❑ Volume _____

        ❑ Permit agency _____

    ❑ Process discharge

        ❑ Volume _____

        ❑ Permit agency _____

    ❑ Storm-water discharge

        ❑ Volume _____

        ❑ Permit agency _____

❑ Describe type(s) of pretreatment prior to discharge (such as oil/water separation, coagulation/precipitation, filtration, ion exchange, carbon treatment, etc.)

Industrial Wastewater Info

❑ List major process wastewater sources, date begun discharging, gallons/day (GPD):

    ❑ Sources

    ❑ Date

    ❑ GPD

❑ List of pollutants from industrial wastewater sources listed above:

    ❑ 1. Metal:

        ❑ Chrome ❑ Nickel ❑ Copper   ❑ Lead ❑ Zinc ❑ Other

    ❑ 2. Toxic Organic

    ❑ 3. Oil and Grease

    ❑ 4. PH

    ❑ 5. BOD

    ❑ 6. Solids:

        ❑ Settleable ❑ Suspendable ❑ Dissolved

    ❑ 7. Other: _____

❏ Regulatory contact (please provide the name, title, affiliation, and telephone number of local, state, or federal officials who are regularly involved in wastewater discharge/pretreatment issues at the plant):

❏ Has the facility been cited for violation of water pollution control regulations in the past three years? If yes, please describe:

Hazardous and Solid Waste Data Sheet

Plant Name:
Address:
Contact Person(s):
Date:

Section 1 — Hazardous Wastes

❏ EPA I.D. #

❏ Describe the types of hazardous waste activities conducted at the plant in the following sections:

  ❏ **Generator** (List the types of wastes generated by name of EPA code, and the average pounds generated per month):

  ❏ **Storer** (List the types of waste, by name or EPA code, that are stored on-site in drums, tanks, etc., for greater than 90 days, and the maximum quantity in storage at any time in pounds):

  ❏ **Treater**: (List the types of wastes, by name or EPA code, that are treated to the point where they no longer meet the definition of hazardous waste, the treatment methods utilized, and the maximum quantity treated per month):

  ❏ **Disposer:** (List the types of wastes, by name or EPA code, that are disposed of on-site, the disposal methods, and the quantity disposed monthly):

  ❏ **Reclaimer**: (List the types of wastes, by name or EPA code, that are reclaimed on-site, and the monthly quantity):

❏ If hazardous wastes are stored, treated, disposed of, or recycled off-site, please complete the following for all sites used currently and in the past:

  ❏ Site name

  ❏ Location

  ❏ Type and volume of waste site

  ❏ Currently used or date last used

Section 2 — Non-hazardous Wastes

Type/Composition

❑ 1. General/commercial

    ❑ Volume _____

❑ 2. Industrial (i.e., paint filter/sludge/rejects; oil no combined with PCB, etc.)

    ❑ Volume _____

❑ 3. Other

    ❑ Volume _____

Method of Disposal:

❑ On-site ❑ Off-site ❑ Both

❑ Dump/landfill

    ❑ Volume _____

❑ Incineration

    ❑ Volume _____

❑ Other

    ❑ Volume _____

❑ Locations of off-site waste disposal sites (list name and address):

❑ Regulatory contact (please provide the name, title, affiliation, and telephone number of local, state, or federal officials who are regularly involved in hazardous and solid waste issues at the plant):

❑ Has the facility been cited for violation of hazardous or solid waste regulations in the past three years? If yes, please describe:

Miscellaneous Information Data Sheet

Plant name:
Address:
Contact Person(s):
Date:

Section 1 — Underground Tanks and Piping

❑ Does the facility have any underground storage tanks?:

    ❑ Yes ❑ No ❑ Don't know

❑ If yes, how many?

    ❑ Are they active? ❑ Inactive?

❑ If yes, on a separate sheet, please provide the following information for each tank: size (in gallons), construction material age, and which tanks have cathodic protection or secondary containment.

❑ Does the facility have:

    ❑ Underground piping

        ❑ Yes ❑ No ❑ Don't know

    ❑ Sewer lines

        ❑ Yes ❑ No ❑ Don't know

    ❑ Sumps

        ❑ Yes ❑ No ❑ Don't know

Section 2 — Polychlorinate Biphenyls (PCBs)

❑ Does the facility have any PCB transformers or capacitors in service at the site?

    ❑ Yes ❑ No ❑ Don't know

❑ Does the facility have any PCB-contaminated transformers or capacitors in service at the site?

    ❑ Yes ❑ No ❑ Don't Know

❑ Does the facility have any PCB-contaminated transformers or capacitors that are out of service and in storage at the site?

    ❑ Yes ❑ No ❑ Don't know

Pre-audit Information Collection Checklist

Information to be Collected

A. Air Emissions

1. Copies of all current air permits

    ❑ Available (❑ Included ❑ Not included) ❑ Not available ❑ Not applicable

2. Air monitoring data for the past 12 months

    ❑ Available (❑ Included ❑ Not included) ❑ Not available ❑ Not applicable

3. Air emission inventory

    ❑ Available (❑ Included ❑ Not included) ❑ Not available ❑ Not applicable

4. Air emission reports submitted to regulatory agencies for the past 12 months

    ❑ Available (❑ Included ❑ Not included) ❑ Not available ❑ Not applicable

5. Copies of any violation notices received in the past three years

    ❑ Available (❑ Included ❑ Not included) ❑ Not available ❑ Not applicable

B. Wastewater

1. Copies of all EPA or municipal sewer permits

    ❑ Available (❑ Included ❑ Not included) ❑ Not available ❑ Not applicable

2. Copies of discharge monitoring data for last two years for flow and permit parameters

   ❏ Available (❏ Included ❏ Not included) ❏ Not available ❏ Not applicable

3. Any complete (organic and inorganic) analyses of process, cooling, or storm water streams

   ❏ Available (❏ Included ❏ Not included) ❏ Not available ❏ Not applicable

4. Water use records for the past 12 months

   ❏ Available (❏ Included ❏ Not included) ❏ Not available ❏ Not applicable

5. Copies of any violation notices received in the past three years

   ❏ Available (❏ Included ❏ Not included) ❏ Not available ❏ Not applicable

C. Hazardous Wastes

1. RCRA permits

   ❏ Available (❏ Included ❏ Not included) ❏ Not available ❏ Not applicable

2. Hazardous waste manifests for the past 12 months

   ❏ Available (❏ Included ❏ Not included) ❏ Not available ❏ Not applicable

3. Copies of preparedness and prevention/contingency plans

   ❏ Available (❏ Included ❏ Not included) ❏ Not available ❏ Not applicable

4. Waste analysis data for all hazardous waste streams

   ❏ Available (❏ Included ❏ Not included) ❏ Not available ❏ Not applicable

5. Latest generators report to EPA/state

   ❏ Available (❏ Included ❏ Not included) ❏ Not available ❏ Not applicable

6. Copies of any notices of involvement at "Superfund" sites

   ❏ Available (❏ Included ❏ Not included) ❏ Not available ❏ Not applicable

7. Copies of any violation notices received in the past three years

   ❏ Available (❏ Included ❏ Not included) ❏ Not available ❏ Not applicable

8. Copy of the waste minimization plan

   ❏ Available (❏ Included ❏ Not included) ❏ Not available ❏ Not applicable

D. Tanks

1. A listing of all aboveground storage tanks which includes: capacity, contents, use, and volume capacity of secondary containment system

   ❏ Available (❏ Included ❏ Not included) ❏ Not available ❏ Not applicable

2. A copy of the underground tank registration form(s) submitted to any authority

   ❏ Available (❏ Included ❏ Not included) ❏ Not available ❏ Not applicable

3. A copy of the site's Spill Prevention Control and Countermeasure (SPCC) plan

   ❏ Available (❏ Included ❏ Not included) ❏ Not available ❏ Not applicable

E. Polychlorinate Biphenyls (PCBs)

1. A copy of an annual PCB report

 ❏ Available (❏ Included ❏ Not included) ❏ Not available ❏ Not applicable

2. PCB test results from analysis on electrical equipment

 ❏ Available (❏ Included ❏ Not included) ❏ Not available ❏ Not applicable

3. Copies of any violation notices received in the past three years

 ❏ Available (❏ Included ❏ Not included) ❏ Not available ❏ Not applicable

F. Groundwater

1. Well construction diagrams for on-site water supply or groundwater monitoring wells

 ❏ Available (❏ Included ❏ Not included) ❏ Not available ❏ Not applicable

2. Water quality analysis from water supply or groundwater monitoring wells for the past 12 months
 ❏ Available (❏ Included ❏ Not included) ❏ Not available ❏ Not applicable

G. Industrial Hygiene

1. Copies of OSHA or insurance carrier inspection reports for the past three years

 ❏ Available (❏ Included ❏ Not included) ❏ Not available ❏ Not applicable

2. Copy of the facility safety/health manual

 ❏ Available (❏ Included ❏ Not included) ❏ Not available ❏ Not applicable

3. Copies of material safety data sheets (MSDS) for all materials used at the site

 ❏ Available (❏ Included ❏ Not included) ❏ Not available ❏ Not applicable

4. Copies of any violation notices received in the past three years

 ❏ Available (❏ Included ❏ Not included) ❏ Not available ❏ Not applicable

SECTION3

ISO 14001 Environmental Management System Self-Assessment Checklist

The Global Environmental Management Initiative (GEMI) — a non-profit organization of leading companies dedicated to helping business achieve environmental, health, and safety excellence — has developed a comprehensive self-assessment checklist for use by any company, any size, seeking to implement ISO 14001. The checklist and primer, published in March 1996, aims at improving facility managers' understanding of the requirements and elements of the environmental management system outlined in the ISO 14001 draft international standard.

Through the collaborative efforts of its members, GEMI promotes a worldwide business ethic for environmental management and sustainable development through example and leadership.

Some 40 pages long, the checklist is available by contacting the address below. It was written by several Fortune 500 company members, among others, and is designed to allow for a rapid self-assessment of an organization or facility to determine how closely existing management practices and procedures correspond to the elements of the standard. The criteria of the draft standard have been rephrased in the format of a simple questionnaire, with a three-part scoring system. In addition to a brief guide to self-scoring, a fuller description of what is required by the standard's criteria is included in the appendix.

In this format, even with limited background knowledge of the ISO 14001 standard, a facility or other business manager can quickly review existing operations to determine how they measure up to the standard. This in turn can serve as the starting point of a "gap analysis" to identify management tools or system elements that might usefully be implemented in the organization to help improve overall environmental performance.

GEMI's member companies as of March 1996 were:

AT&T; Allied Signal Inc.; Amoco Corp.; Anheuser-Busch Companies; Apple Computer Inc.; Bristol-Myers Squibb Company; Browning-Ferris Industries; The Coca-Cola Company; Colgate-Palmolive Company; Coors Brewing Company; Digital Equipment Corp.; The Dow Chemical Company; Duke Power Company; The DuPont Company; Eastman Kodak Company; Florida Power & Light; Georgia-Pacific Corp.; Halliburton Company; Hughes Electronics Corp.; Johnson & Johnson; Merck & Company, Inc.; Olin Corp.; The Procter & Gamble Company; The Southern Company; Tenneco; Union Carbide Corp.; WMX Technologies Inc.

Global Environmental Management Initiative (GEMI)
2000 L Street NW, Suite 710
Washington, D.C. 20036
Tel: 202-296-7449; Fax: 202-296-7442
E-mail: GEMI@worldweb.net
Internet: http://www.gemi.org

U.S. Sentencing Commission Guidelines and EPA Audit Policies

U.S. Sentencing Commission Guidelines

The following material comes from the U.S. Sentencing Commission's *Guidelines Manual*, published in 1991. While not explicitly mentioning environmental management systems, the guidelines instruct judges to provide some measure of leniency when sentencing organizations that have an "effective program to detect and prevent violations of the law." (§8C2.5.f)

Part Q - Offenses Involving the Environment

1. Environment

§2Q.1.1. Knowing Endangerment Resulting From Mishandling Hazardous or Toxic Substances, Pesticides or Other Pollutants

(a) Base Offense Level: 24

Commentary

Statutory Provisions: 33 U.S.C. § 1319(c)(3); 42 U.S.C. § 6928(e).

Application Note:

1. If death or serious bodily injury resulted, an upward departure may be warranted. See Chapter Five, Part K (Departures).

Background: This section applies to offenses committed with knowledge that the violation placed another person in imminent danger of death or serious bodily injury.

Historical Note: Effective November 1, 1987.

§2Q.1.2. Mishandling of Hazardous or Toxic Substances or Pesticides: Recordkeeping, Tampering, and Falsification

(a) Base Offense Level: 8

(b) Specific Offense Characteristics

(1) (A) If the offense resulted in an ongoing, continuous, or repetitive discharge, release, or emission of a hazardous or toxic substance or pesticide into the environment, increase by 6 levels; or

(B) if the offense otherwise involved a discharge, release, or emission of a hazardous or toxic substance or pesticide, increase by 4 levels.

(2) If the offense resulted in a substantial likelihood of death or serious bodily injury, increase by 9 levels.

(3) If the offense resulted in disruption of public utilities or evacuation of a community, or if cleanup required a substantial expenditure, increase by 4 levels.

(4) If the offense involved transportation, treatment, storage, or disposal without a permit or in violation of a permit, increase by 4 levels.

(5) If a recordkeeping offense reflected an effort to conceal a substantive environmental offense, use the offense level for the substantive offense.

(6) If the offense involved a simple recordkeeping or reporting violation only, decrease by 2 levels.

Commentary

Statutory Provisions: 7 U.S.C. §§ 136j-136l; 15 U.S.C. §§ 2614 and 2615; 33 U.S.C. §§ 1319(c)(1), (2), 1321(b)(5), 1517(b); 42 U.S.C. §§ 300h-2, 6928(d), 7413, 9603(b), (c), (d); 43 U.S.C. §§1350, 1816(a), 1822(b). For additional statutory provision(s), see Appendix A (Statutory Index).

Application Notes:

1. "Recordkeeping offense" include both recordkeeping and reporting offenses. The term is to be broadly construed as including failure to report discharges, releases, or emissions where required; the giving of false information; failure to file other required reports or provide necessary information; and failure to prepare, maintain, or provide records as prescribed.

2. "Simple record keeping or reporting violation" means a recordkeeping or reporting offense in a situation where the defendant neither know nor had reason to believe that the recordkeeping offense would significantly increase the likelihood of any substantive environmental harm.

3. This section applies to offenses involving pesticides or substances designated toxic or hazardous at the time of the offense by statute or regulation. A listing of hazardous and toxic substances in the guidelines would be impractical. Several federal statutes (or regulations promulgated thereunder) list toxics, hazardous wastes and substances, and pesticides. These lists, such as those of toxic pollutants for which effluent standards are published under the Federal Water Pollution Control Act (e.g., 33 U.S.C § 1317) as well as the designation of hazardous substances under the Comprehensive Environmental Response, Compensation an Liability Act (e.g., 42 U.S.C. § 9601(14),), are revised from time to time. "Toxic" and "hazardous" are defined differently in various statutes, but the common dictionary meaning of the words are not significantly different.

4. Except when the adjustment in subsection (b)(6) for simple recordkeeping offenses applies, this section assumes knowing conduct. In cases involving negligent conduct, a downward departure may be warranted.

5. Subsection (b)(1) assumes a discharge or emission into the environment resulting in actual environmental contamination. A wide range of conduct, involving the handling of different quantities of materials with widely differing propensities, potentially is covered. Depending upon the harm resulting from the emission, release or discharge, the quantity and nature of the substance or pollutant, the duration of the offense and the risk associated with the violation, a departure of up to two levels in either direction from the offense levels prescribed in these specific offense characteristics may be appropriate.

6. Subsection (b)(2) applies to offenses where the public health is seriously endangered. Depending upon the nature of the risk created and the number of people placed at risk, a departure of up to three levels upward or downward may be warranted. If death or serious bodily injury results, a departure would be called for. See Chapter Five, Part K (Departures).

7. Subsection (b)(3) provides an enhancement where a public disruption, evacuation or cleanup at substantial expense has been required. Depending upon the nature of the contamination involved, a departure of up to two levels either upward or downward could be warranted.

8. Subsection (b)(4) applies where the offense involved violation of a permit, or where there was a failure to obtain a permit when one was required. Depending upon the nature and quantity of the substance involved and the risk associated with the offense, a departure of up to two levels either upward or downward may be warranted.

9. Where a defendant has previously engaged in similar misconduct established by a civil adjudication or has failed to comply with an administrative order, an upward departure may be warranted. See §4A1.3 (Adequacy of Criminal History Category).

Background: This section applies both to substantive violations of the statute governing the handling of pesticides and toxic and hazardous substances and to recordkeeping offenses. The first four specific offense characteristics provide enhancements when the offense involved a substantive violation. The last two specific offense characteristics apply to recordkeeping offenses. Although other sections of the guidelines generally prescribe a base offense level of 6 for regulatory violations, §2Q1.2 prescribes a base offense level of 8 because of the inherently dangerous nature of hazardous and toxic substances and pesticides. A decrease of 2 levels is provided, however, for "simple recordkeeping or reporting violations" under §2Q1.2(b)(6).

Historical Note: Effective November 1, 1987.

§2Q1.3. Mishandling of Other Environmental Pollutant: Recordkeeping, Tampering, and Falsification

(a) Base Offense Level: 6

(b)   Specific Offense Characteristics

(1) (A) If the offense resulted in an ongoing, continuous, or repetitive discharge, release, or emission of a pollutant into the environment, increase by 6 levels; or

(B) If the offense otherwise involved a discharge, release, or emission of a pollutant, increase by 4 levels.

(2) If the offense resulted in a substantial likelihood of death or serious bodily injury, increase by 11 levels.

(3) If the offense resulted in disruption of public utilities or evacuation of a community, or if cleanup required a substantial expenditure, increase by 4 levels.

(4) If the offense involved a discharge without a permit or in violation of a permit, increase by 4 levels.

(5) If a recordkeeping offense reflected an effort to conceal a substantive environmental offense, use the offense level for the substantive offense.

Commentary

Statutory Provisions: 33 U.S.C. §§ 403, 406, 407, 411, 1319(c)(1), (c)(2), 1415(b), 1907, 1908; 42 U.S.C. § 7413. For additional statutory provision(s), see Appendix A (Statutory Index).

Application Notes:

1. "Recordkeeping offense" includes both recordkeeping and reporting offenses. The term is to be broadly construed as including failure to report discharges, releases, or emissions where required; the giving of false information; failure to file other required reports or provide necessary information; and failure to prepare, maintain, or provide records as prescribed.

2. If the offense involved mishandling of nuclear material, apply §2M6.2 (Violation of Other negligent conduct, a downward departure may be warranted.

4. Subsection (b)(1) assumes a discharge or emission into the environment resulting in actual environmental contamination. A wide range of conduct, involving the handling of different quantities of materials with widely differing propensities, potentially is covered. Depending upon the harm resulting from the emission, release or discharge, the quantity and nature of the substance or pollutant, the duration of the offense and the risk associated with the violation a departure of up to two levels in either direction from that prescribed in these specific offense characteristics may be appropriate.

5. Subsection (b)(2) applies to offenses where the public health is seriously endangered. Depending upon the nature of the risk created and the number of people placed at risk, a departure of up to three

levels upward or downward may be warranted. If death or serious bodily injury results, a departure would be called for. See Chapter Five, Part K (Departures).

6. Subsection (b)(3) provides an enhancement where a public disruption, evacuation or cleanup at substantial expense has been required. Depending upon the nature of the contamination involved, a departure of up to two levels in either direction could be warranted.

7. Subsection (b)(4) applies where the offense involved violation of a permit, or where there was a failure to obtain a permit when one was required. Depending upon the nature and quantity of the substance involved and the risk associated with the offense, a departure of up to two levels in either direction may be warranted.

8. Where a defendant has previously engaged in similar misconduct established by a civil adjudication or has failed to comply with an administrative order, an upward departure may be warranted. See §4A1.3 (Adequacy of Criminal History Category).

Background: This section parallels §2Q1.2 but applies to offenses involving substances which are not pesticides and are not designated as hazardous or toxic.

Historical Note: Effective November 1, 1987. Amended effective November 1, 1989 (see Appendix C, amendment 205).

§2Q1.4. Tampering or Attempted Tampering with Public Water System

(a) Base Offense Level: 18

(b) Specific Offense Characteristics

(1) If a risk of death or serious bodily injury was created, increase by 6 levels.

(2) If the offense resulted in disruption of a public water system or evacuation of a community, or if cleanup required a substantial expenditure, increase by 4 levels.

(3) If the offense resulted in an ongoing, continuous, or repetitive release of a contaminant into a public water system or lasted for a substantial period of time, increase by 2 levels.

(4) If the purpose of the offense was to influence government action or to extort money, increase by 6 levels.

Commentary

Statutory Provision: 42 U.S.C. § 300i-1.

Application Note:

1. "Serious bodily injury" is defined in the Commentary to §1B1.1 (Application Instructions).

Historical Note: Effective November 1,1987. Amended effective November 1, 1989 (see appendix C, amendment 206).

§2Q1.5. Threatened Tampering with Public Water System

(a) Base Offense Level: 10

(b) Specific Offense Characteristic

(1) If the threat or attempt resulted in disruption of a public water system or evacuation of a commu-

nity or a substantial public expenditure, increase by 4 levels.

(c) Cross Reference

(1) If the purpose of the offense was to influence government action or to extort money, apply §2B3.2 (Extortion by Force or Threat of Injury or Serious Damage).

Commentary

Statutory Provision: 42 U.S.C. § 300i-1.

Historical Note: Effective November 1, 1987. Amended effective November 1, 1989 (see Appendix C, amendment 207.

§2Q1.6. Hazardous or Injurious Devices on Federal Lands

(a) Base Offense Level (Apply the greatest):

(1) If the intent was to violate the Controlled Substance Act, apply §2D1.9 (Placing or Maintaining Dangerous Devices on Federal Property to Protect the Unlawful Production of Controlled Substances);

(2) If the intent was to obstruct the harvesting of timber, and property destruction resulted, apply §2B1.3 (Property Damage or Destruction);

(3) If the offense involved reckless disregard to the risk that another person would be placed in danger of death or serious bodily injury under circumstances manifesting extreme indifference to such risk, the offense level from §2A2.2 (Aggravated Assault);

(4) 6, otherwise.

Commentary

Statutory Provision: 18 U.S.C. § 1864.

Background: The statute covered by this guideline proscribes a wide variety of conduct, ranging from placing nails in trees to interfere with harvesting equipment to placing anti-personnel devices capable of causing death or serious bodily injury to protect the unlawful production of a controlled substance. Subsections (a)(1)-(a)(3) cover the more serious forms of this offense. Subsection (a)(4) provides a minimum offense level of 6 where the intent was to obstruct the harvesting of timber and little or no property damage resulted.

Historical Note: Effective November 1, 1989 (see Appendix C, amendment 208). Amended effective November 1, 1990 (see Appendix C, amendment 313).

§8C2.5. Culpability Score

(a) Start with 5 points and apply subsections (b) through (g) below.

(b) Involvement in or Tolerance of Criminal Activity

If more than one applies, use the greatest:

(1) If—

(A) the organization had 5,000 or more employees and

(i) an individual within high-level personnel of the organization participated in, condoned, or was willfully ignorant of the offense; or

(ii) tolerance of the offense by substantial authority personnel was pervasive throughout the organization; or

(B) the unit of the organization within which the offense was committed had 5,000 or more employees and

(i) an individual within high-level personnel of the unit participated in , condoned, or was willfully ignorant of the offense; or

(ii) tolerance of the offense by substantial authority personnel was pervasive throughout such unit,

add 5 points; or

(2) If

(A) the organization had 200 or more employees and

(i) an individual within high-level personnel of the organization participated in, condoned, or was willfully ignorant of the offense; or

(ii) tolerance of the offense by substantial authority personnel was pervasive throughout the organization; or

(B) the unit of the organization within which the offense was committed had 200 or more employees and

(i) an individual within high-level personnel of the unit participated in, condoned, or was willfully ignorant of the offense; or

(ii) tolerance of the offense by substantial authority personnel was pervasive throughout such unit,

add 3 points; or

(4) If the organization had 50 or more employees and an individual within substantial authority personnel participated in, condoned, or was willfully ignorant of the offense, add 2 points; or

(5) If the organization had 10 or more employees and an individual within substantial authority personnel participated in, condoned, or was willfully ignorant of the offense, add 1 point.

(c) Prior History

If more than one applies, use the greater:

(1) If the organization (or separately-managed line of business) committed any part of the instant offense less than 10 years after (A) a criminal adjudication based on similar misconduct; or (B) civil or administrative adjudication(s) based on two or more separate instances of similar misconduct, add 1 point; or

(2) If the organization (or separately-managed line of business) committed any part of the instant offense less than 5 years after (A) a criminal adjudication based on similar misconduct; or (B) civil or administrative adjudication(s) based on two or more separate instances of similar misconduct, add 2 points.

(d) Violation of an Order

If more than one applies, use the greater:

(1) (A) If the commission of the instant offense violated a judicial order or injunction, other than a violation of a condition of probation; or (B) if the organization (or separately-managed line of business) violated a condition of probation by engaging in similar misconduct, i.e., misconduct similar to that for which it was placed on probation, add 2 points; or

(2) If the commission of the instant offense violated a condition of probation, add 1 point.

(e) Obstruction of Justice

If the organization willfully obstructed or impeded, attempted to obstruct or impede, or aided, abetted, or encouraged obstruction of justice during the investigation, prosecution ,or sentencing of the instant offense, or, with knowledge thereof, failed to take reasonable steps to prevent such obstruction or impedance or attempted obstruction or impedance, add 3 points.

(f) Effective Program to Prevent and Detect Violations of Law

If the offense occurred despite an effective program to prevent and detect violations of law, subtract 3 points.

Provided, that this subsection does not apply if an individual within high-level personnel of the organization, a person within high-level personnel of the unit of the organization within which the offense was committed where the unit had 200 or more employees, or an individual responsible for the administration or enforcement of a program to prevent and detect violations of law participated in condoned, or was willfully ignorant of the offense. Participation of an individual within substantial authority personnel in an offense results in a rebuttable presumption that the organization did not have an effective program to prevent and detect violations of law.

Provided, further, that this subsection dw s not apply if, after becoming aware of an offense, the organization unreasonably delayed reporting the offense to appropriate governmental authorities.

(g) Self-Reporting, Cooperation, and Acceptance of Responsibility

If more than one applies, use the greatest:

(1) If the organization (A) prior to an imminent threat of disclosure or government investigation; and (B) within a reasonably prompt time after becoming aware of the offense, reported the offense to appropriate governmental authorities, fully cooperated in the investigation, and clearly demonstrated recognition and affirmative acceptance of responsibility for its criminal conduct, subtract 5 points; or

(2) If the organization fully cooperated in the investigation and clearly demonstrated recognition and affirmative acceptance of responsibility for its criminal conduct, subtract 2 points; or

(3) If the organization clearly demonstrated recognition and affirmative acceptance of responsibility for its criminal conduct, subtract 1 point.

Commentary

Application Notes:

1. "Substantial authority personnel," "condoned," "willfully ignorant of the offense," "similar misconduct," "prior criminal adjudication," and "effective program to prevent and detect violations of law," are defined in the Commentary to §8A1.2 (Application Instruction - Organization).

2. For purposes of subsection (b), "unit of the organization" means any reasonably distinct operational component of the organization. For example, a large organization may have several large units such as divisions or subsidiaries, as well as many smaller units such as specialized manufacturing, marketing,

or accounting operations within these larger units. For purposes of this definition, all of these types of units are encompassed within the term "unit of the organization."

3. "High-level personnel of the organization" is defined in the Commentary to §8A1.2 (Application Instructions - Organizations). With respect to a unit with 200 or more employees, "high-level personnel of a unit of the organization" means agents within the unit who set the policy for or control that unit. For example, if the managing agent of a unit with 200 employees participated in an offense, three points would be added under subsection (b)(3); if that organization had 1,000 employees and the managing agent of the unit with 200 employees were also within high-level personnel of the entire organization, four points (rather than three) would be added under subsection (b)(2).

4. Pervasiveness under subsection (b) will be case specific and depend on the number, and degree of responsibility, of individuals within substantial authority personnel who participated in, condoned, or were willfully ignorant of the offense. Fewer individuals need to be involved for a finding of Pervasiveness if those individuals exercised a relatively high degree of authority. Pervasiveness can occur either within an organization as a whole or within a unit of an organization. For example, if an offense were committed in an organization with 1,000 employees but the tolerance of the offense was pervasive only within a unit of the organization with 200 employees (and no high-level personnel of the organization participated in, condoned, or was willfully ignorant of the offense), three points would be added under subsection (b)(3). If, in the same organization, tolerance of the offense was pervasive only within a unit of the organization with 200 employees but the tolerance of the offense was pervasive only within a unit of the organization with 200 employees (and no high-level personnel of the organization participated in, condoned, or was willfully ignorant of the offense), three points would be added under subsection (b)(3). If, in the same organization, tolerance of the offense was pervasive throughout the organization as a whole, or an individual within high-level personnel of the organization participated in the offense, four points (rather than three) would be added under subsection (b)(2).

5. A "separately-managed line of business," as used in subsections (c) and (d), is a subpart of a for-profit organization that has its own management, has a high degree of autonomy from higher managerial authority, and maintains its own separate books of account. Corporate subsidiaries and divisions frequently are separately-managed lines of business. Under subsection (c), in determining the prior history of an organization with separately-managed lines of business, only the prior conduct or criminal record of the separately-managed line of business involved in the instant offense is to be used. Under subsection (d), in the context of an organization with separately-managed lines of business, in making the determination whether a violation of a condition of probation involved engaging in similar misconduct, only the prior misconduct of the separately-managed line of business involved in the instant offense is to be considered.

6. Under subsection (c), in determining the prior history of an organization or separately-managed line of business, the conduct of the underlying economic entity shall be considered without regard to its legal structure or ownership. For example, if two companies merged and became separate divisions and separately-managed lines of business within the merged company, each division would retain the prior history of its predecessor company. If a company reorganized and became a new legal entity, the new company would retain the prior history of the predecessor company. In contrast, if one company purchased the physical assets but not the ongoing business of another company, the prior history of the company selling the physical assets would not be transferred to the company purchasing the assets. However, if an organization is acquired by another organization in response to solicitations by appropriate federal government officials, the prior history of the acquired organization shall not be

attributed to the acquiring organization.

7. Under subsections (c)(1)(B) and (c)(2)(B), the civil or administrative adjudication(s) must have occurred within the specified period (ten or five years) of the instant offense.

8. Adjust the culpability score for the factors listed in subsection (e) whether or not the offense guideline incorporates that factor, or that factor is inherent in the offense.

9. Subsection (e) applies where the obstruction is committed on behalf of the organization; it does not apply where an individual or individuals have attempted to conceal their misconduct from the organization. The Commentary to §3C1.1 (Obstructing or Impeding the Administration of Justice) provided guidance regarding the types of conduct that constitute obstruction.

10. The second proviso in subsection (f) contemplates that the organization will be allowed a reasonable period of time to conduct an internal investigation. In addition, no reporting is required by this proviso if the organization reasonably concluded, based on the information then available, that no offense had been committed.

11. "Appropriate governmental authorities," as used in subsections (f) and (g)(1), means the federal or state law enforcement, regulatory, or program officials having jurisdiction over such matter. To qualify for a reduction under subsection (g)(1), the report to appropriate governmental authorities must be made under the direction of the organization.

12. To qualify for a reduction under subsection (g)(1) or (g)(2), cooperation must be both timely and thorough. To be timely, the cooperation must begin essentially at the same time as the organization is officially notified of a criminal investigation. To be thorough, the cooperation should include the disclosure of all pertinent information known by the organization. A prime test of whether the organization has disclose all pertinent information is whether the information is sufficient for law enforcement personnel to identify the nature and extent of the offense and the individual(s) responsible for the criminal conduct. However, the cooperation to be measured is the cooperation of the organization itself, not the cooperation of individuals within the organization. If, because of the lack of cooperation of particular individual(s), neither the organization nor law enforcement personnel are able to identify the culpable individual(s) within the organization despite the organization's efforts to cooperate fully, the organization may still be given credit for full cooperation.

13. Entry of a plea of guilty prior to the commencement of trial combined with truthful admission of involvement in the offense and related conduct ordinarily will constitute significant evidence of affirmative acceptance of responsibility under subsection (g), unless outweighed by conduct of the organization that is inconsistent with such acceptance of responsibility. This adjustment is not intended to apply to an organization that puts the government to its burden of proof at trial by denying the essential factual elements of guilt, is convicted, and only then admits guilt and expresses remorse. Conviction by trial, however, does not automatically preclude an organization from consideration for such a reduction. In rare situations, an organization may clearly demonstrate an acceptance of responsibility for its criminal conduct even though it exercised its constitutional right to a trial. This may occur, for example, where an organization goes to trial to assert and preserve issues that do not relate to factual guilt (e.g., to make a constitutional challenge to a statute or a challenge to the applicability of a statute to its responsibility will be based primarily upon pretrial statements and conduct.

14. In making a determination with respect to subsection (g), the court may determine that the chief executive officer or highest ranking employee of an organization should appear at sentencing in order

to signify that the organization has clearly demonstrated recognition and affirmative acceptance of responsibility.

Background: The increased culpability scores under subsection (b) are based on three interrelated principles. First, an organization is more culpable when individuals who manage the organization or who have substantial discretion in acting for the organization participate in, condone, or are willfully ignorant of criminal conduct. Second, as organizations become larger and their managements become more professional, participation in, condonation of, or willful ignorance of criminal conduct by such management is increasingly a breach of trust or abuse of position. Third, as organizations increase in size, the risk of criminal conduct beyond that reflected in the instant offense also increases whenever management's tolerance of that offense is pervasive. Because of the continuum of sizes of organizations and professionalization of management, subsection (b) gradually increases the culpability score based upon the size of the organization and the level and extent of the substantial authority personnel involvement.

Historical Note: Effective November 1, 1991 (see Appendix C, amendment 422).

§8C2.6. Minimum and Maximum Multipliers

Using the culpability score from §8C2.5 (Culpability Score) and applying any applicable special instruction for fines in Chapter Two, determine the applicable minimum and maximum fine multipliers from the table below.

Culpability Score	Minimum Multiplier	Maximum Multiplier
10 or more	2.00	4.00
9	1.80	3.60
8	1.60	3.20
7	1.40	2.80
6	1.20	2.40
5	1.00	2.00
4	0.80	1.60
3	0.60	1.20
2	0.40	0.80
1	0.20	0.40
0 or less	0.05	0.20

Figure D.1

Commentary

Application Note:

1. A special instruction for fines in §2R1.1 (Bid-Rigging, Price-Fixing or Market-Allocation Agreements Among Competitors) sets a floor for minimum and maximum multipliers in cases covered by that guideline.

Historical Note: Effective November 1, 1991 (see Appendix C, amendment 422).

SECTION 2
U.S. Sentencing Commission Draft Guidelines on Organizational Environmental Violations

The following is a set of amendments to the U.S. Sentencing Guidelines submitted in 1993 by 12 former officials of the Department of Justice's Environment and Natural Resources Division and the Office of General Counsel of the US Environmental Protection Agency. The amendments were in response to draft organizational guidelines for environmental crimes developed by the US Sentencing Commission's Advisory Working Group on Environmental Sanctions (see above). The advisory group was addressing perceived gaps in the guidelines. The signatories state that they do not believe the guidelines require extensive re-haul, but that their amendments would strengthen organization environmental violations adequately. As of March 1996, these were still in draft form and expected to be considered before 1998.

Appendix

Brief Explanation and Mockup of Structure for Setting a Base Fine for Environmental Organizational Offenders

We provide the following in order to show with some specificity how a sentencing scheme based on the concepts we have articulated might look. Given the relatively limited period of time that we were given to analyze and prepare comments to the Advisory Group, we believe this to be a reasonable estimate of how to address the offenses at issue. It is certainly open to refinement. If the Advisory Group wishes, we would be happy further to develop the language, commentary, and explanatory rationale.

The base fine scenario reflects offense levels tied to specific gradations of culpability and a general range of offense levels to be applied to foreseeable harm. Ultimately, suitable offense levels for each gradation of foreseeable harm could be designated as experience develops. The remainder of the existing organizational sentencing scheme should generally be applied as written, except for those few aspects identified above which require specific comment or amendment addressing areas of particular significance in environmental cases.

A. Knowing Endangerment Offenses

A knowing endangerment is an offense committed with knowledge that the violation placed another person in imminent danger of death or serious bodily injury. As we indicated in our comments, knowing endangerments represent a fairly discrete and more specifically defined category of environmental criminal offenses. The statutory maximum is $1,000,000.

To maintain consistency with the general organizational sentencing scheme, the base fine range must be selected so as to ensure that the statutory maximum will be assessed in the most egregious instances of organizational culpability, but nevertheless allow for substantial mitigation where the organization is virtually free from blame for the act of its employee. The calculus for achieving such a result is relatively straightforward.

Under the existing organizational guidelines, the fine is determined by first deriving a base fine from a table that corresponds to the offense level for the underlying individual violation. §8C2.4(d). The base fine figure is then multiplied by a factor that corresponds to an organizational "culpability score" — essentially a measure of the severity of imputed corporate liability. Section 8C2.6 establishes a multiplier range of 2 to 4 for instances of maximum corporate culpability, based on a culpability score of 10 or more "points."[1] Working backward from those multipliers, in order to arrive at a figure of $1,000,000 in cases where organizational culpability for a knowing endangerment is at its apex, the base fine should be set at no more than $250,000. The corresponding offense level would therefore be 17. This would result in an overall guideline fine range of $500,000 to $1,000,000 for a relatively significant organizational role in the offense.[2] In determining the fine within the range, the court would follow the policy statement provisions in §8C2.8. The court would then proceed to consider any other appropriate provisions from Chapter 8.

B. Major Statutory Environmental Offenses

As noted in our comments, setting the base fine for the major statutory environmental offenses requires consideration of a broad array of culpability and foreseeable harm scenarios, but the same basic principle used for calculating knowing endangerments can be employed here as well.

The maximum statutory fine for most environmental organizational felonies is $500,000 (under the Alternative Fines Act). With that as a benchmark, the maximum base fine for an environmental felony amount should be $125,000. This would produce a substantial overall guideline fine range of $250,000 to $500,000 for the most serious environmental offenses.[3] Consistent with the existing scheme, the minimum base fine should remain at $5,000 for the least serious felony circumstances. Judges should be asked to work within this $5,000 to $125,000 range when weighing the combination of factors listed below. Where a negligence or strict liability misdemeanor count is involved, the range should be reduced to $2,500 to $62,500.

Base Fine for Environmental Offenses

For environmental offenses, the factors to be used in setting the base offense level should be 1) the degree of culpable knowledge of the defendant combined with 2) the harm foreseeable to the defendant as described below.

In exceptional cases involving egregious organizational misconduct and massive harm, the court may determine the base fine in accordance with §8C2.4(a)(1), (a)(2), and (c).

Culpable Knowledge

The degrees of culpable knowledge attributable to the organization committing the underlying offense are as follows:

- Strict Liability
  - — Offense level: 0
- Negligence/Collective knowledge
  - — Offense level: 1
- Knowing offense committed with or without knowledge of legal requirement with reasonable effort to comply including informing the government
  - — Offense level: 2
- Knowing offense committed with lack of knowledge of legal requirement
  - — Offense level: 3

- Knowing offense committed with knowledge of legal requirement with reasonable effort to comply but not informing the government

  — Offense level: 4

- Knowing offense committed with willful blindness to legal requirement

  — Offense level: 5

- Knowing offense committed with knowledge of particular legal requirement without reasonable effort to comply

  — Offense level: 6

Background: For the third level of culpable knowledge (the one that warrants an offense level of 2) to be applicable, one would expect that for an offense committed with knowledge of the legal requirements the organizational defendant would immediately inform the government. For an offense committed without knowledge of applicable legal requirements, one would expect the organizational defendant to have informed the government promptly upon discovery of the violations.

Harm Foreseeable at Time Offense was Committed

The foreseeable harm given weight at sentencing should be limited to those emissions or discharges of pollutants or hazardous waste management practices which would have been enjoined if they were known to the government before they took place and which would have resulted in demonstrable harm to people or the environment.

— Offense level: 0-9

In assessing the nature and scope of foreseeable harm, the court should consider the following:

- Extent of Harm to People

The nature of demonstrable harm to people could include: permanent or life-threatening bodily injury, serious bodily injury, bodily injury, adverse health effects. The court should also consider the number of persons actually affected or at demonstrable risk of being affected. An increase in the base fine may be warranted where the threatened harm actually transpired and was serious.

- Extent of Harm to the Environment

There are a great variety of potential scenarios of potential environmental harm, ranging from relatively minor, temporary losses of biota to massive, permanent ecological despoliation.

- Harm foreseeable to reasonably competent person

If the harm foreseeable to a reasonably competent person in the position of the employee(s) who committed the violation is significantly greater than the harm foreseeable to the employee(s), an increase in the base fine amount may be warranted.

Background: The threshold definition of "harm" for the purposes of sentencing accounts for the fact that organizations are allowed, pursuant to permit, regulation, or without regulation, to emit or discharge pollutants and dispose of waste as a necessary part of otherwise acceptable economic activity. The government's or the court's decision not to enjoin otherwise violative emissions should be viewed as a reliable indicator that, on balance, the social utility to allowing a violation to occur or continue outweighs the incremental "environmental loading" that might happen prior to correction of the violation. If the event would not have been enjoined or, in the case of an ongoing emission, was not enjoined, then no additional weight should be added to the base fine culpable knowledge determination.

Under the structure, recordkeeping and reporting offenses do not require special treatment per se. Those recordkeeping or reporting offenses that are related to the perpetuation of violations giving rise to foreseeable harm would be regarded the same as any other offense that leads to or exacerbates foreseeable harm. Those that lead to no foreseeable harm should be treated like any other "purely regulatory" situations.

C. Modifications to Existing Adjustment Factors

1. <u>Collateral Consequences of a Conviction</u>: The following should be added to application note 3 to Section 8C2.8: "In an environmental case in which the conviction will result in an organization being barred from government contracting, a downward departure may be warranted."

2. <u>Prior Enforcement History:</u> The following should be added to application note 7 to Section 8C2.5: "In an environmental case, civil or administrative adjudications based on principles of strict liability or based purely on the doctrine of respondeat superior should not be counted as 'similar misconduct'".

3. <u>Remedial Costs</u>: Section 8C4.9 should be amended as follows: If the organization has paid off, has agreed to pay, or can show that it will be liable for remedial costs .... In such a case, a substantial fine may not be necessary in order to achieve adequate punishment and deterrence. This frequently may be an element of environmental cases.

SECTION 3
U.S. Environmental Protection Agency —
1986 *Environmental Auditing Policy Statement*

The following is the EPA's first policy on environmental auditing, published in 1986. It encourages the use of environmental auditing to help companies "achieve and maintain compliance" and identify environmental hazards.

25004 Federal Register/Vol. 51, No. 131/Wednesday, July 9, 1986/Notices

Environmental Protection Agency

[OPPE-FRL-3046-6]

Environmental Auditing Policy Statement

Agency: Environmental Protection Agency (EPA)

Action: Final Policy Statement

Summary: It is EPA policy to encourage the use of environmental auditing by regulated entities to help achieve and maintain compliance with environmental laws and regulations, as well as to help identify and correct unregulated environmental hazards. EPA first published this policy as interim guidance on November 8, 1985 (50 FR 46504). Based on comments received regarding the interim guidance, the Agency is issuing today's final policy statement with only minor changes.

This final policy statement specifically:

• Encourages regulated entities to develop, implement and upgrade environmental auditing programs;

• Discusses when the Agency may or may not request audit reports;

- Explains how EPA's inspection and enforcement activities may respond to regulated entities' efforts to assure compliance through auditing;
- Endorses environmental auditing at federal facilities;
- Encourages state and local environmental auditing initiatives; and
- Outlines elements of effective audit programs.

Environmental auditing includes a variety of compliance assessment techniques which go beyond those legally required and are used to identify actual and potential environmental problems. Effective environmental auditing can lead to higher levels of overall compliance and reduced risk to human health and the environment. EPA endorses the practice of environmental auditing and supports its accelerated use by regulated entities to help meet the goals of federal, state and local environmental requirements. However, the existence of an auditing program does not create any defense to, or otherwise limit, the responsibility of any regulated entity to comply with applicable regulatory requirements.

States are encouraged to adopt these or similar and equally effective policies in order to advance the use of environmental auditing on a consistent, nationwide basis.

Dates: This final policy statement is effective July 9, 1986.

For further information contact: Leonard Fleckenstein, Office of Policy, Planning, and Evaluation, 202-382-2726; or Cheryl Wasserman, Office of Enforcement and Compliance Monitoring, 202-382-7550.

Supplementary Information:

Environmental Auditing Policy Statement

I. Preamble

On November 8, 1985 EPA published an Environmental Auditing Policy Statement, effective as interim guidance, and solicited written comments until January 7, 1986.

Thirteen commenters submitted written comments. Eight were from private industry. Two commenters represented industry trade associations. One federal agency, one consulting firm and one law firm also submitted comments.

Twelve commenters addressed EPA requests for audit reports. Three comments per subject were received regarding inspections, enforcement response and elements of effective environmental auditing. One commenter addressed audit provisions as remedies in enforcement actions, one addressed environmental auditing at federal facilities, and one addressed the relationship of the policy statement to state or local regulatory agencies. Comments generally supported both the concept of a policy statement and the interim guidance, but raised specific concerns with respect to particular language and policy issued in sections of the guidance.

A. General Comments

Three commenters found the interim guidance to be constructive, balanced and effective at encouraging more and better environmental auditing.

Another commenter, while considering the policy on the whole to be constructive, felt that new and identifiable auditing "incentives" should be offered by EPA. Based on earlier comments received from

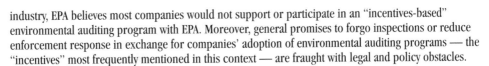

industry, EPA believes most companies would not support or participate in an "incentives-based" environmental auditing program with EPA. Moreover, general promises to forgo inspections or reduce enforcement response in exchange for companies' adoption of environmental auditing programs — the "incentives" most frequently mentioned in this context — are fraught with legal and policy obstacles.

Several commenters expressed concern that states or localities might use the interim guidance to *require* auditing. The Agency disagrees that the policy statement opens the way for states and localities to require auditing. No EPA policy can grant states or localities any more (or less) authority than they already possess. EPA believes that the interim guidance effectively encourages voluntary auditing. In fact, Section II.B. of the policy states: "because audit quality depends to a large degree on genuine management commitment to the program and its objectives, auditing should remain a *voluntary* program."

Another commenter suggested that EPA should not expect an audit to identify all potential problem areas or conclude that a problem identified in an audit reflects normal operations and procedures. EPA agrees that an audit report should clearly reflect these realities and should be written to point out the audit's limitations. However, since EPA will not routinely request audit reports, the Agency does not believe these concerns raise issues which need to be addressed in the policy statement.

A second concern expressed by the same commenter was that EPA should acknowledge that environmental audits are only part of a successful environmental management program and thus should not be expected to cover every environmental issue or solve all problems. EPA agrees and accordingly has amended the statement of purpose which appears at the end of this preamble.

Yet another commenter thought EPA should focus on environmental performance results (compliance or non-compliance), not on the processes or vehicles used to achieve those results. In general, EPA agrees with this statement and will continue to focus on environmental results. However, EPA also believes that such results can be improved through Agency efforts to identify and encourage effective environmental management practices, and will continue to encourage such practices in non-regulatory ways.

A final general comment recommended that EPA should sponsor seminars for small businesses on how to start auditing programs. EPA agrees that such seminars would be useful. However, since audit seminars already are available from several private sector organizations, EPA does not believe it should intervene in that market, with the possible exception of seminars for government agencies, especially federal agencies, for which EPA has a broad mandate under Executive Order 12088 to provide technical assistance for environmental compliance.

B. Requests for Reports

EPA received 12 comments regarding Agency requests for environmental audit reports, far more than on any other topic in the policy statement. One commenter felt that EPA struck an appropriate balance between respecting the need for self-evaluation with some measure of privacy, and allowing the Agency enough flexibility of inquiry to accomplish future statutory missions. However, most commenters expressed concern that the interim guidance did not go far enough to assuage corporate fears that EPA will use audit reports for environmental compliance "witch hunts." Several commenters suggested additional specific assurances regarding the circumstances under which EPA will request such reports.

One commenter recommended that EPA request audit reports only "when the Agency can show the information it needs to perform its statutory mission cannot be obtained from the monitoring, compliance or other data that is otherwise reportable and/or accessible to EPA, or where the Government deems an audit report material to a criminal investigation." EPA accepts this recommendation in part. The Agency believes it would not be in the best interest of human health and the environment to commit to making a "showing" of a compelling information need before ever requesting an audit report. While EPA may normally be willing to do so, the Agency cannot rule out in advance all circumstances in which such a showing may not be possible. However, it would be helpful to further clarify that a request for an audit report or a portion of a report normally will be made when needed information is not available by alternative means. Therefore, EPA has revised Section III.A., paragraph two and added the phrase: "and usually made where the information needed cannot be obtained from monitoring, reporting, or other data otherwise available to the Agency."

Another commenter suggested that (except in the case of criminal investigations) EPA should limit requests for audit documents to specific questions. By including the phrase "or relevant portions of a report" in Section III.A., EPA meant to emphasize it would not request an entire audit document when only a relevant portion would suffice. Likewise, EPA fully intends not to request even a portion of a report if needed information or data can be otherwise obtained. To further clarify this point EPA has added the phrase, "most likely focused on particular information needs rather than the entire report," to the second sentence of paragraph two of final Section III.A. now reads: "EPA's authority to request an audit report, or relevant portions thereof, will be exercised on a case-by-case basis where the Agency determines it is needed to accomplish a statutory mission or the Government deems it to be material to a criminal investigation. EPA expects such requests to be limited, most likely focused on particular information needs rather than the entire report, and usually made where the information needed cannot be obtained from monitoring, reporting or other data otherwise available to the Agency."

Other commenters recommended that EPA not request audit reports under any circumstances, that requests be "restricted to only those legally required," that requests be limited to criminal investigations, or that requests be made only when EPA has reason to believe "that the audit programs or reports are being used to conceal evidence of environmental non-compliance or otherwise being used in bad faith." EPA appreciates concerns underlying all of these comments and has considered each carefully. However, the Agency believes that these recommendations do not strike the appropriate balance between retaining the flexibility to accomplish EPA's statutory missions in future, unforeseen circumstances, and acknowledging regulated entities' need to self-evaluate environmental performance with some measure of privacy. Indeed, based on prime informal comments, the small number of formal comments received, and the even smaller number of adverse comments, EPA believes the final policy statement should remain largely unchanged from the interim version.

C. Elements of Effective Environmental Auditing

Three commenters expressed concerns regarding the seven general elements EPA outlined in the Appendix to the interim guidance.

One commenter noted that were EPA to further expand or more fully detail such elements, programs not specifically fulfilling each element would then be judged inadequate. EPA agrees that presenting highly specific and prescriptive auditing elements could be counter-productive by not taking into account numerous factors which vary extensively from one organization to another, but which may still result in effective auditing programs. Accordingly, EPA does not plan to expand or more fully detail these auditing elements.

Another commenter asserted that states and localities should be cautioned not to consider EPA's auditing elements as mandatory steps. The Agency is fully aware of this concern and in the interim guidance noted its strong opinion that "regulatory agencies should not attempt to prescribe the precise form and structure of regulated entities environmental management or auditing programs." While EPA cannot require state or local regulators to adopt this or similar policies, the Agency does strongly encourage them to do so, both in the interim and final policies.

A final commenter thought the Appendix too specifically prescribed what should and what should not be included in an auditing program. Other commenters, on the other hand, viewed the elements described as very general in nature. EPA agrees with these other commenters. The elements are in no way binding. Moreover, EPA believes that most mature, effective environmental auditing programs do incorporate each of these general elements in some form, and considers them useful yardsticks for those considering adopting or upgrading audit programs. For these reasons, EPA has not revised the Appendix in today's final policy statement.

D. Other Comments

Other significant comments addressed EPA inspection priorities for, and enforcement responses to, organizations with environmental auditing programs.

One commenter, stressing that audit programs are *internal* management tools, took exception to the phrase in the second paragraph of section III.B.1 of the interim guidance which states that environmental audits can 'complement' regulatory oversight. By using the word 'complement' in this context, EPA does not intend to imply that audit reports must be obtained by the Agency in order to supplement regulatory inspections. 'Complement' is used in a broad sense of being in addition to inspections and providing something (i.e., self-assessment) which otherwise would be lacking. To clarify this point EPA has added the phrase "by providing self-assessment to assure compliance" after "environmental audits may complement inspections" in this paragraph.

The same commenter also expressed concern that, as EPA sets inspection priorities, a company having an audit program could appear to be a 'poor performer' due to complete and accurate reporting when measured against a company which reports something less than required by law. EPA agrees that it is important to communicate this fact to Agency and state personnel, and will do so. However, the Agency does not believe a change in the policy statement is necessary.

A further comment suggested EPA should commit to take auditing programs into account when assessing all enforcement actions. However, in order to maintain enforcement flexibility under varied circumstances, the Agency cannot promise reduced enforcement responses to violations at all audited facilities when other factors may be overriding. Therefore, the policy statement continues to state that EPA may exercise its discretion to consider auditing programs as evidence of honest and genuine efforts to assure compliance, which would then be taken into account in fashioning enforcement responses to violations.

A final commenter suggested the phrase "expeditiously correct environmental problems" not be used in the enforcement concept since it implied EPA would use an entity's record of correcting nonregulated matters when evaluating regulatory violations. EPA did not intend for such an inference to be made. EPA intended the term "environmental problems" to refer to the underlying circumstances which eventually lead up to the violations. To clarify this point, EPA is revising the first two sentences of the paragraph to which this comment refers by changing "environmental problems" to "violations and underlying environmental problems" in the first sentence and to "underlying environmental problems" in the second sentence.

In a separate development EPA is preparing an update of its January 1984 *Federal Facilities Compliance Strategy*, which is referenced in section III.C. of the auditing policy. The Strategy should be completed and available on request from EPA's Office of Federal Activities later this year.

EPA thanks all commenters for responding to the November 8, 1985 publication. Today's notice is being issued to inform regulated entities and the public of EPA's final policy toward environmental auditing. This policy was developed to help (a) encourage regulated entities to institutionalize effective audit practices as one means of improving compliance and sound environmental management, and (b) guide internal EPA actions directly related to regulated entities' environmental auditing programs.

EPA will evaluate implementation of this final policy to ensure it meets the above goals and continues to encourage better environmental management, while strengthening the Agency's own efforts to monitor and enforce compliance with environmental requirements.

II. General EPA Policy on Environmental Auditing

A. Introduction

Environmental auditing is a systematic, documented, periodic, and objective review by regulated entities[4] of facility operations and practices related to meeting environmental requirements. Audits can be designed to accomplish any or all of the following: verify compliance with environmental requirements; evaluate the effectiveness of environmental management systems already in place; or assess risks from regulated and unregulated materials and practices.

Auditing serves as a quality assurance check to help improve the effectiveness of basic environmental management by verifying that management practices are in place, functioning and adequate. Environmental audits evaluate, and are not a substitute for, direct compliance activities such as obtaining permits, installing controls, monitoring compliance, reporting violations, and keeping records. Environmental auditing may verify but does not include activities required by law, regulation or permit (e.g., continuous emissions monitoring, composite correction plans at wastewater treatment plants, etc.). Audits do not in any way replace regulatory agency inspections. However, environmental audits can improve compliance by complementing conventional federal, state and local oversight.

The appendix to this policy statement outlines some basic elements of environmental auditing (e.g., auditor independence and top management support) for use by those considering implementation of effective auditing programs to help achieve and maintain compliance. Additional information on environmental auditing practices can be found in various published materials.[5] Environmental auditing has developed for sound business reasons, particularly as a means of helping regulated entities manage pollution control affirmatively over time instead of reacting to crises. Auditing can result in improved facility environmental performance, help communicate effective solutions to common environmental problems, focus facility managers' attention on current and upcoming regulatory requirements, and generate protocols and checklists which help facilities better manage themselves. Auditing also can result in better-integrated management of environmental hazards, since auditors frequently identify environmental liabilities which go beyond regulatory compliance. Companies, public entities and federal facilities have employed a variety of environmental auditing practices in recent years. Several hundred major firms in diverse industries now have environmental auditing programs, although they often are known by other names such as assessment, survey, surveillance, review or appraisal.

While auditing has demonstrated its usefulness to those with audit programs, many others still do not audit. Clarification of EPA's position regarding auditing may help encourage regulated entities to establish audit programs or upgrade systems already in place.

B. EPA Encourages the Use of Environmental Auditing

EPA encourages regulated entities to adopt sound environmental management practices to improve environmental performance. In particular, EPA encourages regulated entities subject to environmental regulations to institute environmental auditing programs to help ensure the adequacy of internal systems to achieve, maintain and monitor compliance. Implementation of environmental auditing programs can result in better identification, resolution and avoidance of environmental problems, as well as improvements to management practices. Audits can be conducted effectively by independent internal or third-party auditors. Larger organizations generally have greater resources to devote to an internal audit team, while smaller entities might be more likely to use outside auditors.

Regulated entities are responsible for taking all necessary steps to ensure compliance with environmental requirements, whether or not they adopt audit programs. Although environmental laws do not require a regulated facility to have an auditing program, ultimate responsibility for the environmental performance of the facility lies with top management, which therefore has a strong incentive to use reasonable means, such as environmental auditing, to secure reliable information of facility compliance status.

EPA does not intend to dictate or interfere with the environmental management practices of private or public organizations. Nor does EPA intend to mandate auditing (though in certain instances EPA may seek to include provisions for environmental auditing as part of settlement agreements, as noted below). Because environmental auditing systems have been widely adopted on a voluntary basis in the past, and because audit quality depends to a large degree upon genuine management commitment to the program and its objectives, auditing should remain a voluntary activity.

III. EPA Policy on Specific Environmental Auditing Issues

A. Agency Requests for Audit Reports

EPA has broad statutory authority to request relevant information on the environmental status of regulated entities. However, EPA believes routine Agency requests for audit reports[6] could inhibit auditing in the long run, decreasing both the quantity and quality of audits conducted. Therefore, as a matter of policy, EPA will not routinely request environmental audit reports.

EPA's authority to request an audit report, or relevant portions thereof, will be exercised on a case-by-case basis where the Agency determines it is needed to accomplish a statutory mission, or where the Government deems it to be material to a criminal investigation. EPA expects such requests to be limited, most likely focused on particular information needs rather than the entire report, and usually made where the information needed cannot be obtained from monitoring, reporting or other data otherwise available to the Agency. Examples would likely include situations where: audits are conducted under consent decrees or other settlement agreements; a company has placed its management practices at issue by raising them as a defense; or state of mind or intent are a relevant element of inquiry, such as during a criminal investigation. This list is illustrative rather than exhaustive, since there doubtless will be other situations not subject to prediction, in which audit reports rather than information may be required.

EPA acknowledges regulated entities need to self-evaluate environmental performance with some measure of privacy and encourages such activity. However, audit reports may not shield monitoring, compliance, or other information that would otherwise be reportable and/or accessible to EPA, even if there is no explicit 'requirement' to generate that data.[7] Thus, this policy does not alter regulated entities, existing or future obligations to monitor, record or report information required under environmental statutes, regulations or permits, or to allow EPA access to that information. Nor does this policy alter EPA's authority to request and receive any relevant information—including that contained in audit reports—under various environmental statutes (e.g., Clean Water Act section 308, Clean Air Act sections 114 and 208) or in other administrative or judicial proceedings.

Regulated entities also should be aware that certain audit findings may by law have to be reported to government agencies. However, in addition to any such requirements, EPA encourages regulated entities to notify appropriate State or Federal officials of findings which suggest significant environmental or public health risks, even when not specifically required to do so.

B. EPA Response to Environmental Auditing

1. General Policy

EPA will not promise to forgo inspections, reduce enforcement responses, or offer other such incentives in exchange for implementation of environmental auditing or other sound environmental management practices. Indeed, a credible enforcement program provides a strong incentive for regulated entities to audit.

Regulatory agencies have an obligation to assess source compliance status independently and cannot eliminate inspections for particular firms or classes of firms. Although environmental audits may complement inspections by providing self-assessment to assure compliance, they are in no way a substitute for regulatory oversight. Moreover, certain statutes (e.g. RCRA) and Agency policies establish minimum facility inspection frequencies to which EPA will adhere.

However, EPA will continue to address environmental problems on a priority basis and will consequently inspect facilities with poor environmental records and practices more frequently. Since effective environmental auditing helps management identify and promptly correct actual or potential problems, audited facilities, environmental performance should improve. Thus, while EPA inspections of self-audited facilities will continue, to the extent that compliance performance is considered in setting inspection priorities, facilities with a good compliance history may be subject to fewer inspections.

In fashioning enforcement responses to violations, EPA policy is to take into account, on a case-by-case basis, the honest and genuine efforts of regulated entities to avoid and promptly correct violations and underlying environmental problems. When regulated entities take reasonable precautions to avoid noncompliance, expeditiously correct underlying environmental problems discovered through audits or other means, and implement measures to prevent their recurrence, EPA may exercise its discretion to consider such actions as honest and genuine efforts to assure compliance. Such consideration applies particularly when a regulated entity promptly reports violations or compliance data which otherwise were not required to be recorded or reported to EPA.

2. Audit Provisions as Remedies in Enforcement Actions

EPA may propose environmental auditing provisions in consent decrees and in other settlement negotiations where auditing could provide a remedy for identified problems and reduce the likelihood of similar problems recurring in the future.[8] Environmental auditing provisions are most likely to be proposed in settlement negotiations where:

- A pattern of violations can be attributed at least in part to the absence or poor functioning of an environmental management system; or

- The type or nature of violations indicates a likelihood that similar noncompliance problems may exist or occur elsewhere in the facility or at other facilities operated by the regulated entity.

Through this consent decree approach and other means, EPA may consider how to encourage effective auditing by publicly owned sewage treatment works (POTWs). POTWs often have compliance problems related to operation and maintenance procedures which can be addressed effectively through the use of environmental auditing. Under its National Municipal Policy EPA already is requiring many POTWs to develop composite correction plans to identify and correct compliance problems.

C. Environmental Auditing at Federal Facilities

EPA encourages all federal agencies subject to environmental laws and regulations to institute environmental auditing systems to help ensure the adequacy of internal systems to achieve, maintain and monitor compliance. Environmental auditing at federal facilities can be an effective supplement to EPA and state inspections. Such federal facility environmental audit programs should be structured to promptly identify environmental problems and expeditiously develop schedules for remedial action.

To the extent feasible, EPA will provide technical assistance to help federal agencies design and initiate audit programs. Where appropriate, EPA will enter into agreements with other agencies to clarify the respective roles, responsibilities and commitments of each agency in conducting and responding to federal facility environmental audits.

With respect to inspection of self-audited facilities (see section III.B.1 above) and requests for audit reports (see section III.A above) EPA generally will respond to environmental audits by federal facilities in the same manner as it does for other regulated entities, in keeping with the spirit and intent of Executive Order 12088 and the EPA Federal Facilities Compliance Strategy (January 1984, update forthcoming in late 1986). Federal agencies should, however, be aware that the Freedom of Information Act will govern any disclosure of audit reports or audit-generated information requested from federal agencies by the public.

When federal agencies discover significant violations through an environmental audit, EPA encourages them to submit the related audit findings and remedial action plans expeditiously to the applicable IPA regional office (and responsible state agencies where appropriate) even when not specifically required to do so. EPA will review the audit findings and action plans and either provide written approval or negotiate a Federal Facilities Compliance Agreement. EPA will utilize the escalation procedures provided in Executive Order 12088 and the EPA Federal Facilities Compliance Strategy only when agreement between agencies cannot be reached. In any event, federal agencies are expected to report pollution abatement projects involving costs (necessary to correct problems discovered through the audit) to EPA in accordance with OMB Circular A-106. Upon request and in appropriate circumstances, EPA will assist affected federal agencies through coordination of any public release of audit findings with approved action plans once agreement has been reached.

IV. Relationship to State or Local Regulatory Agencies

State and local regulatory agencies have independent jurisdiction over regulated entities. EPA encourages them to adopt these or similar policies, in order to advance the use of effective environmental auditing in a consistent manner.

EPA recognizes that some states have already undertaken environmental auditing initiatives which differ somewhat from this policy. Other states also may want to develop auditing policies which accommodate their particular needs or circumstances. Nothing in this policy statement is intended to preempt or preclude states from developing other approaches to environmental auditing. EPA encourages state and local authorities to consider the basic principles which guided the Agency in developing this policy:

- Regulated entities must continue to report or record compliance information required under existing statutes or regulations, regardless of whether such information is generated by an environmental audit or contained in an audit report. Required information cannot be withheld merely because it is generated by an audit rather than by some other means.

- Regulatory agencies cannot make promises to forgo or limit enforcement action against a particular facility or class of facilities in exchange for the use of environmental auditing systems. However, such agencies may use their discretion to adjust enforcement actions on a case-by-case basis in response to honest and genuine efforts by regulated entities to assure environmental compliance.

- When setting inspection priorities regulatory agencies should focus to the extent possible on compliance performance and environmental results.

- Regulatory agencies must continue to meet minimum program requirements (e.g., minimum inspection requirements etc.).

- Regulatory agencies should not attempt to prescribe the precise form and structure of regulated entities' environmental management or auditing programs.

An effective state/federal partnership is needed to accomplish the mutual goal of achieving and maintaining high levels of compliance with environmental laws and regulations. The greater the consistency between state or local policies and this federal response to environmental auditing, the greater the degree to which sound auditing practices might be adopted and compliance levels improve.

Dated: June 28, 1986.

Lee M. Thomas

Administrator

Appendix — Elements of Effective Environmental Auditing Programs

Introduction

Environmental auditing is a systematic, documented, periodic and objective review by a regulated entity of facility operations and practices related to meeting environmental requirements.

Private sector environmental audits of facilities have been conducted for several years and have taken a variety of forms, in part to accommodate unique organizational structures and circumstances. Nevertheless, effective environmental audits appear to have certain discernible elements in common with other kinds of audits. Standards for internal audits have been documented extensively. The elements outlined below draw heavily on two of these documents: *Compendium of Audit Standards* (1983, Walter Willborn, American Society for Quality Control) and *Standards for the Professional Practice of Internal Auditing* (1981, The Institute of Internal Auditors Inc.). They also reflect Agency analyses conducted over the last several years.

Performance-oriented auditing elements are outlined here to help accomplish several objectives. A general description of features of effective, mature audit programs can help those starting audit programs, especially federal agencies and smaller businesses. These elements also indicate the attributes of auditing EPA generally considers important to ensure program effectiveness. Regulatory agencies may use these elements in negotiating environmental auditing provisions for consent decrees. Finally, these elements can help guide states and localities considering auditing initiatives.

An effective environmental auditing system will likely include the following general elements:

I. Explicit top management support for environmental auditing and commitment to follow-up on audit findings. Management support may be demonstrated by a written policy articulating upper management support for the auditing program and for compliance with all pertinent requirements, including corporate policies and permit requirements as well as federal, state and local statutes and regulations.

Management support for the auditing program also should be demonstrated by an explicit written commitment to follow-up on audit findings to correct identified problems and prevent their recurrence.

II. An environmental auditing function independent of audited activities. The status or organizational locus of environmental auditors should be sufficient to ensure objective and unobstructed inquiry, observation and testing. Auditor objectivity should not be impaired by personal relationships, financial or other conflicts of interest, interference with free inquiry or judgment, or fear of potential retribution.

III. Adequate team staffing and auditor training. Environmental auditors should possess or have ready access to the knowledge, skills, and disciplines needed to accomplish audit objectives. Each individual auditor should comply with the company's professional standards of conduct. Auditors, whether full-time or part-time, should maintain their technical and analytical competence through continuing education and training.

IV. Explicit audit program objectives, scope, resources and frequency. At a minimum, audit objectives should include assessing compliance with applicable environmental laws and evaluating the adequacy of internal compliance policies, procedure, and personnel training programs to ensure continued compliance.

Audits should be based on a process which provides auditors: all corporate policies, permits, and federal, state, and local regulations pertinent to the facility; and checklists or protocols addressing specific features that should be evaluated by auditors.

Explicit written audit procedures generally should be used for planning audits, establishing audit scope, examining and evaluating audit findings, communicating audit results, and following-up.

V. A process which collects, analyzes, interprets and documents information sufficient to achieve audit objectives. Information should be collected before and during an onsite visit regarding environmental compliance(1), environmental management effectiveness(2), and other matters(3), related to audit objectives and scope. This information should be sufficient, reliable relevant and useful to provide a sound basis for audit findings and recommendations.

a. Sufficient information is factual, adequate and convincing so that a prudent, informed person would be likely to reach the same conclusions as the auditor.

b. Reliable information is the best attainable through use of appropriate audit techniques.

c. Relevant information supports audit findings and recommendations and is consistent with the objectives for the audit.

d. Useful information helps the organization meet its goals.

The audit process should include a periodic review of the reliability and integrity of this information and the means used to identify, measure, classify and report it. Audit procedures, including the testing and sampling techniques employed, should be selected in advance to the extent practical, and expanded or altered if circumstances warrant. The process of collecting, analyzing, interpreting, and documenting information should provide reasonable assurance that audit objectivity is maintained and audit goals are met.

VI. A process which includes specific procedures to promptly prepare candid, clear and appropriate written reports on audit findings corrective actions, and schedules for implementation. Procedures should be in place to ensure that such information is communicated to managers, including facility and corporate management, who can evaluate the information and ensure correction of identified problems. Procedures also should be in place for determining what internal findings are reportable to state or federal agencies.

VII. A process which includes quality assurance procedures to assure the accuracy and thoroughness of environmental audits. Quality assurance may be accomplished through supervision, independent internal reviews external reviews, or a combination of these approaches.

Footnotes to EPA Policy Appendix

1) A comprehensive assessment of compliance with federal environmental regulations requires an analysis of facility performance against numerous environmental statutes and implementing regulations. These statutes include:

- Resource Conservation and Recovery Act
- Federal Water Pollution Control Act Clean Air Act,
- Hazardous Materials Transportation Act,
- Toxic Substances Control Act,
- Comprehensive Environmental Response Compensation and Liability Act,
- Safe Drinking Water Act,
- Federal Insecticide, Fungicide and Rodenticide Act,
- Marine Protection Research and Sanctuaries Act,
- Uranium Mill Tailings Radiation Control Act.

In addition, state and local government are likely to have their own environmental laws. Many states have been delegated authority to administer federal programs. Many local governments' building, fire, safety and health codes also have environmental requirements relevant to an audit evaluation.

2) An environmental audit could go well beyond the type of compliance assessment normally conducted during regulatory inspections, for example, by evaluating policies and practices, regardless of whether they are part of the environmental system or the operating and maintenance procedures. Specifically, audits can evaluate the extent to which systems or procedures:

1. Develop organizational environmental policies which; a. implement regulatory requirements; b. provide management guidance for environmental hazards not specifically addressed in regulations;

2. Train and motivate facility personnel to work in an environmentally-acceptable manner and to understand and comply with government regulations and the entity's environmental policy;

3. Communicate relevant environmental developments expeditiously to facility and other personnel;

4. Communicate effectively with government and the public regarding serious environmental incidents:

5. Require third parties working for, with or on behalf of the organization to follow its environmental procedures;

6. Make proficient personnel available at all times to carry out environmental (especially emergency) procedures;

7. Incorporate environmental protection into written operating procedures;

8. Apply best management practices and operating procedures including "good housekeeping" techniques;

9. Institute preventive and corrective maintenance systems to minimize actual and potential environmental harm;

10. Utilize best available process and control technologies;

11. Use most-effective sampling and monitoring techniques test methods recordkeeping systems or reporting protocols (beyond minimum legal requirements);

12. Evaluate causes behind any serious environmental incidents and establish procedures to avoid recurrence;

13. Exploit source reduction, recycle and reuse potential wherever practical; and

14. Substitute materials or processes to allow use of the least-hazardous substances feasible.

3) Auditors could also assess environmental risks and uncertainties.

SECTION 4
U.S. Environmental Protection Agency — 1995 *Incentives For Self-Policing: Discovery, Disclosure, Correction and Prevention of Violations*

The following policy statement from EPA outlines possible incentives to regulated entities that to voluntarily discover, and disclose and correct regulatory violations.

Agency: Environmental Protection Agency (EPA)

Action: Final Policy Statement

Summary: The Environmental Protection Agency (EPA) today (December 22, 1995) issues its final policy to enhance protection of human health and the environment by encouraging regulated entities to voluntarily discover, and disclose and correct violations of environmental requirements. Incentives include eliminating or substantially reducing the gravity component of civil penalties and not recommending cases for criminal prosecution where specified conditions are met, to those who voluntarily self-disclose and promptly correct violations. The policy also restates EPA's long-standing practice of not requesting voluntary audit reports to trigger enforcement investigations. This policy was developed in close consultation with the U.S. Department of Justice, states, public interest groups and the regulated community, and will be applied uniformly by the Agency's enforcement programs.

Dates: This policy is effective 30 days after publication.

For further information contact: Additional documentation relating to the development of this policy is contained in the environmental auditing public docket. Documents from the docket may be obtained by calling 202-260-7548, requesting an index to docket #C-94-01, and faxing document requests to 202-260-4400. Hours of operation are 8 a.m. to 5:30 p.m., Monday through Friday, except legal holidays. Additional contacts are Robert Fentress or Brian Riedel, at 202-564-2280.

Supplementary information:

I. Explanation of Policy

A. Introduction

The Environmental Protection Agency today issues its final policy to enhance protection of human health and the environment by encouraging regulated entities to discover voluntarily, disclose, correct and prevent violations of federal environmental law. Effective 30 days from today, where violations are found through voluntary environmental audits or efforts that reflect a regulated entity's due diligence, and are promptly disclosed and expeditiously corrected, EPA will not seek gravity-based (i.e., non-economic benefit) penalties and will generally not recommend criminal prosecution against the regulated entity. EPA will reduce gravity-based penalties by 75% for violations that are voluntarily discovered, and are promptly disclosed and corrected, even if not found through a formal audit or due diligence. Finally, the policy restates EPA's long-held policy and practice to refrain from routine requests for environmental audit reports.

The policy includes important safeguards to deter irresponsible behavior and protect the public and environment. For example, in addition to prompt disclosure and expeditious correction, the policy requires companies to act to prevent recurrence of the violation and to remedy any environmental harm which may have occurred. Repeated violations or those which result in actual harm or may present imminent and substantial endangerment are not eligible for relief under this policy, and companies will not be allowed to gain an economic advantage over their competitors by delaying their investment in compliance. Corporations remain criminally liable for violations that result from conscious disregard of their obligations under the law, and individuals are liable for criminal misconduct.

The issuance of this policy concludes EPA's eighteen-month public evaluation of the optimum way to encourage voluntary self-policing while preserving fair and effective enforcement. The incentives, conditions and exceptions announced today reflect thoughtful suggestions from the Department of Justice, state attorneys general and local prosecutors, state environmental agencies, the regulated community, and public interest organizations. EPA believes that it has found a balanced and responsible approach, and will conduct a study within three years to determine the effectiveness of this policy.

B. Public Process

One of the Environmental Protection Agency's most important responsibilities is ensuring compliance with federal laws that protect public health and safeguard the environment. Effective deterrence requires inspecting, bringing penalty actions and securing compliance and remediation of harm. But EPA realizes that achieving compliance also requires the cooperation of thousands of businesses and other regulated entities subject to these requirements. Accordingly, in May of 1994, the Administrator asked the Office of Enforcement and Compliance Assurance (OECA) to determine whether additional incentives were needed to encourage voluntary disclosure and correction of violations uncovered during environmental audits.

EPA began its evaluation with a two-day public meeting in July of 1994, in Washington, D.C., followed by a two-day meeting in San Francisco on January 19, 1995 with stakeholders from industry, trade groups, state environmental commissioners and attorneys general, district attorneys, public interest organizations and professional environmental auditors. The Agency also established and maintained a public docket of testimony presented at these meetings and all comment and correspondence submitted to EPA by outside parties on this issue.

In addition to considering opinion and information from stakeholders, the Agency examined other federal and state policies related to self-policing, self-disclosure and correction. The Agency also considered relevant surveys on auditing practices in the private sector. EPA completed the first stage of this effort with the announcement of an interim policy on April 3 of this year, which defined conditions under which EPA would reduce civil penalties and not recommend criminal prosecution for companies that audited, disclosed, and corrected violations.

Interested parties were asked to submit comment on the interim policy by June 30 of this year (60 Fed.Reg 16875), and EPA received over 300 responses from a wide variety of private and public organizations. (Comments on the interim audit policy are contained in the Auditing Policy Docket, hereinafter, "Docket".) Further, the American Bar Association SONREEL Subcommittee hosted five days of dialogue with representatives from the regulated industry, states and public interest organizations in June and September of this year, which identified options for strengthening the interim policy. The changes to the interim policy announced today reflect insight gained through comments submitted to EPA, the ABA dialogue, and the Agency's practical experience implementing the interim policy.

C. Purpose

This policy is designed to encourage greater compliance with laws and regulations that protect human health and the environment. It promotes a higher standard of self-policing by waiving gravity-based penalties for violations that are promptly disclosed and corrected, and which were discovered through voluntary audits or compliance management systems that demonstrate due diligence. To further promote compliance, the policy reduces gravity-based penalties by 75% for any violation voluntarily discovered and promptly disclosed and corrected, even if not found through an audit or compliance management system.

EPA's enforcement program provides a strong incentive for responsible behavior by imposing stiff sanctions for noncompliance. Enforcement has contributed to the dramatic expansion of environmental auditing measured in numerous recent surveys. For example, more than 90% of the corporate respondents to a 1995 Price-Waterhouse survey who conduct audits said that one of the reasons they did so was to find and correct violations before they were found by government inspectors. (A copy of the Price-Waterhouse survey is contained in the Docket as document VIII-A-76.)

At the same time, because government resources are limited, maximum compliance cannot be achieved without active efforts by the regulated community to police themselves. More than half of the respondents to the same 1995 Price-Waterhouse survey said that they would expand environmental auditing in exchange for reduced penalties for violations discovered and corrected. While many companies already audit or have compliance management programs, EPA believes that the incentives offered in this policy will improve the frequency and quality of these self-monitoring efforts.

D. Incentives for Self-policing

Section C of EPA's policy identifies the major incentives that EPA will provide to encourage self-policing, self-disclosure, and prompt self-correction. These include not seeking gravity-based civil penalties or reducing them by 75%, declining to recommend criminal prosecution for regulated entities that self-police, and refraining from routine requests for audits. (As noted in Section C of the policy, EPA has refrained from making routine requests for audit reports since issuance of its 1986 policy on environmental auditing.)

1. Eliminating Gravity-Based Penalties

Under Section C(1) of the policy, EPA will not seek gravity-based penalties for violations found through auditing that are promptly disclosed and corrected. Gravity-based penalties will also be waived for violations found through any documented procedure for self-policing, where the company can show that it has a compliance management program that meets the criteria for due diligence in Section B of the policy.

Gravity-based penalties (defined in Section B of the policy) generally reflect the seriousness of the violator's behavior. EPA has elected to waive such penalties for violations discovered through due diligence or environmental audits, recognizing that these voluntary efforts play a critical role in protecting human health and the environment by identifying, correcting and ultimately preventing violations. All of the conditions set forth in Section D, which include prompt disclosure and expeditious correction, must be satisfied for gravity-based penalties to be waived.

As in the interim policy, EPA reserves the right to collect any economic benefit that may have been realized as a result of noncompliance, even where companies meet all other conditions of the policy. Economic benefit may be waived, however, where the Agency determines that it is insignificant.

After considering public comment, EPA has decided to retain the discretion to recover economic benefit for two reasons. First, it provides an incentive to comply on time. Taxpayers expect to pay interest or a penalty fee if their tax payments are late; the same principle should apply to corporations that have delayed their investment in compliance. Second, it is fair because it protects responsible companies from being undercut by their noncomplying competitors, thereby preserving a level playing field. The concept of recovering economic benefit was supported in public comments by many stakeholders, including industry representatives (see, e.g., Docket, II-F-39, II-F-28, and II-F-18).

2. 75% Reduction of Gravity

The policy appropriately limits the complete waiver of gravity-based civil penalties to companies that meet the higher standard of environmental auditing or systematic compliance management. However, to provide additional encouragement for the kind of self-policing that benefits the public, gravity-based penalties will be reduced by 75% for a violation that is voluntarily discovered, promptly disclosed and expeditiously corrected, even if it was not found through an environmental audit and the company cannot document due diligence. EPA expects that this will encourage companies to come forward and work with the Agency to resolve environmental problems and begin to develop an effective compliance management program.

Gravity-based penalties will be reduced 75% only where the company meets all conditions in Sections D(2) through D(9). EPA has eliminated language from the interim policy indicating that penalties may be reduced "up to" 75% where "most" conditions are met, because the Agency believes that all of the conditions in D(2) through D(9) are reasonable and essential to achieving compliance. This change also responds to requests for greater clarity and predictability.

3. No Recommendations for Criminal Prosecution

EPA has never recommended criminal prosecution of a regulated entity based on voluntary disclosure of violations discovered through audits and disclosed to the government before an investigation was already under way. Thus, EPA will not recommend criminal prosecution for a regulated entity that uncovers violations through environmental audits or due diligence, promptly discloses and expeditiously corrects those violations, and meets all other conditions of Section D of the policy.

This policy is limited to good actors, and therefore has important limitations. It will not apply, for example, where corporate officials are consciously involved in or willfully blind to violations, or conceal or condone noncompliance. Since the regulated entity must satisfy all of the conditions of Section D of the policy, violations that caused serious harm or which may pose imminent and substantial endangerment to human health or the environment are not covered by this policy. Finally, EPA reserves the right to recommend prosecution for the criminal conduct of any culpable individual.

Even where all of the conditions of this policy are not met, however, it is important to remember that EPA may decline to recommend prosecution of a company or individual for many other reasons under other Agency enforcement policies. For example, the Agency may decline to recommend prosecution where there is no significant harm or culpability and the individual or corporate defendant has cooperated fully.

Where a company has met the conditions for avoiding a recommendation for criminal prosecution under this policy, it will not face any civil liability for gravity-based penalties. That is because the same conditions for discovery, disclosure, and correction apply in both cases. This represents a clarification of the interim policy, not a substantive change.

4. No Routine Requests for Audits

EPA is reaffirming its policy, in effect since 1986, to refrain from routine requests for audits. Eighteen months of public testimony and debate have produced no evidence that the Agency has deviated, or should deviate, from this policy.

If the Agency has independent evidence of a violation, it may seek information needed to establish the extent and nature of the problem and the degree of culpability. In general, however, an audit which results in prompt correction clearly will reduce liability, not expand it. Furthermore, a review of the criminal docket did not reveal a single criminal prosecution for violations discovered as a result of an audit self-disclosed to the government.

E. Conditions

Section D describes the nine conditions that a regulated entity must meet in order for the Agency not to seek (or to reduce) gravity-based penalties under the policy. As explained in the Summary above, regulated entities that meet all nine conditions will not face gravity-based civil penalties, and will generally not have to fear criminal prosecution. Where the regulated entity meets all of the conditions except the first (D(1)), EPA will reduce gravity-based penalties by 75%.

1. Discovery of the Violation Through an Environmental Audit or Due Diligence

Under Section D(1), the violation must have been discovered through either a) an environmental audit that is systematic, objective, and periodic as defined in the 1986 audit policy, or b) a documented, systematic procedure or practice which reflects the regulated entity's due diligence in preventing, detecting, and correcting violations. The interim policy provided full credit for any violation found through "voluntary self-evaluation," even if the evaluation did not constitute an audit. In order to receive full credit under the final policy, any self-evaluation that is not an audit must be part of a "due diligence" program. Both "environmental audit" and "due diligence" are defined in Section B of the policy.

Where the violation is discovered through a "systematic procedure or practice" which is not an audit, the regulated entity will be asked to document how its program reflects the criteria for due diligence as defined in Section B of the policy. These criteria, which are adapted from existing codes of practice such as the 1991 Criminal Sentencing Guidelines, were fully discussed during the ABA dialogue. The criteria are flexible enough to accommodate different types and sizes of businesses. The Agency recognizes that a variety of compliance management programs may develop under the due diligence criteria, and will use its review under this policy to determine whether basic criteria have been met.

Compliance management programs which train and motivate production staff to prevent, detect and correct violations on a daily basis are a valuable complement to periodic auditing. The policy is responsive to recommendations received during public comment and from the ABA dialogue to give compliance management efforts which meet the criteria for due diligence the same penalty reduction offered for environmental audits. (See, e.g., II-F-39, II-E-18, and II-G-18 in the Docket.)

EPA may require as a condition of penalty mitigation that a description of the regulated entity's due diligence efforts be made publicly available. The Agency added this provision in response to suggestions from environmental groups, and believes that the availability of such information will allow the public to judge the adequacy of compliance management systems, lead to enhanced compliance, and foster greater public trust in the integrity of compliance management systems.

2. Voluntary Discovery and Prompt Disclosure

Under Section D(2) of the final policy, the violation must have been identified voluntarily, and not through a monitoring, sampling, or auditing procedure that is required by statute, regulation, permit, judicial or administrative order, or consent agreement. Section D(4) requires that disclosure of the violation be prompt and in writing. To avoid confusion and respond to state requests for greater clarity, disclosures under this policy should be made to EPA. The Agency will work closely with states in implementing the policy.

The requirement that discovery of the violation be voluntary is consistent with proposed federal and state bills which would reward those discoveries that the regulated entity can legitimately attribute to its own voluntary efforts.

The policy gives three specific examples of discovery that would not be voluntary, and therefore would not be eligible for penalty mitigation: emissions violations detected through a required continuous emissions monitor, violations of NPDES discharge limits found through prescribed monitoring, and violations discovered through a compliance audit required to be performed by the terms of a consent order or settlement agreement.

The final policy generally applies to any violation that is voluntarily discovered, regardless of whether the violation is required to be reported. This definition responds to comments pointing out that reporting requirements are extensive, and that excluding them from the policy's scope would severely limit the incentive for self-policing (see, e.g., II-C-48 in the Docket).

The Agency wishes to emphasize that the integrity of federal environmental law depends upon timely and accurate reporting. The public relies on timely and accurate reports from the regulated community, not only to measure compliance but to evaluate health or environmental risk and gauge progress in reducing pollutant loadings. EPA expects the policy to encourage the kind of vigorous self-policing that will serve these objectives, and not to provide an excuse for delayed reporting. Where violations of reporting requirements are voluntarily discovered, they must be promptly reported (as discussed below). Where a failure to report results in imminent and substantial endangerment or serious harm, that violation is not covered under this policy (see Condition D(8)). The policy also requires the regulated entity to prevent recurrence of the violation, to ensure that noncompliance with reporting requirements is not repeated. EPA will closely scrutinize the effect of the policy in furthering the public interest in timely and accurate reports from the regulated community.

Under Section D(4), disclosure of the violation should be made within 10 days of its discovery, and in writing to EPA. Where a statute or regulation requires reporting be made in less than 10 days, disclosure should be made within the time limit established by law. Where reporting within ten days is not practical because the violation is complex and compliance cannot be determined within that period, the Agency may accept later disclosures if the circumstances do not present a serious threat and the regulated entity meets its burden of showing that the additional time was needed to determine compliance status.

This condition recognizes that it is critical for EPA to get timely reporting of violations in order that it might have clear notice of the violations and the opportunity to respond if necessary, as well as an accurate picture of a given facility's compliance record. Prompt disclosure is also evidence of the regulated entity's good faith in wanting to achieve or return to compliance as soon as possible.

In the final policy, the Agency has added the words, "or may have occurred," to the sentence, "The regulated entity fully discloses that a specific violation has occurred, or may have occurred ..." This change, which was made in response to comments received, clarifies that where an entity has some doubt about the existence of a violation, the recommended course is for it to disclose and allow the regulatory authorities to make a definitive determination.

In general, the Freedom of Information Act will govern the Agency's release of disclosures made pursuant to this policy. EPA will, independently of FOIA, make publicly available any compliance agreements reached under the policy (see Section H of the policy), as well as descriptions of due diligence programs submitted under Section D.1 of the Policy. Any material claimed to be Confidential Business Information will be treated in accordance with EPA regulations at 40 C.F.R. Part 2.

3. Discovery and Disclosure Independent of Government or Third Party Plaintiff

Under Section D(3), in order to be "voluntary", the violation must be identified and disclosed by the regulated entity prior to: the commencement of a federal state or local agency inspection, investigation, or information request; notice of a citizen suit; legal complaint by a third party; the reporting of the violation to EPA by a "whistleblower" employee; and imminent discovery of the violation by a regulatory agency.

This condition means that regulated entities must have taken the initiative to find violations and promptly report them, rather than reacting to knowledge of a pending enforcement action or third-party complaint. This concept was reflected in the interim policy and in federal and state penalty immunity laws and did not prove controversial in the public comment process.

4. Correction and Remediation

Section D(5) ensures that, in order to receive the penalty mitigation benefits available under the policy, the regulated entity not only voluntarily discovers and promptly discloses a violation, but expeditiously corrects it, remedies any harm caused by that violation (including responding to any spill and carrying out any removal or remedial action required by law), and expeditiously certifies in writing to appropriate state, local and EPA authorities that violations have been corrected. It also enables EPA to ensure that the regulated entity will be publicly accountable for its commitments through binding written agreements, orders or consent decrees where necessary.

The final policy requires the violation to be corrected within 60 days, or that the regulated entity provide written notice where violations may take longer to correct. EPA recognizes that some violations can and should be corrected immediately, while others (e.g., where capital expenditures are involved), may take longer than 60 days to correct. In all cases, the regulated entity will be expected to do its utmost to achieve or return to compliance as expeditiously as possible.

Where correction of the violation depends upon issuance of a permit which has been applied for but not issued by federal or state authorities, the Agency will, where appropriate, make reasonable efforts to secure timely review of the permit.

5. Prevent Recurrence

Under Section D(6), the regulated entity must agree to take steps to prevent a recurrence of the violation, including but not limited to improvements to its environmental auditing or due diligence efforts. The final policy makes clear that the preventive steps may include improvements to a regulated entity's environmental auditing or due diligence efforts to prevent recurrence of the violation.

In the interim policy, the Agency required that the entity implement appropriate measures to prevent a recurrence of the violation, a requirement that operates prospectively. However, a separate condition in the interim policy also required that the violation not indicate "a failure to take appropriate steps to avoid repeat or recurring violations" — a requirement that operates retrospectively. In the interest of both clarity and fairness, the Agency has decided for purposes of this condition to keep the focus prospective and thus to require only that steps be taken to prevent recurrence of the violation after it has been disclosed.

6. No Repeat Violations

In response to requests from commenters (see, e.g., II-F-39 and II-G-18 in the Docket), EPA has established "bright lines" to determine when previous violations will bar a regulated entity from obtaining relief under this policy. These will help protect the public and responsible companies by ensuring that penalties are not waived for repeat offenders. Under condition D(7), the same or closely-related violation must not have occurred previously within the past three years at the same facility, or be part of a pattern of violations on the regulated entity's part over the past five years. This provides companies with a continuing incentive to prevent violations, without being unfair to regulated entities responsible for managing hundreds of facilities. It would be unreasonable to provide unlimited amnesty for repeated violations of the same requirement.

The term "violation" includes any violation subject to a federal or state civil judicial or administrative order, consent agreement, conviction or plea agreement. Recognizing that minor violations are sometimes settled without a formal action in court, the term also covers any act or omission for which the regulated entity has received a penalty reduction in the past. Together, these conditions identify situations in which the regulated community has had clear notice of its noncompliance and an opportunity to correct.

7. Other Violations Excluded

Section D(8) makes clear that penalty reductions are not available under this policy for violations that resulted in serious actual harm or which may have presented an imminent and substantial endangerment to public health or the environment. Such events indicate a serious failure (or absence) of a self-policing program, which should be designed to prevent such risks, and it would seriously undermine deterrence to waive penalties for such violations. These exceptions are responsive to suggestions from public interest organizations, as well as other commenters. (See, e.g., II-F-39 and II-G-18 in the Docket.) The final policy also excludes penalty reductions for violations of the specific terms of any order, consent agreement, or plea agreement. (See, II-E-60 in the Docket.) Once a consent agreement has been negotiated, there is little incentive to comply if there are no sanctions for violating its specific requirements. The exclusion in this section applies to violations of the terms of any response, removal or remedial action covered by a written agreement.

8. Cooperation

Under Section D(9), the regulated entity must cooperate as required by EPA and provide information necessary to determine the applicability of the policy. This condition is largely unchanged from the interim policy. In the final policy, however, the Agency has added that "cooperation" includes assistance in determining the facts of any related violations suggested by the disclosure, as well as of the disclosed violation itself. This was added to allow the agency to obtain information about any violations indicated by the disclosure, even where the violation is not initially identified by the regulated entity.

F. Opposition to Privilege

The Agency remains firmly opposed to the establishment of a statutory evidentiary privilege for environmental audits for the following reasons:

1. Privilege, by definition, invites secrecy, instead of the openness needed to build public trust in industry's ability to self-police. American law reflects the high value that the public places on fair access to the facts. The Supreme Court, for example, has said of privileges that, "[w]hatever their origins, these exceptions to the demand for every man's evidence are not lightly created nor expansively construed, for they are in derogation of the search for truth." United States v. Nixon, 418 U.S. 683 (1974). Federal courts have unanimously refused to recognize a privilege for environmental audits in the context of government investigations. See, e.g., United States v. Dexter, 132 F.R.D. 8, 9-10 (D.Conn. 1990) (application of a privilege "would effectively impede [EPA's] ability to enforce the Clean Water Act, and would be contrary to stated public policy.")

2. Eighteen months have failed to produce any evidence that a privilege is needed. Public testimony on the interim policy confirmed that EPA rarely uses audit reports as evidence. Furthermore, surveys demonstrate that environmental auditing has expanded rapidly over the past decade without the stimulus of a privilege. Most recently, the 1995 Price Waterhouse survey found that those few large or mid-sized companies that do not audit generally do not perceive any need to; concern about confidentiality ranked as one of the least important factors in their decisions.

3. A privilege would invite defendants to claim as "audit" material almost any evidence the government needed to establish a violation or determine who was responsible. For example, most audit privilege bills under consideration in federal and state legislatures would arguably protect factual information — such as health studies or contaminated sediment data — and not just the conclusions of the auditors. While the government might have access to required monitoring data under the law, as some industry commenters have suggested, a privilege of that nature would cloak underlying facts needed to determine whether such data were accurate.

4. An audit privilege would breed litigation, as both parties struggled to determine what material fell within its scope. The problem is compounded by the lack of any clear national standard for audits. The "in camera" (i.e., non-public) proceedings used to resolve these disputes under some statutory schemes would result in a series of time-consuming, expensive mini-trials.

5. The Agency's policy eliminates the need for any privilege as against the government, by reducing civil penalties and criminal liability for those companies that audit, disclose and correct violations. The 1995 Price Waterhouse survey indicated that companies would expand their auditing programs in exchange for the kind of incentives that EPA provides in its policy.

6. Finally, audit privileges are strongly opposed by the law enforcement community, including the National District Attorneys Association, as well as by public interest groups. (See, e.g., Docket, II-C-21, II-C-28, II-C-52, IV-G-10, II-C-25, II-C-33, II-C-52, II-C-48, and II-G-13 through II-G-24.)

G. Effect on States

The final policy reflects EPA's desire to develop fair and effective incentives for self-policing that will have practical value to states that share responsibility for enforcing federal environmental laws. To that end, the Agency has consulted closely with state officials in developing this policy, through a series of special meetings and conference calls in addition to the extensive opportunity for public comment. As a result, EPA believes its final policy is grounded in common-sense principles that should prove useful in the development of state programs and policies.

As always, states are encouraged to experiment with different approaches that do not jeopardize the fundamental national interest in assuring that violations of federal law do not threaten the public health or the environment, or make it profitable not to comply. The Agency remains opposed to state legislation that does not include these basic protections, and reserves its right to bring independent action against regulated entities for violations of federal law that threaten human health or the environment, reflect criminal conduct or repeated noncompliance, or allow one company to make a substantial profit at the expense of its law-abiding competitors. Where a state has obtained appropriate sanctions needed to deter such misconduct, there is no need for EPA action.

H. Scope of Policy

EPA has developed this document as a policy to guide settlement actions. EPA employees will be expected to follow this policy, and the Agency will take steps to assure national consistency in application. For example, the Agency will make public any compliance agreements reached under this policy, in order to provide the regulated community with fair notice of decisions and greater accountability to affected communities. Many in the regulated community recommended that the Agency convert the policy into a regulation because they felt it might ensure greater consistency and predictability. While EPA is taking steps to ensure consistency and predictability and believes that it will be successful, the Agency will consider this issue and will provide notice if it determines that a rulemaking is appropriate.

II. Statement Of Policy: Incentives For Self-Policing

Discovery, Disclosure, Correction and Prevention

A. Purpose

This policy is designed to enhance protection of human health and the environment by encouraging regulated entities to voluntarily discover, disclose, correct and prevent violations of federal environmental requirements.

B. Definitions

For purposes of this policy, the following definitions apply:

"Environmental Audit" has the definition given to it in

EPA's 1986 audit policy on environmental auditing, i.e., "a systematic, documented, periodic and objective review by regulated entities of facility operations and practices related to meeting environmental requirements."

"Due Diligence" encompasses the regulated entity's systematic efforts, appropriate to the size and nature of its business, to prevent, detect and correct violations through all of the following:

a) Compliance policies, standards and procedures that identify how employees and agents are to meet the requirements of laws, regulations, permits and other sources of authority for environmental requirements;

b) Assignment of overall responsibility for overseeing compliance with policies, standards, and procedures, and assignment of specific responsibility for assuring compliance at each facility or operation;

c) Mechanisms for systematically assuring that compliance policies, standards and procedures are being carried out, including monitoring and auditing systems reasonably designed to detect and correct violations, periodic evaluation of the overall performance of the compliance management system, and a means for employees or agents to report violations of environmental requirements without fear of retaliation;

d) Efforts to communicate effectively the regulated entity's standards and procedures to all employees and other agents;

e) Appropriate incentives to managers and employees to perform in accordance with the compliance policies, standards and procedures, including consistent enforcement through appropriate disciplinary mechanisms; and

f) Procedures for the prompt and appropriate correction of any violations, and any necessary modifications to the regulated entity's program to prevent future violations.

"Environmental audit report" means the analysis, conclusions, and recommendations resulting from an environmental audit, but does not include data obtained in, or testimonial evidence concerning, the environmental audit.

"Gravity-based penalties" are that portion of a penalty over and above the economic benefit., i.e., the punitive portion of the penalty, rather than that portion representing a defendant's economic gain from non-compliance. (For further discussion of this concept, see "A Framework for Statute-Specific Approaches to Penalty Assessments", #GM-22, 1980, U.S. EPA General Enforcement Policy Compendium).

"Regulated entity" means any entity, including a federal, state or municipal agency or facility, regulated under federal environmental laws.

C. Incentives for Self-Policing

1. No Gravity-Based Penalties: Where the regulated entity establishes that it satisfies all of the conditions of Section D of the policy, EPA will not seek gravity-based penalties for violations of federal environmental requirements.

2. Reduction of Gravity-Based Penalties by 75%: EPA will reduce gravity-based penalties for violations of federal environmental requirements by 75% so long as the regulated entity satisfies all of the conditions of Section D(2) through D(9) below.

3. No Criminal Recommendations:

(a) EPA will not recommend to the Department of Justice or other prosecuting authority that criminal charges be brought against a regulated entity where EPA determines that all of the conditions in Section D are satisfied, so long as the violation does not demonstrate or involve:

i) a prevalent management philosophy or practice that concealed or condoned environmental violations; or

ii) high-level corporate officials' or managers' conscious involvement in, or willful blindness to, the violations.

(b)   Whether or not EPA refers the regulated entity for criminal prosecution under this section, the Agency reserves the right to recommend prosecution for the criminal acts of individual managers or employees under existing policies guiding the exercise of enforcement discretion.

4. No Routine Request for Audits: EPA will not request or use an environmental audit report to initiate a civil or criminal investigation of the entity. For example, EPA will not request an environmental audit report in routine inspections. If the Agency has independent reason to believe that a violation has occurred, however, EPA may seek any information relevant to identifying violations or determining liability or extent of harm.

D. Conditions

1. Systematic Discovery: The violation was discovered through:

a) an environmental audit; or

b) an objective, documented, systematic procedure or practice reflecting the regulated entity's due diligence in preventing, detecting, and correcting violations. The regulated entity must provide accurate and complete documentation to the Agency as to how it exercises due diligence to prevent, detect and correct violations according to the criteria for due diligence outlined in Section B. EPA may require as a condition of penalty mitigation that a description of the regulated entity's due diligence efforts be made publicly available.

2. Voluntary Discovery: The violation was identified voluntarily, and not through a legally mandated monitoring or sampling requirement prescribed by statute, regulation, permit, judicial or administrative order, or consent agreement. For example, the policy does not apply to:

a) emissions violations detected through a continuous emissions monitor (or alternative monitor established in a permit) where any such monitoring is required;

b) violations of National Pollutant Discharge Elimination System (NPDES) discharge limits detected through required sampling or monitoring;

c) violations discovered through a compliance audit required to be performed by the terms of a consent order or settlement agreement.

3. Prompt Disclosure: The regulated entity fully discloses a specific violation within 10 days (or such shorter period provided by law) after it has discovered that the violation has occurred, or may have occurred, in writing to EPA;

4. Discovery and Disclosure Independent of Government or Third Party Plaintiff: The violation must also be identified and disclosed by the regulated entity prior to:

a) the commencement of a federal, state or local agency inspection or investigation, or the issuance by such agency of an information request to the regulated entity;

b) notice of a citizen suit;

c) the filing of a complaint by a third party;

d) the reporting of the violation to EPA (or other government agency) by a "whistleblower" employee, rather than by one authorized to speak on behalf of the regulated entity; or

e) imminent discovery of the violation by a regulatory agency;

5. Correction and Remediation: The regulated entity corrects the violation within 60 days, certifies in writing that violations have been corrected, and takes appropriate measures as determined by EPA to remedy any environmental or human harm due to the violation. If more than 60 days will be needed to correct the violation(s), the regulated entity must so notify EPA in writing before the 60-day period has passed. Where appropriate, EPA may require that to satisfy conditions 5 and 6, a regulated entity enter into a publicly available written agreement, administrative consent order or judicial consent decree, particularly where compliance or remedial measures are complex or a lengthy schedule for attaining and maintaining compliance or remediating harm is required;

6. Prevent Recurrence: The regulated entity agrees in writing to take steps to prevent a recurrence of the violation, which may include improvements to its environmental auditing or due diligence efforts;

7. No Repeat Violations: The specific violation (or closely related violation) has not occurred previously within the past three years at the same facility, or is not part of a pattern of federal, state or local violations by the facility's parent organization (if any), which have occurred within the past five years. For the purposes of this section, a violation is:

a) any violation of federal, state or local environmental law identified in a judicial or administrative order, consent agreement or order, complaint, or notice of violation, conviction or plea agreement; or

b) any act or omission for which the regulated entity has previously received penalty mitigation from EPA or a state or local agency.

8. Other Violations Excluded: The violation is not one which (i) resulted in serious actual harm, or may have presented an imminent and substantial endangerment to, human health or the environment, or (ii) violates the specific terms of any judicial or administrative order, or consent agreement.

9. Cooperation: The regulated entity cooperates as requested by EPA and provides such information as is necessary and requested by EPA to determine applicability of this policy. Cooperation includes, at a minimum, providing all requested documents and access to employees and assistance in investigating the violation, any noncompliance problems related to the disclosure, and any environmental consequences related to the violations.

E. Economic Benefit

EPA will retain its full discretion to recover any economic benefit gained as a result of noncompliance to preserve a "level playing field" in which violators do not gain a competitive advantage over regulated entities that do comply. EPA may forgive the entire penalty for violations which meet conditions 1 through 9 in section D and, in the Agency's opinion, do not merit any penalty due to the insignificant amount of any economic benefit.

F. Effect on State Law, Regulation or Policy

EPA will work closely with states to encourage their adoption of policies that reflect the incentives and conditions outlined in this policy. EPA remains firmly opposed to statutory environmental audit privileges that shield evidence of environmental violations and undermine the public's right to know, as well as to blanket immunities for violations that reflect criminal conduct, present serious threats or actual harm to health and the environment, allow noncomplying companies to gain an economic advantage over their competitors, or reflect a repeated failure to comply with federal law. EPA will work with states to address any provisions of state audit privilege or immunity laws that are inconsistent with this policy, and which may prevent a timely and appropriate response to significant environmental violations. The Agency reserves its right to take necessary actions to protect public health or the environment by enforcing against any violations of federal law.

G. Applicability

1. This policy applies to the assessment of penalties for any violations under all of the federal environmental statutes that EPA administers, and supersedes any inconsistent provisions in media-specific penalty or enforcement policies and EPA's 1986 Environmental Auditing Policy Statement.

2. To the extent that existing EPA enforcement policies are not inconsistent, they will continue to apply in conjunction with this policy. However, a regulated entity that has received penalty mitigation for satisfying specific conditions under this policy may not receive additional penalty mitigation for satisfying the same or similar conditions under other policies for the same violation(s), nor will this policy apply to violations which have received penalty mitigation under other policies.

3. This policy sets forth factors for consideration that will guide the Agency in the exercise of its prosecutorial discretion. It states the Agency's views as to the proper allocation of its enforcement resources. The policy is not final agency action, and is intended as guidance. It does not create any rights, duties, obligations, or defenses, implied or otherwise, in any third parties.

4. This policy should be used whenever applicable in settlement negotiations for both administrative and civil judicial enforcement actions. It is not intended for use in pleading, at hearing or at trial. The policy may be applied at EPA's discretion to the settlement of administrative and judicial enforcement actions instituted prior to, but not yet resolved, as of the effective date of this policy.

H. Public Accountability

1. Within 3 years of the effective date of this policy, EPA will complete a study of the effectiveness of the policy in encouraging:

a) changes in compliance behavior within the regulated community, including improved compliance rates;

b) prompt disclosure and correction of violations, including timely and accurate compliance with reporting requirements;

c) corporate compliance programs that are successful in preventing violations, improving environmental performance, and promoting public disclosure;

d) consistency among state programs that provide incentives for voluntary compliance.

EPA will make the study available to the public.

2. EPA will make publicly available the terms and conditions of any compliance agreement reached under this policy, including the nature of the violation, the remedy, and the schedule for returning to compliance.

I. Effective Date

This policy is effective thirty days from today.

Dated:

Steven A. Herman

Assistant Administrator for Enforcement and Compliance Assurance

FOOTNOTES — SECTION 2

1 Because the highest culpability score that could be assessed in aggravation is 17 points, the 10 point threshold for receiving the maximum multiplier range allows for a number of differing scenarios that could result in the maximum fine.

2 Full organizational mitigation would still result in a fine range of $12,500 to $50,000.

3 Full organizational mitigation would still result in a fine range of $6,250 to $25,000.

FOOTNOTES — SECTION 3

4 "Regulated entities" include private firms and public agencies with facilities subject to environmental regulation. Public agencies can include federal, state, or local agencies as well as special-purpose organizations such as regional sewage commissions.

5 See e.g., "Current Practices in Environmental Auditing," EPA Report No. EPA-230-08-85-008, February 1984; "Annotated Bibliography on Environmental Auditing," Fifth Edition, September 1985, both available from: Regulatory Reform Staff, PM-223, EPA, 401 M Street SW, Washington, DC 20480.

6 An "environmental audit report" is a written report which candidly and thoroughly presents findings from a review conducted as part of an environmental audit as described in section II.A. of facility environmental performance and practices. An audit report is not a substitute for compliance monitoring reports or other reports or records which may be required by EPA or other regulatory agencies.

7 See, for example, "Duties to Report or Disclose Information on the Environmental Aspects of Business Activities." Environmental Law Institute report to EPA, final report, September 1985.

8 EPA is developing guidance for use by Agency negotiators in structuring appropriate environmental audit provisions for consent decrees and other settlement negotiations.

Surveys

Many independent surveys were conducted between 1994 and 1995 to gauge interest in ISO 14001 and related topics. Among the consulting firms, private companies, and various associations compiling these surveys were Price Waterhouse, Arthur D. Little, Dun and Bradstreet, Quality Systems Update, *and Apple Computer. The surveys showed a strong interest in developing and implementing EMS initiatives and environmental auditing programs in North America and the U.K.; however, the results confirmed the "wait-and-see" attitude many companies have taken regarding certification to the draft standard.*

SECTION 1
Surveys Show Interest in EMS Despite Impediments

from International Environmental Systems Update, February 1996

1,500+ Sites Considered; Suppliers Not Targeted

Survey results show companies in the U.S., Canada, and the U.K. have a strong interest in EMS initiatives but are not racing toward certification.

Apple Computer's Environmental Health & Safety Division, Arthur D. Little Inc., an international consulting firm, and Dun and Bradstreet/*Quality Systems Update* (QSU) conducted surveys of all sizes of companies to determine degrees of ISO 14000 awareness and interest.

Apple's survey focused on identifying trends in ISO 14000 programs in the U.S. A.D. Little conducted one survey looking at all the specific EMS voluntary standards — ISO 14001, BS 7750, and EMAS — in the U.K., and another looking at environmental management in general in the U.S. and Canada.

Dun and Bradstreet, in partnership with *Quality Systems Update*, an ISO 9000 newsletter published in Fairfax, Va., surveyed companies registered to the quality management system standard to determine their plans regarding ISO 14001 implementation.

The surveys confirmed earlier survey information compiled throughout 1995 by several management firms and associations, including Price Waterhouse, Lloyds Register Quality Assurance, Grant Thornton, and the National Association for Environmental Management. These organizations' surveys revealed that the majority of U.S. companies were interested in ISO 14000 but were taking a wait-and-see approach to certification, and in many cases to implementation as well.

Waiting for Joneses

According to Corky Chew, regulations and strategic issues manager with Apple, Apple's survey took place in late 1995 and included 99 U.S. businesses: 63 U.S. TAG members and 36 members of the West Coast Working Group — a group of west coast companies who meet periodically to discuss issues relating to ISO 14000.

The respondents, which included representatives from electronics, manufacturing, pharmaceutical, and the engineering/consulting fields, together were considering more than 1,330 U.S. sites for ISO 14001 implementation and an additional 280 sites in other parts of the world.

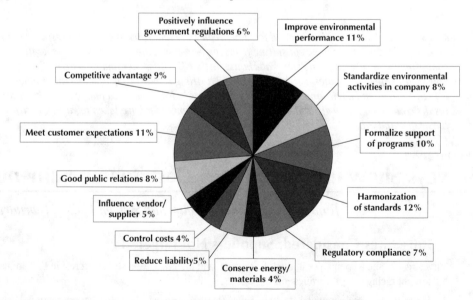

Figure E.1 — What do you see as the benefits of ISO 14000? (source: Apple, Inc.)

"We did not draw a fine level of detailed analyses from the raw data we gathered but tried to get a better idea of who was doing what among a nationally representative sample of companies," explained Chew.

The majority of U.S. companies surveyed wanted to learn more about what their customers are demanding, what their competitors are doing, and what's going on in the foreign marketplace before jumping in the arena, Chew said. They were aware that Europe and the Pacific Rim countries were far ahead of the U.S. in adopting voluntary standards.

"Companies are massaging their existing EMS programs, preparing to conform during 1996," said Chew. Companies, especially small and medium-sized enterprises (SMEs), were hesitant about ISO 14001 because they foresaw high initial costs, an added level of regulatory conformance, and additional work and resources for first becoming certified.

The survey also highlighted what Chew saw as an obstacle — A.D. Little's survey characterized this as the "green wall" — to certification: the ongoing mentality in many U.S. companies that establishing and maintaining an EMS was purely an environmental health and safety (EHS) responsibility, not that of all employees.

"The entire organization should be active and involved, including upper management. ISO 14001 should permeate throughout an entire organization . . . as it does with ISO 9000," said Chew.

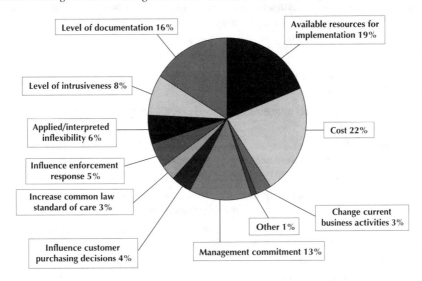

Figure E.2 — What are your concerns regarding ISO 14000? (source: Arthur D. Little, Inc.)

Certification Drivers

The Apple results also showed the following:

- Companies said reasons for certifying under ISO 14001 were customer demand (26%), competitive advantage (24%), improving an existing EMS (21%), public relations (11%), influencing government regulations (9%), and streamlining existing programs (7%).

- Equal value was placed on what most viewed as the benefits of certification, which included standards harmonization, improved environmental performance, formalizing support programs, competitive advantage, customer satisfaction, regulatory compliance, and good public relations.

- If ISO 14000 implementation were to take place today (in late 1995), the majority of companies (48%) would target a specific facility, location, or operation; 22% would implement the standard on a company-wide basis; 17% would go after specific business units; while 13% didn't know.

- 65% of the companies had not formed a formal organization to address ISO 14000.

- A majority (76%) did not plan on requiring vendors/suppliers to be ISO 14000 certified.

- 38% of those surveyed felt they were well-informed on ISO 14000; 32% said they had a working knowledge; 26% know the basic elements; while 4% know very little.

- 33% said they would tailor their ISO 14000 program similar to their ISO 9000 program, although 33% of the companies are not ISO 9000 certified.

EMS Initiatives

A majority of the 84 blue-chip companies surveyed in the U.K. by A.D. Little said that adopting one or more of the environmental management initiatives would be important to future business success. The prevalent belief among these companies was that the voluntary standards — ISO 14001, BS 7750, and EMAS — could demonstrate "due diligence," offer a competitive advantage in certain markets, improve quality, and reduce environmental management costs, according to an A.D. Little spokesperson.

Other results showed:

- 86% of all respondents were tracking development of ISO 14001, while 83% are following BS 7750 and EMAS developments.

- Although 10% of respondents were already certified to BS 7750, the majority (60%) surveyed viewed ISO 14001 as important.

- About a quarter of the respondents said they planned to obtain third-party recognition to one of the EMS initiatives; half said they were not planning to seek third-party recognition under any of the initiatives.

- Regardless of whether they aimed for third-party certification, 85% of the respondents said that it was important or potentially important that their EMS be consistent with a leading initiative.

- 86% of the companies were ISO 9000 certified; of these, 50% said they intended to integrate environmental management with their quality management system.

"Clearly companies are extremely interested in these [EMS] initiatives and what they can mean to business, but certification can be a complicated and time-consuming process," said Tim Sunderland, senior consultant with A.D. Little. "Many companies have a lot of homework to do to decide how best to approach this issue, and which initiatives best meet their particular needs."

Environmental/Business Integration Roadblock

A "green wall" between the environmental and business staffs of many companies created a "major roadblock" to managing corporate environmental issues successfully, according to A.D. Little's survey of North American businesses. A.D. Little surveyed environmental, health, and safety managers from 185 corporations in the U.S. and Canada — representing a broad cross-section of products and services.

The majority of respondents cited several problems that often impede their ability to improve their companies' environmental management. These included:

- a lack of integration between environmental and business issues in the company;
- cost and resource issues;
- organizational difficulties;
- complexity of regulations; and
- their own failure to convince management that environment is an important business issue.

"Getting around, over, or through the green wall is clearly the concern of environmental managers in a large number of companies," said Robert Shelton, director of EHS Consulting at A.D. Little. "Managing transition is a major challenge, but it may be the single most important strategic activity undertaken in the next few years."

The survey showed that only 4% of the respondents said environmental issues were managed as part of the business team. However, 27% indicated they were increasingly managing environmental issues as part of the business management and decision-making responsibility.

Shelton noted that, while some companies did include the environmental function as a critical part of the business process, more businesses needed to "view the environment as a potential business opportunity, not just a liability that the environmental staff worries about.

"Environmental managers also need to shift their self-image and operating style from technical advisors to business strategists . . . and begin to reduce the barriers to collaboration with other business functions if the environment is ever to find its rightful place in corporations."

ISO 9000 Companies Looking at ISO 14001

According to the D&B/*QSU* survey, about 31% of 1,880 ISO 9000 certificate holders in the U.S. said they planned to seek ISO 14001 certification.

While 48% of those registered to the quality management system standard still had no ISO 14001 certification plans, the fact that about one third of the respondents showed an interest was "significant" since the standard was still in draft form, according to *QSU*. Most of those eyeing certification had not set a date for actual registration.

The survey of ISO 9000 sites also found:

- U.S. companies were spending less annually on ISO 9000 registration (an average of $187,000 as compared with $245,200 in 1993) but actual savings on registration was down to $117,000 in 1995 from $179,000 in 1993. This result varied based on different tracking techniques, according to the survey.
- ISO 9000 registration took about 15 months to be completed, as compared with about one year in 1993.
- 85% of the respondents said they passed their registration audits for ISO 9000 on their first try.
- The majority (77%) said quality was their primary reason to be ISO 9000 certified, although market advantage and customer demands were also important.
- Internal benefits of ISO 9000 certification included better documentation, higher quality awareness among employees, and more efficient internal communication.

For more information on the *QSU*/Dun & Bradstreet survey, contact *Quality Systems Update*, Irwin Professional Publishing, 11150 Main Street, Suite 403, Fairfax, VA 22030; tel: 703-591-9008; fax: 703-591-0971.

For more information on the Apple survey, contact the regulations and strategic issues manager, Apple Computer, Inc., EHS, 20450 Stevens Creek Blvd., Cupertino, CA 95014; tel: 408-974-8667; fax: 408-974-1950.

For more information on A.D. Little's surveys, contact Corporate Marketing and Communications, A.D. Little Inc., Acorn Park, Cambridge, MA 02140; tel: 617-498-5896; fax: 617-498-7161.

SECTION 2
Most Surveyed U.S. Firms Have Environmental Audit Programs

from International Environmental Systems Update, May 1995

U.S. companies would conduct environmental audits more frequently if they were assured the results would not be used against them, according to a Price Waterhouse LLP survey released April 7, 1995. But nearly all firms with business outside the U.S. conduct such audits, the survey found.

This information came as the U.S. Environmental Protection Agency (EPA) was studying how environmental management systems (EMSs) and self-audits can be used in EPA enforcement programs. The Price Waterhouse study, titled *The Voluntary Environmental Audit Survey of U.S. Businesses*, also coincided with the development of the three ISO auditing standards — ISO 14010, ISO 14011, and ISO 14012.

"This survey was designed to measure compliance auditing within companies of all sizes; much different from the ISO standards being developed that are primarily directed at auditing EMSs," said Dean Petracca, national director of environmental services at Price Waterhouse.

Not surprisingly, several of the survey sponsors were directly involved in drafting the auditing standards and many were members of the U.S. Technical Advisory Group to TC 207 on EMSs.

Results

Of the 369 companies participating in the survey, 75 percent had environmental auditing programs in place, according to the results. Most of these companies indicated that the reason for audits was "good business or assurance reasons, or because they seek to be proactive in their environmental management," according to Robert Jonardi, director of Price Waterhouse's Environmental Services Group.

The primary reason for a company's conducting audits was potential for improvement to its overall environmental management program. Only about 10 percent of the companies were motivated to perform audits in response to the 1986 EPA auditing policy statement that gave companies credit for self-audits. (See Handbook Appendix D for text of EPA auditing policies.)

"Environmental auditing is an important topic for U.S. businesses," said Jonardi. "About 60 percent of the companies that conduct audits have formal company policy statements on this procedure, usually signed by a board member, the CEO, or company president."

He said more than 95 percent of the companies that conduct audits reported that management awareness had improved as a result of these audit programs.

Further Findings

Jonardi listed some of the other findings from the survey:

- more than 70 percent of companies with environmental auditing programs said the audits had significantly improved the company's regulatory compliance;

- nearly 50 percent said auditing improved employee awareness, diligence, and compliance with company policy and procedures;

- about 43 percent of companies that conduct audits considered the information to be attorney-client privileged or protected by the work-product doctrine — a subset of attorney-client privilege that covers actual documentation information;

- 25 percent of the companies that conduct environmental audits had been approached by outside parties attempting to obtain the results; and

- audit data were obtained by outside parties from 15 percent of the companies.

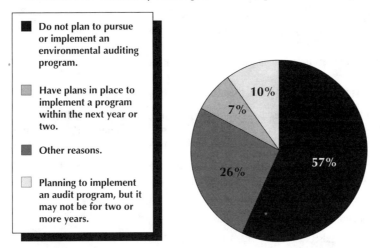

Figure E.3 — Future plans regarding auditing for companies that do not audit (source: The Voluntary Environmental Audit Survey of U.S. Businesses)

The chemicals and petrochemicals industry comprised 31 percent of the respondents, with remaining responses distributed "rather evenly" from other industries, said Jonardi.

"Companies were more likely to audit if they had greater sales, more employees, or a greater number of facilities," according to the survey.

"We found that companies with environmental audit programs in place don't want outsiders coming in; they want to fix it themselves," Jonardi said.

The survey found that 88 percent of those companies with both domestic and international operations performed environmental audits. The number was significantly lower for companies with solely domestic concerns — only 59 percent of these companies performed audits.

"The larger and more extensive a company's operations, the more likely they are to audit," Jonardi explained.

The aerospace and defense equipment, electric and gas utilities, and the forest and paper industries all reported more than a 90 percent environmental audit rate. On the other end the food, beverage, and tobacco industry reported a 50 percent audit rate.

"Companies that did not conduct environmental audits primarily stated that their products and processes did not have significant environmental impacts," he said.

Companies that did not conduct audits named several concerns as reasons:

- budget constraints;
- potential for competition to discover audit results;
- concern that results could be used against the company; and
- risk that they would find items requiring Securities and Exchange Commission reporting.

For those companies with environmental auditing programs in place, several explanations were given for not auditing on a more frequent basis. Among them were the following:

- limited company resources prohibited frequent audits;
- audit information could be used in a citizen suit, toxic tort litigation, civil or criminal suit, or enforcement actions; and
- the company was already performing a sufficient number of audits.

Survey Targets Array of Companies

The survey targeted companies with at least 100 employees and annual sales of $10 million or more. Price Waterhouse mailed more than 1,800 copies of the survey in the last week of January 1994. The survey was conducted at the request of representatives from the regulated community.

Another requirement for inclusion in the survey was that the company must perform some level of manufacturing or be in one of the following industry groups:

- aerospace or defense equipment;
- business services or supplies;
- chemicals or petrochemicals;
- construction or building materials;
- consumer durable or nondurable goods;
- electric or gas utilities;
- electronics, computers, or electrical equipment;
- energy production or petroleum refining;
- food, beverages, or tobacco;
- forest or paper products;
- healthcare products or packaging;
- industrial or farm equipment;
- metals or mining; and
- travel or transportation services.

"These manufacturing groups were selected for this study because they would be prime candidates for environmental auditing programs and they represented many of the industrial sectors included among the Environmental Protection Agency's regulated sector index," said Jonardi.

Law firms, information services, banking or financial services, healthcare providers (unless they operate hospitals), insurance companies, merchandise retailers, entertainment, and government entities were excluded from the survey.

Sponsors

The sponsors of the survey included:

- BF Goodrich Co.;
- Eli Lilly & Co.;
- Texas Instruments;
- the Environmental Auditing Roundtable;
- the Compliance Management and Policy Group with representatives from the American Petroleum Institute, the Chemical Manufacturers Association, and AT&T, among others; and
- the Coalition for Improved Environmental Audits with representatives from the American Automobile Manufacturers Association, Bell Atlantic Corporation, and Dow Chemical Co.

"I think this clearly shows who is driving the international standards process," said Jonardi. "Larger companies with extensive overseas interests seem to be the ones taking the most interest."

SECTION 3
Inside the Price Waterhouse Survey

from International Environmental Systems Update, May 1995

The Voluntary Environmental Audit Survey of U.S. Businesses conducted by Price Waterhouse LLP was divided into four sections with a total of 73 questions.

Section I of the survey was a basic information outline that included the name of company, parent company, and permission to use the participant's name in a published list.

The second section of the survey asked about domestic and international operations; annual sales; and approximate number of domestic and international employees.

Non-Auditing Companies

Questions directed toward companies that did not perform environmental audits constituted the next section of the survey. The questions included:

- Why does your company not have an environmental auditing program? Answers ranged from a belief that processes and products had insignificant environmental impacts to saying auditing was too expensive.
- What are your future plans with regard to environmental auditing? The majority of the participants indicated they did not plan to pursue or implement an environmental auditing program.

Once these two questions were answered companies without auditing programs were asked to not finish the survey.

Companies with Auditing Programs

The three sub-sections of Section IV of the survey were devoted solely to those companies that have an audit program in place and as a result conduct frequent environmental audits.

The survey used the EPA's 1986 Environmental Auditing Policy to define the term "environmental auditing." 📖 (See Handbook Appendix D for a draft of this policy.) It stated: "environmental auditing is a systematic, documented, periodic, and objective review by regulated entities of facility operations and practices related to meeting environmental requirements. Audits can be designed to accomplish any or all of the following: verify compliance with environmental regulations [compliance audits]; evaluate the effectiveness of environmental management systems already in place; or assess risk from the regulated and unregulated materials and practices."

The section posed questions including:

- In what year was your environmental auditing program established?

- What are the company's reasons for performing environmental audits?

- Have compliance audit findings ever been involuntarily disclosed or discovered?

- Has the EPA or a state regulatory agency ever requested the company's audit reports?

Some questions focused on the number of U.S. and international facilities the company had audited in the past two years and whether or not steps were taken to ensure the "independence" of the auditors. Others asked companies about the scope of their environmental audits and the review process for the results. Reporting and control questions rounded out the survey.

For more information, contact Price Waterhouse LLP, 1301 K Street, NW, 800W, Washington, DC 20005-3333; tel: 202-414-1355; fax: 202-414-1301.

Related Standards and Guides

As ISO Technical Committee 207 develops the ISO 14000 series of environmental standards, numerous other standards, guides, and reports exist, were under revision, or were being developed in early 1996. These documents have varying impacts on the ISO 14000 series. Some are directly related and others can be used as tools to augment an EMS or a company's overall management system.

The first section in this appendix lists key ISO/IEC guides by topic. Many country standards bodies have developed their own versions of quality management system standards or EMS standards. We have included only those deemed to have played a role in ISO 14000 standards development.

All ISO/IEC Documents can be obtained from your country's ISO member body. ▢ (See Appendix B for a list of ISO member bodies.) In the U.S., standards may be purchased from:

- *American National Standards Institute*
  11 West 42nd St.
  New York, NY 10036
  Tel: 212-642-4900
  Fax: 212-398-0023

- *American Society for Quality Control*
  611 East Wisconsin Ave.
  Milwaukee, WI 53201
  Tel: 414-272-8575
  Fax: 414-272-1734

- *American Society for Testing and Materials*
  100 Barr Harbor Dr.
  W. Conshohocken, PA 19428
  Tel: 610-832-9500
  Fax: 610-832-9555

- *NSF International*
  P.O. Box 130140
  Ann Arbor, Michigan 48113
  Tel: 313-769-8010
  Fax: 313-769-0109

British national standards can be purchased from:

- *British Standards Institution*
  389 Chiswick High Road
  GB-London W4 4AL
  Tel: +441-81-996-9000
  Fax: +441-81-996-7400

Canadian national standards can be purchased from:

- *Canadian Standards Association*
  178 Rexdale Boulevard
  Etobicoke, Ontario M9W-2R3
  Tel: 416-747-4044
  Fax: 416-747-2475
  Internet: http://www.csa.ca

Irish national standards can be purchased from:

- *National Standards Authority of Ireland*
  Glasnevin
  Dublin-9
  Tel: +353-1-837-0101
  Fax: +353-1-836-9821

French national standards may be purchased from:

- *Association Française de Normalisation*
  Tour Europe
  F-92049 Paris La Défense Cedex
  Tel: +33-1-42-91-5555
  Fax: +33-1-42-91-5656

SECTION 1
Key ISO/IEC Guides

Definitions

Guide 2: 1991* — General Terms and Their Definitions Concerning Standardization and Related Activities

ISO 8402 — Quality Management and Quality Assurance — Vocabulary

Supplier's Declaration

Guide 22: 1982* — Information on Manufacturer's Declaration of Conformity with Standards or Other Technical Specifications

Testing

Guide 25: 1990* — General Requirements for the Competence of Calibration and Testing Laboratories

Inspection

Guide 39: 1988 — General Requirements for the Acceptance of Inspection Bodies

Guide 57: 1991 — Guidelines for the Presentation of Inspection Results

Certification

Guide 7: 1982 — Requirements for Standards Suitable for Product Certification

Guide 23: 1982 — Methods of Indicating Conformity with Standards or Other Technical Specifications

Guide 27: 1983** — Guidelines for Corrective Action To Be Taken by a Certification Body in the Event of Misuse of Its Mark of Conformity

Guide 28: 1982 — General Rules for a Model Third-Party Certification System for Products

Guide 40: 1983* — General Requirements for the Acceptance of Certification Bodies

Guide 44: 1985 — General Rules for ISO or IEC International Third-Party Certification Schemes for Products

SECTION 2
Quality Management Systems

ISO/IEC Guide 48: 1986 — Guidelines for Third-Party Assessment and Registration of a Supplier's Quality System

CASCO Draft 227 — General Requirements for Bodies Operating Assessment and Certification/Registration of Quality Systems

ISO/ 9000-1 — Quality Management and Quality Assurance Standards — Part 1: Guidelines for Selection and Use

ISO/DIS 9000-2 — Quality Management and Quality Assurance Standards — Part 2: Generic Guidelines for the Application of ISO 9001, ISO 9002, and ISO 9003

ISO/CD 9000-3 — Quality Management and Quality Assurance Standards — Part 3: Guidelines for the Application of ISO 9001 to the Development, Supply, and Maintenance of Software

ISO 9001 — Quality Systems — Model for Quality Assurance in Design/Development, Production, Installation, and Servicing

ISO 9002 — Quality Systems — Model for Quality Assurance in Production and Installation

ISO 9003 — Quality Systems — Model for Quality Assurance in Final Inspection and Test

ISO 9004-1 — Quality Management and Quality System Elements — Part 1: Guidelines

ISO 9004-8 — Quality Management and Quality System Elements — Part 8: Guidelines on Quality Principles and Their Application to Management Practices

ISO 10005 — Quality Management — Guidelines for Quality Plans

ISO/CD 10006 — Quality Management — Guidelines for Quality Assurance for Project Management

ISO 10007 — Quality Management — Guidelines for Configuration Management

ISO/WD 10011 — Guidelines for Auditing Quality Systems (Revision of ISO 10011-1, 10011-2, and 10011-3)

ISO 10012-1 — Quality Assurance Requirements for Measuring Equipment — Part 1: Metrological Confirmation System for Measuring Equipment

ISO/DIS 10012-2 — Quality Assurance Requirements for Measuring Equipment — Part 2: Control of Measuring Processes

ISO 10013 — Guidelines for Developing Quality Manuals

ISO/CD 10014 — Guide to Economics of Quality Management

ISO/NWI 10015 — Continuing Education and Training Guidelines

ISO/NWI 10016 — Inspection and Test Records — Presentation of Results

ISO/NWI 10017 — Guide to the Application of Statistical Techniques in the ISO 9000 Family of Standards (Future Type 3 Technical Report)

SECTION 3
Environmental Management Systems

American Society for Testing and Materials (ASTM) PS 11 — Practice for Environmental Regulatory Compliance Audits

ASTM PS 12 — Guide for Study and Evaluation of an Organization's Environmental Management System

British BS 7750 — Environmental Management Systems

Canadian CSA Z750 — Voluntary Environmental Management System

French X30-300 — Analyse de Cycle de Vie

ANSI/ISO 14001-1996 — Environmental Management Systems — Specification with Guidance for Use

ANSI/ISO 14004-1996 — Environmental Management Systems — General Guidelines on Principles, Systems, and Supporting Techniques

ANSI/ISO 14010-1996 — Guidelines for Environmental Auditing — General Principles on Environmental Auditing

ANSI/ISO 14011-1996 — Guidelines for Environmental Auditing — Audit Procedures — Auditing of Environmental Management Systems

ANSI/ISO 14012-1996 — Guidelines for Environmental Auditing — Qualification Criteria for Environmental Auditors

ISO 14015 — Environmental Assessments of Entities and Sites (EASE)

ISO 14020 — Goals and Principles of All Environmental Labeling

ISO 14021 — Environmental Labels and Declarations — Self Declared Environmental Claims

ISO 14024 — Environmental Labels and Declarations — Environmental Labeling Type I — Guiding Principles and Procedures

ISO 14025 — Type III Labeling (technical report)

ISO 14031 — Evaluation of Environmental Performance

ISO 14040 — Environmental Management — Life-Cycle Assessment Principles and Framework

ISO 14041 — Environmental Management Life Cycle Assessment — Goal and Scope Definition and Inventory Analysis

ISO 14042 — Environmental Management Life Cycle Assessment — Life Cycle Impact Assessment

ISO 14043 — Environmental Management Life Cycle Assessment — Life Cycle Interpretation

ISO 14050 — Environmental Management — Terms and Definitions

ISO Guide 64 (formerly ISO 14060) — Guide for the Inclusion of Environmental Aspects in Product Standards

SECTION 4
Accreditation

American National Standards Institute — National Accreditation Program: Policy and Procedures***

ISO/IEC Guide 43: 1984 — Development and Operation of Laboratory Proficiency Testing

ISO/IEC Guide 58: 1993 — Calibration and Testing Laboratory Accreditation Systems — General Requirements for Operation and Recognition

ISO CASCO Draft Guide 226— General Requirements for Assessment and Accreditation of Certification/ Registration Bodies

Registrar Accreditation Board — Guide for Accreditation of Registrars for Environmental Management System***

SECTION 5

Occupational Health and Safety Management Systems

British BS 8800 — Guide to Occupational Health and Safety Management (formerly BS 8750)

Accreditation and Certification Bodies

While ISO 14001 was not a final International Standard in early 1996, several certification bodies were offering certificates to companies complying with the Draft International Standard version of the standard. In addition, only a few accreditation bodies had developed criteria for accrediting certification bodies to offer environmental management system certification. In the United States, as in several other countries, accreditation criteria were only just being approved.

We have included here the names of accreditation bodies known to be developing or to have developed EMS accreditation criteria as of early 1996. We have only published the names of accredited certification bodies. Readers should be aware that most ISO 9000 certification bodies, along with a few other groups, have indicated they will seek accreditation in due course. This list is only the beginning.

SECTION 1
Accreditation Bodies

As of March 1996

Australia/New Zealand

Joint Accreditation Society of Australia and New
Zealand
51 Allara St.
Canberra, ACT 2608
Tel: +61-6-276-1156
Fax: + 61-6-276-2041

Austria

Federal Ministry for Economic Affairs
Landstasser Haupstrasse 55-57
1031 Vienna
Tel: +43-1-711-02-352
Fax: +43-1-714-3582

Belgium

Belcert
Ministry of Economic Affairs
Division Quality/Accreditation Service
Boulevard E Jacqmain 154
Brussels 1210
Tel: +32-2-206-4111
Fax: +32-2-206-5744

Canada

Standards Council of Canada
45 O'Connor Street, Suite 1200
Ottawa, Ontario K1P 6N7
Tel: +613-238-3222
Fax: +613-995-4564

Denmark

Danish Agency for Development of Trade and
Industry
Tageusvej 137
2200 Copenhagen 2
Tel: +45-35-86-8686
Fax: +45-35-86-8687

Finland

Centre for Metrology and Accreditation
Box 239
FI 00181 Helsinki
Tel: +358-0-61671
Fax: +358-0-6167341

France

Comité Francaise d'Accreditation (COFRAC)
37 rue de Lyon
75012 Paris
Tel: +33-1-44-68-82-20
Fax: +33-1-44-68-82-21

Germany

Deutscher Akkreditierungerat
c/o Trägergemeinschaft für Akkreditierung
Postfach 70 12 61
60591 Frankfurt
Tel: +49-69-63-00-91-11
Fax: +49-69-63-00-91-44

Greece

Hellenic Organization for Standardization
Odos Acharnon 313
111 Athens
Tel: +30-1-201-5125
Fax: +30-1-202-0776

Iceland

Löggildingarstofan
Box 8114
128 Reykjavik
Iceland
Tel: +354-568-1122
Fax: +354-568-5998

Ireland

Irish National Accreditation Board
35-39 Shelbourne Rd. Ballsbridge
Dublin 4
Tel: +353-1-668-6977
Fax: +353-1-668-6821

Italy

Sistema Nazionale per l'Accreditament degli
Organismi de Cerificazione
Via Battietotti Sassi 11
20133 Milano
Tel: +39-2-719-202
Fax: +39-2-719-055

Japan

Japan Accreditation Board
Akasaka Royal Block Annex
G-18 Akaska #7 Chome-Minato-ku
Tokyo 107
Tel: +81-3-5561-0375
Fax:+81-3-5561-0376

Mexico

Dirección General de Normas
Calle Puente de Tecamachalco No 6
Lomas de Tecamachalco
Sección Fuentes
Naucalpan de Juárez
53 950
Tel: +52-5-729-9300
Fax: +52-5-729-9484

The Netherlands

Raad voor Accreditatie (RvA)
Radboudkwartier 223
Postbus 2768
3500 GT Utrecht
Tel: +31-30-239-45-00
Fax: +31-30-239-45-39

Norway

Norsk Akkreditering
Box 6832, St. Olav's Plass
0130 Oslo 1
Tel: +47-222-00226
Fax: +47-222-07772

Portugal

Insituto Portgues de Qualidade
Rua C à Avenida dos Trés Vales
2825 Monte da Caparies
Tel: +351-1-294-8201
Fax: + 351-1-294-8202

Spain

BNAC
Serrano, 240 7th floor
28016 Madrid
Tel: +34-1-457-9687
Fax: +34-1-458-6280

Sweden

Swedish Board for Accreditation and Confor-
mity Assessment
Box 878
SB-501 15 Boras
Sweden
Tel: +46-33-17-7700
Fax: +46-33-10-1892

Switzerland

Eidgenossisches Amt für Messwesen (EAM)
Lindenweg 50
8084 Wabern
Switzerland
Tel: +41-31-963-3111
Fax: +41-31-963-3210

United Kingdom

United Kingdom Accreditation Service (UKAS)
Audley House
13 Place St. London SW1B 5HS
Tel: +441-71-233-7111
Fax: +441-71-233-5115

United States

American National Standards Insitiute
11 West 42nd Street
New York, New York 10036
Tel: +212-642-4900
Fax: +212-398-0023

Registrar Accreditation Board
611 East Wisonsin Ave.

Milwaukee, WI 53201
Tel: +414-272-8575
Fax: +414-272-1734

SECTION 2
COFRAC Accredited Certification Bodies (France)

As of March 1996

Association Francaise pour l'Assurance de la Qualite

116 Avenue Aristide
Briande Box DP 40
Bagneux 92224, France
Tel: +33-1-461-13737
Fax: +33-1-461-13710
Scope of accreditation:
Environmental Management System Certification

Ascert International

4547 Avenue Carnot
Cachen 94230, France
Tel.: +33-1-461-57060
Fax: +33-1- 461-57069
Scope of accreditation:
Environmental Management System Certification

Bureau Veritas Quality International

Immeuble Apollo
10 Rue Jacques Daguerre
Rueil Malmaison 92565, France
Tel: +33-1-471-44330
Fax: +33-1-471-44325
Scope of accreditation:
Environmental Management System Certification

Det Norske Veritas

10 Rue Lionel Terray
Rueil Malmaison 92508, France
Tel.: +33-1-471-49929
Fax: +33-1-470-84294
Scope of accreditation:
Environmental Management System Certification

Lloyds Register Quality Assurance

32 Rue Caumartin
Paris 75009, France
Tel.: +31-1-474-26030
Fax: +31-1-474-21058
Scope of accreditation:
Environmental Management System Certification

SECTION 3
RvA Accredited Certification Bodies (The Netherlands)

As of March 1996

Bureau Veritas Quality International Ltd.

70 Borough High Street
SE1 1XF London, United Kingdom
Tel: +441-71-378-8113
Fax: +441-71-378-0309

Scope of accreditation:

- in combination with quality system certification: environmental management system according to BS 7750;

- quality system certification based on the ISO 9000 series; and

- safety checklist.

Det Norske Veritas Industry B.V.

Haastrechtstraat 7
P.O. Box 9599
3007 AN Rotterdam, The Netherlands
Tel: +31-10-479-8700
Fax: +31-10-479-6768

Scope of accreditation:

- quality system certification based on the ISO 9000 series;

- product certification of wind turbines;

- environmental management system certification according to BS 7750; and

- safety checklist.

KPMG Certification

P.O. Box 74103
1070 BC Amsterdam, The Netherlands
Tel: +31-20-656-8751
Fax: +31-20-656-8750

Scope of accreditation:

- quality system certification based on the ISO 9000 series; and

- environmental management system certification according to BS 7750.

Lloyds Register Quality Assurance

Wellesley Road
Croyden CR9-2DT, United Kingdom
Tel: +441-816-886-882
Fax: +441-816-818-146

Scope of accreditation:

- quality system certification based on the ISO 9000 series; and

- environmental management system certification according to BS 7750.

NV Kema

Department KCS/KKS
P.O. Box 9035
6800 ET Arnhem, The Netherlands
Tel: +31-85-569111
Fax: +31-85-515606

Scope of accreditation:

- product certification for the electrotechnical industry;

- product certification: declarations of conformity according to European directives;

- Dutch eco-label ("Milieukeurmerk");

- certification of design: electrotechnical industry;

- certification of environmental management systems; and

- quality system certification based on the ISO 9000 series.

NV Kiwa

P.O. Box 70
2280 AB Ryswyk, The Netherlands
Tel: +31-70-395-3535
Fax: +31-70-395-3420

Scope of accreditation:

- QSC Certification ISO 9000;

- EMSC Certification BS 7750;

- Process Certification: Asbestos Removal;

- Repair of concrete constructions;

- Safety constructions;

- Certification of design or prototype for the area "water, building, and environment;" and

- Product certification for the area "water, building and environment."

SECTION 4
UKAS Accredited Certification Bodies (U.K.)

As of March 1996

Aspects Certification Services Ltd.

864 Birchwood Boulevard
Birchwood, Warrington
Cheshire WA3 7QZ, United Kingdom
Tel: +441-925-852-851
Fax: +441-925-852-857

Scope of accreditation:

- Environmental Management Systems

British Approval Service for Electric Cables

Silbury Ct.
360 Silbury Blvd.
Milton Keynes MK9 2AF, United Kingdom
Tel: +441-908-691121
Fax: +441-908-692722

Scope of accreditation:

Factors engaged in the design, manufacture, and distribution of:

- copper and aluminum rod;
- copper and enamelled wire;
- copper and fiber cable;
- extrusion and molding; and
- ancillary components (to cable).

British Standards Institution

Linford Wood
Milton Keynes MK14 6LL, United Kingdom
Tel: +441-908-220-908
Fax: +441-908-228-726

Scope of accreditation:

Environmental Management Systems

Bureau Veritas Quality International Ltd.

70 Borough High Street
London SE1 1XF, United Kingdom
Tel: +441-71-378-8113
Fax: +441-71-378-0309

Scope of accreditation:

Environmental Management Systems

Construction Quality Assurance Ltd

Barnby House
Barnby Gate
Newark
Notts NG24 1PZ, United Kingdom
Tel: +441-636-708-700
Fax: +441-636-708-766

Scope of accreditation:

Environmental Management Systems

Det Norske Veritas Quality Assurance Ltd.

Palace House
3 Cathedral Street
London SE1 9DE, United Kingdom
Tel: +441-71-357-6080
Fax: +441-71-357-6048

Scope of accreditation:

Environmental Management Systems

Electricity Association Quality Assurance Ltd.

30 Millbank
London SW1P 4RD, United Kingdom
Tel: +441-71-344-5947
Fax: +441-71-828-9237

Scope of accreditation:

Environmental Management Systems

Intertek Services Corporation

313 Speen St., Suite 200
Natick, Massachusetts 01780, United States
Tel: 508-647-5147
Fax: 508-647-6714

Scope of accreditation:

- Chemical (Organic, Inorganic, Specialities, Petrochemical, Agrochemical);
- Rubber and Plastics;
- Materials (Textile, Furniture, Leather);
- Utilities (Waste Management: treatment, storage, disposal, and incineration; Energy/ Power Generation, Transmission, and Distribution;
- Manufacturing;
- Automotive;
- Mechanical Engineering (Fabricated metal products, Industrial machinery); and
- Electronics (Semiconductors, Major appliances, Computers).

Lloyd's Register Quality Assurance Ltd.

Hiramford
Middlemarch Office Village
Siskin Drive
Coventry CV3 4FJ, United Kingdom
Tel: +441-203-639-566
Fax: +441-203-639-493

Scope of accreditation:

Environmental Management Systems

Professional Environmental & Caring Services (QA) Ltd.

Resource House
144 High Street
Rayleigh
Essex SS6 7BU, United Kingdom
Tel: +441-268-770-135
Fax: +441-268-774-436

Scope of accreditation:

Environmental Management Systems

SGS Yarsley International Certification Services Ltd.

Trowers Way, Reddhill
Surrey RH1 2JN, United Kingdom
Tel: +441-737-768-445
Fax: +441-737-770-973

Scope of accreditation:

Environmental Management Systems

Trada Certification

Stocking Lane, Hughenden Valley
High Wycombe
Buckinghamshire HP14 4NR, United Kingdom
Tel: +441-494-565-484
Fax: +441-494-565-487

Scope of accreditation:

Environmental Management Systems

SECTION 5
EAM Accredited
Certification Bodies (Switzerland)

As of March 1996

Schweiz Vereinigung für Qualitats und Management Systeme

Industriestrasse 1
3052 Zollikofen, Switzerland
Tel: +41-31-911-4801
Fax: +41-31-911-3455

Scope of accreditation:

Environmental Management Systems

SGS International Certification Services AG

Technopark
Pfingstweidstrasse 30
8005 Zurich, Switzerland
Tel: +46-1-445-1680
Fax: +46-1-445-1688

Scope of accreditation:

Environmental Management Systems

Document Comparison Chart

Even though BS 7750, (the British national EMS standard), the Eco-Management and Audit Scheme (EMAS — a European Union regulation), and ISO 14001 have common elements, there are still subtle differences. Some will have no impact on your EMS. Other differences, however, could have profound ramifications, depending on where your site is located.

One concern many companies have is how to integrate their ISO 9001 quality management system (QMS) with their EMS. While the ISO 14000 series is based in large part on the ISO 9000 series, some areas of difference remain.

The following chart is designed to help you pinpoint the similarities and differences among ISO 14001, BS 7750, EMAS, and ISO 9001 and aid you in your implementation strategy.

ISO 14001	ISO 9001	BS 7750	EMAS (Annex 1 of EMAR)
Scope: Specifies voluntary EMS requirements without stating specific environmental performance criteria. Enables an organization to formulate policy and objectives while considering legislative requirements and information about significant environmental impacts.	Scope: Specifies quality system requirements for use where a supplier's capability to design and supply conforming product needs to be demonstrated.	Scope: Specifies voluntary requirements for the development, implementation, and maintenance of an EMS, without stating specific environmental performance criteria. Requires organizations to formulate policies and objectives taking into account information about significant environmental effects.	(EMAR Article 1) Objectives: Eco-management and audit-scheme established to evaluate and improve the environmental performance of companies performing industrial activities; participation is voluntary.
4.0 EMS requirements: An organization shall establish and maintain an EMS to be certified.	4.0 Quality system requirements (Contained in all of Section 4).	4.1 EMS requirements: An organization shall establish and maintain an EMS to be certified. Must have a documented system and procedures and effective implementation of those procedures.	(EMAR Article 3) EMAS Requirements: For a site to be registered, company must have a verified policy programme, EMS review or audit procedure, and environmental statement.
4.1 Environmental policy: Management shall define and ensure policy appropriateness, continual improvement and public awareness; provide framework for policy review, documentation, implementation, maintenance and communication.	4.1.1 Quality policy: Supplier's management shall define, document, implement, and maintain its policy and objectives.	4.2 Environmental policy: Management shall define, document policy and ensure it is relevant, communicated, implemented, maintained, made public, and continually improved; shall publish objectives, define environmental activities, and show how objectives will be made public.	Annex I.A.1, 2, 3, 4: Environmental policies: Company policy shall be in writing, periodically reviewed, revised, and communicated to employees and public by management; policy shall specify objectives.
4.2 Planning	4.2.3 Quality Planning	No Similar Title	No Similar Title
4.2.1 Environmental aspects shall be considered when setting environmental objectives; shall establish updated procedures to identify environmental impacts.	Supplier shall define and document how the requirements for quality shall be met.	4.4. Environmental effects: 4.4.1 Communications shall be established concerning effects; 4.4.2 Environmental effects evaluation and register: effects shall be identified and register shall be maintained.	Annex I.B.3: Environmental effects: Activities shall be evaluated and significant effects compiled in a register.

ISO 14001	ISO 9001	BS 7750	EMAS (Annex 1 of EMAR)
4.2.2 Legal and other requirements shall be identified and made accessible.	4.4.4 Design input requirements shall include applicable statutory and regulatory requirements.	4.4.3 Register of legislative, regulatory, and other policy requirements shall be established and maintained.	Annex I.B.3: Register of legislative and other policy requirements shall be established and maintained.
4.2.3 Objectives and targets shall be consistent with environmental policy, including commitment to prevention of pollution.	4.1.1 Quality policy shall include quality objectives and commitments.	4.5 Environmental objectives and targets shall be consistent with environmental policy, and quantify continual improvement commitment over time.	Annex I.A.4: Environmental objectives shall be consistent with environmental policy and quantify continual improvement commitment over time.
4.2.4 Environmental management program(s) shall include designation of responsibility and timeframe for achieving objectives and targets.	4.2.2 Quality system procedures shall prepare and effectively implement quality system and documented procedures.	4.6 Environmental management program shall include designation of responsibility and the means for achieving targets.	Annex I.A.5: Environmental program for the site shall include designation of responsibility and the means for achieving objectives.
4.3 Implementation and operation	4.1.2 Organization	4.3 Organization and Personnel	Annex I.B.2: Organization and Personnel
4.3.1 Structure and responsibility shall be defined, documented and communicated; resources made available and a management representative appointed to ensure standard's implementation.	4.1.2.1 Responsibility and authority shall be defined and documented by key quality personnel. 4.1.2.3 Management representative appointed to ensure quality system is established.	4.3.1 Responsibility, authority and resources shall be defined and documented with sufficient personnel; problems/solutions identified, verified and controlled. 4.3.3 Management representative appointed to ensure standard's implementation.	Annex I (B) 2: Responsibility and authority shall be defined among key personnel Management representative appointed for ensuring EMS.
4.3.2 Training, awareness, and competence of personnel dealing with EMS policies and procedures shall be established and maintained. 4.3.3 Communication regarding EMS policy, both internal and external, shall be maintained and documented.	4.18 Training of personnel on activities affecting quality shall be established, maintained, and documented. 4.1.2.3 (note 5) establishes a liaison with external parties by management.	4.3.4 Personnel, communication and training on environmental policy and procedures; records of training shall be maintained.	Annex I.B.2: Personnel, communication and training on environmental policy and procedures; documents shall be maintained of all communications.

ISO 14001	ISO 9001	BS 7750	EMAS (Annex 1 of EMAR)
4.3.4 EMS Documentation shall be maintained. 4.3.5 Document Control to ensure location, review, and relevance.	4.2.1 Quality System, General: Supplier shall establish, maintain and document a quality system and a quality manual. 4.5 Document and data control.	4.7 Environmental management manual and documentation shall be maintained, reviewed, and checked for relevance; manual shall cover both normal and abnormal activities.	Annex (I) B 5: Environmental Management documentation records shall be established to present/record EMS policy and objectives.
4.3.6 Operational control shall be identified and documented regarding operations and procedures related to suppliers and contractors as they impact environmental policy.	4.2.2 Quality system procedures 4.6 Purchasing 4.3 Contract review 4.4 Design control 4.6 Purchasing 4.7 Control of customer-supplied product 4.8 Product identification and traceability 4.9 Process control 4.15 Handling, storage, packaging, preservation and delivery 4.19 Servicing	4.8.1, 2 Operational control to ensure activities, procedures, and work instructions — dealing with procurement and suppliers — shall be monitored and coordinated. 4.3.5 Contractors shall be aware of EMS requirements.	Annex I.B.4: Operational control shall establish operating procedures affecting environment; includes documentation, monitoring, and procedures dealing with procurement and contracted activities.
4.3.7 Emergency preparedness and response procedures to prepare for and prevent accidents and emergency situations shall be reviewed, revised, and tested.	Not Applicable	4.4.2 Environmental effects evaluation and register (paragraph two) shall include procedures arising from accidents and emergency situations.	Annex I.C.9: Prevention and limitation of environmental accidents shall be addressed. Annex I.C.10: Contingency procedures in cases of environmental accidents shall be addressed.
4.4.1 Monitoring and measurement procedures shall be established and documented to identify the key operations impacting environment and evaluate compliance with legislation and regulations.	4.10 Inspection and testing 4.11 Control of inspection, measuring and test equipment 4.12 Inspection and test status 4.20 Statistical Techniques.	4.8.3 Verification, measurement, and testing compliance with specified requirements shall be documented and maintained to assess all relevant activities.	Annex I.B.4: Monitoring procedures shall be maintained to ensure policy requirements are being met, documented, and each relevant activity is assessed.

ISO 14001	ISO 9001	BS 7750	EMAS (Annex 1 of EMAR)
4.4.2 Non-conformance and corrective and preventive action shall be established to define responsibility and handle nonconformance; changes resulting from mitigating action must be recorded.	4.13 Control of nonconforming product shall be maintained to ensure it is prevented from unintended use. 4.14 Corrective and preventive action must be taken to ensure quality; changes must be recorded.	4.8.4 Non-compliance and corrective action shall be defined, procedures established and maintained; and controls applied and changes recorded.	Annex I.B.4: Non-compliance and corrective action: noncompliance shall be identified, evaluated, corrected, and controled and any changes recorded.
4.4.3 Records including training, audits and review, shall be maintained to demonstrate conformance.	4.16 Control of quality records shall be maintained to demonstrate compliance and show effective operation; records shall be kept and made available to customer.	4.9 Environmental management records, including procurement, audit and review records, shall be maintained to demonstrate compliance and made available both internally and externally.	Annex (I).B.5: Environmental management documentation records shall be maintained and recorded to present and document policy, and demonstrate EMS compliance.
4.4.4 EMS audit shall be conducted periodically to determine proper conformity, implementation, and maintenance and results shall be provided to management, and shall be based on relevance of activity.	4.17 Internal quality audits shall be performed to verify whether quality activities and results comply and are effective; carried out periodically by independent personnel and recorded and reviewed.	4.10 Environmental management audits shall be maintained to determine conformity, effectiveness of EMS. 4.10.1 General 4.10.2 Audit program 4.10.3 Audit protocols and procedures	Annex I.B.6: Environmental audits shall be done periodically concerning conformance, effective implementation, of EMS policy.
4.5 Management review shall be done periodically of EMS to ensure effectiveness and adequacy; shall address possible need for changes and be documented.	4.1.3 Management review shall be performed at defined intervals to ensure effectiveness of quality policy; records shall be maintained.	4.11 Environmental management reviews of EMS to satisfy standards, ensure effectiveness shall be conducted; review shall be documented, done at regular intervals and address need for changes.	Annex I.D: Good Management Practices based on "principles of action" in environmental policy, shall be checked regularly and ensure continual improvement. Annex I.B.1: Environmental policy, objectives, and programmes shall be periodically reviewed and revised at top level.

North American Standards Organizations

SECTION 1
United States

American National Standards Institute

11 West 42nd St.
New York, New York 10036
Tel: 212-642-4900
Fax: 212-642-4969
Internet: http://www.ansi.org

The ANSI Federation, organized in 1918, is made up of manufacturing and service businesses, professional societies and trade associations, standards developers, academia, government agencies, and consumer and labor interests, all working together to develop voluntary national consensus standards. In early 1996, ANSI had more than 1,700 members.

ANSI's mission is to enhance both the global competitiveness of U.S. business and the quality of life in the U.S. It accomplishes this by promoting and facilitating voluntary consensus standards and conformity assessment systems and protecting their integrity. It considers its mission very relevant to today's business community and to all segments of the U.S. economy.

American Society for Quality Control

611 East Wisconsin Ave., P.O. Box 3005
Milwaukee, Wisconsin 53201-3005
Tel: 414-272-8575; 800-248-1946 (in U.S.)
Fax: 414-272-1734
Internet: http://www.asqc.org

ASQC is the leading quality improvement organization in the United States, with more than 130,000 individual and 1,000 sustaining members worldwide in early 1996. A not-for-profit professional association headquartered in Milwaukee, Wisconsin, ASQC carries out a variety of professional, educational, and informational programs. ASQC's vision is to be the world's recognized champion and leading authority on all issues related to quality.

ASQC was founded in 1946 with the merger of several local quality societies. These groups were formed to share information about statistical quality control after classes on that subject were held during World War II to improve and maintain the quality of defense materials. Most of the quality methods now used throughout the world — including statistical process control, quality cost measurement and control, total quality management, failure analysis, and zero defects — were initiated by ASQC members.

ASQC's mission is to facilitate continuous improvement and increased customer satisfaction by identifying, communicating, and promoting the use of quality principles, concepts, and technology; and thereby be recognized throughout the world as the leading authority on and champion for quality.

American Society for Testing and Materials

100 Barr Harbor Dr.
West Conshohocken, Pennsylvania 19428
Tel: 610-832-9500
Fax: 610-832-8666
Internet: http://www.astm.org

Organized in 1898, ASTM has grown into one of the largest voluntary standards development systems in the world.

ASTM is a not-for-profit organization that provides a forum for producers, users, ultimate consumers, and those having a general interest (representatives of government and academia) to meet on common ground and write standards for materials, products, systems, and services. From the work of 132 standards-writing committees, ASTM publishes standard test methods, specifications, practices, guides, classifications, and terminology.

ASTM's standards development activities encompass metals, paints, plastics, textiles, petroleum, construction, energy, the environment, consumer products, medical services and devices, computerized systems, electronics, and many other areas. ASTM headquarters has no technical research or testing facilities; such work is done voluntarily by 35,000 technically qualified ASTM members located throughout the world.

More than 9,100 ASTM standards are published each year in the 71 volumes of the *Annual Book of ASTM Standards*. These standards and related information are sold throughout the world.

NSF International

P.O. Box 130140
Ann Arbor, Michigan 48113-0410
Tel: 313-769-8010
Fax: 313-769-0109
Internet: http://www.nsf.com

NSF International (NSF) is a private, independent, not-for-profit organization that develops and maintains voluntary standards using a unique consensus procedure involving all interested parties — regulatory, user, and producer — at all stages of the process. NSF was chartered in 1944 with a vision and mission for public service.

In addition to standards activities, NSF provides conformity assessment through established programs of evaluation and testing, including toxicological risk assessments; product certification, with authorized use of formally registered Marks; facilities compliance audits; and follow-up testing and audits, as evidence of continued standards compliance.

NSF's continuing goal is mission-related, "to provide clients and the general public with objective, high-quality, timely third-party services at acceptable cost."

SECTION 2
Canada

Canadian Standards Association

178 Rexdale Blvd.
Etobicoke, Ontario M9W-1R3
Tel: 416-747-4044
Fax: 416-747-2475
Internet: http://www.csa.ca

For more than 75 years, the Canadian Standards Association (CSA) has been developing product and service standards, guidelines, codes, and other documents, as well as seminars and educational services.

In addition, it provides extensive testing, certification, and verification services. An independent, not-for-profit organization with proven management systems and a large international network of volunteers, CSA provides a neutral forum in which business, industry, governments, and consumers can work together to produce consensus documents that meet their collective needs.
With offices across Canada, Europe, and the Far East, CSA plays a key role in developing solutions.

Standards Council of Canada

45 O'Connor St., Suite 1200
Ottawa, Ontario K1P 6N7
Tel: 613-238-3222
Fax: 613-995-4564
Internet: info@scc.ca

The Standards Council of Canada (SCC) Act was given royal assent in 1970. The SCC is a crown corporation, the national coordinating agency for standardization, bringing together into a national standards system established organizations involved in the preparation of voluntary standards for application in both the private and public sectors, and in testing and certification.

The objects of the SCC, as set forth in the Act, are to foster and promote voluntary standardization in fields relating to the construction, manufacture, production, quality, performance, and safety of buildings, structures, manufactured articles, and products and other goods, including components thereof, not expressly provided for by law, as a means of advancing the national economy, benefiting the health, safety, and welfare of the public, assisting and protecting consumers, facilitating domestic and international trade, and furthering international cooperation in the fields of standards.

SECTION 3
Mexico

Dirección General de Normas

Calle Puente de Tecamachalco No. 6
Lomas de Tecamachalco
Sección Fuentes
Naucalpan de Juárez
53 950
Tel: +52-5-729-9300
Fax: +52-5-729-9484

The Dirección General de Normas (DGN) of the Ministry of Trade and Industrial Development, created by decree in 1943, is the official body in charge of standardization activities in Mexico. It promotes the development of standards through several committees and subcommittees working in the main fields of industry. It also carries out metrological activities, especially dealing with secondary standards and technical studies as an industrial support activity. It is also in charge of the official guarantee mark, Norma Oficial Mexicana (NOM), and the compulsory standard official mark, which are government certification marks for products of certified quality.

In addition, DGN is the representative of Mexico at the International Conference on Laboratory Accreditation and counts quality control promotion activities as one of its main duties.

The DGN is a founding member of ISO and Comisión Panamericana de Normas Tecnicas, and is a member of the Codex Alimentarius Commission.

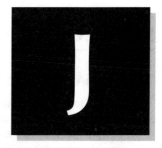

Software and Training Resources

Many high-tech software development and environmental consulting firms have begun creating software tools to help organizations meet EMS implementing challenges. Some, but not all, are based on ISO 14001. Other packages use different approaches, including life-cycle costing and database management techniques to help companies identify and quantify environmental aspects and impacts.

Other packages allow users to track conformance to the various ISO 14001 requirements specifically. These packages also give hints and tips on implementation.

Another area of growth in ISO 14000 information is the Internet. Already in early 1996, several organizations had home pages on the World Wide Web, and there were two mailing lists devoted to ISO 14000 and related issues.

One caveat, however, is that the information found on the Internet is subject to rumor and inaccuracy. You must be sure to verify information from a newsgroup or Web site before using it to make the types of business decisions ISO 14001 implementation calls for.

Following is information available as of March 1996 on software and Internet sites that readers may want to explore. It was provided by the companies and was not tested by the publisher of this book. New products and services appear regularly, so this information is only a beginning. Also included is a list of companies known to be providing training on ISO 14001. This information does not imply endorsement in any way by the publisher, authors, or editors of this handbook.

SECTION 1
Software

ChemAcct®

One tool to help organizations conduct short- and medium-term planning is a program called *Environmental Performance Manager (EPM)* by Conpro Corp. and Trigon Engineering Consultants Inc. This is a combination of software and consulting services designed to provide users with a tool to conduct medium-term planning using projections of energy and environmental costs.

EPM provides a platform for making business decisions using environmental performance evaluations and life-cycle assessments. *EPM* uses a "what-if" approach to project costs into the future, allowing companies to do strategic planning based on environmental factors and move beyond simply filling out forms and attempting to maintain compliance with regulations.

The software for *EPM, ChemAcct®*, is a client-server, data warehouse application designed to run on many different platforms, including UNIX-based systems, Windows PCs and Macintoshes, and with many different database engines such as Oracle, Informix, and Sybase.

For more information, contact Bob Heinz, Trigon Engineering Consultants, P700 Blue Ridge Rd. Suite 101, Pylon Commercial Park, Raleigh, NC 27606; tel.: 919-755-5011; fax: 919-755-1414.

SimaPro

SimaPro 3.1 is available from Pre Consultants in The Netherlands. SimaPro is life-cycle assessment (LCA) software designed to allow users to model and study the interaction between their product and the environment. The software package allows users to describe a complex product and its life cycle as a set of materials and processes.

SimaPro's features include:

- the ability to add new products to the life cycle of the main product to study, for example, packaging alternatives;

- waste treatment scenarios to study various disposal strategies;

- impact assessment with characterization, normalization, and weighting; and

- a database that can handle processes with multiple outputs.

SimaPro is available in two single-user versions and a network version for the IBM (DOS) platform. A demonstration version of SimaPro is available on the World Wide Web. The Uniform Resource Locator (URL) address is: http://www.ivambv.uva.nl/pre/simapro.html.

For more information, contact Michiel Oele, Pre Consultants, Bergstraat 6, 3811 NH Amersfoort, The Netherlands; tel: +31-33-461-1046; fax: +31-33-465-2853; e-mail: pre@sara.nl.

QSAS-14000

Quality Technology Company markets QSAS-14000, a self-assessment software tool for environmental management systems. The software package, designed to allow the user assess to its EMS in a cost-effective manner, features:

- a questionnaire related to the ISO 14001 sections;
- three-dimensional charts;
- a "user-friendly" interface;
- printable reports; and
- a quick-access toolbar.

Quality Technology Company is a consulting firm in the quality and environmental areas and also sells software for other management standards.

For more information, contact Krista Osterman, Quality Technology Company, 1611 Tower Rd., Schaumberg, IL 60173; tel: 708-884-1900, ext. 116; fax: 708-884-7280.

Intelex 14000

Intelex Press Inc. has announced the development of a software system designed to help review, build, and manage environmental management systems following ISO 14001, BS 7750, and Eco-Management and Audit Scheme standards.

Intelex 14000 allows the user to track progress through the development, implementation, and improvement stages of an EMS. Along with databases designed to track and record events required by the standards, the package contains a reference section which includes examples, checklists, and Canadian laws and regulations.

Intelex 14000 is available in a Windows-based format, in both single-user and network versions. A demonstration version may be downloaded from the World Wide Web at http://www.intelex.com/intelex.

For more information or to order Intelex 14000, *contact Brenda Shepley, customer service, Intelex, 93 Skyway Ave., Suite 101, Etobicoke, Ontario, Canada, M9W 6C7; tel: 416-679-0119; fax: 416-679-0168, e-mail: intelex-info@intelex.com.*

SECTION 2
World Wide Web

ISO Online — http://www.iso.ch

This World Wide Web site covers the whole range of ISO activities. Sections include a listing of ISO member bodies, technical committees, and an events calendar. The site also contains links to other standards-related web sites.

SM Stoller — http://www.stoller.com

This site has an ISO 14000 section that features the latest news on ISO 14000 and related issues provided by CEEM Information Services. It also contains background on SM Stoller.

Roy F. Weston — http://www.rfweston.com

This site contains information on ISO 14000 and Roy F. Weston's projects in the area of sustainable development. Roy F. Weston is a multifaceted environmental services consulting firm.

ISO 14000 InfoCenter — http://www.iso14000.com

This site features a question-and-answer section on ISO 14000 and a listing of other ISO 14000 resources, both print and electronic. This site is part of the Environmental Industry Web Site (URL: http://www.enviroindustry.com), managed by HomePage Associates.

ANSI Online — http://www.ansi.org

This site contains information on the American National Standards Institute and standards-related activities.

ASTM Home Page — http://www.astm.org

This site contains information on the American Society for Testing and Materials, one of the administrators of the U.S. Technical Advisory Group to TC 207.

ASQC Home Page — http://www.asqc.org

This site contains information on the American Society for Quality Control, one of the administrators of the U.S. Technical Advisory Group to TC 207.

CSA Home Page — http://www.csa.ca

This site contains information on the Canadian Standards Association, the administrators of TC 207. One section of the site contains information on ISO 14000.

EPA Home Page — http://www.epa.gov

This site contains a comprehensive listing of EPA intiatives, regulations, and contact information. The site also contains links to the EPA regional offices and other governmental web sites.

NSF Home Page — http://www.nsf.com

This site contains information on NSF International and some of its pilot projects in the environmental management systems area. NSF is one of the administrators of the U.S. Technical Advisory Group to TC 207.

SECTION 3
ISO 14000 Discussion Groups and Other Mailing Lists

As of early 1996, there were two major mailing lists for ISO 14000 information. To subscribe, follow these steps:

1) Send an e-mail message only to "majordomo@quality.org" (no quotes) with the following text only in the body of the message: "subscribe iso14000" (no quotes).

2) Send an e-mail message only to "listserv@vm1.nodak.edu" (no quotes) with the following command in the body of the message (filling in your first and last name): "subscribe QUEST first name last name" (no quotes).

The major USENET discussion group for ISO 14000 is "sci.environment." Other areas where ISO 14000 has popped up are "misc.industry.quality" and "talk.environment."

Other Web sites, mailing lists, and discussion groups are always forming.

SECTION 4
Training Resources

Arthur D. Little, Inc.

Acorn Park
Cambridge, MA 02149-2390
Tel: 617-498-5000
Fax: 616-498-7200

American Institute of Chemical Engineers (AIChE)

AIChExpress Service Center
345 E. 47th Street
New York, NY 10017
Tel: 800-AIChemE, 800-242-4363
Fax: 212-705-8400

AIG Consultants Ltd.

Pier House
Wallgate, Wigan
Lancashire   WN3 4AL
United Kingdom
Tel.: +441-942-826-539
Fax: +441-942-824-030

American Society for Quality Control

611 E. Wisconsin Ave.
Milwaukee, WI 53201-3005
Tel: 414-272-8575
Fax: 414-272-1734

American Society for Testing and Materials (ASTM)

100 Barr Harbor Drive
West Conshohocken, PA 19428
Tel: 610-832-9500
Fax: 610-832-9555

Business and the Environment

1909 E. Orange Dr.
Phoenix, AZ 85016
Tel: 414-569-1890
Fax: 414-569-1890

B-K Education Services

2505 Locksley Dr.
Grand Prarie, TX 75050
Tel.: 214-660-4575
Fax: 214-641-1327

Butler Quality Services

110 Summit Ave.
Montvale, NJ 07645
Tel: 800-624-5892
Fax: 201-307-0212

Bureau Veritas Quality International

555 E. Ocean Blvd. Suite 310
Long Beach, CA 90802
Tel: 310-983-7290
Fax: 310-983-7293

Chemical Engineering

McGraw Hill
1221 Avenue of the Americas
New York, NY 10124
Tel: 212-512-3997
Fax: 212-512-4762

CEEM Inc.

10521 Braddock Rd.
Fairfax, VA 22032
Tel: 703-250-5900; 800-745-5565
Fax: 703-250-5313

Corinne Fleming Associated Limited

9 Orme Ct.
London W2 4RL
Tel: +441-712-431-033
Fax: +441-717-924-267

Chemical Week

888 Seventh Ave., 26th Floor
New York, NY 10106-2698
Tel: 212-621-4971; 800-278-7549
Fax: 212-621-4970/4949

Ga. Tech Economic Development Institute

Center for International Standards and Quality
O'Keefe Bldg. Room 143
Atlanta, GA 30332-0800
Tel: 404-894-0968
Fax: 404-894-1192

Det Norske Veritas

4546 Atlanta Highway
Loganville, GA 30249-2637
Tel: 404-466-2208; 800-0486-4524
Fax: 404-466-4318; 404-466-0066

Executive Enterprises, Inc.

22 West 21st St.
New York, NY 10010-6990
Tel: 800-831-8333
Fax: 212-645-8689

Environmental Management Consultants

PO Box 2087
Huntington Station
Shelton, CT 06484
Tel: 800-388-3941, 203-924-9544
Fax: 203-924-2194

Environmental Resource Center

101 Center Pointe Dr.
Cary, NC 27513
Tel: 919-469-1585; 800-537-2372
Fax: 919-469-4137

Excel Partnership Inc.

75 Glen Rd.
Sandy Hook, CT 06482
Tel: 203-426-3281; 800-374-3818
Fax: 203-426-7811

Government Institutes, Inc.

4 Research Pl., Suite 200
Rockville, MD 20850
Tel: 301-921-2345
Fax: 301-921-0373

Grant Thornton LLP

500 Pillsbury Center North
200 South Sixth Street
Minneapolis, MN 55402-1459
Tel: 612-332-0001
Fax: 612-322-8361

IBC USA Conferences, Inc.

225 Turnpike Rd.
Southborough, MA 01772
Tel: 508-481-6400
Fax: 508-481-4473

ICF Kaiser

9300 Lee Highway
Fairfax, VA 22031
Tel.: 800-791-9607; 703-934-3293
Fax: 703-934-3420

Institute for International Research

708 Third Ave. 2nd Floor
New York, NY 10017
Tel: 800-999-3123
Fax: 800-959-9644

International Standards Initiative

P.O. Box 1202
Issaquah, WA 98027-1202
Tel: 206-392-7610
Fax: 206-392-7630

Inchcape Testing Services

313 Speen St., Suite 200
Natick, MA 01780
Tel: 508-647-5147, 800-810-1195
Fax: 508-647-6714, 800-813-9287

Lloyds Register Quality Assurance

33-41 Newark St.
Hoboken, NJ 07030
Tel: 201-963-1111
Fax: 201-963-3299

Miller-Rettew

119 South Centerville Rd.
Lancaster, PA 17603
Tel: 717-295-7764
Fax: 717-295-7640

Marsden Environmental International

37 The Oval, Tickhill
Doncaster DN11 9HF
United Kingdom
Tel / Fax: +441-302-752123

Omni Tech International, Ltd.

2715 Ashman Street
Midland, MI 48640
Tel: 517-631-3377
Fax: 517-631-7360

Productivity Improvement Centre

9901 E. Valley Ranch Pkway, Suite 2000
Irving, TX 75063
Tel: 800-263-3735
FaX: 905-721-3339

Quality Management Institute

2 Roberts Speck Parkway
Suite 800
Mississauga, Ontario L4Z 1H8 Canada
Tel: 800-465-3737

Quality Management International

Exton Square Pkwy
P.O. Box 271
Exton, PA 19341
Tel: 800-971-4001
Fax: 800-611-4004

Quality Systems Development/ L. Marvin Johnson & Assoc., Inc.

105 Woodside Ct.
Leitchfield, KY 42754
Tel: 502-257-9997
Fax: 502-257-2740

Qualified Specialists, Inc.
13231 Chapion Forest Dr. Suite 104
Houston, TX 77069
Tel: 713-444-5366
Fax: 713-444-6127

Quality Systems Integrators

60 Pottstown Pike Suite 8
P.O. Box 91
Eagle PA 19480
Tel: 610-458-0539
Fax: 610-458-7555

Quality Technology Company

1161 Tower Road
Schaumburg, IL 60173
Tel: 708-884-1900
Fax: 708-884-7280

Quality Assurance Services

1 The Crescent,
Homebush
NSW 2140
Australia
Tel.: +61-02-746-4945
Fax: +61-02-746-8460

Stat-A-Matrix

One Quality Pl.
Edison, NJ 08820
Tel: 908-548-0600
Fax: 908-548-4085

SGS International Certification Services, Inc.

Meadows Office Complex
301 Route 17 N.
Rutherford, NJ 07070
Tel: 201-935-1500
Fax: 201-935-4555

S.M. Stoller Corporation

5700 Flatiron Parkway
Boulder, CO 80301-5718
Tel: 303-449-7220
Fax: 303-443-1408

Technical Management Consulting

PO Box 325
New Milford, NJ 07646
Tel: 201-837-5934
Fax: 201-837-8893

The Victoria Group

10340 Democracy Lane, Suite 204
Fairfax, VA 22030
Tel: 800-845-0567, 703-691-8484
Fax: 703-691-2542

Yankee Engineering Services

580 Main Street
Bolton, MA 01740
Tel: 508-568-2866, 508-568-2376
Fax: 508-568-3704

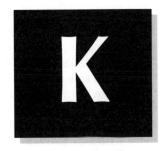

Contributor Biographies

John Audley

John Audley is an assistant professor of environmental policy and political economy at Purdue University. From 1991 until July 1993, he was the Sierra Club's program director for Trade and the Environment, where he participated in the policy process concerning the North American Free Trade Agreement (NAFTA), the Uruguay Round of the General Agreement on Tariffs and Trade, and the discussions between the Trade and Environment Working Groups at the Organization for Economic Cooperation and Development. Audley has testified before Congress on numerous occasions on the relationship between trade rules and environmental protection and has published a number of articles on the relationship between environmental interests and trade policy. He has recently completed a book manuscript entitled *Environmental Interests in the North American Free Trade Agreement*.

Audley was a regional manager of a multinational company that has supplied packaging equipment to businesses operating in Mexico under the Border Industrialization Program, 1987-1989.

Audley has a Ph.D. from the University of Maryland, an M.A. from the University of Arizona, and a Master's degree in international management from the American Graduate School of International Management (Thunderbird), Phoenix, Arizona. Audley can be reached at Purdue University: *Tel: 317-494-7599.*

Mark B. Baker

Mark Baker is special projects manager and editor for CEEM Information Services where he develops and launches ancillary products and publications including books, video training programs, special reports, and directories. Since joining CEEM, he has developed the *ISO 14000 in Focus* video training package and *The ISO 14000 Handbook*. For 10 years prior to becoming a professional projects manager, Baker developed curricula and taught fiction and expository writing, British, American, and world literature, and English as a Second Language courses in the Fairfax County public school system in Virginia. He received a B.A. in English from East Carolina University and an M.A. in English and writing instruction from George Mason University. CEEM Inc. is a member of the U.S. TAG to ISO TC 207 and ISO TC 176. *Tel: 800-745-5565; 703-250-5900.*

Thomas Bartel

Thomas Bartel is a corporate regulatory affairs manager for Unisys Corporation, based in the Phoenix, Arizona, office. He heads up the corporation's Environmental Stewardship Program, which includes development and implementation of corporate environmental policies and standards and administration of the Unisys ISO 14000 EMS program. Bartel is a U.S. Technical Advisory Group delegate to TC 207 and serves as a commissioner of the Commission on the Arizona Environment. In addition, he is a task force member on the U.S. EPA Common Sense Initiative — Computers & Electronic Sector.

Christopher L. Bell

Christopher Bell is a partner practicing environmental law with the Washington, D.C., office of the law firm Sidley & Austin. Bell has participated in administrative and civil litigation and criminal enforcement investigations, and has counseled clients regarding CERCLA (Superfund), RCRA (waste), TSCA (chemicals), the Clean Water Act, the Clean Air Act, FIFRA (pesticides), OSHA (safety), and product-related issues. Bell's practice includes client training, advice on managerial aspects of environmental compliance, and the design and conduct of audits. Bell has worked on several international projects for both U.S. and foreign clients involving facility and product-related matters, and environmental management and auditing.

Bell is a member of the U.S. delegation to ISO TC 207 and one of the lead negotiators for the ISO 14001 EMS specifications document, environmental performance evaluation, life-cycle assessment, and terms and definitions.

Bell is the co-author of the *RCRA Compliance and Enforcement Manual* by Shepard's/McGraw-Hill, and has published several articles in the U.S. and abroad.

Bell graduated magna cum laude with the Order of Coif from the University of Michigan Law School in 1985, and joined Sidley & Austin after a two-year clerkship with a federal judge. In addition, Bell has several years of manufacturing experience, is a past member of the Society of Manufacturing Engineers, and is a certified Manufacturing Technician.

Michelle Blazek

Michelle Blazek is an environmental consultant for the AT&T Environmental, Health and Safety Process. From 1994-1996, she was the project manager for AT&T's worldwide ISO 14000 effort, providing technical assistance on environmental issues to AT&T factories, and was a representative for AT&T on U.S. Environmental Protection Agency regulatory reengineering initiatives. As part of the AT&T Environmental and Safety and Engineering Center she conducted audits for AT&T factories, service centers, and research and development laboratories in the U.S. and Europe.

Prior to joining AT&T in 1991, Blazek worked in the Waste Management Division of Killam Associates, Millburn, New Jersey, on a wide range of jobs including environmental permitting, investigation and remediation.

Blazek has a B.S. in civil engineering and engineering and public policy from Carnegie Mellon University, Pittsburgh, Pennsylvania.

Marilyn R. Block

Marilyn R. Block, president of MRB Associates, specializes in designing, implementing, and evaluating environmental management systems that demonstrate leadership and improve environmental performance.

Block is actively involved with the work of ISO/TC 207. She serves as one of the U.S. delegates on environmental management principles, systems, and supporting techniques.

Before establishing MRB Associates, Block held senior positions with several environmental consulting firms. Most recently, she was deputy director of the Environmental Policy Center, Law Companies Group Inc., where she established and managed the firm's TQEM practice. She was actively involved with the Global Environmental Management Initiative (GEMI), a coalition of 27 leading companies that foster environmental excellence by businesses worldwide.

Prior to joining Law Companies, Block was vice president of ICF International Inc. (now ICF Kaiser International). In that position, she helped companies create pro-environmental strategic plans. She also helped corporations within a diverse array of industries identify new business opportunities, new markets, and new products that reflect emerging environmental trends.

Block earned her B.S., M.Ed., and Ph.D. at the University of Maryland. She is a delegate with the U.S. TAG to ISO TC 207 and a member of the Environmental Auditing Roundtable, and the National Association of Environmental Professionals. *MRB Associates, 6824 Tammy Court, West Bethesda, MD 20817; tel: 301-469-8405; fax: 301-365-4635.*

Roger Brockway

Roger Brockway has been environmental manager at the United Kingdom Accreditation Service (UKAS), formerly the National Accreditation Council for Certification Bodies, since 1993.

Brockway is chairman of the European Accreditation Working Group on environmental matters and is a member of the U.K. government's Advisory Group on Eco-Management and Audit.

Previously, Brockway worked in the European Commission in Brussels on the mutual recognition of testing and certification for the single European market, and before that he was employed by the British Standards Institution on legal and quality matters. *UKAS, Audley House, 13 Palace Street, London, SW1E 5HS, United Kingdom; tel: 011-44-171-233-7111; fax: 011-44-171-233-5115.*

John R. Broomfield

John Broomfield is the president and CEO of Quality Management International Inc. This firm is a dual accredited (RAB and IRCA) trainer of system auditors and comprises accomplished instructors, advisors, and registered lead auditors. He has more than 20 years' experience in management systems on environmental and transportation projects in Europe, Saudi Arabia, Asia, the Falkland Islands, Africa, the United States, and elsewhere.

Broomfield is active on the U.S. Technical Advisory Groups to TC 207 and TC 176. He is a visiting lecturer on systems standards (including ISO 9000 and ISO/DIS 14000) to the Heinz School of Public Policy and Management at the Carnegie Mellon University in Pittsburgh. He is an invited speaker to a wide range of public events. Broomfield has been registered as a Lead Systems Auditor by the International Register of Certificated Auditors since 1989.

Broomfield is a senior member of the Institute of Industrial Engineers and a member of the American Society for Quality Control.

Broomfield has a Master's degree in management (including construction, environmental studies, and materials protection) from Loughborough University and is an Associate of that university. *Tel: 800-971-4001; fax: 800-614-4004.*

Linda G. Brown

Linda Brown is a co-founder and vice president of communications at Scientific Certification Systems Inc. (SCS). Before teaming up to form SCS, Brown worked in Atlanta as a federal programs specialist for International Systems Inc., a consulting firm advising cities and countries across the country on a variety of federal grants programs. In this position, she worked with clients to develop projects designed to improve the health and environment of their communities, and prepared grant proposals in areas ranging from health care services and urban planning to environmental issues. Brown later served as co-editor for two monthly trade magazines before pursuing her graduate studies at Stanford.

Among Brown's recent articles and presentations addressing the subjects of life-cycle assessment, environmental management, and eco-profile labeling are *Life-Cycle Assessment: An Evolving Environmental Management Tool* and *P2SC: Pollution Prevention South Carolina*, co-authored with Rebecca Ward, to be published in spring 1996.

Brown has a B.A. in English and political science from Emory University, Atlanta, 1979, and an M.A. in journalism, Stanford University, Palo Alto, 1982. *Scientific Certification Systems, Ordway Building Suite 109, One Kaiser Plaza, Oakland, CA 94612-3601; tel: 510-832-1415; fax: 510-832-0359.*

Laura B. Campbell

Laura B. Campbell is the senior legal officer in the United Nations Environment Programme's regional office for North America in New York and has worked on trade and environmental matters since 1994. Before joining UNEP's New York office, she was the deputy coordinator of the Ozone Secretariat in Nairobi from 1992-1994.

Prior to joining the United Nations Environment Programme, Campbell worked as an attorney with major U.S. law firms in Washington, D.C., and New York for seven years, practicing international trade, and environmental and banking law. She also worked as a biologist and, later, as an enforcement attorney, for the U.S. Environmental Protection Agency.

From 1983-1986, Campbell was a Fulbright research fellow at the University of Tokyo, Faculty of Law, researching environmental law and policy in Japan, China, and Southeast Asia.

Since 1987, Campbell has been an adjunct professor of international environmental law at the George Washington University in Washington, D.C. *UNEP, 2 United Nations Plaza, Rm. DC 2-0803, New York, NY 10017; tel: 212-963-8142; fax: 212-963-7341.*

Joseph Cascio

Joseph Cascio is the vice president of environmental management systems for the Global Environment and Technology Foundation. From 1970 to 1996, Cascio was program director, environmental, health and safety standardization at the IBM Corporation. He holds the chairmanship of the U.S. Technical Advisory Group to TC 207. He is affiliated professionally with the American Society for Quality Control (ASQC), the American Society for Testing and Materials (ASTM), and the Institute of Electrical and Electronics Engineers (IEEE,) Environment, Health and Safety Committee.

Cascio was the principal author of the International Chamber of Commerce (ICC) Business Charter for Sustainable Development in 1991. Cascio has also authored numerous articles and papers on standards, standardization, and public policy. He is the principal author of *ISO 14000: A Guide to the Environmental Management Standards*, and editor of *The ISO 14000 Handbook* by CEEM Information Services. Cascio has delivered more than 200 presentations on standards, standardization, and public policy subjects at various national and international fora.

Cascio holds a B.S. in engineering from Polytechnic University of New York in 1966 and an M.S. in management from University of Southern California in 1971. He also received a J.D. in law from Fordham Law School in 1976.

Craig Diamond

Craig Diamond manages a variety of projects for NSF International's Environmental Management Systems Program, including two multi-industry EMS pilot programs and an EMS/pollution prevention project with the metal finishing industry. He is a delegate to the U.S. Technical Advisory Group to TC 207 and speaks frequently on ISO 14000 and EMS implementation issues.

NSF International is a not-for-profit company that specializes in standards development and certification in the areas of public health and the environment. Prior to coming to NSF in 1994, Diamond was a program consultant at the World Wildlife Fund in Washington, D.C., where he helped coordinate regional and national initiatives to promote pollution prevention in agriculture.

Diamond holds a B.S. in biology from Tufts University and a Master's degree in public policy from the University of Michigan. *NSF International, 3475 Plymouth Road, Ann Arbor, MI 48105.*

Tom Donlon

Tom Donlon, an independent consultant, writes and edits for various companies in the Washington, D.C. area. Some projects in the past two years have included writing, editing, and revising training courses for

Fortune 500 companies with an association in Leesburg, Virginia. From 1992 to 1995, Donlon was part of an aviation technical writing team at Washington Dulles International Airport for a Federal Aviation Administration contract to develop aviation safety inspector handbooks.

Donlon received an M.F.A. in creative writing from the American University in Washington, D.C., in 1984 and has published stories, articles, and poems in literary journals, newspapers, and newsletters. From 1988-92, he taught freshman writing at Shepherd College in Shepherdstown, West Virginia. He is a member of the Bookend Poets of Shepherdstown and conducts poetry readings and seminars.

Ira Feldman

Ira Feldman is president of gt strategies + solutions, a management consulting practice that emphasizes ISO 14000 implementation as a component of a proactive compliance approach to corporate environmental programs. In addition, he is the senior advisor to the chairman of the National Environmental Policy Institute (NEPI), a bipartisan environmental policy "think tank" based in Washington, D.C.

Feldman co-chairs the ISO 14000 Legal Issues Forum, an initiative jointly sponsored by the U.S. TAG, the Environmental Law Institute, and the American Bar Association. He is a U.S. delegate to TC 207 SC4 on environmental performance evaluation and SC6 on terms and definitions.

Formerly, Feldman was special counsel at U.S. Environmental Protection Agency Headquarters. In that position he served as director of the Environmental Leadership Program and chair of the task force that revised the EPA voluntary audit policy.

Feldman completed a combined B.A./M.S. program at the University of Pennsylvania. He holds his J.D. from Columbia University. He is admitted to the bar in Washington, D.C., and New York.

gt strategies + solutions, 1300 Connecticut Ave., NW, Suite 1000, Washington DC 20036; tel.: 202-530-9770; fax: 202-530-9772.

Bob Ferrone

Bob Ferrone is president of The Ferrone Group, based in Waltham, Massachusetts, specializing in the integration of industrial design engineering, quality, manufacturing, and environmental management systems toward improved environmental and quality performance. The Ferrone Group provides training and technical support to companies preparing for ISO 14001, including integrating ISO 9000 quality and environmental management systems. Ferrone is a lead instructor for the CEEM Inc. ISO 14001 courses and a delegate to the U.S. Technical Advisory Group to TC 207.

Until late 1995, Ferrone was vice president, Environmental Management Systems for Excel Partnership Inc. For many years, Ferrone was a consulting engineer for Digital Equipment Corporation and led company-wide efforts on ISO 9000 certification through the Office of Corporate Quality and Technology. He has extensive consulting experience working with Fortune 500 companies developing innovations in quality and environmental management systems. During 1992-93, Ferrone led a consortium of 14 electronics companies conducting a study of the environmental aspects of a computer workstation, and played a lead role in the work of the Council on Office Product Energy Efficiency and the development of EPA's Energy Star Computer Program. He is a member of the board of the IEEE Environmental Committee and an advisor to environmental programs at Tufts University and the University of Massachusetts. *The Ferrone Group, 87 Lura Lane, Waltham, MA 02154; Tel: 617-894-6657.*

David J. Freeman

David Freeman is a partner and head of the Environmental Department at Battle Fowler, a 125-lawyer firm based in New York City. He is a delegate to the U.S. TAG to TC 207 and serves on the SubTAGs for auditing, labeling, and life cycle assessment. He is also a co-chair of the TAG's Ad Hoc Forum on Legal Issues. He has written and spoken extensively on ISO-related topics.

Freeman's other areas of expertise include negotiation and supervision of hazardous waste cleanups; litigation of federal and state Superfund cases; implementation of environmental audits and compliance programs; negotiation of environmental issues in transactions involving contaminated property; and advice regarding asbestos, lead, radon, and other "indoor air" issues.

Freeman received his undergraduate and law degrees from Harvard. Prior to entering private law practice, he was a legislative aide to U.S. Senator Frank Moss and a trial attorney with the Federal Trade Commission's Division of National Advertising. *Battle Fowler LLP, 75 E. 55th Street, New York, NY 10022; tel: 212-856-7000; fax: 212-339-9150.*

Marie Godfrey

Marie Godfrey is a consultant/project manager for Franklin Quest Consulting Group, formerly Shipley Associates. She helps clients communicate more productively by actively leading analyses of systems and processes, and facilitating prototyping sessions, workshops, and training.

Godfrey leads teams in creating traditional and on-line quality documentation systems, from individual manuals to entirely integrated systems of many documents, depending on the needs of the client. Work with clients is generally collaborative so that clients learn how to produce quality documents specific to their organizations.

Godfrey is a trained ISO 9000 lead auditor and has completed training in ISO 14000. Her experience includes work with pharmaceutical companies, major telecommunications firms, oil and gas companies, banking firms, and a variety of manufacturers. She is principal author of several workshop manuals including *Documenting Quality Systems*, *Managing Document Development*, and *Scientific Thinking and Writing*.

Godfrey received her undergraduate degree from the University of Connecticut and her Ph.D. from Johns Hopkins University.

Peter Goosen

Peter Goosen is a chemical engineer. Since 1991 he has been manager of accreditation with the Dutch Council for Accreditation, or Raad voor Accreditatie (RvA), formerly Raad voor Certificatie. He has performed a vast number of accreditation assessments worldwide. He developed the RvA accreditation scheme for certification bodies operating environmental management systems, and is chairman of the task force that set up the EAC guidelines for that sector.

Goosen started his professional career with Euratom, the nuclear research organization of the European Community. He then joined a multinational Dutch chemical company where he was involved in applied product and process development. Related to his studies in economics, he spent several years in the business development and marketing area of the company. From 1983 he worked for the Occupational

Health and Safety Bureau of the Dutch government and was an advisor to the Dutch authorities and the European Commission in environmental issues.

Goosen is a member of numerous national and international working groups, including the EAC, IAF, and standardization committees in the field of environmental management systems and occupational health and safety. He is a member of the ISO Committee on Conformity Assessment (CASCO) study group in the environmental field.

Barbara B. Haas

Barbara Haas is the director of the National Wildlife Federation's (NWF's) Corporate Conservation Council, a position she has held since 1982. Additionally, she is an active member of the U.S. TAG to TC 207 and a member of the Chairman's Advisory Group.

Before joining NWF, Haas served as the special assistant to the Assistant Secretary for Fish and Wildlife and Parks in the U.S. Department of the Interior. She is a member of several boards, including the Boards of Trustees of the Sierra Club Legal Defense Fund and the National Park Trust.

Gregory J. Hale

Gregory Hale is associate editor of *International Environmental Systems Update*, a monthly newsletter covering the ISO 14000 series of standards published by CEEM Information Services. He is also an associate editor of *Integrated Management Systems Update*, a monthly newsletter on environmental, health and safety, quality, and financial management systems. Hale communicates regularly with representatives from industry, government, management consulting services, and public interest groups worldwide concerning management systems activities. He is an observing delegate to the U.S. TAG to TC 207 and a member of the Environmental Auditing Roundtable. He speaks to U.S. audiences on ISO 14000 implementation.

Hale has published articles in several management publications, including *Quality Progress Magazine*, *Quality Digest*, and *Quality Magazine*.

He received his B.A. in journalism from Radford University in 1994.

Caroline G. Hemenway

Caroline G. Hemenway, vice president and publisher of CEEM Information Services, a division of CEEM Inc., has more than 18 years' experience in publishing. She has covered business, the environment, medicine, and federal and local government for news services, newspapers, magazines, and newsletters.

At CEEM Hemenway is responsible for the development, management, and profitability of all CEEM's publications and multimedia products. Her focus at CEEM is to provide readers with practical, accurate, timely, independent, and comprehensive management systems information.

Hemenway launched the *International Environmental Systems Update* monthly newsletter in 1994 and *ISO 14000 In Focus* video training in 1995 for CEEM in response to heavy demand from business for information on the ISO 14000 series of international environmental management system standards. In 1996, she launched *Integrated Management Systems Update* on environmental, health and safety, quality, and financial management systems, and *The ISO 14000 Handbook*, among other products. She speaks on ISO 14000 and related topics to audiences nationwide.

As executive editor at CEEM from 1991 to 1994, Hemenway managed the company's newsletters and launches, including *Quality Systems Update* and *Aboveground Tank Update*, which she edited until they were divested recently. She is a delegate from CEEM Inc. to the U.S. TAGs to ISO TC 207 and TC 176.

Hemenway has a B.A. in journalism and political science from the George Washington University, and has won several journalism honors.

Patrick F. Hoy

Patrick F. Hoy is the Environmental Manager for SGS-Thomson Microelectronics, Inc., San Diego and Phoenix semiconductor operations. Hoy was responsible for preparing the Rancho Bernardo site for the EMAS and ISO 14001 certification. Hoy is also responsible for ensuring compliance with applicable federal, state, and local environmental rules and regulations.

Prior to joining ST, Hoy managed the Risk Management and Prevention Program for the County of San Diego Hazardous Materials Management Division. Hoy received his B.S. in biochemistry from California Polytechnic University at San Luis Obispo and an M.B.A. from National University. He is a certified hazardous materials manager (CHMM).

Hoy offers special thanks to Joe Hess, Dames & Moore project manager. Hess was instrumental in the development of the environmental manual for SGS-Thomson, and provided peer review of the contribution.

Rozell Hunter

Rod Hunter practices law in the Brussels office of Hunton & Williams, where he has been based since 1989. Hunter advises clients on trade barrier issues raised by E.U. and national environmental legislation (e.g., product "take-back" initiatives, and substance restrictions); E.U. and national chemical environmental and occupational health and safety law on industrial operations; organizing corporate international environmental management and compliance efforts; and environmental issues in business transactions.

Hunter co-authored the Environmental Law Institute's *EC Environmental Law Deskbook* and regularly contributes feature articles on E.U. affairs and on environmental law to *The Wall Street Journal Europe*. He also serves as director of Regulatory Studies at the Centre for the New Europe (CNE), an independent Brussels-based think tank.

Before joining Hunton & Williams, Hunter served during 1988 as Associate to the Chief Justice of Australia, Sir Anthony Mason. Prior to that, he clerked for a year for U.S. Circuit Judge Boyce Martin, of the Sixth Circuit Court of Appeals. He served during 1982 and 1983 in Washington, D.C., as an aide to U.S. Senator John Warner. Hunter received his law degree from the University of Virginia (J.D., 1986), where he served on the managing board of the *Virginia Law Review*.

Raymond W. Kane

Raymond Kane is an engineer with Environmental Management Consulting and a leading national expert in the field of environmental compliance management, auditing, and program development with almost 20 years' experience. He is a principal author in the widely used text *Environmental Audits, 6th Edition* , and has authored more than 20 papers and articles on environmental compliance.

Kane has directed environmental audit and compliance management programs for numerous Fortune 500 companies, including Kodak, Philip Morris, Sandoz, GE, Air Products, and Eaton Corp. He also developed the first environmental audit programs for the U.S. Air Force and the National Institutes of Health and was the project director of one of the first SEC-mandated environmental audits of Occidental Petroleum Corp. in 1980. He is listed in "Who's Who" in the Environmental Registry and was awarded "Distinguished Instructor" from Government Institutes Inc. He is a member of the U.S. TAG delegation to ISO TC 207.

Kane graduated from Villanova University with a Bachelor's and Master's degree in civil/environmental engineering and is a registered professional engineer. *Environmental Management Consulting, Executive Commons, 175 Strofford Avenue Suite 1, Wayne, PA, 19087; tel: 610-975-4405; fax: 610-687-7860.*

Robert Kloepfer

Robert Kloepfer is vice president of Haley & Aldrich's Environmental, Health & Safety Management Consulting Group. An environmental professional with more than 16 years' experience in government, industry, and consulting, his expertise lies in helping clients design, develop, and implement systems to maximize environmental compliance, risk control, and efficiency. He has extensive experience developing and managing multimedia environmental compliance and management systems audits, and has designed and managed audits for clients in the aerospace, utility, automotive, biomedical, insurance, and petroleum industries, among others. In addition, Kloepfer's other areas of expertise include environmental due diligence for real property transactions and corporate acquisitions, facility siting, and environmental impact assessment, environmental communications, and training.

Kloepfer is an active member of the U.S. TAG to TC 207. He is a frequent lecturer, and has published several recent papers and articles on ISO 14000 and the underlying principles and systems of environmental management. He is also active in the Environmental Auditing Roundtable.

Kloepfer received an M.S. in environmental policy and management from the University of Michigan and a B.S. in environmental resource management from Allegheny College. *Haley & Aldrich, Inc., 110 National Drive, Glastonbury, CT 06033; tel: 203-659-424;, fax: 203-659-4003.*

C. Foster Knight

Knight is Managing Director of Knight & Associates, a consulting group specializing in environmental management, law, and technology. Knight & Associates is helping companies in the U.S. and Mexico develop corporate environmental strategies and management systems and provide training and technical assistance on ISO 14001 planning and implementation. It also assists companies with appropriate use of information technologies for environmental management.

Knight is an environmental attorney with more than 20 years' experience in the environmental field working in government (policy and enforcement) and industry. He is the former environmental counsel to Digital Equipment Corporation, responsible for worldwide environmental compliance management systems. Earlier, he was deputy general counsel of the President's Council on Environmental Quality and a deputy attorney general in the California Attorney General's Environmental Unit. He is bilingual in Spanish and English and recently taught seminars on environmental management systems (and ISO 14000) to industry managers in Mexico. Knight teaches courses for CEEM Inc. on implementing and auditing ISO 14001. He was an early participant in the U.S. Technical Advisory Group to TC 207 and a current delegate. He is a graduate of Yale University and the University of California, Berkeley, School of Law.

Knight & Associates, Environmental Management, Law & Technology, 16 Hillside Avenue, Winchester, MA 01890; Tel: 617-721-6454; Fax: 617-721-0838; email: CKnight747@aol.com.

Jennifer L. Kraus

Jennifer L. Kraus is the program director for Environmental Management Services with Dames & Moore, an international environmental consulting firm. Kraus specializes in providing strategic environmental management and planning services to clients in the United States and Mexico. Since joining the firm in 1990, she has managed multidisciplinary environmental projects for clients in the U.S. and Mexico. Projects include compliance audits, environmental management system planning, hazardous waste management, hazardous materials management and training, NPDES stormwater permitting and compliance, and spill prevention and contingency planning.

Prior to joining Dames & Moore, Kraus managed the Environmental Resources Management Program for General Dynamics Electronics Division in San Diego. While with GD she was responsible for ensuring compliance with applicable federal, state, and local environmental rules and regulations, and for implementing the company's proactive environmental program. Before joining GD she served as safety engineer with Litton Industries.

Kraus received her B.S. in biology from Princeton University and a Masters in Public Health from UCLA. She is a Registered Environmental Assessor (REA) with the state of California and a certified hazardous materials manager (CHMM).

Philip A. Marcus

Philip Marcus is vice president at ICF Kaiser Incorporated and is professionally affiliated with the American Society for Quality Control. He is competent in the development of EMSs, which improve compliance and competitive advantage for Fortune 500 corporations, including benchmarking, strategic plans, worldwide standards of practice, program support tools, product evaluation, environmental performance evaluation, and total quality environmental management programs. Marcus has been an author of over 20 publications and numerous presentations to professional societies dealing with environmental management systems, performance measures, international environmental trends, waste disposal, etc. He is a member of U.S. ANSI delegation to ISO TC 207 and is a U.S. technical expert to ISO TC 207 Subcommittee 1, Environmental Management Systems, 1993-present. Marcus also is a member of an ANSI-designated U.S. panel to interpret the terms of the ISO 14001 standard. He has participated in drafting ISO 14004.

Marcus has a B.A. in biological conservation from the University of Wisconsin, an M.S. in environmental planning from the University of Wisconsin, and an M.B.A. from the University of Illinois.

John E. Master

John E. Master is a retired executive from ARCO Chemical Company, currently a consultant to the Chemical

Manufacturers Association (CMA). He is responsible for the chemical industry participation in the international environmental management standards development process, and also assists in integrating Responsible Care® with the standards. He is a member of the Chairman's Advisory Group to the U.S. TAG to TC 207 and chairs the U.S. SubTAG for Environmental Performance Evaluation. He serves as the lead U.S. expert on EPE to TC 207 SC 4.

Master worked with ARCO Chemical Company and its predecessor, Sinclair Oil, from 1957 until 1995. He has a strong process and project background, as well as extensive technical and operations management experience including several years as corporate manager of engineering and environment. In his last assignment, he was director of environment, health, and safety at ARCO Chemical, responsible for worldwide performance improvement programs in the safety, health, and environmental area.

From 1983 to 1987 Master served on the director's board of the engineering and construction contracting division of the American Institute of Chemical Engineers, and served as chairman in 1985/86. He has also chaired CMA's Engineering Advisory Committee (1986-88) and its International Affairs Committee (1992-94). Master received his B.S. in chemical engineering from Yale University.

Lelia M. McAdams

Lelia McAdams is technical manager of the corporate EH&S engineering group at Lucent Technologies, formerly AT&T Microelectronics.

From 1993 to 1996 McAdams was technical manager with the Environmental Strategic Planning Department of AT&T's Corporate Environmental & Safety Engineering Center. The department was responsible for tracking emerging global or regional environmental and energy issues that may affect multiple AT&T business units; participating in legislative, regulatory, and standards development processes; developing corporate environmental/energy policies, standards, and goals; and developing and coordinating deployment of certain AT&T environmental/energy programs.

Since joining AT&T in 1987, McAdams spent six years in the Corporate Environmental Engineering Department as senior engineer/distinguished member of technical staff responsible for RCRA and waste management consultation, program coordination, and legislative review and advocacy. She also coordinated the formation of a cross-business unit environmental and safety compliance team in Mexico and was responsible for addressing shareholder issues relating to operations in Mexico. McAdams has a B.S. in civil engineering from the University of Dayton.

AT&T separated into three separate companies in 1996, forming AT&T, Lucent Technologies, and NCR.

Jean H. McCreary

Jean McCreary is a lawyer with Nixon, Hargrave, Devans & Doyle, LLP, in its Environmental Practice Group. She chairs the group's preacquisition, compliance, and asset-based lending audit practice, which is supported by in-house technical professional auditors. McCreary has coordinated and conducted environmental compliance and preapplication audits throughout the United States and internationally.

McCreary serves as president of the Environmental Auditing Roundtable, the world's largest and oldest professional organization for environmental auditors. She currently chairs the committee developing the U.S. position on general auditing principles in the U.S. TAG to TC 207. She served as the U.S. expert on ANSI/ISO 14010 at the ISO TC 207 meeting in Oslo, Norway, in 1995.

McCreary has been appointed as a representative of auditor interests by ANSI to serve on the 18-member EMS Council. The council is developing the American National Accreditation Program to accredit registrars, certifiers of auditors, and providers of training programs for ISO 14000.

McCreary graduated from the University of Rochester and obtained her J.D. at the University of Florida College of Law. She is a member of the bar in New York and Florida. *Nixon, Hargrave, Devans & Doyle, Clinton Square, PO Box 1051, Rochester, NY 14603; tel: 716-263-1611; fax: 716-263-1600.*

Annette D. McCully

Annette McCully has steadily expanded the range of her capabilities over the last twenty years to include regulatory research and documentation, project coordination, policy development, construction safety, health promotion, health care reform and research, malpractice/insurance issues, medical ethics, and technical writing. Her degree project on the group dynamics of small group decision making in health care cost containment provided the skills for her to effectively coordinate complex, unwieldy documentation and large groups of reviewers.

Her experience in developing corporate safety, health, and environmental policy and procedures for major corporations enables her to know which regulations are required and how these apply. When regulations must be applied to multiple sites and varying work processes as in the aerospace and construction industries, she has successfully coordinated and developed documentation appropriate for all sites and conditions. She has written on a regular basis for *Northwest Physician* and *Enviro* magazines. She is also a west coast correspondent for *International Environmental Systems Update*.

Samantha Munn

Samantha Munn is the manager for Environmental Systems Business Development for Inchcape Testing Service/Intertek Services and leads the ISO 14001 certification program. Prior to this, Munn held positions with the British Standards Institution, the U.K.'s national standards body, working on the U.K.'s software TickIt scheme, the development of the U.K.'s EMS standard, BS 7750, and eventually as BSI's business development officer in the U.S.

Munn spent three months in Africa as a conservation volunteer conducting environmental research for The Society for Environmental Exploration. She is a participating delegate to ISO TC 207. Munn is a London University Honors graduate of zoology, and is an associate environmental auditor with EARA. *Inchcape Testing Services/Intertek, 313 Speen Street, Natick, MA 01760; tel: 800-810-1195; fax: 800-813-9287.*

Cynthia Neve

Cynthia Neve is an ISO Consultant with The Victoria Group. In this capacity, she is responsible for developing and presenting workshops and courses regarding ISO 14000, as well as consulting on the proposed standard. Before this, she was a senior consultant for AT&T's Environmental and Safety organization based in Basking Ridge, New Jersey. Her background includes experience as an ISO 9000 Quality Consultant/Trainer and Field Quality Manager responsible for vendor management activities, determining the need for and implementing Quality Improvement Programs, and providing technical support to field quality associates. An ASQC Certified Quality Auditor, Neve has chaired and performed quality system audits, as well as participated with the AT&T Quality Registrar in assessment of companies in a variety of industries.

Marissa A. Perrone

Marissa Perrone is president of ECO-TRADE Consulting, based in Philadelphia. Consulting services include conducting training, preparing analytical pieces, and developing business strategies for companies seeking to export abroad. Clients include industry, environmental organizations, and government agencies. Perrone has authored articles in the field of trade and the environment in various publications (i.e., *The Environmental Law Reporter; In Business; Export Today*).

Perrone formerly served as deputy director for Trade and Environment Affairs for the Office of the United States Trade Representative in Washington, D.C., 1992-93. Under the Bush and Clinton administrations, she assisted in developing U.S. policy on environmental issues in the Uruguay Round of the General Agreement on Tariffs and Trade and in NAFTA. Perrone also served as a budget policy analyst for the Secretary of the U.S. Department of Commerce, 1990-91.

Perrone has been an active delegate to the U.S. TAG to ISO TC 207. Since 1994, she has served as a member of the New Jersey Commission on National Service. She has an M.B.A. in international business and economic development and a B.S. in marketing from the University of Maryland at College Park, Maryland. *Eco-Trade Consulting, 4000 Bell Atlantic Tower, 1717 Arch Street 37th Floor, Philadelphia, PA 19103-2793.*

Edwin Pinero

Edwin Pinero is a certified professional geologist and special projects manager with EnSafe, an environmental and safety designs consulting firm based in Memphis, Tennessee. He has more than 14 years' experience in the environmental field, ranging from offshore oil exploration to providing expert testimony on the siting of landfills.

Pinero has worked closely in negotiations with local, state, and federal government. He has conducted scores of environmental studies, including compliance audits, site assessments, contaminant transport studies, and remediation projects and is well aware of the environmental challenges facing industry today.

Pinero is active in numerous legislative work groups affiliated with organizations such as the Pennsylvania Chamber of Business and Industry, and conducts training seminars on environmental compliance and management issues. He is also a delegate to the U.S. TAG to ISO TC 207 and the leader of SubTAG 2, Taskgroup 4, which is working on environmental site assessment standards.

Pinero has received lead auditor training for EMSs. *EnSafe, 5724 Summer Trees Drive, Memphis, TN. 38134; tel: 901-372-7962; fax: 901-372-2454.*

Elizabeth A. Potts

Elizabeth Potts is president of ABS Quality Evaluations Inc., an accredited third-party registrar of management systems for a variety of standards including the ISO 9000, QS 9000, and ISO 14000 standards. She was most recently employed as the quality assurance manager for the American Gas Association Laboratories where she was responsible for product certification follow-up inspections, ISO 9000 quality system registrations, and internal quality control program development. Previously, Potts was employed as a quality control manager with Babcock & Wilcox, where she developed and implemented quality control programs for nuclear reactor components and other defense-related components.

Potts is a delegate to the U.S. TAG to ISO/TC 176 on quality assurance and quality management. Potts is a member of the Board of Directors of the Registrar Accreditation Board (RAB). She is also a registered ASQC Certified Quality Auditor (#445), and an IQA Registered Assessor. Potts is a chemical engineering graduate from the University of Illinois and also holds an M.B.A. from Ashland (Ohio) University. *ABS Quality Evaluations, Inc., 16855 Northchase Drive, Houston TX 77060-6008; tel: 713-874-6528; fax: 713-874-9564.*

Richard G. Quick

Richard Quick is a senior industrial hygienist with the Lucent Technologies (formerly AT&T) Corporate Environmental, Health, and Safety Organization. He is a certified industrial hygienist and a certified safety professional.

Since joining AT&T in 1987, Quick's responsibilities have included developing corporate safety and health practices and goals, performing worldwide safety and health internal audits, and participating in the regulatory standards development process. He has also developed and delivered safety and health workshops for company locations in the Asian, Latin American, and European regions. Recently, Quick has managed the implementation of the AT&T Corporate Safety Goal: participation in the OSHA Voluntary Protection Program (VPP). In this role, Quick has performed numerous VPP self-assessments, application reviews, and OSHA VPP Onsite Review consultations.

Quick received a B.S. degree in environmental science from Rutgers University-Cook College and an M.S. degree in occupational safety and health from Temple University.

Stanley Rhodes

Since founding Scientific Certification Systems in 1984, Stanley Rhodes has taken the lead in the development of several major certification endeavors in the areas of food, safety, forestry, and environmental claims certification. He has spearheaded SCS's development of a comprehensive life-cycle assessment program to assist companies in gauging the environmental burdens associated with their production systems, and to identify strategies for continuous environmental improvement through product design and process improvement innovations. SCS's efforts have led to the creation of the Certified Eco-Profile (internationally recognized as a "Type III" label), an environmental performance-based information disclosure labeling system for both products and services. In addition, he has authored numerous documents, and has conducted seminars and workshops, on both international eco-labeling and LCA.

Rhodes is a U.S. delegate to ISO TC207. He participates as a U.S. expert delegate on life-cycle assessment, where he has participated actively in examining the technical feasibility of using inventory analysis for impact and risk assessment, and standardizing impact assessment. Rhodes is also the acting U.S. vice-chairman to the Subcommittee on Environmental Labeling.

He has a B.S. in chemistry from the University of California, Berkeley, and a Ph.D. in organic chemistry from Purdue University. *Scientific Certification Systems, Ordway Building Suite 109, One Kaiser Plaza, Oakland, CA 94612-3601; tel: 510-832-1415; fax: 510-832-0359.*

Brian P. Riedel

Brian Riedel is counsel for EPA's Office of Planning and Policy Analysis (OPPA), which serves the assistant administrator for Enforcement and Compliance Assurance (OECA). Riedel is the OECA lead on enforcement and compliance matters relating to ISO 14001 standards for environmental management systems. He is a member of the U.S. Technical Advisory Group (TAG) to ISO Technical Committee 207 on environmental management.

Riedel is also co-author of EPA's interim and final environmental self-policing policies. He is co-chair of the Quick Response Team responsible for making recommendations regarding interpretation and application of the interim and final policies to cases. Before moving to EPA, Riedel practiced environmental law with the Washington, D.C., law firm of Newman & Holtzinger.

He received his J.D. from the University of Wisconsin and A.B. from the University of Michigan.

Connie G. Ritzert

Connie Ritzert, an environmental issues manager with Alcoa, has more than 30 years' technical and management experience, more than 25 of which have been in the environmental field. Her current responsibilities focus on environmental management and risk assessment. Her original academic background is in chemistry (Baylor University), but her varied experience includes R&D management, product evaluations, business management, regulatory compliance, materials recovery operations, environmental consulting, water and waste treatment, analytical chemistry, and site investigations. She has been a speaker on dozens of platforms on subjects as diverse as waste minimization in the metal finishing industry, colloidal silica in reverse osmosis systems, and implications of the U.S. experience for emerging Australian environmental regulations.

Ritzert also has 25 years of experience in consensus standards development and has served on the board of directors of ASTM and as chairman of the board of the Institute for Standards Research. She is an active participant in the U.S. TAG to ISO TC 207. She has been a U.S. delegate to all three of the TC 207 international meetings and serves as a U.S. expert in TC 207 SC4 on EPE. In her current position with Alcoa, she is developing and deploying environmental management guidance to Alcoa business worldwide.

Michael A. Ross

Michael A. Ross is CEO and principal consultant of Ross Ltd., Quality & Environmental Consulting. For the past 25 years, he has assisted numerous clients in performing environmental compliance audits and evaluations at their facilities; worked closely with state and federal EPAs at the project and program levels; and directed and coordinated client companies' program development in environmental compliance and management. Ross has been an active participant in the U.S. TAG to TC 207 for since 1993. He also is a delegate to the TAG to ISO TC 176 on quality management and quality assurance. *Ross, Ltd., 310 Hale Meade Road, Gray, TN 37615-4636; tel: 423-283-0875; fax: 423-283-0875.*

Dawne Schomer

Schomer is a member of the Corporate Environmental, Safety and Health Team of Texas Instruments Inc. located in Dallas, Texas. She currently manages the EHS Audit Program and the EHS Systems Program.

Schomer is serving the environmental community as co-leader of the Workgroup on Auditor Qualifications for the U.S. delegation to ISO TC 207. During 1994-1995, she vice-chaired the Standards Conformance and Registration Advisory Group, which provided research and advice to the U.S. TAG on the issues of ISO 14000 certification and registration.

Schomer participates in the Environmental Auditors Roundtable and was 1994-95 co-chair of the EAR Auditor Qualifications/Training Workgroup.

Schomer has been an environmental auditor since 1985 with experience in semiconductors, defense systems electronics, printed circuit board manufacturing, and microcircuit processor plating. She has served in the capacity of site environmental engineer, corporate environmental specialist, environmental/safety and facilities manager, and as supervisor of a municipal industrial wastewater pretreatment program.

Schomer received her B.S. in environmental management from the University of Houston, at Clear Lake, Texas, and her M.S. in environmental science from the University of Texas at Arlington. *Texas Instruments, Incorporated, 13532 N. Central Expressway M/S 56, PO Box 655012, Dallas, TX 75265; tel: 214-997-5153; fax: 214-997-2626.*

Sachin Shah

Sachin Shah is the assistant editor for CEEM Information Services. He writes news stories and manages regular features in *International Environmental Systems Update* and *Integrated Management Systems Update*. He is a member of the Institute of Electrical and Electronics Engineers Environment, Health, and Safety Committee. In addition, he is responsible for CEEM's ISO 9001 quality management system implementation.

Shah holds a B.A. in political science from Mary Washington College in Fredericksburg, Virginia.

Cornelius C. "Bud" Smith, Jr.

Bud Smith is the director of environmental management services at ML Strategies Inc. He brings more than 25 years of legal and management experience with environmental, health, and safety (EH&S) issues. He is recognized for his development, integration, and implementation of innovative and cost-effective EH&S compliance and management systems. Smith advises and assists clients in the consumer products, pharmaceutical, chemical, automobile, paper, aluminum, and other manufacturing and service industries on environmental compliance and other environmental management issues. Project activities include benchmarking, policy and procedures development, strategic planning reviews, training, development and implementation of self-assessment, auditing and performance evaluation tools, and conducting environmental aspects/impacts and gap analyses.

Smith is a leader of the U.S. TAG to ISO TC 207. He is a member of the TAG Chairman's Advisory Group, chairman of its Environmental Auditing SubTAG, and a member of its EMS, labeling, environmental performance evaluation, and life-cycle analysis SubTAGs. He also serves as a member of the TAG's Liaison

Group with the U.S. TAG to TC 176, and the ANSI ASC Z-1 Standards Group Leadership Council and Environmental Subcommittee. Smith has published and lectured widely on EH&S management topics. He received his B.S. from Holy Cross College and his J.D. from New York University.

Turner T. Smith, Jr.

Smith is a partner in the Washington, D.C., office of Hunton & Williams, an international law firm with more than 500 attorneys and offices in nine U.S. cities, and Brussels, Hong Kong, and Warsaw. Head of his firm's international environmental law practice, Smith has specialized in energy and environmental law for more than 25 years and was the first managing partner of the firm's Brussels office. Smith's current practice centers on international environmental and energy law, and involves policy, transactional, and litigation work, including advice concerning the European Union's environmental laws and those of its member states, environmental laws in Central and Eastern Europe and the former Soviet Union, Latin American environmental law, U.S. environmental and energy law, and the impact of environmental law and liabilities on business and financial transactions. Recently his practice has focused on corporate environmental management issues, advising companies on international environmental law, major environmental rulemakings, and regulatory reform matters.

A graduate of Princeton University and Harvard Law School, Smith has written and lectured extensively on European and American environmental law, has testified before the U.S. Congress, the United Kingdom's House of Lords, and the Royal Commission on Environmental Pollution.

Denise A. St. Ours

Denise St. Ours, a contributing editor for CEEM Information Services, reports and writes news articles for CEEM's publications, including its two newsletters — *International Environmental Systems Update* and *Integrated Management Systems Update*.

St. Ours has a B.S. in political science at the University of Virginia and did graduate work in publishing at the George Washington University. She began her career in journalism with *US News & World Report* and *USA Today*, and then worked as public relations director for the Epilepsy Association of the Eastern Shore.

Nancy Evans Stuckwisch

Nancy Evans Stuckwisch lives in Mobile, Alabama, where she works as an independent consultant and has formed TECHNE Environmental Consulting. She was one of the earliest participants in the ISO 14000 process for the U.S. environmental community. Through her participation with the U.S. TAG to TC 207 she continues to work to bring a stakeholder perspective to the table.

At an earlier stage of her career Stuckwisch worked with a national environmental organization as project coordinator in a division working with senior executives from corporate America on emerging issues of mutual concern such as international trade and the environment and environmental justice.

Stuckwisch has an M.A. in war studies from King's College, London, and M.S.C. in environmental management from the London School of Economics. She is currently working on her Ph.D. thesis on energy policy and the environment at the Sary School.

Joel Urman

Joel Urman has worked for the IBM Corporation for nearly 30 years, the last 10 of which have focused on national and international standardization and conformity assessment as IBM's program director of standards. He is on the IBM corporate standards staff and is IBM's representative on several committees of ANSI, Accredited Standards Committee X3 on Information Technology, and the U.S. TAG to TC 207. During his career with IBM he has held jobs in marketing, technical support, data security, and telecommunications policy.

As the chair of ANSI's ICAC, Urman leads the committee responsible for developing U.S. input to the International Organization for Standardization's committee on conformity assessment, ISO/CASCO. He is a delegate to the U.S. TAG to JTC 1's Special Working Group on Conformity Assessment (SWG-CA), and serves as a U.S. delegate to international meetings of the SWG-CA.

Urman has had considerable international experience. From 1987-1992, he was on assignment for IBM in Tokyo, Japan, where he was involved in standards, telecommunication policy, and government relations in Asia. Before that, his responsibilities included IBM standards activity in Latin America.

Urman has a B.S. in engineering and an M.B.A. degree from U.C.L.A. *IBM, 500 Columbus Avenue, Thornwood, NY 10594; fax: 914-742-6747.*

Heather F. Villavicencio

Heather Villavicencio is an editorial assistant at CEEM Information Services. Along with her work on *The ISO 14000 Handbook*, she does editorial work for *International Environmental Systems Update* and *Integrated Management Systems Update*. She holds a B.A. in English from George Mason University in Fairfax, Virginia.

John Wolfe

John Wolfe is the manager of ICF Kaiser International, Inc.'s, Canadian office. Before joining Kaiser, an international consulting group, he was director of the business management systems program, research and development, for the Canadian Standards Association in Toronto. In addition, he was secretary to TC 207 for the Standards Council of Canada, which held the ISO secretariat.

Wolfe serves on the board of directors of the Canadian Environmental Auditors Association and the Major Industrial Accident Council of Canada. He belongs to a number of associations, councils, and steering committees that deal with environmental matters. He has led Canada's delegation on private-sector environmental standards and conformity assessment programs, and the trilateral NAFTA discussions coordinated by the Standards Council of Canada, among others.

Wolfe holds a Master's degree in business administration from York University and a Master's degree in environmental science from Trent University.

Glossary and Acronyms

SECTION 1
Glossary

Accreditation — Procedure by which an authoritative body formally recognizes that a body or person is competent to carry out specific tasks. (ISO/IEC Guide 2)

Accreditation Body — Body that gives formal recognition that a body or person is competent to carry out specific tasks.

Accreditation Criteria — Set of requirements that is used by an accreditation body, to be fulfilled by a conformity assessment body in order to be accredited. (ISO/IEC Guide 2)

Accreditation System — System that has its own rules of procedure and management for carrying out accreditation.
Note — Accreditation of conformity assessment bodies is normally awarded following successful assessment and is followed by appropriate surveillance. (ISO/IEC Guide 2)

Accredited Body — Body to which accreditation has been granted. (ISO/IEC Guide 2)

Allocation — Technique for partitioning the inputs and outputs of a system among products. (ISO 14040)

Ancillary Material — Material input that is used by the unit process producing the product, but is not used directly in the formation of the product. (ISO 14040)

Applicant — Legal entity applying for an environmental label for a product or a range of products and that undertakes the compliance with ecological and product function criteria and the certification and costs involved in the application and awarding of the label. (ISO 14024)

Assessment — An estimate or determination of the significance, importance, or value of something. (ASQC Quality Auditing Technical Committee)

Assessment Body — Third party that assesses products and registers the quality systems of suppliers.

Assessment System — Procedural and managerial rules for conducting an assessment leading to the issue of a certification document and its maintenance.

Audit — A planned, independent, and documented assessment to determine whether agreed-upon requirements are being met. (ASQC Quality Auditing Technical Committee)

Audit Conclusion — Professional judgment or opinion expressed by an auditor about the subject matter of the audit, based on and limited to reasoning the auditor has applied to audit findings. (ISO 14010)

Audit Criteria — Policies, practices, procedures, or requirements against which the auditor compares collected audit evidence about the subject matter. (ISO 14010)

Audit Evidence — Verifiable information, records, or statements of fact. (ISO 14010)

Audit Findings — Results of the evaluation of the collected audit evidence compared against the agreed audit criteria. (ISO 14010)

Audit Program — The organizational structure, commitment, and documented methods used to plan and perform audits. (ASQC Quality Auditing Technical Committee)

Audit Team — Group of auditors, or a single auditor, designated to perform a given audit; the audit team may also include technical experts and auditors in training. (ISO 14010)

Auditee — Organization to be audited. (ISO 14010)

Auditor (environmental) — Person qualified to perform environmental audits. (ISO 14010)

Body — Legal or administrative entity that has specific tasks and composition.
Note — Examples of bodies are organizations, authorities, companies, and foundations. (ISO/IEC Guide 2)

Certificate [of conformity] — Document issued under the rules of a certification system, indicating that adequate confidence is provided that a duly identified product, process, or service is in conformity with a specific standard or other normative document. (ISO/IEC Guide 2)

Certification — Procedure by which a third party gives written assurance that a product, process, or service conforms to specified requirements. (ISO/IEC Guide 2)

Certification Body — Body that conducts certification of conformity.

Certification System — System that has its own rules of procedure and management for carrying out certification of conformity. (ISO/IEC Guide 2)

Certifier — *See certification body.*

Certified — The EMS of a company, location, or plant is certified for conformance with ISO 14001 after it has demonstrated such conformance through the audit process. When used to indicate EMS certification, it means the same thing as registration.

Client — Organization commissioning the audit. (ISO 14010)

Comparative Assertion — Environmental claim made publicly regarding the superiority of one product versus a competing product that performs the same function. (ISO 14040)

Compliance — An affirmative indication or judgment that the supplier of a product or service has met the requirements of the relevant specifications, contract, or regulation; also the state of meeting the requirements. (ANSI/ASQC A3) (*See also conformance.*)

Conformance — An affirmative indication or judgment that a product or service has met the requirements of the relevant specifications, contract, or regulation; also the state of meeting the requirements. (ANSI/ASQC A3) (*See also compliance.*)

Conformity Assessment — Conformity assessment includes all activities that are intended to assure the conformity of products or systems to a set of standards. This can include testing, inspection, certification, quality system assessment, and other activities.

Continual Improvement — Process of enhancing the environmental management system to achieve improvements in overall environmental performance, in line with the organization's environmental policy. Note — The process need not take place in all areas of activity simultaneously. (ISO 14001)

Contractor — The organization that provides a product to the customer in a contractual situation. (ISO 8402)

Convention — A customary practice, rule, or method. (ASQC Quality Auditing Technical Committee)

Corrective Action — An action taken to eliminate the causes of an existing nonconformity, defect, or other undesirable situation in order to prevent recurrence. (ISO 8402)

Customer — Ultimate consumer, user, client, beneficiary, or second party. (ISO 9004-3)

Data Quality Indicators — Measures that characterize attributes of data or data sets. (ISO 14040)

Degree — Recognized national or international degree, or equivalent qualification, normally obtained after secondary education, through a minimum of three years' formal full-time or equivalent part-time study. (ISO 14012)

Design Review — A formal, documented, comprehensive, and systematic examination of a design to evaluate the design requirements and the capability of the design to meet these requirements and to identify problems and propose solutions. (ISO 8402)

Economic Benefit Component — The economic advantage a violator gains through noncompliance.

Environmental Audit — A systematic, documented, periodic and objective review by regulated entities of facility operations and practices related to meeting environmental requirements.

Elementary Flow — Any flow of raw material entering the system being studied and that has been drawn from the environment without previous human transformation; any flow of material leaving the system being studied, and that is discarded into the environment, without subsequent human transformation. (ISO 14040)

EN 45000 — A series of standards set up by the EC to regulate and harmonize certification, accreditation and testing activities. Guides for assessment and accreditation of certification bodies and guides for bodies operating product certification systems were published in Fall 1995.

Environment — Surroundings in which an organization operates, including air, water, land, natural resources, flora, fauna, humans, and their interrelation.
Note — Surroundings in this context extend from within an organization to the global system. (ISO 14001)

Environmental Aspect — Element of an organization's activities, products, and services that can interact with the environment. (ISO 14001)

Environmental Audit — Systematic, documented verification process of objectively obtaining and evaluating audit evidence to determine whether specified environmental activities, events, conditions, management systems, or information about these matters conform with audit criteria, and communicating the results of this process to the client. (ISO 14010)

Environmental Claim — Any environmental declaration that describes or implies by whatever means the effects that the raw material extraction, production, distribution, use, or disposal of a product or service has on the environment. This applies to effects that are local, regional, or global, and the environment that an individual lives in, affects, or is affected by. (ISO 14021)

Environmental Impact — Any change to the environment, whether adverse or beneficial, wholly or partially resulting from an organization's activities, products, or services. (ISO 14001)

Environmental Label/Declaration — Claim indicating the environmental attributes of a product or service that may take the form of statements, symbols, or graphics on product or package labels, product literature, technical bulletins, advertising, publicity, etc. (ISO 14020)

Environmental Labeling–Type I — Multiple criteria-based, third-party voluntary environmental labeling program. (ISO 14024)

Environmental Management System(EMS) — Organizational structure, responsibilities, practices, procedures, processes, and resources for developing, implementing, achieving, reviewing, and maintaining the environmental policy. (ISO 14001)

EMS Audit — A systematic and documented verification process to objectively obtain and evaluate evidence to determine whether an organization's environmental management system conforms to the EMS audit criteria set by the organization, and to communicate the results of this process to management. (ISO 14001)

EMS Audit Criteria — Policies, practices, procedures, or requirements, such as covered by ISO 14001, and, if applicable, any additional EMS requirements against which the auditor compares collected evidence about the organization's EMS. (ISO 14011)

Environmental Indicator — Expression that is used to provide information about environmental performance or the condition of the environment.
Note — The expression can be relative or absolute. (ISO 14031 WD 4) *Formerly environmental performance indicator*

Environmental Objective — Overall environmental goal, arising from the environmental policy, that an organization sets itself to achieve, and that is quantified where practicable. (ISO 14001)

Environmental Performance — The measurable results of the environmental management system, related to an organization's control of its environmental aspects, based on its environmental policy, objectives, and targets. (ISO 14001)

Environmental Performance Evaluation — Process to measure, analyze, assess, report, and communicate an organization's environmental performance against criteria set by management. (ISO 14031 WD 4)

Environmental Policy — Statement by the organization of its intentions and principles in relation to its overall environmental performance, which provides a framework for action and for the setting of its environmental objectives and targets. (ISO 14001)

Environmental Target — Detailed performance requirement, quantified wherever practicable, applicable to the organization or parts thereof, that arises from the environmental objectives and that needs to be set and met in order to achieve those objectives. (ISO 14001)

Explanatory Statement — Any further explanation that is needed so that an environmental claim can be properly understood by a purchaser or consumer.

Finding — A conclusion of importance based on observation(s). (ASQC Quality Auditing Technical Committee)

Follow-up Audit — An audit whose purpose and scope are limited to verifying that corrective action has been accomplished as scheduled and to determining that the action effectively prevented recurrence. (ASQC Quality Auditing Technical Committee)

Function — Performance characteristic.

Functional Unit — Measure of performance of the main functional output of the product system. (ISO 14040)

Gravity-Based Penalty — The "seriousness" or "punitive" portion of a penalty.

Interested Party — Individual or group concerned with or affected by the environmental performance of an investigation.

Inputs and Outputs — Material or energy that crosses a unit process boundary.
Example — Materials may include raw materials, products, emissions, and waste. (ISO 14040)

Inspection — Activities such as measuring, examining, testing, and gauging one or more characteristics of a product or service and comparing these with specified requirements to determine conformity. (ISO 8402)

Interested Party — Individual or group concerned with or affected by the environmental performance of an organization. (ISO 14001)

Joint Assessment — Cooperative assessments resulting in formal mutual recognition of certifications.

Lead Auditor (environmental) — Person qualified to manage and perform environmental audits. (ISO 14010)

Licensee — A party authorized by a practitioner to use an environmental label. (ISO 14024)

Life Cycle — Consecutive and inter-linked stages of a product system, from raw material acquisition or generation of natural resources to the final disposal. (ISO 14040)

Life-Cycle Assessment (LCA) — Compilation and evaluation, according to a systematic set of procedures, of the inputs and outputs of materials and energy and the potential environmental impacts of a product system throughout its life cycle. (ISO 14040)

Life-Cycle Characterization — Element of the life-cycle impact assessment phase in which the potential impacts associated with the inventory data in each of the selected categories are analyzed. (ISO 14040)

Life-Cycle Classification — Element of the life-cycle impact assessment phase in which the inventory parameters are grouped together and sorted into a number of impact categories. (ISO 14040)

Life-Cycle Impact Assessment — Phase of life-cycle assessment aimed at understanding and evaluating the magnitude and significance of the potential environmental impacts of a product system. (ISO 14040)

Life-Cycle Interpretation Phase of life-cycle assessment in which a synthesis is drawn from the findings of either the inventory analysis or the impact assessment, or both, in line with the defined goal and scope. (ISO 14040)

Life-Cycle Inventory Analysis — Phase of life-cycle assessment involving compilation and quantification of inputs and outputs for a given product system throughout its life cycle. (ISO 14040)

Life-Cycle Valuation — Element of the life-cycle assessment involving compilation and quantification of inputs and outputs, for a given product system throughout its life cycle.

Mark of Conformity — Protected mark, applied or issued under the rules of a certification system, indicating that confidence is provided that the relevant product, process, or service is in conformity with a specific standard or other normative document. (ISO/IEC Guide 2)

Nonconformity — The nonfulfillment of a specified requirement. (ISO 8402)

Notified Body — A notified body is a testing organization that has been selected to perform assessment activities for (a) particular directive(s). It is approved by the competent authority of its member state and notified to the European Commission and all other member states.

Organization — Company, corporation, firm, enterprise, or institution, or part or combination thereof, whether incorporated or not, public or private, that has its own function and administration. (ISO 14001)

Organizational Structure — The responsibilities, authorities, and relationships, arranged in a pattern, through which an organization performs its functions. (ISO 8402)

Package/Packaging — A material or item that is used to protect or contain a product during transportation, storage, or marketing.

Practitioner — Third party body that operates an environmental labeling program. (ISO 14024) Individual or group of people that conducts a life-cycle assessment study. (ISO 14040)

Prevention of Pollution — Use of processes, practices, materials, or products that avoid, reduce, or control pollution, which may include recycling, treatment, process changes, control mechanisms, efficient use of resources, and materials substitutions. (ISO 14001)

Procedure — A specified way to perform an activity. (ISO 8402)

Process — A set of interrelated resources and activities that transform inputs into outputs. (ISO 8402)

Product — Any good or service. (ISO 14024)

Product Category — Group(s) of products that have equivalent functions. (ISO 14024)

Product Environmental Criteria — Set of qualitative and quantitative technical requirements that the applicant, product, or product category shall meet to be awarded an environmental label. Product criteria include ecological and product function elements. (ISO 14024)

Product System — Collection of materially and energetically connected unit processes that performs one or more defined functions. (ISO 14040)

Protocol Agreement — An agreement signed between two organizations that operate in different but complementary fields of activity and that commit themselves to take into account their respective assessment results according to conditions specified in advance.

Purchaser — The customer in a contractual situation. (ISO 8402)

Qualified Environmental Claim — An environmental claim which is accompanied by an explanatory statement that describes the limits of the claim.

Qualification Process — The process of demonstrating whether an entity is capable of fulfilling specified requirements. (ISO 8402)

Quality System — Organization structure, procedures, processes, and resources needed to implement quality management. (ISO 8402)

Raw Material — Primary or secondary recovered or recycled material that is used in a system to produce a product. (ISO 14040)

Raw Material Acquisition — Activities associated with the production and delivery of raw materials. (ISO 14040)

Recognition agreement — An agreement that is based on the acceptance by one party of results, presented by another party, from the implementation of one or more designated functional elements of a conformity assessment system. (ISO/IEC Guide 2)

Registrar — *See certification body.*

Registration — Procedure by which a body indicates relevant characteristics of a product, process, or service, or particulars of a body or person in an appropriate, publicly available, list. (ISO/IEC Guide 2)

Registration Body — *See certification body.*

Registration System — System having its own rules of procedure and management for carrying out the assessment leading to the issuance of a registration document and its subsequent maintenance. (ISO/IEC Guide 2)

Requirements of Society — Requirements including laws, statutes, rules and regulations, codes, environmental considerations, health and safety factors, and conservation of energy and materials. (ISO 9004-3)

Resource Productivity Framework — A systematic approach to environmental issues and opportunities in the entire value chain of the enterprise.

Responsible Care® — Comprehensive guidelines for environmental management systems adopted by Chemical Manufacturers Association (CMA) in 1988. Participation by individual businesses is an obligation of membership in the CMA.

Root Cause — A fundamental deficiency that results in a nonconformance and must be corrected to prevent recurrence of the same or similar nonconformance. (ASQC Quality Auditing Technical Committee)

Secondary Education — That part of the national educational system that comes after the primary or elementary stage, but that is completed immediately prior to entrance to a university or similar establishment. (ISO 14012)

Self-Declaration Environmental Claims — An environmental claim that is made without independent third party certification, by manufacturers, importers, distributors, retailers, or anyone else likely to benefit from such a claim. (ISO 14021)

Service — The result generated by activities at the interface between the supplier and the customer and by supplier internal activities to meet the customer needs. (ISO 8402)

Service Delivery — Those supplier activities necessary to provide the service. (ISO 8402)

Site — All land on which the activities under the control of a company at a given location are carried out, including any connected or associated storage of raw materials, byproducts, intermediate products, end products, and waste material, and any equipment or infrastructure involved in the activities, whether or not fixed. Where applicable, the definition of site shall correspond to definitions specified in legal requirements. (ISO/IEC Guide 2)

Specification — The document that prescribes the requirements with which the product or service must conform. (ANSI/ASQC A3)

Stakeholders — Those groups and organizations having an interest or stake in a company's EMS program (e.g., regulators, shareholders, customers, suppliers, special interest groups, residents, competitors, investors, bankers, media, lawyers, insurance companies, trade groups, unions, ecosystems, cultural heritage, and geology).

Subcontractor — An organization that provides a product to the supplier. (ISO 8402)

Subject Matter — Specified environmental activity, event, condition, management system, and/or information about these matters.

Supplier — An organization that provides a product to the customer. (ISO 8402)

Survey — An examination for some specific purpose — to inspect or consider carefully; to review in detail. (ASQC Quality Auditing Technical Committee)

System — Collection of unit processes that, when acting together, perform some defined function. (ISO 14040)

System Boundary — Interface between the product system being studied and its environment or other systems. (ISO 14040)

Technical Expert — Person who provides specific knowledge or expertise to the audit team, but who does not participate as an auditor. (ISO 14010)

Testing — A means of determining an item's capability to meet specified requirements by subjecting it to a set of physical, chemical, environmental, or operating actions and conditions. (ANSI/ASQC A3)

Third Party — Person or body recognized as being independent of the issue involved, as concerns the issue in question.
Note — Parties involved are usually supplier ("first party") and purchaser ("second party"). (ISO/IEC Guide 2)

Transparency — Open and comprehensive presentation of information. (ISO 14040)

Unit Processes — The smallest technical sub-system for which data are collected. (ISO 14040)

Verification — Process of authenticating evidence. (ISO 14010) The act of reviewing, inspecting, testing, checking, auditing, or otherwise establishing and documenting whether items, processes, services, or documents conform to specified requirements. (ANSI/ASQC A3)

Waste — Any output from the product system that is disposed of. (ISO 14040)

SECTION 2
Acronyms

AAEI — American Association of Exporters & Importers

AAMA — American Automobile Manufacturers Association

AFNOR — French standards organization

AFPA — American Forest and Paper Association

AIHA — American Industrial Hygiene Association

AIST — Japanese Agency of Industrial Science and Technology

ANSI — American National Standards Institute

API — American Petroleum Institute

ASQC — American Society for Quality Control

ASME — American Society of Mechanical Engineers

ASSE — American Society of Sanitary Engineers

ASTM — American Society for Testing and Materials

ATMI — American Textile Manufacturers Institute

AWG — Ad hoc working group

BCCA — Board Committee on Conformity Assessment (within ANSI)

BFI — Browning-Ferris Industries

BPR — Business Process Redesign or Reengineering (from Arthur D. Little)

BSI — British Standards Institution

BVQI — Bureau Veritas Quality International Ltd.

CAA — Clean Air Act

CAG — Chairman's Advisory Group (made up of leadership of TAG to TC 207)

CASCO — ISO Council Committee on Conformity Assessment

CBI — Confederation of Business Industry

CCEI — Central Committee on Environment and Industry

CCIB — Canadian Council for International Business

CD — Committee Draft

CEC — Commission on Environmental Cooperation (within NAFTA)

CEN — Comité Européen de Normalisation (European Committee for Standardization)

CENELEC — Comité Européen de Normalisation Électrotechnique

CFC — Chlorofluorocarbon

CIH — Certified Industrial Hygienist

CISQ — Center for International Standards and Quality, Georgia Tech

CLP — China Light & Power

CMA — Chemical Manufacturers Association

CMS — Corrective Measures Study

CMCEC — Company Member Council Executive Committee

COFRAC — Comité Française d'Accreditation

CQAE — Commission de Qualification des Auditers Environnementaux

CONCAMIN — Mexican National Confederation of Industrial Chambers

CRLRC — Columbia Ridge Landfill and Recycling Center

CSA — Canadian Standards Association

CSBTS — Chinese standards organization

CSP — Certified Safety Professional

CTE — Committee on Trade and the Environment, U.S. Department of Commerce

CWM — Chemical Waste Management

D2D — Design to Distribution Ltd.

DEQ — Oregon Dept. of Environmental Quality

DFE — Design for the Environment

DIN — Deutsches Institut für Normung (German standards organization)

DIS — Draft International Standard

DMR — Discharge Monitoring Report

DOD — U.S. Department of Defense

DOE — U.S. Department of Energy

DOJ — Department of Justice

EA — Environmental Audit; Environmental Auditing

EAC — European Accreditation of Certification

EAF — Environmental Auditing Forum

EAPS — Environmental Aspects in Product Standards

EAR — Environmental Auditing Roundtable

EARA — Environmental Auditors Registration Association

EBRD — European Bank for Reconstruction and Development

EC — European Commission

EEB — European Environmental Bureau

EEC — The European Economic Community. This comprises the EC and EFTA countries.

EFTA — European Free Trade Association. Members as of May 1995 were Austria, Finland, Iceland, Norway, Sweden, and Switzerland

EHS — Environment Health and Safety

EI — Environmental Indicators (formerly EPI)

EIP — Environmental Interested Party

EL — Environmental Labeling; Eco-labeling

ELI — Environmental Law Institute

ELP — Environmental Leadership Program (within EPA)

EMAR — Eco-Management and Audit Regulation (EU)

EMAS — Eco-Management and Audit Scheme (EU)

EMIT — Group — Environmental Measures and International Trade Group

EMS — Environmental Management System

EPA — United States Environmental Protection Agency

EPCRA — Emergency Preparedness and Community Right to Know Act

EPBA — European Portable Battery Association

EPE — Environmental Performance Evaluation

EPI — Environmental Performance Indicator (now EI)

ESA — Endangered Species Act

EU — European Union. Current members are Austria, Belgium, Denmark, Finland, France, Germany, Greece, Ireland, Italy, Luxembourg, The Netherlands, Portugal, Spain, Sweden, and the United Kingdom

EVABAT — Economically Viable Application of Best Available Technology

FDIS — Final Draft International Standard

FTC — Federal Trade Commission

FUNTEC — Mexican Foundation for Innovation and Technology Transfer in Small and Medium Enterprises

GATT — General Agreement on Tariffs and Trade

GEF — Global Environmental Facility

GEMI — Global Environmental Management Initiative

GELN — Global Ecolabeling Network (12 EL programs)

GETF — Global Environmental Technology Foundation

GSA — General Services Administration

HKPC — Hong Kong Productivity Council

IAAR — Independent Association of Accredited Registrars

IAETL — International Association of Environmental Testing Laboratories

IAC — International Advisory Committee (established under board level in ANSI)

IAF — International Accreditation Forum

IATCA — International Auditor and Training Certification Association

ICC — International Chamber of Commerce. An organization based in Paris, France

ICSP — Inter-agency Committee on Standards Policy (within NIST)

IDEM — Indiana Department of Environmental Management

IEA — Institute of Environmental Auditing

IEC — International Electrotechnical Commission

IEEE — Institute of Electrical and Electronic Engineers

IESU — *International Environmental Systems Update*

IISD — International Institute for Sustainable Development

IISI — International Iron and Steel Institute

ILO — International Labor Organization

IMNC — Mexican Institute of Certification and Normalization

IMSU — *Integrated Management Systems Update*

INEM — International Network for Environmental Management

INMETRO — National Institute of Metrology and Standardization

IQA — Institute of Quality Assurance

IRCA — International Register of Certified Auditors

IS — International Standard

ISO — International Organization for Standardization

ITESM — Instituto Technologico Y de Esudios Superiores de Monterey, Mexico

JAS-ANZ — Joint Accreditation System of Australia and New Zealand

JISC — Japanese Industrial Standards Committee

KIAA — Industrial Advancement Administration, Republic of Korea

LCA — Life-Cycle Assessment (or Life-Cycle Analysis)

LRQA — Lloyds Register Quality Assurance Ltd.

MITI — Japanese Ministry of International Trade and Industry

MMS — Mineral Management Service, U.S. Dept of Interior

MOU — Memorandum of Understanding

MRA — Mutual Recognition Agreement

MSDS — Material Safety Data Sheets

NACEC — North American Commission for Environmental Cooperation

NACCB — National Accreditation Council for Certification Bodies (U.K.) (Now UKAS)

NAEM — National Association of Environmental Management

NAFTA — North American Free Trade Agreement

NCSCI — National Center for Standards and Certification Information (within NIST)

NEC — Nippon Electric and Electronics Company

NEMI — National Environmental Management Institute

NEPA — National Environmental Policy Act

NEPI — National Environmental Policy Institute

NGO — Non-Government Organization

NIOSH — National Institute of Occupational Safety and Health

NIST — National Institute of Standards and Technology, U.S. — Department of Commerce

NPDES — National Pollutant Discharge Elimination System

NSFI — NSF International

NTIS — U.S. National Technical Information Service

NVCASE — National Voluntary Conformity Assessment System Evaluation

NWF — National Wildlife Federation

ODA — Ozone Depletion Area

OECD — Organization for Economic Cooperation and Development

OHS — Occupational Health and Safety

OHSMS — Occupational Health and Safety Management Standard

OMA — Office of Multilateral Affairs, U.S. Department of Commerce

OSHA — U.S. Occupational Safety and Health Administration

OWM — Office of Wastewater Management

PASC — Pacific Area Standards Council

PPB — Parts Per Billion

PPM — Parts Per Million

PPM — Production Process Methods

PRBA — Portable Rechargeable Battery Association

PROFEPA — Procuraduria Federal de Proteccion al Ambiente

PSM — Process Safety Management

QEP — Qualified Environmental Professional

QMS — Quality Management System

QSD — Quality Systems Development

QSU — Quality Systems Update

RAB — Registrar Accreditation Board

RCRA — Resource Conservation and Recovery Act

RvA — Raad voor Accreditatie (Dutch Council for Accreditation)

RvC — Raad voor Certificate (Dutch Council for Certification) (Now RvA)

SAA — Australian standards organization

SAC — Supplier Audit and Confirmation Proposal

SAGE — Strategic Advisory Group on Environment (disbanded)

SARA — Superfund Amendments and Reauthorization Act

SC — Subcommittee

SCC — Standards Council of Canada

SCRAG — Standards Conformance Registrar Advisory Group (disbanded)

SECOFI — Mexican commerce department

SEMARNAP — Mexican Department for Environment, Natural Resources and Fisheries

SETAC — Society for Environmental Toxicology and Chemistry

SFM — Sustainable Forest Management

SGE — Special Government Employee

SIC — Standard Industrial Classification code

SIS — Swedish standards organization

SME — Small and Medium-Sized Enterprises

SNV — Swiss standards organization

ST — SubTAG, Subgroup of a TAG

STEP — Strategies for Today's Environmental Partnership

SWG — Subworking Group (U.S. TAG)

TAG — Technical Advisory Group

TBT — Agreement on Technical Barriers to Trade

TC — Technical Committee

TCE — trichlorethylene — a universal solvent used in the electronics industry

TG — Task Group

TMB — Technical Management Board

TRI — Toxic Release Inventory

TSCA — Toxic Substances Control Act

TVA — Tennessee Valley Authority

UKAS — United Kingdom Accreditation Service (See NACCB)

UNCTAD — United Nations Council on Trade and Development

UNEP — United Nations Environment Program

UNIDO — United Nations Industrial Development Organization

USCIB — United States Council on International Business

USTR — Office of the United States Trade Representative

VPP — Voluntary Protection Program (OSHA)

VPPPA — Voluntary Protection Program Participant's Association

WD — Working Draft

WG — Working Group

WTO — World Trade Organization

WWF — World Wildlife Fund for Nature

Index

B

C

I

M

N

Q

QS-9000 245

Qualified environmental auditor 351

Qualified environmental professional 351

Qualitative measurement system 129

Quality 150
   and environmental aspects 112
   and environmental performance 150

Quality management system integration 58, 253

Quality System Assessment Registration (QSAR) 357

Quantitative measurement 129

Quantitative risk assessment 116

Quick, Richard 510

R

 Raad voor Accreditatie (RvA) 358, 359, 363, 366, 373, 488

Raad voor Certificatie 358

RAB 355, 367

Rank Xerox 474

Realized savings 251

Recognition agreement
   definition 349

Records 145, 147
   documentation 186
   ISO 14001
      Section 4.4.3 186
   ISO 9000 companies 187
   SMEs 186

Recycling 116, 499

Reese, Debra 76, 84

Registrar 350
   Definition 349

Registrar Accreditation Board (RAB) 30, 348, 360, 373, 473

Registrar Accreditation Process 366

Registration 331, 350

business considerations 369
business implications 133
Definition 349
third-party 525

Registration body
   Definition 349

Registration or mark 351

Regulatory benefits of certification
   streamlined permitting 400
   benefits for certification 399
   reduced inspections 400
   reporting and monitoring 399

Regulatory compliance audit 302

Regulatory context 390
   certification 391

Regulatory requirements 105

Reinventing the Vehicle for Environmental Management 405

Related issues 273

Relevant function and level 130

Remembering function 283

Reporting 239, 466
   of hazards 506

Resources 62, 119, 145
   productivity 111

Responsibilities 136

Responsible Care®
3, 118, 166, 246, 250, 505, 506, 508
   Community awareness codes 509
   Comparison with ISO 14001 507
   occupational health and safety 509
   product stewardship 509
   six codes of management practices 505

Responsible Care Elements 506
   10 Guiding Principles 506
   6 Codes of Management Practice 507

Reuse 116

Review and improvement
   ISO 14004 189. See also Management Review

Rewards 239

Rhodes, Stanley 280

Riedel, Brian 386

T